W9-ANB-718

Celebrated military historian and television presenter Richard Holmes is famous for his BBC series such as *War Walks* and *Wellington*. He is the author of the bestselling and widely acclaimed *Redcoat* and *Tommy* and more than a dozen other books, including *The Western Front*, *Dusty Warriors* and *Sahib*. He is general editor of the definitive *Oxford Companion to Military History*. He taught military history at Sandhurst for many years and is now a professor at Cranfield University and the Defence Academy of the United Kingdom. He lives near Winchester in Hampshire.

From the reviews of *Marlborough: England's Fragile Genius*:

'Unbeatable military history, with rattling narrative vitality, full of political plots, grand strategy, battlefield carnage and dynastic vainglory, and with a piercing empathy for commanders and cannon fodder alike'
RICHARD DAVENPORT-HINES, *Sunday Telegraph*, Books of the Year

'As comprehensive an account of Marlborough as a single volume can hope to be ... In his descriptions of the great set-piece battles [Holmes's] eye for detail, grasp of subject, deployment of sources, and familiarity with physical terrain, which distinguishes all his military writing, combine to produce as lucid and vivid an account of warfare as one could ask for' *Spectator*

'[Holmes] has certainly done his subject full justice by crafting a quite brilliant, judicious and fully rounded portrait that should go some way to restoring Marlborough's reputation as a truly Great Briton' *Sunday Telegraph*

'Though [Richard Holmes] guides us sure-footedly through the political and diplomatic maze, it is his account of Marlborough's organisation of the army and campaigns, and his lucid descriptions of the battles, that make this work outstanding' *Daily Telegraph*

'Holmes depicts the moral and political landscape of an entire age in this rewarding biography ... [He] is as thrilling on his subject's romantic devotion to his wife ... as he is on the battles'
Sunday Times

'Holmes tells the tale well and fairly, and on the whole elegantly. He has a good eye for the captivating detail and the illuminating quotation. While rightly concentrating on military matters, he fills in the international and political background skilfully ... A thorough and readable book'
Literary Review

RICHARD HOLMES

MARLBOROUGH

Britain's Greatest General

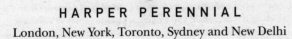

HARPER PERENNIAL

London, New York, Toronto, Sydney and New Delhi

Harper Perennial
An imprint of HarperCollins*Publishers*
77–85 Fulham Palace Road, Hammersmith, London w6 8jb

www.harperperennial.co.uk
Visit our authors' blog at www.fifthestate.co.uk
Love this book? www.bookarmy.com

This Harper Perennial edition published 2009
3

First published in Great Britain by Harper*Press* in 2008

Copyright © Richard Holmes 2008

Richard Holmes asserts the moral right
to be identified as the author of this work

Maps © HarperCollins*Publishers*
designed by HL Studios, Oxfordshire

A catalogue record for this book is available from the British Library

ISBN 978-0-00-722572-9

Set in New Baskerville by
Newgen Imaging Systems (P) Ltd, Chennai, India

Printed and bound in Great Britain by Clays Ltd, St Ives plc

Mixed Sources
Product group from well-managed
forests and other controlled sources
www.fsc.org Cert no. SW-COC-1806
© 1996 Forest Stewardship Council

I am so entirely yours, that if I might have all the world given me, I could not be happy but in your love.

The Hague, 20 April 1703/Ropley, 20 February 2008

CONTENTS

ILLUSTRATIONS

Marlborough and Colonel John Armstrong, his chief engineer, in
  about 1711. *(© Blenheim Palace/The Bridgeman Art Library, London)*
Marlborough in his Garter robes, by Sir Godfrey Kneller. *(© Blenheim
  Palace/The Bridgeman Art Library, London)*
Sarah Churchill, Duchess of Marlborough. *(Attributed to Sir Godfrey
  Kneller/Private collection)*
Marlborough's father, Sir Winston Churchill. Attributed to John
  Michael Wright.
Kneller's portrait of Charles II. *(© Sotheby's/akg-images)*
Winston and Arabella, two of Sir Winston Churchill's children and
  John Churchill's siblings, by Sir Peter Lely. *(Private collection © Peter
  Willi/The Bridgeman Art Library)*
The palace of Whitehall in the reign of Charles II, by Hendrick
  Danckerts. *(Private collection © Ackermann and Johnson Ltd/The
  Bridgeman Art Library, London)*
James Duke of York, later James II, by Sir Peter Lely. *(The Royal
  Collection © 2007 Her Majesty Queen Elizabeth II)*
James Scott, Duke of Monmouth, at the siege of Maastricht in 1673, by
  Jan van Wyck. *(© The National Portrait Gallery, London)*
Barbara Villiers, by Lely. *(Private collection © The Bridgeman Art Library,
  London)*
The wreck of the *Gloucester*, carrying James Duke of York and his
  entourage to Scotland, on 6 May 1682, by Johan Danckerts. *(© The
  National Maritime Museum, London)*
Louis de Dufort-Duras, Earl of Feversham, by John Riley. *(Reproduced by
  kind permission of the Fondazione Palazzo/Archivio Fotografico Coronini
  Cronberg)*
Troops being reviewed on Hounslow Heath in 1688. *(By kind permission
  of the National Army Museum, London)*
King William III, by Lely. *(© The National Portrait Gallery, London)*
Claude Louis Hector, duc de Villars, after Hyacinthe Rigaud. *(Château
  de Versailles © Lauros Giraudon/The Bridgeman Art Library, London)*
Louis XIV playing billiards in 1694. Engraving by Antoine Trouvain.
  (Private collection © Giraudon/The Bridgeman Art Library, London)

The Marlborough family, painted by Johann Baptist Closterman in about 1697. *(© Blenheim Palace/The Bridgeman Art Library, London)*

Holywell House, near St Albans, where the Marlboroughs lived for much of their married lives. *(Courtesy Hertfordshire Archives and Local Studies)*

Sidney, Earl Godolphin. Mezzotint after Kneller, 1705. *(© The National Portrait Gallery/The Bridgeman Art Library, London)*

Queen Anne, by Michael Dahl. *(Private collection © Philip Mould Ltd./The Bridgeman Art Library, London)*

Abigail Hill, later Lady Masham, Sarah Marlborough's cousin, by Kneller. *(Private collection © Philip Mould Ltd./The Bridgeman Art Library, London)*

Sarah Marlborough's elder sister Frances, who married Richard Talbot, Earl of Tyrconnell, by Samuel Cooper. *(© The National Portrait Gallery, London)*

Robert Harley, Earl of Oxford, by Jonathan Richardson. *(Private collection © Philip Mould Ltd./The Bridgeman Art Library, London)*

Prince Eugène of Savoy, by Jacob von Schuppen, 1718. *(© Rijksmuseum, Amsterdam/akg-images)*

John Cutts, 1st Baron Cutts. Mezzotint by John Simon, after Kneller. *(© The National Portrait Gallery, London)*

The axis of Cutts' attack on Blenheim village. *(Michael St Maur Sheil)*

The field at Blenheim, looking east-south-east along the Nebel. *(Michael St Maur Sheil)*

Three panels by Louïs Laguerre depicting the battle of Blenheim. *(By kind permission of the National Army Museum/The Bridgeman Art Library, London)*

Tapestry commissioned by Marlborough to commemorate his victory at Blenheim. *(Image reproduced by kind permission of His Grace the Duke of Marlborough, Blenheim Palace Image Library)*

The old course of the Danube south-east of Sonderheim. *(Michael St Maur Sheil)*

Marlborough and Tallard meeting at Blenheim Engraving after Louis Laguerre. *(By kind permission of the National Army Museum © The Bridgeman Art Library, London)*

William Cadogan, later 1st Earl Cadogan, attributed to Laguerre. *(© The National Portrait Gallery, London)*

Antonie Heinsius, grand pensionary of the Dutch Republic. *(Engraving by H. Pothoven, after G. van der Eikhout © Mary Evans Picture Library)*

Order of Battle for Ramillies. *(From* Campaigns of King William and the Duke of Marlborough, *by Richard Kane, published London 1747, shelfmark 291.g.18, plate XII, The British Library)*

Ramillies seen from Marlborough's approach. *(Michael St Maur Sheil)*

The Tomb of Ottomont, south-west of Ramillies. *(Michael St Maur Sheil)*

François de Neufville, duc de Villeroi, who was defeated by Marlborough at Ramillies. *(Mezzotint © Bibliothèque Nationale, Paris/akg-images)*

The thanksgiving service in St Paul's Cathedral for the victory of Ramillies. *(Maps K. Top.23.36.b, The British Library)*

The siege of Lille, 1708. *(Bibliothèque Nationale, Paris)*

The main gate of the citadel of Lille. *(Michael St Maur Sheil)*

Draft cartel for the exchange of prisoners of war. *(From* Campaigns of King William and the Duke of Marlborough, *by Richard Kane, published London 1747, shelfmark 291.g.18, plate XIV, The British Library)*

Looking southwards along the eastern edge of Sars Wood at Malplaquet. *(Michael St Maur Sheil)*

Dutch infantry of the late seventeenth century, attributed to Everdingen. *(The Royal Collection © 2007 Her Majesty Queen Elizabeth II)*

The standard of the Royal Dragoons. *(From* Drawings of the Colours and Standards of the British Army tempore James II, *Folio 74. The Royal Collection © 2007 Her Majesty Queen Elizabeth II)*

A grenadier of 1st Foot Guards at drill. *(From* The Granadiers Exercise of the Granade *by Bernard Lens, by kind permission of The National Army Museum, London)*

Queen Anne in the House of Lords, by Peter Tillemans (circa 1708–14). *(The Royal Collection © 2007 Her Majesty Queen Elizabeth II)*

High Lodge, Blenheim Park. Engraving by J. Boydell, 1752. *(Maps K. Top XXXV Folio F29, The British Library)*

John, 2nd Duke of Montagu, with his wife, formerly Lady Mary Churchill, and their daughter Lady Mary Montagu. *(Private collection © Philip Mould Ltd/The Bridgeman Art Library, London)*

Marlborough's daughter Henrietta Churchill. Mezzotint by John Smith, after Kneller. *(© The National Portrait Gallery, London)*

Marlborough's grandchildren. Portrait by Bernard Lens. *(The collection at Althorp)*

James FitzJames, Duke of Berwick. Colour lithograph by Sergent-Marceau, after Antoine Louis François. *(Private collection © The Stapleton Collection/Bridgeman Art Library, London)*

Blenheim Palace. *(Painting located at Chartwell Manor, Kent. Photograph by Derek E. Witty © National Trust Photographic Library/The Bridgeman Art Library, London)*

A modern aerial view of Blenheim Palace. *(© Blenheim Palace/The Bridgeman Art Library, London)*

MAPS

Our horsemen had now the better of the fight; but soon we beheld fresh bodies of horsemen, hastening to the relief of their half-defeated squadrons. Marlborough was at the head of this reserve of cavalry . . . I can still see him as, undaunted and serene, he rode forward amid the cheers of his troops, shouting 'Corporal John', the name they had given their hero; he was surrounded by his staff, evidently receiving his commands. I fell on his men with my whole regiment; he narrowly escaped being made prisoner – oh! That heaven was so unpropitious to France – but he was extricated, and my troopers were compelled to retreat.

COLONEL GERALD O'CONNOR, commanding an Irish regiment in French service, Ramillies, 1706

This is a world that is subject to frequent revolutions
SARAH DUCHESS OF MARLBOROUGH

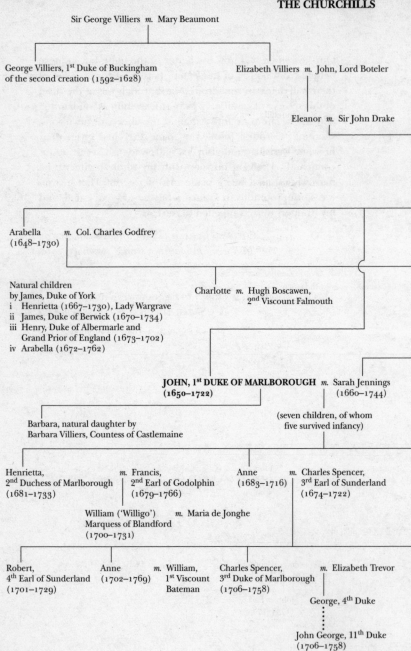

THE CHURCHILLS

Sir George Villiers *m.* Mary Beaumont

George Villiers, 1st Duke of Buckingham
of the second creation (1592–1628)

Elizabeth Villiers *m.* John, Lord Boteler

Eleanor *m.* Sir John Drake

Arabella   *m.* Col. Charles Godfrey
(1648–1730)

Charlotte *m.* Hugh Boscawen,
2nd Viscount Falmouth

Natural children
by James, Duke of York
i   Henrietta (1667–1730), Lady Wargrave
ii   James, Duke of Berwick (1670–1734)
iii Henry, Duke of Albermarle and
     Grand Prior of England (1673–1702)
iv   Arabella (1672–1762)

JOHN, 1st DUKE OF MARLBOROUGH *m.* Sarah Jennings
(1650–1722)   (1660–1744)

Barbara, natural daughter by
Barbara Villiers, Countess of Castlemaine

(seven children, of whom
five survived infancy)

Henrietta,   *m.* Francis,   Anne   *m.* Charles Spencer,
2nd Duchess of Marlborough   2nd Earl of Godolphin (1683–1716)   3rd Earl of Sunderland
(1681–1733)   (1679–1766)   (1674–1722)

William ('Willigo')   *m.* Maria de Jonghe
Marquess of Blandford
(1700–1731)

Robert,   Anne   *m.* William,   Charles Spencer,   *m.* Elizabeth Trevor
4th Earl of Sunderland (1702–1769)   1st Viscount   3rd Duke of Marlborough
(1701–1729)   Bateman   (1706–1758)

George, 4th Duke

John George, 11th Duke
(1706–1758)

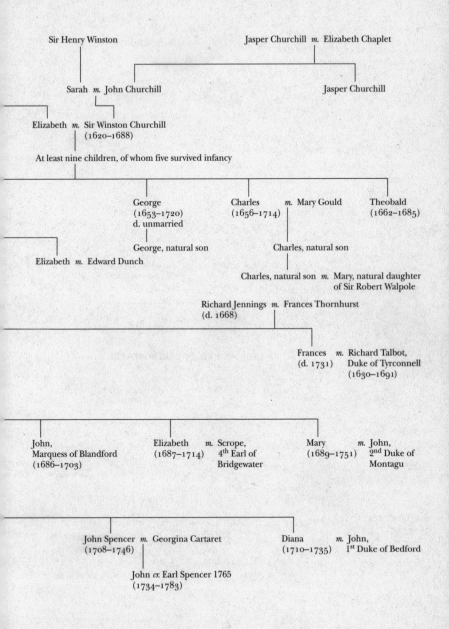

Sir Henry Winston

Jasper Churchill *m.* Elizabeth Chaplet

Sarah *m.* John Churchill

Jasper Churchill

Elizabeth *m.* Sir Winston Churchill
(1620–1688)

At least nine children, of whom five survived infancy

George
(1653–1720)
d. unmarried

Charles   *m.* Mary Gould
(1656–1714)

Theobald
(1662–1685)

Elizabeth *m.* Edward Dunch

George, natural son

Charles, natural son

Charles, natural son *m.* Mary, natural daughter
of Sir Robert Walpole

Richard Jennings *m.* Frances Thornhurst
(d. 1668)

Frances   *m.* Richard Talbot,
(d. 1731)   Duke of Tyrconnell
(1630–1691)

John,
Marquess of Blandford
(1686–1703)

Elizabeth   *m.* Scrope,
(1687–1714)   4th Earl of
Bridgewater

Mary   *m.* John,
(1689–1751)   2nd Duke of
Montagu

John Spencer *m.* Georgina Cartaret
(1708–1746)

Diana   *m.* John,
(1710–1735)   1st Duke of Bedford

John *cr.* Earl Spencer 1765
(1734–1783)

AUTHOR'S NOTE

Pounds, Shillings and Pence

English money at the time in which this book is set was reckoned in pounds, shillings and pence, with twenty shillings to the pound and twelve pence to the shilling: a guinea was worth thirty shillings prior to the recoinage in 1696, and twenty-one shillings thereafter. Simple multiplications do not catch the subtleties of the real value of money, although one reliable source suggests that £1 in 1700 was worth the equivalent of £125 in 2006. Scots money was worth rather less: in 1703 five dragoon broadswords cost £24 Scots, but just £2 Sterling. Soldiers and merchants had to take local currencies as they found them, and relative values were generally on the move. By the beginning of the eighteenth century the French livre was worth about twenty louis d'or, and one of the latter was worth about a guinea. The Dutch guilder contained twenty stivers, and a stiver roughly equated to an English penny. The Spanish pistole, widely used in the Spanish Netherlands, in which so much of Marlborough's campaigning took place, was worth much the same as a louis d'or. There were other currencies about, their value easily reckoned up by those like the jovial Irishman 'Captain' Peter Drake (his rank stemming from self-granted courtesy, not formal commission) with an eye to the main chance. In 1702 he slit a corn bag in Nijmegen castle and found 'a hundred silver ducatoons, value about five shillings and tenpence each, near £30 Sterling'.[1]

Incomes differed hugely. Near the top of the social scale, Sir William Cowper met lord treasurer Godolphin on 11 October 1705 and agreed to become lord keeper 'on condition I had the same money for equipage (£2,000) and salary of £4,000 as my predecessor had, and a peerage next promotion'. Before he could take office he had to swear the oaths of allegiance and supremacy, paying a fee of £26 for each. In the period 1706–08 his income did not fall below £7,000 a year.[2] This was wealth indeed: in 1688 Gregory King estimated the yearly average income of noble families at £3,200 apiece. However, at the height of her power Sarah Marlborough made £9,500 a year from all her court offices (that of groom of the stole alone was worth £3,000), and one apparently well-founded contemporary estimate put her husband's total income in 1704 at the staggering sum of £54,825.[3] The merchant princes of the age, like Sir Peter Vansittart and Sir Theodore Jensen, left fortunes of more than £100,000, and most London merchants of the middling sort, bringing in £200–£400 a year, might leave £5,000–£15,000. It cost perhaps £1,000 to be sworn apprentice to a 'Turkey merchant' trading with the east, £400–£600 to other merchants, and £200–£300 to wholesale dealers like linen drapers.

In 1667 Bab May suggested that £300 a year was quite enough for any country gentleman, coming quite close to Gregory King's 1688 estimate of £450 a year for the average annual income of esquires – the rank between knight and gentleman – and £280 for plain gentlemen.[4] Although King thought that 'persons in greater offices and places' averaged £240 a year, Samuel Pepys, a rising young official, had clearly done rather better. He reckoned himself worth £650 in 1662, £2,164 (and an inherited estate) in 1665, and £6,700 in 1667.

Army pay changed little across the period. A colonel of horse received twelve shillings a day for his colonelcy, plus another ten shillings as captain of a troop in his own regiment (the work was actually done by his captain-lieutenant), and allowances for servants, horses and forage that took him to a total of forty-one shillings a day. Much of this allowance would indeed have been spent, but he could expect to make a profit on the difference between money allocated for clothing and equipping his regiment and that actually laid out: in a dragoon regiment in Anne's reign this might come to £1 per man per year, say £400 a year. Tight-fisted colonels undoubtedly made more, but many took their soldiers' welfare very seriously and made less. Robert Molesworth, a well-to-do Yorkshire squire on a little under £2,000 a year, found his soldier son Dick a constant financial burden. When the young man joined the army 'he must be furnished with a hundred pounds or he cannot stir a step. He has both horses, clothes and equipages to buy.' Even when Dick was a colonel with a regiment of his own his zeal encouraged him 'to lay out £600 above what is allowed him, so well he loves the service'.[5] An infantry captain, with pay and allowances of ten shillings a day, made about the same as Gregory King's 'persons in the law' and 'lesser merchants', well below the standard of a country gentleman, to be sure, but respectably off.

At the bottom of the scale, a private in the infantry (his pay, across the ages, a disgraceful marker of the bottom end of the national salary scale) was entitled to eight pence a day, about £12 a year, but compulsory deductions often reduced that to about four pence 'all found'. Gregory King thought that 'labouring people and outservants' received about £15 a year, and 'cottagers and paupers' just £6.10s. The poor were, at least in theory, maintained by their parishes. The London parish of St Katherine Coleman spent 80 per cent of its revenue on the poor, giving Ellinor Elliston, for example, 2s.6d a week to maintain herself and her two children. It was not even cheap to be in prison. The keeper of Newgate, the worst of London's many prisons, paid £5,000 for his office and recouped his outlay by fleecing those inmates who could afford to pay. 'Garnish money' payable on admission to prison rose from nine shillings to seventeen, and those who did not have the sum to hand were 'presently conveyed to a place they call Tangier, and there stripped, beaten and abused in a very violent manner'.

Peter Drake was sentenced to death as a traitor after his capture aboard the Jacobite privateer *Nightingale* in 1708. He discovered that 'even the condemned are not exempt from extortions in Newgate', and had to pay to have his irons struck off, but was eventually able to enlist the interest of 'six . . . great personages' to gain his pardon. The Roman Catholic captain of the privateer, condemned to die at Execution Dock at Wapping, turned down the prison chaplain's last services. The Reverend Paul Lorrain whined that he was still entitled to his perquisites, but the brave Captain Smith 'took the clergyman by the arm, and bidding him begone, asked if it was a proper time to be talking of perquisites, when he came to exhort him for the good of his soul'.[6] The chaplain had to rub along on the £35 a year he received from the City of London, but boosted this by last-minute tips from the penitent, and the sale of sheets printed, well ahead of the event, with the 'last words' of the condemned: they fetched three to six pence each. The public executioner earned £90 a year. His perquisites included the clothes of his victims, many of whom went to the gallows dressed in fine style, and tips from the Barber-Surgeons Company for helping their servants secure the corpses that were allocated to them for dissection in what was often a ghastly brawl at the foot of the gallows.

Gregory King's estimate, based on hearth-tax returns, suggests that of a total English population that he put at 5,500,520, about 21,500 families (just under 194,000 souls) had a family income of £240 or more. This book is largely peopled by folk who come well into this upper bracket, and the sums that they gambled, drank or spent on luxuries would have been regarded as absurd by that great majority of households getting by on perhaps ten shillings a week. When Marlborough told Godolphin that he should give the bearer of a victorious dispatch no more than £500, it was not a token of the duke's avarice, but a recommendation that would give this officer enough money to buy a good-sized house.

However, things were never as simple as they may seem. People at the bottom of the heap, especially in the country, had recourse to tradition-al acquisitions: cottage vegetable patches, gleaning at harvest-time, penny tips for services like gate-opening or horse-holding. Garments passed down the social scale as they became outmoded or ill-fitting. In London, links were often looser and there was a growing number of out-of-work day labourers, prone to assemble in unstable groups for which contemporaries were just beginning to use the word 'mob' (from *mobile vulgus*, excitable crowd).

Even in cities there was still extra money to be had, sometimes doled out, like the tips bestowed on watchful urchins in modern carparks, to avert mockery or mire. Isabella, Duchess of Grafton in her own right, was married to the High Tory MP Sir Thomas Hanmer, who gave her £500 a year 'pin money' for her domestic expenses. Her account book shows that in early 1712 she spent eighteen shillings on a pair of black silk stockings and a pair of black gloves, £6.19s.9d on ermine, and gave ten shillings to the tooth-cleaner. In February alone she paid chair-men, the bearers of the sedan chairs that were the equivalent of today's taxis, £16.14s, and in March she lost £7.10s.6d to her husband at cards. In March that year 2s.6d was simply 'given to the mob', in 1714 the finder of a lost diamond earring was rewarded with £1.1s.6d, and 'Matt the postillion' received the same sum for finding another missing dia-mond. Isabella also spent fourteen shillings on 'two quarts of usque-baugh', which says nothing about the lady's philanthropy but much about her regard for Scotch whisky.[7] It may also tell us something about her marriage, for her husband extended his fastidious ways to wearing white gloves in the marital bed, and the relationship was not notably passionate.

Official salaries and other payments were often in arrears. Officers might find themselves arrested for debt because their soldiers' subsistence money had not arrived but they had engaged themselves to tavern-keepers or sutlers. The unlucky Colonel Michelbourne spent years in the Fleet prison as a debtor, and at the end of Anne's reign his regiment was still short more than £198,000, owed since the siege of Londonderry in 1690. In 1706 the officers and men of Harvey's

Regiment were still trying to lay hands on back-pay owed since 1689–92.[8] It was not always wise for private individuals to draw debts to the attention of the great. When Peter Drake reminded Colonel Pocock that he owed him money, the colonel roared, '"I'll pay you"; and without saying any more, he fell to caning me.' Drake would have lugged out had they not been in the Duke of Marlborough's quarters, but contented himself with throwing the colonel down and so losing his post as quartermaster: 'I now commenced trooper . . .'[9]

There was irregular inflation during the eighteenth century: prices in 1800 were about half as much again as they had been in 1700. In Marlborough's active career there was fluctuation in both directions: one scholar suggests that £100 in 1701 would have been worth £132 in 1699, £89 in 1705, £135 in 1711 and £95 in 1717.[10] Daniel Defoe maintained that the shortage of domestic servants in London forced up their wages. Writing in 1725 he thought that their pay had risen from thirty to forty shillings a year to £6–£8, and they now expected tips from dinner guests. 'Now they make it a perquisite, a material part of their wages,' he grumbled. 'Nor must their master give a supper, but the maid expects the guests should pay for it, nay, sometimes through the nose.'[11] Peter Drake, by then in the British army and a quartermaster 'responsible for all sutlers and other dealers' in camp, extracted £12–£14 a week from his tenants, but of this 'I had five and thirty shillings only, exclusive of windfalls.'

The staples of life were relatively cheap. In 1714 bread at Greenwich hospital was a penny a pound, and in 1700 a hundred eggs cost 5s.9d at Westminster School, and a pound of cheese was four pence. In 1712 fourteen pounds of 'flesh' cost two shillings at Greenwich hospital, which paid three shillings for fourteen pounds of beef and mutton.[12] Moving up the social scale, a dish of coffee in one of the coffee houses that were even more popular in 1700 than Starbucks and Costa now are, cost a penny halfpenny, and a gallon of claret at Eton College cost seven shillings. After the Methuen Treaty with Portugal, port became cheaper, and this in turn helped bring down the cost of claret: it was just 3s.4d in 1721. A good meal could be eaten in London for a shilling, but John Evelyn might have to pay a guinea or two for dinner at the fashionable Pontack's.

In 1668 Samuel Pepys felt secure enough to buy his own coach, and paid £50 for 'a fine pair' of horses for it. The following year he met his ex-servant Deb, dismissed after Mrs Pepys found him with his hand up her skirt, and gave her twenty shillings after some more inconclusive fumbling down an alley, paying more for past guilt than for present gratification. A guided tour of Oxford cost him £1.2*s*.6*d*, and a barber 2*s*.6*d*. He thought Salisbury 'a great city, I think greater than Oxford', but found it horribly expensive: '£2 5s 6d servants, 1s 6d poor, 1s guide to the stones, 2s poor woman in the street, ribbands 9d, washerwomen 1s . . .'[13] The Earl of Ailesbury's son Lord Bruce, a peer in his own right after the 1712 promotion, paid £8.18*s*.6*d* for his own coronet and £5.15*s*.6*d* for his wife's, and coronation robes cost the couple £6.5*s*.6*d*. In 1703 the architect John Vanbrugh spent £2,000 on the site for a theatre on the west side of the Haymarket, and seven years later Jonathan Swift was paying eight shillings a week for two decent rooms in London. Castle Howard cost the Earl of Carlisle £40,000 to build, the same as the original budget for the Marlboroughs' Blenheim Palace, which eventually cost around £300,000, with Grinling Gibbons alone putting in his bill for over £4,000.

Words and Dates

I have generally modernised spelling and adjusted grammar where the original is too convoluted. It is worth noting that few of those whose words I use wrote what we might now call the Queen's English. If Macaulay complained that Marlborough could not spell simple words in his own language, this observation can be extended across much of the political nation. People wrote words the way they heard them. Charles Mordaunt, Earl of Monmouth, succeeded as Earl of Peterborough in 1697 but always spelt his name Peterbrow. A song lamenting Marlborough's dismissal as captain general managed to rhyme 'now' with 'Marlborough', suggesting that it was actually pronounced 'Marlborow'. Percy Kirke, commander of the Tangier Regiment and moving spirit behind some of the post-Sedgemoor atrocities, actually spelt his first name Piercy, and probably pronounced it that way. Civil War royalists had quipped that their puritan opponents called on the Lord as 'Laard', and Sarah Marlborough, given to beginning her sentences with 'Lord, Lord,' probably sounded rather similar. Alexander Pope tells us precisely what 'tea' rhymed with:

> *Here thou great Anna! whom three realms obey*
> *Does sometimes council take – and sometimes Tea.*

Lady Wentworth, Lord Raby's* doting mother, stretched the language further than most. In August 1703 she told him that 'an extreme wynde has brock one of your winds in your dyning room quite down'. Next year she reported that one of the family pet's litter had found a good home, for 'one of Fubsis puppys the Duke of Boffud has got'. In November 1708 she wrote to lament the death of poor Fubs: 'As it leved so it dyed, full of lov leening its head in my bosom, never offered to snap at any body in its horrid torter but nussle its head to us and look earnestly upon me and Sue.' She later hoped to persuade her son to marry the heiress Lady Mary Villiers, writing:

> Why will you let Lady Mary then goe, she is young, ritch and not unhand-som, sum sey she is pretty; and a vertious lady and of the nobillety, and why will you not trye to gett her.[14]

Most educated folk could speak French, or something very like it. It was the Allied *lingua franca*, and Marlborough usually used it when corre-sponding with his Dutch or German confederates, and it was his sole means of contact with the future George I. It was an age when national-ism was less sharply defined than would be the case even a generation later. There were Huguenot refugees in the British army, Irish Catholics in the French army, and Swiss on both sides. Marlborough's great mili-tary collaborator Prince Eugène of Savoy-Carignan was born in Paris, son of Eugène Maurice, prince of Savoy-Carignan and Duke of Soissons, and Olympia Mancini, a niece of Cardinal Mazarin and once a favourite of Louis XIV's. Louis directed him into the Church, and when the young Eugène approached the king to ask for a commission in the army he was turned down. The reasons for the refusal remain obscure. There were rumours that Eugène had been too fond of other pages at court; his mother, caught up in accusations of witchcraft, was someone the king now recalled with horror, and in any case the lad was shockingly ugly. The refusal infuriated Eugène, who affirmed that: 'No Huguenot expelled by the Revocation of the Edict of Nantes ever cherished a

---

* Thomas Wentworth (1672–1739), soldier and diplomat, 3rd Baron Raby and in 1711 1st Earl of Stratford of the third creation. Scion of a Yorkshire family related to Charles I's favourite, Stratford, he was impeached for his role in negotiating the Treaty of Utrecht, and was created a Jacobite duke in 1722.

stronger hatred against him.' He admitted that he was emotionally engaged in the struggle against France.

> I have entered it on more sides than one; and it is not my fault that I did not penetrate further. But for the English, I should have given law in the capital of the *grande monarque* and shut up his [wife, the former Madame de] Maintenon in a convent for life.[15]

Yet he was always happier in French, the language of his enemies, than in German, and in the polyglot style of the age signed himself Eugenio von Savoye.

If signatures can be one problem, dates are certainly another. Until 1752 Britain used the Julian calendar ('Old Style'), whereas after 1700 all European countries except Russia switched to the Gregorian calendar ('New Style'), which was eleven days ahead of it. Marlborough himself tended to use Old Style wherever he was, until halfway through the Blenheim campaign, when he announced that he would thereafter follow 'the custom of the country' and use New Style when abroad. Some correspondents gave both dates (e.g. August 2/13th) or added either 'OS' or 'NS' to make their meaning clear. I too adhere to the custom of the country, and date documents as their writers would have done: where there is a possibility of confusion I add 'OS' or 'NS' to the date. British contemporaries dated the beginning of each New Year not from 1 January but from 25 March. I follow the generally accepted practice of beginning the New Year on the first day of January.

Lastly, Charles II, James II, William and Mary, and Anne (until the Union of England and Scotland in 1707) ruled the three distinct kingdoms of England, Scotland and Ireland, complete with their own peerages and parliaments. Yet in practice the army in which young John Churchill served included Scots and Irish regiments, and there were Scots and Irish soldiers within nominally English regiments. Although Wales was then subsumed within England, what was to become the 23rd Foot, the Royal Welch Fusiliers, had a decidedly Welsh feel even in Marlborough's lifetime. I therefore write of a British army when contemporaries would have used the term English. To do otherwise would be fair neither to Captain Robert Parker's Irish infantry nor to Lieutenant Colonel Jemmy Campbell's Scots dragoons.

Regiments were generally known by the names of their colonels, and might in consequence change their titles quite often. Some of Marlborough's regiments have clear descendants even in today's abbreviated regimental structure. In other cases successive amalgamations have made the golden thread harder to follow, and in still other cases disbandments after the War of Spanish Succession cut off some of Marlborough's regiments without legitimate issue. This is a matter rightly dear to the hearts of military antiquarians, but I shall rub along without worrying too much about bastion-ended lace here or sea-green facings there. The officers of the age did not wear uniforms as we would understand them, and not least of Marlborough's contributions to the British army was to insist on the officers of horse and foot turning out in red coats. When he was born a red coat did not mean much on a European battlefield: by the time he died it meant a great deal.

Portrait of an Age

Marlborough and the Weight of History

Some will tell you that John Churchill, 1st Duke of Marlborough, was Britain's greatest ever general. John Keegan and Andrew Wheatcroft, two wise judges, affirmed that:

> There was no talent for war which he did not possess. He had imagination and command of detail to plan a grand strategy: he was an able generalissimo of allied armies, always ready to flatter a foreign ruler for some political advantage. His capacity for innovation really lay off the battlefield . . . But his greatest strength lay in his attention to the economic underpinning of the war, and in his concern for the morale and welfare of his men . . . In this combination of military virtues Marlborough's greatness nestled, but most of all in his understanding that the army was precious and that its value resided in the officers and men who made it up.[1]

Winston S. Churchill concluded his six-volume biography of his distinguished ancestor by declaring:

> He had consolidated all that England had gained by the Revolution of 1688 and the achievements of William III. By his invincible genius in war and his scarcely less admirable qualities of wisdom and management he had completed that glorious process that carried England from her dependency upon France under Charles II to ten years' leadership of Europe . . . He had proved himself the 'good Englishman' he aspired to be, and History may declare that if he had had more power his country would have had more strength and happiness, and Europe a surer progress.[2]

Another assessment added private virtue to public achievement to make Marlborough the very model of the Christian soldier:

> He was by nature pure and temperate, kind and brave. He had supreme genius, personal beauty, and the art of pleasing. He was born to shine in courts, and understood the graces of life to perfection. He met with glory and ingratitude, infamy and fame. So, moving splendidly through a splendid world, he saw more fully to the share of most men, of human nature and the human lot.
>
> He was honourable in his public life because he was also honourable in his private life. He was kind and chivalrous abroad, because he was kind and chivalrous at heart, and in his own home, and to his best beloved. He had a deep, strong faith, which never failed him.[3]

Marlborough's contemporary, Archdeacon William Coxe, concluded his three-volume biography, which still repays study, with the lapidary declaration that he was simply: 'THE GREATEST GENERAL AND ... THE GREATEST MINISTER that our country, or any other, has produced.'[4]

In his multi-volume history of the British army published in 1910, Sir John Fortescue, never a man to shy from a harsh verdict when he thought it justified, wrote of how Marlborough's

> transcendent ability as a general, a statesman, a diplomatist and an administrator, guided not only England but Europe through the War of Spanish Succession, and delivered them safe for a whole generation from the craft and ambition of France ...
>
> Regarding him as a general, his fame is assured as one of the greatest captains of all time; and it would not become a civilian to add a word to the eulogy of great soldiers who alone can comprehend the full measure of his greatness.[5]

Fortescue wrote that Marlborough, like Wellington,

> was endowed with a strong common sense that in itself amounted to genius, and possessed in the most trying moments a serenity and calm that was almost miraculous ... With such a temperament there was a bond of humanity between him and his men that was lacking in Wellington. Great as Wellington was, the Iron Duke's army could never have nicknamed him the Old Corporal.[6]

Elsewhere, citing an approving comment in the papers of an officer in Marlborough's army, Fortescue mused: 'What modern decoration (save the Victoria Cross) could compare to a word of hearty praise from Corporal John himself?'[7]

However, it was hard even for Fortescue to ignore the fact that Marlborough had detractors during his lifetime, though he maintained that the duke's 'fall was brought about by a faction, and his fame has remained ever since prey to the tender mercies of a faction'.[8] Some of Marlborough's warmest admirers acknowledge that there was indeed another side to the man. Although Charles Spencer, like Winston S. Churchill, has some of Marlborough's blood in his veins, he is a wise enough historian to admit that:

> It is difficult to understand Marlborough the man. He was enigmatic, focussed, and brilliant. He was also avaricious and – as we know from his correspondence with the Jacobites – capable of double-dealing. However, his men adored him, and they knew his incomparable military worth: they were proud to point out that he never lost a battle, or failed to take a city that he besieged.[9]

Marlborough's abandonment of James II (who had befriended him and raised him to the peerage) in 1688 was a move so significant that one historian has called it 'Lord Churchill's coup'. It led G.K. Chesterton to accuse him of the vilest of betrayals: 'Churchill, as if to add something ideal to his imitation of Iscariot, went to James with wanton professions of love and loyalty, went forth in arms as if to defend the country from invasion, and then calmly handed over the country to the invader.'[10] Marlborough lived on the margins of treason. He never regarded the verdict of 1688 as final, and remained in touch with the Jacobite court for the rest of his life, a process assisted by the fact that one of James's illegitimate sons, James FitzJames, Duke of Berwick, was both Marlborough's nephew and a marshal of France.

Although the circumstances of his upbringing go far towards explaining his notorious cupidity, Marlborough was given to a rapacity remarkable even in a rapacious age, amassing offices which made him one of the richest men in the land. While we must accept stories about his tight-fistedness with caution, for they were circulated by his detractors to damage his reputation, the tale that, after an evening's gaming in Bath, he borrowed the money for a sedan chair but then walked home regardless may indeed be well-founded. Yet he spent enormous sums on building

Blenheim Palace, which still glares out in chilly splendour as his lasting memorial. Though most of the practical work of supervising its construction was left to his wife, who demonstrated that high temper rarely makes a successful contribution to labour relations on a building site, the concept was his, and his pressing on with its construction at a time of crisis in the nation's history showed that selective blindness which sometimes afflicts the great.

Many of Marlborough's advocates argue that, great though his achievements were, he would have been even more successful had he not been 'hampered by the intransigence of the Dutch field-deputies, incompetent civilians attached to the Duke's staff whose agreement in any project had to be obtained before it could proceed'.[11] There is a strongly nationalistic element in much that is written about Marlborough, and in this instance it is worth recalling that an Allied military defeat in Flanders risked having far more effect upon the Dutch than upon the English, conveniently insulated from the armies of Louis XIV by Shakespeare's 'moat defensive'. When Marlborough clashed with the Dutch, as he did from time to time, he was not always right and they were not always wrong, and there were times when he avoided the complicating longueurs of coalition politics by outright deception.

One of the pleasures of the research for this book is that it took me back to G.M. Trevelyan's incomparable trilogy on the reign of Queen Anne. If earnest modern scholars have unearthed evidence which changes some of Trevelyan's findings, few have his ability to bring an age to life. He concluded his assessment of Marlborough's personality by speculating that:

> Perhaps the secret of Marlborough's character is that there is no secret. Abnormal only in his genius, he may have been guided by motives very much like those that sway commoner folk. He loved his wife, with her witty talk and her masterful temper, which he was man enough to hold in check without quarrelling. He loved his country; he was attached to her religion and free institutions. He loved money, in which he was not singular. He loved, as every true man must, to use his peculiar talents to their full; and as in his case they required a vast field for their full exercise, he was therefore ambitious. Last, but not least, he loved his fellow men, if scrupulous humaneness and consideration for others are signs of loving one's fellows. He was the prince of courtesy.[12]

In all this, though, Trevelyan recognised that he was taking issue with his distinguished uncle, whose surname he bore as his own middle name. Thomas Babington Macaulay was a poet (who, if he had never written another word, would surely be remembered for his account of Horatius holding that bridge), politician and the dominant British historian in the mid-Victorian era. Macaulay, argued Trevelyan, 'adopted his unfavourable reading of Marlborough's motives and character straight from Swift and the Tory pamphleteers of the latter part of Anne's reign'. Yet he was

> less often misled by traditional Whig views than by his own over-confident, lucid mentality, which always saw things in black and white, but never in grey . . . He instinctively desired to make Marlborough's genius stand out bright against the background of his villainy.[13]

The villainy, maintained Macaulay, was certainly dark enough. Marlborough was wholly immoral. He 'owed his rise to his sister's shame', and was then 'kept by the most profane, impious and shameless of harlots', Barbara Villiers, Countess of Castlemaine. He was woefully ignorant, and 'could not spell the most common words in his own language'. His avarice knew no bounds, and 'though he drew a large allowance under pretence of keeping a public table, he never asked an officer to dinner'. And he was, quite simply, a traitor, rendering 'wicked and shameful service to the Jacobite cause' by leaking information of a 1694 expedition against Brest so that its troops were slaughtered and its commander, a personal rival, was slain.[14]

This is not the moment to deal with Macaulay's charges in detail, although it is clear that the documents he used to formulate some of them do, in themselves, demonstrate their own falsehood, thereby making Churchill's accusation of 'liar' more appropriate than Trevelyan's defence of his forebear as an honest historian misled by his emotions and his sources. 'Lord Macaulay is not to be trusted either to narrate facts accurately, to state facts truly, or to answer the judgement of history with impartiality,' wrote a barrister who applied his forensic skills to Macaulay's methods, and it is impossible for a modern historian to disagree.[15]

Even though Macaulay erred in his attacks on Marlborough, it is already evident that there is much more to the man than stout hagiography can possibly acknowledge. We might avoid at least part of the problem by concentrating on the military aspects of his career, and by passing rapidly over his early life to see him emerge, full-fledged, as captain general of the English army in the Low Countries. Indeed, David Chandler, one the most gifted historians to write about Marlborough in recent times, sidestepped the issue in his *Marlborough as a Military Commander* by considering the duke in his role as a general, although there are few men less suited to the description 'simple soldier'.[16] To consider Marlborough purely as a general is as misleading as it would be to see, say, Paul McCartney as only a classical composer, Alexander Borodin as just a chemist, or Winston S. Churchill as a simple historian.

Part of my task, then, is to get as close as I can to the man that Churchill loved to call 'Duke John'. However, almost like hunted game that knows its tracks will be followed, Marlborough himself made my task no easier. Although the shelves of the British Library groan beneath the weight of the Blenheim Papers, with thousands of letters showing him in a variety of lights, as husband, lover, courtier, politician, alliance manager, diplomat, commander-in-chief, prosecutor, defendant and even interior designer, he rarely let his mask slip. Wellington is the general to whom he is most often compared, and is the only other British commander who has ever exercised command on sufficient scale, for long enough and in varied enough circumstances for him also to be considered a truly great general. Yet despite his notorious secret-iveness, in his later years Wellington was always prepared to unburden himself to friends or diarists. There was generally an answer to those questions that began, 'Tell me, Duke . . .' and the Wellington of old age tells us, across the nuts and port, about the commander of his youth and middle years. It is just possible that Marlborough might have done the same had he enjoyed a long retirement, marching slowly to meet a sloth-ful death. But even then I doubt it: he was too mindful of those necessary treasons of his early life, too well aware that he had been all things to most men, to let us inside his mind.

Many of my sources will be familiar to those who know the period. I have made extensive use of the duke's own words, going back to the originals in the British Library when I have had to, but also availing myself of Sir George Murray's five-volume edition of Marlborough's dispatches and Henry L. Snyder's three volumes of the Marlborough–Godolphin correspondence. Both Marlborough's quartermaster general (chief of staff by modern standards), William Cadogan, and his private secretary, Adam de Cardonnel, have left papers which throw useful light on the way that Marlborough's headquarters worked.

Viscount Chelsea, heir to the present Earl Cadogan, recently discovered some of his ancestor's papers, and through his kindness I am, I believe, the second historian to consult them. They show just how much routine work Marlborough entrusted to Cadogan, and give early grounds for suspecting that even if command is, in a legal and spiritual sense, indivisible, it is harder than we once thought to see just where Marlborough ended and Cadogan began.

Marlborough's own hold on political power would scarcely have been possible without his wife's intimate relationship with Queen Anne. Sarah Marlborough is rarely much further away from these pages than she was from her husband's thoughts. I have not only used her correspondence, but a good deal of her self-justifying pamphleteering, much of it produced with the aid of collaborators like Bishop Gilbert Burnet, who generally strove to be objective, and her man of affairs, Arthur Maynwaring, who did not. While no assessment of the politics of the age could be complete without taking the duchess's views into account, her words require more caveats than most. Here she is on the subject of Queen Anne, with whom she had once enjoyed a friendship so very close that some writers have detected lesbianism.

> Queen Anne had a person and appearance not at all ungraceful, till she grew exceeding gross and corpulent. There was something of majesty in her look, but mixed with a sullen and constant frown, that plainly betrayed a gloomy soul, and a cloudiness of disposition within. She seemed to inherit a good deal of her father's moroseness, which naturally produced in her the same sort of stubborn positiveness in many cases . . . as well as the same sort of bigotry in religion.
>
> Her memory was exceeding great, almost to wonder, and . . . she could, whenever she pleased, forget what others would have thought themselves obliged by truth and honour to remember, and remember all such things as others would think it an happiness to forget. Indeed she chose to retain in it very little besides ceremonies and customs of courts . . . so that her conversation, which otherwise might have been enlivened by so great a memory, was only made more empty and trifling but is chiefly turning upon *fashions* and rules of precedence, or observations upon the weather, or some such poor topics, without any variety of entertainment.[17]

There are two points of which I have no doubt whatsoever. The first is that the Marlboroughs' relationship, despite its stormy moments, was a genuine love-match. The second is that if there is indeed an afterlife I must look out for squalls soon after crossing the bar, for Sarah was as jealous of her lord's memory as of her own historical reputation.

No student of the period can be unaware of the fact that there are far fewer letter-writers and diarists on hand to describe the War of Spanish Succession than there would be, a century later, to tell us about the Peninsular War. However, there are certainly enough to get us in amongst the powder-smoke. That dour Cameronian Lieutenant Colonel Blackader complains of the army's profanity; Captain Richard Parker takes pride in watching his own Irish soldiers beat their countrymen in French service at Malplaquet; Corporal Matthew Bishop assures us, not once but several times, that Marlborough could not have won the war without him; and Brigadier General Richard Kane warns us of the perils of premature surrender – and the dangers of too resolute a defence.

John Wilson, the 'old Flanderkin Sergeant', recalls attacking the Schellenberg with his front-rank men clutching fascines 'in order to break the enemy's shot in advancing'.[18] Private John Marshall Deane of the 1st Foot Guards recalls that at the same action, 'being strongly entrenched they killed and mortified abundance of our men both officers and soldiers'.[19] Chaplain Josias Sandby maintained a useful journal of the Blenheim campaign, often attributed to Marlborough's chaplain-general Francis Hare. Chaplain Samuel Noyes wrote assiduously to his bishop, hoping no doubt that civil preferment might follow military accomplishment.[20]

On the French side, the Duke of Berwick, illegitimate son of James II by Marlborough's sister Arabella Churchill and probably the most competent of the later Stuarts, published a set of memoirs before he was killed in action. Colonel François de la Colonie commanded a Bavarian grenadier battalion composed of French deserters, and escaped from the storming of the Schellenberg with his coat scorched by musket-fire and his long riding-boots jettisoned to run the better. The Count de Mérode-Westerloo, in the perplexing way of the age a Flemish noble-man but a loyal officer in the army of Louis XIV, tells us what it was like to wake up at Blenheim to see the Allies advancing steadily on the French camp but to find everyone else asleep. Marshal Camille de Tallard, the French commander that day, has left us his own account of the action. He told the French minister of war that he had had a bad campaign plan foisted upon him, and found it impossible to get on with his allies: 'it is a fine lesson that we should only have one man commanding an army, and that it is a great misfortune to have to deal with a prince of the humour of M. the Elector of Bavaria . . .' Having been traduced by his senior colleagues, Tallard tells us that he was then let down by his men: 'The bulk of the cavalry did badly, I say very badly, for they did not break a single enemy squadron.'[21] Sadly, his subordinates did not share his view. Another of those accounts whose writer lamented that his own courage and prescience were not matched elsewhere concluded: 'You know, Sir, better than me whose fault this is.'[22]

'Captain' Peter Drake served in the Spanish, Dutch, English and French armies, often joining one without having completed the tiresome formalities which might properly have accompanied his discharge from another. He was wounded at Malplaquet while serving with the *Maison du Roi*, the French Household Cavalry, and tells us how he owed his life to the duke's humanitarian intervention at the close of that terrible day.

Sicco van Goslinga's *Mémoires relatifs à la Guerre de Succession* show just how unwise it is to follow the prevailing contemporary English view of the Dutch as dour and unhelpful, any more than the Dutch view of the English as dirty and drunken, as necessarily correct. Goslinga, let it be said, is no more inherently trustworthy than any other witness. No contemporary, however influential, had more than a limited view of events. All tended to supplement what they could themselves remember (which might not in itself be accurate) with what they heard from others, who were themselves rarely fully informed. And most, in the way of things, had likes and dislikes which might reflect nothing more than the imponderables of human emotion. However, Goslinga was in the Allied army but not of it, and in regular contact with Marlborough but never dependent on his goodwill for advancement. He saw Marlborough in his depths as well as at his heights: riding out with him to his outposts in the small hours when it seemed certain that the French had trapped him, or sharing the duke's riding-cloak when both lay down to snatch some sleep after a long and successful pursuit.

Goslinga gives us a pen-picture which at last begins to catch some of the light and shade of Marlborough.

Here is his portrait, as far as I am able to paint it. I do not speak of his fortune, nor of the manner in which he began to make it: his conduct towards his great benefactor and his first benefactress are things well known, and add nothing to the matter in hand. He was born a gentleman: his stature was above average and was one of the finest one might see: he had a perfectly beautiful face, with two fine and sparkling eyes of an admirable colour, a pink and white complexion which a woman might envy, and fine teeth . . . He had much spirit . . . very clear and solid judgment, swift and deep penetration, knowing his people well and able to distinguish real merit from false; speaking well and agreeably even in French, which he actually spoke with poor grammar but with a harmonious tone of voice.

On the other hand, Goslinga found him

capable of profound, even the most dangerous deception, which he covers by manners and expressions which seem to express the utmost frankness: he has a boundless ambition, and the most sordid avarice, which influences all his conduct: if he has courage, which he doubtless has, whatever his enemies say, he has certainly not got the firmness of character which makes the real hero . . . He did not know much about military discipline, and gave free rein to the soldier, who committed frightful disorders. He also knew little of the detail of the profession, less than was proper for a commander-in-chief. Here are the weaknesses which, however, do not detract from the rare talents of this really great man.[23]

Some of Goslinga's words find answering echoes elsewhere. The two great English diarists of the age, Samuel Pepys and John Evelyn, both had a view of Marlborough. Pepys, 'sole counsellor' to the newly ennobled George Legge, Lord Dartmouth, on his 1683 fact-finding trip to the English garrison of Tangier, chatted with his master about John Churchill, as he then was. Dartmouth:

tells me of the Duke of York's kindness to him and how Churchill was made what he is by my Lord Rochester, only to lessen him; and that all he knows Churchill rewards himself by, is his lying with their wives, which he says is not certain as to my ladies Rochester and Sunderland.[24]

This was the sort of salacious gossip that Pepys loved, and in part Dartmouth's words no doubt reflect the suspicion of one fast-rising man for another. Yet there were persistent rumours that Churchill turned his remarkable physical attractiveness to his advantage, and he is certainly not the first British commander to profit from being big and bonny; nor, no doubt, will he be the last.

In 1702, well before Marlborough had won his greatest victories, John Evelyn complained of the 'excess of honour conferred by the Queen on the Earl of Marlborough, by making him a Knight of the Garter, and a Duke, for the success of but one campaign', but added: 'He is a very handsome person, well-spoken and affable, and supports his want of acquired knowledge by keeping good company.'[25] In February 1705, just a year before his death, Evelyn visited Lord Godolphin.

> I went to wait on my Lord Treasurer, where was the victorious Duke of Marlborough, who came to me and took me by the hand with extraordinary familiarity and civility, as formerly he was used to do, without any alteration of his good nature. He had a most rich George in a Sardonyx set with diamonds of very great value, for the rest, very plain.* I had not seen him for some years, and believed he might have forgotten me.[26]

This is a telling anecdote. Marlborough's social accomplishments were legendary, and his ability to remember old acquaintances did much to help him. The Earl of Ailesbury remembered that when he was a Jacobite exile and Marlborough was the queen's captain general and Allied commander-in-chief, the duke gave him dinner at his own 'little table' at headquarters, and held his hand for part of the meal, although (and here is another penetrating insight) he ensured that their clasped hands were hidden under a napkin.

Portraits in a Gallery

We can get much closer to our quarry in words than we ever can in pictures. Portraits often deceive, and it is perhaps in the early eighteenth century that the deception is most complete. There are the great men of the age, with well-scrubbed pink-and-white faces, staring complacently at their world from beneath full-bottomed wigs, lips pursed in the half-smile of those who know that life has treated them well. The peruke's

---

* The George referred to here was the Riband Badge of the Order of the Garter, with a central depiction of St George killing the dragon, usually cut in cameo in hard stone, encircled by large rose-cut brilliants, usually diamonds. Sardonyx is a form of onyx in which white alternates with cornelian.

soft curls and the snowy lace of a jabot tumble onto a coat whose stuff and hue betokens the wearer's status: a cleric's black broadcloth, a merchant's prosperous blue or plum, or a soldier's martial red. Peers often wear the ermine of their House, with a coronet denoting their rank (six silver balls on a plain silver gilt circlet for a baron, and on to the chased coronet with its eight strawberry leaves for a duke) dangling from the noble fingers or tossed onto a table just within the picture's frame. In their portraits generals appear in the armour they would never have worn on the battlefield, sometimes with a plumed helmet, as useless then as a general's ivory-hilted dress sword is today, standing in for a peer's coronet.

Women are plump-faced, opulent of bust and shoulders, and usually portrayed with their heads tilted ever so slightly to the right to allow the artist to throw some shadow beneath a soft jawline. Children are rarely allowed much in the way of childhood. Once boys had been breeched, at the age of four or five, they appeared as miniature adults. Johann Baptiste Clostermann's huge family portrait of the Marlboroughs, painted in about 1694, shows the parents and their five children against theatrical drapes. John, later Marquess of Blandford, their eldest son, is stepping up onto the dais, looking back at the artist and gesturing proudly towards his elegant family. He was nine years old at the time.

A year later Nicholas de Largillière painted James II's only legitimate son, James Francis Edward Stuart ('the Old Pretender') and his sister Louisa Maria Theresa. Although the young prince was only seven and his sister just three, both are dressed for court: James is wearing long coat, lace jabot and silk stockings, and Louisa has a dress with a train and the tall *fontange* headdress. William Henry, Duke of Gloucester, was the only one of Queen Anne's many children to live beyond infancy, and was regarded by many as the heir most likely to prevent the restoration of his uncle James II. In 1699 Sir Godfrey Kneller painted him as a warrior prince, with a soldier's cuirass: the boy was ten years old and had just a year to live.

There is enough symbolism to keep costume historians busily engaged for years. Gentlemen advertise their status by wearing swords, the slim, straight-bladed small sword in town and the stubbier hunting sword in the country. Races at Newmarket, then the only major national meeting, were an exception, for folk of all classes met on equal terms, turning out 'suitable to the humour and design of the place for horse sports', with nobody wearing swords. Spurs were important even if there was no evidence of a horse, for they showed that although the sitter might not be riding at the time, he could vault into the saddle at a moment's notice. Not for nothing did the Latin inscriptions on gentry's tomb-stones style a knight as *equitus* and a gentleman as *armiger*. In Charles II's time red shoe-heels – a fashion borrowed, like so much else, from France – suggested noble rank, and the fashion spread so that officers of the Restoration army were as identifiable by their bright heels as their great-grandsons were to be by their epaulettes. The greatest officers of state, like the lord treasurer and secretary of state, carried thin white staffs of office. Sidney, Earl Godolphin, had his made short enough to be carried in a sedan chair, while the Earl of Rochester had his, of the longer variety, carried by a bareheaded footman to allay any doubts about the distinction of his chair's occupant.

A portrait of Sarah, Duchess of Marlborough painted in about 1700 had a gold key added to its waist in 1702. In the interim Sarah had become keeper of the privy purse to the new queen, Anne, and the key confirms the status that her expression already suggests: she is a woman whose beauty is matched, at last, by her wealth and influence. And so pigment is splashed across canvas. Mouths curve like cupid's bow, dogs stare admiringly at masters, steeds curvet without apparent inconvenience to riders, and occasionally, like extras in a drama, lesser mortals gather slain game or ply musket and bayonet amidst the background smoke.

None of this is a great deal of help to historians. Even court artists in England, it is true, could rarely disguise that bulbous blue-eyed, faintly irascible expression that characterised the Hanoverians, any more than their colleagues in Vienna could do much with the Hapsburg jaw. However, artists seldom get us beyond polite generalities. Portraits of Prince Eugène of Savoy-Carignan, Marlborough's great collaborator, give no real sense that he was widely regarded as one of the ugliest men of his age, and almost always had his mouth slightly open. Louis XIV, for all his sneer of cold command, was five feet five inches tall, a full five inches taller than Charles I but an inch and a half shorter than William of Orange – who was four inches shorter than his wife Mary. William himself was, if you will forgive the phrase, no oil painting: he was thin and somewhat hunchbacked, and his face, already striving to accommodate a prominent nose, was heavily pockmarked.

While artists were happy enough to use their skills to reflect status and lineage and to hint at accomplishments and aspirations, in the main they present us with a great number of plump-faced, well-to-do gentle-men in wigs, accompanied by ladies perhaps too generously built for modern taste. Charles II's mistresses were generally Junoesque but pretty, while James II's were as substantial, but so very, very plain that Charles quipped that they had been imposed upon his brother by his confessor as a penance. Sir Peter Lely's portraits, however, make them look so alike that even contemporaries complained:

> Sir Peter Lely when he had painted the Duchess of Cleveland's picture, he put something of Cleveland's face as her languishing eyes into every picture, so that all his pictures had an air of one another, and the eyes were sleepy alike. So that Mr Walker the painter said Lely's pictures were all brothers and sisters.[27]

Century of Revolution

At one level, the barrier that portraiture interposes between us and Marlborough's age is a useful corrective. Philip Guedalla, whose books did so much to arouse my passion for history, wrote of the world 'spinning down the long groove of the eighteenth century'. How wrong he was. The world does not, so to speak, change step as a new century appears, and there is rarely a well-oiled hinge between one epoch and another. Marlborough was in many ways a creature of the seventeenth century, profoundly marked by his family's experience of the Civil War. But his thoughts and character were forming at just the time that the spiritual and political convictions that had made the war possible were changing. Christianity, as Christopher Wren's light and airy churches testify, was becoming more rational and less constricting. The execution of Charles I on the one hand, and the Restoration of his son on the other, left both royalists and radicals aware that God's favour could prove all too transient. Science was fast becoming secularised, and a series of major discoveries, starting with Harvey's work on the circulation of the blood and continuing with the ideas of Newton, Boyle and Hooke, began to replace old mysteries with new rationalism.

This science, however, had yet to transform the economy. Marlborough died while his country was experiencing the first birthpangs of the Industrial Revolution. The road system he knew would have been familiar to his Tudor ancestors: York and Exeter were still over three days' travel from London. John Evelyn's house at Wotton, near Guildford in Surrey, was twenty-six miles from London but was 'so securely placed as if it were 100'. The first turnpike (essentially a toll road) was established in 1663, and there were only seven turnpikes by 1700: the great explosion did not come till after 1750. The intrepid

Celia Fiennes reported in 1698 that her route around England 'was in many places full of holes, though it is served by a bar at which passengers pay a penny a horse to the maintaining of the way'. John Byng, writing a century later, mused:

> I am just old enough to remember turnpike roads, few and bad; and when travelling was slow, difficult and, in carriages, dangerous . . . In the days of bad roads the country could not be stripped of its timber or despoiled of its honesty, cheapness, ancient customs and civility; every gentleman, then, was bowed to with reverence, and 'A good morning to you, master. Good evening. Good journey to you, sir,' were always presented; with every old-fashioned wish, and compliment of the season . . .
>
> Even till lately, there were hollow ways from Grays Inn Lane to Kentish Town, and a long deep water to be waded through from Mother red-Caps in the road to Highgate. All the Hertfordshire roads were deep ravines.[28]

The first breaths of the wind of change could already be felt. The swash and buckle of Restoration drama was light years away from the masques of the early part of the century. The witty and elegant essays of Joseph Addison and Richard Steele are, suggests one editor, like old silver, whose fashion is still well regarded even if its weight is negligible.[29] Political thought was also changing fast. In 1690 John Locke affirmed that 'All men are naturally in a state of perfect freedom to order their actions and dispose of their possessions and persons as they think fit without asking the leave or depending upon the will of any man.' Locke could get away with this in Britain, but these were dangerous ideas elsewhere: the Enlightenment was still two generations away, and few contemporary European monarchs would have tolerated such words.

For some historians the Glorious Revolution of 1688, which saw James II replaced by William and Mary, is the real turning point, although it accomplished less than many contemporaries hoped. For others, though, the real break comes with the Hanoverian succession, which brought George I bloodlessly to the throne in 1714, even though Jacobitism was to remain a threat until the defeat of Charles Edward Stuart, James's grandson the 'Young Pretender', in 1745–46. Were our focus here European rather than more narrowly British then we might see the 1713 Treaty of Utrecht, which ended the War of Spanish Succession, and with it the more extravagant ambitions of Louis XIV, as a sharp bend in history's long and rutted road.

It is not my purpose to answer the undergraduate question as to whether the seventeenth century really ended in 1688 or 1714. Suffice it to say, though, that the most important years of Marlborough's active career lay between these dates, and that he lived through a period of quite extraordinary change and uncertainty. This was much more the case with the military profession than most biographers acknowledge. He was commissioned into an army which, with its pikes, matchlock muskets and lobster-tail helmets, would not have surprised Oliver Cromwell, and he died as captain general of a force whose infantry had made its reputation with those measured volleys that Wellington so admired.

What is history to us was an unknown and challenging future to John Churchill; even to begin to grasp him we must break from what some historians call 'presentism', the inability to see anything save through the lens of the present moment. None of the events of 1688–1714 was predestined. A more adroit James II might have retained the kingdom bequeathed to him by his more supple brother; the 'Protestant Wind' of 1688 might so easily have blown up into a Catholic gale; the cannonball which grazed William III at the Boyne in 1690 might have killed him just as surely as another ball decapitated the very capable Jacobite commander, the marquis de St Ruth, at the deciding moment at the battle of Aughrim the following year.

There were no certainties for a man like John Churchill. He was stripped of all his offices twice in his career, imprisoned in the Tower on the first occasion and effectively exiled on the second. He ran the risk of the battlefield death that snatched so many of his comrades and opponents: at Ramillies a cannonball took the head off his equerry as he held the duke's stirrup for him to mount a fresh charger. He lived in a world where disease was rife and today's hero was tomorrow's corpse. Smallpox was no respecter of persons: King William lost his parents and his wife to the disease, and it carried off Queen Anne's only surviving son the Duke of Gloucester and Marlborough's own heir the Marquess of Blandford. Indeed, of the five children in that carefully posed Clostermann painting of Marlborough's family only two lived beyond their twenties. We must judge Marlborough in the light of his times, not our own, and a biographer's first task must be to sketch out the background to the portrait he is painting.

There are indeed moments when the immediacy of the spoken word strips away the years. The Reverend Andrew Paschall, rector of the Somerset village of Chedzoy, tells us how, when the rebel Duke of

Monmouth's men were first detected in their night attack on the royal army's bivouac at Sedgemoor in 1686, a trooper of the Horse Guards galloped

> full speed to the camp, calls with all imaginable earnestness, 20 times at least, 'Beat your drums, the enemy is come. For the Lord's sake beat your drums.' He then rode back with the like speed the way he had come . . . Now the drums beat, the drummers running to it, even barefoot for haste. All fly to arms.[30]

Yet there are as many times when the period seems more ancient than modern. It is easy to forget how deep the iron of Charles I's execution had entered into the royalist soul. On 17 September 1661 (with young John Churchill still unbreeched) John Evelyn wrote:

> Scot, Scroope, Cook and Jones, suffered for reward of their iniquities at Charing Cross, in sight of the place where they put to death their natural Prince, and in the presence of the King his son who they also sought to kill. I saw not their execution, but met their quarters mangled and cut and reeking as they were brought from the gallows in baskets on the hurdle. Oh the miraculous providence of God![31]

Male traitors were hanged, drawn and quartered, a gruesome process that involved being dragged through the streets on a hurdle, partially strangled, and then castrated and disembowelled. The victim's guts were 'burnt before his face' before he was beheaded and quartered. By 1745 the executioner would customarily leave his victim hanging long enough for him to be unconscious, but as late as 1715 some men were 'bowelled alive and seeing'. The victim's quarters, duly pickled for longevity, were stuck up at suitable points to ensure that the message was widely distributed. When Captain-Lieutenant Sir Thomas Armstrong of the Life Guards was executed as a traitor in 1683 one of his quarters was sent off to Stafford, where he had been Member of Parliament. The monarch might, by exercise of his prerogative, remit the punishment to beheading or simple hanging. At the time of the Popish Plot (1678–81), William, Lord Russell, had argued that the king did not have it in his power to show such leniency, and when he himself was convicted of treason in 1683 he bravely made no personal appeal for clemency. He was granted the favour of the axe, although the executioner botched his job.

Female traitors, whether they were guilty of high treason towards the monarch or petty treason – an act against what was perceived as being the natural order of things, like the murder of a husband or employer – were burnt at the stake. This too might be commuted to beheading (as it was for Alice Lisle, executed in the square at Winchester in 1685), or the executioner might be privately ordered by the sheriff to stab or strangle his victim before the fire took hold. The devout and philan-thropic Elizabeth Gaunt, convicted of harbouring rebels after Monmouth's rebellion in 1685, probably has the dreadful distinction of being the last woman in Britain to be burnt alive by judicial process. She met her end with exemplary courage, but the spectacle was profoundly shocking even to spectators used to brutality. Gilbert Burnet wrote that 'Penn, the Quaker, told me, he saw her die. She laid the straw about her for burning her speedily, and behaved herself in such a manner, that all the spectators melted in tears.'[32]

There was a widespread feeling that such savagery went against the spirit of the age, and James II's inability to understand this was not least amongst the causes of his failure as a monarch. It also ran squarely against what seemed to be natural justice. Lord Grey of Wark, who had commanded Monmouth's cavalry with towering ineptitude, bought his life for a full confession, the surrender of large parts of his estates, and the promise to give evidence against other prominent members of the rebellion. When he testified against Lord Delamere, arraigned before his peers on 16 January 1686, he proved such a poor witness that Delamere got off. The first peer to give his verdict that day was John, Lord Churchill, the junior baron present, who announced: 'Not Guilty, upon my honour.'

The barbarity of gallows, pyre, block and pillory sits uncomfortably alongside the poetry of John Dryden or the witty dramas of Aphra Behn. It was there in the background when Steele sketched out that genial baronet, Sir Roger de Coverly.

> He is now in his Fifty sixth year, cheerful, gay and hearty, keeps a good House both in Town and Country; a great Lover of Mankind; but there is such a mirthful Cast in his Behaviour, that he is rather beloved than esteemed: His Tenants grow rich, his Servants look satisfied, all the young Women profess Love to him, and the young Men are glad of his Company: When he comes into a House he calls the Servants by their Names, and talks all the way up Stairs to a Visit. I must not omit that Sir ROGER is a Justice of the *Quorum*; that he fills a chair at

a Quarter-Sessions with great abilities, and three months ago gain'd
universal Applause by explaining a Passage in the Game-Act.[33]

The Game Act of 1670 limited the right to kill game to those owning
property worth £100 a year, perhaps half of one per cent of the population, and was rigidly enforced by justices of the peace like Sir Roger,
whose helpful legal explanations might have escaped a defendant
who stood to lose the skin off his back if convicted. But it was wholly
consistent with the spirit of the age that Sir Roger spent his morning in
vigorous pursuit of a hare, only, at the very end, to scoop up his exhausted
quarry and release it in his park, where it joined 'several of these
Prisoners of Wars', for he 'could not find it in his heart to murder a
Creature that had given him so much Diversion'.[34]

Sir Roger 'fought a Duel upon his first coming to town', and there too
he was in good company. While Richard Brinsley Sheridan was later to
write of 'sharps and snaps', in our period the flintlock pistol ('snap')
had not yet come of age as a duelling weapon, although Major General
William Stewart and Captain Thomas Bellew agreed to use pistols when
they met in 1700 because both had wounded right hands. Gentlemen
usually went at one another with their small swords, either in the relatively
formal circumstance of a duel, or the wholly casual surroundings of
coffee house, club or street.

Affairs of honour swept up all those who thought, however flimsy the
grounds, that they might have honour to defend. Peter Drake rubbed
along at the very bottom end of gentility, and when he kept the Queen's
Arms tavern near St Clement Danes he 'provided bob-wigs, blue aprons,
etc, proper for the business of a vintner; these I wore at home, but could
not yet leave off the tie-wig and sword when I went abroad'.[35] He duelled
whenever the mood took him. Scarcely had he reached Holland, with
the first of his many regiments, in 1689, than he had cross words with
'one Butler, who was a quartermaster in a regiment of Dutch horse . . .
I ran him in the sword arm, and he ran me through the left breast, and
so we parted, to take care of ourselves.'[36]

Nearer the top end of the social scale, the most celebrated duel of the
age saw the Whig Lord Mohun, a reformed rake who had already twice
been tried by his peers for murder, and the Tory grandee the Duke of
Hamilton (who had sired an illegitimate child on Marlborough's own
bastard daughter), just appointed ambassador to Versailles, meet in
Hyde Park early on the morning of 12 November 1712. Mohun and
Hamilton rushed at one another 'like wild beasts, not fencing or parrying'.

Mohun, run through the chest, was killed on the spot, but he lashed out as he fell and the tip of his small sword opened a vein in Hamilton's arm, leaving him bleeding to death. Their seconds, Major General Macartney (recently dismissed the service for toasting damnation to the new Tory ministry) for Mohun, and Colonel John Hamilton for the duke, had not let time hang heavy on their hands, and were at it too: Hamilton was pinked in the lower leg. Hamilton later claimed that he was holding his wounded principal when Mohun ran up and stabbed the prostrate man, and although the evidence was uncorroborated, Macartney wisely fled abroad. He reappeared after the accession of George I, stood his trial at the King's Bench, and was acquitted.

Officers, with their keen sense of honour and arms conveniently to hand, were always ready to lug out, though the British army never reached the quarrelsome pinnacle of its French opponents. De la Colonie fought his first duel when still a cadet, but his opponent, a lieutenant and assistant adjutant of the Régiment de Navarre, summoned help by yelling '*À moi, Navarre,*' and thus unsportingly turning private squabble into public riot. Peter Drake, then serving in a French regiment, was with 'thirteen friends and bottle companions' when a dispute arose between two of them. They decided on a mass duel, and as they were walking to a suitable ground Lieutenant de la Salle, observing that the numbers were uneven, cheerfully joined the smaller group. For a moment there was a chance of reconciliation, but de la Salle observed that the wine was drawn and they must drink it.

> The fight began, every man tilting at his opponent, and the two principals engaged; and in a short time killed each other. There was another lost on the part for which I fought, and some wounded on both sides; and I had the good fortune to wound and disarm Monsieur de la Salle.[37]

British officers, though, were no slouches. In 1692, when Lord Berkeley's regiment of dragoons was quartered in Louvain a convivial evening at Captain Edward Mortimer's lodgings was interrupted by the drunken arrival of Captain Thomas Lloyd, who had recently left the regiment in disgrace. As the officers walked out across the marketplace, Lloyd blamed Major Giles Spencer for his misfortunes: both men drew, and Lloyd was wounded in the thigh, dying soon afterwards. Spencer was court-martialled, and acquitted on the grounds of self-defence. Two years later, despite the fact that the Allied army was marching flat-out to stop the French from crossing the Scheldt near Oudenarde, Sandy Dundas found time to kill Cornet Conway of Lord Polwarth's Regiment.

In 1699 the foppish young Conway Seymour met Captain George Kirke of the Royal Horse Guards in Hyde Park, and high words were exchanged. Seymour was stabbed in the neck, and seemed likely to recover when he embarked on a debauch which made him vomit, reopening the wound and causing an infection which killed him. Kirke was convicted of manslaughter and 'burned in the hand', branded with a hot iron, a punishment made rather less damaging if one could afford to pay to have the iron dipped in cold water first. He was temporarily suspended from his commission, but went on to be promoted.[38] In 1711 the Duke of Argyll, a member of the anti-Marlborough faction, heard from 'a penny post letter sent him from an unknown hand' that Colonel Court of the foot guards had refused to drink his health, saying, 'Damn him he would not drink the health of a man that changed sides.' When the matter was put to the good colonel he confessed that he had been in drink at the time and had no idea at all what he might have said, but would not deny His Grace satisfaction: 'They fought in Hyde Park, and the Duke disarmed him, and there's an end of the business.'

In 1708 it was said by Ensign Hugh Shaw that the Master of Sinclair, captain-lieutenant in Colonel Preston's Regiment, 'had bowed himself towards the ground for a considerable time altogether' in the hard-fought little battle of Wynendaele. Captain Alexander Shaw, the ensign's older brother, took his sibling's side, but Sinclair killed them both, allegedly by hitting Alexander over the head with a concealed stick before wounding him mortally, and then going on to pistol young Hugh 'before he had time to put himself in a posture of defence'.[39] The case caused serious difficulties, for Sir John Shaw, brother of the two dead men, petitioned the queen, demanding the death penalty, while John Sinclair, eldest son of a Scots peer, was not without clout of his own. The solution was typical of the age. Sinclair was convicted by court-martial on one count of murder, but miraculously escaped from custody. On 26 May 1709 Marlborough wrote to Lord Raby, then ambassador to Berlin.

This will be delivered to Y[our].E[xcellency]. by the Master of St Clair . . . who having had the misfortune to kill two brothers of Sir John Shaw the last campaign in Flanders, for one of which being tried and condemned by a court martial, he has found means to get away, and must now seek employment elsewhere. If Y.E. will please to take him under your protection and recommend him to your court, I shall take it as a particular favour . . . [40]

Influence and Interest

Influence, that glutinous, omnipresent lubricant that the age called 'interest', was never far away, and we cannot hope to understand the period without analysing it. It had a number of components. There was a strong strain of two-way obligation laced with self-interest, with tenants supporting their landlords, officers their colonels, and the heads of families striving to provide for distant relatives. Most contemporaries thought that the process was wholly proper, and the tomb of Elizabeth Bate, widow of the Reverend Richard Bate, who died in 1751 at the age of seventy-four, proudly announced that:

> She was honourably descended
> And by means of her Alliance to
> The illustrious family of Stanhope
> She had the merit to obtain
> For her husband and children
> Twelve several employments
> In Church and State.[41]

Yet even contemporaries, well aware of how the system operated, sometimes thought that it went too far. In 1722 a news-sheet lambasted Robert Walpole, the first man to be widely regarded as prime minister.

> First Lord of the Treasury, Mr Walpole. Chancellor of the Exchequer, Mr Walpole. Clerk of the Pells, Mr Walpole's son. Customs of London, second son of Mr Walpole . . . Secretary of the Treasury, Mr Walpole's brother. Secretary to Ireland, Mr Walpole's brother. Secretary to the Postmaster-General, Mr Walpole's brother in law.[42]

Many posts, lucrative in themselves, brought with them the right to appoint to other posts, and there was a palpable pull-through as interest groups prospered, and its distressing reverse as the fall of powerful patrons sent misfortune knocking on down the line. In 1718 Sir Christopher Wren lost his post as surveyor general as part of a wider redistribution of spoils. Sir John Vanbrugh would not accept the office 'out of tenderness to Sir Christopher Wren', so it went instead to an incompetent nonentity, William Benson.[43]

Sarah Marlborough often repeated that her cousin Abigail Hill, who was to supplant her in the queen's affections, had been raised from nothing by her deployment of interest. Abigail was the daughter of a City merchant 'by a sister of my father', and as soon as Sarah heard that she was in want she sent her ten guineas. When the Duke of Gloucester died Sarah got her £200 a year out of the queen's privy purse, and secured a place in the customs for her son. She recommended Abigail's brother Jack – 'a tall boy, whom I clothed . . . and put to school at St Albans' – to the Duke of Marlborough.

> And although my Lord always said that Jack Hill *was good for nothing* yet to oblige me he made him his aide de camp, and afterwards gave him a regiment. But it was his sister's interest that raised him to be a general, and to command in that memorable [Sarahese for deeply unsuccessful] expedition to Quebec: I had no share in doing him these honours.[44]

As Sarah's interest waned, Abigail's waxed. In 1710 Lord Raby told his brother Peter that 'Lord Powlett has complemented Brigadier Masham [Abigail's husband] by having him chose a member in a borough he controls.' It seems likely that Sam Masham sensibly chose himself, for he became MP for Ilchester at about this time, though the grateful Tories soon ensured that he had the peerage that his wife's new interest demanded.

With Sarah deprived of all her offices she had no interest, and she always respected the few who stood by her in these chilly times. Lady Scarborough wrote to her on 5 November 1711, after Sarah had been succeeded as keeper of the queen's privy purse by the Duchess of Somerset. Sarah annotated the missive: 'A very kind letter when I had lost my interest. This is a very great deal for her to say, for she had a great friendship with the Duchess of Somerset . . .'[45] Lady Hervey, 'who has been a slave to the Duchess of Marlborough', was roundly told by the Duchess of Montagu that she was a fool to waste her time on someone who had no interest.

> Lady Hervey in return in a whole company of ladies told her that might be, but she was honest and had lain with nobody but her own Lord. Her Grace had lain with the Duke of Grafton, and the marshal, so they call Lord Villars . . . The Duchess of Montagu made no reply, but O Lord my Lady is in a passion . . .[46]

Those with interest, however small, were besieged by those who sought favours. In the army, colonels of regiments were essentially proprietors who ran their regiments at a profit, receiving a grant from the government for arms, clothing and equipment and generally spending rather less than the allowance for these items and pocketing the difference. Like many other offices, military and civil, colonelcies were sold by private treaty or bestowed by a grateful government or a commander-in-chief anxious to line his pocket or reinforce his own interest. In September 1700 Lord Raby reported that: 'Lord Portmore has done one good thing for himself, he has sold his regiment for £6000 to Kirk his lieutenant colonel, of a stranger he could have had £7000, as Lord Trelawney told me.'[47]

In 1710 the three disgraced officers Meredith, Honeywood and Macartney were allowed to sell their regiments for half their market value, and Lord Orrery, a political ally of the Duke of Argyll's, was to have Meredith's at a knockdown price, having first sold his own for its full value. Honeywood came close to being let off 'as a young man that might be drawn in . . . He and Macartney are to sell for £2500 and Meredith for £3500 which he can well afford as he can sell his own [regiment] for more money.'[48]

In 1711 Lord Raby decided to seek an ensign's commission (in the ungrammatical idiom of the age, 'to ask a colours') for his schoolboy son George from Colonel Bellew.

> I did design before he went into Ireland to ask a colours for him [George]. He very kindly told me he was to have a regiment, and that when I asked that he would put the Duke of Ormonde [then captain general, who had to ratify the agreement] in mind and desire it might be in his regiment, which was a great favour, for he might be set down for a colonel that would make interest against him . . . If the regiment is broke [disbanded] the year after it is raised, the half pay will keep the boy at school and save me the charge I am now at.[49]

The monarch was the fountain of all interest, and those who could sipped direct from the fountainhead. Thomas Bruce, Earl of Ailesbury, was a well-placed courtier under the later Stuarts and a well-connected exile in the Low Countries after 1688. He recalled that Charles II rarely had time to himself in the jumbled hothouse of Whitehall, but after getting ready for bed,

> according to custom he went to ease himself, and he stayed long generally, he being there free from company, and loved to discourse,

nobody having entrance but the lord and the groom of the bedchamber in waiting, and I desired him to bestow a colours in the Guards on a relative of mine.

'Trouble me not with trifles,' said the king. 'The Colonel will be glad to oblige you therein.'[50] Ailesbury later seems to have repeated the request on behalf of another relative, this time asking 'a colours for him in the Royal Scottish Regiment of Dumbarton'.[51] The earl was very fond of Charles, who 'knew men better than any that hath reigned over us, and when he gave himself time to think, no man ever judged better of men and things'.[52] But being lord of the bedchamber had its disadvantages, for he and the duty groom slept on truckle beds by the king's door, and the monarch's affection for the little spaniels that now bear his name meant that 'a dozen dogs came into our beds'.[53]

On 16–19 July 1693 the *London Gazette*, a news-sheet with official information on its front page and announcements and advertisements on the back, told its readers of

> a small liver coloured Spanish bitch lost from the King's lodgings, on the 11th instant, with a little white on her breast and a little white on the tops of her hind feet. Whoever brings her to Mr Chiffinch's lodgings at the King's Back Stairs, or to the King's Dog-Keeper in Whitehall, shall be well rewarded for their pains.

William Chiffinch had succeeded his brother Thomas as one of the pages of the king's bedchamber and keeper of the king's closet. The page posts were worth about £80 a year in pay and board, with another £47 for livery, fees worth £17 a year and an assortment of tips ('vails') worth perhaps another £120. These lucrative appointments were wholly in the interest of the groom of the stole, and they themselves brought interest of their own.

Will Chiffinch was the only man allowed to enter the king's closet unbidden. His wife received £1,200 a year for showing selected ladies up to the king's quarters, and Will acted as royal informer, organising drinking parties for those who sought access to the king, recording their conversation while himself remaining studiously sober thanks to a concoction called 'Dr Goddard's drops'. He also became surveyor of the king's pictures, had a fine art collection of his own, and sat to the painter John Riley, whose portrait shows a hard, canny face, with smile and frown folded away for easy interchange. Chiffinch's daughter Barbara married the Earl of Jersey, and is nine times removed great-grandmother to Princes William and Harry: interest indeed.

As groom of the king's bedchamber from 1662, Baptist May – always Bab May to his friends – was one step up the court ladder from Will Chiffinch, and no less indispensable. Son of an influential royalist gentleman, he had been in exile with the Duke of York in the Low Countries during the interregnum, and received lucrative offices after the Restoration. May entertained the king and his close friends in his lodgings in Whitehall and St James's, and was allowed more liberties with Charles than most men. In November 1667 the lord chancellor, the Earl of Clarendon, was unseated by a court conspiracy. Samuel Pepys tells us that: 'As soon as Secretary Morrice brought the great seal from my Lord Chancellor, Bab May fell upon his knees and ketched the king about the legs and joyed him, and said that this was the first time he could call him king of England, being freed from this great man.'[54] May was on very good terms with Barbara Villiers, the most powerful of Charles II's mistresses, and in 1665 it was probably her influence that secured him the post of keeper of the privy purse, upon which she immediately made substantial demands. He received 'several parcels of ground in Pall Mall Fields for building thereon a square of thirteen or fourteen good houses'. May became an MP, and his work on Charles II's divorce, a measure abandoned by the king at the last moment, brought him the appointment of ranger of Windsor Great Park. With money rolling in from a variety of sources, May was able to indulge his tastes for art and the breeding of racehorses. Although he fell from favour after Charles's death, May sensed the way the wind was blowing, and in 1695 received £1,000 for his 'loyalty' to William of Orange. This affable old rogue is remembered today by Babmaes Street, a short dogleg kicking down from Jermyn Street towards St James's Square.[55]

On James II's last hurried visit to Whitehall before he fled to France in 1688, the Earl of Mulgrave, lord chamberlain, rightly fearing that this particular fountain would shortly be shut off, asked the king to make him a marquess. 'Good God! What a time you take to ask a thing of that nature,' said James. 'I am just arrived and am all in disorder.' He added that he did not have a secretary to hand, but the ever-helpful earl replied that he had already made out the warrant himself, and a simple signature would do the business. It was, though, too much for the harassed monarch.[56] When Queen Mary died in 1694 her sister Princess Anne, James II's younger daughter, seemed assured of the succession, and Sarah Marlborough saw how her popularity rocketed overnight. Suddenly 'clouds of people' came to pay their respects. This

> sudden alteration . . . occasioned the half-witted Lord Carnarvon to say one night to the princess, as he stood close by her, in the hall, I hope your Highness will remember that I came to visit you, when none of this company did; which caused a great deal of mirth.[57]

The Stuarts created peers as they chose, and had three distinct peerages – of England, Ireland and Scotland – to pick from.[58] James I ennobled a number of good-looking young men, and Charles II usually had a peerage to hand for his mistresses and their offspring. Although Nell Gwyn ('pretty, witty Nell' to the admiring Mr Pepys) was never ennobled, it was said that she held Charles Beauclerk, the elder of her two sons by the king, out of the window when the monarch visited her, lamenting that the infant had no peerage. 'God save the Earl of Burford!' shouted the happy father. James FitzJames, James II's son by Marlborough's sister Arabella, was created Duke of Berwick at the age of seventeen in 1687, and, already a major general in Emperor Leopold's service, was given his own regiment of infantry and in February 1688 was made colonel of the Blues, replacing Aubrey de Vere, Earl of Oxford, who as lord lieutenant of his county had refused James's order to appoint Roman Catholics to public offices, saying: 'I will stand by Your Majesty against all enemies to the last drop of my blood. But this is a matter of conscience and I cannot comply.'[59]

Louis de Duras, marquis de Blanquefort in the French peerage, came to England in the retinue of James, Duke of York, and was given an English peerage as Baron Duras in 1693. He inherited his father-in-law's earldom by special remainder, becoming Earl of Feversham. He was colonel of the King's Troop of Life Guards, and commander-in-chief for the campaigns of 1685 and 1688. He was a nephew of the great Marshal Turenne, and fought under his command in the Dutch War. William gave many of his Dutch followers English or Irish peerages, leading Ailesbury to complain that: 'Dutch Lords come in so thick, and the crown not being limited, it is a melancholy prospect for us English peers.'[60] To avoid creating irritation amongst English peers, monarchs created Irish peerages to reward those for whom an English peerage might have been considered more than they merited. 'In the seventeenth and eighteenth centuries,' write Mark Bence-Jones and Hugh Montgomery-Massingberd, 'Irish peerages were frequently conferred on

English, Welsh or Scots magnates who were not considered to have merited peerages of England or Great Britain; even though they may have had no family connection with Ireland at all.'[61]

The redoubtable John 'Salamander' Cutts, so called because he loved to be where the enemy's fire was hottest, was created Baron Cutts of Gowran in the peerage of Ireland in 1690, and the Huguenot general Henri de Massue, marquis de Ruvigny, was made Viscount Galway in the Irish peerage in 1696. He had the misfortune to be badly beaten by Berwick at the battle of Almanza in 1707, and the mismatch between his name and his title has induced one writer to surmise that there were in fact two generals in command, the marquis de Ruvigny and his colleague Viscount Galway.[62] Summoned to the bar of the English House of Lords to explain his defeat, Galway argued that his halting English and physical infirmities (he had lost a hand in one battle and been cut across the head in another) meant that he could not really explain himself, and the House allowed him to reply in writing.

Some men reached the House of Lords by sheer merit. John Somers was an Oxford-educated lawyer who was one of the counsel for the seven bishops tried before the King's Bench in 1688 for petitioning James II against his Declaration of Indulgence, helped draft the Declaration of Rights, and rose through the ranks of the government's law officers to become lord chancellor as Baron Somers in 1697. Charles Montagu was a Cambridge man who produced a little light poetry before establishing himself as the financial wizard of his age, initiating the national debt, setting up the Bank of England and overseeing a wholesale recoinage in 1695, though he had to raise window tax to pay for it. He was shoved upstairs into the Lords as Baron Halifax when the Tories came to power in 1699, and became an earl, and effectively prime minister, after the accession of George I.

Others rose without visible trace (it is good to note some continuity between this age and our own), often because there was interest to be repaid. Sarah Marlborough maintained that she had only personally asked Anne to create one peer, the result of a long personal obligation, but that she had failed in a subsequent attempt to get Lord Hervey promoted to an earldom. In January 1712 the queen was persuaded to create peers to overcome the Whigs in the Lords. The Tories enjoyed a comfortable majority in the Commons but were defeated in the Lords, and it seemed likely that the government would fall. But the lord treasurer, Robert Harley (whose audibly Welsh background had not prevented him from becoming Earl of Oxford and Mortimer in 1711), and the queen had agreed to create a dozen peers, amongst them the husband of the queen's favourite (and Harley's cousin) Abigail Masham, as well as Harley's son-in-law and another of his cousins. One of the secretaries of state told the queen that although the creation was certainly legal, he 'very much doubted the expediency, for I feared it would have a very ill effect in the House of Lords and no good one in the kingdom'.

Lord Wharton waspishly asked the new peers, when they took their seats, whether, like a jury, they voted by their foreman. Most had adopted grand territorial titles, apparently confusing the Italian-born Duchess of Shrewsbury. 'Madam,' she said to the pious Lady Oxford, 'I and my Lord are so weary of talking politics. What are you and your Lord?' Lady Oxford dourly replied that 'she knew no Lord but the Lord Jehovah'. 'O dear! Madam, who is that?' enquired the duchess innocently. 'I believe 'tis one of the new titles, for I never heard of him before.'[63]

We should not be surprised that the House of Lords grew steadily in size. In 1687 there were twenty-six lords spiritual (archbishops and bishops) and 154 lords temporal at Westminster. By 1714 this had risen to 171 lords temporal and sixteen representative Scots lords, elected by their peers. There was a substantial inflation at the upper end of the peerage, with the record number of forty-four dukedoms in 1726. Degrees in the peerage were a matter of very real concern. The Tory leader Henry St John, ennobled as Viscount Bolingbroke in 1712, regarded the appointment as a slap in the face, for he believed himself entitled to an earldom, like his ally Robert Harley. Earls usually had one or two subsidiary titles, the senior of which was borne as a courtesy title by their eldest son, and their daughters were styled 'Lady'. Sidney Godolphin's granddaughter, who became Duchess of Leeds, cheerfully signed a letter with all her family titles: 'I am, dear sister, affectionately yours, M Leeds, Carmarthen, Danby, Latimer, Dumblin, Osborne.'[64]

The last words of Anne Hyde, James II's first wife, were: 'Duke, Duke, death is terrible, death is very terrible.' An outraged duke, whose wife had tapped him gently with a fan, sharply observed that his first duchess had never taken such a shocking liberty, although 'she was a Percy'.[65] Peers' brothers assiduously made use of their siblings' titles. In 1704 Captain John Campbell wrote to his brother to say that he had survived Blenheim:

> My Lord the post is going this minute so I have no time to write to Willie Primrose's brother [Viscount Primrose] but I beg that your Lordship will be so kind as to tell him that his brother is wounded and without money.

He moved on to become a major in Hepburn's Regiment in the Dutch service, and survived both 'a very critical time' at Ramillies and 'cruel work' at the siege of Lille, but eventually complained that promotion was too slow: 'There is no man of my quality in the island of Britain that hath served so long as captain and major (which is now fourteen years) as I have.'

John Campbell's luck ran out at Malplaquet. His elder brother James, who commanded the Scots Greys with great distinction that day, wrote to tell their brother that:

> Colonel Hepburn's [Regiment] is all cut to pieces the colonel and
> lieutenant colonel is killed our brother John is shot through the arm
> I have seen him this day, his surgeons have very good hopes of him
> and he is very hearty . . .

Despite the rush of claims on his interest produced by heavy casualties amongst senior officers, Marlborough ensured that John received the colonelcy of Tullibardine's Regiment, left vacant by Tullibardine's death at Malplaquet, but he died of his wound. James saw him buried in the Capuchin cloister in Brussels: seventy grenadiers with blazing torches followed him to the grave. 'It is such a great loss that we cannot enough regret,' wrote James. 'This is a prodigious loss to your lordship and me to lose such a brother and comrade I do assure you that he is regretted by every one that knew him.'[66]

William Cadogan, told that he was to be ennobled for his service against the Jacobites in 1715, at once wrote to Marlborough, his patron, to 'beg leave to return my most humble thanks for your great goodness in being pleased to approve of the good success I have endeavoured to render here, and your Grace's representing them so very favourably to his Majesty'. He hoped to style his barony after 'Cadogan, near Wrexham on the borders of Wales', and, reminding Marlborough that he had no son, hoped that the title would be allowed to pass sideways to his brother. 'I humbly beg pardon for mentioning it,' he concluded, 'and entreat your Grace would consider it no more than if I had not.'[67] He was next elevated to an earldom in 1716, after distinguished diplomatic service in Europe, as 'Earl of Cadogan, in Denbighshire, Viscount of Caversham in Oxfordshire; and Baron Oakley, in Buckinghamshire'.[68] The barony did indeed pass on to his brother Charles, and the earldom, with the new viscountcy of Chelsea added, was later revived for his descendants.

Interest was at its most viscid at election time. The House of Commons had 513 Members before union with Scotland in 1707 added forty-five Scots Members, bringing the total to 558, 'knights of the shire' for rural areas and burgesses for the boroughs. Throughout our period the franchise was limited, in the forty English counties, to 'forty shilling freeholders', and in the boroughs to men meeting the appropriate local qualification. For instance, there were 'corporation boroughs', where the corporation – maybe as few as thirteen men or as many as fifty-four – could vote; 'freeman boroughs' where all freemen – like London's 8,000 liverymen – could vote; and 'burgage boroughs' where the franchise was attached to particular parcels of land, leaving Old Sarum in Wiltshire with just ten voters in 1705. Perhaps one man in seven had the vote. There was no secret ballot; most constituencies returned two Members, and many would-be MPs stood for several constituencies at once to allow a greater chance of success. It was to take the Industrial Revolution and the burgeoning of manufacturing centres to render the whole system palpably absurd, with great cities unrepresented while some tiny boroughs, villages then and now, glibly returned their two Members.

There were many 'pocket boroughs', where the electors were so dependent on a major landowner as to be effectively in his pocket, and 'rotten boroughs' where electors cheerfully sold themselves to the highest bidder. Although the high-minded occasionally inveighed against the system, there was no real pressure for change, certainly not from the electors themselves, who stood to gain good dinners and full pockets by its survival. In 1716 the electors of Marlborough sent a flowery petition to Parliament, attacking the Septennial Act and unsuccessfully arguing that triennial Parliaments were 'the greatest security to the preservation of liberty'.

The Earl of Ailesbury's family was Scots by origin and owned land in Bedfordshire, but it had a substantial interest in the Wiltshire constituencies of Marlborough, Great Bedwyn and Ludgershall. With the earl in exile in the Low Countries his son, Lord Bruce, presided over the family's borough-mongering. In November 1701 the economist Charles Davenant, who had already represented the pocket borough of Great Bedwyn, told Bruce that seeking election at Ampthill, also within the family's sphere of influence but less securely in its pocket, would require personal effort and financial outlay: it was therefore too risky for him.

I received the packet from Ampthill, and the letters from there have quite made me lay aside the thought of standing there. Besides, the electors are generally such a corrupt pack of rogues that it is a chance an honest gentleman should represent them. I hope I have done my country so much service that some friend or other will bring me into this Parliament.[69]

In April 1705 Bruce's agent warned him that there was dirty work afoot at Great Bedwyn, where 'three or four score of the voters have received £5 each and have engaged to serve Pollexfen whose agents gave £5 to the women under pretence of their spinning five pounds of wool at 20 shillings a pound'. The night before the election the Whig agents got sixteen of the electors blind drunk, and the candidates' servants kept them under guard until they were frogmarched to the hustings to cast their ballots.

Seven months later the agent wrote to say that another of the Bruce family's bastions was under attack:

I was yesterday at Marlborough and find the [Whig] Duke [of Somerset's] agents very lavish in their expenses and offers. Williams is about paying £30 debts for Solomon Clarke, and almost as much for Flurry Bowshire, so they are wavering. Persons are at work to counter-plot them.

When Lord Bruce asked who this Mr Bowshire might be, his agent answered: 'Flurry Bowshire is he with one eye, and jealous, it is said, of his wife.' Happily, Solomon Clarke, offered £20 and a job as porter by the duke's agent, had turned him down, 'and vowed he would not serve him if he would give him the castle and the barton farm'.[70]

Although candidates and their agents did what they could to make bribery less obvious, elections were regularly overturned when disappointed candidates petitioned the Commons, although, oddly enough, the outcome of the challenge often reflected the political balance of the House. Even 'legitimate' expenses might raise a modern eyebrow. The Tory magnate Sir Edward Seymour was a Member for the city of Exeter in 1688–89. Before the vote he gave the electors a good dinner of the roast beef of old England, 'two pieces of rib-beef weighing 96lb at 3d per lb – £1 4s 6d'. After it he distributed '25 bottles of sherry . . . 11 bottles and one pint of canary . . . 11 bottles of claret . . .' Of the total drinks bill of £3.8s.4d, a mere fourpence was spent on ale.[71]

There was much more to electioneering than simple bribery, for family influence and local allegiances ran strong. Edward Seymour was a prominent figure in the West Country, colonel of the Devon militia, and men spoke of his 'Western Empire'. The Tories certainly had it their own way in Cornwall. The county's sturdy gentry families like the Grenvilles, Slannings and Trevanions had raised some of the very best royalist infantry in the Civil War, and in William's last Parliament only half a dozen of the county's forty-four MPs were whiggish. In Devonshire, however, religious dissent was strong, and the Whigs enjoyed the support of the powerful Russell family.

But the Bishop of Exeter was Sir Jonathan Trelawney, baronet, a local magnate in his own right. He was one of the seven bishops tried for their opposition to James II, but one of the two of this number who were prepared to swear allegiance to William and Mary. He was a Tory by upbringing and conviction, and used his power-base to increase his interest. In 1703 he reminded the Tory Earl of Nottingham, one of the two secretaries of state, that he had secured the election of eleven Tory Members, but nothing had so far been done to relieve his 'numerous family from the burdens of a poor bishopric'. Wondrous to relate, Trelawney soon found himself promoted to the rich see of Winchester, and appointed prelate to the Order of the Garter.

That 'vigorous and attractive debauchee', the Whig leader Thomas, Lord Wharton, had, in contrast, a puritan and parliamentarian background, 'but he owed his scepticism, his engaging manners and his loose morals to the Restoration society in which he had been brought up'. Jonathan Swift, churchman and Tory pamphleteer, hated him 'like a toad', but could not help admiring the way in which Wharton, when vigorously assailed by yet another pamphlet, would tell Swift that he had been 'damnably mauled' by it, but then chat with him as if nothing really mattered. The Tories made repeated attempts to see him off in a duel, but he disarmed their swordsmen one after another, and always spared their lives.

A contemporary gives us a pen-picture of Wharton wielding interest just as deftly as he did his small sword. He recommended two candidates of his own persuasion for the borough of High Wycombe, only to find that:

> Some of the staunch Churchmen invited two of their own party to oppose them and money was spent on both sides . . . They found my Lord Wharton was got there before them and was going up and down the town with his friends to secure votes on their side. The [Tory] gentleman with his two candidates and a very few followers marched

on one side of the street; my Lord Wharton's candidates and a great company on the other. The gentleman, not being known to my Lord or the townsman, joined with his Lordship's men to make discoveries, and was by when my Lord, entering a shoemaker's shop, asked *where Dick was?* The good woman said *her husband was gone two or three miles off with some shoes, but his Lordship need not fear him, she would keep him right. 'I know that,'* says my Lord, *'but I want to see Dick and drink a glass with him.'* The wife was very sorry Dick was out of the way. *'Well,'* says his Lordship, *'how does all thy children? Molly is a brave girl I warrant by this time.' 'Yes, I thank you,'* says the woman. And his Lordship continued: *'Is not Jemmy breeched yet?'*

It was all too much for the principal Tory, who 'crossed over to his friends and cried: *"E'en take your horse and begone; whoever has my Lord Wharton on his side has enough for this election."* '[72]

Whig and Tory

Discussion of the importance of interest has already slid us deep into politics. Political parties as we understand them did not yet exist: there were no formally appointed party leaders, central offices, manifestos, whips or lists of approved candidates. Yet there were most certainly political groupings, and a rancour between them so intense that a Victorian editor of Sarah Marlborough's papers warned his readers that 'It is almost impossible to conceive the bitter hatred which they bear to each other, and the atrocious libels against their leaders which the press sent every day into the world.'[73] I was taught history at a time when Sir Lewis Namier's views on the politics of the age were very much current. He stressed the importance of connections – groupings based on family or interest – rather than party as we would now understand it. Recent research, especially the painstaking work carried out for the monumental *History of Parliament* project (whose *House of Commons 1690–1715* has proved invaluable), now suggests that party was a good deal more important than Namier believed.

So what did Marlborough and his contemporaries understand by parties? As the historian Tim Harris has so brilliantly demonstrated, the political legacy of the Restoration was a complex one. For a start, it was different in England, Ireland and Scotland, for these three kingdoms were united only in the person of the monarch, and presented distinct problems of their own. In England, with whose politics Marlborough was most intimately concerned, there were two broad groups, each composed of men of similar political persuasions but subject to wide internal disagreement.

On the one hand the Whigs (dubbed 'the party of movement' by our Victorian editor, who saw them as the ancestors of the radicals of his own age) had welcomed the return of Charles II but emphasised that he had been called back by Parliament, and believed that the monarch should rule according to law. The Whigs were the least homogeneous of the parties, for they were an alliance of nonconformist churchmen at one end of the spectrum, and grandees at the other, their most notable figures known as the 'Lords of the Junto' in the first decade of the eighteenth century.* The more astute Whig leaders, like Lord Wharton, recognised that if they were to succeed it would be by a political organisation which their rivals lacked. On the other hand the Tories applauded the restoration of a monarch sanctified by God, and although most of them expected him to obey the law, they believed that there were times when he could use his royal prerogative to override it. Some High Tories went further, arguing that he held his throne by divine right and was accountable only to God, and not to man.

Supporters of the established Church, with its bishops and prayer book, tended to the Tory view. Presbyterians and the descendants of the Civil War puritans hoped to see the Church of England reformed before they could work within it. They agreed with the Anglicans in their dislike of separatist sects, but they were generally whiggish in sympathy. Both parties found their views easily misrepresented by opponents, and the pamphleteering of the age, unshackled by the removal of censorship in 1695, left no stone unhurled when it came to blackguarding opponents: the Tories were Popish and autocratic, seeking to turn England into Louis XIV's France, while the Whigs were nonconformist republicans who would bring back the dark days of the interregnum.

In addition to declared Whigs and Tories, there were always some 'Queen's Servants', who were inclined to support the government of the day. These were often numerous enough to swing the balance of the Commons, and Marlborough and Godolphin could scarcely have survived without the support of these gentlemen, most of whom were moderate Tories by persuasion. Service officers were often MPs: over

---

* They included Somers, Montagu (Halifax), Wharton and Russell (Orford). The word 'Junto' is derived from the Spanish *junta*.

the period 1660–1715 the Commons never had fewer than between 12 and 18 per cent of its members in the army or the navy. James II's tendency to reward the political opposition of officers by removing their commissions meant that, in his reign and immediately after it, most officer MPs tended to be Tories. By 1702, though, most of them, like generals William Cadogan, George Macartney and Francis Palmes, were Whigs. John Webb, the victor of Wynendaele, was a Tory, and his fellow Tories made much of the fact that he had allegedly received scant recognition for his victory. In his private correspondence Marlborough professed disdain for party politics so often that one believes him. Given a choice, he would probably have been a moderate Tory, while Sarah, never one for half-measures, saw all Tories as closet Jacobites, and lost no opportunity to tell Queen Anne of the danger they posed. Whatever else united John and Sarah, it was certainly not politics.

There is no simple political map of the England of Marlborough's day. Country squires like Sir Roger de Coverly were proverbially Tory, and the *Spectator*'s engaging sketches of the good-natured baronet show a man who behaved, in his own little kingdom, much as a benevolent monarch might act on a bigger stage. The parish clergy, whose comfortable liaison with the squirearchy produced the squarson, that hybrid of squire and parson who was more comfortable on his hunter than in his pulpit, were usually Tory, though Low Church bishops often tilted the political balance in the Lords in favour of the Whigs.

The City of London, so important to Parliament's success during the Civil War, was firmly Whig. What Trevelyan called 'the middling classes of society . . . rich merchants, small shopkeepers, freehold yeomen, artisans and craftsmen' were whiggish, as were those, like younger sons and merchants trading overseas, who found 'antique custom and privilege' more hindrance than help.[74] There were great noble houses on both sides, sometimes as much because of traditional rivalries and an eye for the main chance as because of genuine political conviction, and in terms of 'wantonness, unbelief and faction' there was little to choose between the High Tory Henry St John, champion of the bishops, and the Whig Lord Wharton, mainstay of the dissenters.[75] Indeed, our earnest Victorian believed that it was all about interest: 'The leading men of all parties aimed chiefly at getting into high places.' Nor should we discount the way that the terms 'Whig' and 'Tory' became tribal markings, with the smoky little loyalties of club, coffee house and hunting field holding men together, like a covey of partridges in the same patch of stubble.

There was political movement too. During the last four years of his reign, in the early 1680s, Charles II managed to appeal to opinion in the wider political nation 'out of doors', reaching out past the Whigs in Parliament to find a solid majority of royalists in the country at large, encouraging meetings and addresses which undercut the Whigs' claim to be speaking for the people. In contrast, Whig grandees like Wharton recognised that their own party, an essentially disparate alliance, could only hope to win if it emphasised its agreement on the key issues of the day: religious toleration for all Protestants; war with France; union with Scotland; and the Hanoverian succession. Although the Tories constituted a 'solid phalanx' based on the Church and landed interest, they were divided on all these issues.

The fact that the war was financed largely by a land tax of four shillings in the pound meant that however much Sir Roger and his cronies revelled in the spectacle of the French, widely regarded as England's natural enemies, getting a good drubbing, they became increasingly concerned that their own broad acres were paying for it. It was easy enough to put this out of their minds 'while Marlborough and Galway beat/The French and Spaniards every day'. But as the Allies' early successes were followed by disaster in Spain and apparent stalemate in the Low Countries, so the Tories became increasingly sure that the war was neither in the nation's interest, nor – perhaps more to the point – in their own.

Ruling the country actually involved a good deal more than securing a majority in Parliament, for what Tim Harris calls the 'social history of politics' reveals that, in order to make its writ run, any government needed to control

> peers, gentry and merchants at the top level who served as Lord Lieutenants [of counties], deputy Lieutenants, grand jurors, JPs, mayors and common councilmen, down to the men of lesser social standing who served as petty jurors, militiamen, tax assessors, churchwardens, overseers, vestrymen, constables and other parish and ward officers.[76]

In this context Sir Roger's neighbour, hacking into the county town with his spaniel at his side, was scarcely less important than the baronet himself. He was

> a Yeoman of about an hundred Pounds a year, an honest man: He is just within the Game-Act, and qualified to kill an Hare or a Pheasant . . .

He would be a good neighbour if he did not destroy so many partridges: in short, he is a very sensible man; shoots flying; and has been several Times Foreman of the Petty-Jury.[77]

Successive governments used their interest to try to ensure a favourable balance of power locally, in particular by removing those justices of the peace – in default of a paid bureaucracy the keystones of local administration – who were known to oppose their policy. This straightforward spoils system found supporters at both political extremes, but the majority, like Queen Anne herself, correctly feared that it caused local instability and increased political rancour. It is always as well to remember that while Marlborough's England could be threatened, cajoled and bribed, it could not be coerced, and that solid and unremarkable truth, however elusive it might have seemed in Whitehall, underlies the febrile politics of the period.

1

Young Cavalier

Faithful but Unfortunate

It was 26 May 1650. Charles I had been beheaded on a scaffold outside the Banqueting House in Whitehall only sixteen months before, and England was a republic. True, it was not a very happy republic. The House of Commons, summoned by Charles in 1640, had long ago lost its royalists, had more recently been stripped of its Presbyterian Members, and was now too obviously the mere rump of its former self. The House of Lords had been abolished. There was no sense of political equilibrium. On the one hand there were complaints that those 'persons of condition' upon whom so much of the practical exercise of local government depended had simply withdrawn from active participation in it. On the other, although the army had put down Leveller mutinies in the spring of 1649, there were many who thought that England was nothing like republican enough.

These were uncertain times for everyone, and downright difficult ones for those who had demonstrably been on the wrong side in the recent Civil War. Fate chose this unpropitious moment to provide a son for a West Country gentleman called Winston Churchill, sometime captain of horse in the king's army, and his wife Elizabeth. They named him John, for his paternal grandfather.

Winston and Elizabeth had married across the jagged political divide of the 1640s. John Churchill the elder was a prosperous lawyer, a member of the Middle Temple, and Deputy Registrar of Chancery before the Civil War, who had bought an estate at Newton Montacute in the parish of Wootton Glanville, near Sherborne in Dorset. Aged about sixty, he was too old to be in arms, but like Robert Browning's 'Kentish Sir Byng' he 'stood for his king/bidding the cropheaded Parliament swing' and served as one of Charles's commissioners. When he came to terms with the victorious parliamentarians he pleaded that he had broken his allegiance to the king in November 1645, after the decisive battle of Naseby but before the surrender of Oxford, the royalist capital, in May the following year. He was fined £440 in addition to the £400 he had already paid, and having thus 'compounded' with the victors he was allowed to keep his estate.

John Churchill had not simply bought his way into the gentry with money made in law, but had wed wisely too. In 1618 he married Sarah, daughter of a Gloucestershire knight, Sir Henry Winston, in the City church of St Stephen's Walbrook, and the couple's son Winston was born in 1620. Winston had been a student at St John's College Oxford and, like his father, was destined for a career in the law, for he joined Lincoln's Inn in January 1637. The Civil War changed his life. He joined the royalist army on the outbreak of war in 1642, and was the storybook cavalier: an early portrait shows a self-confident young man with luxuriant shoulder-length hair and a bright doublet with slashed sleeves, and, typically, he became a captain of cavalry.[1] Captain Churchill has left us no account of his service, but a brother officer, Captain Richard Atkyns of Prince Maurice's Regiment, a Gloucestershire gentleman whose background was much like Churchill's, remembered how the King's Horse, threadbare West Country regiments riding up from Devizes and a fresh brigade hurtling down from Oxford, between them beat Sir William Waller's cavalry on Roundway Down on 13 July 1643. The royalists called it 'Runaway Down', as well they might, for they broke the roundhead horse and sent some of them tumbling to ruin down the steep western edge of the down.

> I cannot better compare the figure of both armies than to the map of the fight at sea, between the English and the Spanish Armada . . . for though they were above twice our numbers; they being six deep, in close order and we but three deep, and open (by reason of our sudden charge) we were without them at both ends . . . No men ever charged better than ours did that day, especially the Oxford horse, for ours were tired and scattered, yet those that were there did their best.[2]

Winston Churchill's parliamentarian accusers maintained that he was still in the field against them in December 1645, and in the winter of 1649 he was duly charged with 'delinquency'. He fought a stiff rearguard action, trying both to haul in money owed him by others and to delay the government's case against him, no doubt hoping that if it eventually went against him he would have some money for the fine.

He could delay the evil day but not avoid it, and on 29 April 1651 the Commissioners for Compounding ordered that:

> Winston Churchill of Wootton Glanville in the county of Dorset, gent. do pay as a fine for his delinquence the sum of four hundred and four score pounds; whereof four hundred and forty-six pounds eighteen shillings is to be paid into the Treasury at Goldsmith's Hall, and the thirty-three pounds two shillings received already by our treasurer Mr Dawson of Sir Henry Rosewell in part of the money owing by him to John Churchill, father of the said Winston, is hereby allowed of us in part of the said four hundred and four score pounds.[3]

Although the fine was severe enough for a gentleman worth £160 a year, he had paid it by the end of 1651. However, he could not afford to house his family, and we know that he was on bad terms with his stepmother, whom his father had married in 1643, for there was eventually to be an acrimonious squabble over John Churchill's will.[4] Instead, he turned to his mother-in-law, Eleanor, Lady Drake, widow of a Devonshire gentleman, Sir John Drake of Ashe, and daughter of John, Lord Boteler of Bramfield. The Drakes were a substantial Devonshire gentry family, with connections by marriage to the Cornish Grenvilles, and were of the same tribe, though a different branch, as the Elizabethan seaman Sir Francis Drake. Indeed, one of the Musbury Drakes, from whom Sir John Drake descended, had knocked down Sir Francis for daring to use the armorial wyvern that he believed to be his by right.[5]

Lady Drake lived at Ashe House, a substantial Elizabethan E-shaped building in the parish of Musbury, on the right of the main road winding south from Axminster. She was 'of good affection' to the Parliament, had 'animated her tenants in seven adjoining parishes' to its cause, and her son John was serving with its forces. She feared a royalist descent upon Ashe and asked the local parliamentarian garrison of Lyme to send troops. They duly arrived, but before they could fortify the place a royalist force under John, Lord Poulett, leader of the Somerset royalists, arrived and took the house. Poulett's men fired the chapel and an adjoining wing, and 'stripped the good lady, who, almost naked and without shoe to her foot but what she afterwards begged, fled to Lyme for her safety'.[6]

No sooner had Eleanor Drake arrived at Lyme than it was besieged by Prince Maurice, one the king's nephews and brother of the better-known Rupert. The royalists hoped for help from a fleet commanded, in the topsy-turvy way of the loyalties of the day, by the grandson of Lady

Drake's sister, James Ley, Earl of Marlborough. The earl remained in the Channel Islands, and the siege was raised when the Earl of Essex's main parliamentarian army arrived in the West Country in 1644, enabling Lady Drake to get to London where, on 28 September, she was allocated the house of Sir Thomas Reynell, a gentleman then in arms for the king. When he came to terms with Parliament and compounded for his house in 1646 he accused Lady Drake of wrecking the place in search of concealed treasure, but she continued to live there for some time, herself pursuing compensation from Lord Poulett for the substantial damage his men had inflicted on her own house. In the spring of 1648 she was awarded £1,500, but £500 of this was still owing in July 1650, possibly because Poulett himself had died in 1649.

We cannot be wholly certain of Eleanor Drake's residence at this time. There is an argument that Ashe House had been too badly damaged to be habitable, and that in consequence she moved to her son John Drake's house at Great Trill, in the parish of Axminster. The question is anything but academic. As Winston Churchill was living with his mother-in-law, Ashe House and Great Trill vie for the honour of being the birthplace of the future Duke of Marlborough. However, the parish register of St Michael's church Musbury tells those who can penetrate its spidery scrawl: 'John the son of Mr Winston Churchill, born the 26th day of May 1650,' and the majority of scholars, including Archdeacon Coxe, whose life overlapped the duke's, agree that it was indeed in Ashe House that John Churchill first saw the light of day.[7]

Winston and Elizabeth Churchill had at least nine children. Four sons, Winston (b.1649), Henry, Jasper and Mountjoy, died in infancy or youth. Theobald, born in Dublin in 1662, took holy orders and died in 1685. The remaining four children, Arabella (1647–1730), John, the subject of this book (1650–1722), George (1653–1710) and Charles (1656–1714) all enjoyed careers which abutted on their better-known brother's, and we will hear from them later.[8] The circumstances of John Churchill's childhood are largely surmise, for he himself tells us nothing of it. The anonymous author of *The Lives of the Two Illustrious Generals*, published in 1713, assures us that:

> He was born in the time of the grand rebellion, when his father siding with the royal party against the usurpers, was under many pressures, which were common to such as adhered to the king. Yet, notwithstanding the devastations and plunderings, and other nefarious practices which were daily committed by the licentious soldiery, no care was omitted

on the part of his tender parents for a liberal and gentle education. For he was no sooner out of the hands of women than he was given into those of a sequestered clergyman, who made it his first concern to instil sound principles of religion into him, and that the seeds of humane literature might take deeper root, and he from a just knowledge of the omnipotence of the creator, might have a true sense of the dependence of the creature.[9]

Things were certainly not easy for the king's supporters. In 1656 an abortive royalist rising in the south was led by Colonel John Penruddock, who surprised the judges at Salisbury and got as far as South Molton in Devon before he was surrounded and captured. This encouraged Oliver Cromwell, searching fruitlessly for some enduring constitution, to divide England and Wales up into twelve military districts, each under a major general charged with enforcing not only security but also laws against drunkenness and sexual licence. The rule of the major generals was paid for by a 'decimation tax' of 10 per cent on royalists. Although the troops of horse who enforced the central government's will on the regions were sometimes brutal, they were generally 'honest and efficient'. There was little of the plundering and devastation that our anonymous author complains of, and certainly no licentiousness from these psalm-singing bigots whose efforts did so much to instil in contemporaries a deep hatred of military rule and a suspicion of standing armies.

While Cromwell's Protectorate fumbled on in its quest for a settlement, Winston Churchill – called to the bar in 1652, though he made no use of it and did not keep term – remained at Ashe, living in the part of the house left unburned by Lord Poulett's men, in an atmosphere redolent of old dogs and young children, painfully aware that he had backed the wrong horse. He busied himself with the family genealogy, discovering, at least to his own satisfaction, an ancestor who had come over with William the Conqueror, and edging gingerly past the decided possibility that his great-great-great-grandfather had been a blacksmith who had married his employer's widow. Sarah Marlborough was forthright about all this, and in 1736 commented on Thomas Lediard's biography of her husband that:

> This history takes a great deal of pains to make the Duke of Marlborough's lineage very ancient. This may be true for aught I know; but it is no matter whether it be true or not in my opinion, for I value nobody for another's merit.[10]

There was, sadly, no denying either the fact that the Drakes were a more substantial family, or that without Lady Drake's generosity Winston Churchill would have no roof over his head. We simply cannot be sure what all this meant in terms of the relationship between Winston Churchill, his growing family and his mother-in-law: young John was certainly proud enough of the Drake connection to take the title of his own earldom from that of Eleanor's sister's royalist husband.[11] However, he was brought up in a household that demonstrated all too clearly the consequences of being on the losing side and having neither money nor influence: in this respect the child was father to the man.

The King Comes Home in Peace Again

Oliver Cromwell, almost broken by the agonising death of his favourite daughter, died in September 1658, leaving not the stable settlement he had so craved, but a shifting and unstable coalition headed, at least in name, by his son Richard. In an air of worsening political breakdown General George Monck, commander of the army in Scotland but a Devonian by ancestry, who had served the king until his capture in 1646, marched southwards, reaching London in February 1660. He dissolved Parliament, no less than the reinstated Rump of the Long Parliament which had met before the Civil War, and issued writs for another, for which royalists would be allowed to vote. Monck now began to receive letters written to him by the exiled Charles II, but there was still no certainty that the monarchy would be restored.

The Declaration of Breda, issued by Charles on 4 April, made known the conditions on which he would accept restoration to his father's throne. He proposed to take 'possession of that right which God and nature hath made our due', guaranteed a general pardon to all who returned to 'the loyalty and obedience of good subjects', apart from those specifically excepted by Parliament, and promised a free Parliament and 'liberty to tender consciences, and that no man shall be disquieted or called in question for differences of opinion in matters of religion which do not disturb the peace of the kingdom'. The army would receive arrears of pay, and there was an attempt to reassure landowners, great and small, by affirming that grants and purchases of estates made 'in the continued distractions of so many years and so many and great revolutions' would be determined by Parliament.[12]

The declaration and accompanying letters were received by the new 'Convention' Parliament, which declared the monarchy restored, and

Charles duly returned to the royal palace of Whitehall on 29 May 1660, his thirtieth birthday. 'All the world in a merry mood,' wrote Samuel Pepys, 'because of the king's coming.'[13] John Evelyn was even more elated.

> I stood in the Strand and beheld it, and blessed God. And all this was done without one drop of blood shed, and by that very army which rebelled against him; but it was the Lord's doing, for such a Restoration was never mentioned in any history ancient or modern, since the return of the Jews from their Babylonish captivity; nor so joyful a day and so bright ever seen in this nation, this happening when to expect or effect it was past all human policy.[14]

The vast quantity of scholarly work produced since Samuel Rawson Gardiner wrote on the subject over a century ago has not diluted the fundamental truth of his assertion that: 'The majority of political Englishmen . . . thought that Charles II ought to be their king.'[15] The issues which were to bedevil the whole of John Churchill's career were not about monarchy as opposed to republicanism, but about the nature of that monarchy. In this sense the Declaration of Breda was a carefully drafted compromise. It spoke of the authority conferred on Charles by 'God and nature', but recognised that much of the implementation of that authority was a matter for Parliament.

In the short term, though, the Restoration changed the fortunes of the Churchill family at a stroke. A gleeful Winston immediately published *Divi Britannici: Being a remark upon the lives of all the kings of this isle*, a joyfully uncritical celebration of monarchy. He was elected MP for Weymouth in 1661, sitting for that constituency in the 'Cavalier Parliament' which lasted till 1679, and going on to represent Lyme from 1685 until his death in 1688. Winston enjoyed the patronage of Sir Henry Bennet (Lord Arlington from 1663), also an Oxford man and a Civil War royalist. He had taken a sword-cut across the face (an occupational hazard for a cavalryman, and precisely the reason why sensible folk, roundhead or cavalier, wore a lobster-tail pot with a sliding noseguard) in a skirmish near Andover in 1644, and habitually wore a black plaster which concealed the wound but, in so doing, advertised its recipient's loyalty. Arlington accompanied the royal family in exile, where he became secretary to James, Duke of York, and after the Restoration he went on to be a major political figure, not least because of his ability to select (and, so some averred, sample in advance) ladies who might meet his master's generous tastes.

We do not know what brought Arlington and Churchill together, but we can make an educated guess. They had overlapped at Oxford, though they were in different colleges, and they both fought in the south-west, so it is just possible to think of a friendship forged in an Oxford ale-house and continued through the hack-and-gallop affair at Andover; and Arlington was anxious to build up his own client base in the West Country. Thanks to Arlington's patronage, in 1661 Winston Churchill became a commissioner of the Court of Claims and Explanations (Ireland), a body charged with reviewing the redistribution of land in Ireland during the Civil War and the Protectorate. In 1664 he became junior clerk comptroller to the Board of Green Cloth, a committee taking its name from the baize-covered table at which its members sat, which audited the expenses of the royal household and exercised administrative jurisdiction within royal palaces. On 12 June 1681, for example, with a proper regard for interior economy, the board ordered that: 'The Maids of Honour should have cherry tarts instead of gooseberry tarts, it being observed that cherries are three pence a pound.' In 1664 Winston was knighted, and he had already been authorised to add an augmentation to his cherished coat of arms, 'for his service to the late king as captain of horse, and for his present loyalty as a member of this House of Commons'. His arms bore the motto *Fiel pero desdichado*, 'Faithful but Unfortunate'.

Winston might more accurately have described himself as faithful but busy. In 1662 he departed for Ireland, where young John attended the Dublin Free Grammar School. He returned to England in 1664, and it seems safe to surmise that John came with him, to become one of the 153 scholars at St Paul's School. It is certain that Sir Winston bought a house in the capital, for Sarah Marlborough later recalled John showing her the family home in the City of London. The early records of St Paul's School were destroyed in 1666, during the Great Fire, but a copy of Vegetius' *De Re Militari*, with an annotation certifying that it was from that book that 'John Churchill, scholar of this school, afterwards the celebrated Duke of Marlborough, first learnt the elements of the art of war', survived.

Winston S. Churchill wondered how 'our hero was able to extract various modern sunbeams from this ancient cucumber'.[16] However, Professor Philip Sabin has recently suggested that military history might indeed be the most important legacy of the ancient world. While Vegetius' first two books are perhaps of little value to succeeding ages, his third, in which he sums up Roman strategy, tactics and logistics, has been hailed as 'the foundation of military learning for every European commander from William the Silent to Frederick the Great'. He emphasised the importance of seeking information to dispel the fog of war, while at the same time concealing one's own strength and plans. Vegetius dealt with the principles of war fought for limited objectives, by no means an inapt comparison with the wars of the early eighteenth century. 'Consult with many on proper measures to be taken, but communicate the plans you intend to put in execution to few, and those only of most assured fidelity,' he suggested. 'Or better,' he added, 'trust no one but yourself.'[17] There could scarcely be a better description of John Churchill's approach to generalship.

In 1665, with John still at school, his sister Arabella was appointed a maid of honour to the Duchess of York, wife of the king's brother James. Given the close relationship between York and Arlington, and the latter's role as royal pander, what followed soon afterwards should come as no surprise. Winston called on the fashionable portraitist Sir Peter Lely, and at some time in the very early 1660s Lely painted his eldest son Winston and his daughter Arabella in neo-classical dress. At this time Arabella was perhaps fourteen years old, and her remorselessly flat-chested portrait gives little hint that she was soon to prove irresistibly attractive to the Duke of York.

In 1659 James had contracted a secret marriage to Anne Hyde, daughter of Charles II's adviser Edward Hyde, who as Earl of Clarendon was to dominate politics in the period 1660–66. Of the children she bore him only two, Mary (b.1662) and Anne (b.1665), survived infancy. The marriage was formalised in London in 1660, but James's eyes and hands were for ever wandering, and he embarked on a series of affairs. In 1665 the gossipy Pepys identified a lady who 'is said to have given the Duke of York a clap upon his first coming over'; the following year the eager duke was said to be 'desperately in love with Mrs Stewart', and on Easter Day 1669 Pepys, now frankly alarmed rather than merely gossipy, complained that the royal lecher 'did eye my wife mightily'.[18] We might style James gourmand rather than gourmet, and his taste in ladies, like his religion, was Catholic. Catherine Sedley, one of his mistresses, confessed that: 'We are none of us handsome, and if we had wit, he has not enough to discover it.'[19]

Arabella Churchill was described by one contemporary as having a face of no more than ordinary feminine beauty, which made her a good deal more attractive than many of James's ladies, but a very pretty figure. We are told that the ducal party was riding to a greyhound meet near

York when Arabella's horse bolted. She fell, and the Duke of York found her unconscious and dishevelled: the fact that underwear was not in general use at the time may well have increased the joy of his discovery. Arabella bore James at least four children, Henrietta FitzJames (b.1667), James FitzJames, later Duke of Berwick (b.1670) and, after Anne Hyde's death in 1671 and James's marriage to Mary of Modena in 1673, Henry FitzJames, later Duke of Albemarle (b.1673), and Arabella FitzJames (b.1674).

Lord Macaulay, whiskery jowls quivering, thundered that the complaisant John Churchill stood dishonoured by his sister's behaviour, though Sarah Marlborough acidly wondered quite what 'he could do when a boy at school to prevent the infamy of his sister'. Sir Winston could do little, even if he had the inclination to make the attempt, because in 1665 he was sent back to Ireland, leaving his family behind in London. At about this time John went to court as page to the Duke of York, and in 1667 he begged his patron for an ensign's commission in the foot guards, which was duly granted on 14 September that year. There was no formal uniform for army officers at this time, but the guards, like the rest of the infantry, wore red, and young John would have turned out in a knee-length red coat with broad blue turned-back cuffs and a good deal of gold lace. It would have taken rare perception to have guessed just how much lustre he would bring to coats like that and the men who wore them.

The Army of Charles II

The army that John Churchill joined was the product of an uneasy union between George Monck's regiments, which represented the New Model Army, instrument of parliamentarian victory in the Civil War, and the force of exiled royalists maintained by Charles in the Low Countries. In 1660 Monck, now the well-pensioned Duke of Albemarle in reward for his services, began the disbandment of his troops as their arrears of pay were met, and by Christmas that year only two regiments of this remarkable army remained: his own foot, the 'Coldstream Regiment', and his own regiment of horse. A force of around 6,000 foot and six hundred horse was maintained in Dunkirk, consisting partly of ex-parliamentarian soldiers and partly of royalists, including Lord Wentworth's regiment of foot guards.

It soon became clear to Charles that he could not afford to maintain Dunkirk, and in 1662 he sold it to France. Some of the troops went to the North African city of Tangier, which had come to the crown as part of the dowry of Charles's queen, Catherine of Braganza. Others went off to fight in Portugal, and still others were disbanded in Dunkirk or joined the French army as mercenaries: Lord Wentworth's guards returned to England in 1662, and were amalgamated with Colonel John Russell's 1st Foot Guards in 1665.

Charles did not share the widespread mistrust of standing armies, and Gilbert Burnet maintains that lord chancellor Clarendon agreed that such a force was needed to protect the king from riots and risings.

> And there was great talk of a design, as soon as the army were disbanded, to raise a force that should be so chosen and modelled that the King might depend upon it; and that it should be so considerable, that there might be no reason to apprehend tumults any more.[20]

However, the Earl of Southampton, the lord treasurer, feared that while the New Model's men had been 'sober and religious' the king's would perforce be brutal and licentious, and the probable instrument of royal despotism. One of Samuel Pepys's drinking companions certainly agreed with him:

> They go with their belts and swords, swearing and cursing, and stealing – running into people's houses, by force oftentimes, to carry away something. And this is the difference between the temper of one and the other.[21]

Charles's army was small – 6,000 strong at its peak – and it would have been a wise man who predicted that it would eventually grow into a force of European stature. There were many who argued, throughout his reign and beyond it, that the Trained Bands of the City of London and the county militias, their officers appointed by local potentates and their men selected by ballot from lists provided by parish constables, were sufficient guarantee of domestic security. On 1 January 1661, however, a small armed group of no more than fifty Fifth Monarchy men under 'Venner the cooper' seized the north gate of St Paul's. A plucky watchman cried out that he was for King Charles. They replied that they were for King Jesus, and piously shot him through the head. Venner's men went on to beat both a detachment of musketeers sent across from the guard on the Royal Exchange, and the lord mayor's own troop of City militia, before making off to Highgate. Running short of food, they returned to the City on the fourth. It took the king's Life Guard and 'all the City Regiments' to subdue them: ten were taken and twenty killed. Thomas Venner was wounded, but lived long enough for rope and bowelling knife.

Charles had already raised a regiment of foot guards commanded by John Russell, one of the Duke of Bedford's grandsons and a steadfast Civil War royalist. The king had brought a Life Guard of horse across with him in 1660, but it had subsequently been reduced in size and the residue sent to Dunkirk. As a consequence of Venner's rising the officers and men of Albemarle's Coldstream regiment of foot were disbanded (thus meeting the letter of the agreement that specified that the old army was to disappear) and then immediately re-enlisted. In 1684 a royal ruling made this 'new' regiment junior to Russell's 1st Foot Guards, but the Coldstreamers made clear their disapproval by adopting the motto *Nulli Secundus*, second to none. Members of the 1st Foot Guards helpfully translated this as 'second to one' or 'better than nothing'.[22] The Life Guards were brought back from Dunkirk and augmented into three troops – the King's, the Duke of York's and the Lord General's, with a Scots troop raised soon afterwards. At the same time Aubrey de Vere, Earl of Oxford, raised a regiment of horse, properly the Royal Regiment of Horse Guards but known, from the colour of their uniforms, as the 'Oxford Blues'. This was based on a parliamentarian regiment, brought up to strength with royalist volunteers.

This process gave Charles II guards, both horse and foot, and with them came the realistic prospect of preserving order in the capital and escorting the monarch when he travelled in the country. There were also a number of isolated non-regimented garrison companies in key strongholds like Portsmouth, Dover and Hull, all now commanded by officers of suitable royalist credentials. Although the small standing armies of each of Charles's kingdoms were theoretically separate, 'In practice,' as John Childs tells us, 'all three were interdependent and formed part of the same large whole. Soldiers from Scotland and Ireland were raised to serve on the English establishment whenever forces were needed for foreign service.'[23]

Charles expanded his army beyond this tiny kernel for two reasons. Firstly, there were the demands of his foreign policy, and as John Churchill was to find himself swept up in the wars that this provoked, we need to grasp its essentials. The treaty of 1661, which established the conditions for Charles's marriage to the Portuguese Princess Catherine of Braganza, brought England the North African city of Tangier, intermittently under siege by the Moors, and it required garrisoning. Amongst troops raised for this dangerous task was the Queen's Foot, which went on to become the 2nd of Foot, the Queen's Royal Regiment, whose paschal lamb badge can still be found on the buttons of its lineal descendant, the Princess of Wales's Royal Regiment. A brigade of one regiment of cavalry and two of infantry also served in Portugal itself in 1662–68.

Then there were forces needed for war on the Continent. A dominating influence across the whole of John Churchill's active career was the desire of the French monarch Louis XIV to extend the borders of France and secure influence across a wider Europe. However, for much of Charles's reign the government pursued a pro-French policy. This undoubtedly reflected Charles's personal inclination. His mother Henrietta Maria was French, his sister Henriette-Anne was married to the Duke of Orléans, and his personal religious beliefs drew him strongly towards Catholicism. In 1670 the secret Treaty of Dover, pushed on by some of Charles's advisers (including Winston Churchill's patron Lord Arlington, who had succeeded the fallen Clarendon), provided for an alliance between Britain and France. Charles affirmed that he was 'convinced of the truth of the Roman Catholic religion and resolved to declare it and reconcile himself with the Church of Rome as soon as the welfare of his kingdom will permit'. Louis XIV would send 6,000 soldiers to help him against any recalcitrant subjects, and would provide Charles with £140,000, half payable in advance of his declaration. Amongst the treaty's other clauses was one which bound the two kings to declare war on the States-General of the United Provinces, and others which determined the arrangements for this war – including a generous annual subsidy for the British. Henriette d'Orléans visited her brother in 1670 and persuaded him to defer his declaration of Catholicity until after the war had begun.

In fact Charles did not need much convincing, for, with that finely-tuned survival instinct which his brother so signally lacked, he recognised that such a pronouncement would be profoundly unpopular, and he was reconciled to the Roman Catholic Church only on his deathbed. A bogus treaty, which excluded the awkward clause committing Charles to Catholicism, was signed in December by five of his ministers – Clifford, Arlington, Buckingham, Ashley Cooper and Lauderdale – whose initials conveniently made up the word cabal, or conspiracy, giving us some indication of what many of their contemporaries thought of them and their policy.[24]

As a consequence of this policy, a brigade of infantry served alongside the French army against the Dutch in 1672–78. It included the Earl of Dumbarton's Scots Regiment, which was to become the Royal Scots, the 1st of Foot, and the senior line infantry regiment in the British army, rejoicing in the nickname 'Pontius Pilate's bodyguard'.* There was also the Duke of Monmouth's Royal English Regiment, an Irish regiment under Sir George Hamilton (replaced, when he was killed at Saverne in 1676, by Colonel Thomas Dongan), assorted cavalry, and further infantry battalions which were broken up, on their arrival in France, to reinforce existing units. We shall see more of this brigade later.[25]

The government's policy of war against the Dutch in alliance with the French was not popular, not least because many Englishmen regarded the Dutch as good fellow-Protestants who were, into the bargain, the doughtiest of adversaries at sea. England pulled out of the Third Dutch War in 1674, and with the fall of the cabal soon afterwards the Earl of Danby, the king's new chief minister, gradually redefined foreign policy so as to align England with Holland and against France. Charles was uneasy about the arrangement, but his sister Henriette's untimely death removed what might have proved an insuperable obstacle. In 1677 the Dutch stadholder William of Orange, fast emerging as the chief obstacle to Louis' ambitions, married the Duke of York's daughter Mary. The jocular Charles was on hand to help the happy couple to their bridal bed, and as he drew the curtains around it he improved the tender moment with his expert advice: 'Now, nephew, to your work! Hey! St George for England!'[26]

On 31 December 1677 England signed a treaty with the Dutch, agreeing to work towards a general peace on the basis of French surrender of key fortresses in the Low Countries, to recall British troops from French service, and to send men to fight alongside the Dutch and their allies the Spanish, who were, through most of the period covered by this book, *de jure* rulers of the Spanish Netherlands, that broad and often contested

---

* In the seventeenth century the regiment's ancestor, Hepburn's Regiment, in French service, was in dispute with the Régiment de Picardie over the dates of their respective foundations. In the process, the Scots claimed to have been on duty when Christ was crucified.

strip of territory between France and Holland. A further treaty was not ratified by the English, and Charles then characteristically attempted to avoid both breaking his agreement with France and actually entering the war on the other side. Eventually, in 1678, a force of almost 18,000 men was ready, part of it composed of regiments recalled from French service, and part from regiments newly raised for the war. The force was disbanded in 1679 without having been in action, but the experience of getting it to Flanders, sustaining it in the theatre of operations and bringing it back to England was useful for the future. In addition to this expeditionary force, genuinely part of the British army, there were also British troops, including a high proportion of Scots, in Dutch service too.

We can already discern, from the very beginning of John Churchill's career, the second reason for Charles's expansion of his army. He was besieged by Civil War royalists, many of them awash with extended families, who sought places for themselves and their adherents as a reward for past services and, by unspoken implication, a guarantee of future loyalty. Although in 1661 Parliament had undertaken to raise £60,000 to pay former officers of the royalist armies, there was precious little available for those who had served as junior officers. John Gwyn had been a captain in the Civil War and then a lieutenant in the royalist army in Flanders before the Restoration. After it he found himself on half-pay in Dunkirk, in a garrison full of ex-parliamentarians, and with two of his 'familiar associates' decided to visit the governor and offer to serve as private soldiers. At that stage infantry regiments contained both pikemen and musketeers, and a gentleman would naturally prefer, as Shakespeare had put it, to 'trail the puissant pike'.

> Then I went with them to the Governor, as he was marching at the head of fifteen hundred men, and told him they were officers of His Majesty's Regiment of Guards, gentlemen, and brave fellows; and that they and myself would own it an honour to take our pikes upon our shoulders, and wait upon him that day. He returned as many grateful expressions unto us, as if it had been the highest obligation that was ever put upon him, and he would not take us from our command.[27]

By the time Gwyn wrote his memoirs, though, he was serving as a gentleman trooper in the King's Troop of Life Guards, then commanded by the Duke of Monmouth. Although a trooper in the Life Guards received four shillings a day, compared to the 2s.6d paid to a trooper in a line cavalry regiment, it is clear that Gwyn hoped for promotion, and that the prefatory letters opening his memoirs were (apparently fruitless) pleas for assistance. He told Charles II that he had 'faithfully spent my prime years in your service', and evidently hoped for more than a billet in the Life Guards. There were thousands of John Gwyns in the England of the 1660s (one contemporary survey identified 5,353 former officers), all clamouring for jobs, and the expansion of the army could gratify at least some of them.

Much as they might have resented the comparison, army officers had at least something in common with the keeper of Newgate prison, for their offices, like his, were generally bought and sold. Indeed, one historian has suggested that the purchase of commissions 'operated to its greatest extent' in the Restoration army.[28] Any appointment or promotion required royal permission, and an officer either joining for the first time or being promoted paid a set fee to the secretary at war and negotiated the price payable to the officer he replaced. Commissions in units raised for short conflicts like the 1677–78 expedition were cheap but a poor long-term investment, while, at the other extreme, colonelcies of well-established regiments were hugely expensive. Charles gave Colonel John Russell £5,100 for the 1st Foot Guards in 1672, and then presented the regiment to one of his illegitimate brood, the Duke of Grafton, who had no military experience at all but rather enjoyed being a colonel.

The rules governing the purchase of commissions changed from time to time, and in 1684 the whole practice was outlawed, but with or without official approval it clinked cheerfully on. There was no reason why young men needed to understand their profession before buying their way into it: some young officers could not 'relieve a guard without arousing the merry glee of spectators'. Moreover, there were many gentlemen 'whom nothing but captaincies would contest', thus leaving a residue of subalterns who frequently saw ignorant men buy their way in above them. One of the disappointed tells us that:

> the subaltern . . . let him be never so diligent, faithful and industrious; nay never so successful too; and although he has spent so much of his own money in carrying arms . . . or in small posts, as would have bought a company; yet if he has not the

ready – he must be sure to find one that has put over his head; and too often one that neither is, nor ever will make a soldier.[29]

However, the system, such as it was, was in a state of evolution, and during John Churchill's career there were attempts to prevent the worst abuses: for instance, the commissioning of youths and children was theoretically banned in 1705. Churchill, as we shall see, had his own firm views on the subject, and it was at least in part thanks to his efforts that, between the reigns of Charles II and George I, a career in the army came increasingly to offer genuine professional advancement rather than sporadic achievement based on money and patronage, inflated by wartime promotion but imperilled by peacetime reductions. Yet throughout the period many officers, especially those in the most recently raised regiments, which would be the first to go on the outbreak of peace, were uncomfortably aware that the spectre of compulsory retirement on half-pay always beckoned:

> *This week we shine in scarlet and in gold*
> *The next, the cloak is pawned, the watch is sold.*

Court and Garrison

None of this was yet of much concern to Ensign Churchill of the 1st Foot Guards, commissioned without purchase by the kindly intervention of James, Duke of York. He carried his company's colour (until about 1690 each company of foot had a colour of its own, and thereafter most regiments had a royal colour and a colonel's colour) and watched the pikemen and musketeers of his company, now in the proportion of about one pikeman to four musketeers, stepping through their stately evolutions. Their captain enjoined them to 'Have a care: shoulder your pikes and muskets; to your right hand, face; to your front, march.' Off they stepped, stiff-legged, slow, and mighty proud of themselves, with the captain and half the musketeers at their head, the ensign and his colour in the middle with the pikes, then the remainder of the musketeers and last of all the lieutenant, with a keen eye on the alignment of the ranks and the behaviour of the men.

The foot guards were quartered in and around the capital, even then easily the largest city in the kingdom, with a population of more than 300,000 souls (almost one in sixteen of the total English population of over five million), and growing all the time to outstrip Paris in 1700 and

Constantinople in 1750.[30] It straggled along the north bank of the Thames, then crossed only at London Bridge, though there was a ferry between Westminster and Lambeth, long replaced by Lambeth Bridge but remembered by Horseferry Road, that now leads onto it. The City itself, the ancient commercial heart of London, comprised the original square mile bounded by the Roman walls, with Blackfriars to its west and Southwark just across London Bridge. To its west lay Westminster, approached by the Strand, which took the traveller to Charing Cross, whence King Street ran slightly north of the line of the modern Whitehall to Westminster Hall, where Parliament met.

The palace of Whitehall, frequented by John Churchill for much of this period, was the monarch's principal residence. It stretched along the river for about half a mile, just a little to the north of the present Embankment, which was reclaimed in the nineteenth century. The traveller arriving by King Street from the City would enter the precincts of the palace by the Holbein Gate, with the Banqueting House to his left and a muddle of galleries and apartments around the little Pebble Court behind it. As he passed on through Holbein Gate our traveller would cross the north side of the Privy Garden, with a run of buildings on his right which from 1664 included quarters for a permanent guard of fifty private gentlemen of the Life Guards. Entry to St James's Park, where the king loved to walk briskly with a selection of his dogs and to which access was strictly controlled, was monitored by these troopers, and passes to the park were much coveted.

This cavalry guardhouse stood for nearly a century; the present one, called Horse Guards like its predecessor, dates from the 1750s. Leaving through King Street Gate, and now conscious of Westminster Hall and the Abbey filling his horizon, the traveller would see a scattering of more apartments and the royal bowling green to his left. The whole place was a mixture of medieval and more modern, with Inigo Jones's great Banqueting House, built for Charles's grandfather James I to replace an earlier building destroyed by fire, as its most striking feature.

Court life mixed formality and practicality. Samuel Pepys was predictably gratified to see a royal mistress's petticoats hanging out to dry in the Privy Garden, though the vision gave him rather lurid dreams. Privacy could be rare. When Margaret, wife of John Churchill's future political ally Sidney Godolphin, was dying of puerperal fever in 1678, her shrieks rang out right across the palace's riverfront. Many marriages of the period were made by conniving old men in smoky rooms, but this had been a love-match, and the distraught Godolphin wrote that his loss was 'never to be supplied this side of heaven'.[31] He never remarried.

John Evelyn admired Charles, that 'prince of many virtues', but complained that:

> He took delight in having a number of little spaniels follow him and lie in his bed-chamber, where he often suffered the bitches to puppy and give suck, which rendered it very offensive, and indeed made the whole court nasty and stinking.[32]

Royal mistresses, in 'unimaginable profusion', according to the strait-laced Evelyn, might be ushered in via Whitehall Stairs from the river, or up the backstairs from Pebble Court, with the more permanent fixtures actually housed within the palace, though safely away from the queen's apartment, just off the gallery where Pebble Court and the Privy Garden met. The place was full of courtiers, place-holders and hangers-on, sleeping (and sometimes pissing) where they could, and hoping to make themselves indispensable to Charles. He was 'easy of access', and

> had a particular talent in telling a story, and facetious passages, of which he had innumerable; this made some buffoons and vicious wretches too presumptuous and familiar, not worth the favour they abused.[33]

Gilbert Burnet was less impressed by the monarch's skill as a raconteur. 'Though a room might be full when the king began one of his stories,' he wrote, 'it was generally almost empty before he finished it.'[34]

This royal rabbit-warren was badly damaged by fire in January 1698, and the Banqueting House was one of the few buildings to survive. Christopher Wren was told that 'His Majesty desires to make it a noble palace, which by computation may be finished in four years.' But there was never enough money, and although 'the spectre of a grand palace at Whitehall haunts English architectural history in the seventeenth century', the ghost never assumed substantial form.[35] After the destruction of Whitehall the court moved to St James's and Kensington Palaces in London. Charles liked Windsor Castle, with its romantic wooded sur-roundings, and William III was very taken by Hampton Court, where he was able to create gardens like those he so loved at Het Loo.

As a page John Churchill was a regular visitor to the Duke of York's apartments, at the palace's south-west corner. He also called on his second cousin once removed, conveniently lodged nearby. Barbara

Villiers had been born in 1640, the second child of Lord Grandison, and in 1659 she married the lawyer Roger Palmer, later Lord Castlemaine. She had already enjoyed a vigorous affair with the Earl of Chesterfield ('the joy I have of being with you last night, has made me do nothing but dream of you'), and in February 1661 she gave birth to her first daughter by Charles II. John Churchill was often to be found in her lodgings (alongside the King Street Gate till 1663, and near the Holbein Gate thereafter), eating sweets and chatting. Winston S. Churchill is at pains to persuade us that:

> Very likely she had known him from his childhood. Naturally she was nice to him, and extended her powerful protection to her young and sprightly relation. Naturally, too, she aroused his schoolboy's admiration. There is not . . . the slightest ground for suggesting that the beginning of their affection was not perfectly innocent and such as would normally subsist between a well-established woman of the world and a boy of sixteen, newly arrived at the Court where she was dominant.[36]

Much later in Marlborough's life, when his enemies were anxious to do him whatever damage they could, the author of a scurrilous account of the court life of the period suggested that even at this stage Barbara Villiers aroused a good deal more than John Churchill's admiration. We cannot be sure when his relationship with Barbara became more than neighbourly, and it may well be that things began perfectly innocently, as Winston S. Churchill suggests. But we can be sure of two things. Firstly, John Churchill was not simply one of the most attractive men of his day, but became an ardent lover whose correspondence with his wife testifies to a healthy sexual appetite, even if we cannot produce a respectable source for Sarah's enthusiastic: 'My Lord home from the wars this day, and pleasured me, his boots still on.'[37] Secondly, his relationship with Barbara did indeed blossom into an affair, and she was to bear him a daughter, also called Barbara, in July 1672.

To the Tuck of Drum

By that time, however, John Churchill had most certainly become a man of the world. It was common for young officers to serve on campaign or on warships of the fleet as volunteers, even if their own regiments were not involved. There is circumstantial evidence that in 1668–70 he served in the garrison of Tangier. Some contemporaries believed that either the roving eye of the Duchess of York or Churchill's relationship with Barbara Villiers caused tension at court, and that 'the jealousy of one of the royal brothers was the cause of his temporary banishment'. Archdeacon Coxe thought the story absurd, for Churchill was not away from court for long, and was, so Coxe argued, recalled by the Duke of York.[38]

Tangier lay in a hollow under the hills of the Barbary coast in North Africa, and came under intermittent attack by local Moors, as cunning as they were cruel. In 1663 the governor, the Earl of Teviot, was killed when a hitherto-successful sortie pushed on too far and was swamped by superior numbers. In 1678 the Moors took two outlying forts, but in 1680 the beleaguered garrison sallied out to inflict such a serious defeat on the Moors that they were able to negotiate a truce that lasted four years. Yet it was clear that the place had no lasting value, and the 1683 mission led by Lord Dartmouth, with Pepys as his henchman, concluded that the city should be given up, and so it was, after the destruction of the Mole, built with much trouble and expense in a vain effort to turn the place into a usable port.

Tangier was hot and uncomfortable: when Pepys was there he was 'infinitely bit by chinchies', presumably the local mosquitoes, from whom he gained some refuge only by covering his face and hands before going to sleep. He hated the place. There was 'no going by a door but you hear people swearing and damning, and the women as much as the men'.[39] The behaviour of the governor, Colonel Percy Kirke, appalled him.

> I heard Kirke, with my own ears walking with him and two others to the Mole . . . ask the young controller whether he had had a whore yet, since he came into the town, and that he must do it quickly or they would all be gone on board the ships, and that he would help him to a little one of his own size . . . [40]

When a drunken soldier reeled into the governor as he walked in the street, Kirke simply said, ' "God damn me, the fellow has got a good morning's draught already," and so let him go without a word of reprehension.'[41]

Apart from a letter of 1707 in which he complained that Brabant in flaming June was as hot as the Mediterranean in August, we have no idea what Churchill made of the place. We do know, however, that there was fighting afoot, and it is reasonable to assume that his baptism of fire came in skirmishes under the walls of the city. In August 1671 Sir Hugh Cholmley described how:

> [The Moors] lodge their ambushes within our very lines, and sometimes they killed our men as they passed to discover, which they continually do without any other danger than hazarding a few shots, whilst they leap over the lines and run into the fields of their own country. This insecurity makes men all the more shy in passing about the fields, and cannot be prevented but by walling the lines about.[42]

Life was decidedly martial. The whole garrison paraded at seven or eight in the morning for an hour's drill, after which guards were posted and duties allocated. The young Churchill would have grasped the essentials of his profession in a way that would scarcely have been possible with the staid finery of 1st Foot Guards in St James's Park or at the Tower of London. In March 1670 Lord Castlemaine, Barbara Villiers' husband, told Lord Arlington that he had great hopes that Tangier might become 'a bridle for the pirates of Barbary', and 'neither is it a little honour for the Crown to have a nursery of its own soldiers, without being altogether beholding to our neighbours for their education and breeding'.[43]

On 21 March 1670 Charles signed a document acknowledging that Sir Winston Churchill was still owed £140 for his work in Ireland, noting that Winston had given John precisely this sum 'for & towards his equipage & other expenses in the employment he is now forthwith by our command to undertake on board the fleet in the Mediterranean sea'. Charles wished 'to give all due encouragement to the forwardness of the early affections of John Churchill', and ordered that Sir Winston's arrears should be paid forthwith.[44] We can see from this that Sir Winston was yet again short of money, and that John Churchill was certainly not out of royal favour.

One of the illusory attractions of Tangier was that it might provide a base for putting pressure on the rulers of Algiers and Salee, whose enterprising corsairs ravaged trade in the Mediterranean and the Atlantic, and in 1687 even pushed up into the Channel, where they took two mail packets and carried a hundred passengers off into slavery. In 1669 Sir Thomas Allen blockaded Algiers, and he tried again in 1670; this time John Churchill was embarked with the fleet. The

Lord High Admiral's Regiment of Foot, its colonel James, Duke of York, had been formed in 1664, but other marine regiments were no sooner raised than disbanded: two had been sharply cut back after the humiliating Dutch raid into the Medway in 1667. In 1672 Prince Rupert raised a marine regiment for the Third Dutch War, but it was disbanded in 1674.

This meant that the task of providing marines to the fleet had to be shared out amongst the army's infantry regiments, and normally every one of them had two of its companies embarked, rotating them from time to time. The soldiers provided unskilled labour (and no doubt much innocent mirth) during voyages, lined ships' rails with their muskets in action, and could be sent ashore to destroy fortifications or harbour facilities. The practice seems to have been popular with sailors but less so with soldiers, not least because the army and navy ran incompatible accounting systems, leading to repeated difficulties over pay, allowances and rations.[45]

Thomas Allen's blockade of Algiers in 1670 was no more fruitful than his efforts the previous years. Indeed, it was to take another century and a half for the menace of Barbary pirates to be brought under control by repeated international action which, amongst other things, put 'the shores of Tripoli' into the US Marine Corps' hymn. We cannot say whether John Churchill saw any action or not, and certainly he was back in England by 1671, when Sir Edward Spagge caught seven Algerine cruisers in Bougie Bay and burnt them all.

My Lady Castlemaine

Perhaps John Churchill and Barbara Castlemaine had already become lovers before he set off for Tangier, but more probably, as Winston S. Churchill suggests, it was his reappearance at Whitehall 'bronzed by African sunshine, close-knit by active service and tempered by discipline and danger' that did the trick. He certainly fought a duel with the future Lord Herbert of Cherbury at this time, getting run through the arm but pinking his opponent in the thigh. Whatever the reason for the fight, Churchill had the best of the propaganda. Sir Charles Lyttelton told a friend: 'Churchill has so spoke of it, that the King and the Duke are angry with Herbert. I know not what he [Churchill] has done to justify himself.'[46]

Barbara Castlemaine had a hearty sexual appetite. Even in her sixties, by then Duchess of Cleveland in her own right, she conducted what turned out to be a bigamous marriage with Robert 'Beau' Fielding. She had not lost her taste for elegant men. For his part Fielding hoped to marry money, somehow forgetting that he had recently wed a Mary Wadsworth, imagining her to be a wealthy widow called Mrs Deleau. He certainly did not help matters by sleeping with Barbara's granddaughter Charlotte Calvert, and the furious duchess duly sued him for adultery, ensuring that his explicit love letters were read out in court and subsequently published.

By the time of John's return to court Barbara Castlemaine had lost her place as the king's acknowledged mistress. Charles had insisted on her appointment as lady of the bedchamber to Catherine of Braganza when she arrived from Portugal, warning: 'Whosoever I find to be my Lady Castlemaine's enemy in this matter, I do promise upon my word to be his enemy as long as I live.'[47] She played a leading role at court, formed an alliance of mutual self-promotion with Sir Peter Lely (some of whose impact upon English portraiture we have already seen), and bore the king several children: Anne (b.1661), Charles, 2nd Duke of Cleveland and 1st Duke of Southampton (b.1662), Henry, Duke of Grafton (b.1663, though the king seems to have harboured some reservations about his paternity), Charlotte (b.1664) and George, Duke of Northumberland (b.1665). Charles was fond of his children, and had Catherine of Braganza been able to give him any, this story might have been very different. 'He loves not the queen at all,' thought Pepys, 'but is rather sullen to her, and she by all accounts incapable of any children.' In contrast, 'The king is mighty kind to these bastard children and at this day will go at midnight to my Lady Castlemaine's nurses and take the child and dance it in his arms.'[48]

By 1667 Barbara Castlemaine's name had been linked with that of Henry Jermyn, courtier, dandy and successful property developer, and what one royal biographer calls Charles's 'generous affection' had been warmly engaged by a maid of honour, Frances Stuart.[49] That year Barbara was rumoured to be pregnant, and demanded that the king acknowledge the child, but he protested that he had not slept with her for the past six months. There was also a court rumour that he had nearly caught her with Henry Jermyn, who 'was fain to creep under the bed into her closet' to avoid royal detection. In January 1668 the king's affair with the actress Mary Davis was widely known, but although Lady Castlemaine moved out of Whitehall into Berkshire House, opposite St James's Palace, bought for her by the king, she remained on good terms with Charles, who paid her frequent visits. Her lovers during this period seem to have included the rope-dancer Jacob Hall, the actor Charles Hart, the playwright William Wycherley and, last but not least, Ensign John Churchill.

She was definitively supplanted in the king's affection by Louise de Kéroualle, Duchess of Portsmouth, in 1671–72, but succeeded, largely because of the king's regard for his children, in retaining significant influence at court. She was created Duchess of Cleveland in 1670, and her boys were granted arms testifying to their royal connection. In 1676 she left for Paris, to oversee the education of her daughters, and on her return to England in 1682 she found that her former power had evaporated. An ill-starred affair with the actor Cardell Goodman, not long before the no less unlucky marriage to Beau Fielding, made her something of a figure of ridicule. She died of dropsy in October 1709.

Some of John Churchill's biographers see his affair with Barbara Castlemaine as simply a young man's dalliance with an attractive and experienced older woman, but there is much more to it than that. Castlemaine was strong-willed and hot-tempered, capable of telling Charles that she would bring a child 'into Whitehall gallery and dash the brains of it out before the King's face' unless he acknowledged paternity. She was a major political figure, deploying her formidable interest against all who crossed her. Castlemaine was an implacable enemy of Lord Clarendon, who as lord chancellor repeatedly opposed the king's largesse towards her. When he left Whitehall in disgrace he saw her with Arlington and Bab May 'looking out of her open window with great gaiety and triumph, which all people observed'.[50]

Her relationship with her kinsman George Villiers, Duke of Buckingham, was more changeable, and was enlivened by a public spat in 1668–69 when Buckingham engaged Lady Hervey to undermine Castlemaine, only to be decisively outmanoeuvred himself. She had declared her conversion to Roman Catholicism in 1663, and favoured the French party at court, giving the French ambassador useful information on the attitude of the king and his ministers. Finally, she was a consummate accumulator of grants and pensions, and by 1674 she was worth, in theory, £12,000 a year. We should not concern ourselves with speculation about what Ensign Churchill might have learnt in the bedroom, though A.L. Rowse is doubtless right to call it ' a very liberal education', but he was certainly in a position to learn much about the manipulation of interest at court.[51]

Despite the family's first successes after the Restoration, the Churchills were not well off, and John had not been able to buy promotion in the army. His relationship with Barbara changed all that. She gave him a present of £5,000, which he immediately converted into an annuity of £500 a year. The 4th Earl of Chesterfield, whose grandfather had been one of Barbara's first lovers, benevolently attributed the gift simply to Churchill's delightful manners and appearance.

> Of all the men that I ever knew in my life (and I knew him extremely well) the late Duke of Marlborough possessed all the graces in the highest degree, not to say engrossed them; and indeed, he got the most by them, for I will venture (contrary to the custom of profound historians, who always assign deep causes for great events) to ascribe the better half of the Duke of Marlborough's greatness and riches to those graces . . . while he was an Ensign of the Guard, the Duchess of Cleveland . . . struck by those very graces, gave him five thousand pounds, with which he immediately bought an annuity for his life, of five hundred pounds a year of my grandfather [the Marquess of] Halifax, which was the foundation of his subsequent fortune. His figure was beautiful, but his manner was irresistible, by either man or woman.[52]

Others ascribe the gift to an occasion when Churchill's quick-wittedness prevented embarrassment. He was in bed with Barbara when the king arrived, and immediately jumped out of her window and made off across the courtyard: thus the payment was less for services rendered in bed than for alacrity in getting out of it. A similar version of the story has the Duke of Buckingham, then at odds with Barbara, pay a servant £100 for information on the lovers' next tryst, and ensure that the king called on her at the worst possible moment. After Barbara's prevarication over lost keys, Churchill was discovered naked in her wardrobe, and both he and Barbara knelt to beseech the monarch's forgiveness. 'Go; you are a rascal,' said Charles, 'but I forgive you because you do it for your bread.' Winston S. Churchill speculates that 'It may be that the two stories are one, and that untrue.' But there is nothing inherently improbable in the encounter, and the words are very much in Charles's tone. Moreover, by this stage his relationship with Barbara had cooled to one of friendship for the mother of part of his extensive brood, and, a serial adulterer himself, he could be generous in accepting the infidelities of others.[53]

Yet there is room to doubt just how far this generosity went in Churchill's case, for we will see very shortly that he was in 'the king's displeasure' at just this time.

Churchill never formally acknowledged his daughter with Barbara Castlemaine. She was styled Lady Barbara Palmer (for she was, in theory, an earl's daughter, even if Roger Palmer did not actually sire any of his wife's brood), though she was sometimes called Lady Barbara Fitzroy. However, Charles II never bestowed on her the surname which he gave to the acknowledged bastards that Barbara bore him, deliberately leaving her 'without a token of royal bounty'. Her mother was either remarkably thick-skinned or had a broad sense of humour, because she took the child to Paris in 1676 and installed her in the Convent of the Immaculate Conception of Our Lady in the rue Charenton. There, as the years went by, this witty and well-connected nun was visited by British travellers. Among them was James Douglas, Earl of Arran, heir to the Duke of Hamilton. Douglas had married Lady Susan Spencer in 1688, and John Evelyn thought him 'a sober and worthy gentleman'. When he visited the convent in 1690 the lure of young Barbara, who had evidently inherited some of her mother's temperament, proved too much for him, and she bore him a son, Charles Hamilton, on 20 March 1691. The boy (who took to styling himself the comte d'Arran) was sent off to live with his grandmother in Walpole House, Chiswick Mall, and Barbara ended her days as abbess of the Priory of St Nicolas in the Normandy town of Pontoise. James Douglas duly succeeded to his father's dukedom, but was killed in that desperate duel with Lord Mohun.[54]

The Dutch War

John Churchill's affair with Barbara Castlemaine took place against a background of rising international tension. The Treaty of Dover had, as we have seen, bound Charles to support Louis XIV in his attack on the Dutch. Louis was characteristically pleased with himself in poising a mighty war machine over the heads of the Dutch. 'After having taken precautions of all sorts,' he wrote with his usual immodesty,

> as much by alliances as raising troops, magazines, warships, and great sums of money . . . I made treaties with England, the Elector of Cologne, the bishop of Munster . . . also with Sweden, and to hold Germany in check, with the Dukes of Hanover and of Neuburg and

with the Emperor . . . I made my enemies tremble, astounded my neighbours, and brought despair to my foes . . . All my subjects supported my intentions . . . in the army with their valour, in the kingdom with their zeal, in foreign lands with their industry and skill; France has demonstrated the difference between herself and other nations.[55]

It is easy to be attracted by the splendour of Versailles, the spectacle of the French court, or the saga of Louis and his mistresses, and to forget just what a challenge this devout and opinionated monarch presented to Europe.[56] By invading Holland in the spring of 1672 he sought to improve upon the terms of the Treaty of Aix la Chapelle of 1668, which had given France useful gains on her northern frontier but had also left Dutch garrisons in Spanish-owned 'barrier fortresses' in an effort to restrict further French expansion. Louis' apologists suggest that he launched the Dutch War in 1672 not simply because of 'wounded pride or . . . insupportable arrogance', though even they can scarcely deny a fair measure of both these commodities, but because France had good reason to control the 'gates' of the kingdom, especially Antwerp, and to achieve the 'annihilation' of the Dutch commercial fleet.[57]

To do this he presided over a nation whose nobility was largely exempt from taxation, and where famines (long unknown in England) regularly killed tens of thousands: perhaps 800,000 were to die in the severe winter of 1709. Judicial torture, outlawed in England and soon to be abolished in Scotland too, was routine in French criminal investigations. A shocked John Evelyn watched a suspect who had refused to confess to theft racked, a process which 'severed the fellow's joints in a miserable sort, drawing him out at length in an extraordinary manner'. The victim then had two buckets of water poured down his throat 'with a horn (just such as they use to drench horses with)', but still denied his guilt. The affronted investigator told Evelyn that under these circumstances they could not hang the fellow, but could at least pack him off as a galley-slave, 'which is as bad as death'.[58]

The 'affair of the poisons', which diverted Louis' court in the 1670s, eventually saw thirty-four people executed and almost as many sent to the galleys or banished. When the marquise de Brinvilliers was executed for widespread poisoning, after the customary tortures, the cultured Madame de Sévigné complained that the crowd around her pyre was so great that she had, disappointingly, only been able to catch a glimpse of the victim's mobcap.[59] A sketch by Charles le Brun of the marquise on her way to execution shows a plump face exhausted by pain. Nancy Mitford suggested that Mme de Brinvilliers' 'appalling tortures' were 'probably no worse . . . than those she had inflicted'.[60] But one did not have to be a murderer to come to a bad end: a scurrilous cartoon of Louis' equestrian statue in the place des Victoires, depicting the king being led in chains by four mistresses, earned hanging for the printer, the bookseller and, for good measure, the printer's apprentice too.[61]

The republic which so affronted Louis was a federation of seven of the seventeen provinces of the Low Countries which had been under Spanish rule, and was governed by the States-General of the United Provinces, to which individual provinces sent delegates. The grand pensionary was its chief executive, and for some time successive ruling princes of Orange had been both stadholder (effectively an appointed constitutional monarch) and captain general. The British are fond of calling William of Orange, formally given both these offices in 1672, 'Dutch William'. However, his principality of Orange was actually on the southern Rhône, his mother was Mary, daughter of Charles I and Henrietta Maria, he had inherited some German blood from his grandfather William the Silent, French blood came through his maternal grandfather, Scots blood from his maternal great-grandfather, James I, and Danish blood through the latter's wife, Anne of Denmark. If he was Dutch it was by birth, residence and the most passionate conviction. Some have hailed him as 'the First European', and it was certainly thanks in part to his efforts that Louis' imperial dreams were to evaporate.

The first French attacks went unsurprisingly well, the Dutch frontier garrisons being overwhelmed with scarcely a shot fired. The Dutch government offered to make peace on generous terms, but Louis, beset by the blindness that so often afflicts dictators, rejected its offer. A riot in The Hague saw the grand pensionary, Jan de Witt, and his brother murdered by the mob, and now, under the determined leadership of William, the Dutch settled to their task. They opened their dykes, flooding thousands of acres of fertile land, and when the French began the systematic destruction of Dutch towns resistance only deepened.

If the Dutch had begun the war at a disadvantage on land, they enjoyed a comfortable supremacy over the French at sea, and this is what the Treaty of Dover was intended to counteract. Charles repudiated his debts by declaring a Stop of the Exchequer in January 1672, issued a Declaration of Indulgence, granting toleration to both dissenters and Roman Catholics, the following month, and looked forward to the

French subsidies which would enable him to fight a war, and, so he hoped, strengthen his army, without needing to ask Parliament for funds. The English and French fleets met at Portsmouth in May, and then cruised round to the coast of Suffolk, hoping to bring the Dutch to battle and then land troops in Zealand.

Ensign Churchill's company of 1st Foot Guards, one of those embarked on the fleet, was aboard the Duke of York's flagship *Prince*. On 28 May the Dutch under Admiral de Ruyter found the Allies at anchor in Southwold Bay, expecting an attack, with the French in a single squadron on the south of the line and two English squadrons to the north, and the wind coming in from the east-north-east, giving the Dutch the advantage. When the Dutch came into sight, with sixty-four ships to the Allies' eighty-two, the Duke of York led the English off northwards against the main body of the Dutch, but failed to make his intentions clear to the French, who sailed southwards and engaged the weaker Dutch vanguard.

The English lost their battle. Lord Sandwich, vice-admiral of the kingdom and Samuel Pepys's patron, who commanded the leading squadron, was killed, and his flagship *Royal James* was burnt. *Prince* was in the thick of things, as Captain John Narborough tells us.

> His Royal Highness went fore and aft in the ship and cheered up the men to fight, which did encourage them very much . . . Presently when [Captain] Sir John Cox was slain I commanded as captain, observing his Royal Highness's commands in working the ship, striving to get the wind of the enemy. I do absolutely believe no prince upon earth can compare with his Royal Highness in gallant resolution in fighting his enemy, and with so great conduct and knowledge in navigation as never any general understood before him. He is better acquainted in these seas than many masters which are now in the fleet; he is general, soldier, pilot, master, seaman; to say all, he is everything that man can be, and most pleasant when the great shot are thundering about his ears.[62]

Prince lost her captain and a third of her complement, and was so badly damaged that James shifted his flag to *St Michael*, and when she too was too badly mauled to serve as flagship he shifted it again to *London*. The French had done rather better, but there was a bitter dispute between two French admirals, and the whole episode was discouraging.

We might pause to consider how the battle reflected on James. That he had been brave is beyond question. But the fleet he commanded, drawn up in the expectation of battle, had been beaten, with loss, by a significantly inferior force. When he set off on the port tack with his two northernmost squadrons he did not order the French to follow. Perhaps, as the naval historian N.A.M. Rodger surmises, he might have thought it too obvious to suggest. However, it was his duty to have either agreed on a standard operating procedure or to have sent the appropriate signals. John Narborough became Rear Admiral Sir John Narborough soon after the action thanks to James's patronage, and we can scarcely blame him for describing his patron's behaviour in the best possible light. After the battle there was a disagreeable bout of 'blame the foreigner', and what was evidently a lost battle could be attributed to French negligence or cowardice. In fact James's behaviour should not escape censure: one does not become a successful admiral simply by being brave.

Whatever the reasons for the defeat in Southwold Bay, it is evident that John Churchill, war hero or not, did not stand high in royal favour. On 25 October 1672 Sir Winston Churchill told the Duke of Richmond that:

> My poor son Jack, that should have waited on Your Excellency thither, has been very unfortunate ever since in the continuation of the king's displeasure, who, notwithstanding the service he did in the last fight, whereof the Duke [of York] was pleased to give the King a particular character, would not give him leave to be of the Duke's bedchamber, although his highness declared he would not dispose of it to anyone else. He has been pleased since to let him have my cousin Vaughan's company, but with confinement to his country quarters at Yarmouth.[63]

The Lord Admiral's Regiment had lost four of its captains at Southwold Bay, and on 13 June John Churchill was commissioned into one of the vacancies. This left the unlucky Lieutenant Pick, once his superior in his company of 1st Foot Guards, pressing Lord Arlington's under-secretary for a captaincy, promising him £400 once his commission arrived, though there is no evidence that it ever did.

Captain John Churchill was now confined to his regiment's garrison at Great Yarmouth, which was convenient for rapid embarkation aboard the fleet but rather less handy for access to the capital, and had been denied the post as gentleman of the bedchamber to the Duke of York. The inference is clear: Charles wanted him out of Whitehall. Barbara might no longer be the king's favourite, but for a handsome young officer to get her with child was too much even for the merry monarch. Years later the Duchess of Portsmouth sent Churchill a rich snuffbox in memory of their (unspecified) association, and it is possible that the young cavalier had been fishing in forbidden waters again. Promoting Churchill out of the Foot Guards and into the Lord Admiral's Regiment also made perfect sense, for the Lord Admiral's was already warned for foreign service. Even so, John set off for the Continent well in advance of his regiment, and in June 1673 he was with the Duke of Monmouth's party of gentleman volunteers, supported by thirty troopers of the Life Guards, in the trenches before Maastricht, besieged by Louis in person. There, a determined garrison disposed of a variety of ingenious contrivances which were a good deal more unpleasant even than the disapproval of Charles II.

The Imminent Deadly Breach

Fortification and siegecraft had a grammar of their own, which John Churchill was now beginning to learn. The military historian David Chandler has observed that during the period 1680–1748 there were 167 sieges to 144 land engagements in Europe, and the Earl of Orrery affirmed in 1677: 'We make war more like foxes than lions; and you have twenty sieges for one battle.'[64] The high walls of medieval castles had offered but a poor defence against gunpowder, and this period saw the apogee of the new artillery fortification, the speciality of military engineers like the Frenchman Sebastien le Prestre de Vauban and his Dutch rival Menno van Coehoorn. The bastion, an arrow-shaped work jutting out from the main curtain wall of a fortress, was the key to the system. The cannon mounted on it could fire, from its flanking ramparts, along the wall and, from the ramparts on its angled faces, could sweep the gently-sloping glacis on the other side of the broad ditch protecting the brick or ashlar scarp, the wall which shored up the squat, solid mass of bastion and curtain. A 'covered way' enabled men to walk in safety along the top of the counterscarp, the wall which propped up the far side of the ditch, and a palisade of sharpened stakes protected the covered way against an enemy who might have fought his way up the glacis.

Outworks, like the half-moon-shaped demi-lune or ravelin, could be used to keep the attacker out of reach of bastion and curtain, and the hornwork, sometimes called a crownwork because of its spiky plan, might cover an attractive approach or an exposed suburb. A variety of ingenuity was employed to make life unpleasant for the attacker. Caponiers, hutch-like works whose name came from the Spanish for chicken house, sat smugly in the ditch, ready to blast storming parties who hoped to cross it. Tenailles were banks of earth rising up out of the ditch just in front of the curtain to prevent the attacker's artillery pounding the base of the wall. Ditches themselves might be wet, which made it hard for attackers to mine beneath them, but were prone to icing over in the winter and were smelly in the summer. Or they might be dry, in which case they were often provided with countermine galleries sneaking off below the glacis in the hope of allowing the defending engineers to interrupt the attackers' attempts at mining.

Faced with this intractable low-lying geometry, the attacker, having first ensured that he had his slow-moving battering train of siege guns to hand, would encircle the fortress, digging 'lines of circumvallation' to keep off raiding parties from the outside. At an early stage he would summon the fortress to surrender, but a cool-headed governor would usually reject such impertinence. When the Dutch were besieging Maastricht in 1676 the governor, Count Calvo, entered into the spirit of the witty exchanges that were common at this stage in the siege. George Carleton, then serving as a gentleman volunteer in the Prince of Orange's Foot Guards, tells us that:

> The governor, by a messenger, intimating his sorrow that we had pawned our guns for ammunition bread [the siege train was late in arriving], answer was made that in a few days we hoped to give him a taste of the loaves which he should find would be sent him into the town in extraordinary plenty . . . I remembered another piece of raillery which passed some days after between the Rhinegrave and the same Calvo. The former sending him word that he hoped within three weeks to salute the governor's mistress within the place, Calvo replied that he would give him leave to kiss her all over if he kissed her anywhere in three months.[65]

The attacker formally began the siege by 'breaking ground' (*tranchée ouverte*), commencing his first line of trenches facing the part of the fortress he planned to assail. From this 'first parallel' zig-zag saps were pushed out, until a second parallel could be dug; more sapping would lead to a third. While the attacker's engineers were busy grubbing their way forward, cannon would be mounted just forward of the parallels to bring fire to bear on the chosen front. A clear bell-like ring announced a direct hit on the exposed muzzle of a defending cannon, probably sending it spinning from its carriage, to the discomfiture of its detachment. Eventually, having first sent gusts of grapeshot scudding up the glacis to weaken the palisade, the attacker would try to storm the covered way.

This is where grenadiers came into their own. The hand grenade, its name deriving from the Spanish for pomegranate, which the little projectile resembled, was carried by specialist infantrymen who wore crownless caps rather than the more common tricorn hats, which made it easier for them to sling their muskets across their backs, leaving both hands free to light the fuse on their grenade before hurling it. The process required strength and courage, and by this time grenadiers, usually recruited on the basis of one company in each battalion, were the elite of the infantry. Although grenades could be used in a variety of circumstances, it was in the attack on the covered way that they were indispensable. The song 'The British Grenadiers' describes the process perfectly.

> Whene'er we are commanded to storm the palisades
> Our leaders march with fusees and we with hand grenades
> We throw them from the glacis, about our enemies' ears,
> Sing tow row, row, row, row, the British Grenadiers.

A good deal could go amiss long before the victorious grenadiers fell to 'drowning bumpers' and tow-row-rowing. A Scots grenadier, Private Donald McBane, was about to hurl his grenade over the palisades at Maastricht when it exploded

> in my hands, killing several about me, and blew me over the palisades; burnt my clothes so that the skin came off me. I . . . fell among Murray's Company of Grenadiers, flayed like an old dead horse from head to foot. They cast me into the water to put out the fire about me.[66]

George Carleton was part of a 'forlorn hope' (two sergeants and twenty grenadiers, a captain and fifty musketeers, and then a party carrying empty sandbags) sent to rush a breach in one of Maastricht's bastions. They got into the work well enough, but then:

> One of our own soldiers aiming to throw one [grenade] over the wall into the counterscarp among the enemy, it so happened that he unfortunately missed his aim, and the grenade fell down again on our side of the wall, very near the person who fired it. He, starting back to save himself, and some others who saw it fall doing the like, those who knew nothing of the matter fell into a sudden confusion . . . everybody was struck with a panic fear, and endeavoured to be the first who should quit the bastion . . . [67]

There was, though, a silver lining to this dark cloud: an ensign in Sir John Fenwick's Regiment was killed in the scuffle, and Carleton received the vacancy.

Once the grenadiers had duly taken the covered way, the attacker would 'crown' the spot with gabions, great wicker baskets filled with earth, and would then haul up his heavy guns to thunder out across the ditch at the base of the scarp. His gunners would try to adjust their fire so as to make a cannelure – a long groove – cutting through the retaining masonry, and eventually gravity would assert itself and the whole mass of scarp and rampart would tumble down into the ditch. To be deemed practicable for assault the breach had to be wide enough for two men to walk up it side by side without using their hands. The great Vauban would often check practicability himself, creeping forward after dark and scrambling back like some great earthy badger, muttering, '*C'est mûre, c'est bien mûre.*'[68]

The establishment of a practicable breach was usually the sign for the defender's drummers to beat the chamade, requesting a parley, or for the attacker to formally warn the governor that, with a practicable breach in his wall and assault imminent, he should give in at once to avoid a needless effusion of blood. If a town was taken by storm the attacking troops could not be expected to respect either the possessions of the inhabitants or the virtue of their womenfolk, and a sensible governor would make what terms he could, although usually the longer he left the negotiation the worse the deal he could expect. The garrison of a fortress taken by storm could expect no mercy, a practice designed to discourage pointless last-ditch defence and reflecting the very real difficulty of controlling maddened troops who had just come boiling into the town through a defended breach.

Of course there were variations to this theme. A fortress might be taken by a *coup de main*, perhaps with a group of picked men in civilian clothes making their way covertly into the place and then suddenly opening a gate to admit troops hiding just outside. In 1702 the Bavarians took Ulm by this method, but a subsequent Austrian attempt against Maubeuge miscarried when a French sentry beat a particularly sullen 'peasant' in a line of carts awaiting entry, only for the man (in fact an infantry major) to lose his temper and grab a musket from under the hay on his cart, killing the sentry but alerting the garrison. While the siege was in progress each side would drop mortar bombs onto the other, and sometimes a lucky hit on a magazine would end the struggle at a stroke: in 1687 the Venetian siege of the Acropolis at Athens was decided by two mortar bombs which caused extensive damage to the Parthenon, then used by the Turks to store gunpowder. Sorties might set back the progress of the siege by wrecking trenches and carrying off or breaking engineers' tools; mines could engulf whole bastions and discourage even the stoutest governor, or either side might run out of food or water.

In general, though, a siege, as Captain Churchill was now beginning to discover in the trenches before Maastricht, was rather like a formal dance, in which everyone stepped out to a rhythm they understood, with engineers calling out the time and gunners providing the percussion. Vauban reckoned that the average siege, if there was such a thing, would run for thirty-nine days from *tranchée ouverte* to the attacker's formal entry after terms had been agreed. In April 1705 Louis XIV gently reminded his governors that they were expected to put up a proper defence, not merely surrender on terms as soon as the outworks were lost:

> Despite the satisfaction I have derived from the fine and vigorous defence of some of my fortresses besieged during this war, as well as from those of my governors who have held their outworks for more than two months – which is more than the commanders of enemy fortresses have managed when besieged by my arms; nevertheless, as I consider that the main defences of my towns can be held equally as long as the outworks . . . I write you this letter to inform you that in the circumstances of your being besieged by the enemy it is my intention that you should not surrender until there is a breach in the main body of the *enceinte*, and until you have withstood at least one assault . . . [69]

On the other side of the lines, Brigadier General Richard Kane commended Captain Withers of Calthorp's Regiment, who in 1696, 'being posted in a chateau with only six men', faced the French off for several hours. When he saw that they were preparing to storm, he beat the chamade and received the same terms as much bigger garrisons which had surrendered without firing a shot. This ought to show officers, declared Kane,

> that they be not too forward in delivering up places committed to their charge; nor yet too foolhardy in standing out till an attack is begun, for then it will be too late. I mean, the attacking a breach, or such works as may be easily carried, especially when there is not a considerable force to oppose.

In 1695 the Allied governors of Dixmude and Diest were court-martialled for premature surrender. Nobody expected 'that they should stand a general assault, for the design . . . was only to keep the enemy employed as long as they could'. The Danish Major General Elnberger, governor of Dixmude, admitted that 'a panic seized him, which he could not get over, nor account for', and he was beheaded 'by the common executioner of the Danish forces' in November, after William of Orange had confirmed his sentence. He had served blamelessly for forty years until this single error of judgement cost him his life. The commanding officers who signed the capitulation with him lost their commissions, as did Brigadier O'Farrell, 'a man of long service, who had always behaved well' but had surrendered tiny Diest without even a show of resistance.[70]

Besiegers had their own hierarchy, with a general of the trenches doing duty for a day at a time, assisted by a trench major to oversee daily routine. The French, with their British allies, opened their trenches before the Tongres gate of Maastricht on the night of 17–18 June 1673, and a week later they were ready to assault a hornwork and ravelin in front of the gate. The Duke of Monmouth was trench general that day, and his contingent took part in the assault: Captain Churchill, it was said, planted a colour on the ramparts of the outwork. The night was spent consolidating the captured position, and Monmouth's men had scarcely retired to their tents after dawn the next day when the thud of a mine and an outbreak of firing announced that the governor, Jacques de Fariaux, a French gentleman in Dutch service, had mounted a sortie and recaptured the ravelin. Monmouth at once sent word to a nearby company of the French king's *Mousquetaires Gris*, commanded by Charles de Batz de Castelmore, comte d'Artagnan, and set off hot-foot for the ravelin.

Colonel Lord Alington was an eyewitness to what happened next, as he told Lord Arlington.

> After the duke had put on his arms [i.e. body armour], we went not out at the ordinary place, but leapt over the bank of the trenches, in the face of our enemy. Those that happened to be with the duke were Mr Charles O'Brien, Mr Villiers, Lord Rockingham's two sons, and Capt Watson their kinsman, Sir Tho Armstrong, Capt Churchill, Capt Godfrey, Mr Roe and myself, with the duke's two pages and three or four more of his servants, thus we marched with our swords in our hands to a barricade of the enemy's, where only one man could pass at a time. There was Monsieur d'Artagnan with his musketeers who did very bravely. This gentleman was one of the greatest reputation in the army, and he would have persuaded the duke not to have passed that place, but that being not to be done, this gentleman would go along with him, but in passing that narrow place was killed with a shot in his head, upon which the duke and we passed there where Mr O'Brien had a shot through his legs. The soldiers at this took heart the duke twice leading them on with great courage; when his grace found the enemy begin to retire, he was prevailed with to retire to the trench, the better to give his commands as there should be occasion. Then he sent Mr Villiers to the king for 500 fresh men and to give him an account of what had passed. When those men came, the enemy left us without any further disturbance . . . Some old commanders say, this was the bravest and briskest action that they had seen in their lives, and our duke did the part of a much older and more experienced general, and the king was very kind to him last night.[71]

Fariaux was a wily campaigner, and had stood siege five or six times before. Louis, in overall command, noted that he 'was used to dealing with narrow approach trenches which were untenable against the smallest sortie' – which had probably encouraged his sortie against the Tongres gate outworks – but saw that he could not cope with Vauban's new technique of moving forward in sweeping parallels 'almost as if we were drawn up for a field battle'. Having secured the outworks in front of the Tongres gate the French allowed Fariaux to capitulate, and on

1 July his 3,000 survivors marched out with the honours of war – drums beating, colours flying, musketeers with their slow-matches alight and bullets in their mouths, and all ranks with their 'bag and baggage' – with safe conduct to the nearest Dutch garrison.[72]

The Handsome Englishman

On their return to Whitehall at the close of the campaigning season that autumn Monmouth presented John Churchill to the king as 'the brave man who saved my life', which seems to have been instrumental in restoring him to royal favour. As succeeding events were to show, Monmouth was not the brightest of Charles's bastards. Although Monmouth was the monarch's eldest son, by the 'actress' Lucy Walter (who even Charles could not bring himself to ennoble), when Gilbert Burnet asked the king if it might not be wise to legitimise him and make him his successor instead of his Roman Catholic brother James, Charles 'answered him quick that, well as he loved him, he had rather see him hanged'.[73] However, Monmouth's approval strengthened Churchill's hand. Barbara Castlemaine had borne him a daughter the previous summer and, we may conclude, was now helping him financially; the Duke of York, already favourably disposed to his former page and having an affair with his sister, had seen him fight bravely at Southwold Bay; and now Monmouth told his indulgent father that John Churchill had saved his life. This was interest in full spate, and it would have been astonishing had our hero not been swept onwards by it.

There was, though, a sudden faltering in the flood. Early in 1673 Charles had to summon his Parliament to ask it for money to fight the Dutch War. He found it in a predictably curmudgeonly frame of mind. The war and the French alliance were unpopular, and the Declaration of Indulgence, which Charles had issued by virtue of his royal prerogative, was seen (perfectly rightly, in view of what we now know of the Treaty of Dover) to be giving encouragement to Roman Catholics. Although Parliament was prepared to grant him funds for the war, it did so at the price of his withdrawal of the Declaration of Indulgence and, even worse from the royal standpoint, passed the Test Act. The Corporation Act of 1671 had already prescribed that all members of corporations, besides taking the Oath of Supremacy, were to take communion according to the rites of the Church of England. The Test Act compelled all office-holders, military or civil, to 'declare that I do believe that there is not any transubstantiation in the sacrament of the Lord's Supper', and to take Anglican communion within three months. In 1678 the Act was extended, compelling all peers and MPs to make a declaration against transubstantiation and invocation of saints.

The Duke of York was an early casualty, and resigned all his offices. Prince Rupert headed the commission which took on his work as lord high admiral, and was already at sea with the fleet. He had failed to defeat the Dutch in two clashes in the Schoonevelt, and on 11 August his Allied fleet had the worst of a two-day battle against de Ruyter off Texel. Rupert had never much liked the French alliance, and lost little time in telling his countrymen what they already believed: that the French were useless at sea. Admiral d'Estrées had let him down, and the spectacle of d'Estrées blaming failure on his own second in command (who, in the great tradition of punishing the poorly-connected guiltless, was promptly clapped into the Bastille) made matters worse. The alliance was dead on its feet, but it was not until early 1674 that peace was made, although its terms allowed British troops who were serving as French-paid auxiliaries to remain on the Continent.

While all this was in progress the cabal fragmented, and by the end of the year Charles's new chief minister was his lord treasurer, Sir Thomas Osborne, known to posterity, by the title he soon acquired, as the Earl of Danby. Parliament, irritated by James's marriage to Mary of Modena, a Roman Catholic princess, and by the news of his conversion to Catholicism, debated a Bill for securing the Protestant religion by preventing any royal prince from marrying a Catholic without its consent. That summer Charles prorogued it, declaring that he would rather be a poor king than no king, and relying on the attentive Danby to improve his finances.

Charles had sent 6,000 men to France after the outbreak of the Dutch War, and after the conclusion of peace in 1674 much of this force remained in France, now under French pay and command, and connected with Britain only through recruiting. Its plight was made even more bizarre by the fact that the old Anglo-Dutch brigade in Dutch service, its members formally summoned back by Charles in 1672, was still soldiering on, with many of its British-born officers and men having become naturalised Dutchmen. There were awkward scenes in Brussels in 1679 when officers of the Anglo-Dutch brigade tried to find recruits amongst the British battalions that were then leaving for home after their stint in French service.

The British brigade sent to France in 1672 was commanded by the Duke of Monmouth, commissioned as a French lieutenant general, but, much as he enjoyed diverting scrambles like the siege of Maastricht, he exercised no overall command, for the regiments of his brigade were spread out across the Flanders and Rhine fronts. His colonels were, in consequence, very powerful men, and Robert Scott of the Royal English Regiment held his own courts-martial, appointed officers as he pleased, and happily swindled officers and men of their pay. Amalgamations and reductions were frequent, and in early 1674 Bevil Skelton's Regiment was merged with the Earl of Peterborough's Regiment to emerge as the 1st Battalion of the Royal English Regiment.[74] On 19 March 1674 a newsletter from Paris announced:

> Lord Peterborough's Regiment, now in France, is to be broken up and some companies of it joined to the companies that went out of the Guards last summer, and to be incorporated into one regiment, and to remain there for the present under the command of Captain Churchill, son of Sir Winston.[75]

His colonelcy, of course, was French, and his English rank did not begin to catch up for almost another year, when he became lieutenant colonel of the Duke of York's Regiment.

Much of the British brigade was destined to serve on France's eastern borders against the German coalition forces of the Emperor Leopold I and the Elector of Brandenburg, whose entry into what had begun as a Dutch war reflected the way in which it was tilting out of Louis' control. The French army on this front was commanded by Marshal Henri de la Tour d'Auvergne, vicomte de Turenne. Turenne was arguably the greatest captain of his age, and might have done even better during this war had it not been for his long-standing quarrel with the marquis de Louvois, Louis' formidable war minister.

When Field Marshal Lord Wolseley wrote his biography of Marlborough more than a century ago, he concluded that Turenne had been 'tutor in war' to the young Jack Churchill.[76] We know that Turenne called him 'the handsome Englishman'. There is also a story, widely repeated though without a reliable primary source to back it up, that, when a French colonel was forced back from a position, Turenne bet that Churchill, with fewer men under his command, would retake it: he won his money.[77]

On 16 June 1674 Turenne fought the emperor's army at Sinsheim, roughly midway between Philippsburg on the Rhine and Heilbronn on the Neckar. Both sides were roughly equal in numbers, and the Imperialists were strongly posted behind the River Breusch, on a slab of high ground. Turenne managed to turn both enemy flanks by making good use of unpromising terrain, getting his men onto the plateau by 'a narrow defile on one side and a steep climb on the other'.[78] Even French sources suggest that it was the disciplined fire of the British infantry that checked the counterattacks of Imperialist cuirassiers.[79] The careful historian C.T. Atkinson noted that Churchill's regiment was not present at the battle, but it is clear that both Churchill and his fellow colonel, George Hamilton of the Irish Regiment, accompanied Lord George Douglas, who had been sent off to reconnoitre with 1,500 musketeers and six light guns.

Serving as a volunteer, with no formal command responsibility, Churchill would have had the opportunity to see just how Turenne went about his business, and the French army, at around 25,000 men, was small enough for a well-mounted observer to follow its movements closely. The essence of Turenne's success at Sinsheim was his swift reading of the ground to see what chance it gave him to get at the enemy, and the routes he selected had not been identified by the Imperialists as likely avenues of approach. The French commemorative medal for the battle bore the words *Vis et Celeritas* (vigour and speed), which might so easily have been Churchill's own watchwords.[80]

By the time that Turenne had moved south to fight the battle of Ensheim, on 4 October 1674, in weather which worsened from drizzle to a downpour, Churchill's regiment was indeed present with the main French army. The fight hinged on possession of a little wood on the Imperialist left, eventually carried by the French, though with great bloodshed. Churchill's men fought their way through it, overran a battery, and cleared the Imperialist infantry from 'a very good ditch' which they then occupied, obeying the orders of 'M. de Vaubrun, one of our lieutenant generals' to hold that ground and advance no further. 'I durst not brag too much of our victory,' wrote our young colonel, 'but it is certain that they left the field as soon as we. We have three of their cannon, several of their colours and some prisoners.' Louis de Duras (later Earl of Feversham) commanded a troop of Life Guards at that battle, and was eventually to assume command of the British brigade. He declared that 'No one in the world could have done better than Mr Churchill could have done and M de Turenne is indeed very well pleased with all our nation,' and Turenne's official dispatch paid handsome tribute to Churchill and his men.[81] In his report to Monmouth, Churchill recorded the loss of eleven of his twenty-two officers, but added that Monmouth's own regiment of horse had fared far worse, losing its lieutenant colonel and almost all its officers killed or wounded, as well as half the troopers and several standards. He was anything but an uncritical admirer of Turenne's, though, and admitted that 'half our foot was posted so that they did not fight at all'.[82]

On 5 January 1675 Turenne won the battle that decided the campaign. He pulled back from the Rhine near Haguenau, and allowed many of his officers (including Louis de Duras) to take leave in Paris, giving the impression that he had ended the campaign, for armies usually slunk into winter quarters in October and emerged from their hibernation in April. But in fact he swung in a long fish-hook march round the Vosges, through Epinal and the Belfort gap, to find his opponents relaxed in their winter quarters near Colmar – and what better place to relax, with so much of the golden bitter-sweet Gewürztraminer conveniently to hand? Although the Imperialists managed to rally and face him at Turckheim, he kept them pinned to their position by frontal pressure before sending an outflanking force through the rough country on their left. Turenne took the village of Turckheim after a stiff tussle in which British musketry proved decisive, and went on to drive his opponents from Alsace. In July that year Turenne was killed by a cannonball, a loss that France could ill afford.

The campaign certainly showed Churchill the crueller side of war. In the summer of 1674 Turenne's men ravaged the Palatinate as they marched through it. This was done partly to obtain supplies and partly to prevent the Imperialists from obtaining them, but also, as Turenne told the Elector Palatine, who complained about the sufferings of his people, because the local populace attacked stragglers and isolated groups, murdering soldiers with the most appalling cruelty.[83] Turenne's harsh treatment of the Palatinate was not on the same scale as the deliberate destruction of the whole area seven years later, on the specific orders of Louis XIV, but even so the damage was frightful. Archdeacon Coxe quotes a letter written to Churchill from Metz in 1711 in which the widow Saint-Just thanks him because 'The troops who came and burnt everything around my land at Mezeray in the plain spared my estate, saying that they were so ordered by high authority.'[84]

If there had been any doubts about where John Churchill stood in royal favour, his campaigning under Turenne resolved them. His English lieutenant colonelcy had materialised in early 1675, and three years later he was appointed colonel of one of the regiments of foot to be raised, not this time to support the French, but to help defend the Dutch: the realignment of English foreign policy was now complete. There is, though, no evidence that Churchill's new regiment was ever actually formed. His colonelcy (carefully dated a day after that of George Legge, who was to be Pepys's master on the Tangier mission) was simply a device to ensure that John Churchill had 'precedence and pay equivalent to the very important work he was now called upon to discharge'. He had reached a key break in his career, and was striding out to bridge the narrow gap between soldiering and diplomacy: the young cavalier had come of age.

2

From Court to Coup

Love and Colonel Churchill

John Churchill was in love. Sarah Jennings, the object of his affections, had been born on 5 June 1660, the week after Charles II returned from exile.[1] Her father, Richard Jennings, came from a family of Somerset gentry which had moved up to Hertfordshire and lived at Holywell House near St Albans. Richard's father had been high sheriff of the county and MP for St Albans. He himself sat for the same constituency, and had supported John Pym, one of the leaders of the opposition to Charles I in the early days of the Long Parliament, but had later, as a member of the Convention Parliament, backed the return of Charles II.

Although Richard Jennings was in theory a wealthy man, with perhaps £4,000 a year from property in Hertfordshire, Somerset and Kent, his estates were encumbered with debt and he had many younger siblings who had to be provided for. Sarah was the youngest of five children, with two brothers and two sisters, and it may have been the strains of a large family and hopeless debts that drove her parents to split. She moved to London with her mother Frances, who sought (unavailingly) to rescue her dowry from the shipwreck of Richard's finances. In 1673 Sarah followed her sister Frances into the household of the Duchess of York. Frances had served James's first wife Anne Hyde until her death in 1671, and soon became a maid of honour to Mary of Modena. The comte de Gramont called her 'la belle Jenyns', who was as lovely as 'Aurora or the promise of spring'. It speaks volumes for her determination that she resisted the Duke of York's roving eye and busy hands, but remained on sufficiently good terms to get her sister a place in the household.

In 1668 Richard Jennings died, and Sarah's mother, who inherited little but his creditors, moved into an apartment in St James's Palace with her daughters. The scurrilous Mrs Manley, author of *The New Atlantis*, a Tory scandal-sheet, was later to accuse her of witchcraft. She was like 'the famous Mother Shipton, who by the power and influence of her magic art had placed her daughter in the Court'.[2] There are too many contemporary complaints about Mrs Jennings for us to attribute them simply to political malice. She was certainly evil-tempered, may actually have been unhinged, and some suggested that she dabbled in the black arts and the procurement of that commodity most sought after by the court, pretty girls. In any case, the maids of honour were hardly above suspicion. Samuel Pepys grumbled that they bestowed their favours as they pleased without anyone taking any notice, and Frances and a friend once amused themselves by dressing up as orange sellers (a common cover for prostitution) and standing outside a playhouse to accost two gentlemen of their acquaintance. They were given away by their expensive shoes.

Sarah met John towards the end of 1675, and they began to dance together at balls and parties. Sarah had a blazing row with her mother at about this time, and eventually Mrs Jennings was 'commanded to leave the court and her daughter in it, notwithstanding the mother's petition, that she might have her girl with her, the girl saying she is a mad woman'. Theirs was a relationship which prospered only at a distance, and attempts at reunion regularly resulted in hot words. Some time after her marriage, after yet another furious argument in which she urged her mother to get into the coach and not freeze to death outside it, Sarah affirmed that 'I will ever be your most dutiful daughter, whatever you are to me.'[3]

Just as John Churchill's character was shaped by growing up in straitened circumstances, so Sarah's was influenced by her own experience of poverty, genteel though it was, and by her inability to tolerate her mother's company, however much both of them genuinely hoped that their next meeting would bury bad feelings for ever. We often pay out in adult life the coins we receive as children, and in Sarah's tumultuous relationship with her mother we have a foretaste of her dealings with her own daughters. Sarah was certainly beautiful, not with the classical good looks of her sister Frances, but with that thin edge of imperfection that men often find even more attractive. She had long fair hair that she always made the most of, full, firm lips, a naturally pink complexion, and a nose that turned up, ever so slightly, at its tip.

Even at the age of sixteen she had unstoppable determination and a flaming temper. There is a great deal about Sarah Marlborough that is hard to admire, but the three centuries that separate us cannot dull the impact of this outspoken, uncontrollable and self-willed beauty. One can see why, once John Churchill had met her, he never thought seriously about marrying anybody else, and we can never practically separate John Churchill, soldier and politician, from John Churchill, husband and lover, nor usefully speculate on what he might or might not have become without Sarah. One incident throws their relationship into sharp perspective. When Marlborough was captain general of Queen Anne's armies and one of the most important men in the kingdom, he entered Sarah's dressing room to tell her that Sidney Godolphin, the lord treasurer, was going to dine with them. She was brushing a hank of her yellow hair over one shoulder and, furious at having her evening spoiled, seized a pair of scissors and cut it off, then flounced out in a fury. He picked up the severed tress, tied it up with ribbon, and kept it in his strongbox until he died. She found it there, and it broke her heart.

Some of the letters written during their courtship have survived. All are undated, most are from John to Sarah, and she herself assures us that the correspondence started when she was not more than fifteen. She told him to burn her letters, and he seems to have obeyed her, because the eight that survive are only copies. Sarah, in contrast, kept his letters and read them from time to time, and when she had only a year to live, wrote on one: 'Read over in 1743 desiring to burn them, but I could not do it.' His letters, in black ink and a slightly sloping hand, show all the symptoms of courtly love. 'You are, and ever shall be, the dear object of my life,' he tells her, 'for by heavens I will never love anybody but yourself.' In another he assures her:

> If your happiness can depend upon the esteem and love I have for you, you ought to be the happiest thing breathing, for I have never loved anybody to the height I do you. I love you so well that your happiness I prefer much above my own; and if you think meeting me is what you ought not to do, or that it will disquiet you, I promise you I will never press you more to do it. As I prefer your happiness above my own, so I hope you will sometimes think how well I love you; and what you can do without doing yourself an injury, I hope you will be so kind as to do it – I mean in letting me see that you wish me better than the rest of mankind; and in return I swear to you that I never will love anything but your dear self, which has made so sure a conquest of me that, had I the will, I will not have the power ever to break my chains. Pray let me hear from you, and know if I shall be so happy as to see you tonight.[4]

He gave her presents. First she had a choice of two puppies, and then he sent her a waistcoat: 'I do assure you there is not such another to be had in England.'[5] From what we already know of Sarah we will not be surprised to hear that there were rows. 'To show you how unreasonable you are in accusing me,' he wrote, in a letter which still bears red seals and threads of green ribbon,

> I dare swear you yourself will own that your going from me in the Duchess's drawing-room did show as much contempt as was possible. I may grieve at it, but I will no more complain when you do it, for I suppose it is what pleases your humour . . . Could you see my heart you would not be so cruel to say I do not love you, for by all that is good I love you and only you. If I may have the pleasure of seeing you tonight, please let me know, and believe that I am never truly pleased but when I am with you.[6]

This correspondence dates from 1675–76, after John's service under Turenne in Alsace and the Palatinate. However, it is hard to be sure of exact dates. Courtin, the French ambassador in London, had kept Louvois apprised of the goings-on at court, and when there was first talk of John Churchill commanding a French regiment, Louvois advised against it, arguing that Churchill's real concern at that moment was 'to give more satisfaction to a rich and faded mistress' rather than to serve his own royal master, undoubtedly a reference to his relationship with Barbara Castlemaine. Some time later, Courtin reported that 'Mr Churchill prefers to serve the very pretty sister of Lady Hamilton than to be lieutenant colonel of Monmouth's regiment.' In 1665 Frances Jennings had married Sir George Hamilton, Marlborough's fellow colonel, who commanded the Irish Regiment until his death in action in 1676. Winston S. Churchill dates Courtin's second letter to November 1676. It raises the question as to why Churchill might have been interested in being lieutenant colonel to Monmouth, at best a sideways move in the hierarchy, but it does suggest that he was now so heavily preoccupied with Sarah that he was unwilling to accept a full-time command appointment.[7]

Several things blocked the path of true love. First, John Churchill's relationship with Barbara Castlemaine was common knowledge at court, and Courtin reported to Paris that Sarah's parents had refused their consent to her marriage with John. This cannot be true, for Sarah's father was long dead, but it may well reflect the opposition of Sarah's mother. Next, Sir Winston and Lady Churchill were firmly against the union. They hoped that John would marry another of the maids of honour, Catherine Sedley, daughter and heiress to the wealthy Sir Charles Sedley. Her portrait suggests that she was by no means as attractive as Sarah (the attentive Courtin called her 'very rich and very ugly'), and she certainly had a caustic wit. It may be that rumours linking her name with John's were the reason for Sarah's accusation in the last of his letters quoted above. Catherine eventually became yet another of James's mistresses, though when Queen Mary reminded her of the fact after 1688 she riposted: 'Remember, ma'am, if I broke one of the commandments *with* your father, you have broken another *against* him.'[8]

Mrs Manley, writing long after the event, with the intention of damaging the Marlboroughs' reputation and making money, provided two alternative versions of how John ended his relationship with Barbara Castlemaine and married Sarah. The first has him provide a virile 'body double' who, his face concealed, tumbled the ever-ready Barbara, enabling a supposedly furious John to catch the lovers *in flagrante*. The second has Sarah replace Barbara in bed before one of John's visits. This time the lovers are caught by Sarah's mother, who insists upon marriage to save her daughter's honour and promptly produces a priest. Both stories are wholly improbable. Barbara had enjoyed a long sexual relationship with John and borne him a child, so the story of the body double is scarcely convincing. The stage-managing of the second scenario would have been difficult: how did Sarah gain access to Barbara's bed, and where were priest and mother concealed?

The truth of this blazing courtship may actually be gleaned from the surviving love letters. Sarah told John that: 'If it were true that you have that passion for me which you say you have, you would find out some way to make yourself happy – it is in your power.'[9] In other words, if he really loved her then he should marry her or end the relationship. This clearly failed to move him (perhaps his parents, at this very moment, were reminding him how Catherine Sedley's fortune would secure his future), and in another letter Sarah warned him: 'As for seeing you, I am resolved I never will in private nor in public if I could help it.'[10] Things went from bad to worse, and the affronted colonel wrote to Elizabeth Mowdie, Sarah's waiting woman:

> Your mistress's usage to me is so barbarous that sure she must be the worst woman in the world, or else she would not be thus ill-natured. I have sent a letter which I desire you will give her. It is very reasonable for her to take it, because it will then be in her power never to be troubled with me more, if she pleases. I do love her with all my soul,

but will not trouble her, for if I cannot have her love, I shall despise her pity. For the sake of what she has already done, let her read my letter and answer it, and not use me thus like a footman.[11]

Sarah responded that she had done nothing to deserve the sort of letter he had written her, and told him that it was entirely up to him whether or not he saw her, though she would be 'extremely pleased' if he decided against it.

The correspondence thundered on like the most obdurate battle between resolute opponents, with Sarah yielding nothing and John returning to the attack with as much determination. Even when they seemed to have agreed on marriage, John feared that the sudden reappearance of Sarah's sister Lady Hamilton would wreck his plans; but Sarah assured him that he had nothing to fear if his intentions were honourable, and he should not worry that her sister's arrival could 'make any change in me, or that it is in the power of anybody to alter me but yourself'.[12] We know that John formally asked the Duchess of York to consent to the marriage, and we can presume that both Sarah's mother and his own parents agreed.

Sir Winston had his own reasons for giving consent, just as he had for pressing the advantages of the Sedley connection. The old cavalier was broke again, and could survive only if John agreed to give up his inheritance so that Sir Winston could sell off some property to pay his debts. A Sedley marriage would have prevented the need for this, and if we need further evidence of the intensity of John's love for Sarah it is that he was prepared to give up his family estate for her. Even Macaulay was reluctantly prepared to admit that he must have been 'enamoured indeed' to let so much money slip past him. True, their poverty was relative, for he had his army pay and the £500 a year interest on the 'infamous wages' he had received from Barbara. Moreover, Mary of Modena had been charmed by the couple, and with her interest firmly engaged they married, probably in her apartments, in the winter of 1677–78. Colonel and Mrs Churchill could not afford to buy a suitable house, so they stayed in his lodgings in Jermyn Street (five doors along from St James's, not far from where Wilton's restaurant now dispenses its matchless Dover Sole) when he was in London, and she spent a good deal of time in Dorset with Sir Winston and Lady Churchill. Although her circumstances were not precisely the same as those in which her husband had grown up, it is not hard to see how the episode helped sharpen her desire to make money.

John Churchill, a full colonel in the English army from early 1678, was now a senior liaison officer, his tasks part-military and part-diplomatic, negotiating with the Dutch about arrangements for accommodating the British troops who were now on their way to Flanders to fight against the French as a result of the English government's political realignment. He was very much in the Duke of York's mind, and enjoyed a measure of devolved authority. In April that year the Duke of York told William of Orange, concerned about a French attack on Bruges, held by four British battalions, that 'Churchill will speak to you more at large about it.' Churchill was well aware that although the majority of Englishmen, and indeed the Duke of York himself, were in favour of vigorous prosecution of the war, the king himself was not.

In September 1678 he was back in Flanders, this time as a brigadier of foot, his command consisting of two battalions of foot guards, and a battalion each of the Holland, the Duchess's and Lord Arlington's regiments. However, he knew that peace negotiations were under way at Nijmegen, and doubted if he would actually get into action. 'You may rest satisfied that there will be certain peace in a very few days,' he told Sarah.

> The news I do assure you is true; therefore be not concerned when I tell you that I am ordered over and that tomorrow I go. You shall be sure by all opportunities to hear from me, for I do, if possible, love you better than I ever did. I believe it will be about the beginning of October before I shall get back, which time will appear like an age to me, since in all that time I shall not be made happy with the sight of you. Pray write constantly to me. Send your letters as you did before to my house, and there I will take order how they shall be sent off to me. So, dearest soul of my life, farewell.
>
> My duty to my father and mother and remember me to everybody else. Tuesday night. My will I have here sent you for fear of accident.

Sarah later endorsed the letter: 'Lord Marlborough to ease me when I might be frightened at his going into danger.'[13] Her sister's husband, George Hamilton, had been killed in action, and she knew that status was no guarantor of safety.

Politics, Foreign and Domestic

John was perfectly right about the peace. The Treaty of Nijmegen ended Louis' Dutch War. If he fell short of his aim of 'annihilating' the Dutch,

Louis had improved his position along the frontier with the Spanish Netherlands, annexed Franche-Comté, and made important gains in Lorraine. Moreover, although Europe was to remain at peace for the next ten years, during this time Louis strengthened his hand by a variety of means. Some territories were declared to be *réunis à la couronne*, often on flimsy legal pretext; others were purchased from local rulers anxious to deal soon rather than fight later, and still others were simply occupied. Of special importance were Strasbourg, and its bridgehead Kehl, just across the Rhine, gateway into the Empire, and Casale on the Po, bought from the Duke of Mantua, on the edge of the Spanish-held Duchy of Milan. The industrious Vauban busied himself remodelling captured fortresses, and laying out his *pré carré*, a double line of strongholds, on the northern frontier. Although the army was reduced after the peace, thirty-six battalions were ready for immediate service and cadres were kept in place to aid rapid expansion. Louis believed that his ambitions had been checked temporarily, not halted for ever, and at once began to use diplomacy in an effort to dismantle the hostile coalition before he tried again. His interventions in English politics were designed to break the link between England and Holland. Nijmegen was not really a peace, more a ten years' truce.

The historian Keith Feiling affirmed that the Earl of Danby's four years in office were 'the most constructive of the reign, illustrating the forces which, beneath the surface of faction, were making a real advance'.[14] Danby did wonders for the English royal finances, and helped lay the foundations of a civil service, with Samuel Pepys rebuilding the fleet and William Blathwayt bringing the beginnings of order to the administration of the army. The foundation of the Royal Hospitals at Chelsea and Kilmainham, in 1682 and 1684 respectively, showed that the nation was beginning to glimpse the debt it owed to its soldiers, though to this day it has never recognised it fully.

Danby was close to being a real prime minister, and based himself on support in a carefully-managed Parliament, where interest was slapped on with a trowel, and in the wider nation. But if he could usually push through the king's business, he could not prevent politics from becoming rancorously factional, and the terms 'Whig' and 'Tory' date from about this period. The Whigs were named after the radical kirk faction in Scotland, the word itself deriving from the shout of *whiggam* used by drovers to hasten their horses. A Tory was an Irish outlaw, for it was alleged that the Duke of York relied for his support on Irish papists.

Louis may not have beaten the Dutch, but he certainly did for Danby. The ink was no sooner dry on the Treaty of Nijmegen than the Whigs, fearing that Charles would use his army to enforce Catholicism at home, demanded its disbandment. Danby's opponents Shaftesbury and Russell were liberally provided with French gold and used it to buy votes, while the French ambassador helped them discredit Danby by demonstrating that, for all his anti-French and Protestant rhetoric, he had actually been receiving French subsidies. It was the end of Danby, at least for the moment: he was impeached for intriguing with foreign powers and imprisoned in the Tower, where he remained till 1684, when Charles granted him a pardon.

The fall of Danby was subsumed within a greater crisis. In September 1678 a clergyman turned adventurer named Titus Oates revealed details of a 'Popish Plot' to murder the king and install the Duke of York in his place. Some fragments of truth seemed to make the rest of the story credible, and a new Parliament met in 1679 in a mood of Protestant hysteria. Charles tried to govern through a council that now included Monmouth and the opposition leaders. It produced a plan designed to limit the powers of a Catholic monarch, but the Commons went further, and drew up a Bill to exclude James from the succession. Monmouth, 'our beloved Protestant Duke', was the darling of the opposition: he hinted that there was a 'black box' whose contents proved that Charles had married his mother in exile. Charles's latest mistress, Louise de Kéroualle, Duchess of Portsmouth, was seen as further evidence of francophilia at court, and when Nell Gwyn was held up by the mob at Oxford in 1681 she went straight to the crowd's heart by yelling: 'Pray, good people, be civil. I am the *Protestant* whore.'

The Popish Plot and the Exclusion crisis dominated politics till 1683, and there were times when it did indeed seem as if ''41 is come again'. Charles weathered the storm because of his courage and sharp political acumen, so often cloaked in indolence or the pursuit of pleasure. The Earl of Ailesbury thought that the king 'knew men better than any that hath reigned over us, and when he gave himself time to think, no man ever judged better of men and of things'.[15] Although Charles may be censured for letting innocent men face a traitor's death when he knew them to be guiltless, perhaps their lives were the price he paid for his throne. In 1681 he deftly summoned a new Parliament to the old royalist stronghold of Oxford, broke the back of the opposition, and dissolved Parliament: he did not summon another. A supportive public reaction enabled him to attack some of his most prominent opponents, and the fictitious Popish Plot was replaced, in 1683, by real attempts on his life. The Earl of Shaftesbury, the most dangerous of the opposition leaders, fled abroad, and the discovery of the Rye House conspiracy to murder Charles and his brother on their way back from Newmarket races saw the Earl of Essex kill himself in the Tower and Lord Russell leave it to be beheaded on Tower Hill.

None of this was comfortable for John Churchill, and we must now see how his own career flew in these gusty winds. He had been made gentleman of the bedchamber to the Duke of York in 1673, and master of his wardrobe in 1679. He and Sarah were too firmly linked to the Yorks not to share the battering they took, and in 1679 they joined James, judiciously exiled by his brother, first in The Hague and then in Brussels, where they lived in the same house that had been occupied by Charles before his restoration. James began to make plans to settle there indefinitely, first calling for his fox-hounds and then for his daughter, Princess Anne. When Charles fell ill that autumn his advisers felt that James should be on hand in case he died, and Churchill, in England at the time, was sent to bring him over. No sooner did they arrive than Charles recovered, and his advisers now determined that James should return to Brussels.

John, in the meantime, was sent to Paris to further negotiations for a subsidy from Louis, which would help Charles survive without calling another Parliament, and thus reduce the risk of an Exclusion Bill being passed. He was authorised to tell the French that his master would henceforth support the interests of Louis, and apologise for his support for William of Orange, not least for letting his daughter Mary marry the man. The negotiations failed because Louis would not offer sufficient money, for he was doing perfectly well in suborning the opposition, and John was soon back with his master in Brussels. But James had had enough of the place, and obtained his brother's leave to live in Scotland. He travelled to London, and then went overland to Edinburgh, taking thirty-eight days for the journey. John accompanied him, but Sarah, heavily pregnant, stayed behind in their Jermyn Street apartment.

They corresponded fondly. John unsuccessfully begged Sarah not to let her sister Frances marry a former suitor, Lieutenant Colonel Richard Talbot, an Irish Roman Catholic gentleman who had the character-forming distinction of having escaped from Drogheda when Cromwell stormed the place in 1649, and was himself caught up on the fringes of the Popish Plot. James later made Dick Talbot Earl of Tyrconnell and his viceroy in Ireland, and with the defeat of the Jacobites the Tyrconnells went into exile.[16] Lady Tyrconnell makes one more brief entry on history's stage. When James was beaten by William of Orange on the Boyne in 1690 he rode hard for Dublin, where Frances congratulated him on arriving so well in advance of his men, and offered him food. He replied that after such a breakfast he had no stomach for his dinner.

When James was summoned south by his brother in early 1680 John went with him, and urged Sarah to:

> Pray for fair winds, so that we may not stay here, nor be long at sea, for should we be long at sea, and very sick, I am afraid it would do me great hurt, for really I am not well, for in my whole lifetime I never had so long a fit of headaching as now: I hope the red spots of the child will be gone against I see her, and her nose straight, so that I may fancy it be like the mother, so I would have her be like you in all things else.[17]

They were destined for cruel disappointment, for little Harriet (or Hariote, as her delighted father spelt her name) died in infancy, whether because those red spots were harbingers of something sinister, or for one of a dozen other reasons we cannot say.

James spent the summer of 1680 in London, and Charles hoped that he might be able not to order his brother into exile again. The Duke of York's uncertain future made it hard for him to secure an appointment for his young protégé. Although the governorship of Sheerness, command of the Lord Admiral's Regiment, and even the post of ambassador to France or Holland were spoken of, James was determined not to be separated from Churchill if he went into exile again. He was right to be concerned, for Charles feared that a new Parliament, due to meet on 21 October, would prepare a second Exclusion Act, and might even impeach his brother. The council was divided in its opinion, and James himself was all for facing down the opposition, and blamed the Earl of Halifax and the Duchess of Portsmouth for recommending his departure, but he reluctantly heeded his brother's command to go back to Scotland. This time the Churchills could go north together, and they reached Leith after five days' voyage.

James was not simply exiled to Edinburgh but was, by virtue of letters patent which John Churchill brought up to him in June 1681, the king's commissioner in Scotland and effectively its viceroy. He had arrived in the aftermath of a rising by Covenanters, Lowland opponents of the episcopacy which had returned to Scotland with the Restoration.

Monmouth had beaten them decisively at Bothwell Bridge near Glasgow in June 1679, doing much for his own reputation south of the border, but not snuffing out their resistance, which remained especially strong in the south-west. Many leading Covenanters fled to Holland, where they joined English opposition leaders who had escaped Charles's reassertion of his authority, and, ironically, were soon joined by Monmouth himself, exiled at last by his exasperated father.

James persevered in the persecution of the Covenanters, often using Catholic highlanders as his chosen instruments, and there are those who see in his policy in Scotland in 1681–82 a foretaste of what he would have done in England after 1685 had he been given the chance. Judicial torture was still legal in Scotland, although it had to be authorised by the council. Gilbert Burnet, no unbiased critic, suggested that while most members of the council would have avoided watching a man being 'struck in the boots', as wedges were hammered in between an iron boot and his foot, James observed the process with 'unmoved indifference'. The martyrology inevitably generated by this sort of conflict inflated some of the atrocities committed by the government and its supporters, but there is no doubt that some of James's adherents plied boot, thumb-screws and smouldering cord with inventive zeal.

Churchill's attitude to James's policy in Scotland at this time helps us understand the process which was to lead to his decisive breach with his patron in 1688. James was anxious to be permitted to return to England, and early in 1681 sent Churchill to London to urge Charles not to allow Parliament to sit, to make an alliance with France, whose resultant sub-sidy would enable him to rule without Parliament, and then to summon him homewards. Churchill did his best for his master, but made it clear that he did not support James's blustering threats to raise Catholic Scots and Irish to support him, which, after all, was precisely what many of his English opponents expected him to do.

When she was an old woman, Sarah recalled how much she and her husband had hated the persecution of the Covenanters.

I have cried at some of these trials, to see the cruelty that was done to some of these men only for their choosing to die rather than tell a lie. How happy would this country be if we had more of these sort of men! I remember the Duke of Marlborough was mightily grieved one day at a conversation he had heard between the Earl of Argyll . . . and the Duke of York. The Duke of Marlborough told me he never heard a man speak more reason than he [i.e. Argyll] did to the Duke and after he had said what he at first resolved, the Duke would never make an answer to anything, but 'You shall excuse me, my Lord, You shall excuse me, my Lord,' and continued so for a long time . . . I remember the Duke of Marlborough told me when we were in Scotland, there came a letter from Lewis the Grand to the Duke of York, writ by himself; which put all the family [i.e. household] into a great disorder, for nobody could read it. But it was enough to show that there was a strict correspondence between the Duke and the King of France.[18]

We must be cautious about accepting Sarah's recollections at face value, for she could see, just as well as we can, how evidence of John's growing concern at James's policy might mitigate his action in 1688.

Yet her words cannot be brushed aside as the mutterings of a partisan octogenarian, for they are corroborated by those of John himself. James's chief advisers at this time were Churchill, George Legge, later Lord Dartmouth, and the Duke's brother-in-law Laurence Hyde, later Earl of Rochester.[19] All agreed that James's position would be much improved if he would consent to attend Anglican service, and the Earl of Halifax, the most supple of Charles's ministers, warned that unless James complied 'his friends would be obliged to leave him like a garrison one could no longer defend'. In September 1681 Churchill told Legge that they had failed to persuade James. 'You will find,' he wrote glumly, 'that nothing is done in what was so much desired, so that sooner or later we must all be undone . . . My heart is very full, so that should I write to you of the sad prospect I fear we have, I should try your patience.'[20]

James soon found himself in conflict with the Earl of Argyll, who made his feelings clear by opposing a clause in the Scottish Test Act which sought to exempt members of the royal household from taking the Protestant oath of allegiance. Argyll swore the oath of allegiance himself, but qualified it by adding 'so far as is consistent with the Protestant religion', and went on to put his objections to the Test in writing. In December 1681 he was tried for treason, and James helped ensure that he was condemned to death. Churchill wrote at once to James's private secretary Sir John Werden, an old friend, urging that James should show mercy, and received a hopeful reply: 'now (in regard to your old friendship, which you put me in mind of) I hope he will have the King's pardon and the effects of his bounty, and hereafter in some measure deserve both'.[21] Argyll escaped from Edinburgh Castle shortly afterwards, and Churchill wrote at once to George Legge, hoping that the escape would not be taken too seriously. It was certainly not in the government's interest to execute Argyll, for a treason conviction meant that his lands and hereditary jurisdictions were already forfeit. But now, in the Low Countries with so many of the opposition leaders, he was another of James's embittered opponents, and when Monmouth rose against James II in 1685 he led a rebellion in the western Highlands but was speedily captured and, this time, beheaded.

As early as 1681 Churchill grasped the essence of what would eventually ruin James. He was usually physically courageous and, as a recent biographer observes, 'had high standards of honour and integrity, from which he deviated only rarely'.[22] Yet the Earl of Ailesbury, who risked life and fortune for James, wrote that Charles II 'was a great master of king-craft and I wish to God that his royal father and brother had been endowed with the same talent and for the same motives'. James, he thought, 'wanted for nothing but the talent of his royal brother'.[23] His religious conviction hardened moral courage but dissolved pliability, and as king he was to display 'political incompetence' laced with 'sheer bad luck'.[24] Ultimately he lacked judgement, and those who, like John Churchill, owed their rise to his patronage, feared even before he ascended the throne that his fall would eventually encompass their own. James was impossible to steer, and much later, in the draft of a memoir ghosted by Gilbert Burnet, Sarah argued that he had been undone by flattery: 'I saw poor K James ruined by this that nobody would honestly tell him of his danger till he was past recovery: and that for fear of displeasing him.'[25]

James was allowed to return to England in the spring of 1682, and set off from Leith for Yarmouth on 4 May, with Churchill among his entourage. Sarah remained in Edinburgh. On 19 July 1681 she had given birth to a daughter, Henrietta, who was baptised at St Martin-in-the- Fields on the twenty-ninth, and then left in Jermyn Street in the care of a nurse. John Churchill had not yet seen her. After a stormy four-day voyage they arrived in Yarmouth, and went by road to Norwich and thence to Newmarket, where Charles was enjoying the horseracing. While they were there John wrote to tell Sarah, still in Edinburgh, that he had just received a letter from London saying that Henrietta was very well. 'Everybody seems to be very kind to the Duke,' he added, hoping that his recall would be permanent, enabling the Churchills to move back to London. Indeed it was. Charles asked his brother to return to Scotland, wind up his affairs there and return with his wife and youngest daughter, Anne.

The ducal party sailed from Margate on the frigate *Gloucester* on 4 May accompanied by a small squadron, including the yacht *Catherine* with Samuel Pepys aboard: he had hoped to sail with the duke but the cramped conditions aboard *Gloucester* made this impossible. Early on the morning of their second day at sea, while most of the passengers were asleep, *Gloucester* struck the sandbank known as Lemon and Ore off Cromer on the Norfolk coast. After hanging on to the sandbank for some time she slipped off into deep water and sank almost immediately. The ship's pilot, Captain Ayres, was court-martialled and sentenced to perpetual imprisonment for negligence, and Pepys told his old associate Will Hewer that Ayres was doubly guilty because 'Sir John Berry, his master, mates, Col Legge, the Duke himself' had all agreed that the squadron should stand out further from the land. Although the sea was calm and there were ships in close company, there may have been as few as forty survivors from perhaps three hundred passengers and crew.

The loss of the *Gloucester* was soon politicised. Some, of a Tory persuasion, maintained that James did his best to save the vessel, and Sir John Berry, the vessel's captain, affirmed that his sailors were so devoted to the duke that 'in the midst of their affliction and dying condition [they] did rejoice and thank God that his royal highness was preserved'. Others, of a more whiggish view, had James leading the rush for the only available lifeboat, shouting, 'Save the dogs and Colonel Churchill.' Gilbert Burnet, in this latter camp, wrote:

> The Duke got into the boat: and took good care of his dogs and some unknown persons who were taken, from that earnest care of his, to be his priests: the long boat went off with very few in her, though she might have carried off above eighty persons more than she did. One hundred and fifty persons perished, some of them men of great quality.[26]

Lord Ailesbury, writing from the opposite viewpoint and with personal knowledge of many of the key players, also thought things were mishandled: 'The Duke went into the shallop, calling out for Churchill, he being so greatly in favour.' Ailesbury agreed that the boat could certainly have taken more passengers. Thomas Jermy, foot huntsman to the duke, managed to creep under the stern seat where he lay doggo and was mistaken for baggage. When the oarsmen discovered him they were so furious that they would have thrown him overboard had James not interceded.[27]

Samuel Pepys was an eyewitness, and saw that the one available boat, which had been taken astern below the windows of the duke's cabin, was sent off with the duke and John Churchill in her 'to prevent his being oppressed with men labouring their escapes'. George Legge told his son that there had certainly been avoidable delay. He had pressed the duke to get into the boat, but James first argued that he needed to stay to help save the ship, and then ordered his heavy strongbox to be loaded. The resolute Legge, who had been responsible for getting the boat round to the ship's stern, bluntly asked James what the box might contain that could possibly be worth a man's life, and James replied that he would rather hazard his own life than lose the box. Eventually only a few of the duke's closest adherents got into the boat, and it is unlikely that there were many priests amongst them: Father Ronché, the queen's almoner, swam for his life and found a plank to cling to. There may indeed have been dogs in the lifeboat, but we know that at least one went overboard, for the duke's physician, Sir Charles Scarburgh, found himself earnestly disputing the possession of a plank with the creature Mumper (evidently not a King Charles spaniel, but something of a more martial stamp), who was eventually rescued.

Sarah, commenting on Thomas Lediard's biography of her late husband, recalled that John had

> blamed the Duke to me excessively for his obstinacy and cruelty. For if he would have been persuaded to go off himself at first, when it was certain the ship could not be saved, the Duke of Marlborough was of the opinion that there would not have been a man lost. For though there was not enough boats to carry them all away, all those he mentions were drowned by the Duke's obstinacy in not coming away sooner.[28]

Sarah remembered that John had told her that the duke had given him his sword to prevent the boat from being stormed by panic-stricken men, and Sir John Berry agreed that Churchill had kept the boat free from intruders.

James himself told William of Orange that 'considering the little time the ship was above water after she struck first', the loss of life might reasonably have been greater, and if he had known that Ayres had survived the wreck he would 'have been hanged up immediately, according to the custom of the sea'. Some other accounts emphasise that there was a delay between first impact and sinking, and if this is so one might conclude that James's hesitation prevented more passengers from getting aboard the lifeboat, and his insistence that the ship might yet be saved probably delayed the issuing of an early order to abandon her. However, we cannot be certain how long *Gloucester* remained on the sandbank before slipping to her doom. Winston S. Churchill, with his own reasons for emphasising the delay, suggests that it was 'about an hour', but Sir John Berry, an eyewitness, though with a reputation at risk, recalled how 'for a moment or two she beat upon the sands; then a terrible blow knocked off her rudder and tore her side open'.[29]

The loss of life was certainly not all James's fault: more seamen and passengers might have survived had they been able to swim. The tubby Sir John stayed on his quarterdeck until the vessel sank, and then swam to the *Happy Return*, which had anchored just short of the sands. The duke's equerry Edward Griffin saved himself by clinging to a chicken-coop, and the Marquis of Montrose was hauled from the sea into James's boat. Among those lost were Lords Roxborough and O'Brien and a number of gentlemen, including Laurence Hyde's brother James, the ship's lieutenant, and it was this loss of genteel life (almost like a micro-cosm of the *Titanic*) that struck contemporaries. Pepys was 'sensible of God's infinite mercy', for he had no doubt that he would have drowned had he been aboard *Gloucester*: 'For many will . . . be found lost as well or better qualified to save themselves by swimming than I might have been.'[30] James ordered donations to the widows and orphans of the drowned seamen, but there can be no doubt that the episode had done little to enhance his status in the eyes of many of those close to him.

The duke and his party set off for England aboard the aptly named *Happy Return* on 15 May. The journey was an unpleasant one for Mary of Modena, so heavily pregnant that she had to be hoisted aboard in a chair-lift. The homeward voyage took twelve days, and it may be that its discomfort contributed to the premature birth of Charlotte Mary, who lived only till October. Just over a month after her death, on 21 December 1682, John was rewarded for his services with the barony of Churchill of Aynmouth in the peerage of Scotland. This made him a Member of the Edinburgh Parliament, which then sat in the great hall known as the Parliament House off the High Street. There the three estates, nobles, barons and burgesses, debated and voted together as a single chamber.[31] In view of Churchill's work over the past three years the grant of a Scots peerage was not as puzzling as it might seem. Although it was not of as much practical value as a seat in the English House of Lords, it was certainly more dignified than an Irish peerage, proverbially the cheapest coinage available to reward supporters of the government.

Domestic Bliss, Public Prosperity

Lord and Lady Churchill settled in Holywell House, Sarah's family home near St Albans. John's income – now increased by his appointment to the virtual sinecure of command of the Third Troop of Life Guards on £1 a day – had been sufficient to enable him to buy Frances Tyrconnell's share of the Jennings family home in 1681, and three years later the Churchills demolished the old house and built a new one, with elegant gardens and fish ponds. It was their favourite home. Sarah said in 1714 that however ordinary it might be, she would not part with it for any she had seen on her travels, and on St George's Day 1703 John wrote whimsically to her that: 'This being the season I hear the nightingales as I lie in my bed I have wished them with all my heart with you, knowing how you love them.'[32]

Churchill resumed court life with enthusiasm. Charles had long forgiven him for his affair with Barbara Castlemaine, and he was now one of the king's regular tennis partners. He shared this honour with Louis de Duras, his comrade in arms from the Alsace campaign, who had now inherited his father-in-law's peerage and become Earl of Feversham, and Sidney Godolphin: they were 'all so excellent players that if one beat the other 'tis alternatively'. Godolphin, born on the family estate at Helston in Cornwall in 1645, was a short, ungainly and rather taciturn man. His poet grandfather had died fighting for the king in a West Country skirmish, and his father Francis – who sired no fewer than sixteen children – had raised a regiment of royalist foot.[33] Like Sir Winston Churchill, Sir Francis Godolphin was rewarded after the Restoration, and in 1662 young Sidney became a royal page. He had married Margaret Blagge in 1675, though he lost her, all too early, to puerperal fever. John Evelyn wrote that 'She was the best wife, the best friend, the best mistress, that husband ever had,' and he saw how Sidney, 'struck with unspeakable affliction, fell down as dead'.[34] Their surviving child, Francis, was to marry the Marlboroughs' daughter Henrietta in 1698.

Godolphin became MP for the family borough of Helston in 1668, and cut his teeth on a variety of diplomatic missions over the next decade. He was at once unobtrusive and indispensable: Charles II quipped that he was 'never in the way and never out of the way'. In 1679 he joined Sunderland and Laurence Hyde in the short-lived governing group unkindly known as 'the chits' for the youth and inexperience of its members, but he managed to retain royal favour during the Exclusion crisis, possibly because he was ill at several crucial moments. Hyde, holding the important post of lord treasurer, became Earl of Rochester in 1682, and two years later he was, as Halifax put it, 'kicked upstairs' to the less demanding job of lord president of the council. Godolphin, raised to the peerage as Baron Godolphin of Rialton, replaced him. With the accession of James II in 1685 he became lord chamberlain to the queen, and when she attended chapel was 'accustomed . . . to give her his arm as far as the door'. He sided with James in 1688 but soon made his peace with William and Mary.

Godolphin was to become Churchill's principal political ally, and the Marlborough–Godolphin correspondence, so painstakingly transcribed by Henry L. Snyder, remains 'one of the most famous and important in English history'.[35] Snyder's work corrects most of the errors in dating and transcription which, initially made by Archdeacon Coxe, were sometimes perpetuated by Winston S. Churchill. The letters illuminate several non-martial aspects of Churchill's career, not least in his dealings with the Dutch, and reveal what Snyder calls his 'essential timidity and the extreme care he took to obtain authority for his every action'.[36] This correspondence did not begin in earnest till 1701, when both Churchill and Godolphin were in positions of substantial influence, but it is surely right to see in the correspondence of prime minister and commander-in-chief a reflection of a much earlier friendship.[37]

A measure of Churchill's favour was his appointment, on 19 November 1683, as colonel of a regiment which had begun its life as the Tangier Horse and was now known as the King's Own Regiment of Dragoons. The post, held in plurality with command of the Life Guards troop and the colonelcy of foot, was worth another fifteen shillings a day in pay and allowances. Dragoons derived their name from the fact that they originally carried a 'fire and cock' musket – a weapon, like its users, called *dragon* in French – which was a primitive form of flintlock, rather than the matchlock musket of Civil War infantry. They were mounted, though traditionally on cheaper steeds than cavalry proper: the New Model's cavalry horses cost £8–£10 apiece, but half that sum would buy a dragoon nag.

Dragoons originally fought on foot, with their horses simply providing them with tactical mobility or, as their enemies alleged, enabling them 'to be fitter to rob and to pillage'.[38] They sometimes fought on horseback even during the Civil War, and after it they gradually ascended to be cavalry proper, although the whole process was to take them at least a century. The *Military Dictionary* of 1702 described them as:

> Musketeers mounted, who sometimes serve a-foot, and sometimes a-horseback, being always ready upon anything that requires expedition, as being able to keep pace with the horse, and do the service of foot. In battle, or upon attacks, they are commonly the *Enfants Perdus*, or Forlorn [Hope], being the first that fall on. In the field they commonly encamp either at the head of the army, or on the wings, to cover the others, and be the first at their arms.[39]

Churchill was an infantry officer, and his appointment as a colonel of dragoons was seen by his enemies almost as a breach of natural law. There was some whinnying:

> *Let's cut our meat with spoons!*
> *The sense is as good*
> *As that Churchill should*
> *Be put to command the Dragoons.*[40]

He made a good start with his regiment, however, issuing the men with new red coats faced with blue, and keeping the annual cost of each troop down to £2,200, evidence of his 'careful administration'. Churchill's lieutenant colonel was Lord Cornbury, grandson of Edward Hyde, Earl of Clarendon, Charles's first chancellor, and so nephew to the Duke of York's deceased wife Anne Hyde. It was to prove a portentous connection.

There were limits to royal benevolence. When somebody suggested that Churchill might make a good ministerial colleague for Sunderland, Charles replied bluntly that 'he was resolved not to have two idle Secretaries of State'. Churchill was certainly much preoccupied with rebuilding Holywell House, and with his growing family. Another daughter, Anne, was born in 1684, John (a son at last) followed in 1686, Elizabeth in 1687, Mary in 1689 and Charles, who lived for only two years, in 1690. There is no evidence, during the early 1680s, of a man eaten up by ambition. He had his peerage and a colonelcy, stood high in royal favour, and perhaps Charles's suggestion of temporary indolence is not unfair, for he was still a young man but not now in much of a hurry. Indeed, if anyone in the family was making the running at this period it was not John, but Sarah.

Sarah Jennings had first met Lady Anne, youngest daughter of James, Duke of York and Anne Hyde, at Whitehall when Sarah was ten and Anne only six, and they appeared together in a court production of the masque *Calisto* in December 1674. They had seen a good deal of one another in Scotland, and in 1680 Sarah was on hand when Anne was involved in a controversial relationship with John Sheffield, Lord Mulgrave, a great favourite of the king's but, at thirty-five, almost twice her age. Although London gossips suggested that Mulgrave had seduced her 'so far as to spoil her marrying to anyone else', Mulgrave had probably done no more than write letters 'intimating too near an address to her'. He was exiled to Tangier, but went on to hold high office under James II, William III, who made him Marquess of Normanby, and Queen Anne herself, who created him Duke of Buckingham.[41]

The Mulgrave affair both accelerated efforts to get Anne suitably married, and, as the historian Edward Gregg is right to suggest, 'underlined – and perhaps contributed to' a growing divergence between Anne and her elder sister Mary, whose hints of displeasure at Anne risking her reputation were not welcomed by someone who did not believe that she had done anything at all to contribute to the scandal. Bruised by her sister's priggishness, and thrust on inexorably towards an arranged marriage, Anne became increasingly attracted to the beautiful, intelligent and witty Sarah. Their friendship was to be so closely interwoven with John Churchill's own rise that we cannot hope to tease the strands apart. Nor can we be certain of the precise nature of the relationship, because Sarah, who wrote most about it, did so mainly after the burning affection of its early years had frozen into mutual contempt.

We have two main difficulties. The first is that it is never easy for men to grasp the depth and intensity of the love that can exist between women. Even the most heterosexual of men usually know that they have bonds of affection with other men that are indeed 'passing the love of women', even if they are not always comfortable in talking about them. Yet it is hard for them to acknowledge that women can have relationships which are as profound, partly because of men's fear that women's affection is in some way finite, and that the emotion which binds them to other women must necessarily limit that available for commitment to men.

Our second problem is that the relationship between Anne and Sarah has now become part of the battlefield of sexual politics. Some lesbian authors have suggested that the relationship was indeed lesbian, and that it is only the gender-centric perversity of the historical establishment that has prevented a proper acknowledgement of the fact that European courts at this time were full of girls and women in loving physical relationships, and historians who deny it are simply revealing their inherent homophobia.

It is important to understand that correspondence may mislead us. In a letter whose sheer nobility mists one's eyes even today, Margaret Godolphin told Jael Boscawen, her sister-in-law, 'My dear, believe me, that of all earthly things you were and are most dear to me.' She evidently did not mean that she loved Jael more than she loved Sidney, for 'Nobody ever had a better or half so good a husband.' Yet her affection for Jael went beyond this happiest of marriages. So: 'Not knowing how God Almighty may deal with me . . . as in case I be to leave the world, no earthly thing may take up my thoughts,' it was to Jael she wrote just before her confinement, bidding farewell to mortality and putting her affairs in order.[42] When Anne's sister Mary wrote breathlessly, 'What can I say more to persuade you that I love you with more zeal than any lover and I love you with a love that was never known by man I have for you an excess of friendship more of love than woman can for woman and more love ever than the constant lover had for his mistress . . .' she was in fact writing to Frances Apsley, daughter of the Duke of York's treasurer.[43] Both women enjoyed happy marriages. Just before her own marriage Anne also wrote to Frances, in a letter veiled in classical allegory: 'Your Ziphares [Anne] changes his condition yet nothing shall ever alter him from being the same to his dear Semandra [Frances] as he ever was.'

Women often wrote passionately to one another, even if there was nothing physical in their relationship. One of Sarah's biographers, Ophelia Field, declares that 'it can never be certain what unlabelled feelings – feelings which Sarah would manipulate skilfully in later life – existed between the two. For now, it is enough to emphasise that Sarah and Anne were not entirely innocent of what their words might mean if history happened to eavesdrop.'[44] When we do listen at history's keyholes, let us do so as honestly as we can, neither making the easy assumptions that such whispers might imply today, nor putting our characters on a political stage which is our creation, not theirs.

There can be no doubting Anne's need for female affection. Sarah became her lady of the bedchamber in 1683 on Anne's marriage to Prince

George of Denmark, replacing Mary Cornwallis, of whom Charles II said that 'No man ever loved his mistress as his niece Anne did Mrs Cornwallis.'[45] When Sarah lost her hold on Anne's affection she did not simply alienate Anne by her filthy temper and overbearing behaviour, but because she was insidiously outmanoeuvred by Abigail Masham.

Sarah's own account of her friendship with Anne is best encapsulated in *An Account of the Conduct of the Dowager Duchess of Marlborough from her first coming to court . . .* , although so much of what she wrote in later life, on her own account or in collaboration with associates like Bishop Burnet, in some way reflects the catastrophic end of that relationship. She claimed that she wrote the book knowing that 'I am coming near my end, and very soon there will be nothing of me but a *name*', and wanted to comment on 'the successful artifice of Mr Harley and Mrs Masham in taking advantage of the Queen's passion for what she called *the church* to undermine me in her affections'.[46]

Sarah made much of her early friendship with Anne: 'We used to play together when she was a child, and even then she expressed a particular fondness for me.' This gave her an important advantage, accentuated by the fact that the manners of the Countess of Clarendon, first lady of the bedchamber, 'could not possibly recommend her to so young a mistress: for she looked like a mad-woman, and talked like a scholar'.[47] Sarah maintained that flattery was 'falsehood to my trust, and ingratitude to my greatest friend; and that I did not deserve so much favour, if I could not venture the loss of it by speaking the truth'. Kings and princes, she believed, generally thought that the dignity of their position would be eroded by friendship with an inferior. 'The Princess had a different taste,' she wrote. 'A friend was what she most coveted: and for the sake of friendship (a relation which she did not disdain to have with me) she was fond even of that *equality* which she thought belonged to it.' They eventually decided to address one another by assumed names.

> Morley and Freeman were the names her fancy hit upon; and she left me to choose by which of these I would be called. My frank, open temperament naturally led me to pitch upon Freeman, and the Princess took the other; and from time to time Mrs Morley and Mrs Freeman began to converse as equals, made so by affection and friendship.[48]

There were other nicknames too: William of Orange, whom neither much liked, was 'Mr Caliban'.

An unpublished account of this period written in the third person by Sarah much later tells us how:

she now began to employ all her wit and all her vivacity and almost all her time to divert, entertain and serve the Princess; and to fix that favour, which one might now easily observe to be increasing more towards her each day. This favour quickly became a passion; and a passion which possessed the heart of the Princess too much to be hid. They were shut up together for many hours daily. Every moment of absence was counted a sort of tedious, lifeless state. To see the Duchess was a constant joy; and to part with her for never so short a time, a constant uneasiness; as the Princess's own frequent expressions were. This worked even to the jealousy of a lover. She used to say that she desired to possess her wholly: and could hardly bear that she could escape, from this confinement, into other company.[49]

In another account, this time part of Sarah's published campaign to defend her reputation, she maintains that all Anne's friendships 'were flames of extravagant passion, ending in indifference or aversion'. She 'seemed to inherit a good deal of her father's moroseness', thought Sarah, 'which naturally produced in her the same sort of stubborn positiveness in many cases, both ordinary and extraordinary, as well as the same sort of bigotry in religion'.[50]

In July 1683 the eighteen-year-old Anne was married to Prince George of Denmark. John Evelyn thought that 'He had the Danish countenance, blonde, of few words, spoke French but ill, seemed somewhat heavy, but reported to be valiant, and indeed he had bravely rescued and brought off his brother the King of Denmark in a battle against the Swedes.'[51] The arrangement suited Louis XIV, who hoped to see the two naval powers united against the Dutch, as well as James, who was trying to limit the influence of his other son-in-law, William of Orange. Negotiations were handled by Anne's uncle Laurence, now Earl of Rochester, and secretary of state Sunderland. They drove a hard bargain: James gave the couple £40,000 in capital and £5,000 a year. Anything else had to come from Prince George's personal estates, and he was expected to reside in England. The Danish ambassador suggested to his French colleague that it would suit them all if Anne and George could be given precedence in the succession over William and Mary, but the Frenchman replied that hereditary right could not be brushed aside like this.

Charles II deftly summed up George, saying: 'I have tried him drunk and I have tried him sober and there is nothing in him.' He was indolent and good-natured, devoutly Protestant (a Lutheran, and so, in

English terms, a dissenter rather than an Anglican, which made him an 'occasional conformist' to the services of the established Church), wholly free from scandal, and as wholly devoted to Anne, who bore him child after stillborn child in an almost annual succession of perhaps as many as seventeen pregnancies, although Anne's predisposition towards false pregnancies make it impossible to be sure. The best estimate is probably twelve miscarriages, one stillbirth and four children who died young. Only one of their children, William, Duke of Gloucester (1689–1700), survived early childhood. Notwithstanding Anne's relationship with Sarah this was a happy marriage, and Anne always acknowledged that though she might be queen, George was head of the household. In 1708 she nursed him through his last illness, and his death

> flung the queen into an unspeakable grief. She never left him till he was dead, but continued kissing him till the very moment the breath went out of his body, and 'twas with a very great deal of difficulty my Lady Marlborough prevailed upon her to leave him.[52]

Just as there is no reason to doubt Anne's affection for her husband, so too we can see why Anne expected more emotional engagement than he was able to offer, and understand how Sarah fitted into this relationship. Ophelia Field's suggestion that 'the marriage contained many of the qualities of a friendship while Sarah's relationship with Anne was developing into a fraught romance' seems exactly right.[53]

It is an index of the Churchills' position that John had been sent to Denmark to bring George to England for his wedding, and when it was decided that the prince's prickly private secretary, Christian Siegfried von Plessen, should be sent back to Denmark, it was John who made the arrangements and Sarah's brother-in-law Colonel Edward Griffith who replaced Plessen. Anne and her husband were given apartments known as the Cockpit in the Palace of Whitehall, across King Street from the Privy Garden, just to the west of Horse Guards. Adjacent parts of the palace were occupied by the secretaries of state, and it is no coincidence that Downing Street, so close to the Cockpit, has now assumed its importance. With King Street acting as a firebreak the Cockpit survived successive fires, and Anne remained there until ordered to quit by her sister.

A Cockpit circle was quickly scribed out. Near its centre were John and Sarah Churchill, with John's brothers, Captain George Churchill of the Royal Navy and Lieutenant Colonel Charles Churchill (who had once served as a page to Prince George's brother King Christian), Colonel John Berkeley, of Anne's dragoon regiment, and his wife Barbara, daughter of Lady Villiers, who had been the princess's governess. Sir Benjamin Bathurst, comptroller of the household, was now married to Frances Apsley. The Duke of Grafton, one of Charles's bastards by Barbara Castlemaine, was a regular visitor, as were the Marquess of Ossory (who succeeded as Duke of Ormonde in 1688) and the Earl of Drumlanrig (Marquess of Queensberry in 1695). Robert and Anne Spencer, Earl and Countess of Sunderland, were on the outer edge of the circle. They were close to the Churchills, and Anne Churchill was to marry their eldest son Charles, but, because of Sunderland's support for the Exclusion Bill, Anne never really trusted him.[54] Sarah was promoted to first lady of the bedchamber when Lady Clarendon went off to Ireland with her husband, who had been made its lord lieutenant.

Because Sarah travelled with Anne, and John with the Duke of York, they were often separated, and some of their letters survive. In a note which seems to predate the birth of their daughter Anne on 27 February 1684 by perhaps six months, sent by an 'express' courier rather than a regular post, John wrote:

> I had writ to you by the post, but that I was persuaded this would be with you sooner. You see I am very just in writing, and I hope that I shall find by the daily receiving of yours that you are so. I hope in God you are out of all danger of any miscarrying, for I swear to you I love you better than all the rest of the world put together, wherefore you ought to be so just as to make me a kind return, which will make me much happier than aught else in this world can do. If I can get a passage a Sunday I will come, but if I cannot I shall be with you a Monday morning by nine of the clock; for the Duke will leave this place by six. Pray [give] my most humble respects to your fair daughter, and believe me what I am with all my heart and soul,
>
> Yours . . . [55]

The Churchills' settled world was rocked by the king's unexpected death. In the winter of 1684–85 Charles had been troubled with the gout and could not take his usual exercise, but spent a good deal of time in his laboratory, trying to find a process for the fixing of mercury. He ate less than he once had and 'drank only for his thirst', but still took a turn to the Duchess of Portsmouth's apartments after his supper. On the morning of 2 February 1685 he rose after a restless night, and sat down to the barber, 'it being shaving day' – even monarchs were shaved only two or three times a week. He had scarcely sat down when he had 'an apoplectic fit' and fell into Lord Ailesbury's arms. Dr Edmund King, on hand to deal with a sore heel, bled him at once. Charles endured the ministrations of his doctors, which almost certainly accelerated his death, for five days.

On 5 February, when it was clear that his brother was dying, James asked him if he wished to be reconciled to the Roman Catholic Church, and Charles eagerly assented. Finding an English-speaking priest was not easy, for all Queen Catherine's priests were Portuguese. Quite fortuitously, Father John Huddlestone, who had helped Charles escape after the battle of Worcester in 1651, was in the palace and was brought into Charles's bedchamber by a secret door which, in its time, had doubtless fulfilled less noble purposes.[56]

Charles died well. He apologised to the crowd of assembled courtiers and functionaries for being such an unconscionably long time about it, begged the queen's forgiveness, commended the Duchess of Portsmouth to James's care and urged his listeners: 'Let not poor Nelly starve.' Early on the morning of 6 February he asked for his curtains to be drawn so that he might see one more dawn, and he died at noon. 'He was ever kind to me,' lamented John Evelyn, 'and very gracious upon all occasions, and therefore I cannot, without ingratitude, but deplore his loss, which for many respects as well as duty I do with all my soul.'[57]

The Churchills stood high in the favour of the new king, James II. John was confirmed in his appointments and sent off to Paris, ostensibly to formally notify Louis XIV of the succession but actually to ask for money. In fact Paul Barillon, the French ambassador, had already presented James with 500,000 livres (perhaps £10 million), so John's instructions were changed while he was on his way, and he was simply to thank Louis for this handsome gift. Gilbert Burnet maintains that while he was in France John Churchill met the Protestant soldier and diplomat Henri de Massue, marquis de Ruvigny, whom he already knew from Charles's negotiations with the French in 1678, and warned him that 'If the King was ever prevailed upon to alter our religion he would serve him no longer, but would withdraw from him.'[58]

We must be as cautious about Burnet's assertions, made from the Whig standpoint, as we should be about Lord Ailesbury's, imbued as they are with Jacobite sympathies. However, it is evident that religion was already an issue dividing the Cockpit circle from James's court. Sarah maintains that James had tried to shift Anne from her firm Anglicanism 'by putting into her hands some books and papers', and in 1679 Dick Talbot, now her brother-in-law, 'took pains with me, but without any effect, to persuade me to bring over the Princess to their Catholic purpose'.[59] A secret French report of 1687 was to suggest that Anne was heavily influenced by Sarah, 'whom she loves tenderly', and this helped keep her away from court so that her father could not speak to her about religion.[60]

Monmouth's Rebellion

Even if there was palpable tension between court and Cockpit in early 1685, it did not prevent James from settling old debts. On 14 May that year John Churchill was created Baron Churchill of Sandridge in Hertfordshire, and so had a seat in the House of Lords, which was to meet later that month for the first time in the new reign. He also became a governor of the Hudson's Bay Company. The first session of the new, staunchly Tory-Anglican English Parliament was overshadowed by rebellion, led in Scotland by the Earl of Argyll, who had lived in the Low Countries since his escape from Edinburgh Castle, and in England by the Duke of Monmouth, also in exile, but likely to have been allowed back home had Charles not died. Monmouth, born in Rotterdam in April 1649, was an experienced soldier, handsome and staunchly Protestant. He maintained that Charles had actually been married to his mother, Lucy Walter, but he had never been the Whigs' candidate to supplant James at the time of the Exclusion Crisis: they preferred his niece Mary. Exiled following his involvement in the Rye House plot of 1683, Monmouth had been at the centre of a web of radical discontent in the Low Countries, and his invasion in 1685 was widely expected. Argyll and Monmouth might have had a better chance had they been able to coordinate their activities, but even so neither insurrection attracted the widespread popular support that might have posed a serious challenge to the government. Argyll may have assembled as many as 2,500 men, and Monmouth perhaps 7,000 at the peak of his success.

When we are considering John Churchill's motivation in 1685 and 1688 it is important to recognise some simple truths. In 1685 James had not attracted the suspicion which dogged him by 1688. The army was loyal to its leaders, and they were loyal to James. Neither Argyll's nor Monmouth's expedition was a well-planned military invasion with reserves of arms to equip supporters, or serious external support. In 1685 neither invasion had a realistic prospect of success, and men like John Churchill, who lived their lives on the basis of rational calculation, would not support Monmouth or Argyll. Furthermore, Churchill had served under Monmouth, and this experience, far from increasing his regard for 'the Protestant duke', had demonstrated some of Monmouth's frightening unsteadiness.

Monmouth arrived in Lyme Bay on 11 June, to be told that the Somerset militia were already in arms and the Duke of Albemarle (George Monck's son), lord lieutenant of Devon, was calling out his militiamen. An attempt to fire a warning shot from the guns protecting Lyme Regis had failed ridiculously when it transpired that neither powder nor shot was available. Soon Monmouth himself landed on the beach that now bears his name, thanked God for his safe arrival, and ordered his banner – with the words *Fear nothing but GOD* on a background of Leveller green – to be unfurled. The town's mayor set off for Honiton, whence he wrote to the king to say that he thought Monmouth was ashore with three hundred men, and went on to report to Albemarle. Two local royalists saw what had happened and rode hard for London, where they sought out their MP.

By a remarkable coincidence Sir Winston Churchill was Member for Lyme, and so it was that James was roused at four on the morning of 13 June by John Churchill, who, as a lord of the bedchamber, had ready access to the royal bedroom, accompanied by his father and the two loyalists. The latter were rewarded with £20 apiece, and even before he had taken any formal advice, James ordered Churchill to ride westwards with four troops of the Oxford Blues and four of his own regiment of dragoons. Percy Kirke, of Tangier fame, was to join him with five companies of the Queen Dowager's Regiment of Foot as soon as he could.

Whatever his personal failings, Monmouth was a competent soldier. He realised that he needed to raise troops as quickly as he could, and spent the first few days issuing the weapons he had landed with and procuring more locally. There was a clash with some militia horse in Bridport, but the militia proved less aggressive than Monmouth had feared. This gave him the opportunity to form his infantry into five regiments, known (like the regiments of the London Trained Bands) as Red (the Duke of Monmouth's own), White, Blue, Green and Yellow, with an independent company of Lyme men. The horse formed a single body under Lord Grey, who had been handicapped by having his second in command, Andrew Fletcher, arrested for murder after pistolling Monmouth's treasurer, Thomas Dare, in a squabble over a requisitioned charger.

Although the insurrection is now locally described as 'the Pitchfork Rebellion', many of the rebels were decently armed with matchlock muskets brought across from Holland, or seized from militia armouries and private houses. Scythe blades were requisitioned and mounted on eight-foot poles, and James himself believed that each of the rebel regiments had a company of scythe-men taking the place of grenadiers. The historian Peter Earle points out that the rank and file of Monmouth's army tended to be 'tradesmen, such as shopkeepers or artisans', solid West Country dissenting folk, rather than general or farm labourers. Most were well established in their professions, and it was rare for father and son to enlist together, or for brothers to serve side by side: wise families insured against failure.

There were exceptions. Abraham Holmes, a former officer of the New Model Army, commanded the Green Regiment. He was to lose his son, a captain in his own regiment, in a skirmish at Norton St Philip, and was badly wounded at Sedgemoor, where he cut off his own mangled arm. He scorned to plead for his life, telling his judges: 'I am an aged man, and what remains to me of life is not worth a falsehood or a baseness. I have always been a republican, and I am one still.' When the horses which were to have dragged him to the place of execution would not budge (Holmes thought that an angel was blocking their way) he walked to his death with a firm step. He apologised to the spectators, whose mood quickly changed from derision to admiration, for his slowness in mounting the scaffold. 'You see,' said the old warrior, 'I have but one arm.'

Cobbling together an army, however promising some of its raw material, is never an easy task. One of Monmouth's colonels, Nathaniel Wade, tells us just how hard things were even when his opponents were simply those good-natured countryfolk of the Dorset militia. On 14 June he took about five hundred infantry, notionally supported by Lord Grey with forty horse, to attack Bridport.

We advanced to the attack of the bridge, to the defence of which, the [militia] officers had with much ado prevailed with their soldiers to stand. Our foot fired one volley upon them, which they answered with another, and killed us two men of the foot; at which my Lord Grey and the horse ran till they came to Lyme, where they reported me to be slain, and all the foot to be cut off. This flight of Lord Grey so discouraged the vanguard of the foot, that they threw down their arms and began to run; but I bringing up another body to their succour, they were persuaded to take up their arms again . . . [The enemy] contented themselves to repossess the town, and shout at us out of musket-shot; and we answered them alike, and by this bravo having a little established the staggering courage of our soldiers we retreated in pretty good order with 12 or 14 prisoners and about 30 horses.[61]

The first clash of a campaign often sets the tone of what follows, and here we see in microcosm the story of Monmouth's defeat. His cavalry was poor, which tells us more about the difficulty of getting untrained horses to fight in rank and file than it does about the courage of the rebel troopers or the quality of some of their officers. His infantry was better, but only massed formation and brave leadership would nerve it to its task. Monmouth must have recognised that his men could not face regular troops in open field in broad daylight. Like a powerful but clumsy fighter facing a more skilled opponent, his only chance was to move fast and get in close: inaction would ruin him.

On 15 June Monmouth pounced on Axminster, dispersing the Devon and Somerset militia who were trying to rendezvous there before moving on to attack Lyme. He then marched north to Chard and Ilminster, his ranks swelled by local volunteers and disenchanted militiamen, reaching Taunton, where he was proclaimed king in the marketplace, on the eighteenth. Optimistically signing himself 'James R', he asked both Albemarle and Churchill to join him. Monmouth and Albemarle were old drinking companions, but Albemarle's dignified reply informed Monmouth that 'I never was, nor ever will be, a rebel to my lawful King, who is James the second.'[62] John Churchill did not enter into a correspondence which, one way or another, might have been misconstrued, but sent Monmouth's letter on to London.

Churchill had reached Bridport with his weary cavalry and dragoons on the seventeenth. His first report, written that day, warned James very frankly that:

we are likely to lose this country [i.e. the West Country] to the rebels, for we have those two [Devon and Somerset militia] regiments run away a second time . . . there is not any relying on these regiments that are left unless we had some of your Majesty's standing forces to lead them on and encourage them; for at this unfortunate news I never saw people so much daunted in my life.[63]

He also drafted a letter to the Duke of Somerset, lord lieutenant of that county, urging him to send 4,000 men to Chard and Crewkerne, and saying that he would do his best to support them if Monmouth took advantage of the collapse of the militia by marching straight for

London. The government was already doing its best to guard against a sudden thrust at the capital, concentrating the militia of Surrey, Oxfordshire and Berkshire at Reading to cover the Great West Road, and ordering the Duke of Beaufort to assemble the militia of Gloucestershire, Hereford and Monmouthshire to protect Bristol, which was believed to be Monmouth's preferred target.

None of this would beat Monmouth, but it would give the royal army time to concentrate. The Earl of Dumbarton's Regiment set off with a train of artillery from the Tower of London, and Colonel Charles Trelawney's Regiment, commanded by its lieutenant colonel, Charles Churchill, accompanied a smaller train from Portsmouth. James recalled the English and Scots regiments in Dutch service: William of Orange was not only happy to release them but, possibly fearing that his own prospects in England would be compromised if Monmouth succeeded, volunteered to command them himself, an offer James felt able to decline.

Churchill, with his advance guard, hung on to the rebels like a terrier locked on to a burglar's ankle. He reached Chard on 19 June, and sent out a strong patrol of the Blues under Lieutenant Philip Munnocks. Near Ashill, three miles from Ilminster, it met 'about the like number of sturdy rebels, well armed, between whom there happened a very brisk encounter'. Churchill's men had the best of the first clash, but the rebel patrol was supported by a stronger force and the Blues fell back, leaving their officer 'upon the place, shot in the head and killed on the first charge'.[64] Churchill told the Duke of Somerset that he intended to follow Monmouth 'so close as I can upon his marches', and suggested that the duke should get Albemarle to join him because the latter's militiamen would not be able to keep pace with Churchill's horse.

This advance guard of cavalry was 'to be commanded by our trusty and wellbeloved John Lord Churchill in all things according to the rules and discipline of war', and Churchill had been appointed brigadier general for the purpose.[65] However, he was not entitled to give orders to the lords lieutenant, magnates like the Dukes of Somerset and Albemarle who were responsible for the county militias and commissioned their officers. He may have had a professional soldier's grasp of tactics, but as the most junior baron in the House of Lords he was simply not in their league. On or about the eighteenth James decided to appoint Louis de Duras, Earl of Feversham, his lieutenant general for the campaign. Feversham was 'to command in chief wherever he is, the militia as well as the King's forces'.[66]

There is no foundation for suggestions that this reflected a sudden loss of confidence in Churchill on James's part. Churchill had only been appointed to head the advance guard, and command of the whole royal army evidently required a more senior officer. Not only has Winston S. Churchill's assertion that Churchill 'resented his supersession, and he knew it could only come from mistrust' little contemporary foundation, but to maintain that 'this snub . . . eventually turned Churchill from loyalty to the Stuart kings' stretches the evidence to breaking point.[67] It was only later in the campaign, when he thought that Feversham was inclined to favour Colonel Theophilus Oglethorpe and to ignore his own contribution to the early stages of the campaign, that Churchill's irritation can be detected.

On 21 June Percy Kirke joined a wholly unsnubbed Churchill at Chard with five companies of his regiment, having marched 140 miles in

The Sedgemoor Campaign

eight days. This now gave Churchill a small combined-arms brigade, and he told the Duke of Somerset that 'I have enough forces not to apprehend [fear] the Duke of Monmouth, but on the contrary should be glad to meet with him and my men are in so good heart.'[68] Although Churchill was not to know it at the time, Feversham was making good speed into the West Country, travelling with the remaining troops of the Life Guards and Royals, as well as the Horse Grenadiers, who looked 'very fierce and fantastical' with their moustaches and grenadier caps, even if their complicated drill made experienced officers grumble that no good would come from combining grenade-throwing with galloping about on horseback.

Feversham marched from London to Maidenhead on 20 June, reached Newbury the next day and joined the Dukes of Beaufort and Somerset at Bristol on the twenty-third. He had slipped Colonel Oglethorpe, with a party of Life Guards and Horse Grenadiers, off to his left flank by way of Andover and Warminster in case Monmouth tried to break eastwards between Churchill and his own force. There can be no faulting Feversham's performance in the early stages of the campaign. He reached Bristol in time to thwart Monmouth, and screened his open flank as he marched. We cannot say for certain how close the militia were to total collapse, but a fragmentary undated letter from the Duke of Somerset to either Albemarle or Churchill shows the state he was in:

> I do desire your Lordship to come away towards me with what forces you have, for I have only one regiment and one troop of horse which I am afraid will hardly stand because the others have showed them the way to run, the enemy is now at Bridgwater, which is ten miles of where I am, and that if your Lordship does not march to Somerton . . . [69]

Monmouth might conceivably have beaten Feversham to Bristol, but he was raising troops as he advanced, so could not achieve Feversham's turn of speed. As generations of holiday-makers know to their cost, the dryness of West Country summers cannot be guaranteed, and now the weather conspired against the soldiers on both sides. Nathaniel Wade recorded that on 22 June the rebels marched to Glastonbury on 'an exceeding rainy day' and quartered their infantry in the abbey and churches, making 'very great fires' to dry them out. On that day a patrol of the Oxford Blues, scouting out from Langport, met a stronger party of rebel horse and 'beat them into their camp', and the Portsmouth train of artillery, which had reached Sherborne with its escorting infantry of Trelawney's Regiment, was ordered forward to Somerton by Churchill. This further

Marlborough gestures towards a plan of the fortress of Bouchain held up by Colonel John Armstrong, his chief engineer. His wife Sarah observed that the portrait, of about 1711, was 'as like him as I ever saw'.

Marlborough triumphant:
the duke in his Garter robes,
by Sir Godfrey Kneller.

Royal favourite, resolute Whig,
turbulent wife: Sarah Churchill,
Duchess of Marlborough.

Country gentleman and captain of horse, faithful but unfortunate: Marlborough's father, Sir Winston Churchill.

Kneller's portrait of Charles II allows a hint of the monarch's natural affability and political judgement to shine through its formal setting.

Two of Sir Winston Churchill's children and John Churchill's siblings. On the left is Winston, who died young, and on the right is Arabella, who blossomed into a royal mistress before enjoying a happy marriage to Colonel Charles Godfrey.

Hendrick Danckerts' painting of the palace of Whitehall from St James's Park in the reign of Charles II shows the Banqueting House (extreme left) and, beneath the steep roof on the right, the Cockpit, where Princess Anne was to live. Charles loved to walk briskly in the park with his dogs.

James, Duke of York, later James II. James was Marlborough's patron, but they differed over religion: James was a staunch Catholic and Marlborough a committed Anglican. Even James's supporters recognised that he lacked the political wisdom of his elder brother Charles.

James Scott, Duke of Monmouth, one of Charles II's illegitimate brood, seen here at the siege of Maastricht in 1673. On the left a heavy gun fires from between two large gabions, wicker baskets filled with earth.

My Lady Castlemaine: Barbara Villiers painted by Sir Peter Lely as St Catherine of Alexandria. She was arguably the most powerful of Charles II's mistresses, and bore the young John Churchill a daughter, also called Barbara.

The wreck of the *Gloucester*, carrying James, Duke of York and his entourage to Scotland, on 6 May 1682. She hung on the sandbank for an indeterminate time, and then slipped off to founder in deeper water, with great loss of life.

Louis de Dufort-Duras, Earl of Feversham. A Huguenot nobleman, he commanded the royal army in both 1685 and 1688.

Troops being reviewed on Hounslow Heath in 1688. James II hoped that the camp would not simply increase the standard of his army's training, but would also overawe opposition in the capital. About one-third of the infantry still carried the pike.

King William III by Sir Peter Lely, displaying the court painter's tendency to flatter his sitter.

The testy Claude Louis Hector, duc de Villars, was arguably Marlborough's most formidable opponent. A determined general with a natural penchant for the offensive, his achievements might have been greater had it not been for the shackles imposed on him by Versailles.

Louis XIV playing billiards in 1694. Amongst his entourage is the ingratiating Michel Chamillart, soon to become both controller-general of finances and minister of war. He failed to curb the king's warlike tastes or to institute effective economic reform.

The Marlborough family, painted by Johann Baptist Closterman in about 1697. John, later Marquess of Blandford, stands on the right, gesturing towards (from right to left) Anne, Henrietta, Sarah, Mary, Elizabeth and Marlborough himself. Marlborough told the artist: 'It has given me more trouble to reconcile my wife to you than to fight a battle,' and indeed Sarah does not look pleased.

increased the strength of his brigade, and on 23 June he told the nervous Duke of Somerset that he hoped to persuade Feversham to join him at Wells and fight Monmouth before he reached Bristol.

Feversham, however, had decided to head straight for Bristol, and reached it with his leading horse on the twenty-third, leaving the bulk of his infantry slogging out behind him along the Great West Road. Then, on the twenty-fourth, still before Bristol was firmly secured, the leading cavalry troop of Monmouth's advance guard rushed the Avon bridge at Keynsham, only five miles away, and drove off the party of militia horse protecting civilian workmen who were damaging the bridge so as to prevent the rebels from crossing. It took Monmouth's inexperienced officers the best part of twenty-four hours to get their men across the river and formed up in Sydenham Mead on the far bank. Monmouth decided to attack Bristol that night, and we cannot tell how its defenders, the Duke of Beaufort's Gloucester militia, would have performed if put to the test. But the filthy weather induced Monmouth's men to recross the river: a local royalist heard shouts of 'Horse and away' as they broke for cover. Those who could took shelter in the houses of Keynsham, and others were in the nearby fields 'refreshing themselves'. The posting of sentries was not accorded high priority.

Feversham had spent much of the twenty-fourth at Bath, and when he heard that Monmouth had seized Keynsham bridge he sent Oglethorpe, who had commanded his flank-guard on the march west, to investigate. The Horse Grenadiers, at the head of Oglethorpe's detachment, were as poor at their scouting as Monmouth's men were at their sentry duty, and had actually reached the centre of Keynsham before the rebels turned out of the houses and opened fire. The royalists eventually had the better of the skirmish, with an anonymous rebel reporting: 'They did us mischief, killed and wounded about twenty men, whereas we killed none of theirs, only took four prisoners and their horses, and wounded my Lord Newburgh, that it was thought mortal.'[70] Oglethorpe, who had immediately charged to rescue the beleaguered Horse Grenadiers, actually lost two men killed and four wounded, and was in no position to force the issue. However, one of the captured troopers told Monmouth that Feversham's main body was not far behind, and Monmouth resolved to fall back, along the south bank of the Avon, to Bath.

Monmouth reached Bath on the twenty-fifth, but the militia garrison refused to open the gates, and shot his messenger. He then headed south, for Frome, and on the evening of the twenty-sixth the royal army, now lacking only the guns from the Tower of London and their escorting companies of Dumbarton's Regiment, linked up in the city. Churchill had marched in from the west, pausing briefly near Pensford to hang 'Jarvis the feltmaker', a Yeovil radical whose commission as a captain in the rebel army did not save him, though he died 'obstinately and impenitently', and we should remember him for that.

The astute historian John Tincey complains that Churchill had not managed to stop Monmouth's march on Keynsham, and that had Bristol fallen its loss might have been laid at his door. Yet from the start of the campaign it had been Churchill's plan to hang on to Monmouth's flanks and rear: his getting ahead of the rebels only made sense if Feversham joined him, which is precisely what he had hoped for on 23 June. When Feversham decided instead to head straight for Bristol it was reasonable for Churchill to assume that the earl would watch his own front. The fact that Feversham had indeed begun to break down Keynsham bridge shows that he understood its importance, even if those hapless lads of the Gloucester militia did not.

The campaign was now reaching its climax. Monmouth's first option had been to march straight for London, sustained as he hoped by a vast and unstoppable popular rising. When, disobligingly, this support failed to materialise, he sought to base himself on Bristol (whence he could communicate with supporters elsewhere in the country), strengthen and train his army, and only then head for the capital. With the swing away from Bristol his campaign had teetered beyond its culminating point, and he was fast running out of options. Feversham, for his part, had never planned to fight until his army was complete, and time was now on his side.

Poor scouting led the royal army, heading south on Monmouth's heels, into an unplanned clash at Norton St Philip on 27 June. Its advance guard received a bloody nose, staunched only by the arrival of Churchill, who 'secured the mouth of the lane with his dragoons and lined the hedges on each side with foot', providing a secure base which enabled Feversham to extricate himself. Despite this brief setback, Feversham remained determined to maintain close contact with Monmouth, whose army, suffering the effects of repeated bad weather and evident failure, was haemorrhaging deserters. Monmouth briefly considered trying to sidestep Feversham by making for Warminster and then heading for London, but Feversham got wind of this from sympathisers and deserters, and marched from Bradford on Avon early on 29 June to block the rebels' route at 'Westbury under the Plain'.

The train of artillery at last arrived on the thirtieth, and Feversham then edged south-westwards, gently shadowing Monmouth, whose numbers shrank daily. On 4 July Churchill wrote to Lord Clarendon from Somerton. He was now evidently as anxious about his career as he was about the outcome of the campaign. He told Clarendon that:

> nobody living can have been more observant than I have been to my Lord Feversham . . . in so much that he did tell me he would write to the King, to let him know how diligent I was, and I should be glad if you would let me know if he has done me that justice. I find, by the enemy's warrant to the constables, that they have more mind to get horses and saddles than anything else, which looks as if he has a mind to break away with his horse to some other place and leave his foot entrenched at Bridgwater, but of this and all other things you will have it more at large from my Lord Feversham, who has the sole command here, so that I know nothing but what it is in his pleasure to tell me, so that I am afraid of giving my opinion freely, for fear it should not agree with what is the King's intentions, and so expose myself. But as to the taking care of the men and all other things that is my duty, I am sure nobody can be more careful than I am; and as for my obedience, I am sure Mr Oglethorpe is not more dutiful than I am . . . [71]

Oglethorpe, scion of a Yorkshire royalist family, also enjoyed the personal favour of James II. His conduct so far had kept him in Feversham's eye, and at this juncture there was every chance that he would emerge with at least as much credit as Churchill. In the event Oglethorpe made significant mistakes at Sedgemoor but did indeed prosper. He stayed loyal to James in 1688 and refused to swear allegiance to William till 1696, thus destroying his military and political career. One of his sons, James Edward, went on to found the American state of Georgia; another, Lewis, was mortally wounded when Marlborough stormed the Schellenberg in 1704.

However, in 1685 all this lay in the future. When Churchill told Clarendon, 'I see plainly that the trouble is all mine and the honour will be another's,' he was at least as suspicious of Oglethorpe as he was of Feversham. He was Feversham's second in command, but was kept in the dark as to his plans, while the cavalry pursuit was entrusted to Oglethorpe, leaving Churchill with command of the foot. He was actually promoted major general in July, though he probably did not know of his good fortune till after Sedgemoor had been fought.

It was to Sedgemoor that Churchill's steps now turned. While the royal army was at Somerton news arrived that the rebels were fortifying Bridgwater, where they had arrived on 3 July, as if they proposed to make their stand there. One of Feversham's officers had ridden over the moor, and suggested that there was a good campsite on its edge, near the village of Westonzoyland. The royal army arrived there on Sunday, 5 July, and William Sparke, a local farmer, climbed the tower of Chedzoy church to see it moving into camp. He dispatched his herdsman, Benjamin Godfrey, to tell the Duke of Monmouth what had happened.[72] The citizens of Taunton had firmly informed Monmouth that he would not now be welcome to return, and he had decided to march northwards once more, heading yet again for Keynsham bridge and Bristol. However, Godfrey's news induced him to change his mind. He determined to mount a night attack on the royal army, interviewed Godfrey, and may well have spoken to William Sparke and climbed Chedzoy tower to see the ground for himself. So much of what happened that busy afternoon has become the stuff of legend, but one credible story has Monmouth spot the colours of Dumbarton's Regiment, which had fought under his command in France and 'by which he had been extremely beloved'. He told one of his officers, 'I know these men will fight and if I had them I would not doubt of success.'[73]

The field of Sedgemoor is a squarish slab of tussocky lowland, each of its sides roughly three miles long. The Bussex Rhine, marking its southeast border, oozed into the River Parrett, its south-west edge, two miles from Westonzoyland. North-east of the village the Bussex Rhine joined the Black Ditch, the north-eastern boundary of the battlefield. The smaller Langport Rhine curled out like a comma from the Black Ditch just south of the cornfields bordering Chedzoy. The main road to Bristol from Bridgwater, marking the north-west edge of the field, ran across the moor via the 'Long Causeway'. Just over two miles from the town the 'Short Causeway' carried a track to Chedzoy, out on the moor. Another metalled road curled from Westonzoyland to Bridgwater by way of Panzoy Farm.

On 4 July Captain Coy's troop of the Royal Dragoons flicked forward towards Bridgwater, met a strong body of Monmouth's horse and got off 'without any considerable damage on either side'. Feversham seems to have believed that the main body of the rebels would stand siege in Bridgwater, for he sent word to Bath to hasten the arrival of his 'mortar piece', no real use to him in the field but able to pitch its explosive shells over walls. His men went into camp just north of Westonzoyland, with the Bussex Rhine between them and Bridgwater, a little over three miles away.

Recent research suggests that the Bussex Rhine was perhaps eight and a half metres wide but, in the area of the battlefield, only thirty centimetres deep. Much bigger rivers have had less momentous consequences.

Feversham's infantry pitched their tents in a single line behind the Bussex Rhine, leaving enough ground between camp and ditch for them to form up in line of battle. The cannon were on the infantry's left, 'fronting the great road' to make it easier to get them on the move again next morning, and the horse and dragoons were quartered in Westonzoyland. The official account of the battle emphasises the trouble that Feversham took to guard against surprise. Captain Coy's dragoons watched the crossings of the River Parrett at Barrow Bridge and Langport to the army's left rear. The road to Bridgwater was soundly

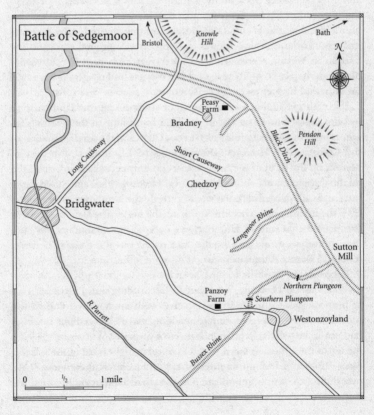

Battle of Sedgemoor

picketed. Captain Upcott of the Oxford Blues had a 'grand guard' of forty troopers, essentially a stationary sentry-party, out on the moor beyond Panzoy Farm. There were forty musketeers of the Foot Guards behind the walls of a sheep fold ('walled man-high') further towards Bridgwater, with plenty of sheep ticks and few opportunities for tow-row-rowing. Finally, a party of a hundred men of the Blues and fifty dragoons under Lieutenant Colonel Sir Francis Compton was further forward still, providing sentries and small patrols to screen the moor and able to fall back onto the musketeers and the cavalry grand guard if they came under pressure.

Given Feversham's assumption, shared by Churchill, that the rebels might try to get their horse away, probably to the north, Theophilus Oglethorpe had put a small patrol out onto the Bridgwater–Bristol road, and posted another party on the Langmoor Rhine, and then rode up to the top of Knowle Hill. Feversham visited 'his sentries, together with his grand and out guards', at about eleven and then retired to his quarters in Westonzoyland, where he was to sleep on a camp bed set up in the parlour at Weston Court. He had every reason to turn in with confidence: perhaps 250 of his seven hundred horse and dragoons were now on duty, and he had taken all reasonable precautions against surprise.

His infantry battalions were camped in order of seniority. Dumbarton's was the senior line regiment in the field but junior to the guards regiments present, two battalions of 1st Foot Guards and a single battalion of the Coldstream.[74] However, Dumbarton's took station at the post of honour on the right of the line, almost certainly because it furnished the infantry grand guard, with perhaps a hundred of its soldiers standing to their arms all night. This party would provide the little force's right markers if the infantry had to assemble during the night. The vicar of Chedzoy maintained that one of Dumbarton's company commanders was sure that the rebels would attack, and had paced out the ground between tents and Bussex Rhine and warned his men to be ready.

There seems, however, to have been little sense that there was any real danger. Edward Dummer, a gunner in the artillery train, recorded that 'a preposterous confidence of ourselves with an undervaluing of the rebels that many days before had made us make such tedious marches had put us into the worst circumstances of surprise'. Writing in 1718, an officer of the Blues declared that 'On Sunday night most of the officers were drunk and had no manner of apprehension of the enemy.'[75] We may doubt whether a tiny village like Westonzoyland actually contained sufficient alcohol to induce widespread drunkenness, even if the royal army was unfamiliar with the foot-tangling attributes of the local cider. But it is safe to assume that, apart from the occasional edgy Scot, most of Feversham's officers yawned confidently to their beds.

Monmouth's army moved out of Bridgwater on the Long Causeway at about eleven o'clock that night. It did not take the Short Causeway out to Chedzoy, the easiest route onto the moor, but turned eastwards in the direction of Peasy Farm to march parallel with the Black Ditch towards the royal army's right flank. Theophilus Oglethorpe, up on Knowle Hill and preoccupied with the Bristol road, saw nothing of this. To make matters worse, after dark he had pulled in his standing patrol from the Langmoor Rhine, leaving a gap through which Monmouth slipped. He discovered what had happened some time later, when he took a patrol towards Bridgwater to satisfy himself that the rebels were still there. He just missed the tail end of Monmouth's marching army, and only when he reached Bridgwater did he learn that the rebels had left the town.

At about the same time that Oglethorpe realised the scale of his failure, Monmouth was getting his men across the Langmoor Rhine, and confirming his plan with his senior commanders. Lord Grey was to take the cavalry over the northern plungeon (ford) over the Bussex Rhine, swing round into Westonzoyland and spread havoc through the royal camp. The infantry, marching onwards in column, would halt opposite the royalist foot, turn left into line, and attack a camp already rocked by the irruption of the rebel horse. It was not a bad plan, and even in the small hours of 6 July it might still have worked. However, as the rebels picked their way over the Langmoor Rhine in the misty half-light, a shot rang out.

We cannot be sure who fired it. Captain John Hucker of Monmouth's horse maintained at his trial that he shot deliberately, to betray the attack, but his tale was as unconvincing then as it is now, and they hanged him anyway. It was probably one of Compton's troopers, out creasing the moor, who fired his pistol in the air the minute he saw columns of rebel infantry on the move, and then rode towards Chedzoy to find Compton himself. Compton sent at least one trooper to camp to raise the alarm, and as he spurred towards Westonzoyland he collided with part of the rebel horse. Lord Grey had predictably missed the northern plungeon and had turned north of the Bussex Rhine rather than south of it, so was now separated from the royal camp by a belt of water which was effectively impassable to poorly trained cavalry in the dark.[76] There was an inconclusive scuffle in which Compton was shot in the chest, but the damage was done.

Behind the Bussex Rhine the king's infantry had turned out of their tents to form up on the open ground south of the ditch. Their drums were now beating. Some regiments had been issued with new flintlock fusil, but others had the older matchlock, and the glow of match-cord flickered out along the line as the corporals, whose job it was to keep a light handy, lit their men's matches. The official account tells of 'my Lord Churchill having command of the foot and seeing every man at his post doing his duty', and the infantry's swift response to the alarm speaks loudly for its training and discipline, and his precautions. All chance of surprise, and with it Monmouth's battle, was now lost.

Most of Grey's horsemen crossed Dumbarton's front unengaged by yelling out that they were militia horse under Albemarle. But when challenged by 1st Foot Guards (commanded by Monmouth's half-brother the Duke of Grafton), some replied with the rebel field-word 'Monmouth and God with us,' and both battalions of 1st Foot Guards in turn replied with a volley, as did the right-hand companies of the Coldstream. This was too much for Grey's men, who broke back across the moor, some of them colliding with the two rearmost regiments of foot, the Blue and the White, which were forming up after crossing the Langmoor Rhine. The three remaining regiments, Red, Yellow and Green, managed to get into line 'but not in good order', just across the Bussex Rhine from the royal army's right flank.

The rebel gunners had trundled three small field guns all the way from Bridgwater, and now swung them into action between the Yellow and Green regiments towards the left of Monmouth's line. The rebels got to within 'half musket shot' of their enemies (Nathaniel Wade thought that the Red Regiment was within thirty or forty paces of the Bussex Rhine), stood their ground, and fired. Monmouth's cannon, manned by Dutch professionals, made better practice than his infantry, most of whom, like many soldiers in battle for the first time, shot too high. Sending blasts of case-shot across the Bussex Rhine, the guns were soon doing serious damage to Dumbarton's men and the right-hand battalion of 1st Foot Guards. Churchill, having satisfied himself that his line was properly drawn up, sent one troop of the Royal Dragoons across to the southern plungeon, and directed Lord Cornbury to take two more across to the right to support Dumbarton's. He also ordered three light field guns to take station on the right of Dumbarton's and pushed another three forward to join the first battalion of 1st Foot Guards. There is a pleasing story that Dr Peter Mews, Bishop of Winchester, a Dorset man who was accompanying the army, used his carriage horses to tug at least one of the guns into action. He had been a royalist captain during the Civil War and had fought in Holland after it, and was just the sort of prelate who saw no harm in praising God and passing the ammunition, but it is impossible to confirm the tale.

Cornbury's dragoons, probably dismounted, were in action against the Green regiment on Monmouth's left. They hit its colonel, Abraham Holmes, killing his horse beneath him and leaving him badly wounded on the ground. Churchill crossed the ditch nearby when the infantry eventually moved forward and asked Holmes, 'Who art thou?' Holmes replied glumly that he was not in a condition to tell. By this time some of the royal horse had mounted and ridden out of Westonzoyland to attack the right flank of Monmouth's infantry. There is a possibility that they missed their way in the dark, swung back too close to the royal line and were duly shot at by their own infantry, but we cannot be sure.

When Feversham reached the field he divided his horse into two groups, and sent them out across the two plungeons to threaten the rebel flanks, probably ordering them not to charge until it was light enough for them to see what they were doing. Oglethorpe, on the right, spurred on anyhow, collided with a party of rebel horse and was then beaten off with loss when he charged one of the rebel foot regiments. While the horse were getting out onto the moor, Churchill shifted Trelawney's and Kirke's, who had nothing to shoot at, across to the right, although by the time they came up with Dumbarton's the sun was beginning to rise and the battle was entering its last phase. With daylight reducing the risk of further 'friendly fire' incidents the royalist horse charged the retreating rebel infantry. The guns were swiftly overrun, and the rebel foot, struggling off as best it could, was soon swamped. Churchill quickly pushed the grenadier companies of his infantry across the Bussex Rhine to support the horse. The grenadiers of Dumbarton's took Monmouth's own banner, whose motto *Fear nothing but GOD* might have seemed ironic to the rebel survivors now running for their lives to escape the broadswords of the pursuing horsemen.

Oglethorpe was sent post-haste to London with news of the victory: his mistakes had not cost him Feversham's favour. Churchill rode straight for Bridgwater, which opened its gates at once. The settling of accounts began early: on 7 July a Dutch gunner and a deserter who had fought for the rebels were hanged in front of the whole army. That hard man Percy Kirke, now appointed brigadier to command both his own regiment and Trelawney's, was left behind to secure prisoners and ensure that the dead were properly buried. Sedgemoor had cost the royal army about thirty killed, and another 206, most of them from Dumbarton's and 1st Foot Guards, were to receive pensions for wounds received. At least 1,400 rebels had been killed in the fighting and pursuit.

Monmouth was captured, dressed in shepherd's clothes, on 8 July. He had already been condemned by Act of Attainder, but cravenly begged the king for his life: James observed that he 'did not behave himself so well as I expected nor as one ought who had taken upon him to be king'.[77] He had recovered his courage by the time he was taken to Tower Hill for execution the next day but, despite a substantial tip of six guineas, with the promise of another six from a servant after the job was done, Jack Ketch, the executioner, failed to kill him with his first three hacks. He then threw down his axe and declared that he could not go on, but the furious crowd urged him to put Monmouth out of his misery. Another two blows failed to sever the duke's head, and the executioner eventually worried it off with his knife. Ketch had to be escorted from the scene to protect him from the mob.

The trials of captured rebels began at Winchester in late August, and thereafter the 'Bloody Assizes', supervised by George, Lord Jeffreys, the lord chief justice, worked its sanguinary way across the West Country. Something over three hundred rebels were hanged, drawn and quartered, their executions taking place across the region and their quartered bodies distributed even more widely. Almost nine hundred were sentenced to transportation to the West Indies as unpaid labourers for four years, a term of exile soon increased to ten years. Churchill's biographers whisk him back to London immediately after the battle, but in late September Jeffreys wrote to tell the king that Churchill, 'who was upon the place', would tell him what had been done to snuff out rebellion in Taunton, a comment that makes sense only if Churchill had first witnessed Jeffreys' bloody handiwork and then returned to London.[78] The property of traitors was forfeit to the crown, and some of it was passed on as reward to the victors of Sedgemoor. Feversham, made a Knight of the Garter, received the estates of the executed Alice Lisle, and Churchill was given the very considerable property of John Hacker, captain of rebel horse and prosperous Taunton businessman.

Churchill emerged from the campaign with great credit. Of his possible rivals, Theophilus Oglethorpe had not fulfilled his promise as a cavalry leader, and Percy Kirke was to establish an unpleasant (though probably exaggerated) reputation for casual brutality as he snuffed out the embers of the rebellion with his tough Tangier veterans, known ironically, from their paschal lamb emblem, as Kirke's Lambs. However, Churchill's role in the battle became politicised almost immediately, and too many of his biographers have taken contemporary polemic for historical fact. Feversham, a royal favourite and a Frenchman by birth, was not popular at a time when the French were seen as natural enemies. His depiction in the Duke of Buckingham's play *The Battle of Sedgemoor* (which manages to combine both anti-French and anti-Irish prejudice) is valuable only as evidence of perennial English suspicion of Johnny Foreigner.

> A pox take de Towna vid de hard Name: How you call de Towna, De Breeche? . . . Ay begarra, Breechwater; so Madama we have intelegenta dat de Rebel go to Breechwater; me say to my Mena, Match you Rogua; so we marsha de greata Fielda, beggar, de brave Contra where dey killa de Hare vid de Hawk, beggar, de brav Sport in de Varld.[79]

Feversham was a naturalised Englishman, had lived in England for over twenty years, and spoke the language well.

Thomas Lediard's whiggish biography of Marlborough (1736) quotes an unknown author who affirms that Feversham 'had no parties abroad, he got no intelligence, and was almost surprised, and like to be defeated, when he seemed under no apprehension, but was abed without any care or order'. We have already seen how Feversham's precautions were wholly professional. Had Oglethorpe not shifted the crucial picket Monmouth's advance would have been detected sooner, but as it was Compton's screen did precisely what was expected of it. The Reverend Andrew Paschall heard from a church official in Westonzoyland that an unnamed lord sought a local guide to take him away from the battle, but it is impossible to link this firmly to Feversham, though some have tried. There were repeated suggestions that Feversham, a Frenchman and thus by definition a fop, took a long time to dress after the alarm was given and insisted on breakfasting before leaving his quarters. The most that we can say is that he had been injured by a falling timber in one of the Whitehall fires and had subsequently been trepanned: this might have made it harder for his servants to wake him.

Winston S. Churchill claimed that:

> Nothing could free the public mind from the fact that Churchill had saved and won the battle. The whole Army knew the facts. The officers included the Household troops, the Guards, and all the most fashionable soldiers about the court. They all said what they thought.

Feversham's martial achievements became a laughing-stock . . . The impression that this slothful foreigner was slumbering on his couch and that the vigilant Englishman saved the situation had more truth in it than the popular version of many historical events.[80]

If these well-placed officers did indeed know discreditable facts about Feversham, and trailed them about court, we may wonder why James appointed him to command his army in 1688 when the threat was infinitely more serious.

Feversham does not have to be a villain for Churchill to be a hero. Whatever the rumours of drunkenness or lack of vigilance, the royal infantry, his prime responsibility as the army's second in command, was camped in good order with well-understood alarm drills, and Dumbarton's provided an alert grand guard which established the right marker for its battle line. Once the fight was joined, Churchill shifted dragoons to both flanks, and paid special attention to his right, where Dumbarton's Scots were under pressure. He moved his two left-hand regiments off to the right some time afterwards, but by this time the rebel attack was broken. John Tincey, whose recent scholarly account of Sedgemoor comes as close as we can hope to being definitive, reckons that: 'By the time Feversham arrived the battle was won and he had little to do but, with the dawn, to organise the pursuit of a beaten enemy . . . Sedgemoor may not have been John Churchill's most spectacular victory, but it must rightfully be considered to be his first.'[81]

Uneasy Lies the Head

Any historian surveying the next three years must account for the fact that the nations which applauded the defeat of Monmouth and Argyll in 1685 offered remarkably little support for James II in 1688. For Churchill's biographers the task is even more specific: what made a man who acknowledged himself to owe everything to James, and who had helped keep him on the throne in 1685, betray him in his hour of need? We have the usual clash of polemics. James II's many critics see him as a monster bent on imposing Roman Catholicism on his three kingdoms and obliterating those legal defences which stood in his way. In contrast, the Jacobite *Life of James II*, based partly on his own memoirs, maintained that James was a benevolent and paternalistic figure who

had given all the marks of love, care and tenderness of his subjects, that could be expected from a true father of his people: he had . . .

encouraged and increased their trade, preserved them from taxes, supported their credit, [and] made them a rich, happy and more powerful people than they had ever appeared in the world.[82]

It is perhaps easiest to see 1685–88 as a sequence of interlinked royal miscalculations, in which maladroitness and bad luck loomed larger than malice or cruelty; and though James won most of the individual legal battles he lost the war. The Bloody Assizes had the effect (not wholly unlike the Dublin executions of 1916) of alarming many moderate men who had never wished the rebels well but did not relish the severities meted out to them. James's own overt Roman Catholicism, the arrival in London of a papal nuncio and the apparent influence of James's Jesuit confessor Father Petre created tension in themselves. They were, though, made far more disturbing to Protestants by the fact that in 1685 Louis XIV revoked the Edict of Nantes, which had given religious toleration to his Protestant subjects, and embarked upon a policy of forced conversion which drove tens of thousands of Huguenots into exile with dreadful stories to tell.

John Evelyn was shocked by what he heard.

The French persecution of the Protestants raging with the utmost barbarity, exceeded even what the very heathens used; innumerable persons of the greatest birth and riches leaving all their earthly substance and barely escaping with their lives, dispersed through all the countries of Europe. The French tyrant abrogated the Edict of Nantes . . . on a sudden demolishing all their churches, banishing, imprisoning and sending to the galleys all the ministers; plundering all the common people, and exposing them to all sorts of barbarous usages by soldiers sent to ruin and prey upon them; taking away their children; forcing people to mass, and then executing them as relapsers . . . [83]

In the spring of 1686 English congregations were asked to contribute to a fund for the exiles. This 'was long expected, and was at last with difficulty procured to be published, the interest of the French ambassador obstructing it'. The government ordered a book detailing the outrages inflicted on the Huguenots to be burnt by the common hangman, but even Evelyn, a committed royalist, thought that this was 'no refutation of any facts therein' but simply showed the French ambassador's 'great indignation at the pious and truly generous charity of all the nation'.[84]

Between 50,000 and 80,000 Huguenots arrived in England, where

they were generally welcomed as fellow Protestants, even by the constric-
tive guilds of the City of London, for the skills they brought. The tales they
told confirmed the worst English fears of an absolute monarchy with the
stink of incense in its nostrils. Martha Guiscard of Fleet Street 'came out
of France, because Jean Guiscard, her father, was burnt at Nérac,
accused of having irreverently received the host'. A wealthy gentleman
who had to 'abandon a great estate [was] condemned to be hanged: and
his house demolished, and his woods destroyed'.[85] Gilbert Burnet saw all
this as 'a real argument against the cruel and persecuting spirit of
popery, wherever it prevailed . . . the French persecution came very
seasonably to awaken the nation'.[86] Another contemporary observer
thought that: 'The whole of Europe . . . is inundated with the enemies
of Louis XIV since the expulsion of the Huguenots,' and even Marshal
Vauban lamented that France's loss included 'sixty millions of money,
nine thousand sailors, twelve thousand tried soldiers, six hundred
officers, and its most flourishing manufacturers'.[87]

English concern at the persecution of the Huguenots had two
specific aspects. First, it was carried out without regard to class or wealth:
indeed, it was the threat to 'their property, rights or privileges' that
persuaded many Huguenot noblemen to give up their religion. To
nervous Protestant gentlemen across the Channel, the process posed a
revolutionary threat to the established social as well as religious order.
Second, the regular army was the chosen instrument of terror. Dragoons
were often quartered on Huguenot villages with licence to behave abom-
inably, giving the process the name of the *dragonnades* and founding the
verb 'to dragoon' in the English language. Armed resistance was crushed
remorselessly: the marquis de Louvois told a military commander to
'cause such destruction in the area' that the example would teach other
Huguenots 'how dangerous it is to rise against the King'.[88]

Just as the abused often go on to be abusers, Huguenot exiles were not
slow to take vengeance on those they believed responsible for their plight.
At the Boyne in 1690 the Duke of Schomberg, himself a Huguenot, and
a marshal of France before his exile, shouted to a shaky Huguenot regiment: '*Allons, messieurs, voilà vos persecuteurs*' – 'Come, gentlemen, there
are your persecutors' – and it immediately rallied. Conversely, some of the
Wild Geese, Irish soldiers who left to serve in France after the collapse of
the Jacobite cause in Ireland, behaved just as badly to French Protestants
as English Protestants had to them. James's illegitimate son the Duke of
Berwick played a prominent part in suppressing a Protestant insurrection
in Languedoc, and assures us that he had a brisk way with prisoners:

'Revarelle and Catinat, who had been grenadiers in the troop, were burnt alive, on account of the horrid sacrileges they had been guilty of. Villar and Jonquet were broken on the wheel . . .'[89]

James quickly dissolved Parliament. He then proceeded to use the royal prerogative to dispense Roman Catholics from the Test Act, with a packed bench of judges finding in his favour in the collusive test case of Godden *v.* Hales in 1686.* He broke the Anglican monopoly of education by enabling Oxford fellows who became Catholics to retain their posts, and then imposed a Catholic president on Magdalen, the richest of Oxford's colleges. County lieutenancies and magistrates' benches were disproportionately reinforced by Catholics, and City livery companies and town councils across England saw the government's opponents ejected. When the Duke of Somerset refused to conduct the public ceremonial for the reception of the papal nuncio on the ground that it was illegal, James replied: 'I am above the law.' 'Your Majesty is so,' replied the duke, 'but I am not.' He was dismissed from all his offices. Although the process worked almost as much to the advantage of Dissenters as it did to that of Catholics, it affronted Tory Anglicans in England and Protestants of the established Church in both Scotland and Ireland.[90] James was alienating the very people who had backed his brother.

In May 1688 James found himself in a direct confrontation with Archbishop Sancroft and six bishops who refused to have an Indulgence, suspending the Test Act and allowing public Catholic worship, read from every pulpit. Tellingly, they would have been joined by Peter Mews, once a captain of royalist horse and a Sedgemoor veteran, had he been well enough to attend the crucial meeting. The bishops were arrested for seditious libel, and when they refused to give bail, arguing that, as peers, they did not need to do so, they were sent to the Tower. It gave the worst possible impression, and even the soldiers on guard there shouted 'God bless the bishops.' At their trial they argued that the Indulgence violated the law, which could only be changed by Parliament, and were acquitted. That night there were bonfires and fireworks across London, and even a number of symbolic pope-burnings. It was a substantial public rebuff for James.

---

* Colonel Sir Edward Hales, a Roman Catholic, was accused by his coachman, Arthur Godden, of holding a commission without taking the oaths of Supremacy and Allegiance. Convicted at Rochester assizes, Hales was successful in his appeal to the King's Bench, which agreed that the king could legally dispense him from these requirements.

Although James's approach to his armed forces was but one aspect of his general policy, the importance of the army as a means of repression in both interregnum England and Louis XIV's France gave it particular prominence. Monmouth's rebellion had illustrated the frailty of county militias, and James allowed the militia to wither on the vine during his reign, a fact which may actually have worked to his disadvantage in 1688. He maintained his regular English military establishment at just short of 20,000, the figure it had risen to as a result of the rising. He did not substantially raise it till the spring of 1688, when he recalled the Anglo-Dutch brigade, sending one each of its regiments to England, Ireland and Scotland. With the fear of Dutch invasion that autumn he added extra troops to existing establishments and raised new regiments, giving his English army a theoretical strength of something over 34,000 men. Even this was not an unreasonably large force for a country the size of England: the French had some 100,000 regulars at the same time, and even little Hesse-Cassel had more than 10,000.[91] Such comparisons, however, were not uppermost in the minds of James's parliamentary critics, who were reluctant to maintain the army even at its October 1685 size: this hostility led James to prorogue and eventually to dissolve Parliament.

The establishment of a Roman Catholic troop of Life Guards accorded with James's policy of assisting his Catholic subjects as best he could, although the Earl of Ailesbury maintained that its captain was so venal that he would gladly have enlisted a Turk if he had the £40 entrance fee to hand. What caused more concern was James's use of the prerogative to enable Catholic officers to serve, and indeed Sir Edward Hales, defendant in Godden *v.* Hales, was a colonel of infantry. Modern research has not identified that swelling torrent of Catholic officers described by some contemporaries, and even the 1688 expansion did not take the proportion above 11 per cent. There were, naturally enough, regimental exceptions: Sir Edward Hales's Regiment had sixteen Catholics out of thirty-seven officers.

Perhaps more serious was James's practice of depriving officers who opposed him in Parliament in 1685, or who subsequently crossed him, of their commissions. They were not always replaced with Catholics, but lost the money they had paid for their commissions, and he was thus 'attacking the sanctity of property and acting without tact'.[92] Overall, between the spring of 1685 and the autumn of 1688 James had increased the size of the English army and done much to improve its efficiency. Yet in the process he had 'disobliged' many Protestant career officers. This might not, in and of itself, have turned them into rebels. But as they glanced across St George's Channel, as Englishmen so often have, they saw a truly alarming process at work: the wholesale purging of the Irish army and its replacement by a Catholic force.

The Irish army was theoretically distinct from its English and Scots cousins. It was not only smaller and far worse equipped than the English army, but traditionally reflected the ascendancy of the Protestant minority over the Roman Catholic majority. James sought to reform it for two reasons: it urgently needed bringing up to date, and it was only fair, as he put it, 'that the roman catholics, who had tasted so deeply of his sufferings, should now, in his prosperity, have at least a share of his protection'.[93] It would have been a dangerous enough task in the first place, and for James to entrust it to Dick Talbot, Earl of Tyrconnell and Sarah Churchill's brother-in-law, made it explosive.

Tyrconnell, appointed lieutenant general in Ireland in 1685, and then lord lieutenant in place of Clarendon in January 1687, was the scion of an 'old English' family that had been settled in Ireland for centuries. Proud, prickly and presumptuous, he quickly set about dismissing Protestant officers from the militia and regular army alike and replacing them with 'old English' Catholic officers, and jettisoning Protestant rank and file in favour of Catholics. Robert Parker, one of the best witnesses for Marlborough's campaigns, was a Protestant from Kilkenny who had joined the Irish army as a private in 1683, but in the summer of 1687 Tyrconnell held a great review on the Curragh of Kildare and young Parker found himself dismissed. He was on his way to join the Dutch army in 1688, but a chance encounter with his old company commander in London saw him back in the army after the Glorious Revolution, in Lord Forbes' Regiment of Foot, later the Royal Regiment of Ireland.[94]

We can be sure that it was never Tyrconnell's plan to create an Irish Catholic army which could be shipped across to coerce the English. He was far more interested in redistributing power in Ireland, and it is even possible that, after the death of James II, he wished to declare Ireland an independent state. Although his 'new modelling' drew in a few experienced professional officers, it had little time to take effect, and so the Irish army of 1688 was in fact far worse trained than the force that Tyrconnell had begun to reform three years before. Moreover, even if James and Tyrconnell never intended to use the Irish Catholic army in

England, Protestant Englishmen were wholly unconvinced. Yet again, as they saw it, property rights and religious sensibilities were trampled upon, and God alone knew where the business would stop. Even the *London Gazette*, the government's own information organ, became infected by the prevailing sense of near-panic:

> Bristol, March 6 [1688]. There are arrived in all these Western parts great multitudes of disaffected English protestants from Ireland, whose condition is most deplorable; from whom we have an account that at Dublin the Protestants were all disarmed. And their horses taken from them, and many of them plundered and cruelly treated by the soldiers, who had likewise seized both the cathedrals and the college; and all ships and passengers bound for England were stopped, and their goods and plate that was found on board taken away. In Munster, Leinster and Connaught the protestants are disseized of their inheritances, as well as plundered of their arms, horses and goods, and many of the chiefest amongst them imprisoned . . . [95]

Just as Tyrconnell's camps on the Curragh were intended to bring his army together for training (as well as to expel Protestants), so James's annual military camps on Hounslow Heath had a purpose that was in part innocent. The heath, conveniently midway between Windsor and Whitehall, stood at the intersection of the Great West, Great North and Portsmouth roads, and an army based there could respond to landings in any direction. The camp also represented an opportunity to draw regiments together from individual garrisons and carry out standardised drill and some large-scale training. There was a mock fort, stormed regularly to the delight of spectators, and a chance for officers, when they could drag themselves away from London (captains were only expected to inspect their men every three days or so), to grasp the rudiments of *An Abridgement of the English Military Discipline*, a 1686 update of a drill-book first issued under Charles II. Simply getting regiments from across the land into camp on the right day showed the growing maturity of the army's fledgling central administration, with William Blathwayt and his clerks coordinating arrivals. Once the troops were in camp, James personally took a close interest in their dress, drill and training.

There was more to Hounslow Heath than solid military preparation. The camp also served to show the City of London that there were troops near at hand, and there were, as John Evelyn tells us, 'many jealousies and discourses of what was the meaning of this encampment'.[96] James saw the camp, at least in part, as a means of rattling the coercive power at his disposal in its scabbard. There were certainly times when he was prepared to use his army to dragoon opposition, and we should not be surprised that Londoners feared that they would be next. Trelawney's Regiment was quartered in Bristol in 1685 and 1686 because of the city's whiggish sympathy, and dragoons were posted to Lancaster, Warrington, Liverpool and Preston, though not in 'the honest town of Wigan'. There were cases when soldiers arrived to help towns elect the right Members of Parliament, and were sometimes given voting rights to help the process along.[97]

A combination of factors – amongst them the replacement of some officers of the English army, the purging of the Irish army, fears about the army's role as a political instrument, and mistrust of James's policy overall – helped focus a military conspiracy against him. In the case of some officers, like Churchill and the Earl of Craven, colonel of the Coldstream Guards and Carolina proprietor, opposition to the king was sharpened by fears that his policies were damaging their interests in North America. In February 1687 Churchill, as a governor of the Hudson's Bay Company, delivered to the king the company's formal complaint that nothing was being done to protect the North American colonies from French encroachments. The historian Stephen Saunders Webb may overstate the case when he declares that Churchill was 'the leading exponent of English imperial expansion'. There is, though, no doubt that his belief that English interests in North America were not well served by royal policy was another significant difference between himself and James, and that his views were shared by the influential, efficient and upwardly mobile Blathwayt.[98]

Those involved in the conspiracies against James II risked their lives and fortunes, and so took good care to minimise written evidence of their deeds, thus complicating the historian's task. We can easily enough say what the conspiracy was not. There was no attempt to subvert the majority of the army's officer corps, still less its rank and file. There was never any hope of using the army in a military coup to overthrow the king. In fact the bulk of James's army never directly opposed him, but the military conspiracy ensured that it was unable to fight against William of Orange because of the paralysing defection of its leaders. This defection, organised by men close to James, who knew his failings, fatally loosened his grip on power. It is possible that a stronger character would have withstood the repeated hammer blows of personal betrayal, but James did not. The flaws in his character, so clearly revealed during his brief reign, would destroy him.

Bishop Burnet, who had close connections to some of those involved, believed that at the heart of what he called 'the design' were 'three of the chief officers of the army, Trelawney, Kirke and the Lord Churchill. They all went into it, and Trelawney engaged his brother, the bishop.'[99] Ailesbury, on the other side of the fence, agreed with this. He tells us that he and Feversham went to the king, and begged him

> to clap up seven or eight of the heads of them and with the most humble submission I ventured to name the Prince of Denmark, the Dukes of Ormonde and Grafton, Lord Churchill, Mr Kirke, Mr Trelawney &c., but as it was found, and fatally, that the king could not resolve and, if he had, in all probability the army would have stood by him.[100]

There were two nerve centres of conspiracy. The 'Treason Club', whose members met at the Rose Tavern on Russell Street in Covent Garden to smoke, drink and mutter, included a number of whiggish professional soldiers and politicians like Richard Savage, Viscount Colchester, Thomas Wharton (later to inherit his father's peerage and emerge as a Whig grandee) and Thomas Langston, sometime major of Churchill's Royal Dragoons and now commanding Princess Anne's Horse. Charles Godfrey, who had served with Churchill in France and later married his sister Arabella, kept Churchill abreast of movements in the Rose.

The 'Tangerines' were the other main group, although the term strictly speaking comprised all Tangier veterans, given to musing on old times over their tokay and damning the government. Key conspirators included Percy Kirke and Charles Trelawney, as well as Langston, a Tangier veteran and intermediary with the Treason Club. Another Tangerine was John Cutts, a veteran of the Imperial service, where he had been the first man to plant a standard on the walls of Buda, a wholly characteristic act for a man soon to be known as 'Salamander', after the mythical creature which lives in fire. He had just published a book of *Poetical Exercises* and was a lieutenant colonel in the Anglo-Dutch Brigade, providing useful contact with disaffected officers in that body.

Some regiments were, naturally, more disaffected than others. The officers of 1st Foot Guards, who might have been expected to provide a mainstay for the regime, seem to have followed the lead of their colonel, the Duke of Grafton, who was not simply a member of the Cockpit circle but Barbara Villiers' son, and who felt that his performance in 1685 had been poorly rewarded. He was governor of the Isle of Wight, and one of his captains, Lionel Copley, was deputy governor of the important port and arsenal of Hull.[101] There were a number of naval officers like George Byng, Mathew Aylmer and Arthur Herbert in the conspiracy, but it was naturally more difficult to get naval plotters together.

Neither of these groups turned its attention to practical treason till the summer of 1688, as they could do little until they knew that William was indeed planning to invade. Events moved fast that summer. On 10 June 1688 James's queen gave birth to a son, rendering the temporising policies of men like Halifax irrelevant, for there was now a good chance that James would have a successor who would not reverse his policies. Churchill, we are told, 'was summoned to attend' the birth as a witness, but although he was 'sent for in a very particular manner . . . he had received some intimations before, and was purposely out of the way'.[102] The bishops were acquitted on 30 June, and on that very day the Earls of Devonshire, Danby and Shrewsbury, Bishop Compton, Edward Russell and Henry Sidney, sent a letter to William of Orange assuring him that 'nineteen parts of twenty' throughout the kingdom wanted a change in government, and 'much the greatest part of the nobility and gentry' were 'as much dissatisfied'. If William acted quickly, they were confident that the army would not fight because its members were 'so discontented'.[103]

The army was in camp on Hounslow Heath, and conditions for spreading discontent amongst selected officers could scarcely have been better. Indeed, James's own policy of canvassing officers for their support for repeal of the Test Acts actually worked against his own interests. The majority of army officers, then as now, were apolitical, and resented being invited to make political choices either way. When James asked Captain Sandys of the Blues, who had fought bravely at Sedgemoor, what he thought of the repeal, the captain replied gruffly: 'I understand Your Majesty well enough. I fear God and honour the king, as I ought, but I am not a man that is given to change.'[104]

By mid-1688 the fact that the Prince of Orange was considering an invasion was an open secret. On 19 August Dr Tenison, Archbishop of Canterbury, warned John Evelyn that 'there would suddenly be some great thing discovered. This was the Prince of Orange intending to come over.'[105] On 18 September Evelyn reported that 'the Dutch make extraordinary preparations both at sea and land', and on 7 October he declared that:

To such a strange temper, and unheard of in former times, was this poor nation reduced, and of which I was an eyewitness. The apprehension was (and with reason) that His Majesty's forces would neither at land or at sea oppose them with that vigour requisite to repel the invader.[106]

John Churchill was at the very centre of the plot, and this is not a comfortable admission for some biographers. Winston S. Churchill, indeed, described the conspiracy against James as 'The National Counter-Plot' so as to stress both its national and its reactive character. Like most of the professional soldiers involved in it, Churchill relied primarily upon his army pay, and so the much-feared purge of the English army after the Irish model would strike at his fundamental interests. He had already seen loyal men who obstructed James have their careers blasted. Then, in early 1688 the Earl of Oxford, 'the noblest subject in England and, as Englishmen loved to say, in Europe', refused, as lord lieutenant of Essex, to appoint Catholics to public office. 'I will stand by your Majesty against all enemies to the last drop of my blood,' he declared. 'But this is a matter of conscience and I cannot comply.' He was deprived of his county lieutenancy and of the colonelcy of the Blues, where the Duke of Berwick replaced him.

In the fate of men like Somerset and Oxford, grandees who could survive well enough without royal favour, Churchill sensed a foretaste of his own. He was not willing to become a Catholic, and had told James so, though in less jocular terms than Percy Kirke, who warned the surprised monarch that he had given the Emperor of Morocco first refusal, and so if he was going to convert to anything it would be to Islam. One evening before dinner in the autumn of 1685, we are told, James and Churchill walked round the Deanery Garden at Winchester. James had that day been carrying out the traditional ceremony of touching those afflicted by scrofula, known as the King's Evil, and at Winchester he had performed the ceremony attended by Catholic priests.

James asked Churchill what he thought people made of his carrying out the ceremony in this way. Churchill replied that they feared it might be paving the way for the restoration of Catholicism. The angry James snapped back that he had given his word that all he sought was religious toleration. Churchill then said:

What I spoke, sir, proceeded purely from my zeal for your majesty's service, which I prefer above all things next to that of God, and I humbly beseech your majesty to believe no subject in all your three kingdoms would venture further than I would to purchase your favour and good liking; but I have been bred a Protestant, and intend to live and die in that communion; above nine parts of ten of the whole people are of that persuasion, and I fear (which excess of duty makes me say) from the genius of the English nation, and their natural aversion to the Roman Catholic worship, some consequences which I dare not name, and which it creates in me a horror to think of.

James then said deliberately:

I tell you, Churchill, I will exercise my own religion in such a manner as I shall think fitting. I will show favour to my Catholic subjects, and be a common father to all my Protestants of what religion soever: but I am to remember that I am King, and to be obeyed by them. As for the consequences, I shall leave them to Providence, and make use of the power God has put into my hands to prevent anything that shall be injurious to my honour, or derogatory to the duty that is owing to me.

James did not speak to Churchill again that night, but during dinner he had a long conversation with Dr Maggot, the dean of Winchester, about Passive Obedience. 'I myself,' wrote the anonymous author of this source, 'was a stander by and heard it; without knowing the occasion of it at the time, till the Lord Churchill told me what words had happened between the King and him.'[107]

It is as difficult for us now as it was for contemporaries to judge precisely where, in these matters, conscience left off and self-interest began. Amongst the conspirators were some men who were devout, and others (with Percy Kirke as the most notable example) who were not. If the evidence of his abundant correspondence is any guide, Churchill was sincere in his commitment to Anglicanism. In accordance with the spirit of the age, he tried not to march or fight on Sundays, repeatedly affirmed his trust in God and the need to thank Him publicly for His mercies. Twenty years later, in a dark moment before Oudenarde, ill and at a tactical disadvantage, he was discovered by Sicco van Goslinga earnestly at prayer at one o'clock in the morning. In December 1687 Sarah told Mary of Orange that 'Though he [Churchill] will always obey the King in all things that are consistent with religion – yet, rather than change that, I daresay that he will lose all his places and all that he has.'[108] Churchill did not only *believe* that James was wrong: he *thought* that the monarch's policy would either wreck his own career or generate a wider insurrection. In the latter event he did not wish to be on the losing side, for he had seen, in his own father's case, just what that involved.

He was certainly anxious not to break cover too soon. In February 1688 James decreed that the Duke of Berwick's Regiment of Foot, in garrison at Portsmouth, was to enlist some Irish recruits who were surplus to requirements elsewhere. The regiment's lieutenant colonel and five of the twelve company commanders begged instead that 'we may have leave to fill up our companies with such men of our nation as we judge most suitable to the king's service and to support our honours'. The officers were tried by court-martial at Windsor Castle, and all lost their commissions. Seven of their brother officers resigned in sympathy, and over a hundred private soldiers seized the opportunity to desert. The incident was not in fact a sign of James's intention to pack English regiments with Irish recruits, but to an army that was already suspicious of royal intentions it looked very much that way.

Churchill sat on the court-martial and voted for the death penalty. By doing so he gave a public affirmation of his loyalty to James, but because courts-martial voted in reverse seniority, with the most junior voting first, he knew that his apparent severity would not actually imperil the lives of the accused. However, he was aware that one of the officers on trial, John Beaumont, was an active plotter and must have been worried that his premature action would risk wider disclosures. Churchill, as we shall see, was responsible for remodelling the army after the Revolution of 1688, and saw that Beaumont was promoted to colonel while at least three of the cashiered captains became lieutenant colonels.

In all this dangerous work Churchill was aided and abetted by his wife. There is a very close correlation between the predominantly Tory Cockpit circle and the often whiggish army conspirators. Henry Compton, the suspended Bishop of London, was not only a signatory of the invitation to William of Orange but a confidant of the Cockpit. In the late summer of 1688 he travelled widely, winning over his nephew the Earl of Northampton, the Earl of Dorset, Lord Grey de Ruthin and the Earl of Manchester.[109] At the very heart of the Cockpit was Princess Anne, who assured her elder sister Mary, William of Orange's wife:

> I hope you don't doubt that I will ever be firm to my religion whatever happens . . . I must tell you that I abhor the principles of the Church of Rome as much as it is possible for any to do, and I as much value the doctrine of the Church of England. And certainly there is the greatest

reason in the world to do so, for the doctrine of the Church of Rome is wicked and dangerous, and directly contrary to the Scriptures, and their ceremonies – most of them – plain, downright idolatry.[110]

Anne was already as close to Sarah Churchill as she was distant from her father, and the events of the mid-1680s strengthened the former tie as they further unravelled the latter. Anne's two young daughters, Anne and Mary, died from smallpox early in 1687, and for some weeks Prince George hovered on the brink of following them. The Catholic faction at court began to discuss her remarriage to a suitable Catholic prince, and when the distraught Anne asked her father for permission to visit Mary at The Hague, James, with a typical show of paternal firmness which emerged as intolerance, refused it. Anne immediately warned her sister, in just the tone used by the army conspirators, that if things went on like this no Protestant would be able to live in England. Anne had also come to hate her stepmother, not least because of her evangelising zeal for her religion, and in May 1697 she told Mary: 'She pretends to have a good deal of kindness to me but I doubt it is not real, for I never see proofs of it, but rather the contrary.'[111]

Suspecting that their father's agents would interfere with their letters, the royal sisters took to corresponding through the Dutch ambassador Everaarde van Weede, Heer van Dijkveld, who was himself hard at work gleaning news of English political opinion for his master, and who maintained contact with Princess Anne through the medium of John Churchill. By now James suspected both Anne's increasing political influence and the strength of her affection, which he called 'a boundless passion', for Sarah. In mid-1687 Louis XIV's special envoy reported that Anne's main advisers were now working for William, and Churchill, in his opinion, 'exerts himself more than anyone for the Prince of Orange. Lord Godolphin, who is in all the secret councils, opposes nothing, but plays the good Protestant and always keeps a back door open for access to the Prince of Orange.'[112]

Her stepmother's successful pregnancy, which came to term on 10 June, infuriated Anne, who had by now lost her own two daughters and suffered two miscarriages, and she saw in the infant Prince James Francis Edward an heir who would not only supplant the claims of Mary and herself, but who might also continue James's policy. She complained to Mary that simply being in London was an agony, because 'The Papists are all so very insolent that it is insupportable living with them.'[113] By this time Anne's resentment of her father's policies had gone beyond mere criticism, and the Cockpit circle had a conspiracy of its own, aimed at ensuring that Anne escaped from London to join one of the provincial risings planned to accompany a Dutch invasion.

Although Sarah Churchill was later to argue in *The Conduct of the Duchess of Marlborough* that the princess's hurried departure from London in the middle of the 1688 campaign was 'a thing sudden and unconcerted', it is clear that she and her husband had thrown their hands in with the plotters some time before.[114] Sarah admitted that John 'made settlements to secure his family in case of misfortunes', and in a letter he sent to the Prince of Orange by way of Henry Sidney on 27 July 1688 he formally bound himself to William:

> Mr Sidney will let you know how I intend to behave myself: I think it is what I owe to God and my country. My honour I take leave to put into your Royal Highness's hands, in which I think it safe. If you think there is anything else that I ought to do, you have but to command me, and I shall pay an entire obedience to it, being resolved to die in that religion that it has pleased God to give you both the will and power to protect.[115]

There are times when a nation holds its breath. In the autumn of 1688 England was gripped by rumour and counter-rumour. The French, hands imbued with the blood of Huguenots, were on their way; the Irish were poised to invade. There would be a general massacre of Protestants, and the Church and the constitution would be toppled. Only the arrival of that Protestant hero, William of Orange, could avert catastrophe. On 7 October John Evelyn inhaled the stink of panic:

> Hourly expectation of the Prince of Orange's invasion heightened to that degree that his Majesty saw fit to abrogate the commissions for the dispensing power (but retaining his right still to dispense with all laws) and restore the ejected Fellows of Magdalen College. In the mean time he called over 5000 Irish, and 4000 Scots, and continued to remove Protestants and put in Papists at Portsmouth and other places of trust, and retained the Jesuits about him, increasing the universal discontent. It brought people to so desperate a pass, that they seemed passionately to long for and desire the landing of that Prince whom they looked on to be their deliverer, praying

incessantly for an east wind, which was said to be the only hindrance of his expedition . . . [116]

A popular song honed the edge of unrest. Its snappy little tune is often ascribed, without evidence, to Henry Purcell, and the lyrics are attributed, with as little solid basis, to Lords Wharton and Dorset. If we imagine Tom Wharton scratching a quill in the fug of the Rose Tavern, trying out the couplets on his cronies, then we are stretching history, though not conjecture, too far. The words, which come in many versions, are in cod-Irish, and are meant to be those of a Catholic welcoming recent changes. The doggerel *Lillibulero bullen a la* was repeated after each line, and the refrain *Lero, lero, lillibulero/lillibulero bullen a la/Lero, lero, lillibulero/lillibelero bullen a la* followed each couplet.

> *Ho! Brother Teague, dost hear the decree?*
> *Dat we shall have a new deputy?*
>
> *Ho! By my shoul, it is de Talbot,*
> *And he will cut all de Englishmen's throats . . .*
>
> *And de good Talbot is made a Lord,*
> *And with brave lads is coming abroad.*
>
> *Who all in France have taken a sware,*
> *Dat day will have no Protestant heir.*
>
> *Arragh! But why does he stay behind?*
> *Ho! By my shoul, 'tis a Protestant wind!*
>
> *But see, de Tyrconnell is now come ashore,*
> *And we shall have commissions galore.*
>
> *And he dat will not go to mass,*
> *Shall be turned out, and look like an ass.*
>
> *But now de heretics all go down,*
> *By Creish and St Patrick, the nation's our own.*
>
> *Dare was an old prophesy found in a bog,*
> *Dat we shall be ruled by an ass and a dog.*
>
> *And now dis prophesy is come to pass,*
> *For Talbot's de dog, and James is de ass.*

'Lillibulero' was sung in taverns, brayed tunelessly in the street, and whistled by folk with time on their hands. Two and a half centuries later, when the BBC World Service wanted a signature tune it chose 'Lillibulero'. It is said that James really knew that there was a military conspiracy when he heard the sentry at his door quietly whistling the song which was to sing him out of three kingdoms. In this atmosphere of incipient panic and growing military preparation John, Lord Churchill, prepared to roll fate's dice, and knew that anything but a six would ruin him.

3

The Protestant Wind

On 5 November 1688 William of Orange landed at Torbay. His *Declaration . . . Of the Reasons Inducing him to Appear in Arms in . . . England*, issued at The Hague on 30 September, furnished the public justification for his invasion: it accused James's advisers of seeking to overturn the laws and liberties of the three kingdoms, to introduce arbitrary government and an illegal religion. It affirmed that William did not seek the crown for himself, but sought only to have 'free and lawful' Parliaments elected in England and Scotland. He had sailed with a fleet of forty-nine warships and over four hundred transports, many of them very small, commanded by Sir Arthur Herbert, rear admiral of England until replaced earlier that year by the Catholic Roger Strickland.

James's fleet was commanded by the Earl of Dartmouth, and the military conspiracy had done its best to erode the reliability of his captains. However, the conspiracy appears to have been a good deal less effective afloat than it was ashore, and it seems fair to conclude that James's navy would have fought had it been given the chance. It was not, because the same Protestant wind that blew William's fleet along the Channel kept Dartmouth's warships in the Gunfleet, on the Essex side of the Thames estuary. James had specifically warned him that he risked being 'surprised while there by the sudden coming of the Dutch fleet, as being a place he cannot well get out to sea from, while the wind remains easterly', but the cautious Dartmouth stayed where he was. He actually saw the outer fringe of William's fleet sailing southwards on 3 November, but they were directly to windward and, with the tide at low ebb, Dartmouth could not weather the nearby sandbanks. N.A.M. Rodger is right to attribute William's success in the naval part of the operation to 'wind and tide' rather than to disaffection, although, of course, in the backwash of that success the naval conspiracy grew enormously.[1]

William was taking an extraordinary risk in invading at the season of equinoctal gales, and a rueful Dartmouth told his royal master, "Tis strange that such mad proceedings should have success at this time of year.'[2] The Prince of Orange knew that time was of the essence. That summer Louis XIV had invaded the archbishopric of Cologne and large tracts of the Rhineland, his armies trampling on with that brutal disregard for life and property which had become their hallmark. Louis had already put increasing pressure on the Dutch, seizing Dutch shipping in foreign ports in September, and he eventually issued a formal declaration of war on 26 November. This actually strengthened William's hand, because even the anti-Orange faction in the States-General now rallied, as good Dutchmen, behind him.

Elsewhere French miscalculation helped ensure that a majority of European states were now opposed to Louis, while his Turkish allies were making heavy weather against the Imperialists. The autumn of 1688 found the major part of the French fleet in the Mediterranean ready to act against Pope Innocent XI (perhaps as odd an opponent for a Most Christian King as the Turks were a puzzling ally) and the French army committed in the Rhineland. This situation would not last, and William knew it. He did not simply need to invade before James had discovered the military conspiracy and proceeded against its leaders: he had to strike before the French had rebalanced so as to attack Holland, compelling him to devote his efforts to domestic defence, not foreign adventures.

William's army consisted of Dutch regulars reinforced by English, Scots, Irish, Huguenot, German, Swiss, Finnish and Swedish regiments; there was even a two-hundred-strong black contingent of Dutch Surinamese soldiers. Nevertheless, with a maximum strength of perhaps 20,000, it was very small, and its cavalry would take some time to reach full efficiency as its horses recovered from the voyage. The royal army was at least one-third bigger, and as the events of 1685 had shown, a landing in the West Country could be effectively contained by troops marching in from the east. The great truth about William's invasion is simple. It could not rely on seeking decision by battle: William, an experienced general, knew that he could scarcely hope to pull off some stunning masterstroke, with his small polyglot force, against a bigger professional army fighting on home ground. His manifesto to the British army argued that no 'false notion of honour' should prevent its members from considering 'what you owe to Almighty God and your religion, to your country and to yourselves, and to your posterity, which you, as men of honour, ought to prefer to all private considerations and engagements whatsoever'.[3]

William must have been sure, well beyond the balance of probabilities, that the enemy army would disintegrate without fighting. Both Macaulay and Trevelyan argued that his victory was largely a matter of luck. In contrast, George Hilton Jones, writing in 1990, with much more evidence of the military conspiracy at his disposal, argued that James's 'religious and foreign policies had isolated him beyond hope of recovery . . . His nerve would break when he saw his position so unbalanced that a token expedition would suffice to topple it.'[4]

That was certainly what Captain Isaac Dupont de Bostaquet, a Huguenot cavalry officer with William's army, thought. His fellow countrymen who had been dispossessed by Louis XIV saw this as a crusade. 'Most of the refugees bore arms,' he wrote, 'and officers as well as others went to The Hague to give their names to be enrolled in this holy war.' He found south-west England 'the most inhospitable land in the world', and was astonished, when he visited his first Anglican church, to see 'that so much of the outward appearance of Popery had been retained'. However, 'We had orders to pay wherever we went,' which he knew from his own former service was not the French army's way. In Exeter 'the inhabitants received us with great cheers', and there was real confidence that James would not intervene. 'Rumour was that he was marching towards us,' recalled Bostaquet, 'but did not dare to attack because he did not trust his army which was deserting him.' In contrast, on William's side 'every man hastened on as if to certain victory'.[5]

William arrived in Exeter on 9 November. Although the corporation tried to keep him out and the clergy refused to read his *Declaration* from the pulpit, as Bostaquet has told us, the townspeople greeted him rapturously. He remained there for nearly a fortnight, receiving a number of peers and gentlemen, and encircling Plymouth, whose garrison was to surrender without firing a shot. The Duke of Beaufort's Gloucestershire militia, loyal to James, arrested Lord Lovelace and some of his supporters after a brief fracas, but elsewhere the mood of the West Country, angered but not cowed by the royal reaction to Monmouth's rising, was very encouraging for William.

James ordered his army to concentrate on Salisbury Plain, with a cavalry screen under Sir John Lanier probing forward to find William's outposts. By 15 November the Earl of Feversham, James's captain general, was there with something over 20,000 men, and more still coming in.

Many royal soldiers were already tired, for it was a long march for men from Scotland and Ireland, and it was scarcely encouraging to hear, long before the concentration was complete, that the first desertions had taken place: on 13 November Lord Cornbury and Colonel Thomas Langston, both close associates of Churchill, went over to William.

What was meant to be the mass desertion of an entire elite cavalry brigade of Lanier's covering force misfired, partly because neither Cornbury of the Royal Dragoons nor Lieutenant Colonel Compton of the Blues got their men to follow them, although the more forceful Langston took most of the Duke of St Albans' Horse into the Dutch lines. John Churchill's nephew and James's illegitimate son, the nine-teen-year-old Duke of Berwick, had just arrived in Salisbury. He galloped after the brigade as soon as he heard that it had left for Warminster and claimed to have 'rallied the fugitives, and brought the four regiments back to Salisbury, of which there were only about fifty troopers or dragoons, and a dozen officers missing'.[6] Burnet calls Berwick 'a soft and harmless young man . . . much beloved by the king', but it is clear that had more of James's commanders shown his spirit the campaign's outcome might have been different.[7]

The fact that billets had been reserved for the entire brigade in William's lines speaks volumes for the degree of coordination that existed. Even if the Williamites were disappointed by the actual number of deserters, the episode broke the ice, and there was a steady trickle of desertion thereafter, with officers and men slipping away to join William, each separate desertion contributing to the air of mistrust which overhung James's army like a pestilential miasma. The Whig politician Sir Richard Onslow, whose annotations are printed in the 1833 edition of Burnet's *History of His Own Times*, maintained that even at this early stage James's personal morale was crushed by the desertions: 'This ruined him, for I have been well assured that had he shown any courage and spirit upon the occasion his army would have fought the Prince of Orange.'[8] Lord Ailesbury also reckoned that the rot spread from the top, and that the royal army could have fought: 'Of both horse and foot the common men were well intended to the King's service, and most of the lower rank of officers, some general officers, colonels, etc, the same.'[9]

One of the few flashes of resistance was sparked by a man with an abundance of fighting spirit. Patrick Sarsfield was an Irish Catholic Life Guards officer. Berwick called him 'a man of an amazing stature, utterly void of sense, very good natured and very brave'. He met an Anglo-Dutch detachment at Wincanton on 20 November. When its officer declared that he was for the Prince of Orange, Sarsfield declared: 'God damn you! I'll prince you,' and promptly pistolled him. He had the better of the fight, but pulled back when enemy reinforcements appeared.

John Churchill had been promoted lieutenant general on 7 November, two days after the landing. He joined the king, who had already been dismayed by the news of the first desertions, at Windsor, and on the seventeenth the royal party set off for Salisbury. Princess Anne was poised to play her own part in the betrayal, and on the eighteenth she told William:

> I shall not trouble you with many compliments, only in short assure you, that you have my wishes for your good success in this so just an undertaking; and I hope the Prince [George] will soon be with you to let you see his readiness to join with you . . . He went yesterday with the King towards Salisbury, intending to go from thence to you as soon as his friends thought it proper. I am not certain if I shall continue here, or remove into the City; that shall depend upon the advice my friends will give me; but wherever I am, I shall be ready to show you how very much I am your humble servant.[10]

Both Prince George and John Churchill expected that their wives would escape from Whitehall before they themselves abandoned James, but events moved on more quickly than they expected. That autumn James was suffering from repeated nosebleeds, so copious and severe that some saw them as a sign of divine displeasure. Charles II had been similarly afflicted in moments of stress, and they may have been a family weakness. One eyewitness admitted:

> I can never forget the confusion the court was in . . . The king knew not whom to trust and the flight was so great that they were apt to believe an impossible report just brought in that the Prince of Orange was come with twelve thousand horse between Warminster and Salisbury . . . Everybody in this hurly-burly was thinking of himself and nobody minded the king, who came up to Dr Radcliffe and asked him what he thought was good for the bleeding of the nose.

James was 'much out of order, looks yellow and takes no natural rest'.[11] A visitor to Salisbury

> saw King James ride backwards and forward continually with a languishing look, his hat hanging over his eyes and a handkerchief continually in one hand to dry the blood of his nose for he continually bled. If he and the soldiers did chance to hear a trumpet or even a post-horn they were always upon a surprise, and all fit to run away, and at last they did so. All the nights there was nothing but tumult and every question that was asked 'Where are the enemy?' 'How far off are they? 'Which way are they going?' and such like.[12]

At a council of war on 23 November Churchill and Grafton both recommended an advance, while Feversham spoke in favour of retreat, and James agreed. However, James seems to have accepted Churchill's offer to go and inspect the outposts that night. Both James and the Duke of Berwick were later to maintain that this was simply an excuse to hand over James to the Williamites, or even to murder him: 'A scheme was laid, and the measures taken up by Churchill and Kirke, to deliver the king up to the Prince of Orange.'[13] We cannot tell whether this is true, although if so it would have required very slick coordination. More seriously, it would have involved Churchill in the face-to-face betrayal of his patron, which would have been wholly out of character.

There was no precedent for such confrontation in his past career, and indeed, he did his best to remain on terms of a kind with James and his son for the rest of his life. Early that December, when Clarendon told Churchill that James had informed his supporters in the House of Lords that a kidnap had been intended, he 'denied it with many protestations, saying that he would venture his life in defence of his person; that he would never be ungrateful to the King; and that he had never left him, but that he saw our religion and country were in danger of being destroyed'.[14] It is easy to dismiss this as the self-exculpatory whining of a successful traitor, but it goes straight to the heart of Churchill's dreadful dilemma.

There was to be no kidnap, for no sooner had James agreed to the visit than he was overwhelmed by another nosebleed, and muttered, through his bloody handkerchief, that he was going back to London. Until that moment Churchill, for all his treasonable correspondence with William, may still have suspected that the royal army would receive the forceful leadership which might even now have enabled it to shake off its malaise. But it was now abundantly clear that James could not provide that leadership. He had abandoned his only reasonable war plan, and was about to abandon his army.

Yet even in his despair James could still lash out. When Percy Kirke, commanding a mixed brigade of horse and foot at Warminster, refused, with a temporising excuse, to obey an order to fall back on Devizes, James had him arrested and sent back under escort to Andover. Many of the brigade's officers, including Lieutenant Colonel Charles Churchill and his colonel, Charles Trelawney, deserted anyway. There was now no doubt that James was going to lose, and with Kirke under suspicion and his own brother gone, John Churchill cannot have hoped to escape arrest much longer. Early on the morning of Sunday, 24 November, Churchill, the Duke of Grafton and Colonel John Berkeley, with perhaps four hundred officers and men, set off for Crewkerne, some fifty miles away. It was about twelve miles from William's headquarters at Axminster, so close to Churchill's birthplace. Prince George and the Duke of Ormonde joined them the following night. Although James bravely quipped that the loss of a stout trooper would have hurt him more than the defection of Prince George, the Danish envoy reported that when he interrupted mass to give James the bad news he was profoundly shocked.

Churchill left a letter for James trying to explain his decision.

Sir,

Since men are seldom suspected of sincerity, when they act contrary to their interests, and though my dutiful behaviour to Your Majesty in the worst of times (for which I acknowledge my service is much over-paid) may not be sufficient to incline you to charitable interpretation of my actions, yet I hope the great advantage I enjoy under Your Majesty, which I own I would never expect in any other change of government, may reasonably convince your majesty and the world that I am actuated by a higher principle, when I offer that violence to my inclination and interest as to desert Your Majesty at a time when your affairs seem to challenge the strictest obedience from all your subjects, much more from one who lies under the greatest personal obligations to Your Majesty. This, sir, could proceed from nothing but the inviolable dictates of my conscience, and a necessary concern for my religion, (which no good man can oppose), and with which I am instructed nothing can come in competition. Heaven knows with what partiality my dutiful opinion of Your Majesty has hitherto represented those unhappy designs which inconsiderate and self-interested men have framed against Your Majesty's true interest and the Protestant religion; but as I can no longer join with such to give a pretence of conquest to bring them to effect, so I will always with the hazard of my life and fortune (so much Your Majesty's due) to preserve your royal person and lawful rights, with all the tender concerns and dutiful respect that becomes, sir, Your Majesty's most dutiful and most obliged subject and servant,

CHURCHILL[15]

It must, by any standards, have been an agonising letter to write. In it Churchill acknowledged that he was James's creature, and surmised that he could not expect to prosper as well under any future government, although at the time nobody can have been sure what that might be. It was then perfectly possible that James might have remained king, though with sharply circumscribed powers, and in that case Churchill's desertion must have been fatal to his prospects, as he himself implied: had he been certain that William and Mary would indeed succeed James then the first part of the letter would have been palpably absurd. His supporters would maintain that he was sincere in stressing the inviolable dictates of conscience and a necessary concern for religion, while his critics saw the whole document as transparent cover for self-seeking treason. 'Churchill, as if to add something ideal to his imitation of Iscariot,' thundered G.K. Chesterton (who, as a Roman Catholic, was *parti pris* in this debate), 'went to James with wanton professions of love and loyalty, went forth in arms as if to defend the country from invasion, and then calmly handed the country over to the invader.'[16]

A middle course might be fairer. All Churchill's life, both before and after the events of that rainy autumn, shows us a man whose experience of being on the losing side convinced him that it should not be repeated. In this he had much in common with many contemporaries who, like the vicar of Bray, would trim their sails to suit the wind. We have already seen that his suspicions of James's maladroitness went back at least ten years, and that, whatever we may make of the commitment to Protestantism expressed in his letter, he was not prepared, as some of his countrymen were, to become a Roman Catholic. He thought that James, a winner in 1685, had become a loser by 1688, and was probably close to what Matthew Glozier identified as the bedrock of the army of his age, those 'professional gentlemen officers in search of a livelihood, in conditions which did not unduly compromise their religious and social consciences', who thought much the same.[17] John Childs has a similar view of the bonds of professional identity which linked the wider army conspirators. Without the contribution made by the deserters in 1688, he suggests, 'unconscious and vaguely dishonourable though it was, William might very well have been without any English army at all in the spring of 1689'.[18]

Churchill remained in treasonous contact with the Jacobites for the rest of his life. This is not because he was ideologically Jacobite (had he been so, then surely the moment to show his zeal would have been in 1688) but because he was never a man to burn his bridges. Yet we cannot doubt the contact. For instance, in February 1716, not long before Churchill suffered the first of his disabling strokes, an agent wrote to the Earl of Mar, leader of the 1715 Jacobite rebellion, to say that Captain David Lloyd, another agent, had delivered a letter from the Old Pretender, James II's eldest son, to Churchill,

> to whom Davie downright forced his way. Mark [Marlborough] read the letter with respect. Davie urged and enforced the argument with tears, and drew tears from the other, who protested before God that he intended to serve Mr Keith [the Old Pretender] and would do it, and that his nephew [the Duke of Berwick] knew he intended it and in what manner. But that at present he cannot help some things. That he expects his nephew himself will come ere long, and that in the meantime Mr Keith should handsomely parry a little, and avoid a decision, till matters can be prepared.[19]

The Duke of Berwick later confirmed to Mar that: 'Mark has been, it's true, for these many years in correspondence with his nephew, and has always given assurances of his zeal for Mr Keith, but to this hour has never explained in what manner he intends it.'[20] Berwick has it in a nutshell. It was never *quite* the right time, and the manner in which Churchill was to offer assistance to exiled king and pretender was never clear: but he was to go to his grave without ever wholly disowning the Jacobites.

In one sense it is not certain that Churchill was so very different to many of the senior army officers of our own generation. Few of these thought that the invasion of Iraq in 2003 was a good idea, and many went much further in private, arguing that it was possibly illegal and unlikely to be successful in the long term. But soldiering was their job, and there was certainly ample short-term satisfaction to be had from doing what they were paid to do, deposing a monstrous tyrant, and genuinely trying to make *their* bit of Iraq a better place in the process. Never underestimate the professional soldier's desire to be exactly that, and do not expect that he will emerge with more credit from his moral contradictions than John Churchill did from his. It may not be easy to admire Churchill's desertion of James, but it is less hard to understand it, and many, in all soul and conscience, would not have acted differently.

On 25 November James issued orders that Sarah Churchill should be put under house arrest in the Tyrconnells' lodgings in St James's Palace, while the wife of Colonel Berkeley, who had also abandoned James, should be confined to her father's London house. Happily for the conspirators, news that James was on his way back to London reached the capital before the arrest orders. This 'put the Princess into a great fright', said Sarah. 'She sent for me, told me her distress, and declared, that rather than see her father she would jump out of a window.' Sarah went to Bishop Compton, who was hiding in Suffolk Street, and they arranged an escape plan. The princess retired to bed as usual on the evening of the twenty-fifth, locking the door of her chamber and telling her staff that she was not to be disturbed.

Early on the morning of 26 November Anne, accompanied by Sarah and Mrs Berkeley, slipped down some newly-built back stairs and walked through the mud of Piccadilly (in which the princess lost a shoe) to a carriage containing that unlikely pair, Bishop Compton and Charles Sackville, Earl of Dorset. Dorset had been one of the most notorious rakes at Charles II's court but remained curiously popular: 'My Lord Dorset might do anything,' complained the Earl of Rochester, 'and is never to blame.' He had never enjoyed James's favour, largely because of a vicious lampoon on Catherine Sedley, the girl John Churchill's parents had so wanted him to marry. Dorset was committed to the plot against James, and the fugitives spent their first day at his house, Copt Hall, near Epping in Essex. They then moved on to Castle Ashby, near Northampton, ancestral home of Compton's nephew the Earl of Northampton, another of the plotters. They had originally planned to hurry on to York, now secured for William by the Earl of Danby, but by now felt that they had outrun any pursuit, and proceeded to Nottingham by easy stages.[21]

When James reached London he was shocked to find Anne gone. 'God help me!' he cried. 'Even my children have forsaken me.'

Lord Mulgrave, his chamberlain, argued that even the desertion of James's officers was as nothing when compared to the evidence of common purpose between Anne, Mary and William. He did not simply nurse a particular grievance against John Churchill, but believed that Anne's escape had been organised by Sarah. By now it was evident that there would be no real campaign. Orders telling the garrison of Portsmouth to stock up for a siege simply increased the flow of desertions, and James had lost the war he never fought.

Most historians take the view that Feversham, useless from the start, was paralysed by James's departure. It is, though, possible that Feversham had sniffed the way the wind was blowing. He was a Huguenot, and although he had left France long before the Revocation of the Edict of Nantes he could never return there. If he wished to enjoy his English estates, he would need to make his peace with whoever sat on the throne after 1688, and like Churchill, he could not be sure who this might be. When Percy Kirke arrived at his headquarters under arrest, Feversham at once released him and allowed him to join William. This was not the act of an officer who thought that he might yet be on the winning side, but rather of someone anxious to make his peace with the victor, whoever he was.

The campaign ended more in farce than tragedy, with cities, towns and garrisons declaring for William, and marching parties of loyal troops finding themselves swamped in a hostile countryside. By mid-December the remains of James's army, thoroughly disheartened, was cooped up around Windsor and Uxbridge. Shortly before fleeing to France, James sent Feversham a badly-worded letter which included the sentence, 'I do not expect you should expose yourselves by resisting a foreign army and a poisoned nation.' Feversham saw this as an instruction to disband the army, and set about doing so, although his orders reached only a small proportion of the soldiers still loyal to James. Elsewhere there were murderous attacks on Catholic officers and men, and the Protestant residue of Lord Forbes's Regiment, left behind in Colnbrook after the departure of the disbanded Catholics, averted a large-scale attack by fiercely anti-Catholic local people only by demonstrating, to a helpful local minister, how well the men could recite the responses of the Anglican liturgy. Disintegration was not what William wanted, for he hoped to use the English army in his struggle against Louis XIV, and when Feversham went to Windsor on 18 December to invite William to make his formal entry into London he found himself arrested. William soon forgave him and made him master of the Royal Hospital of St Catherine, near the Tower of London.

James made one attempt to flee to France on 10 November, but was caught by some Faversham fishermen, who, taking him for an escaping Jesuit, behaved with such effrontery that they were later specifically exempted from the general pardons promised by the exiled king. Lord Ailesbury found him with several days' growth of beard, looking, he thought, like Charles I at his trial. He had James shaved and gave him a clean shirt, and for a moment it seemed that he might just re-establish himself. But most of his former supporters had now abandoned him, William wanted him out of the country, and James himself was anxious to join his queen in France. He repeatedly inveighed against the traitorous Churchill as he travelled from Ambleteuse, on the Channel coast, to St Germain en Laye, which was to house his exiled court.

Settling the Crown

A Convention Parliament met in January 1689. The Commons eventually concluded that James had effectively abdicated, while some of the Lords maintained that he had deserted, and that Mary was already queen by hereditary right. William and Mary were eventually declared joint monarchs, with succession going to whichever of them survived. Thereafter the crown would pass to their children, though it was most unlikely that they would have any, and then to Anne and her children. Anne later referred to this agreement as her 'abdication', and Churchill and Dorset carried word of it to the Lords on 6 February. In conversation with Halifax, now one of his most trusted advisers, William acknowledged that he had depended upon the Churchills to secure this agreement.

> [William] said that Lord Churchill could not govern him nor my lady, the Princess his wife, as they did the Prince and Princess of Denmark.
>
> This showed 1. that Lord Churchill was very assuming, which he did not like; 2. It showed a jealous side of the Princess, and that side of the house.
>
> . . . The foregoing discourse happened upon the occasion of its being said that Lord Churchill might perhaps prevail with the Princess of Denmark to give her consent [for William to precede her in the succession]. That made the sharpness; it seems that there was not compliance, etc.[22]

Sarah, for her part, believed that William, now safely on the throne, thought that 'the Prince and Princess were more use than they ever were likely to be again'.[23]

The Churchills, on the winning side in the autumn of 1688, were beginning to drift slowly towards uncomfortable middle ground by the following spring, and soon passed beyond it to more wintry headlands. Quite possibly the tension between William and Churchill was founded in the very act of Churchill's betrayal of James, for however much it suited William, it was not an encouraging precedent. Ailesbury thought that although 'the king was in a manner necessitated to make use of [Churchill's] services . . . at heart he never esteemed him'.[24] Some myths, though, can be jettisoned easily enough. The Jacobite *Life of James II* has Churchill greeted, on his arrival at the Williamite camp in October 1688, by William's second in command, Frederick Schomberg, soon to be Duke of Schomberg in the English peerage, with the words that 'He was the first lieutenant general he had ever heard that had deserted from his colours.' Schomberg was a professional soldier who had been a marshal of France until the Revocation, and who would soon die in battle fighting French and Irish soldiers on the Boyne. He was unlikely to criticise another officer for changing sides because of religious scruple. Moreover, Churchill had a portrait of Schomberg painted to hang at Holywell, an improbable act had Schomberg offered him such an insult.

However, Churchill's conduct in the House of Lords during the succession debate cannot have pleased William. Although he signed the Act of Association, by which seventy peers bound themselves to support the principles of William's declaration, in January 1689, he voted for the extreme Tory solution to the constitutional puzzle, a regency which would govern on behalf of James, who, as lawful king, could not be deposed. This was certainly the solution then favoured by Princess Anne, who was pregnant again, and who was, so Clarendon thought, worried about 'anything that should be of prejudice to her and her children'. The following month, when the Lords voted in favour of having a monarch rather than a regent, Churchill was absent, pleading sickness.

However, once the settlement had been agreed, Princess Anne made it clear that she supported it. Her friends were rewarded. Prince George was made Duke of Cumberland, which gave him a seat in the House of Lords. Churchill was elevated to the earldom of Marlborough on 9 April 1689, two days before the coronation of William and Mary, in recognition of the part he had played in undermining the morale of James's army and in helping persuade Anne to agree to the constitutional settlement. He was also sworn of the Privy Council, and made a gentleman of the king's bedchamber.

Marlborough, as we can at last call him, carried out his first official acts for his new sovereigns by assisting in the remodelling of the army, an urgent task if the damage done by Feversham's disbandment was to be rectified, diehard Jacobites removed and reliable officers promoted. There was a measure of urgency, as regiments were already being shipped abroad for the opening of the 1689 campaigning season, though there was no formal declaration of war between England and France in May. There was one major mutiny, tragically amongst the Scots veterans of Dumbarton's Regiment, who at first refused to go abroad. Other regiments trailed such a comet's tail of deserters as they marched for ports of embarkation that they were disbanded and their remaining soldiers posted to more reliable units.

Some officers resigned, either because they remained loyal to James or because they had simply had their fill of soldiering. Others were fingered as unreliable by resolute Williamites in their regiments. Major James Maitland of the Scots Guards kept his battalion well in hand as it marched to Ipswich, where secretary Blathwayt ordered him to 'send an account in writing of what may concern the regiment and of what officers are removing and fit to be preferred'. Old loyalties were rewarded: the Earl of Oxford became colonel of the Blues again, and Lieutenant Colonel John Coy (a Tangier veteran whom we last saw as a dragoon captain at Sedgemoor, covering the Parrett bridges) was promoted to the vacancy created when his Irish Catholic colonel, Richard Hamilton, was imprisoned in the Tower. William courted some senior professionals who had the experience to help the army through its travails. Our old acquaintance Colonel Theophilus Oglethorpe was pressed to declare for William and Mary, but retired coolly to his house at Godalming in Surrey, and soon added to the growing number of officers and ex-officers arrested later that year on suspicion of Jacobitism.

Ailesbury, with his own axe to grind, tells us that he asked Schomberg for a commission, but Schomberg sent his secretary to tell him that 'The army is new modelling, and all is done in the Prince's closet . . . My Lord Churchill proposes all, I am sent for to say the General consents, and Monsieur Bentinck is the secretary for to write all.'[25] John Childs devotes the whole of an illuminating chapter to this process, and argues that Marlborough and the king were pushing in the same direction: 'William desired a professional and loyal officer corps while Churchill wanted to build up his own circle of clientage by drawing on his contacts among the professionals.'[26] Neither William nor Schomberg knew the personalities involved, and as the senior serving officer of James's old army, Marlborough had a key role to play.

Ailesbury predictably goes on to say that Marlborough was primarily interested in making money. 'The harvest my Lord Churchill made by this was vast,' he writes, 'for all was sold.'[27] This must be treated with some caution, not least because Marlborough himself was ordered to the Continent on active service that spring, and much of the practical work of remodelling was completed by a commission 'for reforming abuses within the army', whose military members included Major General Sir John Lanier, Major General Percy Kirke and Brigadier General Charles Trelawney. Moreover, while Marlborough knew the army's senior officers, so great an influx of junior officers was required that much of the work was done by busy regimental colonels: the Earl of Meath found forty-one new officers for the future Royal Regiment of Foot of Ireland.

However, even by 1689 the image of the Marlboroughs as unfailingly rapacious was already firmly established. Ailesbury walked round the garden at Holywell with Sarah Marlborough a year later. 'Lord,' said Sarah, with her favourite beginning-of-sentence emphasis, 'they keep such a noise at our wealth. I do assure you that it doth not exceed seventy thousand pounds, and what will that come to when laid out in land, and besides we have a son and five daughters to provide for.'[28] She and John were now thinking far beyond the modest accomplishments of the early years of their marriage: their ambitions were fast becoming dynastic.

Little Victory

Marlborough was a natural choice to command the British force of 8,000 men sent to the Low Countries in the spring of 1689. He was senior and experienced, and William might have thought it safer to send him to the Continent rather than to Ireland, where James had arrived in March, in case his newly professed loyalty became strained. Marlborough's contingent formed part of the small army commanded by Georg Friedrich, Prince of Waldeck, intended to hold in check a French army of around 40,000 under Marshal d'Humières, which had moved into the southern portion of the Spanish Netherlands at the beginning of May. The main French effort was to be made on the Rhine, and d'Humières was simply bidden to remain where he was. Waldeck, with roughly the same number of men, felt unable to dislodge him.

Marlborough had made his mark even before his men had fired a shot in anger. The events of the past six months had left the army confused and humiliated. In many regiments officers and men had not yet got to know one another; William's preference for all things Dutch was especially galling to the foot guards, who saw the Dutch Blue Guards replace them on duty in London, and there were still some Jacobites in the army who, usually when in drink, noisily aired their affection for James II. Desertion, that running sore of the armies of the age, was a major problem, and was not helped by the ease with which an agile man could slip between allied or even enemy contingents, scooping an enlistment bonus every time he did so. Many observers believed that the débâcle of 1688 was a fair comment on the British army, and we cannot blame them. Even Waldeck, not history's liveliest general, thought that Marlborough's soldiers suffered from 'sickness, slackness, wretched clothing and the worst of shoes'.

The campaign that follows is Marlborough in miniature. He had three months to train and discipline his army before exposing it to the test of battle. He drilled it hard, worked tirelessly at getting uniforms, arms and equipment into order, and by July Waldeck was reporting to William that he could not 'sufficiently praise the English', and that he found 'the whole so well ordered that I have admired it, and I can say that Monsieur Milord Marlbrouck and the Colonels have shown that their application has had a good effect'.[29]

On 26 August Waldeck crossed the Sambre near Charleroi and camped, some ten miles further south, just north of the small walled town of Walcourt. He probably did so simply to give a fresh opportunity to his foraging parties. These were not small groups of soldiers striving to buy or steal food for themselves (although some men seized any opportunity to take extra rations or even to desert), but organised parties bent on collecting hay for the cavalry. At this time of the year hay had already been mown, but earlier in the season they would have been compelled to cut grass themselves. The armies of the age usually contained two horses (mounts for the cavalry and officers as well as draught animals for guns and wagons) for every three men. A force the size of Waldeck's needed to find some 25,000 pounds of hay a day during the campaigning season, and it was impractical to carry it long distances. Like sharks, constantly on the move to keep water passing through their gills, the armies of the era needed to amble across the landscape to bring fresh forage within their reach.

Armies engaged in foraging were axiomatically vulnerable. D'Humières had, in any case, recently been reinforced, and as soon as he saw that Waldeck had his foragers out he attacked them. On 27 August a single British battalion under Colonel Hodges was posted in the valley about two miles south of Walcourt to act as a rallying point for the foragers, and there were Dutch horse and dragoons further south. As the French advanced northwards the Allied cavalry patrols fell back in contact with them, giving the foragers time to get away. Marlborough rode forward at about 10 a.m. to find Hodges' men, who had 'lined some convenient hedges', in good order but under growing pressure, though happily the ground did not allow the French to hook round on either side of the battalion. With the aid of some cavalry of his own, he brought Hodges back, first to a watermill halfway to Walcourt, and then right back to join the rest of his force, on the high ground just east of Walcourt itself, though not before Lieutenant Colonel Graham and Captain Davison had been mortally wounded and about thirty men killed.

At this stage d'Humières could quite well have broken off the action without discredit: if he had failed to catch the foraging parties he had at least brought the process to a premature halt. But, inflamed by the clash so far and unaware that Waldeck had now concentrated his whole army in and around Walcourt (the great hill on the town's east not only offered excellent fields of fire to Marlborough's guns, but screened from view the troops behind it), he pressed his attack. It is possible that the poor reputation then enjoyed by British troops induced him to take risks he might have deemed inappropriate with others. The defences of Walcourt itself were old and ramshackle, and the place was held by a single Luneburg regiment. A determined party of *Gardes Français* piled faggots against the town's gates and tried to set them alight, but Waldeck reported that 'most of them were killed'. At about 2 p.m., Brigadier General Thomas Tollemache took his own Coldstream Guards and a German battalion into the town to strengthen its garrison, and further French assaults were beaten off with heavy loss.

Marlborough was to become a master of feeling the balance of a battle, and Walcourt helped him develop this quality. When d'Humières' men were played out by successive attacks on the town, Waldeck ordered a counterattack. At about 6 p.m. Major General Slangenberg's Dutch infantry went forward on his right, and on his left Marlborough person-ally led the Life Guards and the Blues in a charge that broke the leading French infantry (the French acknowledged six guards battalions 'for the most part ruined') and decided the battle at a stroke. He would have done even more damage had d'Humières' cavalry commander, Claude de Villars (a veteran of the siege of Maastricht, where he and Marlborough had been on the same side), not led his own horsemen into the battle to help the beaten infantry limp away. The French lost perhaps as many as 2,000 men (including a brigadier general and the colonel of the *Royal-Champagne* infantry regiment) and six guns to no more than three hundred Allied casualties.

Although Waldeck was not able to mint any larger currency from this little victory, and the campaign ended with inconclusive countermarching and cannonading, he praised Marlborough to William in the most glowing terms, adding: 'I would never have believed that so many of the English would show such a *joie de combattre.*'[30] His formal report to the States-General noted: 'All our troops showed a great courage and desire to come to a battle; and particularly the English, who were engaged in this action, behaved themselves very well.'[31] A delighted William told Marlborough: 'It is to you that this advantage is principally owing,' and gave him the colonelcy of an infantry regiment (later the Royal Fusiliers) as a reward. D'Humières, in contrast, dubbed *le maréchal sans lumière* by his unhappy subordinates, never again enjoyed operational command. When the tide of war lapped across the same region in 1690 that frail but energetic warrior Marshal Luxembourg was in charge. He first trounced Waldeck at Fleurus, and went on to win a string of victories which did much for flagging French morale.

Court and Country

While Marlborough was winning laurels abroad, at home Sarah was in the eye of a rising storm, whipped up by the personal rivalry which was characteristic of court life. In this case it involved the children of Sir Edward and Lady Villiers. They were distant relatives of the Marlboroughs, and the children had been playmates of Queen Mary. In 1685 Willem Bentinck, William's closest adviser, had been sent to England to congratulate James on his succession. Anne had warned him to 'check the insolence' of one of the Villiers girls, Elizabeth, now William's mistress, to her royal sister Mary. As Bentinck was then married to Elizabeth's sister Anne he did not much appreciate the mission, and there was thereafter friction between Anne and Bentinck, created Earl of Portland in 1689.

Anne Bentinck died in 1688, but her sister Barbara was married to the Colonel Berkeley who had deserted with Marlborough in 1688, and who inherited the barony of Fitzharding two years later. The Fitzhardings moved away from Anne's sphere of influence into the Villiers camp, and had become a conduit of confidential leaks from the Cockpit by early 1692. Sir Edward Villiers, brother of Barbara and Anne, was created Earl of Jersey and given a series of jobs which his 'very ordinary talents' did not warrant.[32] Marlborough, in turn, got on badly with Portland: whether he simply fell into a line of battle already drawn up by Anne or had more personal causes for dislike it is hard to say.

William resented the fact that he was essentially an elected king, and that Anne's claim to the throne was better than his own. Moreover, though the conspiracies of the 1680s had drawn Anne and Mary together, they were actually very dissimilar, as Sarah Marlborough tells us:

> It was indeed impossible that they should be very agreeable compan-
> ions to each other because Queen Mary grew weary of anybody who
> would not talk a great deal; and the Princess was so silent that she
> rarely spoke more than was necessary to answer a question.[33]

Anne was happily married, while Mary's relationship with William (who had not only had mistresses but was so close to male favourites that there were suggestions of homosexuality) was less idyllic. Small wonder, as Sarah said, that there was 'visible coldness' between the sisters by mid-1689.

First there was a dispute over accommodation at court. The Cockpit had been settled on Anne and her heirs by Charles II, and in early 1688 she had also been given the Duchess of Portsmouth's elegant apartment nearby. She hoped to extend into lodgings close at hand which had, however, been promised to the Earl of Devonshire, who refused to give them up. Anne also hoped that she would be allowed Richmond Place, where she had spent much of her childhood, but this had been allocat- ed to another Villiers sister, Catherine, marquise de Puissiers, who would not budge. In September 1689 the young Duke of Gloucester came close to death with what may have been an asthma attack, and Anne, fearing for her son's health if he remained in grimy Whitehall, rented Lord Craven's house in Kensington, near Kensington Palace, which was being remodelled as the London residence of William and Mary: William's creaky lungs could not abide Whitehall. In 1690 Anne and George also took on Campden House in Kensington, and the burden of these properties told heavily on their limited income.

Anne had hoped for some of the private estate owned by her father, but William managed this himself and kept the income, though he thoughtfully gave almost 88,000 acres in Ireland to Elizabeth Villiers. Prince George was no less disgruntled. In July 1689, at William's behest, he had relinquished some of his Danish properties to help bring about peace between Denmark and Sweden, and was promised that England and Holland, between them, would pay him. However, he had to wait ten years for his money. Anne, meanwhile, argued that as heir to the throne she should be given a parliamentary grant, and a motion for this had been introduced in the Commons in March.

Anne's friends argued that she deserved £70,000 a year, her more moderate supporters thought that £50,000 would do, while William's adherents maintained that it was a thoroughly dangerous precedent, and that Anne should rely on William's generosity. In mid-December William did his best to scotch the debate, and sent Shrewsbury and Wharton, two of his ministers, to persuade Anne to withdraw. Marlborough had returned to England at the end of the campaigning season, and Shrewsbury called on him first. Marlborough 'begged he would not own [i.e. admit] he found him, his wife would by no means hear of it, but was like a mad woman and said the Princess would retire if her friends would not assist her'.[34] On 18 December Anne was duly voted £50,000 a year. Sarah visited Lord Rochester to ask him whether he thought Anne should press for more, but Rochester replied that she should be satisfied with her £50,000 and, moreover, should take it any way William and Mary wished to pay her. In a memorandum of 3 March 1690 Queen Mary suggested that their government was opposed not only by a republican party and a Jacobite party, but 'I have reason to fear that my sister is forming a third.'[35]

Things got steadily worse. When William set off for Ireland in June 1690 to deal with James, Prince George went on campaign with him as a private gentleman at his own expense. Although George was an experienced soldier, William took no notice of him, refused to let him ride in his coach and, as Sarah put it, treated him as if he were a page of the back stairs. When William and George returned to London that autumn, not long before Anne gave birth to another short-lived child, George decided that since he could not endure William's snubs on another land campaign, he would join the fleet as a gentleman volunteer. William went off to the Continent in early 1691, leaving orders with Mary that George was not to serve. Mary first tried to get Sarah to use her influence with Anne to torpedo the project, but eventually she had to send formal instructions via Lord Nottingham that George should not be allowed to proceed. His baggage, already loaded aboard *St Andrew*, had to be disembarked.

All of this helped drive Anne closer to Sarah. Although Sarah suggests that they took to calling one another 'Mrs Morley' (the queen) and 'Mrs Freeman' (Sarah) before 1685, one of Sarah's biographers points out that it was not until 1691 that there is evidence of these names being used in letters.[36] In June that year Anne pressed Sarah to accept from her a pension of £1,000 a year, and Sarah, having first consulted Godolphin, accepted. Godolphin ('Mr Montgomery' in Anne/Sarah cant), who had been Marlborough's tennis partner when both were rising young courtiers, was now in favour with William, who made him first a commissioner of the Treasury and then its first lord. William wrote to him in the franglais which was his *lingua franca*: '*Je vous asseure que je* shrink *aussi bien que vous quandt je considere l'etat ou est le Treusuri et les fachesues affairs que nous aurons aparement cette hyver . . .*'[37] However, while Godolphin worked tirelessly at the Treasury on William's behalf, he was also close to the Cockpit circle. To make assurance doubly sure, he was in contact with the Jacobites too: and so was Marlborough.

In January 1691 Marlborough and Godolphin were walking together in St James's Park when they were approached by Henry Bulkeley, an Irish peer's son who had been master of the household to both Charles II and James II, and whose daughter Anne was to marry Marlborough's nephew the Duke of Berwick in 1700. They would have known Bulkeley well, and can have had little doubt of his sympathies. He invited them to dinner at his lodgings, where he found Godolphin uncommunicative. Marlborough, in contrast, was loquacious, and Bulkeley

> was hugely surprised to find him in appearance the greatest penitent imaginable; he begged him to go to the king and acquaint him with his sincere repentance, and to intercede for mercy, that he was ready to redeem his apostasy with the hazard of his utter ruin, his crimes appearing so horrid to him that he could neither sleep nor eat but in continual anguish . . . [38]

Godolphin's biographer is right to observe that this is based on the Jacobite *Life of James II*, and that any original papers that might have supported it would have been lost, with the rest of James's documents, at the time of the French Revolution. However, for him to argue that the incident is improbable because 'nothing could be less in keeping' with all that we know of the characters of Godolphin and Marlborough is no real defence, because we have evidence from other sources that both did indeed have dealings with the Jacobites. We may challenge the detail of words reported, for which there is indeed no corroboration, but neither the incident itself nor the general tone of Marlborough's speech is inherently improbable.

His actions in 1688 make it unlikely that Marlborough was a convinced Jacobite, and his long history of relations with Jacobite agents may, at one level, be seen simply as evidence of the desire (which he shared with a large proportion of the political nation) not to finish up on the wrong side if there was another change of regime. The prospect of such a change seemed far greater at the time than we might think now, aware as we are of the personal unpopularity of James II, the limited appeal of Jacobitism in Britain and the wholesale penetration of James's apparatus by William's agents. There were suggestions (which came to nought because James and his wife would never countenance them) that if their son the Prince of Wales was brought up as a Protestant he might eventually succeed, for in logic his claim to the throne would trump Anne's.

A deep level of subtlety certainly applied to Marlborough's dealings with the Jacobites in the 1690s. Not only did he go some way towards insuring himself against a possible Stuart restoration, but he helped give James and his advisers the impression that it would be better to deal with Anne than with William. In July 1692 the Jacobite agent David Lloyd delivered a letter from Anne to her father. It was dated December 1691, and embodied 'a sincere and humble offer of my duty and submission to you', and concluded not simply by asking pardon, but by speaking generously of Mary of Modena, so recently the wicked stepmother.[39] James was not disposed to believe Anne in any event, and the apparent change of heart towards his wife can scarcely have been likely to allay his suspicions. Moreover, some English Jacobites took the view that Marlborough's own opposition to some of William's policies, most notably his use of foreign generals, sprang from self-interest and the desire to support Anne, not from any deeply-held Jacobitism.

Irish Interlude

All this took place against a backcloth of war. James had landed at Kinsale on the southern coast of Ireland on 12 March 1689 with some British supporters and a contingent of French troops, and marched straight to Dublin, where he summoned a Parliament. Most of the country had already been secured by Tyrconnell, but James was unable to take the two northern strongholds of Londonderry and Enniskillen, and his supporter Lord Mountcashel (once, as Colonel Justin McCarthy,

Marlborough's comrade in arms in France) was beaten and captured at Newtownbutler. In August Schomberg arrived with a Williamite army, and landed at Carrickfergus, where, so Isaac Bostaquet tells us, the first officer killed, by a cannon-shot, was a Roman Catholic lieutenant in the Dutch Guards. Schomberg took Carrickfergus Castle and then moved southwards as far as Dundalk, facing James's main army, which had pushed up to Drogheda. A filthy autumn and sickness in camp may have killed as many as a quarter of Schomberg's men, and in October both sides fell back to winter quarters.

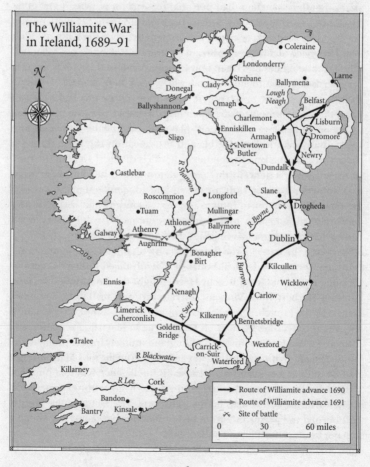

The Williamite War
in Ireland, 1689–91

Route of Williamite advance 1690
Route of Williamite advance 1691
Site of battle

0   30   60 miles

William was not pleased with the progress of events. His wider responsibilities meant that he was reluctant to go to Ireland himself, but he concluded that 'nothing worthwhile would be done' unless he was there to do it. He left the government in the hands of Mary and a council of nine, of whom Marlborough, appointed commander-in-chief in England on 3 June, was one. William arrived at Carrickfergus in June 1690, and on 1 July he forced the crossing of the Boyne just upstream of Drogheda.

William's Dutch Guards marched to the river's edge with their fifes and drums playing 'Lillibulero', and the Huguenots and Enniskilleners attacking alongside them had personal reasons for wanting to win that day. Although the Jacobites fought back hard, killing Schomberg in a mélêe on the far bank, once the Williamites were across in strength, both near Drogheda and further upstream at Rossnaree, the defence collapsed. One Jacobite officer described how his men 'took to their heels, no officer ever being able to stop the men after they were broken . . . some throwing away their arms, others even their coats and shoes to run lighter'. James himself made commendably rapid progress to Dublin, where on 2 July he gave another display of those qualities that made him such a hard man to love. He blamed his defeat on the Irish. 'When it came to a trial,' he lamented, 'they basely fled the field and left the spoil to the enemy . . . henceforth I never determine to head an Irish army, and do now resolve to shift for myself and so, gentlemen, must you.'[40] He left Ireland, never to return, and we may forgive the Irishmen who continued to fight with him with more courage than he deserved for calling him *Seamus an Chaca*, James the Shithead.

Although the battle of the Boyne has now attained iconic status, it was not then decisive. Indeed, although it had advanced William's cause in Ireland, a naval battle off Beachy Head, fought the day before, had seen Admiral Herbert (now Viscount Torrington) and his Dutch comrades beaten by the French. The balance of power at sea was not reversed until the Anglo-Dutch naval victory off La Hougue in May 1692 rendered any French-backed Jacobite invasion of England unlikely for the moment. In June William, writing in his usual execrable French, told Marlborough that he did not fear a landing because his intelligence had told him that there were no troops embarked on the French fleet, but expected that French frigates would snap up his transports. The fact that the French had burned the pretty little town of Teignmouth but dared not attempt a major landing seemed to confirm this.

In August 1690, with William bogged down in the siege of Limerick,

Marlborough suggested a project which, he believed, would win the war in Ireland. He asked the Council to be allowed to take most of the regular troops out of the country and attack the main Jacobite ports of Cork and Kinsale, thus cutting off Tyrconnell from further French reinforcements. Marlborough had already fallen out with Danby, the Council's leading member, who opposed his attempt to get his sailor brother George promoted to rear admiral. 'If Churchill have a flag,' he said, 'it will be called flag by favour, as his brother is called the general of favour.'[41] The Council turned down his plan, but the queen forwarded it to William, who on 14 August approved the scheme, authorising Marlborough to take 4,900 infantry. He would have to take his own supply of ammunition and use the ships' guns, for none could be spared from Limerick, although sufficient cavalry would be sent down. The weather, William emphasised, was the thing to watch.

Mary was deeply concerned, telling her husband that although she hoped the expedition would succeed, 'I find, if it do not, those who have advised it will have an ill time, all except Lord Nottingham being very much against it.'[42] Marlborough left on 17 September, reached Cork on the twenty-first and, after his ship's guns had silenced a battery, landed safely at West Passage, seven miles east of the city. He quickly pushed on to encircle it.

He now found that the operation's complexion had darkened. William had abandoned the siege of Limerick after the enterprising Patrick Sarsfield raided his artillery park, and returned to England. Marlborough had asked particularly to be reinforced by English troops under Kirke, and there were plenty available. However the Dutch general Godert de Ginkel, left in command, sent 5,000 Danish, Dutch and Huguenot troops, and with the Danes came their commander, Prince Ferdinand William of Württemberg, junior to Marlborough as a lieutenant general but claiming, by virtue of his birth, to take command. Marlborough (or perhaps a Huguenot brigadier) suggested a compromise whereby the two generals would command on alternate days, and on his first day in command courteously gave 'Württemberg' as the password.

Winston S. Churchill maintains that the arrival of foreign troops was simply a ploy to prevent the English from carrying off the glory. The historian Matthew Glozier, however, with better access to the documents, goes further. The presence of the foreign troops, he argues, 'was as much political as strategic. William's cabinet had resolved to ruin Churchill if the Irish campaign failed, and it was partly the result of this antipathy which demanded the presence of foreign troops.'[43] Either way, Marlborough was engaged upon his first independent command with an Irish winter on its way, the French fleet at sea, and grudging political support.

With Württemberg duly mollified the siege of Cork went on apace. A breaching battery was speedily established, and it soon knocked a hole in the eastern wall. Early on the afternoon of 27 September, when the tide had receded, enabling his forlorn hope to cross the south branch of the River Lee with its fast-flowing water up to their armpits, Marlborough ordered an attack. The attackers reached a ditch close under the city walls, and were at once reinforced by the bulk of the English foot. The Danes, attacking across the north branch of the Lee, also made good progress. Cannon pecked away at the walls, mortars on bomb-vessels lobbed their shells into the town, and the defenders knew that an assault could not be far away. The city's governor, Roger Macelligott, mindful of the fate of Drogheda a generation before, surrendered on terms which left his 4,000-man garrison prisoners of war but guaranteed the safety of the Roman Catholic clergy in Cork and ensured that most of the Williamite army would not enter the city. There was an echo of the past. The forlorn hope had been commanded by the Duke of Grafton, and his officers included Lord Colchester, Charles Churchill, Colonel John Greville and Captain Stafford Fairburne, all army conspirators in 1688. Grafton was mortally wounded, and died eleven days later.

Kinsale was a different matter. Marlborough arrived there on 29 September, and by 15 October his breaching batteries had done good work. But the place was very much stronger than he had expected, winter was closing in, and there were rumours that Sarsfield was on his way with a relieving force. By mid-October Marlborough had successfully stormed a 'weak old fort' across the River Bandon from the main defences, and breached the walls of Fort Charles; he was, though, happy enough to let the garrison of 11,000 men march out with the honours of war, and to proceed unmolested to Limerick, before he attempted a storm. The governor, Sir Edward Scott, who had been governor of Portsmouth in 1688, was driven through the breach in his carriage to make the point that the gap was indeed practicable and his surrender was not in the least premature.

Although Marlborough's capture of Cork and Kinsale did serious damage to Jacobite ambitions in Ireland, it did not end the war. Tyrconnell returned in May 1691 with a new French commander, the marquis de St Ruth. It was 'like pouring brandy down the throat of a dying man', and the Jacobite cause flared back into life. On 12 July St Ruth, with the whole Jacobite army of 20,000 men, took up a well-chosen position at Aughrim, where he faced Ginkel with about 17,400 men.

Aughrim was no easy victory. Ginkel's frontal attack bogged down in the face of dogged resistance, for the Jacobite infantry, holding a line of ditches, 'would maintain one side until our men put their pieces over the other, and then, having lines of communication from one ditch to another, they would presently post themselves again and flank us'. When a counterattack rolled Ginkel's centre right back to his gun-line the exuberant St Ruth yelled, '*Le jour est à nous, mes enfants*,' words of encouragement which might have cheered his Irish peasant infantry less than he expected. The Williamites then staked everything on an attack on St Ruth's right, and as he was galloping across the peat to meet it a cannonball clipped off his head. His lifeguard wheeled about and left the field at once, followed by the rest of the horse: it may be no accident that their commander later received a pension from William. 'And so,' wrote a bitter infantryman, 'let them keep their priding cavalry to stop bottles with.' The Jacobites were cut to pieces as they fled: one Williamite saw their dead lying 'like a great flock of sheep scattered up and down the country for almost four miles round'.[44]

The Jacobite survivors fell back to Limerick, where Tyrconnell was felled by a stroke. Early in October Ginkel gave them generous terms, allowing the French to go home, accompanied by Irish Jacobites who wished to serve King Louis. He agreed that Jacobite estates would not be confiscated, and that Roman Catholics would endure 'not less toleration' than they had enjoyed under Charles II. The Treaty of Limerick was not ratified: a million and a half acres were confiscated, and penal laws were to bear down harshly on Catholics and Protestant dissenters alike.

Marlborough hoped that his successes at Cork and Kinsale would bring him the office of master general of the ordnance, left vacant by Schomberg's death, but it went instead, for no clearly discernible reason, to the civilian Henry Sidney. There was talk of a dukedom, although at this stage Marlborough felt that he lacked sufficient estate to support the title. He certainly hoped to receive the Garter, for Anne begged it on his behalf, though without success. William maintained that 'No officer now living who has seen so little service as my Lord Marlborough is so fit for great commands,' but there was no visible sign of royal favour. C.T. Atkinson argues that Marlborough 'bitterly resented' the lack of additional tangible reward as 'a further proof of ingratitude, if not jealousy', and that it was this that drove him 'to make his peace with the man to whose overthrow he had contributed so largely'.[45]

Like many other senior officers, Marlborough resented the pre-eminence of foreign generals, just as English peers complained at the influx of foreigners into the Lords: Bentinck became Earl of Portland; Ginkel, Earl of Athlone; Ruvigny, Viscount Galway; and Zulestein, Earl of Rochford. 'Under James,' maintains Winston S. Churchill, 'he saw his path blocked by Papists: under William by Dutchmen.'[46] William only really trusted British officers who had served under him in the Anglo-Dutch Brigade. Thus he was prepared to appoint Hugh Mackay – 'the most pious man that I ever knew in a military way', says Burnet – commander-in-chief in Scotland. Mackay was beaten by Viscount Dundee's Jacobites at Killiekrankie in July 1689. This mishap occurred partly because the plug bayonet then in use had to be rammed into the musket's muzzle, and a government foot soldier thus armed was no match for a charging Highlander with broadsword and targe. Happily for Mackay, Dundee was killed in the moment of victory, and with his death the rebellion lost direction: Mackay subdued the Highlands that summer, and went on to distinguish himself at Aughrim.

However, there was no peerage for Mackay, not even an Irish one, and when he commanded the British vanguard against the French at Steenkirk in 1692 he was killed and his men badly mauled because, it was said, Count Solms, a Dutch lieutenant general and William's great-uncle, failed to support him. William had some regard for Thomas Tollemache, a veteran of Walcourt and Aughrim, but there was a nasty scene when Tollemache told William that he was favouring foreigners, and threatened to resign both his major general's post and the colonelcy of the Coldstream. William made him a lieutenant general but never forgave him. In November 1692 there was an acrimonious debate on the subject in the Commons, which revealed that around half the generals for the campaign of 1693 were to be British. The dispute showed Englishmen's suspicions of foreigners and emphasised the way that William was failing to 'oblige' the political nation. Marlborough may have been unusually forward in his resentment at the way foreign generals were preferred to British, but he certainly spoke for a substantial constituency which suspected that William saw Britain simply as another stick with which to beat the French.

There can be no doubting William's need for sticks. That untidy conflict known to historians as the War of the League of Augsburg rumbled on, with occasional naval clashes, skirmishes in North America (where it was called King William's War) and the Caribbean, much marching and countermarching in the Low Countries, the war's main theatre, and rather less in Italy and Spain, subsidiary areas of operations. In many respects it was a forerunner to the War of Spanish Succession, in which Marlborough was to make his reputation, with the French enjoying the advantage of a central position, interior lines of communication, and military reputation, and with William holding together a disparate alliance whose members were always vulnerable to defeat in detail. England's most significant contribution was her navy, but she also furnished a contingent to the main Allied army, usually under William's personal command, in the Low Countries.

The 1691 campaign began early with a French attack on the fortress of Mons in March, while William was busy with an Allied conference at The Hague. Marlborough had been left behind in England to raise recruits, and on 17 February he had written William a grumpy letter which went to the very edge of politeness. 'I here send your majesty a copy of what we have done concerning the recruits,' he wrote.

> I must at the same time take leave to tell your Majesty that I am tired out of my life with the unreasonable way of proceeding of Lord President [Danby], for he is very ignorant of what is fit for an officer, both as to recruits and everything else as to a soldier; so that when I have given such as I think necessary orders, he does what he thinks fit, and enters into the business of tents, arms and the off-reckonings, which were all settled before your Majesty left England, so at this rate business is never done; but I think this all proceeds from, I hope, the unreasonable prejudice he has taken against me, which makes me incapable of doing you that service which I do with all my heart, and should wish to do, for I do with much truth wish both your person and Government to prosper. I hope it will not be long before your majesty will be here, after which I shall beg never to be in England when you are not.[47]

In May William ordered him to the Continent to command the British contingent, sending Tollemache to Ireland to create the vacancy. It was a thoroughly unsatisfactory campaign, for Marshal Luxembourg was more than a match for William. In September, just after William had given command to Waldeck and retired to Het Loo, Luxembourg unleashed Villars' cavalry against the Allied rearguard, trudging along from Leuze to Grammont, cutting it up badly. Marlborough deftly swung the British contingent back to deal with the attack, but the dextrous Luxembourg had disengaged before it could come into action.

This mongrel campaign is noteworthy only because during it William asked Charles Thomas, Prince of Vaudemont, son of the Duke of Lorraine and an experienced Imperialist general, what he made of British commanders. 'Kirke has fire,' said Vaudemont,

> Lanier thought, Mackay skill, and Colchester bravery; but there is something inexpressible in the Earl of Marlborough. All their virtues seem to be united in his single person. I have lost my wonted skill in physiognomy if any subject of your Majesty can ever attain such a height of military glory as that to which this combination of sublime perfections must raise him.

'Cousin,' responded William, 'you have done your part in answering my question, and I believe the Earl of Marlborough will do his to verify your prediction.'[48]

Fall and Rise

At this time, as William must have known, it would have been dangerous to make predictions about Marlborough. William told Gilbert Burnet, a trusted adviser who had landed with him in 1688, that 'he had very good reason to believe that he [Marlborough] had made his peace with King James and was in correspondence with France'.[49] Marlborough was one of the prime movers in the army's opposition to foreign generals, and without the Marlboroughs' support it would have been hard for Anne to maintain her divergent political line. William was fast concluding that Marlborough was a loose cannon who would be safest rolled overboard. Marlborough pressed him to ensure that British troops were commanded only by British officers. On the night of 9 January 1692 Marlborough told Godolphin and Russell that if the king refused he intended to move two resolutions in the Lords. One would deny all foreign officers the right to hold English commissions, and the other would demand the removal of Dutch troops from England.

On the morning of 20 January Marlborough, in his role as a gentleman of the bedchamber, attended the king's rising as usual. Two hours later Nottingham told him, on behalf of the king, that he was dismissed from all his appointments and forbidden the court. Tollemache replaced him on the generals' list, Lord Colchester took over the Royal Dragoons, and George Hamilton, later Earl of Orkney, became colonel of the Royal Fusiliers. The reversal cost Marlborough up to £11,000 a year, and though it did not leave him destitute, it was a shattering blow: the spectre of his father's fate must have grinned impishly through the coal-fuelled smog of Whitehall.

It may be that William had decided, some time previously, to dispose of Marlborough, and that 20 January simply happened to be the chosen day. Marlborough was, after all, not simply prominent in his complaints about the over-use of foreign officers, but isolated, with Russell and Godolphin as his only really close friends. William told Nottingham that he had disgraced Marlborough for fomenting dissension in the army, but added, 'He has rendered such valuable services that I have no wish to press him too hard.'[50] He assured the Elector of Brandenburg's representative that it was a matter of honour which, had the two of them been private gentlemen, could only have been settled by a duel. The historian Stephen Saunders Webb maintains that Marlborough's opposition to foreign generals was the cause of his disgrace: 'He pursued his xenophobic, patriotic programme to immediate disgrace and to ultimate success.'[51]

Alternatively, William might have received some specific intelligence, not long after rising that morning, that provoked him into taking sudden action. A well-placed but anonymous commentator later wrote that

> the Earl's disgrace was not slow, but sudden. He accompanied Lord George Hamilton, afterwards Earl of Orkney, and husband to Mrs Villiers, to King William in the morning, and was well received as usual; yet, within two hours after, the Earl of Nottingham came with a message from the king, saying that he had no further occasion for his services.

He acknowledged that Marlborough 'spoke very freely of the King's partiality to the Dutch, of the several mismanagements in the war, and of some indignities that had been put upon the English abroad'. However, he maintained that William was not capricious, and 'very rarely dismissed his old servants'. The most probable cause of Marlborough's fall, he argued, was the leakage of information about a projected attack on Dunkirk, known only to Marlborough, Portland and Rochford.[52]

In the published version of his *History* Burnet, by then influenced by his friendship with the Marlboroughs, wrote that 'it seems certain that some letter was intercepted, which gave suspicion'. In his own annotations to Burnet, William Legge, 2nd Earl of Dartmouth, argues that the 'true cause of his disgrace' was betrayal from within the Cockpit circle. Marlborough told Sarah of a projected operation against France, and Sarah passed on the news to Lady Fitzharding. Dartmouth maintains that she informed Lord Chelmsford, who in turn told the king.[53] An anonymous well-wisher warned Anne:

> I beg of you for your own sake that you will have a care of what you say before Lady Fitzharding, remember she's Lord Portland's and Betty Villiers' sister. You may depend upon it that these two are not ignorant of what is said and done in your lodgings. Then I leave you to judge whether they make not their court at your expense . . . by exposing you and preserving the king as they call it . . . The King and Queen have been told that there has not passed a day since Lord Marlborough's being out that you have not shed tears . . . If it ended in his turning out he might leave it with patience, but if resolutions hold he will be taken up as soon as the Parliament is up, and if you do not part with his Lady of yourself, you will be obliged to it . . . [54]

The accuracy of these predictions reinforces the veracity of the source. In April Anne herself warned Sarah about Lady Fitzharding.

> I can't end this without begging dear Mrs Freeman to have a care of Mrs Hill [Sarah's MS insertion: 'That was a nickname for Lady Fitzharding'] for I doubt she is a jade and though one can't be sure she has done anything against you, there is much reason to believe she has not been so sincere as she ought, and I am sure she hates your faithful Mrs Morley, & remember none of her family were ever good for anything.[55]

Princess Anne, pregnant yet again, was shocked, not simply by the news of Marlborough's dismissal but by its yet unspoken corollary: Sarah, as the wife of a disgraced man, would be expected not to appear at court again. Only two weeks after the dismissal Anne put convention to the test by taking Sarah with her to a formal reception at Kensington Palace, and sure enough, Mary at once wrote to tell her forcefully that 'never anybody was suffered to live at court in Lord Marlborough's circumstances. I need not repeat the cause he has given the King to do what he has done, nor his unwillingness at all times to come to extremities, though people do deserve it.' Under the circumstances it was 'the strangest thing ever that was done' for Anne to have brought Sarah to the palace: 'it was very unkind in a sister, would have been very uncivil in an equal; and I need not say I have more to claim'. She concluded: ''Tis upon that account I tell you plainly, Lady Marlborough must not continue with you, in the circumstances her lord is . . .'[56]

Anne, furious at the suggestion that she could not choose her own servants, and by being reminded of the duty she owed her sister, slapped off a note to Sarah saying that she would keep her 'in spite of their teeth'. She followed it with a measured letter telling Mary that 'This proceeding can be for no other intent than to give me a very sensible mortification,' and flatly refusing to part with Sarah. The maladroit Lord Rochester, upon whom Mary would rely increasingly heavily after William had departed to the Continent for the campaign of 1692, was summoned to the Cockpit to deliver this missive. Having seen what was in it he felt unable to do so, but advised the queen to expel Anne and her little court from the Cockpit. The lord chamberlain passed on this order, which was manifestly illegal because Anne held the Cockpit's freehold, given her by Charles II.

However, Anne felt that she had no alternative but to comply, and duly moved into Syon House, on the Thames west of London, generously loaned to her by the Duke of Somerset. Her guards were withdrawn, and the Dutch sentries at Whitehall were told that they need no longer 'stand to their arms' for Anne and her husband. Sarah maintained that she was warned by Lady Fitzharding that her continued support for Anne would provoke worse trouble: 'If I would not put an end to measures so disagreeable to the King and Queen, it would certainly be the ruin of my lord, and consequently of all our family.' Indeed, she argued that it was her own closeness to Anne, not any action of her husband's, that had precipitated his fall. 'The disgrace of my Lord Marlborough,' she writes, 'was designed as a step for removing me from her.'[57]

Sarah offered to resign her post with Anne to defuse the crisis, but Anne replied that her mind was made up: 'I am more yours than can be expressed, & had rather live in a cottage with you than reign empress of the world without you.'[58] She followed this with a violent attack on 'that monster . . . that Dutch abortive', and looked forward to the 'sunshine day' of her own succession when she could right the many wrongs that William had done to her country and her friends.[59] In early April Mary called on Anne, now in the last stages of her pregnancy, and as Anne put it 'talked a great deal of senseless stuff'. Anne gave birth to her seventh child, a boy who lived just long enough to be christened George, on 17 April. Having been told that her sister had endured a difficult labour, Mary came to see her again. It was the last time the sisters ever met, and the only account of their conversation comes from Sarah, who heard it from Anne. There was apparently no sympathy for a dangerous labour or a dead child, only a renewed demand for the dismissal of Sarah, reinforced by the same peremptory order given to Prince George as he escorted Mary to her coach.

Rochester tried to broker a reconciliation based on Anne's removal and, when that failed, advised Mary to ban any courtiers from visiting Anne. This was immediately effective, and only two or three Jacobite ladies visited the princess. Sarah observed that the breach between Mary and Anne was welcomed by the Jacobites. When Lady Ailesbury visited Anne, who was still confined to bed, to tell her that a French invasion was imminent and that 5,000 Jacobite soldiers would be ready to escort her to her father, she replied: 'Well, Madam, tell your Lord that I am ready to do what he can advise me to.'[60]

As rumours of invasion reached fever-pitch, the nervous government responded by acting on a letter provided by Robert Young, a former confederate of Titus Oates and already a convicted criminal. He drew the Council's attention to the fact that a treasonable bond of association, signed by Marlborough, Cornbury, Archbishop Sancroft and others, was hidden in a flowerpot at the Bishop of Rochester's house. A search was made, the document was discovered and all the alleged signatories were sent to the Tower.

The Tower of London, where Marlborough found himself in May 1692, was England's principal state prison, though it also did duty as royal menagerie (the largest, most splendidly-endowed male lion in Charles II's time had been called Rowley after his royal master), arsenal, mint and record office. Prisoners of consequence were usually lodged in apartments on either side of Water Lane, the cobbled street just inside the double drum-fronted Byward Tower, or in buildings opening off Tower Green. Their material conditions were often relatively comfortable, and they sometimes had their families with them: Sir Walter Raleigh's son Carew was born in the Bloody Tower in 1605. The Countess of Ailesbury conceived in the Tower, and her husband blamed the fact that the birth wrecked her health on the governor's refusal to allow a midwife to attend her. The comparatively gentlemanly conditions of detention meant that there were some escapes, the last of them in 1716 by the Jacobite Earl of Nithsdale, who slipped out in his wife's clothes.

Marlborough, perhaps understandably, has left no account of his brief stay in the Tower, but the Earl of Ailesbury, mewed up there a few years later after being charged with plotting James's restoration, reports that he was so courteously treated that he gave venison and wine to the captain, lieutenant and ensign of the company on guard. They felt unable to dine with him, but their colonel, the Earl of Romney (Henry Sidney, formerly a Williamite plotter, and now master general of the ordnance and colonel of the 1st Foot Guards), gave an order that was 'gracious and gentlemanlike and entirely suitable to him'. 'Pray go,' he declared, 'and if I was not engaged I would go there also.'[61] Ailesbury walked for five hours a day across his thirty-three-foot room, daily completing fifteen 'London miles' and, because of the numerous nails in the floor, getting through a pair of shoes a fortnight. His stay there was sharpened not only by concern for his own fate (he was released on five recognisances of £10,000 apiece), but by his fears for his fellow prisoner Major General Sir John Fenwick, charged with conspiring to assassinate William, whose quarters were within earshot and who was plainly terrified of what awaited him. He was sentenced to a traitor's death by an Act of Attainder (the last Englishman to be thus condemned), and was beheaded on Tower Green in January 1697. When the time came, though, 'he behaved himself decently, nobly and well'.

Marlborough and his fellow accused were committed 'close prisoners', and visitors required orders from the Earl of Nottingham to get into the Tower. Anne warned Sarah that she and Prince George were likely to be placed under guard if the wind changed, allowing the French fleet, presumably escorting an invasion army, to leave Brest, and urged her to visit as soon as she could, because a meeting might be impossible later. Sarah was already at her wits' end, for her younger son Charles was desperately ill. On 22 May, with his father still imprisoned, Charles died, and was buried without his father at the graveside. On 19 May Admiral Tourville, out from Brest with a following wind and forty-four sail of the line, met Admiral Russell's larger Anglo-Dutch fleet. In a running battle which began rather well for the French off Cape Barfleur, and ended dismally for them in the bay of St Vaast-la-Hougue, Tourville was comprehensively beaten and his flagship *Soleil Royal* destroyed. In fact the victory did not rule out a future French-Jacobite invasion, for the French had made up their losses in two years, but it drew the moment's sting and enabled Mary and her Council to proceed with some judgement.

William had already warned them that the arrests were 'a delicate matter', no doubt fearing that a trial might misfire. Anne assured Sarah on 12 May 'that they cannot keep Lord Marlborough in the Tower longer than the [legal] term, and I hope, when Parliament sits, care will be taken that people are not clapped up for nothing, or else there will be no living in quiet for anybody but insolent Dutch or sneaking mercenary Englishmen'.[62] Marlborough's own confidence stemmed from early recognition that, whatever the government might once have had against him, the evidence which had put him in the Tower would not stand scrutiny. He told Danby, lord president of the Council, that any letter produced to incriminate him 'must and will' be shown to be a forgery. He assured the Duke of Devonshire, lord high steward, that 'any such letter . . . must appear to be forged, and made use of only to keep me in prison'. Finally, he told Halifax that his counsel would move for his Habeas Corpus as soon as the next law term opened. He would demand bail, and urged Halifax to stand by him.[63]

This was not the correspondence of a man who had doubt about the outcome, and the incriminating letter was indeed soon exposed as a forgery, though a very clever one. Marlborough was kept in the Tower till 15 June, when he brought a writ of Habeas Corpus before the Court of the King's Bench. The government demanded bail of £6,000, and when Halifax and Shrewsbury stood surety for him the queen spitefully struck them both from the roll of the Privy Council. Marlborough's name was still on it, and she drew her pen through that too. In October Marlborough pointed out that Robert Young had been convicted of perjury (he later excelled himself and was hanged for coining), and that it was therefore unreasonable to keep him on bail, but the Council would not budge. By now a last attempt at reconciliation between Queen Mary and her sister had failed, and the two rival courts were in a state of 'siege warfare' in which the queen held all the advantages.

Princess Anne had leased Berkeley House in Piccadilly from Lord Berkeley, groom of the stole to Prince George, who was in turn to move into the Cockpit, although it would take some time for the arrangements to be put in train. In mid-August Anne's court left Syon House for Bath, where they discovered that the mayor and corporation had been forbidden from showing them the 'respect or ceremony' owing to members of the royal family without specific leave from the queen. Anne, pregnant yet again, was scornful, and told Sarah that if they expected to get any change out of her by such small-minded behaviour 'they will be mightily disappointed'. Sarah herself blamed this petty-mindedness on Lord Rochester.

> I remember, when he was treasurer, he made his white staff be carried
> by his [sedan] chair-side, by a servant bare-headed; in this, as in other
> things, so very unlike his successor, my Lord Godolphin, who cut his
> white staff shorter than ordinary, that he might hide it, taking it into
> the chair with him.[64]

If Mary and her advisers hoped that all these petty humiliations would
drive a wedge between Sarah and Anne, they were indeed mistaken.
'I hope in Christ you will never think more of leaving me,' wrote Anne,
'for I would be satisfied to do you the least service, and nothing but
death can ever make me part with you. For if it be possible I am every
day more and more yours.'[65]

The Cockpit circle, strengthened by adversity, reunited at Berkeley
House that autumn 'in a companionship of wrath and misfortune', and
now joined by Shrewsbury. Marlborough remained in contact with
Jacobite agents, though we may doubt Lord Ailesbury's claim that this
was now carried out with William's knowledge to assist in his penetration
of Jacobite plans. Sir John Dalrymple, later 1st Earl of Stair and then a
key figure in the Williamite government of Scotland, believed that
Marlborough was now a leading member of the opposition to the king,
and capitalised on the fact that Parliament had been prorogued, and
would not meet till November.

> That interval gave time for Lord Marlborough, who was enraged at
> what he called the King's ingratitude, to the Whigs and to himself, and
> whose favour with the next heir to the throne, high character in his
> profession, and above all whose power of industry and intrigue made
> his influence, though he was only a soldier, and in prison, be felt in
> every line of life in the kingdom, to prepare a regular and concerted
> opposition in Parliament.[66]

Meanwhile the War of the League of Augsburg trudged on. In June
1692 the French took the fortress of Namur on the River Meuse, a
crucial cornerstone to the defence of the Spanish Netherlands, and went
on to beat William at Steenkirk in August, killing both Mackay and
Lanier in the process. When William returned in the autumn he found
that Count Solms' alleged desertion of his leading division at Steenkirk
('Now we shall see how the bulldogs will come off!') had heightened the
animus against foreigners. The Lords grumbled about the detention of
some of their members, and Marlborough was released from bail by the

king's personal intervention, but William gained the subsidies he needed, and set off for another campaign. The battle of Landen, midway between Louvain and Liège in the Spanish Netherlands, fought in July 1693, was vastly more costly than Steenkirk. Like many battles of the age it involved little tactical merit but a good deal of hard pounding, and Luxembourg eventually carried the Allied position by sheer weight of numbers. Solms was mortally wounded, and there was some mean-spirited sneering in the English camp when he did not die with the resolution expected of him. Battles on this scale (there were some 130,000 combatants and 23,000 casualties) simply collapsed the available medical support, and also made it impossible for local inhabitants to give decent burial to the dead. Sicco van Goslinga was there in 1707. 'I saw a grand foraging party on the battlefield of Landen,' he recalled. 'The bones, with which the fields were still scattered, showed what a murderous business it had been.'[67]

The naval victory of La Hougue encouraged William and his advisers to plan an attack on the naval base of Brest, with the dual intention of inflicting further damage on the French fleet and forcing the French to divert troops from the Low Countries to protect a coastline now apparently vulnerable to British and Dutch seapower. Such excursions were popular with the navy, which naturally secured the leading role, and with certain army officers, who hoped that their success in scrambling briskly up some French beach would not be overshadowed by a Dutchman. But their real merit was political: they gratified the trading interest in the Commons, which liked to see the naval cudgel brandished, and they seemed to reflect a genuinely 'English' approach to strategy, rather than the Continental commitment so clearly favoured by William. Many canny contemporaries, however, recognised that they generally accomplished very little, and Shrewsbury admitted to William: 'The designs that we have on foot appear so frivolous that it is not very pleasant writing upon them.'[68]

Given his personal preference for concentrating on the Low Countries the Brest project was never William's first choice, but his attempt to forge a Mediterranean strategy based on the maintenance of a powerful Anglo-Dutch fleet foundered when the huge 'Smyrna convoy' of Dutch and English merchantmen bound for the eastern Mediterranean was ambushed by the French off Cape St Vincent in June 1693. London's losses alone equalled those of the Great Fire of 1666. William and his advisers were vociferously blamed, and the king had to part with Lord Nottingham. A fleet hastily dispatched to round up the

Smyrna survivors and, so William hoped, form the nucleus of his Mediterranean fleet, was devastated by a storm, and so the Brest project emerged, *faute de mieux*, as the great hope of 1694.

It is easiest to tell the end of this disagreeable story first. Admiral Russell sailed from Plymouth on 2 June, and continued southwards with his main fleet after sending a squadron under Rear Admiral Berkeley to take Lieutenant General Tollemache's little army into Camaret Bay on 7 June. As the squadron first stood into the bay the vigorous fire of the batteries covering the approaches to Brest proved that the element of surprise was long lost. That genial hero 'Salamander' Cutts offered to take fifty grenadiers ashore to sample the quality of the fire, of which he was something of a connoisseur. Tollemache affirmed that they could not in honour retreat, and Berkeley felt that he must not disappoint such courage.

On the following day the squadron stood close inshore and took on the batteries, while Tollemache landed, in the teeth of heavy fire, with fifteen hundred men. The attackers were assailed by infantry and cavalry on the beach itself, and attempts to withdraw were frustrated by the fact that the landing had taken place on a falling tide, and few of the boats could be refloated. Tollemache, hard hit, was carried to safety, but his wound became infected and he died in Plymouth: he was buried with his ancestors in the church of St Mary at Helmingham in Suffolk.[69]

William had that year reappointed Shrewsbury as one of his secretaries of state, and immediately after the disaster he told him of his surprise that the attack, which was 'at discretion', and dependent upon the opinion of senior officers on the spot, had not been better reconnoitred, for the French 'were well apprised of our intended attack, and made active preparations for defence; for what was practicable two months ago, was no longer so at present'.[70] It was evident that the French had known about the attack long enough to take steps to meet it, and Macaulay is among those who argue that the project was betrayed by Marlborough in a letter of 4 May 1694 to James II. The charge is very grave: this 'Camaret Bay letter' ensured that the landing failed and that Tollemache, Marlborough's rival, was killed as its direct result.

The origins of the letter and its associated documents lie in the murky world of Jacobite politics. Captain David Lloyd visited London that March and claimed that he was received by Godolphin, Marlborough, Russell and Shrewsbury with protestations of support for the Jacobite cause. Marlborough gave nothing away: indeed, as he was out of office and had recently been accused of treason, it is fair to wonder what information he might have been privy to. Lloyd maintained that Godolphin, who was indeed a minister, told him 'that Russell would infallibly appear before Brest, the land officers believing that the place may be insulted even though the sea officers were of a different opinion', and Lloyd's report on these conversations, some of them so similar that we must suspect collusion, arrived at Versailles on 1 May. However, the plan was 'town-talk in London' some time before this, and we know that the French began to strengthen their defences around Brest on 22 April: Vauban himself arrived there on the twenty-third. A letter written in England on 4 May would have taken some time to reach James at St Germain, and then be passed on to Versailles: it could only have arrived long after preparations to meet the landing were well advanced.

This far, then, even if the Camaret Bay letter is authentic, it was hardly the cause of the reverse. But the currents run deeper still. The letter, now in the Bodleian Library in Oxford, is a French transcription of the original, and is not in Marlborough's hand. It is in the handwriting of David Nairne, James's under-secretary, and its heading affirms that it was translated from a ciphered document sent to France by the Jacobite agent Major General Edward Sackville. The original, if indeed there was one, has never come to light. It is, though, very hard to imagine a man as careful as Marlborough, only recently freed from suspicion of treason, writing a letter which would kill him if it fell into the wrong hands. Winston S. Churchill concludes that 'Such evidence would not hang a dog,' and it is hard to disagree.

Some historians, surmising that there can be no smoke without fire, and aware of Marlborough's other contacts with the Jacobites, have concluded that he probably did write the original letter, though he did so only when he knew that it would be received too late for its information to be of any practical use. John Paget argues that 'his offence seems to have been against James, in seeking credit for a service of no value, [rather] than against William'.[71] C.T. Atkinson agrees that the material Marlborough disclosed was of no value, but nonetheless finds this 'the meanest episode in his career'.[72] Stephen Saunders Webb says that the letter was 'a political ploy, not a betrayal of comrades. Marlborough had made an overdue payment on an unsavoury insurance policy.'[73] They are rather like a shaky bench of magistrates who, unable to resolve a case to their satisfaction, decide to find the defendant guilty but then impose a token punishment. The fact remains that the evidence linking Marlborough with the Camaret Bay letter is slender. The assertion that he hoped to have Tollemache killed is patently ludicrous. How was he to expect that Tollemache, who as overall land commander had good reason to spare himself (and had the Salamander himself to hand for those dangerous tasks at which he excelled), would land with the first wave?

Sir Tresham Lever, Godolphin's biographer, put the whole episode in the context of English politicians seeking to insure themselves against a Jacobite revival. Even if Lloyd's account of his conversations was substantially correct, he argued, his subjects 'were only saying what Lloyd and half England knew already, they only made the statements because they knew they revealed nothing, and they therefore betrayed no secrets of any sort either to the Jacobites or to the French Court'.[74] The recurrent theme of Jacobite complaints against Marlborough was that he promised much but never delivered anything, and we have no reason to suppose that he behaved differently in 1694.

The tide of politics was beginning to turn in Marlborough's favour. When corresponding with William over Camaret Bay, Shrewsbury, back in office but only recently a refugee in the Cockpit circle, wrote:

> Writing upon this subject it is impossible to forget what has here become a very general discourse, the probability and conveniency of Your Majesty receiving my Lord Marlborough into your favour. He has been with me since this news to offer his services, with all the expressions of duty and fidelity imaginable. What I can say by way of persuasion upon this subject will signify but little, since I very well remember when Your Majesty discoursed with me upon it in the spring, when you were fully convinced of his usefulness; but some points remained of a nature too delicate for me to pretend to advise upon, and on which Your Majesty is the only and best judge; who if those could be committed to Your Majesty's satisfaction I can but think he is capable of being very serviceable. It is so unquestionably his interest to be faithful, that single argument makes me doubt it not.[75]

The demise of Tollemache, coming so soon as it did after the deaths of Mackay and Lanier, undoubtedly helped Marlborough's case. William was under continual pressure to employ more British generals, and he had just lost three of his best. Indeed, just as Sir John Moore's death at Corunna in 1809 opened up the field for the future Duke of Wellington, so the fall of that brave and headstrong officer Thomas Tollemache left a yawning gap on the generals' list.

During the Christmas celebrations in 1694 Queen Mary was stricken with smallpox. She rallied briefly, disappointing some Jacobite ladies who had planned a celebratory dinner, and died on 28 December. William was visibly distraught, and the unfeigned intensity of his grief helped Englishmen like him better, for, they now thought, he had really loved their queen, and not simply married her to draw England into a war. William had also, at long last, started behaving like an Englishman. When a Jacobite nobleman rode deliberately into his path on Newmarket Heath, William struck him with his whip, a forceful act which commended him to the squirearchy.

James, in contrast, refused to order court mourning, and his minister Lord Middleton announced coldly that: 'The King, my master, does not consider her his daughter, because she had renounced her being so in such an open manner.' Jacobite hopes that the death of Mary improved their chances were misplaced, not least because there was now an heir apparent who commanded wide support in England.

Anne had tried hard to see her sister before she died, saying that she would 'run any hazard' for a meeting. She made her peace with William on 29 December, saying how much she regretted 'having fallen into her displeasure'. William was not sure what to make of this, but the Archbishop of Canterbury assured him that the quarrel should be settled. Anne, recovering from what seems to have been a phantom pregnancy, was carried in to see William on 13 January. Her guards had already been restored, her sister's jewellery was passed on to her, and she was given St James's Palace to hold court in, for she was now heir to the throne.

Marlborough did not return to favour immediately. In January 1695 Shrewsbury told Russell that

> our friend [Marlborough] who has no small credit with her, seems very resolved to contribute to the continuance of this union . . . I do not see he is likely, at present, to get much by it, not having yet kissed the King's hand, yet the reversion is very fair and very great.[76]

Marlborough duly kissed hands on 25 March. Sarah, however, was much more inclined to bury the hatchet in the head of an adversary than to make peace, and it took her another year to come to terms. Even then, she tells us, 'I believe I should have continued it, but that my Lord Sunderland dissuaded me from it.'[77]

There were fresh Jacobite plots afoot. The Duke of Berwick visited England incognito and met several supporters, but 'they continued firm in their resolution not to rise, till the King of England [James II] had landed with an army'. He agreed with them, for 'In a battle with their raw, undisciplined troops, against a good number of tried and experienced soldiers . . . they must inevitably have been destroyed.'[78] Louis, however, was not prepared to commit troops until a rising was under way. Early in 1696 a group of plotters prepared to attack William at Turnham Green on his return from hunting, but the plot was betrayed and some of those involved were executed. Lord Ailesbury felt that there was something fundamentally sound in popular judgement at moments like this, and that William's advisers were right to punish ringleaders but not to embark upon a witch-hunt. 'They are good at heart,' he wrote,

> and have compassion; and even in tumultuous occasions the mob ever reasons well, and seldom do they rise when not oppressed and weighed down. They have sudden starts . . . hasty enough to go to the execution, but after that some few have suffered, they would cry out 'that is enough, some few must die for example.'[79]

A successful assassination would have triggered an attempted invasion, for the French fleet had concentrated in the Channel and the hopeful James II went to Calais to join the invasion army. But with no assassination, no rising in England and, above all, none of the naval superiority which riveted the whole business together, the moment passed.

Sir John Fenwick's plot for the assassination of William was discovered that summer of 1696 and the accused man, facing a Bill of Attainder which, if passed, would simply declare him a traitor without the necessity for a trial, which would have demanded evidence, accused Marlborough, Russell, Godolphin and Shrewsbury of being in treasonable communication with the Court of St Germain. Shrewsbury privately admitted to William that he had indeed undertaken to help Lord Middleton, a Jacobite relative, and William at once forgave him. A nervous Godolphin resigned from the ministry, suggesting to many (including his biographer) that there was some truth in Fenwick's accusations.

But it was with perfect confidence that Marlborough, speaking coolly and with complete self-possession, told the Lords:

> Nobody can wonder that a man whose head is in danger should try to save himself by accusing others. I assure your Lordships that, since the accession of his present Majesty, I have no intercourse with Sir John on any subject whatever, and this I declare on my word of honour.[80]

The 'impeccably Whiggish' Colonel Godfrey, who had married Marlborough's sister Arabella, spoke warmly on his brother-in-law's behalf, while George Churchill, also an MP, muttered that dead men told no tales and hoped to see Fenwick dealt with, one way or another. Marlborough himself voted for Fenwick's attainder, and helped persuade Prince George, not a regular attender in the Lords, to avail himself of the rights of his English dukedom by going to the House and voting the same way. If there had indeed been an original Camaret Bay letter this would surely have been the moment for the Jacobites to use it: simply hinting that the document might be shown to William would have been sufficient to stop Marlborough in his tracks. The vote was close, and Godolphin voted in Fenwick's favour. Sir John Fenwick was duly beheaded on 28 January 1697, and Marlborough had safely weathered the last of the season's storms.

Even as Fenwick's fate trembled in the balance, the war was drawing to a close, for Louis opened secret peace negotiations with William late in 1696. William's Grand Alliance had been under terrible strain, with Victor Amadeus of Savoy making a separate peace with France in August 1696 and Britain, Holland and France all financially exhausted. The terms of the Treaty of Ryswick, concluded in the autumn of 1697, were essentially a return to the *status quo ante bellum*. The most fundamental exception was Louis' recognition of William and his heirs as *de facto* monarchs of Great Britain, and his promise not to afford assistance, directly or indirectly, to any of William's enemies. Although, as we shall soon see, Louis was perfectly capable of breaking his word, for mere promises did not bind Sun Kings, this provision was nevertheless a turning point in the history of the British Isles, for it finally took them out of the French sphere of influence.

The French gave up the fortresses they had captured in the Spanish Netherlands – Luxembourg, Chimay, Mons, Courtrai, Charleroi, Ath and Dinant. Barcelona, seized in the last year of the war, was also restored to the Spanish. The French obtained legal title to Strasbourg, though they had to give up their other fortresses on the Rhine. The Dutch gained a favourable commercial treaty with France, but the English asked for nothing, believing that 'The balance of trade, as it now stands, is evidently on the English side.'[81] The French merchant fleet had declined from 750 sizeable ships to 533, while the British, despite the damage done by privateers like Jean Bart, was larger at the war's end than its beginning. Perhaps most seriously for the long-term future of Europe, the French were unable to reform their financial institutions, and raised money to fuel the war by selling offices connected with trade, increasing restrictive practices.

England faced a crisis which was no less serious, and brought the fleet to the edge of mutiny. As N.A.M. Rodger has observed, 'All naval activities cost more money than was coming in. There was virtually no long-term system of borrowing, and the short-term credit of the Navy and the government wilted rapidly.'[82] The government revolutionised public finances by introducing the land tax, exchequer bills and the concept of national debt, and in 1694 Charles Montagu set up the Bank of England. Two years later, with the help of John Locke and Isaac Newton, Montagu carried out a total recoinage, getting rid of clipped and counterfeit coins. There was a brief dearth of currency, and the Bank of England, having over-issued its notes, might well have foundered. However, England had begun to initiate the reforms which would give her the financial and economic strength to fight another, even larger, war, and none of Marlborough's achievements on the battlefield would have been possible without them.

In the meantime, though, a Parliament dead-set on making economies pressed for the reduction of the army from its wartime strength of around 90,000 to an establishment of 7,000 in England and 12,000 in Ireland. These were all to be native-born, and the Dutch Guards were sent back to Holland, despite William's plea, in a personally-written note to Parliament, to be allowed to keep them. The capricious English, who had once seen these big men in blue coats as a symbol of Dutch domination, now grew quite fond of them as they marched to the coast. Many of them had married local girls, and somehow it was sad to see them all go.

The men who had fought at Steenkirk and Landen were treated even worse than their descendants who were to fight on the Somme and at Passchendaele, for Britain's national gratitude has all too short a lease. Despite a series of emergency measures, like opening up all trades to ex-officers and soldiers regardless of whether or not they had served an apprenticeship, there was significant unrest, and many ex-cavalrymen, allowed to keep their horses on demobilisation, simply became highway-men. A line of guardhouses, manned by soldiers, was built on the road from London to Kensington to protect travellers from ex-soldiers. The problem of how to deal with them had not been solved by the time recruiting began for the next war.

The recoinage of 1696 strengthened Sarah's position in Anne's household, and it was through this that Marlborough's route back to favour lay. The value of the guinea was reduced from thirty shillings to twenty-one, but Sir Benjamin Bathurst, the comptroller of the household, made up his accounts as if the change had not occurred. Sarah told Anne what had happened, but was urged to say nothing, for 'there is nobody perfect but dear Mrs Freeman'. In April 1697 Sir Benjamin was found to have been selling posts in the household, and although Anne forgave him, this convinced her that she should have 'a Mrs Freeman in every post in my family'.

On 24 July 1696, his seventh birthday, Anne's son the Duke of Gloucester was inducted into the Order of the Garter in a ceremony at Windsor attended by the whole court. In April 1698 William invited Marlborough to become the boy's governor on a salary of £2,000 a year, and soon restored him to both his rank in the army and the Privy Council. When William departed for Holland in July Marlborough was one of the lords justices left running the country in his absence.

Gloucester's miniature court included Gilbert Burnet as his spiritual guide. Burnet had been made Bishop of Salisbury, but his influence at court had diminished with Mary's death. William, who had once valued his advice, had grown tired of his badgering and indiscretions, calling him *ein rechter Tartuffe* (a real religious hypocrite). Shoving him off to the young duke's court suited William, but Burnet himself was not eager to move, and Anne suspected his whiggish principles and maintained that the king appointed him simply in order to be disagreeable to her. At first Burnet was no more enamoured of the Marlboroughs than they were of him, but he soon fell under John Churchill's spell. The published version of his *History*, written after he got to know them, is far more favourable to the Marlboroughs than the original rough draft.

Lord Churchill, the Marlboroughs' surviving son, was master of the horse, one of Burnet's sons was a page to young Gloucester, and Sarah's cousin Abigail Hill, 'daughter of a city merchant by a sister of my father', was laundress to the little court. This, so the waspish Sarah assures us, 'was a good provision for her'. Abigail's parents had died leaving two sons and two daughters, and Sarah used Godolphin's good offices to get one son into the customs house, and the other, Jack, into Gloucester's household and then into the army. After Gloucester's premature death Sarah took Abigail into Anne's household as bedchamber woman. Bedchamber women were personal maids, unlike the ladies of the bedchamber who were social companions and often confidantes. At that stage Abigail's duties were purely domestic, and Sarah had no idea that she was installing within Anne's household a rival who would eventually supplant her.

Marlborough was busy carefully repairing the dynastic damage done by his disgrace. Although he was given no office of state till the summer of 1701, William now consulted him regularly, though Marlborough told Shrewsbury in May 1700 that he still found the king cold towards him. He spoke in the Lords against the wholesale reduction of the army, said nothing about the Dutch Guards, and later declined to join the clamour against the king's grants of Irish land. His eldest daughter Henrietta had married Godolphin's only son Francis in 1699, and his second surviving daughter Anne married Lord Spencer, Sunderland's heir, the following year. It was a controversial match: Spencer was an extreme Whig and made no secret of his republican views. Princess Anne contributed £5,000 towards the bride's portion in each instance, and made both of them ladies of her bedchamber. The resignation of Marlborough's old enemy Portland in the summer of 1700 and his replacement in William's favour by Joost van Keppel, now Earl of Albemarle, helped smooth the upward path. Marlborough crossed the king by supporting Prince George's long-standing claim to the money owed him since 1689, but William soon forgave him, and Anne was delighted by his help, 'it being wholly owing to your & his kindness', she assured Sarah. When William went to Holland in 1700 Marlborough was again appointed one of the lords justices.

Anne suffered another miscarriage on 14 January 1700, producing a boy who was judged to have been 'dead in her a month'. It was probably her seventeenth pregnancy, and was certainly her last. A deeper tragedy followed: on 30 July the ten-year-old Duke of Gloucester died of smallpox. Anne, suggests a biographer, never really recovered from the blow, and thereafter habitually wrote to Sarah as 'your poor unfortunate faithful Morley', a play on the Churchill family motto, 'Faithful but Unfortunate'.[83] Although Gloucester's death deprived Marlborough of his only office, he found himself at the very centre of the discussions on the succession. He was involved, this time on Anne's behalf, in discussions with the omnipresent Jacobite agents (with the customary camouflage of secrecy laced with deception), and it seems likely that Anne was endeavouring to secure her own unopposed succession to the throne on the death of William by implying that the Jacobite claimant (the twelve-year-old James, Prince of Wales) might succeed her. She was probably never serious in this, and most well-placed contemporary observers believed that she was genuinely committed to the official line.

This policy, championed by William and his predominantly Tory ministry, was that the Protestant succession should be assured. They supported the dowager Electress Sophia of Hanover, who, as a granddaughter of

James I, had some of the old Stuart blood in her veins, and who herself had a grandson, the Electoral Prince Georg August. William was now visibly in failing health, and the issue needed speedy resolution. In June 1701 Parliament passed an Act of Settlement which vested the crown in Electress Sophia and her heirs should Anne die without children, as then seemed almost certain.

Marlborough was not simply influential in steering the measure through the Lords, but also supported the election as speaker of the Commons of Robert Harley, a kinsman of Sarah's, and Harley's careful management nudged the Bill through the Commons. The Act did more than determine the succession. It declared that future monarchs must be communicating members of the Church of England, they were forbidden to leave their three kingdoms without permission from Parliament, only the native-born could hold office, and the full Privy Council must consider major matters of policy. The terms, indeed, were so restrictive that Georg August genuinely believed that the measure was designed to make him refuse the crown and thus assure a Jacobite succession. While Anne saw the need for a Protestant succession, she was, and remained throughout her reign, very sensitive about the issue. She wanted no heir apparent looking over her shoulder, and no cloud on the horizon to dim the glory of her own accession, an event that evidently could not be delayed for long.

Europe changed gear with a palpable jerk in 1700–02. The Treaty of Ryswick had delayed but not expunged Louis' plans for dominating Europe. The death of the childless and decrepit Charles II of Spain had been widely anticipated, and negotiations between the major powers considered ways of partitioning the Spanish Empire, in the New World and the Old, so that neither the French nor their potential adversaries gained decisive advantage from it and that whoever succeeded to the throne of Spain (and there were a number of credible claimants) would not immediately join their realm to France or the Empire. Charles died in November 1700, and his will provided for his entire empire to be offered to Louis' grandson Philippe, duc d'Anjou. If Anjou refused it, then it was to go to the Hapsburg Emperor Leopold's younger son, the Archduke Charles. Louis thought for some time before acting, but eventually decided to back his grandson, introducing him to a room full of waiting courtiers and ambassadors with the pregnant words: 'Gentlemen, here is the king of Spain.' The delighted Spanish ambassador whispered that the Pyrenees no longer existed.

The French may genuinely have hoped, as their foreign minister

Colbert de Torcy told William, that this would simply ensure smooth succession and that the two Bourbon kingdoms would remain distinct. However, the French army was now at a high level of readiness, and in February 1701 Louis' troops moved into the barrier fortresses in the Spanish Netherlands with the connivance of the Spanish authorities. William had just issued orders authorising their Dutch garrisons to withdraw, but the French moved too quickly and grabbed them all, releasing them only after a firm line had been established on the Dutch border. Max Emmanuel, Elector of Bavaria, an Allied general in the previous war and now governor of the Spanish Netherlands, threw in his lot with France and departed to Bavaria to raise troops.

It now seemed evident that the French planned a new war, and French and Austrian troops were fighting in Italy by early summer. English public opinion, not for the last time, was resolutely opposed to a fresh Continental commitment, so much so that William told the Dutch grand pensionary Anthonie Heinsius that this blindness to an obvious danger was a punishment from heaven. On 7 September a Treaty of Grand Alliance bound the Emperor Leopold, the Dutch and the British to support the partition of the Spanish Empire with 'satisfactory compensation' for the Hapsburgs, and equally satisfactory arrangements for the maritime powers in the West Indies. Marlborough had negotiated on Britain's behalf. The Dutch had installed him in the beautiful and exotic Mauritshuis in The Hague, and Marlborough, so familiar with courts, was wholly in his element, charming, flattering, wheedling and cajoling, but always ensuring that he sent drafts of the treaty to Whig and Tory leaders so that there could be no suggestion that he was acting without consultation: the lessons of the last decade had been well learned.

Thus far Louis XIV had dominated events, but he now proceeded to make an error so serious that we must surmise that it sprang from genuine conviction, not subtle statecraft. James II's court just outside Paris at St Germain en Laye, with its odour of sanctity and disappointed ambitions, had never been a happy place. In the late 1690s it grew gloomier still. There was never enough money; French neighbours blamed the continuation of the war on Jacobite pressure, and James's apparent support for the assassination of William (who, whatever his status in England, was indisputably stadholder of the United Provinces) looked rather like an attempt to procure the murder of a Christian prince. Many of his Irish troops were disbanded, and veterans of the Boyne, Aughrim and Limerick became brigands or footpads, risking 'death on the wheel or life eked out in the galleys'. James became increasingly preoccupied by the need to preserve his immortal soul, and spent retreats at the wintry monastery of La Trappe. When the Archbishop of Rheims saw the old king shuffling down the steps of Notre Dame de Paris, he pointed out a 'good man' who had 'renounced three kingdoms for a mass'.[84]

James was hearing mass at St Germain in March 1701 when he collapsed with a heavy nosebleed, and he had a stroke that paralysed his right side a week later. He collapsed again in September, and then lay centre-stage for the finest role he ever played, the resolute confrontation of death in the presence of his family and the comfort of his Church. It was the very public nature of this death, with his magnanimous forgiveness of his three greatest foes – the emperor, the Prince of Orange, and Princess Anne – and the selfless fulfilment of the very highest moral duty of a king that impressed Louis. There, in the antechamber to James's room, he recognised the Prince of Wales as James's lawful heir. Men torn between joy and despair cried 'God save the King' when James died in the small hours on 16 September.

English indignation against Louis knew no bounds, and when William dissolved Parliament that month the election produced a House of Commons almost equally divided between Whigs and Tories but united in one thing: support for the war against a perjured king. William did not live long to enjoy the fruition of his life's work. On 21 February 1702 he was hunting in Richmond Park when his horse stumbled on a molehill and threw William, whose collarbone was broken. The injury should not in itself have proved fatal, but William, at fifty-one, was old and tired, and he died at Kensington Palace on the morning of 8 March. It was ironic that a man who had done so much to frustrate French ambitions should end his life with his last words in French: '*Je tire vers ma fin*,' 'I draw near my end.' Bishop Burnet raced across London to throw himself at Anne's feet, 'full of joy and duty', and tell her that her 'sunshine day' had come at last, and she was queen. For Marlborough, already described as her 'grand vizier', the sun could scarcely have beamed more brightly.

4

A Full Gale of Favour

Marlborough was fifty-one years old when he left London for The Hague on 14 March 1702, blown 'by a full gale of favour', to reassure the members of the Grand Alliance that England was steadfast in her commitment. The previous summer William, conscious of his own failing health, had chosen Marlborough to command the twelve battalions sent to the Low Countries and made him ambassador to the Dutch Republic. But if Marlborough was then glad of such important employment, he was now wholly replete with honour and dignity. The queen had made him a Knight of the Garter immediately after her succession, and went on to appoint him captain general of her army and master general of the ordnance. Lord Romney was dispossessed, though the broad arrow from his coat of arms long survived as an emblem of government property. Marlborough was also reappointed ambassador extraordinary and plenipotentiary to the United Provinces, and this post alone was worth £100 a day, with £1,500 to provide for his equipage and £2,500 for the appropriate plate.

The garter was a particular delight, for he had hoped for it, all those years ago, as a reward for Cork and Kinsale. In those days knights of orders of chivalry wore their insignia most of the time, with braid and tinsel stars sewn to garments like cloaks and overcoats. The practice was not always wise. Berwick says that Schomberg was identified by his garter at the Boyne, and an unlucky French officer, writing home after Blenheim, lamented that his Württemberg decoration had drawn Allied cavalrymen like wasps to a honeypot. Within minutes he had 'two sword-cuts to the head, a sword-cut which pierced my arm, the contusion of a ball on the leg, and my horse wounded'. A kindly enemy officer took his remaining pistol and said: 'You are welcome to quarter, follow me, I will get you cared for, and give me your cross.' The Frenchman added glumly that: 'I had the weakness to give him the 134 louis d'or I had in a purse; but anyone else would have done the same to make them well disposed and to avoid being massacred.'[1] It was some time before Marlborough had quite enough stars. As late as April 1704 he asked Sarah to arrange for Salamander Cutts, due back in Flanders, to bring him some extra insignia: 'I desire Lord Cutts to bring me two stars, I having none to put on any clothes I shall make, and if it be not too much trouble to him, a little liquorish and rhubarb.'[2]

Marlborough already had considerable experience of dealing with the Dutch. They appear in many anglophone accounts as dour and curmudgeonly, always anxious to think of a reason for not fighting and a constant thorn in Marlborough's side. Their names and titles were a trial in themselves. The field deputy that Marlborough calls 'Mr Gilder-Malsen' was in fact Adriaen van Borssele van der Hooghe, Heer van Gueldermalsen.*

Many of the differences of opinion between Marlborough and the most indispensable of Britain's allies were rooted deep in that black alluvial soil of the United Provinces. The seven provinces which constituted the Dutch Republic had torn themselves free from Spanish rule by the early seventeenth century, leaving the remaining provinces of the Spanish Netherlands (very roughly modern Belgium and a slice of northern France, which constituted the battleground for most of Marlborough's campaigns) squeezed uncomfortably between the new republic and the rising power of France.

Most Dutchmen regarded French incursions into the Spanish Netherlands, a constant feature of Louis XIV's policy, as fundamentally inimical to the security of their republic, and they were also concerned for the safety of their Dutch-speaking co-religionists in the Spanish provinces of Flanders and Brabant. For just as Huguenots and Catholic Irish were marked by their own deep sense of persecution, so the Duke of Alba's bloody attempt to burn out Dutch Protestantism (he cheerfully told King Philip that he had taken 'eight hundred heads' in Holy Week 1568 alone) left its enduring legacy. Moreover, many Huguenot refugees made their way to the Dutch Republic before setting off

---

* In these pages I generally call Dutch officers by the names used by their British allies, and thus use 'Overkirk' instead of 'd'Auverkerque' or 'Ouwerkerk'; but I realise that this practice may be considered now (as it was then) another symptom of British cultural myopia.

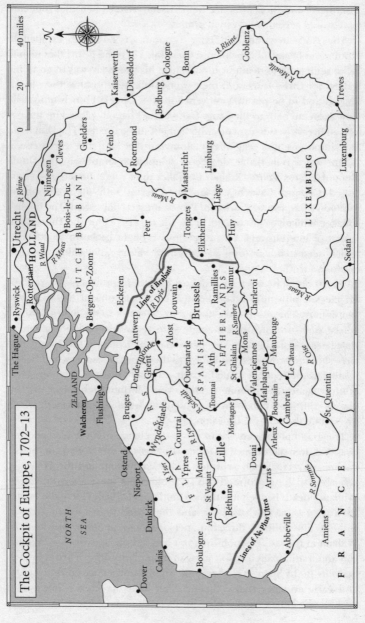

The Cockpit of Europe, 1702–13

elsewhere, and their presence helped assure Dutchmen that rope and pyre would accompany French armies.

The Norman gentleman Isaac Dumont de Bostaquet escaped to Rotterdam by way of Hesdin and Courtrai. There he heard that he had been sentenced to death in his absence: his son-in-law was to go to the galleys for three years, and their womenfolk were to have their heads shaved and to be put in a convent for life.[3] Once a French officer, he now swore an oath to the States-General and happily picked up the pay of 520 livres given to captains who had left the active list. The Dutch did not simply give him religious freedom, but they paid him to exercise it. There was a remarkable degree of religious toleration in the Dutch Republic. Laws against Roman Catholics were not enforced, the established Calvinist Church was on good terms with the francophone Walloon Church, and a variety of Protestant sects flourished. The English Quaker William Penn argued, from his experience of the Dutch, that union of interests and not of opinions brought peace to kingdoms – which seems, in our own age riven by divergent opinion, to be a profound truth.

The Dutch state was a confederacy, each of its provinces governed by an elected provincial estate headed by a paid official known as the pensionary. The provincial estates sent delegates to the States-General, where each province had a single vote regardless of the number of delegates it contributed. The pensionary of Holland, the largest and richest of the provinces, was known as the grand pensionary, and he was as near as the republic came to having a chief executive. The very term confused most Englishmen, and even Marlborough, who worked closely with him, habitually translated the word as 'pensioner', which gives quite the wrong impression.

The grand pensionary was in day-to-day charge of foreign affairs, and presided over the Council of State, whose *greffier* functioned almost as a cabinet secretary. Each province had a stadholder, and the House of Orange had long provided the stadholder for the United Provinces: William's death had left a gap that could not be filled. Few of the estates even tried to elect a successor, and the Dutch were to fight this war without the unifying direction, personal and political, provided by William in the last. Elections in 1702 had left the anti-Orange, republican and traditionally anti-war party in power, but concern about French activities in the Spanish Netherlands, French restrictions on Dutch trade and early evidence that a Spain which toed the French line would exclude the Dutch from trade with its dominions overseas, meant that even anti-Orangists were, in that very Dutch way, not at all keen on the war but determined to prosecute it to a successful conclusion.

The structure of their state, however, made this difficult. There was always tension between the demands of the sea power on which this maritime nation relied, and the armies necessary to seize and retain a barrier between the republic and France. This inevitably played itself out in friction with the British, who complained that the Dutch did not commit sufficient ships to convoy protection, placing an unreasonable burden on the Royal Navy. The Dutch collegiate system of government made even the England of Queen Anne look slick and centralised. There were five independent admiralty boards, whose deputies met to discuss the composition and funding of fleets. The States-General nominated the naval commander-in-chief, but the provincial boards all selected their own admirals. It was not a recipe for clear command and decisive action.

Each provincial estate elected deputies to accompany Dutch armies in the field. Although they were technically civilians, like any sensible gentleman on his travels they carried sword and pistols, and Sicco van Goslinga, the best-known of them, argued that, as direct representatives of the Dutch state, they held residual command authority. Army commanders habitually put major decisions to the vote of a council of war consisting of their senior generals. Even this was rarely a simple process, but Dutch generals could only fight if their field deputies (numbering from six in 1703 to three in 1704 and collectively called 'the deputation') concurred, quite regardless of what an Allied commander-in-chief might wish. Field deputies were not necessarily idle or obstructive, but there would be times when their view of what was best for Zealand or Friesland would not mesh comfortably with a British commander's desire to attack the French that very morning.

Richard Kane of the Royal Regiment of Foot of Ireland believed that in 1702 Marlborough's lack of experience of command on such a scale naturally made the Dutch a little concerned.

My Lord Marlborough knew that the eyes of all the Confederates were upon him, he never having had the like command before, but especially the States General, who purely to oblige the Queen of England, not only placed him at the head of their army, but even the safety of their country in a great measure depended on his conduct. However, as it had always been the practice of that state, even in the King's time, to send two of their Council of State with generals into the field, who always acted in concert, they sent with my Lord two of the most experienced men among them as their Field Deputies, which my Lord could not take ill, since it had been their constant practice, though as he ever did, watched all opportunities to give a bold stroke at his first setting out to fix a reputation.[4]

At precisely the same time Marlborough's private secretary, Adam de Cardonnel, told secretary Blathwayt that bold strokes would be some time in coming.

You will wonder, after what I wrote the last post, to find us on this side of the Meuse; it was then resolved to pass over, but the Dutch are so timorous that they will not venture their army out of sight while the French are so near, and the King of Prussia is of the same opinion, for fear of exposing what is left in the country of Cleve.[5]

Soon afterwards Marlborough admitted to Godolphin that he was finding coalition command harder than he had expected.

I have but too much reason to complain that the ten thousand men upon our right did not march as soon as I sent the orders, which if they had I believe we should have had a very easy victory, for their whole left was in disorder. However, I have thought it very much for her Majesty's service to take no [formal] notice of it, as you will see by my letter to the States. But my Lord Rivers and almost all the general officers of my right were with me when I sent the orders, so that notwithstanding the care I take to hinder it, they do talk.[6]

Anthonie Heinsius, who had become grand pensionary in 1689, had served as Dutch envoy to Versailles after the Peace of Nijmegen. He had no success whatever in persuading the French to relinquish William's principality of Orange, and emerged as an inveterate opponent of French expansionism. He was at first anti-Orangist, but had worked increasingly closely with William, who had persuaded him to become grand pensionary. One historian suggests that after William became king of England Heinsius was effectively his *alter ego*, aware of his deepest thoughts and acting as his most important personal link with the United Provinces. In William's reign the English and Dutch diplomatic services had worked almost as one, though the links unravelled after William's death.

The personal relationship between Marlborough and Heinsius, already well established by 1702, was fundamental to the success of the Grand Alliance. They were very different. Heinsius, born in 1641, was a bachelor of simple tastes, whose crushing workload left him little time for any other interests. Although he was widely respected by his countrymen he could never command the loyalty which had attached to William, and as divergent elements welled up within the United Provinces he drew closer to Marlborough. When Marlborough's grasp on power was fatally weakened in 1711 and the British government was actively considering making a separate peace, it avoided his outright dismissal until the very end of the year because his long friendship with Heinsius helped cloak a policy which would leave the Dutch exposed in the peace negotiations at Utrecht. One of the many anguishes of Marlborough's fall was having to watch, from the sidelines, the shabby treatment of someone who had become an old comrade.

In the spring of 1702, however, the States-General could not have been more supportive. They at once approved Marlborough's demand for the inclusion of 'the expulsion of the pretended Prince of Wales from France' among the articles of the Grand Alliance, and went on to appoint him deputy captain general of their army. The emperor was uneasy about having the Prince of Wales, son of an anointed king, described as 'pretended', but Marlborough made it clear to his ambassador that the clause was fundamental to keeping England in the alliance. Leopold speedily concluded, after speaking to his confessor, that the word could as well mean 'claimant' as 'impostor', and his emissary Count Goes duly signed the article.

The original treaty, duly modified by this new clause, had subsidiary treaties in which members of the alliance contracted to provide specified forces. The Prussians, for instance, agreed to provide two regiments of cavalry at 874 men apiece and five regiments of infantry, each of twelve companies apiece, or 4,255 men in all. The contingent would be paid for half by the English and half by 'their High Mightinesses' of the States-General, and pay was to start immediately the contingent entered Dutch territory. There was a recall clause:

> If the King of Prussia comes to be attacked in his own territory, far away from the Rhine, and should be obliged to demand the return of the said troops, they will be sent back to him immediately, without dispute.[7]

The original document was, naturally enough, in French.

Similar agreements governed the military contributions made to the Grand Alliance by other small states, and it is important to recognise from the outset just how important they were. It was Danish dragoons who began the crumbling of the French position at Ramillies by taking the village of Taviers, and Hanoverian cavalry who pushed the French back across the Norken stream at Oudenarde: the British element in Marlborough's armies was almost always outnumbered by its non-British component. Agreements with Allied contributors required negotiation and re-negotiation, with arrangements for pay and victualling requiring careful attention, for irregularly-paid men often took to looting regardless of whether or not they were on friendly territory. Discipline was a national responsibility, and arrangements would often specify where disciplinary authority ultimately lay. When a British staff officer with a small cavalry escort saw some Danes, accompanied by two officers, engaged in large-scale looting he was wise enough to take no action until British reinforcements arrived. When he handed over the miscreants to a Danish general the officers were at once put in irons, and he was assured that they would be shot forthwith.

Much of Marlborough's time for the next nine years would be taken up with a thousand and one practical issues of coalition warfare. His correspondence files bulge with letters to monarchs, ambassadors and contingent commanders, and his background as courtier and diplomat was every bit as useful as his ability as a soldier. During the campaigning season operational matters were uppermost. When the Imperialist General Thungen was taking charge of the siege of Ulm in August 1704, Marlborough sent him some Prussian reinforcements.

Mr Schlundt, who will have the honour to present this to you, is a colonel of artillery in the service of the King of Prussia, who his Majesty sends with a brigade, specified on the enclosed list, to assist us in our enterprises. He is an officer of merit and experience, and I do not in the least doubt that you will be wholly pleased with him. When you no longer have need of him, I beg you to send him back to me with his men, and to give them wagons and the other necessities for their journey. I wish you, with all my heart, a happy success, and I am, with real esteem and friendship,

Yours, etc,

Marlborough[8]

When the armies were in winter quarters Marlborough's mind ran towards detailed issues of structures and establishments. In December 1706 he told Heinsius:

> You may remember when it was under deliberation at The Hague, I told you my thoughts that it would be both for the service and for the honour of your troops that your squadrons should be of equal force with the rest of the army, therefore I hope the addition of eight men to a troop will meet with no difficulty, and I think you may depend that the Queen will be ready to increase her foot by an equal proportion to the charge you are at; in order whereto I should be very glad if you would send me, as soon as may be, an estimate of the numbers and expense of this augmentation on your part.[9]

Of course his responsibilities did not end there. He was both captain general of the British army and master general of the ordnance, and in consequence in charge not only of the 'marching regiments' of horse and foot, but also of the 'gentlemen of the ordnance', the artillery and engineers, as well as all fortifications and many military supplies. By holding both posts he was able to exercise an almost unmatched degree of control over the British army, but at the cost of mastering yet more detail. In July 1702 he wrote his first formal letter to the principal officers of the ordnance, establishing the policy that was to prevail during his tenure of the post.

> I am obliged to you for your letter of the 30th past, and am very glad to see at the same time that the Queen has thought fit to honour me with an employment of the greatest trust. Her Majesty has been pleased to place me at a board with gentlemen of so much ability and experience, I do not doubt but with your advice and assistance the service will be carried on to Her Majesty's entire satisfaction, and answer the great confidence reposed in us, wherein I shall always be ready to do my part.
>
> I have likewise your letter of the 4th instant relating to the employments that are become void by this new commission and the vacancies that may happen by death or otherwise among the gunners of the garrisons, and other small officers, and in answer must desire that for such vacancies, where Her Majesty's service may require the present filling them up, you will do it without expecting further notice from me;

but for the others, where the delay may be of no prejudice to the service, I should be glad they might be deferred to my return.

As to the storekeeper and gunner of Scarborough, I leave it to you to do therein as upon examination of the complaint you shall find the merit of the case to deserve, either by restoring him or confirming the other who is now acting in his place.[10]

Marlborough did not simply sanction a policy of *laissez-faire*, for as soon as the board drew something to his attention he moved quickly. On 25 August 1707 he wrote from the army's camp in Soignies, just off the 1815 battlefield of Waterloo, to inform the board that:

I have received your letter of the 8th inst. relating to the arms that are making in Holland for the service of Ireland, and send you the enclosed memorial which Lieutenant-General Ingoldsby has delivered to me, wherein he sets forth the extravagant rate demanded for the transport of the said arms, besides five per cent customs demanded on their exportation, and desire you will move the Prince's council to appoint a man of war as soon as any can be spared, to receive the arms in Holland and carry them directly to Ireland to save that expense; in the meantime I shall apply to have the customs taken off. The Lieutenant-General assures me that the arms will be completed within the term of the contract, which he alleged to be eighteen months from the time the advance was made in December last.[11]

Marlborough had firm views on arms and equipment as captain general, and had to ensure, as master general of the ordnance, that these demands were met. When he reached the Continent in 1702 the matchlock musket had all but disappeared from British service, replaced by versions of the flintlock. The socket bayonet, which fitted around the musket's muzzle so that the weapon could be loaded and fired with the bayonet fixed, was fast replacing the inconvenient plug bayonet. The pike, however, was trailed for far longer than we might suppose. In about 1702 Peter Drake was serving in Marlborough's own regiment, having been compulsorily re-enlisted after one of his many desertions. It 'had been commanded by the Marquis [de Puisan], who in coming from Ireland to join his regiment, was lost at sea: upon which it became General Seymour's, and soon after Lord Marlborough's; so that in less than five months we had three colonels'. He had to master pike drill, because

> my size made me a pikeman against my will, though indeed I liked that service, and thought it the most becoming and manly of all. There was an encouragement (to induce a brisk and smart motion in charging) of half a crown to every one that should break a pike in that motion, and I had the good fortune to break two before I left the regiment.[12]

Naturally enough Drake soon deserted, first to a Dutch regiment in Spanish pay, and then to Old Pretender's Life Guard of Horse, having somehow, in the process, changed sides.

As late as 1704 there were evidently not enough muskets for all, and Major General the Earl of Portmore, then at Plymouth, told the Duke of Somerset:

> I have the honour of receiving an order from your Grace directing the storekeeper of this place to deliver 450 firelock in lieu of the like number of pikes which some of the regiments that come from Holland [on their way to Portugal] have, as they say, left behind by his Grace the Duke of Marlborough's allowance.

The storekeeper would not comply unless given a direct order from the ordnance board, because some troops would sail unarmed if he did so.[13]

When Richard Kane wrote his *New System of Military Discipline* after 1714 he observed that a battalion used to form up in three grand divisions, musketeers on the flanks and pikes in the centre, but now, 'since pikes have been laid aside', a new system was required. The abolition of the pike was not universally supported. Lieutenant General Henry 'Hangman' Hawley, a government commander in the 1745 Jacobite rebellion, agreed that Marlborough had been anxious to get rid of the pike. However, he argued, as a professional cavalry officer, that he would be hard pressed to break a battalion of pikemen in good order, and the weapon's long reach might do more harm to his troopers than ill-aimed musketry. Marshal Saxe, who saw his first battle as an Imperialist officer at Malplaquet, always argued that the pike should be retained, because it might be needed one summer's afternoon.

Marlborough was convinced, however, that infantry primarily achieved its effect by fire, and only secondarily by shock, while for cavalry the reverse was true. Kane tells us that he was only prepared 'to allow the horse but three charges of powder and ball to each man for a campaign, and then only for guarding their horses when at grass, and not to be made use of in action'.[14] He believed that cavalry should attack in close order, charging at the last moment so as to preserve alignment but on no account pausing to fire their pistols. The sheer terror of charging squadrons often persuaded their opponents to go 'threes about'. A Royal Dragoon described his first charge: 'We advanced up to them so far as our horses could go with a loud huzzah, but they did not like our appearance, so they did not give us so much as one salute, but all ran in a confused manner away.'[15] Such tactics, in Marlborough's view, demanded that all troopers should wear pistol-proof cuirasses and have a 'secret' (spider-shaped iron lining) in their felt hats. Some Allied horse wore cuirasses anyway, and some Imperialist cavalry had retained the lobster-tailed *zischägge*. However, getting the Dutch to provide their cavalry with body armour required yet more work on Heinsius.

Much of Marlborough's ordnance work could be delegated, but as far as the army's regiments of horse and foot were concerned, a far greater degree of control was required. On 6 April 1704, when he was about to leave Harwich for the Continent, he wrote to Sir Charles Hedges, briefly the sole secretary of state (and a man much disliked by Sarah as having 'no capacity, no quality nor interest') to tell him:

> Herewith I send you a list of general officers to be promoted this year, with a list of officers for the two new regiments of foot to be raised under the command of the Lord Paston and Col Heyman Rooke; as also a fourth list of some officers to be commissioned in the Guards, and the Lord Lucas's regiment, all of which I desire you will lay before Her Majesty and His Royal Highness and prepare commissions thereupon, according to the directions you shall receive in that behalf.
>
> The commissions for the General officers and Brigadiers may bear the date of 1st January last, though it is not intended that those who are to receive pay should commence their allowance before the 1st May next.
>
> I must desire you will remind His Royal Highness, at a proper time, of providing for Mr Montague [Wortley] on the first vacancy of a colours in the Foot Guards.[16]

Hedges was one of the great officers of state, albeit a man frequently in trouble over electoral investigations and a loyal supporter of his own interests, but there is no mistaking Marlborough's peremptory tone.

In contrast, by the same post he winged a letter off to secretary Blathwayt, upon whose judgement he had come to rely, even though he was a veteran of Charles II's administration who was now 'grown somewhat stiff and rusty'.

> I received last night your letter of the 6th, and am just going to embark. I was in hopes I should have taken with me all the troops from home, but I shall be obliged to leave behind me four companies of Sir Richard Temple's, and about fifty dragoons for the next embarkation for the want of part of our shipping . . . I must recommend to you that these, with Farrington's regiment, be all put on board between the 18th and 20th of this month at the farthest, that a convoy may be ready against that time. I shall on this occasion depend upon your care, of which I have had so long experience, and shall always be ready to give you all possible marks of my friendship, and the esteem wherewith I am,
> Sir, yours &c Marlborough[17]

There was never much shelter from the barrage of calls upon his interest. When a lady made a very general demand for a commission for a relative, he professed himself anxious to oblige, but added that it would assist him if she could tell him just which army the youngster had in mind. A bloody battle produced a flurry of requests. On 30 September 1709, in the aftermath of Malplaquet, he told the Duke of Somerset, seeking a regiment for his son Lord Hertford:

> We have only two regiments vacant, that of Brigadier Lalo, and Sir Thomas Prendergast's; the former, which is the eldest of the two, by agreement between the Brigadier and Lord Mordaunt, is to return to his Lordship as soon as peace is made, so that I know not whether Your Grace may be willing Lord Hertford should accept it with that encumbrance; the other is entirely at my disposal, and I will sign no commission till I receive your answer.[18]

Colonel Pennefather was anxious to sell a vacant company in his regiment, and engaged Brigadier Sabine to lobby Marlborough on his behalf. Marlborough could not help him.

> I should willingly have agreed to it were it not for the pressing instances of the Prince of Savoy and others on behalf of Lieutenant Jones, to whom I am therefore obliged to give it, but I have promised the Brigadier that you shall have the benefit of the first that become vacant.[19]

Lord Halifax hoped that Lieutenant Barton might be preferred, 'but there is no vacancy in his regiment, and you are too just to desire I should do it to the prejudice of such as were in the battle'.[20] Marlborough deployed his own interest almost as often, whether it was trying to get a diplomatic post for that convicted duellist the Master of Sinclair, casting his vote as a Scots peer for the election of the Earls of Orkney and Stair as two of the sixteen representative Scots peers sitting at Westminster after the Union, or recommending Mr Abel the singer, 'whose fine voice and manner has not displeased His Imperial Majesty', to that cultured monarch the king of Portugal.[21]

Marlborough's responsibilities immeasurably outweighed those exercised by British commanders-in-chief in the great wars of the twentieth century, for he did not simply execute strategy but helped to determine it. In the context of 1944, for instance, he would have been Eisenhower, Montgomery and Brooke rolled into one. He was able to do this because of his intimate relationship with the man who was as close as politics then allowed to being prime minister. Sidney Godolphin was appointed lord high treasurer on the accession of Anne, and advanced to earl in 1706. He was eventually unseated by the Tories in 1710, a process to which Sarah Marlborough's replacement as Anne's confidante by Abigail Hill (later Lady Masham) contributed. Godolphin was Marlborough's closest friend and political associate, and in 1712 when he was tired, friendless and felt death's fingers groping for him, he went to Marlborough's home, Holywell House, to await the end. 'The Whigs have lost a great support in the Earl of Godolphin,' wrote Richard Swift, by then a Tory pamphleteer. ''Tis good jest to hear the ministers talk of him now with humanity and pity, because he is dead, and can do them no more hurt.'[22]

The fighting in Spain, where British troops were commanded first by Charles Mordaunt, Earl of Peterborough, and then by that rheumy old Huguenot warrior Henri de Ruvigny, Viscount Galway, lay outside the compass of Marlborough's sphere of tactical command. Yet it was never far from his thoughts, for he was concerned that the British army could never be simultaneously strong enough in the Low Countries and the Iberian Peninsula, and that the country's desire to have 'No Peace without Spain' would compel the diversion of resources from the war's main theatre to an important but necessarily subsidiary one. In October 1703 he informed Godolphin:

Mr Secretary [Hedges] sends me word that Lord Nottingham would send me her Majesty's commands concerning the 2,000 men for

Portugal. Not having heard from him, I take it for granted he wrote to me by that packet that is lost. However, I have directed the regiments of Leigh and Lord Baltimore to be ready for to be embarked, which has given so much alarm here, that I had a deputation this day from the States, to represent to me the dangerous consequence of what might happen, by drawing away without their consent any of those troops which were agreed at the beginning of the war . . . [23]

This might almost be Sir John French, writing to Lord Kitchener in the spring of 1915 to say how much the French resented the diversion of British troops to the Dardanelles.

Both of the Marlboroughs had deep reservations about Peterborough. Sarah thought that his 'vileness of soul' had led him into 'a sort of *knight errantry*' with Lord Rivers, himself 'of no better reputation than a common cheat or pickpocket'.[24] Peterborough, initially a Whig, was to win several victories in Spain. The capture of Barcelona owed much to his efforts: when the attackers shrank from the assault on the fort of Montjuich, 'Lord Peterborough . . . fell into the horriblest passion that ever man was seen in, and with a great deal of bravery and resolution, led us back to the part we had quitted.'[25]

However, Peterborough got on badly with other Allied commanders, and suggested a variety of schemes so puzzling that there was reason to believe that he did not in fact wish to see the Archduke Charles installed as king of Spain. Summoned home to explain himself in 1707, he was championed by the Tories, and soon became a member of the opposition to Godolphin and Marlborough. Richard Savage, 4th Earl Rivers, was a general who at first enjoyed Marlborough's patronage, but he too slid across to the opposition, and succeeded Marlborough when he was dismissed as master general of the ordnance. Both were disappointed military commanders who became political opponents, and both, when the dice rolled again, lost their offices under George I and died in exile.

In April 1707 Galway was beaten by Berwick at Almanza and several British regiments were destroyed, and in late 1710 the capitulation of a British force at Brihuega effectively doomed Allied hopes in Spain. Marlborough, as captain general, was part of the opposition's target when the Tory leader Henry St John attacked the government for failing to ensure that the Almanza regiments were up to strength: of almost 30,000 troops on the payroll for Spain fewer than 9,000 had actually been present at the battle. Marlborough was then involved in trying to find extra recruits for 're-forming broken battalions', for influential colonels were not prepared to see their regiments disappear, at precisely the same time that Flanders made its own inexorable demands for man-power and, as a theatre commander in his own right, Marlborough had a campaign to fight.

Gentlemen of the Staff

This workload was unending and potentially crushing, and if its tenor changed between the campaign season and the winter months, its weight scarcely ever receded. Marlborough coped as well as he did not simply because of personal energy and an acute brain, but because the delegation of routine work was fundamental to his style of command. His principal staff officer, 'quartermaster general' in the terminology of the age, was William Cadogan. Cadogan's family was Welsh, but his grandfather had gone to Ireland with Charles I's lord deputy, Thomas Wentworth, Earl of Strafford. He later became a major in the parliament-arian army and served as governor of Trim Castle, whose massy square Norman keep still guards the River Boyne many miles upstream of the battlefield. His son Henry married Bridget, daughter of the regicide Sir Hardress Waller, and they had two sons and two daughters. Henry Cadogan was determined that William, born in 1672, should follow him into the law, and he duly went to Trinity College Dublin, where he met the convivial Lord Raby, subsequently Earl of Strafford.

William Cadogan escaped north when the Jacobites arrived in 1689, and was commissioned as a cornet in the Enniskillen Dragoons. He fought on the Boyne and took part in Marlborough's attacks on Cork and Kinsale. In 1694 he bought a captaincy in Thomas Erle's Regiment of Foot, and was present when William of Orange recaptured Namur the following year. Cadogan went back to the Enniskillen Dragoons as major in 1698, but in 1701 we find him entrusted with the transport of Danish troops to the Low Countries, dealing with issues which went well beyond the responsibilities of the average major. 'I had by the Danish post that came in this morning letters from the Duke of Württemberg and Mr Gregg,' he told secretary Blathwayt,

> which to my very great satisfaction brought an account that the final order was given for the march of the troops and that it would be dispatched by the same post, of which I immediately sent notice to the Danish Commissary General, and to let him know how we were now ready to receive the troops. I have ordered the ships to fall down the

river with the first tide to Gluckstadt, and having before settled everything in relation to the march of the horse, there can be no further delay in this matter.[26]

There is no direct evidence that Cadogan knew Marlborough well because they had served together at Cork and Kinsale. After all, Marlborough was a lieutenant general and Cadogan a cornet, although his huge size did mean that he was a hard man to miss. Winston S. Churchill's assertion that 'they were already old friends' is pure speculation. However, Cadogan had certainly earned Blathwayt's approval by the way he dealt with the Dutch in early 1702, and the circumstances argue strongly for some previous relationship with Marlborough, because that summer he was appointed colonel of foot and quartermaster general on ten shillings a day. Marlborough gained him an extraordinary payment of £175.4s early in 1703, and soon afterwards he was appointed colonel of the Earl of Arran's Regiment of Horse.

Cadogan's career now moved in parallel with Marlborough's. He was promoted steadily, and, like his chief, made a handsome profit from a variety of perquisites and investments. In 1709 he was able to spend over £6,000 buying the Caversham estate near Reading, and his share of what his most recent biographer calls the 'net fraudulent profit' on insider dealing in 1708 alone was over £33,000.[27] In 1706 he slid easily into the House of Commons, in the Whig interest, as Member for Woodstock, a borough firmly in Marlborough's pocket.

If we deplore Cadogan's avarice we cannot but admire his courage. After the fall of Marlborough he must have known that his own future was decidedly cloudy, but he wrote to Robert Harley, now Earl of Oxford and one of the main agents of Marlborough's downfall, asking permission to join him on his travels on the Continent. 'The Duke of Marlborough's ill-health,' he wrote, 'the inconvenience a winter's journey exposes him to, and his being without any one friend to accompany him, make the requesting leave to wait on him an indispensable duty on me, who for so many years have been honoured with his confidence and favour and [owe] all I have in the world to his favour.'[28] He was allowed leave, and was, as he must have expected, dismissed from all his appointments immediately afterwards.

When Marlborough's fortunes turned again, Cadogan shared them. In February 1718, in uneasy combination with the Duke of Argyll, he was commanding the government forces putting down the Jacobite rebellion in Scotland, and heard that he was to receive a peerage.

He wrote to Marlborough at once, to 'beg leave to return my most humble thanks for your great goodness in being pleased to approve of the services I have endeavoured to render here, and Your Grace's representing them so very favourably to His Majesty'.

He hoped to have his barony styled 'of Cadogan, near Wrexham on the borders of Wales'. He reminded Marlborough that he had no son, and had settled his fortune on his brother, and so it would be very generous if the title could slide sideways after his own death. 'I humbly beg pardon for mentioning it,' he wrote, as if they were still back in the old days, as commander-in-chief and quartermaster general, 'and entreat Your Grace to consider it no more than if I had not.'[29] At that time the tiny hamlet of Cadogan was not deemed suitable to sustain a peerage, but when, after a flurry of distinguished diplomatic work, Cadogan was raised to an earldom, he was duly made 'Earl of Cadogan in Denbighshire; Viscount of Caversham in Oxfordshire; and Baron Oakley, in Buckinghamshire'.[30]

Cadogan was big, hard-headed – often with a glass in his hand but rarely in drink – and an inveterate gambler, both at the tables and, less creditably, by advising his London-based business partner to bet on the progress of campaigns. 'They now give 20 Guineas for £100 if either Mons, Charleroi, Lille, Tournai or Namur be not taken by the last of October,' wrote his cautious associate, 'but I won't venture without your advice.'[31] In the autumn of 1707, when Cadogan replaced George Stepney as envoy to the States-General, the same friend wrote to 'congratulate you on two pieces of good news that the town is full of, one that you have won six thousand pistoles at play, and the other that you are to reside at the Hague in the room of Mr Stepney'.[32] Cadogan spoke fluent French, and in 1702 he married Margaretta Munter, a beautiful Dutch heiress, and quickly added both Dutch and German to his languages.

Careful study of both the Cadogan papers and the Marlborough–Cadogan correspondence in the British Library shows the real scale of Cadogan's contribution. First, during the winter months he was in charge of what we would now, less than elegantly, term 'force packaging' and was then called drawing up the order of battle. The Allied forces for the coming campaigning season were divided into brigades, usually on a national basis. Larger formations like divisions did not then exist, but it was customary to divide an army up into formations of the right and left wing, and sometimes to subdivide these further into first and second lines, appointing general officers to command them. Frustratingly for historians, these definitions held good for the whole of a campaign, so it was perfectly possible for the army's right wing to find itself, after a good deal of marching and countermarching, on the left flank of the battle.

The process of drawing up the order of battle needed careful thought, to gratify national preferences and minimise clashes of personalities. Although generals might not always find it easy to ensure that another nation's contingents complied with their orders, the generals of an allied army ranked on a common roll of seniority by the date of their current commission, and it was important to ensure that nations supplying large contingents did not suddenly find themselves commanded by a very senior officer from another, much less significant, force. In August 1703 Marlborough warned Godolphin:

> If I leave the army some time before they go to garrison, it would be for the honour of the English that the right wing should be commanded by an Englishman; and that can't be, there being several lieutenant generals among the foreigners that are elder [i.e. senior] than our lieutenant generals, so that I would beg the favour of the Queen that I might have a commission sent to me for my brother, he being the oldest [English] lieutenant general, to be General of the Foot. I desire that nobody might know of the commission, for if I did not leave the army before they went into garrison, I would not make use of the commission.[33]

When Marlborough went back to England the following month General Charles Churchill duly took command of the right wing of the army, the troops in English pay.

In the winter months Cadogan compiled orders of battle, sent them to England for Marlborough's approval, and then awaited orders for 'assembling the army at the time your Grace is pleased to direct it'. Assembling too early would start the logistic meter ticking too soon, with foraging parties bringing in hay and bread contractors busy. Assembling it too late, though, might mean that the French would be able to steal a march. In April 1709 Cadogan informed Marlborough: 'Fine weather has forwarded everything, and a great deal of the corn which was thought lost begins to spring out again, so that suffering the assembly of the army for eight or ten days is as long as any will require.'[34] On 10 April 1710 he acknowledged receipt of Marlborough's letter of the eighth, and said that he was prepared

> to give *all* orders that may be necessary in your Grace's name. 'Tis with great satisfaction that I acquaint your Grace our magazines and

everything of that kind are in the readiness that could be desired, and due care is taken for the providing wood, straw and [?] in the places the troops encamp at in their passage, what relates to the bread and bread wagons is also requested, so that I hope your Grace on joining the army will find all matters in the forwardness and order you expected.[35]

He did not merely act as the passive instrument of Marlborough's endeavour, but developed operational plans along the lines laid down in outline by his chief. In February 1711 he announced:

I have the honour to enclose to your Grace the memorial I prepared for assembling the army in the middle of April NS [New Style, i.e. according to the Continental calendar] in order to make the siege of Douai. I [have] not entered into any reasons concerning the importance of the design, the facility of the expedition, or the impossibility of the enemy's being able to provide supplies to subsist a body of troops able either to oppose our forming the siege, or to embarrass us by a diversion . . . This project is founded on taking the field on the 10th of April NS and success absolutely depends upon it.[36]

Douai duly fell in June.

Cadogan had prime responsibility for the army's logistics, dealing with the Dutch contractors who supplied bread to the army when it was not so far from its bases that it was forced to bake its own. Roads and waterways alike were his concern. In August 1710 he wrote from Courtrai, possibly to Marlborough's private secretary, to say:

I received at Lille the favour of yours by Colonel Alexander. I have endeavoured to execute his Grace's commands in relation to the bread, and hope such measures as are now taken about that matter, as shall remove all . . . complaint in the future. I was obliged to go beyond St Eloi to meet the artillery boats. I came on with them all night and they are now passing the sluices at Harleseck. They will get this afternoon to Menin, and I hope tonight or tomorrow morning at the camp. If my Lord Duke should not be at home when this comes into your hands, I beg the enclosed may be sent to him.[37]

Cadogan was also Marlborough's intelligence chief. He collated information extracted from prisoners and deserters, and given by officers who had been taken prisoner but were then exchanged. In August 1702, for instance, Lord Mark Kerr, Marlborough's aide de camp, was captured and entertained by the Duke of Berwick, then a lieutenant general, who generously, as one nobleman to another, showed him the French army. The youngster kept his wits about him and reported that the French had seventy-two battalions and 109 squadrons, 'but he says that our battalions are much stronger than theirs'.

In addition to dealing with day-to-day tactical intelligence, Cadogan ran a network of agents in France, especially at the principal seaports. In 1708, for example, his agent at Dunkirk told him that a French fleet was ready to embark fifteen battalions and the Old Pretender in person, and he was informed immediately the fleet sailed northwards. He then sent a sloop, escorted by a fast Dutch privateer, to tell Admiral Sir George Byng what was afoot, and prepared to embark ten British and Dutch battalions for Scotland, the expedition's probable destination, as soon as a convoy arrived.[38] In the event the comte de Forbin, commanding the French squadron, missed his landfall, and by the time he entered the Firth of Forth, his selected objective, Byng was close behind. Forbin did not regard the loss of his little squadron as a price worth paying to get James's force ashore, and he ran for it, losing one ship, the *Salisbury*, captured in 1703, to her namesake HMS *Salisbury* in the pursuit. Forbin had mishandled the expedition, but even if James had landed the countermeasures initiated by Cadogan would probably have doomed the enterprise.

The collation of information gleaned from agents and the interception of mail over the winter months enabled Cadogan to help Marlborough fix his annual campaign plan. At the opening of the 1710 campaigning season he gave Marlborough a full intelligence brief as soon as he arrived, telling him of

> my appointing the several persons I employ, to meet me on Tuesday next at Tournai. As your Grace arrives at Ghent only on Wednesday, I can come from Tournai early on Thursday to met you at Oudenarde and give your Grace an account of all I shall be able to learn of the enemy's strength in the lines . . .[39]

Some of his intelligence was of strategic importance, and went straight to the government. In May 1709, when the French were making discreet overtures for peace, he told Sunderland that three enemy agents with passports from the Dutch had passed through The Hague on their way to Antwerp. One was 'the post-master of Paris; and the other a Spanish courier'. He thought that the third was Marshal Boufflers, travelling incognito. Two days later he confirmed that Torcy, the French foreign minister, had passed through Brussels, and a week afterwards he was able to forward to Sunderland the peace terms Torcy had covertly offered to the Dutch. He was later able to tell Sunderland:

> The last advices from Paris say the Dauphin with the Marshal Villars is to command here next summer, the Duke of Burgundy with the Marshal d'Harcourt on the Rhine, and the Duke of Burgundy in Dauphiné . . .
>   None of the French troops on this frontier have as yet received either money, clothes or recruits, nor is there any appearance of even endeavouring to form such magazines as will be necessary to subsist the troops they must bring into the field to cover their places exposed in Flanders.[40]

Some information was paid for in cash, but there was sometimes a hint of payment in kind. 'You will give me leave to remember my good friend the *Conseiller Intime*,' Cadogan told Marlborough's private secretary in 1705. 'I hope the Tokay and the lady are provided for him as promised.'[41]

Cadogan's practical good sense meant that he was never misled by simple theoretical strengths. Precise organisations varied a good deal, and some regiments (like the four-battalion Régiment du Roi) were very much bigger than others, so the armies of the age reckoned their infantry strength in battalions and their cavalry strength in squadrons. A battalion, usually commanded by a lieutenant colonel, consisted of several companies, and was meant to comprise eight hundred officers and men, while a squadron of cavalry contained two to four troops under a major or a senior captain, and had a strength of perhaps 150 officers and men. Unit numbers, often high at the start of a campaign, tended to fall off as the season wore on because of battle casualties, sickness and desertion. It was easy for one army to have more battalions and squadrons than its adversary, but actually to have fewer soldiers. In June 1707 Cadogan told Raby that Marlborough had one hundred battalions of foot and 164 squadrons of horse facing 120 French battalions and 190 squadrons, but the latter were 'so weak that our troops who are all complete exceed them in number as much as in goodness. I think the King of France does with his troops as his money, makes three hundred men pass for a battalion, as a Louis d'or for Fifteen Livres, and our folly gives this cheat currency.'[42]

Cadogan's officers needed to pay constant attention to the fluctuating strengths of friendly and enemy forces. Amongst the papers of Henry Davenant, English envoy to Frankfurt and Regensburg and one of Cadogan's correspondents, are numerous orders of battle of troops provided by German states, as well as detailed assessments, apparently from a French source, of enemy strengths. French battalions, each of thirteen companies (themselves of forty-five men and three officers apiece), should comprise 624 soldiers, and squadrons, each of four troops of thirty-five men and three officers, should number 152 soldiers. 'But,' added Davenant's French informant, 'as the infantry is not usually fully up to strength, we can reckon the battalion at 550 men at the opening of the campaign,' falling to five hundred or even 450 as it went on.[43]

Cadogan was even more than chief of staff, master logistician and chief of intelligence. When the army was on the move he often commanded the cavalry of the advance guard, moving about half a day ahead of the main body, likely to meet the enemy first and send a contact report back to Marlborough. At Ramillies he found the French deploying for battle, and informed Marlborough, who then hurtled forward to view the ground and make his plans while the army swung along behind. At Oudenarde, the least planned of Marlborough's great battles, Cadogan commanded the whole of the advance guard, horse and foot, took the village of Eyne and then held it against the odds as the French counterattack rolled in. He was indeed a general for all seasons.

In so much of what follows it is sometimes hard to see where Marlborough ended and Cadogan began. Lord Strafford, admittedly a boyhood friend of Cadogan's and a political foe of Marlborough's, told Robert Harley: 'I do believe the greatest part of my Lord Marlborough's victories are owing to him; and even the Pensionary said to me, "Si vous voulez avoir un duc de Marlborough un Cadogan est nécessaire." ' Yet recognising the part played by Cadogan does not diminish Marlborough's stature. He could not be everywhere and do everything, and the careful delegation of responsibility, with authority to back it up, enabled him to shine as commander, alliance manager, administrator and diplomat.

Of course Cadogan could not shoulder his burden alone. His own staff, many of them holding appointments as deputy quartermaster generals, plied devolved authority of their own. Captain Richard King of Lord Orrery's Regiment was authorised in 1707 to draw £100 in his capacity as assistant engineer by the master general of the ordnance, a good example of Marlborough rewarding in one capacity services done to him in another. As one of Cadogan's deputies King was responsible for dealing with civilians who found themselves on the army's line of march. In June 1709 a countess wrote from Malines:

> I hear that you are on the march with the Palatine troops and are likely to pass this town. In that case, Sir, I beg you to remember that we are interested in Bonheiden, where we have meadows which may be greatly damaged by the passage of troops. So, Sir, if you can avoid that route we shall be eternally grateful to you.

She added, 'if you pass by Malines yourself give us at least the pleasure of making use of our house'. Her husband was away at the moment, but sent his best wishes. Ambassador Stepney's secretary, Mr Laws, wrote to ask if two villages near Brussels 'may be entirely spared if possible and left off the routes by which the troops are to return to their winter quarters'. He too was able to hint at some reward, for 'I am employed in this affair by so fair a person that I persuade myself, when you see her, her thanks will be a sufficient recompense for your trouble, though she granted you no other favour.' The implication, of course, is that she might just have other favours in mind.

Captain King also dealt with bread-and-butter letters on Cadogan's behalf. On 13 September 1708 Cadogan asked him to thank an officer 'for his letter and exact account he gave me of everything'. He could not write a decent letter himself because he had been on the move for two days and 'I drop asleep as I write.' King was a colonel in 1711, and squared himself with Marlborough's enemies before his fall. The Hanoverian succession and Marlborough's reinstatement ruined him, and he disappears from history in 1716, blind and searching desperately for a cure.[44]

Most letters from Cadogan are not in his own 'round, half-formed schoolboy's hand, not very beautiful to look at but very easy to read', but are instead the work of clerks or assistants. He generally wrote to Marlborough in his own hand, however, and in February 1716, though a full general and commander-in-chief in Scotland, nonetheless apologised because 'my arm being extremely bruised and my shoulder bone wounded by a fall I got riding from Aberdeen to Montrose obliges me to make use of another hand to write to your Grace'.[45] Similarly, many of Marlborough's letters were written by secretaries or clerks, and his private secretary, Adam de Cardonnel, not only ran his private office in the field but led for the headquarters on many matters that were diplomatic rather than strictly military. Incoming packages of mail from the same source might be divided up between Cadogan and Cardonnel. On 26 June 1710 Cadogan told Marlborough: 'I send Mr Cardonnel by this cover a relating of what was done in the conference here these two days past, by which your Grace will find the present want of the contractors are supplied with an advance of five hundred and fifty thousand guilders . . .'[46]

Adam de Cardonnel, the second son of a Huguenot refugee who had got no further than Southampton, and there prospered, had become chief clerk in the secretary at war's office, and was appointed Marlborough's private secretary early in 1692. During Marlborough's ascendancy he was rewarded by a parliamentary seat at Southampton, eventually being designated secretary of war in place of Walpole in 1710, although he did not actually succeed to the office, for George Granville's Tory friends secured it instead. In February 1712 he was expelled from the House for having accepted an annual sweetener of five hundred gold ducats from Sir Solomon de Medina, the army's main bread contractor. Many MPs had done far worse, but Cardonnel was, as his *Dictionary of National Biography* entry asserts, 'a pawn in a larger political game'. His wife died the following year, and Marlborough, then in exile in Frankfurt, wrote him a touching letter.

> I would have written to you sooner, dear Cardonnel, if I had believed it possible to say anything to lessen your grief; but I think of all the worldly misfortunes, the losing what one loves is the greatest, and nothing but time can ease you. However, I could not deny myself any longer the satisfaction of writing to assure you that I shall always be very sorry for anything that is a trouble to you, and that I long for the opportunity of assuring you myself that I am your humble servant and faithful friend.

He remained Marlborough's secretary until his death in 1719, and was buried in Chiswick, not far from Marlborough's old lover Barbara Castlemaine.

Cardonnel's correspondence, much of it now in the British Library, gives a penetrating view of attitudes at Marlborough's headquarters. In July 1703 he told John Ellis, an under-secretary in London, that both Marlborough and the deputies wanted the Dutch engineer Coehoorn to besiege Ostend, 'but I find 'twill be very difficult to persuade the old gentleman to do his part, so that in all probability we soon return again towards the Maas'. He added: 'My Lord Duke has a very hard task indeed to keep our generals in humour and to prevent their falling out among themselves, particularly Lieut General Slangenburg, who is of a very unhappy temper to command an army.'[47] Although Cardonnel was not a soldier, he ran many of a soldier's risks. On the way to Blenheim in 1704 he reported: 'Our last march was all in fire and smoke. I wish to God it were well over that I might get safe out of this country.' In May 1706 he told Ambassador Stepney that the pursuit after Ramillies had left him 'almost dead with the fatigue of marching, fighting (or at least the fright and apprehension of it) and writing for three days together without any rest'.[48]

The wars of the period were divided into distinct annual campaigns, although on occasion a commander might mount a surprise attack in the winter if he thought the reason good enough. In the winter of 1703–04 Colonel de la Colonie, troubled by the raids of Imperial hussars ('a sort bandit on horseback'), led three hundred of his Bavarian grenadiers and two squadrons of cavalry to the village where they were quartered and took them by surprise in the darkness. The hussars turned out in their shirts, but could offer no effective resistance to men who were not over-anxious to take prisoners. De la Colonie killed four hundred and captured another 140 without the loss of a man. This was, however, exceptional, and generals usually preferred to wait until there was hay for their horses to eat and the roads were firm enough to bear the weight of guns and wagons.

Some Allied contingents simply marched home when the season ended, and the remainder went into garrison in the United Provinces or captured territory of the Spanish Netherlands following plans developed by Cadogan and his staff. British officers tried to get home on leave, to see to family business, sit in Parliament or hunt the fox, for the fox-hunting and campaigning seasons were closely aligned, or simply to recruit. Each March the *London Gazette* gave its call to arms.

It is Her Majesty's Royal Will and Pleasure, that the General Officers, Field Officers, and all others whatever, belonging to the Army in Flanders, do repair forthwith to their respective commands, and not omit the opportunity of the present Embarkation, which is appointed the 15th Instant, upon pain of Her Majesty's highest Displeasure.[49]

Drafts were recruited during the winter to bring regiments up to strength. In November 1711 the *Gazette* told its readers that:

> The Lord High Treasurer of Great Britain, having issued into the hands of the Paymaster-General of Her Majesty's Forces a sufficient sum of money for recruiting the army in Flanders, notice is hereby given to the several agents of the regiments concerned that they do apply for their proportion of what they are to receive thereof, which they are to distribute to the officers of the respective regiments to enable them immediately to proceed upon their service. And the General Officers of the army having allotted what counties each Regiment shall recruit in.[50]

In January 1712 the *Gazette* announced that just a few 'able-bodied men are wanting to supply Her Majesty's Royal Artillery in Flanders', and men wishing to join 'may repair to Colonel Pendlebury, at his house in the Tower, any morning, and shall enter into perfect pay, and have further encouragement'.[51] Elsewhere regimental recruiting parties followed the process so beautifully described in George Farquhar's play *The Recruiting Officer* (1706), with the likes of Captain Plume and Sergeant Kite encouraging men to leave nagging wives, pushy parents or harsh employers and go off to pull down the French tyrant. Kite urges them to meet him 'at the sign of the Spread Eagle, in this good town of Shrewsbury', where they will immediately receive suitable 'relief and entertainment'. He does rather well to recruit five men in a single week, 'the strong man of Kent, the King of the Gypsies, a Scotch pedlar, a Scoundrel Attorney and a Welsh parson'. Plume forces him to release the attorney, for he cannot abide literate men, who are sure to get up petitions.

Desertion was a constant plague, and the *London Gazette* regularly contained descriptions of men who had run from their colours. In October 1704 it announced:

> Deserted out of the Rt Hon the Lord Paston's Regiment in his own company, Rob. Weston, a well-set man, about 5 foot 5 inches high, a fresh complexion, round visaged, aged about 24 years, supposed to be gone to Sheffield in Yorkshire; Rich. Brown, about 5 foot 6 inches high, thin visaged, swarthy complexioned, aged about 22 years, a locksmith; Benj. Lowe and John Tawits, both shoemakers by trade; Rich. Dewberry, aged about 44 years, 5 foot 6 inches high, light brown hair,

bald on his crown, a miller; Steph. Burrel, about 5 foot 5 inches high, aged about 26 years, wears a wig, hath lately had the small-pox, and born at Diss in Norfolk . . . If they will return to the company in 14 days they shall be kindly received; or, whoever apprehends them, so as they may be brought to justice, they shall receive for each man two guineas, to be paid by Mr Rob. Perryman, agent to the said regiment, at his house in Leicester Fields.[52]

The fact that Tilbury was the rendezvous suggests that Paston's men were about to embark for Flanders, though it was late in the year to move a regiment.

Marlborough sometimes spent part of the winter on the Continent, but he normally returned home before the campaign season started, and then left England in March or April, often crossing by yacht from Harwich to Helvoetsluis. Sarah sometimes accompanied him to the port, and Marlborough always felt the separation keenly. 'It is impossible for me to express with what a heavy heart I parted with you,' he told her when he set off for the 1702 campaign.

> I would have given my life to come back but I know my own weakness so much that I darest not for I know I should have exposed myself [revealed his feelings] to the company: I did for a great while with a perspective glass look upon the cliffs in hopes I might have had the sight of you, we are now out of sight of Margate, and I have neither soul nor spirits, but I do at this minute suffer so much that nothing but being with you again can recompense it. If you could be sensible of what I now feel you would endeavour ever to be easy to me, and then I should be most happy, for it is you only that can give me some content . . . [53]

Marlborough normally visited The Hague to see Heinsius and other important officials before setting off south to join the army. Although he sometimes undertook long journeys by coach, on campaign he generally rode, with fresh mounts being provided from a string of horses under the care of his 'gentleman of the horse', Colonel Bringfield, who was killed at Ramillies. On 11 July 1703 he closed a letter to Sarah, written the day before, saying: 'I am just come off my horse where I have been near 14 hours, so that I own to you that I am so weary that I have not spirits to write any more, especially when I know I must be on horseback by three o'clock tomorrow morning.'[54]

At that time European capitals were connected by regular posts, leaving perhaps twice a week, and national authorities then distributed mail internally. London now had a general post office with some forty sorters, and it had recently become possible for 'cross posts' to go between major towns without passing through the capital. On average a postboy would take six days to ride from London to Edinburgh. Posts from London to The Hague and vice versa usually took three days, but bad weather in the Channel could leave a backlog at the ports, and sometimes a packet boat went down in a storm or was snatched by Dunkirk privateers, rather interrupting the mail. An express, the equivalent of modern special delivery, ran outside the times of the normal post, but it too ran the risk of being stopped by bad weather. Really important documents, like first reports of battles, would be sent by hand of an officer, and Marlborough assured Sarah that he would always send her a letter if he had an official courier on the way. Although her fierce temper did not always make her a comfortable spouse, when she wished to be loving she could certainly charm. 'Wherever you are, whilst I have life my soul shall follow you my ever dear Lord Marlborough,' she wrote in 1701–02, 'and wherever I am I shall only kill the time, *with the night that I may sleep* & hope the next day to hear from you.'[55]

The post was notoriously insecure, and many correspondents used simple codes to screen their meaning. Marlborough and his circle replaced names and places by numbers, which changed from time to time. In August 1710, for instance, he gave Sarah instructions about the Woodstock election.

> 39 [Marlborough] shall expect more assistance in 87 [Parliament] from 197 [Cadogan] and 202 [Sir Thomas Wheate, the other MP for Woodstock] than any numbers . . . I do earnestly desire that these two men may be chosen preferable to all others which I desire you will lose no time in acquainting 38 [Godolphin] and that I beg it of him as a particular favour, and that he would take care of securing an election for 202, for 39 does not think it absolutely necessary to have him early in 108 [England] this winter, of which he will take care.[56]

Despite the quality of his staff, his own acumen and growing experience, there were moments when Marlborough found his burden almost intolerable. Sarah's occasional sulks, apparently worsened by the approaching menopause, meant that she was not always as reliable a source of comfort as that other lodestar of Marlborough's existence,

Sidney Godolphin. In the depth of gloom after a battle which failed to materialise because of Allied disobedience, with Sarah ill and no word from her, he told Godolphin: 'I am in so ill humour, that I will not trouble you, nor dare I trust myself to write more. But believe this truth; that I honour, and love you, my Lady Marlborough, and would die for the Queen.'[57]

First Campaign

In 1701 the War of Spanish Succession had opened well for the Allies in Italy, where the Imperialist general Prince Eugène of Savoy had first thrashed Marshal Catinat and gone on to capture his successor, Marshal Villeroi, in a midwinter attack on Cremona. There had been no fighting in the Low Countries, although the initial French incursion into the barrier fortresses had placed them in an advantageous position before a shot had been fired. For the 1702 campaign the French, like their opponents, had to find troops for other theatres of war, and the size of their field armies was reduced by the constant need to garrison fortresses. However, for the first few months of the campaign in the Low Countries the weight of numbers told in their favour.

When Marlborough arrived to take command in July, Marshal Boufflers had just jabbed hard at the main Allied army under the Earl of Athlone (Godert de Ginkel, commanding by virtue of his Dutch commission), which had fallen back on the fortress of Nijmegen. Boufflers was now close to invading the republic's own territory, but Marlborough at once saw that there was nothing to be gained by mere frontal defence. Instead, an Allied crossing of the Meuse below Grave would threaten Boufflers' communications, especially if some simultaneous pressure could be put on the French right on the lower Rhine. Before the Allies could reach a decision on this plan Louis ordered Boufflers to divert a strong detachment to the upper Rhine, giving Marlborough a clear numerical edge. Yet the Dutch were still not confident, and, as Marlborough told Godolphin, 'the fears the Dutch have of Nijmegen and the Rhine, creates such difficulties when we come to take a resolution we were forced to send to the Hague'.[58] He pressed Heinsius hard, telling him:

> It is a shameful thing our lying idle and letting Marshal Boufflers make his detachments for the upper Rhine, that I have no patience . . . Will not Prince Louis of Baden [Allied commander on the upper Rhine]

have great reason to be angry when a superior army does not hinder the enemy from sending detachments nor send none themselves? Till we act offensively, all things must go ill.[59]

The Dutch did not approve the plan till 22 July, and Sergeant John Wilson tells us what happened as soon as Marlborough heard that he could move.

> We continued in this ground without any motion till . . . there was orders to the pontoons to march to the right to lay two bridges over the Maas, as also for the [artillery] train and wheel baggage to march that afternoon by way of . . . Grave. At night there was orders for the quartermaster general, the vanguard and the camp colour men to parade on the right of the front line by four o'clock in the morning and the General to beat at 5.00. Which orders were all punctually obeyed and the army decamped accordingly and that day passed the Maas and advances about two and a half leagues and there encamped. Whereupon the enemy decamped also . . . [60]

This is a classic description of an early-eighteenth-century army at its business. Although the Maas at Grave is a wide and stately river, it was the stock in trade of engineers to bridge it with pontoons, boats carried to the river on carts, floated, anchored and roped together before being turned into bridges by the addition of wooden trackway. Wheeled vehicles and heavy baggage were wisely sent over the fixed bridge in the town. Soldiers, roused from their slumbers by the drag and paradiddle of the general call to arms, drew up in line when the assembly was beaten perhaps half an hour later. Normally the troops to march first were on the right of the line, and included Cadogan with a small cavalry escort, and then the army's vanguard. The camp colourmen were guides from each battalion who carried 'camp colours', small identifying flags which would enable their commanding officers to identify their allocated campsite at the end of the day's march. It was as well to start the whole process as soon as it was light enough to strike camp, to ensure that there was plenty of daylight left when the army reached its next campsite. A river crossing and a march of two and a half leagues (seven and a half miles) was a good day's work.

As soon as the Allies moved, Boufflers behaved just as Marlborough had expected and moved south as quickly as he could, crossing the Meuse at Roermond, now having to march very close to the Allied army and, as Richard Kane saw, 'in great perplexity to get by us'. The little garrison of Gravenbock found itself in the middle of the Allied army, and both sides could hear the other's daily routine. The evening drumbeat of the tattoo, its name derived from the Dutch *doe ten tap toe*, was an instruction for camp settlers to 'turn off the tap' of the wine or beer barrel and for soldiers to turn in. Accurate timekeeping was never easy, and usually a gun was fired from the artillery park to tell regimental drummers to set about their noisy business, as Sergeant Wilson remembered.

> We being then encamped . . . at Gravenbock, the English [artillery] train according to the ancient custom of war, fired the tattoo gun. Upon which all the drums in the army according to order beat off the tattoo and the French garrison in Gravenbock beat their tattoo at the same time, notwithstanding they were within the heart of our camp. Of which my Lord Marlborough being informed, replied with a smile, 'If they beat a tattoo tonight, I'll beat the reveille in the morning.'[61]

Marlborough was not noted for his sense of humour, and he followed this rather crisp quip by immediately constituting a small attacking force, including cannon, an assault party and an unarmed working party under Brigadier Henry Withers, and by dawn the next day the French garrison was encircled by trenches. After a brief exchange of artillery fire the governor offered to surrender with the honours of war.

> But the Brigadier sent them word that they must content to be prisoners at discretion or he would enter the fort sword in hand and neither he nor any of them need expect quarter. Which the governor considered and submitted to be prisoners at discretion. Upon which the command under arms and also the workmen entered the fort and pillaged and made booty of all they could find therein and then demolished the same.[62]

There were several opportunities for a battle on favourable terms for the Allies, but all of them were vetoed by the field deputies, who argued, perhaps rather more reasonably than British historians sometimes suggest, that there was no point in running the risk of a battle unless its outcome was absolutely certain now that the object of the campaign had been achieved and the French had `been drawn away from their borders.

On the first of these occasions Boufflers tried to slip away by using the risky expedient of a night march, having first mounted a grand foraging expedition so that it looked as if he proposed to stay where he was for some time. Marlborough, however, was not taken in, and ordered his men 'to lie on their arms all night'. 'By the time it was day,' recalled Robert Parker,

> their front had entered the heath, and my Lord Marlborough had his men under arms, and just ready to march, when the Field-Deputies came to him, and prayed him to desist. This greatly surprised him, as they had agreed to his scheme the night before: but being a man of great temper and prudence, and being determined not to do anything this first campaign without their approbation, at their earnest entreaty he desisted.[63]

In fact Marlborough was quite content not to fight. He had told Godolphin that his real objective was to 'oblige them to quit the Meuse, by which we shall be able to besiege Venlo', and that is precisely what he now did.[64]

Marlborough began the siege of Venlo, bringing the now redundant garrisons of Nijmegen and Grave, as well as a Prussian detachment from the lower Rhine, down to help. While the besiegers commenced their stately choreography, Marlborough kept a powerful covering force under his hand, and when Boufflers, on orders from Paris, tried to intercept the Allied siege train on its way in from Bois-le-Duc, Marlborough pounced, slipping in between Boufflers and his base, but missing the opportunity of a battle on favourable terms because the Dutch General Opdam did not move as quickly as he had hoped. It was this inaction that gave rise to Marlborough's exasperated letter of 16 August to Godolphin.[65] He was no better pleased with the early stages of the siege, and wrote to Heinsius:

> I think if you had been so lucky as to have left the command of the siege to [the Prussian commander] Baron de Heyden, we should now have been masters not only of this town but of all the Meuse, but as things now are I am apprehensive you may not have the town and may have your army beaten . . . The troops have been before Venlo these eight days, and they now talk of opening trenches two days hence. If this be zeal, God preserve me from being so served as you are, my friend. I take a liberty of writing freely to you . . . I write this by candle light, so that I know not if you will be able to read it.[66]

He reported himself 'very impatient to hear of the cannon being arrived at Venlo', but soon told Godolphin that trenches were open and the batteries installed: the siege had begun in earnest, and he would soon be able to tell him when the campaign would end.

Boufflers made no effort to raise the siege of Venlo. Fort St Michael, described by Robert Parker as 'a regular fortification of five bastions', covered the northern approaches. The attackers pushed their trenches on to the foot of its glacis, and, with a rather suppressed tow row row, the combined grenadiers of Hamilton's brigade were preparing to assault the covered way when that stormy petrel Lord Cutts gleefully informed their officers that if there was any opportunity of continuing beyond their objective they should press right on. 'We all thought these were very rash orders,' grumbled Parker, 'contrary to both the rules of war, and the design of the thing.'

At four in the afternoon the signal for the assault was given. The attackers rushed the covered way, and 'the enemy gave us one scattering fire only, and then ran away'. The grenadiers crossed the ditch and entered a ravelin protecting the curtain wall of the fort itself. The captain and sixty men guarding the ravelin were mostly killed, and the attackers then found a second, smaller ditch between themselves and the curtain. 'They that fled before us,' writes Parker,

> climbed up by the long grass, that grew out of the fort, so we climbed after them. Here we were hard put to it, to pull out the palisades, which pointed down upon us from the parapet; and was it not for the great surprise and consternation of those within we could never have surmounted this very point. But as soon as they saw us at this work, they quitted the rampart, and retired down to the parade [ground] in the body of the fort, where they lied down their arms, and cried for quarter, which was readily granted them.

Parker felt that the whole business had been unaccountably lucky. The retreating French had failed to throw the loose planks of the wooden bridge over the first ditch, 120 feet wide, into the water, and the governor was culpable in not keeping the grass 'close mown, as he ought to have done'. 'In the end,' Parker admitted, 'his Lordship had the glory of the whole action, though he never stirred out of the trenches till it was over.'[67] Richard Kane took much the same view, but added generously that 'the young Earl of Huntingdon', who had come along with Cutts as a volunteer, pluckily kept up with the foremost of the stormers the whole way. The episode did much to establish the reputation of the British troops, 'so that no one there could with modesty express, nor no one that was not believe', the valour of the attackers.[68]

The garrison of Venlo capitulated on 25 September, and marched out a few days later. As soon as he heard the news, Marlborough sent a detachment to snap up the little fortress of Stevensweert, and then moved the Venlo force straight up the Maas to besiege and capture Roermond too. Thus, as he told Godolphin, 'I hope before the end of this month we shall have cleared the Meuse from home to [the Dutch-held fortress of] Maastricht, after which I hope we may have time to force Marshal Boufflers to quit his post at Tongres.'[69]

He did rather better than that. Liège lay on the Maas south of Maastricht, and its commanding geographical position, between the hilly country of the Ardennes and the Eifel to the south and the 'Maastricht appendix' of Dutch territory to the north, made it just as important in 1702 as it was to prove in 1914. As long as the French held it they could move troops freely between Brabant and Flanders on their western flank to their lower Rhine garrisons at Cologne, Bonn and Düsseldorf. From his position at Tongres, the western apex of a triangle whose base was formed by Liège and Maastricht, Boufflers was well-placed to threaten the flank of an Allied advance down the Maas. He probably doubted that Marlborough would try for Liège so late in the season, and when the Allies moved south he botched his attempt to parry them and then, as a delighted Marlborough told Heinsius, 'abandoned Tongres after spending a whole month to fortify it'. The city of Liège had only medieval fortifications, and the city elders wisely opened their gates as soon as the Allies appeared before them.

The citadel, a powerful five-bastioned work on the high ground west of the Maas, staunchly held by Brigadier de Violaine with seven and a half battalions of infantry, was another matter. On 12 October NS it was besieged, and a practicable breach had been made by the twenty-second. Marlborough summoned the governor to surrender on terms, but 'he answered, it would be time enough a month hence, to talk of a surrender'. On 23 October the Allies mounted a general assault and stormed the place after only an hour's fighting. 'Our men gave no quarter for some time,' admitted Parker, 'so that the greater part of the garrison was cut to pieces.'[70] The official bulletin was more circumspect, the attackers 'having after the first fury been very merciful to the enemy'. Marlborough had already written to Lord Nottingham that day, but added a triumphant postscript.

The post being not gone, I could not but open this letter to let you know that, by the extraordinary bravery of the officers and soldiers, the citadel has been carried by storm, and, for the honour of her Majesty's subjects, the English were the first that got upon the breach, and the governor was taken by a lieutenant of Stewart's regiment.[71]

The four-battalion garrison of the nearby Chartreuse, a fortified monastery, were so dismayed by what had happened to the citadel that they surrendered on the twenty-sixth. 'They had liberty to march out with their hands in their pockets,' says Parker, 'and every man was to go where he pleased, by which means the officers carried very few of them home.'[72] The formal surrender terms are actually a good deal more generous. The garrison was allowed to march out 'with arms and baggage, drums beating and matches lit, to be conducted by a sufficient escort to Namur by the shortest route'.[73]

Marlborough still half-hoped to go on and take Huy, but realised that he had done enough, even if unusually he left a small force to take the fortress of Rheinberg in a winter campaign. Although Winston S. Churchill complains that Dutch interference had prevented his distin-guished ancestor from striking one of those 'crashing blows in the field' which became his hallmark, it is difficult to see what battle could have given Marlborough that deft manoeuvre did not. He had ended the risk of direct French attack on the United Provinces and cleared the whole line of the Maas to Liège, a feat so remarkable that it calls to mind Abraham Lincoln's comment about the Father of Waters flowing unvexed to the sea. He had wholly imposed his will on Marshal Boufflers, as the Duke of Berwick acknowledged. Boufflers, Berwick said, was 'in a dreadful embarrassment; though a man of great personal bravery, he stood in fear of the enemy, and on the other hand he knew in what manner he was spoken of both at court and in the army'.[74]

Although the siege of Rheinberg still went on, the army dispersed into winter quarters in the first week of November, and Marlborough set off for England. On 2 November he boarded a large yacht at Maastricht with General Opdam, the two Dutch field deputies and an escort of twenty soldiers. At Roermond they joined Coehoorn, who had a larger boat and a sixty-man escort. After dinner with the Prince of Holstein-Beck, the governor, they continued downstream, with fifty horsemen keeping pace with the boats and closing in to provide security at night. The cavalry escort changed at Venlo, and when the little party was about ten miles below the town it was attacked by a partisan band based on the

French garrison of Guelders, off to the east of the Meuse and not yet reduced.

The attackers were led by Lieutenant Farewell, an Irish deserter from Dutch service who had escaped from Maastricht under accusation of planning to set fire to the magazines. Arson in an artillery park was, by the old laws of war, punishable by being burnt alive, on the cruel logic of the punishment fitting the crime. Indeed, later in the war a French arsonist was 'burnt to death between two fires with every refinement of cruelty'. There is a case for assuming that Farewell, unlike his country-man Peter Drake, was ideologically committed to his cause, but the real story may be more complex. Farewell, who knew the ground well, chose a point where the cavalry escort had to leave the river, pounced on Marlborough's yacht and dragged it to the bank with the rope being used to haul the vessel along the river, fired a volley 'and then threw in several grenades'.

At the time senior officers regularly granted passports to enemy officers and officials, giving them safe conduct through territory in which they might be detained. The system did not simply accord with the age's notion of gentlemanly behaviour, but worked to the advantage of both sides by giving some freedom of movement to senior folk beyond the confines of the battlefield. Although the raiders knew the deputies by sight, and Farewell recognised Opdam, having 'stood sentry a hundred times over his tent', all three had valid passports signed by the Duke of Burgundy. Marlborough had no passport, but one of his clerks, Stephen Gell, quickly slipped him one made out for his brother, Lieutenant General Charles Churchill. The pass was in fact out of date and did not cover transit by water, but after a long discussion Farewell agreed to let Marlborough through, apparently either because of Charles Churchill's pass or by counting him as one of the two secretaries allowed to Field Deputy Gueldermalsen. The raiders took all the money and plate out of the vessel and carried off the escort as prisoners of war, but allowed Marlborough and the Dutchmen to continue.

Robert Parker thought that the partisans were 'more intent on booty than making prisoners', and let them pass 'when they had received a handsome present'.[75] The official bulletin declared that the attackers 'examined the several passports, without knowing my Lord Marlborough'. However, Farewell immediately slipped away from his party and appeared at The Hague, where he received a free pardon and a captaincy in the Dutch army. The Earl of Ailesbury believed that he had betrayed his trust, and would have deservedly been broken on the wheel if the French had ever caught him. He hinted that Marlborough had simply bought off Farewell: 'No doubt he had not the spirit of thrift at the time.'[76]

Marlborough certainly rewarded the quick-thinking Gell with a pension of £50 a year, and obtained him a post in the Exchange of Prisoners Office. The last of the letters printed in Murray's five-volume edition of his dispatches was written in March 1712 when Marlborough was out of office. In it he told Grand Pensionary Heinsius:

> Mr Gill has, I believe, the honour of being known to you, having served us all the war as a commissioner for the exchange of prisoners. Having particular obligations to him as he helped save me from enemy hands when I was captured on the Meuse, I would have much wished to do something for him; but as it is not in my power, please permit me to recommend him to the honour of your protection so that he can obtain some small employment or subsistence at the Hague, where he has lived for forty years.[77]

Marlborough was never a man to forget old obligations.

Empty Elevation

Shortly before Marlborough set off for England, Queen Anne had told Sarah that she knew that her husband 'deserves all that a rich crown can give. But since there is nothing else at this time, I hope you will give me leave as soon as he comes to make him a duke.'[78] Sarah was not convinced that it would be wise to accept. She did not think the family was rich enough to support the title, especially should she produce the numerous sons she might yet be blessed with, which tells us much about her private hopes. 'Though at the time I had myself but one,' she wrote later, 'yet I might have had more, and the next generation a great many.'[79] She told her husband of her misgivings in a letter which has not survived, and he replied from The Hague on 4 November OS: 'I shall have a mind to do nothing but as it may be easy with you. I do agree with you that we ought not to wish for a greater title until we have a better estate.'[80]

Two days later he told her that he had broached the matter with Heinsius, who suggested that he should accept the offer now that it was so clearly connected to a military success, rather than wait till the end of the war. 'He said if it were not done now in the heat of everybody's being pleased with what I had done,' wrote Marlborough, 'it would at any other time be thought the effect of favour, which would not be so great an honour to my family, nor to the Queen's service.'[81] Sarah met Marlborough when he arrived at Margate on 28 November, and they travelled up to London together. The following day the queen told the cabinet that she intended to make Marlborough a duke, and to grant him, for her lifetime, an annual pension of £5,000 from Post Office revenue to enable him to support the dignity, hoping that Parliament would vote him a similar sum. On 2 December she made his promotion public, and eight days later the proposed pension was debated by the Commons.

The Tory majority in the new Parliament had already shown its teeth by voting a congratulatory address which affirmed that 'the vigorous support of Your Majesty's Allies and the wonderful progress of Your Majesty's armies under the conduct of the Earl of Marlborough have signally retrieved the ancient honour and glory of the English nation'. This was anti-Williamite and thus anti-Whig, and a similar address commending the navy's descent on Vigo Bay, where the Spanish treasure fleet was taken, was regarded by Sarah as an affront: how could one naval action take station with a string of successes on land? There was even more to it than that. By commending naval commanders alongside Marlborough, the Tories were making clear their presence for the 'traditional' British strategy based on seapower, rather than a Continental commitment. The queen responded by ordering a victory procession through the City, and Bishop Trelawney preached on Joshua 22: 8–9, 'Return with much riches unto your tents, and with very much cattle, with silver, and with gold, and with brass, and with iron, and with very much raiment: divide the spoil of your enemies with your brethren.'[82]

No amount of public rejoicing could blunt the Tories' assault on the pension proposals, and on 15 December the measure was withdrawn. Anne generously offered the Marlboroughs £2,000 a year from her privy purse, but Sarah, arguing that they had had enough already, turned it down. The episode did much to confirm Sarah in her hatred of the Tories. Her correspondence with Anne already revealed that they were in different political camps. Although Anne 'would never have you & your poor unfortunate faithful Morley differ in opinion in the least thing', she went on to tell Sarah, unusually forcefully, that she quite misunderstood the character of the Whigs and would do better to 'show more countenance' to 'the Church party'. Godolphin regretted that the defeat had been brought about by men he had trusted, Rochester amongst them, and lamented to Harley that he had been beaten in the Commons by 'those of whom I thought we had deserved better'.

There was more choppy water ahead. Parliament quickly granted the queen's request that Prince George should receive £100,000 a year, cheerfully demonstrating that its grudge against Marlborough was political rather than financial. The Whigs in the Lords then attacked a measure which excepted the Prince of Denmark from a clause in the Act of Settlement which would bar naturalised subjects sitting in Parliament or on the Privy Council after a Hanoverian succession. They were led by the Marlboroughs' son-in-law the Earl of Sunderland, and Anne was incandescent. Eventually the clause squeaked by in the Lords by only four votes, and Anne thanked the Marlboroughs for all that they had done to help.

Anne gave a practical sign of her gratitude when the Marlboroughs' daughter Lady Elizabeth Churchill was married to the immensely wealthy Scrope Egerton, 4th Earl of Bridgewater. The queen gave a dowry of £10,000, and Bridgewater was made a gentleman of the horse to Prince George. The Marlboroughs aimed at the senior post of master of the horse, but they failed to secure it for Bridgwater till 1705, when it became all too evident that the incumbent, the Earl of Sandwich, was mentally deranged. The queen also did something for the Duumvirs, as Marlborough and Godolphin were now becoming known, by ordering Rochester to go to Ireland to take up his duties as lord lieutenant, not to reappear at cabinet. When he refused she dismissed him and appointed the Duke of Ormonde in his stead. Rochester at once threw in his lot with the opposition, and inserted a 'tendentious introduction' to the second volume of his father Clarendon's *History of the Great Rebellion*, which appeared in 1703, warning Anne that only adherence to Tory principles could prevent her from sharing the fate of Charles I.

At the beginning of 1703, despite the failure of the attempt to gain a pension from Parliament and some crumbling of Godolphin's political power-base, all seemed set fair for the Duke and Duchess of Marlborough. In February, however, they were struck by a blow from which they never fully recovered. Their eldest son John, so recently made Marquess of Blandford by courtesy title that his proud father still called him 'Lord Churchill', was a sixteen-year-old undergraduate at King's College Cambridge. Even the Marlboroughs' subsequent unpopularity could never induce their many opponents to rake up any mud about young Blandford. 'Notwithstanding his high birth, splendid prospects and courtly education,' says Archdeacon Coxe, 'he set an example of affability, regularity, and steadiness, above his years.'[83] His best friend was Horace Walpole, also of King's, and the two young men spoke about serving together in the cavalry. Blandford wrote to Marlborough asking for a commission in the summer of 1702, and Marlborough sent the letter on to Godolphin, characteristically asking him not to show it to Sarah if he thought it would 'vex' her, but saying that he would 'write what answer she shall think best'. Sarah, like many a worried mother before and since, could not let her son go while he was still so young.

In the winter of 1702–03 Blandford often rode across from Cambridge to stay with Godolphin at Newmarket. Early in 1703 there was smallpox in Newmarket, but Godolphin was sure that the Marlboroughs' son, 'going into no house but mine, will I hope be more defended from it by air and riding, without any violent exercise, than he could be anywhere else'. But shortly after returning to Cambridge from Newmarket in February John was struck down by the disease. Sarah rushed to Cambridge as soon as she heard the news, and the queen, no stranger to this fell illness, sent her own doctors at once. Marlborough wrote to Sarah immediately, dating his letter only 'Thursday, nine in the morning'.

> I have this minute received Mr Godolphin's letter, and have sent to Mr Morta's shop [Daniel Malthus, apothecary to the queen] for what is desired, which is what this messenger will bring. I hope Doctor Hans [Edward Hans, physician to the queen] and Dr Collidon [Sir Theodore Colladon] got to you early this morning. I am so troubled at the sad condition this poor child seems to be in, that I know not what I do. I pray God to give you some comfort in this great affliction. If you think anything under heaven can be done, pray let me know it, or if you think my coming can be of the least use let me know it. I beg I may hear as often as is possible, for I have no thought but what is at Cambridge.[84]

He wrote again that night, telling her:

> I hope the doctors were with you early this morning. If we must be so unhappy as to lose this poor child, I pray God enable us to behave with that resignation which we ought to do. If this uneasiness which I now lie under should last long, I do not think I could live. For God's sake, if there be any hope of recovery let me know it.[85]

The Marquess of Blandford died on the morning of Saturday, 20 February 1703: Marlborough had arrived just in time to join Sarah at his bedside. The death of any child is a tragedy, and the Marlboroughs, like too many of the parents of their age, were already painfully familiar with loss. It hit Marlborough hard. His hopes of founding a dynasty had perished. He quickly made a new will, and begged the queen to allow his dukedom to descend collaterally, hoping at first that it might eventually go to Godolphin's son and his descendants, provided they assumed the name and arms of Churchill. Affairs of state were so pressing that he had little enough time to mourn, for although Cardonnel at once told Heinsius what had happened, he emphasised that 'despite this great misfortune His Excellency will embark in the middle of next week'.[86] When Ailesbury saw him at The Hague soon afterwards Marlborough confessed: 'I've lost what is so dear to me, it is fit for me to retire and not toil and labour for I know not who. My daughters are all married.'[87] In April he wrote wistfully:

> I have seen this day a very great procession, and the thoughts how pleased poor Lord Churchill would have been with such a sight added much to my uneasiness. Since it has pleased God to take him, I do wish from my soul I could think less of him.[88]

If Marlborough, with the mind-filling solace of hard work, was able to rise above his grief, it was much, much harder for Sarah. On 26 February, Godolphin said that he was pleased to hear that 'the drops' seemed to be doing her some good. Marlborough was an even more sedulous correspondent than usual: when he reached Brill after his sea crossing the following month he wrote to say: 'My letter a Tuesday may come as soon as this, but I would not omit this occasion, nor will I ever any that I think may give you the least satisfaction, for the greatest pleasure of my life will be the endeavouring to make you happy.'[89] However, for a time her grief was such that she lost her self-possession: a Westminster schoolboy saw her wandering through the cloisters of the Abbey like a madwoman.

Anne, herself no stranger to this sort of misfortune, did her very best to help. When Sarah left London for Cambridge to attend Blandford, Anne begged her 'for Christ Jesus sake to have a care of your dear precious self', and when she heard that the case was hopeless, prayed 'Christ Jesus comfort & support you under this terrible affliction, & it is his mercy alone that can do it.'[90] The tragedy should have drawn the two women closer together in the sisterhood of shared adversity, but it did not. One contemporary observed: 'We hear the Duchess of Marlborough bears not her affliction like her mistress, if report be true that it hath near touched her head.' Edward Gregg, Anne's masterly biographer, does indeed suggest that the tragedy tipped Sarah's personality over the edge: 'Her wit, which had been sharp, became piercing; her humour, which had been biting, became mordant; her convictions, which had been firm, became absolute; her manner, which had been bold and assured, became precipitous and arrogant.'[91]

There was another element to the tragedy. In her correspondence with Sarah, Anne had always been very forthright about her own periods, sometimes saying that 'Lady Charlotte's' failure to turn up as anticipated suggested that she was pregnant again. We have no evidence that Sarah ever used the same cant with her mistress. Perhaps the letters which did so have simply not survived, but more probably this is yet another example of Anne needing to confide in Sarah far more than Sarah ever needed to confide in her. We cannot describe Sarah's fertility with absolute certainty, but it is clear that in 1702 she certainly hoped to have more children, and likely that she thought herself pregnant in the spring of 1703: she was by then forty-two years old, so it was not an unreasonable hope. It was certainly a hope shared by her husband. 'It was a great pleasure to me when I thought we should be blessed with more children; but as all my happiness centres in living quietly with you, I do conjure you by all the kindness I have for you . . . that you will take the best advice you can for your health,' he assured her.[92] On 17 May he wrote to tell her how delighted he was that 'the troublesome visit' she had experienced the day he left had not recurred, though he was unaware of the real significance of its absence.[93]

As the year went on it became evident that missed and irregular periods denoted, not the chance of giving birth to another son, but the menopause. Jealous (and unfounded) suspicion that the queen was herself pregnant may have contributed to Sarah's refusal to return to London to visit Anne early in 1703, although in fairness she was so deeply distressed at the time that she would not even see her daughters. Early in 1704 her relationship with Marlborough was to break down almost completely. She accused him of infidelity, and he repeatedly wrote to ask what cause she had to treat him as badly as she did. This is creaky ice for a male historian to wander out on, but some comfort may be taken from the fact that Iris Butler suggests, in *Rule of Three*, that sexual jealousy and suspicion of a much-loved partner are common symptoms of women in menopausal age.[94]

All this did not simply affect Sarah's dealings with her husband, but with Queen Anne too. Sarah spent much of 1703 at Holywell or at Windsor Lodge in the Great Park, and did not even appear at court during Prince George's illness that autumn. She deluged the queen with what Gregg calls 'long epistles packed with her own political views', and in May that year ostentatiously called the queen 'your Majesty' in a letter provoking Anne to ask her if anything was wrong. However, Anne still gave her right of refusal when the employment of a maid of honour was being considered. Later that month, when Marlborough, stuck fast in a campaign that was mired by political squabbles, and still conscious of the collapse of his dynastic hopes, first talked of resigning, Anne responded with a warm declaration of support.

> The thoughts that both my dear Mrs Freeman & Mr Freeman seem to have of retiring give me no small uneasiness & therefore I must say something on the subject, it is no wonder at all people in your posts should be weary of the world . . . but give me leave to say, that you should at least consider your faithful friends and poor country, which must be ruined if you should ever put your melancholy thoughts in execution, as for your poor unfortunate Morley she could not bear it, for if you should forsake me, I would have nothing more to do with the world, but make another abdication, for what is a crown, when the support of it is gone. I will never forsake your dear self, Mr Freeman nor Mr Montgomery [Godolphin], but always be your constant faithful servant till death mows us down with his impartial hand.[95]

Anne prorogued her first Parliament at the end of February 1703, and then promoted the Marquess of Normanby (who made his first appearance in these pages as Earl Mulgrave, James II's lord chamberlain) to be Duke of Buckingham, and created four new Tory peers to give their party a working majority in the Lords. She also yielded to Sarah's request to make the Whig John Hervey a baron, the only time, so Sarah claimed, that a peer was created simply to please her. Sarah's letters returned to their familiar theme: that the Tories were simply closet Jacobites. Anne replied, on 11 June, with a measured defence of the Tory role in the Glorious Revolution and the Act of Settlement, and although she admitted that some High Tories were undoubtedly Jacobites, the same could not be said for most of them. Sarah intensified her attack on the Tories in general and Buckingham in particular, and tried to enlist the support of both Godolphin and her husband.

Sarah tried to get Anne to take action over the allegedly incorrect boundaries of the new house Buckingham was building, which was to become the nucleus of Buckingham Palace. She joined a royal visit to Bath rather late in proceedings, and was roundly rebuked by the queen when she complained about a new treaty of alliance with Victor Amadeus, Duke of Savoy, who had once deserted William III. Parliament met again in early November, and there was more tension when the Tories made a second attempt to pass an Occasional Conformity Bill, which would have made life more difficult for those Dissenters who avoided legal discrimination by their 'occasional conformity' to the Church of England. Anne generally favoured the Bill, as she thought that it would strengthen the Church, though she supported her Lutheran husband's right to oppose it. It was probably Prince George's example that encouraged some wavering peers to stay away when the vote was taken. The Tories were furious with Anne, and could not understand how Prince George had absented himself without his wife's support. Marlborough and Godolphin both voted for the Bill, for they could not afford to affront the moderate Tories, upon whose support they relied to secure subsidies with which to continue the war. Yet both were delighted to see it fail.

At home, then, the year 1703 had seen a shift in Sarah's relationship with the queen, subtle, perhaps, but a portent of what was to come. It had also seen Sarah become increasingly extreme in her denunciation of the Tories despite specific warnings from Anne, a confirmed supporter of what she, devout as ever, saw as the Church party. Godolphin was still able to manage Parliament to his advantage, but the Tories had become noticeably stronger. These were gentle judders, not seismic shifts, and they might have been counteracted by a major success on the battlefield. Yet that is precisely what eluded Marlborough in the 1703 campaign.

The 1703 Campaign

The year began just as badly for the Grand Alliance as it did for the Churchill family. Maximilian Emmanuel, Elector of Bavaria and so ruler of the largest and best-armed state in southern Germany, had been a member of the Grand Alliance, and governor of the Spanish Netherlands on behalf of his father-in-law the emperor, in the previous war. However, he had now developed the idea of his own Wittelsbach family competing with the Hapsburgs for the crown of the Holy Roman Empire, and decided to side with Louis XIV. His defection, accompanied by his seizure of Ulm, opened up a new front deep in Germany, and encouraged Louis to make his main effort in the south that year. Marshal Villars was to besiege and capture Kehl, just across the Rhine from Strasbourg, with his manoeuvres covered from the Imperialists by another army under Marshal Tallard in the Lines of Stollhofen, field fortifications covering the gap between the middle Rhine and the Black Forest.

In the Low Countries, Villeroi now had about 60,000 men behind the River Mehaigne, threatening Maastricht, and more in a long line of field fortifications known as the Lines of Brabant, running all the way from Namur to Antwerp, making good use of the river systems, notably the Dyle as it curved between Leau and Tongres. Brigadier the comte de Mérode-Westerloo, who had been born in the Netherlands as a vassal of the Spanish crown and whose Walloon regiment now fought for the French, described the Lines as being

> of prodigious extent, stretching all the way from the Meuse to the Scheldt and thence to the sea, [and] were to my way of thinking more profitable to the purses of the engineers who built them than for the country they were supposed to protect; they really represented a scarecrow for little birds, providing a pretext for those who wished to halt and do nothing. How could anyone guard such an extended system of defences?[96]

Marlborough, on his way back home the previous year, had told Godolphin that the Dutch and British needed to raise another 20,000 men between them, and this was indeed the total agreed in a treaty signed at The Hague the following March. Parliament consented to bear its share of the augmentation only if the Dutch agreed to give up trade with France. Marlborough told Heinsius that he wished 'the troops had been given without any condition', but begged him to persuade the Estates-General to comply, as 'I tremble to think of the consequences that may happen, if this should occasion any coldness between England and Holland.'[97] In practice the troops, four-fifths of them hired from German states, had been obtained before the Dutch actually agreed to suspend trade for a year. In April Marlborough lamented that the French success in southern Germany meant that 'You can have no troops from any prince in Germany but by paying dearly for them, and that they at the same time expect to be protected by your army.'[98]

The Allies met at Wesel, on the Rhine, to discuss strategy in early March. Marlborough had not yet arrived from England, and was represented by Lieutenant General Cutts. Anthonie Heinsius told Marlborough that Cutts would be able to fill in the plan's detail, but briefed him on its outlines. The Allies would besiege Bonn, where Prince Louis of Baden already commanded an Allied detachment, and then do something unspecified in Flanders or Brabant. He added that the effort would demand all the British and Dutch troops that could be made available. The scheme was fleshed out after Marlborough arrived: the capture of Bonn would be followed by a large-scale attempt on Antwerp.

It is clear from this that the general scheme was not Marlborough's, as Winston S. Churchill suggests, but it is perfectly possible that its refinement into the Antwerp design was. He certainly did not favour the attack on Bonn, but told Godolphin that the Allies had made 'so much noise' about it that 'I think it would be scandalous to avoid the making of it now.'[99] On 27 April he wrote from the Allied siege lines before Bonn, where he had taken personal charge of operations, to tell Heinsius 'that Antwerp is a greater security to the States than any other conquest that might be made'. However, he prefaced this with the warning that news from Paris suggested that the French saw Bonn as 'but a feint' and were taking steps to reinforce Antwerp. If they applied their whole strength to the place it might be impossible for him to take it.[100]

Marlborough hoped to be master of Bonn by the end of May, before the French were in the field, though a strong covering force under the Dutch field marshal Hendrik van Nassau, Heer van Ouwerkerk ('Overkirk' to his British allies) had been pushed forward between Liège and Maastricht in case Villeroi stirred early.[101] Villeroi, his army far bigger than Overkirk's, did indeed move sooner than expected, falling on two Allied battalions, one British and one Dutch, at Tongres on 8 May. This little garrison held out for a day before being forced to surrender, but the defence of Tongres gave Overkirk time to concentrate under the guns of Maastricht, 'where he entrenched himself', as Robert Parker tells us.

> Notwithstanding this Villeroi advanced to attack us, and began to cannonade us with great fury; but the cannon of the town, of our camp, and of the Fort of Petersburg, soon made him weary of that work, and obliged him to retire; and upon hearing of the approach of the Duke, he made what haste he could to get within his lines.[102]

Marlborough offered good terms to the garrison of Bonn to ensure its surrender on 15 May, and then marched to join Overkirk, compelling Villeroi to scuttle away.

The fall of Bonn and the relief of Overkirk's force left the Allies free to embark upon their Great Design against Antwerp. Marlborough would certainly have agreed with Mérode-Westerloo's assessment of the Lines of Brabant. The French were not powerful enough to be strong everywhere, and the key to Allied success would lie in concentrating against a chosen point, in this case Antwerp, while manoeuvring elsewhere to prevent the French from reacting to the real threat. This use of manoeuvre in order to unbalance the enemy was an important ingredient of Marlborough's battlefield tactics, with Ramillies as the outstanding example of its success. The method's execution on a large scale, however, hinged on the prompt and unquestioning obedience of orders which must inevitably travel by courier, allowing Marlborough little opportunity for personal intervention with Allied generals who had not yet come to trust him. Moreover, the Allies had to communicate via exterior lines stretched around the great bend of the Dyle, while the French could use interior lines to move directly to any point.

The French defenders of the Lines of Brabant consisted of Villeroi and Boufflers, with sixty battalions and 110 squadrons, in the west, and Count Bedmar, with fifty battalions and ten squadrons, most of them Spanish and spread out in small garrisons, in the east: a small force covered the centre of the Lines. The Allied plan was certainly bold. The attack on Antwerp would be carried out by General Jacob van Wassenaer, Heer von Wassenaer en Obdam ('Opdam' to the British), an experienced Dutch officer who had been promoted full general the previous year. His force would be strengthened by fourteen battalions, released by the fall of Bonn, which would travel by river round to Bergen op Zoom, while another six battalions and fourteen squadrons marched by land. Dutch garrisons in the east would be reduced to strengthen Opdam still further. On 19 May Marlborough wrote to Opdam from Maastricht, saying that he had done his best to ensure that The Hague understood the need to send as many troops as possible to Bergen op Zoom, and begging him to apply pressure of his own.[103]

While the Allied field army under Marlborough, with sixty battalions and 130 squadrons, fixed Villeroi in the east so as to prevent him from helping Bedmar, the venerable siege expert Menno van Coehoorn was to move along the Flanders coast to besiege Ostend, presenting Bedmar with a conflict of priorities. On 23 May, with Villeroi duly fixed near Hannef, Marlborough wrote a long and diplomatic letter to Coehoorn, assuring him that 'I know your experience, your zeal and your good judgement too well not to trust it entirely,' but stressing that the siege of

Antwerp could not begin until Coehoorn had first attacked Ostend.[104] However, he informed Godolphin that he was very worried that Coehoorn would not in fact besiege Ostend as agreed, but would instead make a 'diversion' in Flanders 'which will not oblige them [the French] to make any great detachment'. He believed that Coehoorn simply hoped to force the northern end of the Lines to raise money, 'for as he is the governor of Dutch Flanders he has the tenth of all the contributions'.[105] This was not an unreasonable view, for the Dutch themselves were concerned at Coehoorn's attitude. On 25 June Jacob Hop, the Dutch treasurer general, warned that 'It seems that we cannot justify the conduct of M. Coehoorn, if he pretends to dispute the command of the army in Flanders with his superior [Opdam],' though he agreed that 'It would be irritating enough for a governor of Flanders . . . to have the honour and profit' of the operation taken from him.[106]

There was actually another layer of inter-Allied complexity. The Dutch feared that if Ostend was taken it would finish up in English hands, and would form a bastion of future English trade. On 17 June Marlborough tried to persuade Heinsius that this was not in fact the case. 'I do assure you that [we] are very desirous it should be taken from the French,' he wrote, 'but they would not be masters of it . . . so that you need not apprehend any dispute that might arise upon the taking of this place.'[107] Soon afterwards he warned Heinsius that Coehoorn might be 'disobliged' by one of the generals in Opdam's force, quite possibly Lieutenant General Frederik Johan Baer, Heer van Slangenburg, with whom he was shortly to have a blazing row. He would be happy to meet Opdam's generals at any central spot, but warned that time was being wasted: 'I think the common interest does require that no more time should be lost, but that we either attack Antwerp or Ostend, or else put ourselves on the defensive and send the rest into Germany.'[108] As late as 25 June NS Marlborough still hoped to persuade Coehoorn to besiege Ostend, and sent the baron de Trogne, governor of Liège, to press his case again.

By this time, though, Coehoorn was concerned that his own attack would run into forces released by Villeroi. Marlborough agreed to send some extra troops, repeatedly assured him that Villeroi had not yet moved a detachment westwards, and undertook to keep the French under pressure. It was not until the very end of the month that the Allied right wing at last advanced. Coehoorn and Spaar each pierced the Lines of Brabant to enter the Pays de Waes, the coastal area just west of Antwerp, and Opdam, on the other side of the Scheldt, headed towards Antwerp itself. However, Coehoorn's attack was not serious enough to persuade Bedmar to divide his forces, and on 28 June Marlborough, who had always argued that the project would work only if Bedmar was distracted from Antwerp, told both Coehoorn and Opdam that he would make best speed to join them. On the same day he warned Godolphin that, although he was confident that he had stolen a march on Villeroi, 'we are now got into so enclosed a country' that the French would probably move faster. Worse still, he thought that Villeroi would probably now be able to send a detachment to support Bedmar.

That is precisely what happened. Villeroi had already ordered his central force to join Bedmar, and now he ordered Boufflers to take thirty squadrons of cavalry and thirty companies of grenadiers (five battalions' worth) to make forced marches to the west: Marlborough's spies reported that a foot soldier was mounted behind each horseman to make better time. On 28 June Marlborough warned Opdam that the French were on the move in open country 'where it will be very easy for them, without running any risk, to make detachments'. Villeroi, moving within his own lines, had no shortage of forage, whereas Marlborough, 'our march being upon the heaths', was less well supplied. He assured Opdam that he would be in a position to help him just as soon as he could.[109] The next day he wrote again, begging Opdam to keep him apprised of his movements, and on the thirtieth he admitted that he was a little vexed not to have heard from him for days. On 2 July he assured Heinsius that he was only two days away from Opdam, and urged him to convene a meeting of Allied generals and members of his own government at some suitable place. With the letter signed but not sealed, he added a desperate postscript: 'This minute I am told the postmaster of Breda has written to the postmaster here that Opdam is beaten. I hope it is not true.'[110] He also dashed off a postscript to a letter to Godolphin when he heard the news, saying: 'We have a report come from Breda that Opdam is beat. I pray God it be not so, for he is very capable of having it happen to him.'[111]

Jacob Hop, the Dutch treasurer general, had joined Opdam at the end of June, and told the Estates General that Marlborough had warned them that the French were on the move south of the Lines. A council of war had accordingly decided that Opdam's camp at Eckeren, containing only thirteen battalions and twenty-six squadrons, was dangerously exposed. Opdam's generals got their heavy baggage away towards Bergen op Zoom, and on 30 June, with the French now in sight, they resolved to fall back on Lillo on the Scheldt. 'But that could not be done

Holywell House, near St Albans. Sarah Jennings was born there in 1660, and later bought her sister Frances's share in the property. The Marlboroughs expanded it and lived there for much of their married lives. This engraving dates from 1808, and the house was demolished in 1837.

Marlborough's friend and close political ally Sidney, Earl Godolphin, with his white staff of office as lord treasurer, painted in 1705.

Michael Dahl's portrait shows Queen Anne before she became overweight and dropsical.

Abigail Hill, later Lady Masham, Sarah Marlborough's cousin, who went some way towards supplanting her in Queen's Anne's affections.

Sarah Marlborough's pretty elder sister Frances, who married James II's viceroy in Ireland, Richard Talbot, Earl (and Jacobite Duke) of Tyrconnell.

Robert Harley, Earl of Oxford, who was chiefly responsible for Marlborough's downfall, with the 'Great George' of his Order of the Garter appearing to good effect.

Jacob von Schuppen's 1718 portrait of the highly talented Prince Eugène of Savoy reveals that he was not the most handsome of men. A *zischägge*, the lobster-tailed helmet favoured by Imperialist cavalry, stands by his left hand.

John Cutts, 1st Baron Cutts. Nicknamed 'Salamander' because of his fondness for the hottest fire, Cutts was involved in the military conspiracy against James II. At Blenheim he commanded the assault on Blenheim village on the French right.

Top The axis of Cutts' attack on Blenheim village: the white building in the centre is the *Breisachmüle*.

Middle The field at Blenheim, looking east-south-east along the Nebel, with Unterglauheim, to the left, on the opposite bank. Blenheim village is in the distance, beyond the last tree on the right. Note that the ground falls away from the track towards the river: Allied troops in this area would not have been visible to the French.

Bottom Three panels by Louis Laguerre depicting the battle of Blenheim. On the extreme left, Allied infantry ford the Nebel: note the grenadiers with their mitre caps. In the centre, French cavalry flounder in the Danube; and on the right, Prince Eugène directs the Allied right flank.

Marlborough commissioned ten Brussels-made tapestries which were hung at Blenheim Palace to commemorate his victories. This one seizes the moment when the captured Marshal Tallard (centre, in blue coat) was presented to Marlborough at Blenheim. William Cadogan, the duke's chief of staff, is immediately behind him.

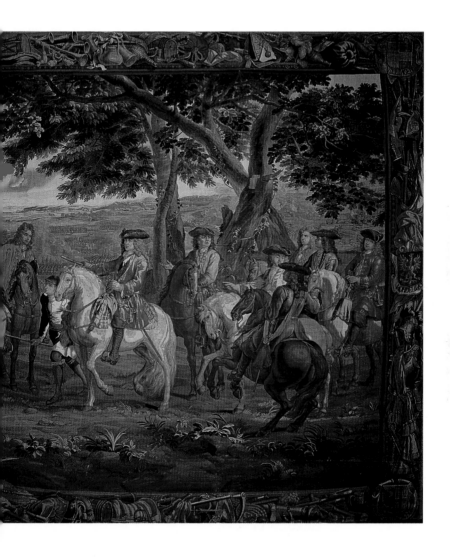

The old course of the Danube south-east of Sonderheim: many French cavalrymen drowned here trying to escape.

An engraving after Louis Laguerre shows Marlborough (left foreground) and Tallard meeting at Blenheim. In the background on the left, fleeing Frenchmen struggle in the Danube.

Above Marlborough's steadfast
Dutch ally Antonie Heinsius,
the republic's grand pensionary,
effectively its head of government.

Left Marlborough's shadow:
William Cadogan, later 1st Earl
Cadogan, quartermaster-general
and the duke's trusted adviser.

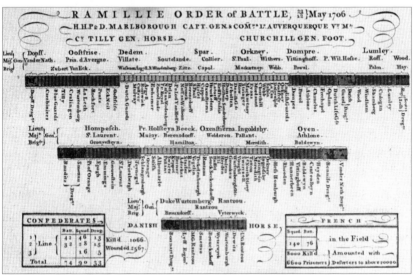

Order of Battle for Ramillies. This is an elegant version of the schematic order of
battle drawn up by quartermaster-generals, with dragoons on the wings, cavalry on the
flanks and infantry in the centre. The command responsibilities of senior officers are
clearly marked.

Above Ramillies seen from Marlborough's approach. The spire on the horizon is Ramillies church: the village lies out of sight, in the valley of the Geete. Orkney's troops, moving from right to left on this side of the far crest, were not visible to the French commanders on the other side of the Geete.

Below The Tomb of Ottomont, south-west of Ramillies. We see it from the direction of the Allied advance towards the end of the battle, when Danish cavalry swept round the French right flank.

so soon but that the enemy appeared both before and behind, and on both sides of us,' wrote Hop to the Estates-General.

> We then engaged with them, and the fight was very furious in several places, lasting from 3 o'clock till it was nearly dark, and frequently with very doubtful success, till at last, by the unwearied bravery (which in truth can never be enough commended) of both your own national troops and those of foreign princes in your service, one of the chief posts by which we must pass to come hither, viz. the village of Oerderen, was forced from the enemy and kept in possession.[112]

Mérode-Westerloo acknowledged that the Allies fought very hard indeed, and saw for himself that Oerderen, through which they had to pass to escape, was the scene of frenzied fighting. His own leading battalion bolted under heavy close-range artillery fire, and although he rallied about three hundred of his men, all was in 'desperate confusion, pikemen picking up muskets and musketeers laying hold of pikes'. Major General Hompesch led a handful of Dutch horsemen in a counterattack which drove back superior numbers of French cavalry. The infantry wilted too, and Mérode-Westerloo could not hold the village without support that never came: 'I never saw a single general officer during the whole affair,' he complained.

> We lost more than 2,000 killed or wounded, although, in fact, we might have made the whole Dutch army prisoners of war for a loss of less than a hundred if only we occupied the line of dykes and pounded them to pieces with cannon . . . But French foolhardiness and I don't know what besides made us muff the opportunity.[113]

Opdam himself had been cut off from his troops, and was first reported missing: Jacob Hop heard that he was a prisoner in Antwerp. It soon transpired, however, that he had made best speed to Breda, whence he gave the Estates-General what Robert Parker called 'a melancholy account of the affair'. Slangenburg took charge of the initial battle and the running fight that followed it, and although Eckeren was scarcely a victory, its results could have been far worse. One byproduct, welcomed by Parker, was that Opdam never received another active command. Marlborough acidly observed that Baron Hop 'had the honour of seeing more of it than the general that should have commanded', and added that the French, who had certainly not done as well as they ought, 'will pretend . . . they had the best of it, and prove it by Opdam's letters'.[114]

The battle of Eckeren left the Great Design in ruins, and worse followed. Marlborough heard that Coehoorn had fallen out with Slangenburg and was thinking of quitting the army. He urged them both to put the public interest before private matters, but Coehoorn, ill and with only a year to live, returned to The Hague. It was in evident despair that Marlborough wrote to Heinsius on 21 July.

> It is impossible the war can go on with success at this rate, if measures must be taken between two armies, and the quarrels and animosities of private people shall make a delay which hinders the whole . . . I know not if I shall outlive this campaign, but I am sure I have not the courage to make another.

He added that his own government was pressing him to send troops to Spain, but he had been able to stave them off for the moment, promising only four battalions of newly-arrived foot and Lord Raby's Dragoons. 'I own to you that I have the spleen to a great degree,' confessed Marlborough, 'which may make me an ill judge of what I write in this letter. I wish it may prove so, and that you may have a glorious campaign.'[115] There was something of the same gloom in a letter to Sarah.

> I find myself daily delaying, so that if I may not have time of living quietly with you, and meddling less with the business of this world, I can't hold long. But of this I shall say a great deal more when I have the happiness of seeing you, which time is passionately wished for by him that loves you above all expression.[116]

A conference at Bergen op Zoom resolved that the Allies would pierce the Lines of Brabant near Antwerp, but Marlborough discovered that neither cannon nor forage was ready, and by the time he reached the Lines, Villeroi and Boufflers were there before him. He still rode forward to see if anything could be done.

> On Friday [27 July NS] I went with 4,000 horse to see the lines. They let us come so near that we beat their outguard home to their barrier, which gave us an opportunity of seeing the lines; which has a ditch 27 foot broad before it and the water in it nine foot deep, so that it is resolved that the armies return to the Meuse, and in the first place

take Huy. Upon the whole matter, if we can't bring the French to a
battle, we shall not do anything worth the being commended.[117]

Huy fell surprisingly quickly, and its garrison, which surrendered as
prisoners of war, gave Marlborough the wherewithal to exchange his
own two battalions taken at Tongres earlier in the year. Already, shaking
off the despair of high summer, he had spotted a new opportunity.
The Lines of Brabant were incomplete between the Mehaigne and the
Meuse, and he proposed piercing them between Leau and the headwaters of the Mehaigne. As this is precisely where he was to penetrate
them in 1706, it is likely that his plan would have succeeded, and that
he would have brought the French to battle.

At a council of war, held at Marlborough's headquarters at Val Notre
Dame, not far from Huy, on 24 August, all the Allied generals present
supported the plan. The Dutch generals, however, would not agree, and
without their consent the operation was impossible. They proposed
instead the siege of Limburg, which Marlborough rightly believed was
so insignificant an objective that it could be fitted in at the end of a
campaign. The senior British, Danish and German generals took the
unusual step of signing a formal document declaring that they believed
that with an attack on the Lines 'We could, with the help of the good
Lord, hope for a victory so complete, and whose consequences would be
so great as not to be predicted.'[118] Marlborough sent a copy of the letter
to Harley, and told Godolphin what had happened, enclosing a copy of
his own letter of well-mannered protest to the Estates-General. He
added that 'I am really tired out of my life,' but concluded by telling
Godolphin that he had, as requested, 'taken care of' one of his clients:
John Yarborough duly became a captain in Hill's Regiment of Foot.[119]

The dispute with the Dutch hit Marlborough hard. He told Godolphin
that he would be home soon, for he had no mind to command an army
that did nothing but eat forage. He added that the whole business 'has
heated my blood so, that I am almost mad with a headache', and railed
against the Dutch generals, some of whom were by then beginning to say
that they would have supported the attack if only they had had more
cannon.[120] He warned Heinsius that Dutch failure to support offensive
action would be used by 'disaffected people in England . . . to convince
our Parliament men that the war ought to be made in other places
and not in this country'.[121] It is clear that his complaint was against the
Dutch generals, not the field deputies, and on 11 October he reported
to Heinsius that 'the Deputies have promised me that they will tell

their generals very plainly that the army must continue in the field all this month'.[122]

Even now, dragging on the fag-end of a wasted campaign, he was still corresponding about the regiments due to be sent to Portugal and the allocation of generals to command them; discussing the state of affairs in southern Germany and northern Italy with a bevy of princelings; lamenting the defeat, in late September, of Count Styrum's Allied army by Villars and Max Emmanuel near a small town called Hochstadt on the Danube; and telling the Duke of Schomberg that he did not think the government would give the generals ordered to Portugal any more than the £10,700 already allocated. There was a little old-world courtliness with his nephew, the Duke of Berwick, whose master of the horse wanted a passport to visit the United Provinces to buy some horses. Indeed, he risked trespassing on this scarred friendship, saying:

> I should be glad . . . if you think it proper, and not otherwise, that you would desire the Maréchal de Villeroi to give me a pass for twenty pieces of burgundy or champagne to come to Huy or Liege, which in that case M. Puech may deliver to Colonel Cadogan when they meet on Thursday at Borchloen.[123]

Even his return to England did not go smoothly. He was marooned at Briel by contrary winds, and eventually reached London, where he landed at Tower wharf on 30 October, just in time to sit in a Parliament which became almost as firmly enmeshed in the Occasional Conformity Bill as he had been in the Lines of Brabant. 1703 could not, by any reasonable definition, be termed a good year.

5

High Germany

Forging a Strategy

The campaign of 1703 in the Low Countries had not been wholly sterile. Bonn had been taken at its beginning, and both Limburg and Guelders fell at its end. Indeed, the grateful Dutch struck a medal with Queen Anne on the obverse and Marlborough on the reverse, with the inscription: 'Victory without slaughter, by the taking of Bonn, Huy and Limburg.' There was no irony in this: gaining territory by manoeuvre remained appealing to the Dutch, who rightly dreaded the consequences of a lost battle. Yet in the winter of 1703–04 it seemed to Marlborough that the war would be lost in Germany long before it could be won in Flanders or Brabant, and the defection of Bavaria meant that the balance of strategic geography for once favoured the French.

How so? The easiest route between France and the litter of small states and the few rather bigger ones that constituted the Germany of the early eighteenth century was what Charles de Gaulle was later to call that 'Fatal Avenue' in which Marlborough had been campaigning for the past two seasons. It was speckled with fortresses, laced with rivers and canals, and offered limited prospects for war-winning advances by either side. Further south, nature splashed forests and rivers across the landscape to make any advance into or from Germany even more difficult. The Ardennes and the Eifel, the south-eastern pivots of Marlborough's operations in 1702–03, were inimical to marching armies, and the valley of the Moselle, which creased their eastern edge, was commanded by the fortresses of Trier, Trarbach and Koblenz. Another slab of forested upland rippled southwards from east of Saarbrücken to the borders of Switzerland, pierced by gaps which were to leave bloody thumbprints on the pages of history: Wissembourg, Saverne and Belfort.

The most promising of these, the Saverne gap, led to Strasbourg, a French city since the Treaty of Ryswick, with its bridgehead Kehl, on the other side of the Rhine, now in French hands too. An advance northwards down the Rhine was blocked by the Lines of Stollhofen, running from the Rhine village of that name to Buhl in the Baden uplands, with the mighty fortress of Landau on the left bank of the Rhine behind them. Easterly routes through the Black Forest were bottlenecks, easily corked by a defender. However, a French army which reached the valley of the Neckar would suddenly find room for manoeuvre, especially into the upper Danube, which then led, by way of Ulm, Donauwörth and Ingolstadt, towards the emperor's capital of Vienna. A jab straight to the pit of the Austrian stomach might, if events in northern Italy turned to the French advantage, be combined with a hook up from Verona and Trento to the Brenner Pass, a classic two-pronged attack which was to be used by Napoleon a century later.

Bavaria was part of a greater Germany largely in a linguistic sense, and with its Roman Catholicism and almost Latin culture, was quite unlike dour Prussia, away in the north with the Baltic on one flank and Russia on another. Elector Max Emmanuel's change of allegiance had suddenly provided Louis with the stepping-stone he needed to get into Germany without a fight, and offered the possibility of cracking the Grand Alliance by striking at its point of natural cleavage along the Danube valley. Louis had long sought to encourage Turkey, still a major military power in Europe and last repulsed from the gates of Vienna in 1683, in order to divert Hapsburg power to the east. During the Nine Years War the Emperor Leopold was forced to juggle his forces between Italy and the Empire on the one hand, and the east on the other. He was fortunate in that Eugène of Savoy, arguably his most capable commander, demolished a large Turkish army at Zenta in September 1697, bringing the Turks to the conference table and leading to the signing of the Peace of Carlowitz in 1699.

However, if Louis had lost one ally he soon gained another. The Hapsburgs, trying to establish a permanent settlement of Hungary, so much of it recently liberated from the Turks, succeeded in inflaming the population by unwise taxation, and irritating the prickly local nobility. In 1703 the patriot leaders Francis Rákóczi and Alexander Károlyi were in large-scale rebellion against the Hapsburgs, and received gilded but empty promises of support from Louis. The Hapsburgs could not afford to send substantial forces against the Hungarian rebels until after Blenheim, in August 1704, and fighting went on till 1711, first under the Emperor Joseph, who succeeded in 1705 but died unexpectedly in 1711, and then under Charles III. Ultimately it was Hapsburg successes in southern Germany and northern Italy that enabled them to move troops eastwards and crush the rebellion. To Marlborough the rebellion was not simply a smoky clash on a distant frontier: it was a major strategic distraction for a crucial ally. There can be no doubting French diplomatic efforts to keep the rebellion alive: when Rákóczi went to Constantinople in 1716, at the request of the Turks, he travelled there from Paris.

The Margrave Ludwig Wilhelm I of Baden, cousin of Eugène of Savoy, was the Allied commander on the upper Rhine. 'Prince Louis' to his British contemporaries and to this author, the margrave was a professional soldier in the emperor's service; his trademark scarlet coat had led the Turks, whom he beat at Slankamen in 1691, to call him the 'red king'. The Allies had reinforced him with troops from the Low Countries, enabling him to take Landau in 1702, but he was beaten by Marshal Villars in something of a pyrrhic victory at Friedlingen soon afterwards. In 1703 he advanced into northern Bavaria in an effort to deal with the Franco-Bavarian army under Villars and Max Emmanuel, but he was soon forced back: it was his subordinate Styrum who had been defeated at Höchstädt on the Danube in September 1703. By the end of the campaign the Franco-Bavarians had captured both Ratisbon on the Danube and Augsburg on its tributary the Lech. However, despite its failure in Bavaria, Prince Louis' army successfully prevented Marshal Tallard from forcing the Lines of Stollhofen, persuading Tallard to operate on the river's left bank and besiege Landau. Louis remained an important strategic asset for the 1704 campaign, essential, as Marlborough assured Heinsius in June that year, for supporting an Allied advance into Germany. 'Prince Lewis will do nothing without first consulting me,' wrote Marlborough, 'and . . . he approves of what I have proposed to him; which is *that he should act on the Iller, at the same time that I do on the Danube, which must necessitate the enemy to divide their army.*'[1]

Marlborough had begun to shift his weight south-eastwards even before the 1703 campaigning season had ended. When the rest of the army went into winter quarters after the fall of Limburg, he sent the Prince of Hesse-Cassel, with twenty-two battalions and thirty squadrons, to recapture Trier and Trarbach on the Moselle. However, Hesse-Cassel tried to make Tallard raise the siege of Landau, and was badly beaten at Speyerbach. Landau duly fell in November, and the Moselle fortresses remained in French hands. In the spring of 1704 Tallard succeeded in getting a substantial convoy of recruits, muskets, cannon and ammunition from Strasbourg to join the Franco-Bavarian army, feinting to deceive Prince Louis and starting the campaign by putting the French at a notable advantage. This contingent formed part of the Franco-Bavarian army which was to be beaten at the battle of Blenheim.

The only setback to France was the defection of the Duke of Savoy to the Allied cause. Prince Eugène had little time for his kinsman.

> Twenty thousand crowns a month from England, twenty thousand more from Holland, four millions for the expenses of the war, a kind of submission amongst all the petty princes of Italy, had more effect than all my eloquence, and converted the Duke of Savoy, for the time being, into the staunchest Austrian in the world. His conduct, which I shall not attempt to justify, reminds me of that formerly pursued by the Dukes of Lorraine, as well as the Dukes of Bavaria. Their geography prevented them from being men of honour.[2]

This at least meant that the French would be unable to advance from northern Italy into the Empire, but given the way the situation in Bavaria had developed, they would scarcely need to.

In the winter of 1703–04 the emperor's ambassador in London, Count Wratislaw, repeatedly pressed Marlborough to relieve the pressure on southern Germany. He had already written to Marlborough to that effect in the summer of 1703, and had again proposed an advance southwards at a conference at Düsseldorf in the autumn. We cannot say, therefore, that the strategic concept for 1704 was Marlborough's, but it was certainly one of the possibilities that he had rolled round his mind before he went to the United Provinces in January that year to discuss strategy. He lamented his departure in a letter to Sarah which juxtaposed the marital and the mundane.

> I never go from you my dearest soul, but I am extremely sensible of my own unhappiness, of not having it in my power to live quietly with you, which is the only thing that can contribute to the ending of my days happily.
>
> The tides fell out so that I did not go from Margate roads till 4 o'clock on Sunday in the afternoon. I never in my life saw so fine an evening, so that we had all the hopes imaginable of a good and quiet passage. But by the time we had got 7 or 8 leagues to sea, the wind began to rise so high that . . . we were forced to take in all our sails, and submit ourselves to be tossed as the wind and sea pleased, which lasted during 7 hours, during which time I was extremely sick . . .

I should be glad if you would get patterns for 7 or 8 pieces of hangings for my bedchamber, when I am in the field. You know my field bed is blue. If I should not be able to write to the Lord Treasurer this post, you will make my excuse. I am, with all the truth imaginable, heart and soul, yours.[3]

Before leaving London he had told Wratislaw that:

It is my intention to induce the Estates-General to decide upon a siege of Landau, or a diversion on the Moselle. I should be very glad to march there myself, but as it is difficult to move the Dutch upon an offensive . . . I should be able to get at the most only 45 battalions and some 60 squadrons for that purpose. Should I take Landau I would supply the Margrave of Baden with as many troops as possible, to enable him to overthrow the Elector of Bavaria.[4]

No sooner had he reached The Hague than he reported to Godolphin that the deputies were 'extremely alarmed' by the news from Germany, and money was so tight that the magazines planned for the coming season had not been filled, and only 60,000 of the 100,000 crowns owed to the Duke of Savoy had been paid. He added that Pierre de Belcastel, a Huguenot in Dutch pay and 'a good officer and a discreet man', had proposed sending aid to the Protestant rebels in the Cevennes so as to divert French strength, although in the event the project foundered because neither the Swiss, who would have supplied the mercenaries needed, nor the Duke of Savoy, through whose territory the expedition would pass, would back it.

For the rest of the trip he told Godolphin nothing of real significance, though there was the usual housekeeping: he agreed that it would indeed be hard to give the major's vacancy in the Blues to anyone but the senior captain. Delayed once again by contrary winds, he told Godolphin that there was no real point in his coming home, as he would have to be on the Continent again so soon, but 'My desire of being with you and Lady Marlborough is such, that I would come, although I were to stay but one day.' He was, though, delighted to hear that his daughter Lady Bridgewater had given birth to a son.[5] But he was gloomy enough at the possibilities for the coming year to tell Sarah:

For this campaign I see so ill a prospect that I am extremely out of heart. But God's will be done; and I must for this year be very uneasy, for in all the other campaigns I had an opinion of being able to do something for the common cause; but in this I have no other hopes than that some lucky accident may enable me to do good.[6]

This is typical of Marlborough. His was not an abstract military brain, but a concrete one: he was always happier dealing with practical problems than with airy conceptions, more confident on the battlefield than in the camp. However, his background as a courtier ensured that only those closest to him ever knew it. In even the darkest hour he was always smiles and politeness, displaying that most attractive of military virtues, grace under pressure.

By early March, however, the design had hardened. First, Marlborough did his best to wreck negotiations between the Elector of Bavaria and the king of Prussia, sending ambassador Stepney to Vienna and thence to Berlin, where he was to 'second my Lord Raby [ambassador to Berlin] in the assurances he has given the king of the great satisfaction her Majesty takes in the zeal he shows for the public'.[7] Cadogan was also in close but rather more light-hearted communication with his old schoolfellow at Berlin, emphasising that plans for the coming year required undivided command. 'Nobody can better judge than your Lordship,' he wrote, 'of the necessity of putting the command into a single hand and the impossibility of doing anything without it. One should think the misfortune of Speyerbach might convince the herring-sellers of the inconveniency which unavoidably attends a distinct right and left wing which is in effect making a great body of men useless at best.' Cadogan added that some verses had come into his hands: 'the ballad is mightily liked', and though 'these on the ladies are not very new' he thought that Raby might be amused by them.[8] Happily they have not survived. He had a lucky escape on his way home when his packet boat was attacked by a Dunkirk privateer which knocked it about with cannonfire. The mail was thrown overboard, and Cadogan emptied his pockets of letters given him by Cutts and Greffier Fagel. The captain and crew manfully refused to strike their colours even as the privateer closed to board. Cadogan was sure that they would be taken, but at the last moment a wind sprang up, enabling the packet to slip away.

On 7 March Marlborough warned Heinsius that 'If England and Holland do not assist the Empire by sending an army early to the Moselle the whole Empire must be undone,' and suggested that he should send his generals to the Meuse to ensure that the army was ready to move in time. He followed up by regretting the death of old Coehoorn, and recommending that it would be no more than justice to give his regiment to one of his sons, for 'had he died one year sooner, any nation might have been proud of such a subject'.[9] There were still major difficulties with the Dutch. Their lieutenant general Johan van Goor, serving under the Margrave of Baden, had fallen out with that gentleman, whom he thought dilatory, and was summoned back to the United Provinces, bringing his men with him. A horrified Wratislaw told Marlborough that this would leave Tallard free to throw 'a new and large reinforcement into Bavaria', and begged him to persuade the Dutch to change their orders. Marlborough said that he would do his best, but begged Wratislaw to accompany him to The Hague to put the case to the Dutch leaders in person.

The outlines of alternative plans were discussed at The Hague in April. Both Prince Louis and the Dutch favoured what we might term the small solution, an offensive in the Moselle valley, linked with an attack on Landau. Marlborough and Prince Eugène, however, favoured the big solution, an advance all the way to the Danube. Archdeacon Coxe suggests a secret understanding on the subject between Marlborough and Eugène, but the written record is silent on the subject. As a senior Imperialist officer Eugène would naturally have found the strategy more appealing than the small solution, and we know that he had a high regard for Marlborough, writing: 'We similarly loved and esteemed each other. He was indeed a great general.'[10] However, that is as far as we can legitimately take the argument, and a long message sent by Marlborough to Eugène in February through the medium of the British ambassador in Vienna does not even mention the Danube strategy.

Indeed, Marlborough's first letters to Godolphin after his return to the Low Countries in April imply that there was no early agreement: the Dutch were unhelpful, and typically, 'my head aches so extremely that I must leave off writing'. His headache was still bad three days later, and news from Germany, suggesting that Tallard and the Elector had just joined forces at Ulm, was likely to worsen it. 'I shall use my utmost endeavours to get them all the help I can from hence,' he wrote, 'being fully persuaded that we shall be undone if we can't get the better of them in that country. I am afraid I shall want the Queen's help in this matter.'[11] He already had broad permission from the cabinet to 'go to the aid of the Emperor', and had discussed the campaign's possible development with Godolphin, but it is not until 18 April OS that he confirmed his plan, although he made it clear that it had not been fully agreed at the Hague conference.

> My intentions are to march all the English to Koblenz, and to declare here that I intend to command on the Moselle; but when I come there to write to the States, that I think it absolutely necessary for saving the Empire to march with the troops under my command to join those in Germany that are in her Majesty's and Dutch pay, in order to take measure with Prince Louis for the speedy reducing of the Elector of Bavaria. The army I propose there would consist of upwards of 40,000 men. If I should act in any other manner than what I now tell you, my design would be immediately known to the French, and these people [the Dutch] would never consent to let so many troops go so far from their frontiers; for the preservation of which and their garrisons, I propose to leave 100 battalions and 110 squadrons . . . What I now write I beg may be known to nobody but her Majesty and the Prince.

He went on to gratefully acknowledge the queen's kindness in making him colonel of 1st Foot Guards.[12] Planning the campaign was exhausting. On 5 May Cadogan told Lord Raby that his work 'has left me hardly time to eat or sleep'. He emphasised that it was 'absolutely necessary to hasten putting into execution the project of reducing the Elector of Bavaria before he can receive a greater succour . . . in order to do it there will be an army left in the Lines of Stollhofen to prevent the French forcing them or passing the Rhine below Philipsburg'.[13]

Despite his desire to conceal his full intentions from the Dutch, Marlborough was open with Heinsius. On 11 May he wrote from Maastricht to say that he had now met Goor, who must logically have been apprised of the plan, for, helpfully, he had proposed that the twenty Dutch cannon at Koblenz should join the march, and on 21 May Marlborough told Heinsius that he hoped to be at Koblenz on the twenty-fifth and then at Mainz on the twenty-ninth. He was confident that if Villeroi shadowed his march with a strong force to the west, as he expected, 'they will hardly be able to leave the name of an army behind them', and that would enable the Dutch to send more troops 'as might make me succeed against the Elector of Bavaria'.[14]

A private shadow hung over public endeavour. By the opening of the campaign Marlborough's relations with Sarah had broken down almost completely, and they were certainly living apart. Although there had already been marked differences of opinion over politics, for John was too much his father's son to approve of Sarah's relentless whiggery, the most probable cause of her coldness was her belief that Marlborough was having an affair. Sarah's biographers suggest that the thirty-year-old Elizabeth Cromwell, wife of Lord Southwell, joint commissioner of the privy seal, was the most probable subject of her ire. It is impossible to say, after this passage of time, whether or not she had cause for it, although the case would fit a diagnosis of menopausal jealousy very closely. On an unspecified date in April, evidently before his departure for the Continent, Marlborough told Sarah:

> Your carriage to me of late is so extraordinary, that I do not know how to behave myself. I thought you used me so barbarously that I was resolved never to send or speak, but I love [you] too well to be able to keep in that resolution. Therefore I desire that you will give me leave to come to you tonight, so that I may know in what it is I have thus offended. I am sure really in thought I have not, for I do love you with all the truth imaginable.

Another letter admitted that:

> As I know your temper, I am very sensible that what I say signifies nothing. However, I can't forebear what I said yesterday, which is that I never sent to her [the unspecified 'mistress'] in my life, and may my happiness in the other world depend upon the truth of this. If there be aught that I could do to let you know my innocency, I should be glad to do it . . . You say that every hour since I came from St Albans has given you fresh assurances of my hating you, and that you know I have sent to this woman. These two things are so barbarous, for I have not for these many years thought myself so happy by your kindness as for these last five or six days, and if you could at that time think I hated you I am most miserable. And for the last which you say you are sure of, may I and all that is dear to me be cursed if ever I sent to her, or have had anything to do with her, or have endeavoured to have.[15]

They were at least communicating by the time he reached The Hague, and he begged her to let him know how she would like him to rewrite his will to reflect Blandford's death: 'As I hope for happiness in the next world and this, I will follow your directions exactly, and take it as kindly as if you have reprieved me from death.'[16] She wrote to him soon afterwards, but 'you write very much with the spleen, which makes me uneasy'. It was not until 24 April that she at last forgave him.

> Your dear letter of the 15th came to me but this minute. My Lord Treasurer's letter in which it was enclosed, by some mistake was sent to Amsterdam. I would not for anything in my power it had been lost, for it is so very kind, that I would in return lose a thousand lives if I had them to make you happy. Before I set down to write this letter I took yours that you wrote at Harwich out of my strong box, and have burnt it; and if you will give me leave, it will be a great pleasure to me to have it in my power to read this dear letter often, and that it may be found in my strong box when I am dead. I do this minute love you better and with more tenderness than ever I did before. This letter of yours has made me so happy, that from my soul I do wish that we could retire and not be blamed . . . I have pressed this business of carrying an army into Germany, in order to have left a good name behind me, wishing for nothing else but good success. I shall now add to that, of having a long life that I may be happy in your dear love.[17]

The Scarlet Caterpillar

The great march began at Bedburg, west of Cologne, on 19 May. The weather had been terrible, but one cavalry officer remembered: 'Notwithstanding the rainy weather that happened at the same time, [the army] made a most glorious appearance.'[18] Marlborough started the march with some 19,000 men in English pay, 5,000 Prussian and Hanoverian troops met him at Koblenz on the twenty-sixth, and other streams flowed in to join the torrent as it rolled southwards. Apart from Marlborough and a few senior officers nobody knew the army's destination. On 11 May he had written to congratulate Henry St John, a protégé of Robert Harley's, who had just taken over from old Blathwayt as secretary at war, telling him that his army would shortly head for the Moselle, but 'I may venture to tell you (though I would not have it public as yet) I design to march a great deal higher into Germany.'[19] There was a two-day halt at Koblenz, 'After which,' says Richard Kane,

> to the surprise of all, we crossed the Moselle and Rhine both at this place, and marched through the country of Hesse-Cassel, where we were joined by the Hereditary Prince of that country with a body of Hessians, which completed the Duke's army to about 40,000. Having

passed through Hesse, we marched through the Electorate of Mainz, and so through the Palatinate of the Rhine, till we came to Heidelberg; here we halted four days, nor was it publicly known, till we came here, what the Duke designed.[20]

The French were as mystified as Captain Kane. Villeroi knew that Marlborough had moved south, and duly shadowed him, but was then ordered by Louis to take station at Offenburg, across the Rhine south-east of Strasbourg, with forty battalions and sixty-eight to seventy squadrons (some of them later sent on to Tallard), and to react as required, blocking Marlborough if he came up the Rhine, turning on him if he entered Alsace, or following him to the Danube. Tallard, with forty battalions and fifty squadrons, was to operate in Bavaria, and Coigny, with a tiny force composed largely of Swiss regiments whose contracts did not oblige them to cross the Rhine, remained in Alsace. Thus while the French were not completely wrong-footed by Marlborough's march, their response at this stage was wholly reactive, and in the event Villeroi was, through no fault of his own, to be no use on either the Brabant or the German front.

Although some historians detect real tension between Marlborough and Overkirk, left behind to command Dutch troops in front of the Lines of Brabant, it is evident that relations between the two generals were actually very good. Cadogan makes it clear that 'Monsieur Overkirk' was the only Dutch general to have backed Marlborough when he wished to penetrate the Lines of Brabant the previous year, suggesting that the real problem was Dutch generals and not field deputies, and that 'the deputies here . . . are extremely for it'.[21] There was a moment of concern in early May when Cardonnel reported to John Ellis, under-secretary of state, that the French

are getting all the boats they can together at Namur and landing cannon with ammunition and instruments for removing of ground and give out that they design to besiege Huy, though 'tis believed they will hardly attempt it, and that they make these preparations rather to hinder or retard our march into Germany.[22]

However, Marlborough correctly deduced that if he moved south Villeroi had no choice but to follow, and on 21 May he assured Overkirk that Villeroi had indeed been ordered to take a very strong detachment from Brabant to follow him wherever he went: as this order had been issued by Louis XIV in person, it is an index of the quality of Marlborough's intelligence. He added in a postscript that this force included thirty-six battalions and forty-five or forty-six squadrons, including the *Maison du Roi*, Louis' household troops: these latter were to be sent on to Tallard in Germany. Three days later he told Overkirk that progress was good, and repeated letters assured Overkirk that operations were going according to plan and that there was no chance of Villeroi breaking back to attack the Dutch in Brabant. Marlborough helped confound confusion by ordering a bridge of boats to be thrown across the Rhine at Philipsburg, implying that Landau might really be his objective, and it was not until he crossed the Main on 3 June that this possibility could be ruled out by the French.

We can see, from the correspondence between Louis and his generals, that they were consistently a move behind Marlborough in the game. On 4 May Louis told Villeroi that enemy movements still did not betray 'their real intentions for the campaign: it seems only, by all the information . . . that they have no other object but a definite concentration in Flanders and Brabant'. Villeroi replied that 'Rumour is rife . . . that they are going to raise a considerable army on the Moselle, and that the Duke of Marlborough will command it.'[23] Tallard and Marsin were concerned about establishing the time and place of their rendezvous, and the only hint that all might not be perfect came when Tallard told Chamillart that his planned manoeuvres in Bavaria, so far from the fount of French strength, might prove tricky 'if things do not turn out as we hope'.[24]

In contrast, throughout this period Marlborough's intelligence network was working flat-out. Although part of the responsibility was Cadogan's, Adam de Cardonnel ran one network through John de Robethon, private secretary to the Elector of Hanover, the future George I. By the time he came to England with his employer Robethon was arguably the most influential of the new king's advisers, and was not a popular figure in his master's new realm. However, during Marlborough's campaigns he was a vital link in an intelligence chain whose length and complexity we can only guess at. Cardonnel gave him accurate appraisals of the state of the French army and the progress of the Allied march. 'The deserters who come in say that all French battalions are very weak despite the recruits who have joined them,' said Cardonnel on 19 June, 'and that sickness is rife amongst the newly-arrived, so that five hundred were buried at Ulm in a single week.' A week later he said that: 'The continual rain which has fallen for fifteen days has greatly inconvenienced our infantry and caused [illegible] sickness amongst them . . . but our cavalry and generally all the other troops in the pay of England and the States are in very good condition.'[25]

The really valuable information flowed the other way. Cardonnel thanked Robethon for letters, now missing, which accompanied 'Mons de Chamillart's Memorial and du Breuil's examination'. Michel de Chamillart was Louis' war minister, who owed his rise at least in part to the fact that he was Louis' billiards partner: 'a hero at billiard, a zero in the ministry' is how a waggish Frenchman described him. It is evident from the letter that his memorandum was nothing less than a summary of royal instructions to the army commanders. 'We find . . . the utmost designs of the enemy in this memorial,' wrote Cardonnel, 'and I hope we shall be able to traverse them.' A French historian of Napoleon's era was exasperated when he described the leaks. 'We must conclude from this significant paper,' he lamented, 'that the feeble Chamillart, occupying the post of Louvois without having either his vigour or his talent, had let himself be robbed of the secret of the campaign plan. Nothing is beyond the reach of the power of gold, and it looks as though Marlborough, although blamed for avarice, knew how to spend money to some point.'[26] Although Cardonnel's letter is as tantalising for what it fails to say as for what it does, the key piece of information seems to have been that French commanders were encouraged to attack the Allies in detail, but not to fight them united. Marlborough was to fail in one of his aims, that of wholly crushing the Bavarians before French reinforcements arrived, but the fact that he knew that the French would only offer battle if the Allies were disunited was of untold value.

The ramifications of the Robethon connection were to spread more widely. First, Marlborough was on warm terms with the Hanoverian court, and enjoyed a good personal relationship with the Elector's son George, who fought under his command at Oudenarde. These relationships played a significant part in Marlborough's helping to ensure the Hanoverian succession on the death of Anne, and the Elector was suitably grateful. Second, Winston S. Churchill's great biography of his ancestor dwelt on the vital importance of this strategic intelligence. It is not too much to argue that it was his gleanings as a historian, as well as his experience as first lord of the admiralty in 1914–15, that encouraged him as prime minister to take the German code ULTRA so seriously, and to insist on seeing original material, not simply summaries.[27]

The march to the Danube was some 250 miles long, and for the most part was conducted through friendly territory. Contracts had been placed for the supply of food, forage and boots along the army's line of march, and Marlborough was scrupulous in assuring local rulers that English gold would pave his way. For example, on 26 May he wrote to the Elector of Mainz, head of the 'circle' of the Rhine, one of the Empire's loose subdivisions.

> Monseigneur,
> Her Majesty the Queen of Great Britain and their High Mightinesses the Estates General having resolved . . . to send an army corps under my orders from the Low Countries, and seeing myself obliged to pass through the Electoral Circle of the Upper Rhine, I beg your Electoral Highness that he will be pleased to give free passage to the above-mentioned troops, and to ensure that supplies can be found on the march, for prompt payment. It would be a great advantage for the troops, and at the same time a solace for the countryside by preventing disorders and foraging, if the forage could be provided with several horses and carts to help the artillery on the road: to which effect officers can be sent in advance to organise things.

He promised that in return for this help, his army would observe 'a very exact discipline'.[28]

For most of the route the horse, with Marlborough himself, followed a different route from the infantry under General Charles Churchill, the duke's brother and 'general of the foot', so as to reduce the drain on local resources. Captain Robert Parker tells how it was for those men in long red coats and white spatterdashes, stepping out in rank and file in the close and comradely world of the marching regiments of foot.

> We frequently marched three, sometimes four days successively, and then halted a day. We generally began our march about three in the morning, proceeded about four leagues, or four and a half each day, and reached our [camping] ground about nine. As we marched through the country of our Allies, commissaries were appointed to furnish us with all manner of necessaries for man and horse; these were brought to the ground before we arrived, and the soldiers had nothing to do, but to pitch their tents, boil their kettles, and lie down to rest. Surely never was a march carried out with more order and regularity and with less fatigue to both man and horse.[29]

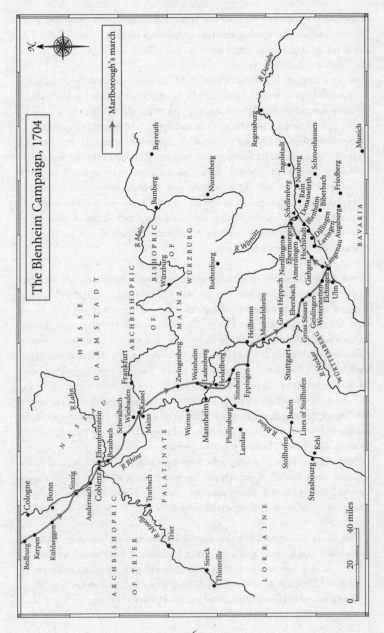

The Blenheim Campaign, 1704

→ Marlborough's march

Sometimes a soldier's view of life reflects his rank, and Sergeant John Wilson was less favourably impressed by the comfort of the march. As the army trudged on from Mainz,

> there falling such a flood of rain by which there came such a torrent of water from the mountains that the roads were rendered so bad that there was no possibility of moving the train [of artillery] . . . the roads were so bad and the ground so boggy . . . that not one piece of cannon could be moved. Upon which there was orders for the country to bring in straw for the men and another day's forage for the horses. And next day fifty men without arms were ordered to go before a mile or two to prepare the way. As the said 50 men of each regiment having repaired the roads, the train was ordered to march gradually after them. Which they did but with a great deal of trouble, they being obliged to put double horses, if not more, to each piece of cannon.[30]

Good generals share sergeants' concerns, and Marlborough too was worried about the weather. On 24 May OS he told Godolphin that the state of the roads meant that the 'cannon and artillery' were now six days behind him, and the Luneburg, Danish and Hessian troops were spread out 'in several quarters', but he hoped to push on to meet Eugène, leaving his brother Charles to bring on the English while the Duke of Württemberg, commander of the Danish contingent, further back still, brought his own men forward.

Even now, with the campaign still far short of any resolution, there was no refuge from administration. The promotion of Dutch generals in Portugal might cause unhappiness in Holland, warned Marlborough. Making Brigadier Harvey a major general might be gratifying to that officer but would not be wise 'when we have colonels in the service elder officers than he is'. Lord Derby, however, should be made a major general, but with the same seniority date as Major General Withers. There were delicate feelings to be salved.

> For want of officers on the march I have been obliged to make Colonel [Archibald] Row a brigadier. He is the eldest colonel we have here, and a very diligent officer, but this will give a just occasion for Colonel Shrimpton of the Guards to desire the like commission, he being an elder colonel than Row, so that I desire they may be dated of the same day . . .

There was at least some good news: he was happy to hear that Godolphin's son had just been made cofferer of the household, and that Lady Henrietta had given him a son.[31]

Captain John Blackader, of what was officially Fergusson's Regiment but was already widely known, by that title by which it would leave its enduring mark on history, as the Cameronians, had already identified that: 'This is like to be a campaign of great fatigue and trouble.' His diary constantly dwells on the unhappy plight of a devout man in a less than devout army.

> Armies which used to be full of men of great and noble souls, are now turned to a parcel of mercenary, fawning, lewd, dissipated creatures; the dregs and scum of mankind: And those who will not fawn and crouch, are made the butt of malice, and oppressed by the joint conspiracy of wicked men.[32]

I am not sure that John Blackader would have approved of Mrs Christian Davies, who had joined the army to look for her husband, who had enlisted when in drink. By 'having been long conversant in the camp, she had lost that softness which heightens the beauty of the fair, and contracted a masculine air and behaviour'. She made a convincing enough dragoon, though she 'narrowly escaped being discovered' when a surgeon investigated a gunshot wound to her hip. She remembered that the army advanced by

> long and tiresome marches, which greatly harassed our foot . . . I cannot help taking notice in this place, though it breaks in upon my narrative, of the Duke of Marlborough's great humanity, who seeing some of our foot drop, through the fatigue of the march, took them into his own coach.[33]

John Marshall Deane, a 'private sentinel' in 1st Foot Guards, and thus close to the bottom of the logistic pile, agreed about the weather.

> One thing observable, it hath rained 32 days together more or less and miserable marches we have had for deep and dirty roads and through tedious woods and wildernesses and over cast high rock and mountains, that it may easily be judged what our little army endured . . . And to help, everything grew to be at an excessive dear rate that there was scarce a living for a soldier and the nearer came every day to the Grand Army the dearer every thing was.[34]

However, the army held up well. Desertion was low, and, despite the bad weather, the army left fewer than 1,000 sick on its line of march.

The careful work of the medical historian Eric Gruber von Arni shows that Marlborough took a great deal of care over the provision for his sick and wounded. A convoy of boats with medical equipment moved up the Rhine and established a transit hospital at Kassel, and then went on up the River Main via Frankfurt to Wertheim, whence it moved by road to establish another transit hospital at Heidenheim. On 22 June Marlborough, ahead with his cavalry, wrote to Charles Churchill, who was with the infantry on the rutted roads behind him.

> I received yesterday yours of the 20th at Blockingen, and having informed myself of the proper place of sending your sick men, I am assured they will be best at Heidenheim, which is not far from you, and therefore desire you will forthwith send them thither in carts with an able surgeon and a mate or two to look after them, and such commission and non-commission officers as you shall think fit, giving them at the same time money for their subsistence.

When he closed the letter 'I long to have you with me, being your loving brother,' he was writing in as much of a professional as a personal sense, for he was increasingly anxious, with hostile territory ahead, to get the army closed up.[35]

On 10 June, at Mundelsheim, sixty miles north-west of Ulm, Marlborough met the Prince Eugène for the first time, and they quickly established that rapport that sometimes unites men who are different in almost all save a driving sense of purpose. Marlborough was tall, handsome and beautifully turned out. He had been a ladies' man in his youth, and was married to a very powerful woman. Eugène was ugly, plainly dressed and had no apparent interest in women: indeed, in his youth there had been rumours that he charged with the lightest of cavalry. Once the cares of office were off his back he seems to have settled down happily enough in some sort of relationship with Countess Eleanora Bethkány, but he believed that there was no point in talking politics to women, for 'They do not have the necessary stability as men, easily become careless, allow their friendship to dictate what they say and therefore you cannot depend on their discretion.'[36] We cannot be sure what Marlborough would have made of this, except perhaps to smile thinly, change the subject, and offer his guest another glass of tokay.

Marlborough was famously soft: Lord Ailesbury complained that he was so kind-hearted that he could not bear to chide a servant or a corporal. His courts-martial often recommended to his mercy men who had broken the letter of the law. For instance, a court-martial felt that Private John Muddey of Captain Alexander Ruthven's company of 1st Foot Guards had not really intended to desert:

> He went from his post without leave, with intent only to visit an acquaintance in Major General Murray's Regiment, but was stopped in the way, and his officer affirming that he is a weak and silly man, and this his first fault.[37]

Muddey was recommended to the duke's mercy, which was unfailingly exercised in these cases. Eugène, in contrast, believed that such generosity weakened discipline. In one instance Marlborough interceded with him for a soldier who had been condemned to death. 'If your Grace has not executed more men than I have done,' said Eugène, 'I will consent to the pardon of this fellow.' It transpired that, for all his generosity, Marlborough had actually hanged more men. 'There, my Lord, you see the benefit of example,' argued Eugène. 'You pardon many, and therefore have to execute many; I never pardon one, therefore few dare offend, and of course but few suffer.'[38] Nicholas Henderson grasps the essentials of the relationship between Eugène and Marlborough:

> The two men were indispensable to each other . . . Not that they were rivals. Their collaboration was constant and selfless. Utterly different in personality and temperament though they were, the two men combined so exquisitely that they were described as 'like two bodies with but a single soul'. On one occasion, at the zenith of their association, a medal was struck likening them to Castor and Pollux.[39]

On 11 June Marlborough and Eugène rode out together on the march towards Heppach, and Marlborough had arranged for the British cavalry, nineteen squadrons strong, to be drawn up by their way. As Winston S. Churchill put it, the men and horses were in perfect condition, 'a little travel stained, rather fine-drawn, but all that soldiers should be'.[40] 'My Lord,' said Eugène, 'I never saw better horses, better clothes, finer belts and accoutrements; but money, which you don't want in England, will buy clothes and fine horses, but it can't buy this lively air I see in every one of these troopers' faces.' 'Sir,' said Marlborough, 'that must be attributed to their heartiness for the public cause and the particular pleasure and satisfaction they have in seeing your Highness.'[41]

If this could be overheard by a nearby chaplain it must have been intended for public consumption, but it was none the worse for that.

Three days later Marlborough and Eugène met Prince Louis at the Inn of the Golden Fleece at Gross Heppach, not far from Stuttgart. They agreed that Prince Louis should remain with Marlborough, with the two generals commanding on alternate days, while Eugène made for the Rhine to hold the Lines of Stollhofen. This was not a question, as some have suggested, of Louis being anxious to move a firebrand out of the way, because Marlborough had told the Prince of Hesse, some days before the meeting, that Eugène's mission had already been fixed in Vienna: 'He is going to command on the Rhine, where his presence is deemed necessary.'[42] It was not an arrangement of Prince Louis' making. Eugène was senior to him in the Imperialist army; Eugène had already told Marlborough something of 'the character of the Prince of Baden, by which I find I must be much more on my guard than if I was with Prince Eugène', and he assured Marlborough that the emperor would not hesitate to replace Louis if the king did not act with vigour in the common cause.

Marlborough and Louis intended to seek out the Elector, who, Marlborough thought, 'will either retire over the Danube or march to his strong camp at Dillengen', and they would act accordingly.[43] Marlborough hoped that, just as the Elector had joined the French cause because of self-interest, he might be induced to leave it for the same reason, and felt that if cuffed hard enough, Max Emmanuel would negotiate. He then pushed on, through those roads that Sergeant Wilson found so tedious, to Gingen near Ulm, where on 26 July reinforcements now brought his strength to ninety-six battalions, two hundred squadrons and forty-eight guns, 80,000 men by the lowest of reckonings. He was delighted to have got his foot and guns in at last, but told both Godolphin and Sarah, to whom he wrote separate letters on the twenty-ninth, that there were still some Danish horse and foot to arrive, and he feared he could not do anything serious until he had them. He added that he was hoping that Charles Hodges, groom of the robes to Queen Anne, would send him the design for a stable for the Ranger's Lodge in Windsor Great Park. 'I should be glad all conveniencies were about it,' he concluded, on one of the last days of relative peace.[44]

He could not but be aware that his own future and that of Godolphin's government teetered in the balance. Thomas Coke wrote to tell him that the squirearchy was pleased to see some stirring in the covert at last: 'The country gentlemen had long groaned under the weight of four shillings in the pound without hearing of a town taken or any enterprise endeavoured.' They were now 'more cheerful in this war' when expeditions were 'carried on so secretly that they are in a manner successful even before the French, so famous formerly for good intelligence, can give a guess where the stroke is likely to fall'.[45] But failure would be harshly punished: 'If he fails,' wrote one critic, 'we will break him up as hounds upon a hare.'

Being Strongly Entrenched: The Schellenberg

The stroke was to fall on Donauwörth, which stands at the confluence of the Danube and the Wörnitz, about midway between Ulm to the west and Ingolstadt to the east. The town itself lay on the low ground on the north bank of the Danube, with a single bridge (and an extra pontoon bridge in 1704) connecting it to Nordheim on the southern bank, and the wooded hills of the Donauwörth Forest rolling off to the north. The town and the river crossing that gave the place its significance were dominated from the east by the Schellenberg, rising over a hundred metres above the height of the river. Near its summit was a three-bastioned earthwork, the *Sternschanze*, built by the Swedes during the Thirty Years War more than half a century before and testifying to the lasting importance of this spot.

That old bruiser Colonel de la Colonie, there with his Bavarian red grenadiers, described the hill as 'oval in plan, with a gentle slope on the southern side, giving very easy communication with Donauwörth; while on the northern side the country is covered with woods and undergrowth, reaching up close to the old entrenchments'.[46] His practised eye noted that the slopes to the north and west, from which the attack would come, were convex, so that attackers were out of sight for most of their climb, only coming into view for the last two hundred paces. Although he would still recognise the place today, he could not but be struck by the fact that the B25 autoroute, the *Romantische Strasse*, hurtles in between the Schellenberg and the town it commands, and the northern suburbs of Donauwörth have spread, on either side of the Kaibach brook, north of the town. The *Sternschanze* is still there, and the whole feature, despite the passage of time, well deserves the caption 'a tough nut to crack'.

On 1 July NS the Allied army marched north-east to Amerdingen, right across the front of the entrenched position at Dillingen, held by the Elector and his French ally Marshal Ferdinand, comte Marsin. Max Emmanuel declined to budge, but, seeing that if the Allies continued to march eastwards they would cross the Danube and be able to manoeuvre on his right and rear, he sent Jean Baptiste, comte d'Arco, to secure Donauwörth with sixteen Bavarian and five French battalions, nine squadrons of French dragoons and eight heavy guns, some 12,000 men. D'Arco was an experienced veteran of Bavarian and Imperial service, who had been made a Bavarian marshal in 1702 and whose support for Max Emmanuel's pro-French policy was to bring him the baton of a marshal of France. He left four French battalions in the town and marched the rest of his men up into the Schellenberg where, with the help of local peasants, they began clearing fields of fire, constructing earthworks and palisades, and connecting the hill to the town itself with a line of trenches protected by gabions, large wicker baskets filled with earth.

Historian James Falkner's soldierly assessment of d'Arco's quandary is wholly logical. D'Arco had three options. He could take his little all-arms force forward and fight a mobile defence, making the Allies pay dearly for the crossings of the Wörnitz, or fire Donauwörth and its magazines and tear down its bridge, depriving the town of strategic purpose. Holding the Schellenberg made sense only if the Elector sent reinforcements and the Allies formed up in the accepted manner before launching a formal attack. This was the option d'Arco selected, and he was not unreasonable in doing so. With every day that passed the Schellenberg would grow stronger, and the Allies would be unlikely to attack it if Max Emmanuel slipped his army along the Danube behind it.

Marlborough's spies and scouts told him what was happening on the Schellenberg, and de la Colonie complained that a corporal in the Electoral Prince of Bavaria's Regiment deserted with full details of defensive preparations. While we must be careful not to make more of the tension between Prince Louis and Marlborough than the evidence warrants, the two men certainly approached war in different ways. Louis tended to be a formalised and reflective commander, and moreover, he had formerly campaigned alongside Max Emmanuel and, as a fellow German prince, was on good personal terms with him regardless of the present political climate. Marlborough, in contrast, needed a quick decision and had no time for niceties. He explained to Godolphin that the Schellenberg

is a hill that commands the town of Donauwörth which passage on the Danube would be very advantageous for us, for I would make a magazine for our army there. If we had the cannon ready we could not fail of taking it. Prince Louis assures me that we shall have 20 pieces of battery here in 4 days, which I am afraid is impossible.[47]

On 1 July Marlborough sent forward Cadogan and Goor, his quartermaster generals, to look at the ground, and he speedily concluded that that he had neither room nor time for manoeuvre. A finger of high wooded ground, then called the Boshberg, pointed southwards from the larger forest to the north, making it impossible to move round the Schellenberg so as to outflank it from the east, while the Kaibach and Wörnitz, with the old defences of the town, made attack from the west impossible. The place had to be carried quickly, because the Elector's quartermasters were already laying out camping grounds south of the Danube in preparation for the arrival of the main army, and this reduced Marlborough's options to the frontal assault which Prince Louis advised most strongly against. He decided to attack on the following day, when it was his turn to command the army, but meanwhile ordered Cadogan to lay out encampments on the Wörnitz west of the town to persuade d'Arco that he proposed to do things by the stately book.

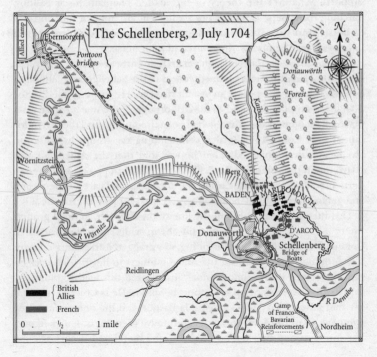

The Schellenberg, 2 July 1704

Allied camp

Ebermorgen

Pontoon bridges

Donauwörth

Kaibach

Donauwörth Forest

Wörnitstein

Berg

BADEN MARLBOROUGH

R Wörnitz

Donauworth

D'ARCO

Schellenberg
Bridge of Boats

Reidlingen

British Allies

French

0   ½   1 mile

Camp of Franco-Bavarian Reinforcements

R Danube

Nordheim

Marlborough threw away the book. He set off at three o'clock on the morning of 2 July with 6,000 foot, made up, as he tells us of 130 men, including ten grenadiers, selected from each Allied battalion, thirty squadrons of horse and dragoons, and three full battalions of Louis' Imperial grenadiers, two German and one Austrian. Eighty men of 1st Foot Guards under Lord Peterborough's eldest boy John, Lord Mordaunt, had volunteered to furnish the 'forlorn hope' which would lead the assault. Marching along 'very difficult' roads they reached the Wörnitz at Ebermorgen at about 1 p.m., and threw pontoons across to support the single existing bridge, but were not all over till three. Behind the stormers came 12,000 Allied infantry in two echelons, under Major General Henry Withers and Count Horn. The cavalry and dragoons, under Lieutenant Generals Lumley and Hompesch, who had marched early with Marlborough, spent part of their time preparing fascines, big bundles of green wood, which were to be used to help fill in entrenchments. The mounted troops then reassembled to form a fourth echelon after the stormers and their two waves of infantry supports. Whatever the theory of the matter, chaplain Josias Sandby, watching from Berg, distinctly saw six lines in all, 'four of foot and two of horse', probably the forlorn hope, the main body of stormers, two lines of infantry supports, dragoons and then horse.

D'Arco heard of Marlborough's march as early as 9 a.m., and spent the day working furiously on the defences of the Schellenberg, although he evidently did not expect an assault that day. He wrote to the Elector asking for support, was told that Marlborough had come so close on a personal reconnaissance that he had been fired upon, and then went for dinner with Colonel du Bordet, commanding the troops in the town. His meal was interrupted when he was told that the Allied advance guard was in the suburb of Berg, which the Bavarian pickets had fired to delay the advance. Telling du Bordet to take special care of the trench and gabion link with the Schellenberg, d'Arco spurred off for the hill.

The attackers formed up on the line of the Kaibach, in dead ground where d'Arco's guns could not hit them, while their own artillery, Colonel Holcroft Blood commanding, was dragged into battery on Berg hill. Although it was hard for the Allied gunners to hit the defences on the crest, many of the rounds which just cleared this feature ploughed into the infantry drawn up in support behind it. De la Colonie said that the first salvo killed 'the Comte de la Bastide and the lieutenant of my company, to whom I was speaking, and twelve grenadiers, knocked over like ninepins; my coat was covered with the blood and brains of these gentlemen . . . the enemy's battery . . . raked us through and through'. He lost eighty men without firing a shot.[48] He was able to take his revenge soon enough. Led by Lieutenant General van Goor in person, the Allied infantry stepped off at about six o'clock, and though they had perhaps four hundred yards to cover they were not visible from the hill for the first two hundred, and de la Colonie remembered, in the quirky way that men recall little things at such times, that he saw their colours breasting the rise first. Coming up the same slope, Sergeant Wilson recalled: 'The front rank had orders for every man to sling his firelock and take a fascine in his arms, in order to break the enemy's shot in advancing. After which we advanced with all the courage and vigour in life.'[49]

The French and Bavarian musketry, delayed so long, was deadly when it came. The defenders had also stockpiled wagonloads of hand grenades, and bowled these underarm downhill, where they burst in the packed ranks of the attackers. As de la Colonie acknowledged, 'The English infantry attacked with all the fury in the world; they showed a terrible determination right up to our parapet, but they met there, to repulse them, at least as much fury and determination as they themselves brought.'[50] The first assault was driven back, and Bavarian grenadiers scampered out of their defences to hurry the broken attackers back down the hill, but were themselves checked by the disciplined fire of the next attacking echelon. The second assault fared no better than the first. This time, as de la Colonie saw, the Allied generals had dismounted and were leading their men forward on foot, but despite hand-to-hand fighting of extraordinary ferocity – de la Colonie witnessed men tearing each other's eyes out with their fingernails – d'Arco's line held, leaving Allied dead piled so high that they topped the fascines protecting his trenches.

Marlborough then ordered his dragoons to dismount and join the assault, and, though somewhat hampered by their big boots and long swords, they went on up the charnel slopes, with the horse, still mounted, closing up behind them. We cannot tell whether, as chaplain Sandby suggests, it was 'their brave example' that animated the infantry, or simply the fact that serried ranks of steady mounted men gave no opportunity for any faint-hearted foot soldiers to scuttle back into the ruins of Berg, that so buttressed the attack that the infantry tried yet again. It was now about seven o'clock: Marlborough's men had suffered very heavily, and there was no apparent progress. Then came a report that some of the attackers, edging away to their right, had found that the trench and gabion line connecting hill and town was not effectively held, and that du Bordet's men were not firing from the loopholes in the old curtain wall round the town, whence musketry might have made any break-through impossible. Marlborough sent an officer to confirm this, and Prince Louis seems to have discovered the lapse at much the same time. His three fine battalions of Imperial grenadiers, all moustaches, match-boxes and mitre caps, were still under his hand in the valley of the Kaibach, and he immediately shoved them into the gap. D'Arco at once counterattacked with some dragoons, whom he had husbanded on the reverse slope, but the grenadiers, coming on briskly to the rattle of their side-drums, brushed them aside.

On the hill Count Maffei, d'Arco's deputy, could not make out the colours and field-signs worn by the advancing troops: the French and their allies generally wore a white ribbon or paper in their hats, and the Imperialists a sprig of greenery. By the time he had realised that they were not reinforcements coming up from the town it was too late: the position was fatally compromised. De la Colonie's men struggled back over the crest in good order but eventually broke. He discovered that the drummer assigned to look after his horse had decamped with the beast. Hit in the jaw, he eventually jettisoned his long riding boots and 'richly laced coat', by now greasy with blood and brains, and scorched by the powder burns of close-range musketry, to swim the Danube to safety. He was in good company: d'Arco also swam for his life, and the pontoon bridge collapsed under the weight of fugitives. Marlborough quickly ordered Brigadier Ferguson, apparently the senior unwounded officer on the hill, to 'keep the foot to their colours' to secure the place, while he unleashed the horse in pursuit, ensuring that d'Arco paid the heavy price of losing a battle with a river at his back.

The battle was shockingly costly, with almost 5,500 Allied casualties and at least 8,000 French and Bavarian, many of them drowned in the Danube. About one-third of the attacking infantry were hit: 1st Foot Guards lost twelve officers and 217 men, the two battalions of Orkney's Regiment (whom we last saw as Dumbarton's, holding the Bussex Rhine half a lifetime ago) thirty officers and 418 men, and Ingoldsby's (later the Royal Welch Fusiliers) sixteen officers and 228 men. Poor Chaplain Noyes of Orkney's reported ruefully that 'We carried the place, but at a cost very dear, the enemy being obstinate . . . we are not yet recovered out of the confusion the death of our friends has put us in.' He thought a good deal of the damage had been done by 'friendly fire'. 'They were in such great numbers combined in the attack,' he wrote, 'that sometimes the hindest firing at random (as on such occasions there is always some confusion) shot those that were before them.' Lieutenant General Lumley told him that 'the Hollanders had not a general officer at present in a condition to lead them'.[51]

The toll of officers was certainly high, and bore eloquent testimony to their courage in leading successive assaults. That resolute Dutchman Johan van Goor was dead, hit in the head at the first assault. He had been acting as Dutch quartermaster general, and Marlborough particularly mourned his loss, for he 'helped me in a great many things, which I am now forced to do myself, till I can find some other officer I can rely on for it'. He now lies in the great church at Nordlingen, with a dignified memorial tablet on the wall. Goor's countryman Major General Beinheim was dead too, and so was the Imperialist major general the Prince of Wolfenbüttel. Prince Louis had been wounded in the foot. Although this was not apparently as serious as the wound suffered by his comrade Count Styrum, shot through the body, it would eventually fester and kill him. Both the Prince of Hesse and Count Horn, who commanded the Württemberg contingent, were also wounded.

On 3 July Marlborough told Sarah that 'We have ruined the best of the Elector's foot,' though the 'English foot has suffered a good deal' in the process. He assured her that all her personal friends were well, apart from Major General Wood and Brigadier General Meredith, both wounded but predicted (correctly) to recover.[52] Private Deane thought that his opponents

> made a brave defence and bold resistance against us as brave and loyal
> hearted gentlemen soldiers ought to for their prince and country . . .
> both English and Dutch behaved themselves to admiration and the
> foreigners, give them their due, did stand like a wall and acted as
> became brave gentlemen and as duty combines a soldier at such a
> juncture, and several general officers they lost in this action and
> abundance of old experienced sentinels. A glorious action it was to be
> sure for this vigorous and bold attack held near 3 hours but with God's
> assistance we driving them out of their works and possessing ourselves
> of them. Our horse likewise pursued and killed abundance of them
> driving several hundreds of them into the River Danube . . .[53]

Chaplain Noyes reported that 'our horse and dragoons hacked them down at a miserable rate . . . but far the greatest part fell into the hands of the [Imperial] hussars who gave no quarter'.[54]

The Allies seized d'Arco's camp that day, with fifteen pieces of cannon (the exuberant Private Deane reported thirty-one guns and a mortar) and abundant baggage and ammunition: the accidental explosion of an underground powder magazine 'did some mischief to a squadron of Dutch dragoons'. On 4 July the garrison of Donauwörth, ordered by the Elector to escape, first firing the town and destroying the bridge, 'durst not stay to execute their design', but left the bridge damaged but still usable, and a rich store of food, powder and 'three great guns'.[55] The Danish contingent under the Duke of Württemberg, twenty-one squadrons and seven battalions, arrived in camp on 5 July, counterbalancing the losses incurred in the storm.

Of Marlborough's admirers, Winston S. Churchill glosses quite quickly over the Schellenberg, possibly because it reminded him too much of what his own generation had so recently lived through. David Chandler, in contrast, suggests that the weakening of the crucial link between town and Schellenberg 'had been Marlborough's intention'.[56] The truth is more complex. At the tactical level the attack on the Schellenberg was necessarily unsubtle. Marlborough did not have the time for a more elaborate plan, and all contemporary accounts emphasise that the discovery of the weak spot was fortuitous, although the Allied reaction was swift and decisive. The battle was, then, no tactical masterpiece: it was won by the sheer courage of the Allied infantry.

However, at what we would now call the operational level, the linking of battles and engagements to form a coherent campaign, the Schellenberg was indeed a masterpiece, and, however dark its hue, it could not have been painted had Marlborough not hustled on to attack before Max Emmanuel had arrived. Sharp offensive action, not for the last time, was the key to his success. As Marlborough pointed out in the many letters he wrote to strengthen his political hand after the action, it was 'a very severe blow' for Max Emmanuel, who had lost some of his finest infantry. The fact that the Elector could not check the Allied foot with his best men in the defences of the Schellenberg cast a long shadow. Donauwörth, taken with so little damage, provided a valuable forward base for the next leg of the campaign. Max Emmanuel could not now prevent the Allies from entering what Marlborough called 'the heart of Bavaria'. Finally, it is very often true that the first major clash of a campaign establishes the pattern of what is to come, and so it was with the Schellenberg.

The Harrowing of Bavaria

Marlborough told Heinsius that he would 'press the Elector' in the hope that he would 'make an accommodation'. Indeed, on 14 July Max Emmanuel agreed that in return for 600,000 crowns a year he would supply the Allies with 12,000 men. But just before signing the definitive treaty, he heard that Tallard was on his way from the Rhine to join him with some 35,000 men, and at once reneged on the deal as being inconsistent with his principles. On 23 July Marlborough told Sarah that he must provoke the Elector into fighting or making peace.

> If he does not his whole country is in our power, for we have it behind us, and he may be sure that if he does not make peace, we will destroy it before we leave. You will, I hope, believe that my nature suffers, when I see so many fine places burnt, or that must be burnt, if the Elector will not hinder it.[57]

A week later he added:

> We sent this morning 3,000 horse to his chief city of Munich, with orders to burn and destroy all the country about it. This is so uneasy to my nature that nothing but an absolute necessity could have obliged me to consent to it, for these poor people suffer only for their master's ambition, there having been no war in this country for above 60 years. Their towns and villages are so clean that you would be pleased with them.[58]

Oddly enough, de la Colonie, who could see the smoke of burning villages from the Electoral palace in Munich, did not believe that the destruction was deliberate. 'I do not say that a few houses were not burnt,' he wrote, 'but the enemy generals did not have the deliberate intention of ordering this; it was the work of marauders in the army who, angry at finding the houses of peasants abandoned and without effects, set fire to some of them.'[59] That was certainly not how Sergeant Wilson remembered his orders. He thought that the army was allowed 'free plunder' in Bavaria, and confirmed that horse were sent out 'to burn and plunder the Elector of Bavaria's country, even to the very gates of Munich'.[60] Mrs Davies, still convincingly disguised as a soldier, admitted that:

we miserably plundered the poor inhabitants of the Electorate; I had left the hospital in time enough to contribute to their misery, and to have a share in the plunder. We spared nothing, killing, burning or otherwise destroying whatever we could [not] carry off. The bells of the churches we broke to pieces, that we might bring them away with us. I filled two bed-ticks [quilt covers], after having thrown out the feathers, with bell-metal, men's and women's clothes, some velvets, and about a hundred Dutch caps, which I had plundered from a shop; all which I sold by the lump to a Jew, who followed the army to purchase our pillage, for four pistoles . . . I got several pieces of plate, as spoons, mugs, cups etc, all which the same conscionable merchant had at his own price.[61]

Chaplain Josias Sandby maintained that the duke ordered the burning to stop, and in any event 'spared the woods, which are stately and numerous in this country. Consisting entirely of tall fir trees and pinastres.' However, another officer recalled how: 'we burnt and plundered almost all the villages right and left, which are indeed very frequent and very fine in this country. In this last march in particular we entirely burnt a mighty pretty village with a noble church and cloister.'[62] Prince Louis, thinking perhaps of his own prosperous villages, found the whole business deeply distasteful, declaring that he wished to fight like a general, not like a hussar.

The Elector, though, would neither fight nor treat, and now Marlborough, so confident after the Schellenberg, was feeling the balance of the campaign tilt against him. He had taken Neuberg and Rain, but his lack of heavy guns at first precluded more serious sieges, and so Munich was invulnerable. He soon knew that Tallard was on his way from the Rhine, with 35,000 men and a huge convoy of provisions, planning to link up first with Marsin's French contingent, entrenched at Augsburg, and then with the Elector, on the move with the remnants of his own army: indeed, on 6 August Tallard joined Marsin at Biberbach on the River Lech near Augsburg. Marlborough had already sent thirty squadrons to help Eugène, who hoped that he might be able both to hold Villeroi in the Lines of Stollhofen and perhaps to block Tallard too. He discovered that he could not do both, left a strong detachment to pin Villeroi to the Lines, and then took the bulk of his army back towards Marlborough's, reaching Höchstädt on the Danube at the end of the first week of August.

Marlborough and Eugène were close enough to support one another by 7 August, and now had a good chance of bringing on the battle they both desired by tempting their opponents to try an attack on either army before they were fully joined. To give themselves another major crossing over the Danube in case the Franco-Bavarians compromised that at Donauwörth, the Allied generals agreed that Prince Louis would turn eastwards to begin the siege of Ingolstadt with 15,000 men, an operation covered from the enemy by the two Allied armies. Several reliable historians argue (as did Mérode-Westerloo at the time) that this was largely a device to get 'the cautious and obstructive Margrave out of the way during the series of bold operations about to commence', and Louis went to his grave three years later believing that the Ingolstadt ploy was really a shabby trick designed to keep him away from the decisive battle.[63]

However, Marlborough assured Heinsius that the siege made perfect sense. The Elector had abandoned Bavaria to join forces with the French, leaving only a few troops in Munich and Augsburg, 'So that Prince Louis will have it in his power during the siege of Ingolstadt to do whatever he pleases with his horse in the country of Bavaria.' Marlborough would reinforce Eugène, and join him with the whole of his army the second he heard that the French had crossed the Danube. The Franco-Bavarians would 'not be able to hinder us from going on with the siege', and if they offered an opportunity for battle he would certainly take it, 'our troops being full of courage and desiring nothing more'.[64] There is no trace of subterfuge here. Prince Louis was a steady and experienced commander who would press the siege of Ingolstadt to its conclusion. Eugène, in any case the senior Imperialist officer in the theatre, was much better suited to a period of swift manoeuvre.

When Marlborough explained his plan to Sarah on 10 August he was clear on its general outline. 'Prince Louis is marched with thirty squadrons and twenty-four battalions to make the siege of Ingolstadt,' he wrote, 'and I have taken measures with Prince Eugène for opposing the Elector and the two marshals.' He lamented that the postmaster at Brill had just told him that five of his letters had gone astray, and 'it would be a cruel thing if, instead of your having them, they should go to France'. This missing mail was less of a risk to Allied security than we might suppose, for the tactical situation in Bavaria would have changed long before the French could react to information gleaned from it.[65] That same day Marlborough assured Heinsius that he would fight if he could: 'The French make their boast of having a great superiority, but I am very confident they will not venture a battle; but if we find a fair occasion, we shall be glad to venture it, being persuaded the ill condition of affairs in most parts requires it.'[66]

On 7 August Eugène, escorted by a single hussar, had ridden south to Marlborough's camp at Friedberg, between the Lech and the Paar east of Augsburg, to a conference with Marlborough and Louis, and then set off back to his own lines. But on the eighth Marlborough heard that the Franco-Bavarian army had 'decamped from Biberbach and were marching towards Lavingen, with a design, as 'tis supposed, to pass the Danube'. Eugène spurred back as soon as he heard, and they agreed 'that he should forthwith be reinforced, and that the whole army should advance nearer the Danube to draw near him if the enemy passed'. He immediately sent Württemberg off with twenty-nine squadrons of horse and ordered 'my brother Churchill' to follow with twenty battalions of foot, all making for newly-established pontoon bridges over the Danube at Merxheim.[67] Eugène slipped back eastwards along the river, as far as the Kessel rivulet, while Marlborough's main body headed first for Rain, where it crossed the Lech, and then moved on for Donauwörth. On the eleventh, as these two great columns neared him, marching separately to make the best use of road-space, Eugène edged back still further, some of his troops going as far as the Schellenberg itself. By about six that evening the armies were united on the line of the Kessel, although it would not be until daybreak that Colonel Blood arrived with the artillery after a march of twenty-four miles.

Even as he was manoeuvring for a handhold with Tallard and the Elector, Marlborough was still dealing with the usual flood of administrative, political and personal correspondence. The Earl of Peterborough was assured that Lord Mordaunt deserved to be 'gratified according to his merit and desire' after his conduct at the Schellenberg, but nothing could be done for the moment. The Duke of Buckingham, Marlborough warned Godolphin, was sure 'to be as troublesome next winter as he can', and Sir John Bland deserved some worthwhile post – he was actually made commissioner for the revenue in Ireland. Godolphin was to be congratulated on his garter, and Sarah on the fact that their grandson William Godolphin had recovered from an illness. On 10 August, with the campaign at last beginning to tilt his way once more, Marlborough congratulated Galway on being appointed to the command in Portugal, and drew his attention to Colonel Richards, who commanded the Portuguese artillery, and deserved Galway's 'favour and protection'. He gave Sarah an early hint that the emperor proposed to offer him a title which would not 'change his name or rank in England' but would be an honour to him and the queen, as 'none ever of his nation have had the like'. Yet the pressures of life were taking their toll. 'My blood is so heated that I have had these last two days a very violent headache,' he told Sarah. 'But not having stirred out of my chamber this day, I find myself much easier.'[68]

A Glorious Victory: Blenheim

The Allies were on the move betimes on 12 August. Marlborough had ordered his regiments to bridge the little Kessel with fascines during the night, and his forces marched westwards parallel with the northern bank of the Danube and halted for the night between the villages of Münster and Tapfheim. Marlborough later admitted that they were 'intending to advance, and take this camp of Höchstädt . . . but found the enemy had already possessed themselves of it, whereupon we resolved to attack them'.[69] He and Eugène climbed the church tower in Tapfheim to view the ground, and then rode forward to the Hühnersberg hill near Wolperstetten. They saw a wide, flat floodplain stretching north from the Danube, now canalised but then curling up in a great bend east of Höchstädt, to the wooded high ground of the Waldberg and the Obere Hölzer, the former a little over four miles due north of the river. On the plain's eastern edge a natural defile, a mile across, between woods and river was dominated by the village of Schwenningen.

Just over a third of the way from Schwenningen to Höchstädt the Nebel brook tottered – in such flat land we can scarcely say it ran – from the slopes of the Waldberg to the Danube. A row of tightly-nucleated villages lay along its line, from Blenheim, on a bend in the Danube, through Unterglauheim and Oberglauheim to Schwemmenbach on the edge of the hills. It was rich farming country, with water rarely far below the surface, but in the summer it provided excellent going for cavalry. The Nebel itself, now cribbed in by modern land drainage, was then more boggy, but could be passed by infantry and cavalry on improvised crossings in most places, although guns would have to use bridges or causeways. One French officer recalled it as 'only a brook two feet wide, which formed a little marsh much dried out because of the great heat, and this deceived our generals who thought it wide'.[70] They might not have thought it so had they taken the trouble to look at it.

Spread across the plain behind the Nebel, and packed into its little villages, were the seventy-eight battalions and 143 squadrons of the Franco-Bavarian army, perhaps 54,000 men in all, with Tallard's wing on the right towards the river and the Elector's and Marsin's army on the left, brushing the high ground with its left cuff. We have seen Marlborough and Eugène manoeuvre with the intention of obtaining the battle they were soon to have: what spirit, then, animated the Franco-Bavarian army? If victory has many fathers, defeat is indeed an orphan, and Camille de Tallard anxiously told Chamillart in his two post-combat reports, written as a prisoner of war, that he had certainly not sired the greatest defeat endured by French arms for a generation: others were to blame. His reports contain a good deal of special pleading, but they do help us understand why the French and Bavarians were sitting about in this natural amphitheatre with the sword of Damocles poised above them.

First, poor logistics ('with no magazine, not even six days' supplies in any place') sharply limited their ability to manoeuvre, just as Marlborough had suspected they would. There had been damaging desertions, especially amongst foreign units. An outbreak of glanders, a deadly and contagious horse-sickness among cavalry units from Alsace, some of whom were now at half-strength, meant that Tallard and Marsin were reluctant to exchange cavalry in case the infection spread, and Tallard had been forced to dismount four regiments (twelve squadrons) of dragoons to give their surviving horses to his cavalry. Worse, Tallard professed 'a total ignorance of the strength of the enemy'. He had no idea that Marlborough and Eugène were fully united and so close. After all, when he had asked if the Höchstädt plain was a safe place to await further reinforcements, 'everyone assured me yes'.

With two marshals of France, a ruling prince and several ambitious lieutenant generals in the field, command was a mite difficult, and the council of war a mere debating chamber.

> This diversity of advice, Sir, which made public what one wished to do, shows us clearly that it is a fine lesson that we should only have one man commanding an army, and that it is a great misfortune to have to deal with a prince of the honour of the Elector of Bavaria, above all when lieutenant generals advised him directly . . . as did certain of M le Maréchal Marsin's army.

The Elector, claimed Tallard, had heard from Donauwörth that they faced only Marlborough and a small advance guard who had joined Eugène, and it would therefore be safe to attack.

On 12 August Tallard ordered the comte de Silly to take a strong party of horse forward to the Reichenbach, beyond Schwenningen, 'in order to take some prisoners, whatever the cost', and so find out how strong Eugène really was. News of this raid arrived when Marlborough and Eugène were at dinner. They thought it an attack on their pioneers, who were at work levelling a 'hollow way' that ran across the army's route just west of the Kessel, and rode forward to see what was happening, ordering their horse to be ready to assist if required. Silly fell back with four prisoners, but neither they nor his scouts gave any warning of what was about to happen. Indeed, there were later suggestions that the prisoners may even have been 'plants', carefully briefed by Cadogan. Tallard himself was worried about the Nebel, and hoped to throw up a battery 'on the main road that crosses the brook', and to dam it near its confluence with the Danube so as to deepen it. The Elector, anxious not to damage the corn, which was ready to be harvested, was against all this, but on the following day, Tallard concludes pathetically, 'those who were against precautions on the previous day sought to make them when there was no more time'.[71]

Marlborough and Eugène, in contrast, were determined to attack, although, with sixty-six battalions and 160 squadrons, they were slightly inferior in strength, with perhaps 50,800 men.[72] They certainly had fewer infantry, but the French were to diminish their advantage in this arm by packing infantry into Blenheim, where their numbers were a source not of strength but of confusion. The Allied numerical advantage in cavalry was especially important in view of the open country, which favoured the mounted arm.

The armies of the age fought in line, although lines tended to be deeper then than they were a generation or two later. The French *Ordonnance* of 1703 still reflected the old days of pike and musket, and decreed that infantry battalions were to form up five deep, although shallower formations were adopted when strengths fell below their establishment figures. In contrast, Richard Kane reflected the best of British practice when he recommended that a battalion of eight hundred men should be drawn up

> three deep, their bayonets fixed on their muzzles, the grenadiers divided on the flanks, the officers ranged in the front; and the colonel, or in his absence the lieutenant colonel (who, I suppose, fights the battalion) on foot, with his sword drawn in his hand, about eight or ten paces in front, opposite the centre, with an expert drum by him. He should appear with a cheerful countenance, never in a

hurry, or by any means ruffled, and to deliver his orders with great calmness and presence of mind.

The commanding officer would divide his battalion into four grand divisions, each of four platoons. These in turn would be subdivided to give three 'firings', although Kane recommended that the front rank might be kept separate to give a fourth 'fire in reserve'. The result of methods like this was to have volleys rolling out regularly from distinct parts of the line, with some loaded muskets (the 'fire in reserve') on hand for an emergency.[73] It was more complex, and certainly required more attention by the officers, than firing by whole ranks ('rank entire'), but was believed to generate a better rate of fire.

The maintenance of a high volume of fire was essential to British infantry tactics in the eighteenth century. In his masterly work *Fit for Service* (1981) J.A. Houlding argued that this 'illustrates the fact that a sound appreciation of the supremacy of firepower over all other forms of combat had been a lesson well learnt by the end of Marlborough's campaigns, and had been taken to heart in the army'.[74] What was really different between Marlborough's battalions at Blenheim and King William's foot ten years before was this 'most formidable and destructive fire' produced by platoon firings. Marlborough took the strongest personal interest in it, and a drill-book of 1708, which enshrined the system in use in his army, was called *The Duke of Marlborough's New Exercise of Firelocks and Bayonets*.

There are good practical reasons to doubt just how long a battalion could maintain its platoon firing in the smoke and din of battle with the enemy's musketry and canister shot winnowing its ranks.[75] Some forty years later an experienced infantry officer wrote of the British foot at Dettingen:

> They were under no command by way of Hyde Park firing, but with the whole three ranks made a running fire of their own accord, at the same time with great judgement and skill, stooping as low as they could, making almost every ball take place . . . The French fired in the same manner, I mean without waiting for words of command, and Lord Stair did often say he had seen many a battle, and never saw the infantry engage in any other manner.[76]

John Dalrymple, 2nd Earl of Stair, fought at Blenheim, and his testimony cannot be brushed aside easily. Even the best infantry could not sustain proper platoon firing for very long, but the impact of no more than half a dozen crisply delivered volleys would break opposing infantry if their morale and training were not up to the strain. Contemporaries were right to warn of the very unpleasant consequences of getting in the way of a French volley fired 'by rank entire', but the deep deployment of French battalions, the wide spacing between their ranks, and, so often, the recent arrival of new recruits, meant that a close-packed British battalion, its men standing shoulder to shoulder and its three ranks 'locked up' one against the other, maintained cohesion better and generated a significantly higher volume of fire than its opponents. In combat the effect of success is cumulative: the side firing fastest and most accurately boosts its own cohesion and confidence, accelerating into a virtuous spiral as its opponents spin round their own vicious circle, losing more men, firing more slowly, and eventually breaking.

The achievement of Marlborough's foot resonated down the ages, and a British officer writing in 1743 told how: 'Our people imitated their predecessors in the late war gloriously, marching in close order, and still kept advancing; for when the smoke blew off a little, instead of being among their living we found the dead in heaps by us: and the second fire turned them to the right about, and upon a long trot.'[77] Platoon firing was the business of Marlburian infantry, and one can almost see them now in the cornfields bordering the Danube, three ranks locked solid, silken colours catching the sun, with the first warning ruffle from the colonel's drummer picked up by drummers along the line, and then those drawling voices, from Cork and Canterbury and Cumberland: 'First firing, make ready. Present. Fire!' Men were already beginning to speak of the canine courage of the British foot, cold resolution coupled with extraordinary ferocity, an impression heightened by their practice of barking out three sharp hurrahs before pressing in with bayonet and butt to take advantage of the damage done by their fire. Many opponents did not care to await their arrival.

If Marlborough believed that firepower was the essence of infantry, he argued that shock action was the soul of cavalry, and trained his horse to eschew squibbing off pistols or carbines before impact, but to charge home at the sort of 'good round trot' that Cromwell's Ironsides had delivered. This was considerably slower than charges would be a century later, when they were delivered 'at the utmost speed of the slowest horse'. Marlborough's method, however, ensured a high degree of control, and at Blenheim Captain Parker and Marshal Tallard both watched, one with elation and the other with growing gloom, the flower of the *Maison du Roi* being seen off by British horse.

Cannon, such a nuisance on the line of march, were generally too cumbersome to move easily about the battlefield. They were usually sited where they could do most damage in the early stages, grouped in small batteries in the battle line. Knowing commanders might clump some of their guns on a suitable piece of high ground: a well-sited sixteen-gun Bavarian battery at Lutzingen helped prop up the Franco-Bavarian left flank at Blenheim. Roundshot, an iron cannonball which spread death and destruction by bounding through the enemy's ranks, was the most common projectile, and there was widespread agreement that no cannon, whatever its calibre, could usefully be employed at a target more than a thousand yards away. Although there were by now a few howitzers about, which fired explosive shells, their primitive fuses and the unreliable casting of their shells meant that they were often rather patchy in their effect. Gunners who lobbed their shells over friendly units would tend to receive forcefully expressed suggestions that they should do something more harmful to the foe and less dangerous to their friends.

In contrast, canister, multiple shot loaded in box, bag or tin, or strapped to a wooden plug the size of the bore, was a real killer. Its range was limited, perhaps three hundred yards at the most, but it could do terrible damage to packed formations at this distance. Canister was the most effective projectile for 'regimental pieces', light guns which kept pace with the infantry, fired from the intervals between battalions and, in their noisy and destructive way, foreshadowed the use of machine-guns two centuries on.

If armies fought in line, they moved in column. The easiest way of deploying from the latter to the former was simply to march onto the field with units destined for the right of the line at the head of the column, to order a right wheel at some suitable point, and then, when the whole army had completed the wheel, to halt it, and order it to turn left into line: this was essentially what the French did at Ramillies. If this was the simplest method of deploying it was easily the least satisfactory, for it required sufficient space to form the whole army up in column of route, a suitable approach on one flank of the field, and time to complete the whole manoeuvre without interference.

We do not use the expression 'give battle' for nothing, for an army in column could usually move faster than an opponent in line. The surest way of avoiding contact with an enemy wheeling into line with all the martial glory of drum ruffles, officers shouting beautifully articulated orders and earnest but profane sergeants urging men to step very, very short on the inner flank, was to march off apace, leaving a few dragoons to hold suitable defiles on the line of withdrawal. It was far better, if the terrain and one's training permitted it, to enter the field in a number of parallel columns. These could still deploy into line by wheeling, but for the best-trained there were more complex procedures available, like the deployment *en tiroir* as units down the column slid out of it to one side or the other, like drawers being pulled out of a chest.

Moving from column into line was always a delicate business, especially if there was a natural obstacle in the way, and the problem for the Allies at Blenheim was that they would reach the Nebel in column and then deploy only after they had crossed it, at their most vulnerable at the very moment that they entered a plateau filled with foes. What Marlborough's reconnaissance on 12 August had almost certainly revealed was that along much of Tallard's front the Nebel was invisible from his campsites. Tallard was certainly right to tell Chamillart that pushing a battery forward to cover the main crossing would have been a good idea, and just as correct to admit that his main line of defence, between Blenheim and the Nebel, was too far back from the obstacle. On the Allied right Eugène was not as fortunate, and this simple piece of geography helped make the battle on his flank a good deal harder than it was for Marlborough on the left, and helps explain why, in essence, there was to be a fixing battle on the Allied right and a striking battle on the left.

The soldiers of the Allied army rose without beat of drum just after midnight on 13 August and, leaving their tents standing, moved out through the Schwenningen defile into the plain, fanning out into eight columns as they did so, with the brigade which had held Schwenningen overnight forming a ninth. Forty squadrons of cavalry screened the advance. Robert Parker recalled that the march started 'by break of day', and at about 6 a.m., well after first light, Marlborough held a brief conference with his generals near Schwenningen, and paid particular attention to the advice of Major General Dubislaw von Natzmer, a Prussian cavalry officer who had been with Count Styrum's force when it was beaten at Höchstädt the previous year, and who knew the ground. Eugène's wing, meanwhile, marched on, along the edge of the forest bordering the plain, while Marlborough's approached the Nebel.

The comte de Mérode-Westerloo, in command of the right wing of Tallard's second line, did not much like the Franco-Bavarian position. He thought that with its left on Lutzingen and its right on the Danube it was far too wide: by pushing the whole line forward, so that the left was on the woods,

> we could have held a far more compact position, with our right still on the Danube . . . and our centre more concentrated. There we could have drawn up three if not four lines of infantry, one behind the other, with our ninety-four guns to the fore, and three or four lines of cavalry to support them in the rear.[78]

However, on the night of the twelfth–thirteenth, Mérode-Westerloo 'sat down to a good hot plate of soup in Blenheim with my generals and colonels' and retired to his camp bed, which had been set up in a barn on the edge of the village, for a good night's sleep.

He was awakened by his head groom at six in the morning.

> The fellow, Lefranc, shook me awake and blurted out that the enemy were there. Thinking to mock him, I asked 'Where? There?' and he at once replied, 'Yes – there – there!' flinging wide as he spoke the door of the barn and drawing my bed-curtains. The door opened straight onto the fine, sunlit plain beyond – and the whole area appeared to be covered by enemy squadrons. I rubbed my eyes in disbelief, and then coolly remarked that the foe must at least give me time to take my morning cup of chocolate.

He rode out as soon as he could, accompanied by his two aides de camp and sixteen spare chargers, and went to the camp, where he found everyone asleep, 'although the enemy was so close that their standards and colours could easily be counted. They were already pushing back our pickets, but nobody seemed worried about it.' He got his regiments mounted as quickly as he could, and soon Tallard galloped by, congratulating him on being so beforehand, and ordered him to get the two cannon salvoes fired to recall the foragers. An aide duly galloped to a nearby battery, 'got himself recognised and obeyed by the gunners, and we soon heard the 24-pounders fire two salvoes'. Across the whole of the Franco-Bavarian camp drums beat up the *générale*, an insistent flurry that their opponents recognised, infantry formed up in rank and file, troopers mounted, and gunners and their teams hauled their pieces forward. Tallard, prescient as ever, had just penned a note to Louis XIV saying that he thought the Allies were falling back on Nordlingen. Why else would they be about so early in the morning?

Chaplain Sandby heard how 'the enemy beat to arms, and fired the signal for the foragers to come in'. He then saw the French and Bavarians

> set fire to the villages of Berghausen, Weilheim and Unterglauheim, and to two mills and some other houses near the [mouth of the Nebel] rivulet. They likewise brought forth their cannon, and planted several batteries along the hill which formed their position.[79]

Tallard posted thirty-six battalions and his twelve squadrons of dismounted dragoons between the Danube and the plain north of Blenheim, and sent two battalions up to his left to support Marsin's fourteen battalions around Oberglauheim. From there twelve more battalions took the line off towards Lutzingen, held by d'Arco and five Bavarian battalions, with another eleven French battalions continuing the line up to the hills on the extreme left. Tallard's own sixty-four squadrons of cavalry were reinforced by sixteen slipped down by Marsin, and the remaining sixty-seven squadrons formed up between Oberglauheim and Lutzingen. At about ten o'clock the Elector and the two marshals met in Blenheim to discuss their plan. Marsin and the Elector resolved to hold as far forward as they could, on the Nebel itself, while Tallard determined to let the Allies cross and then to break them on the west bank. Tallard admitted that the lie of the land was unfortunate: 'The village [Blenheim] was too far from the brook to defend the passage, and too close for us to deploy [all the infantry] in front of it and leave the village behind.' However, he posted two brigades of cavalry with orders 'to move quickly to the brook and charge the enemy before they were formed up'.[80]

The Franco-Bavarian plan was cobbled together at the last moment, but Marlborough's was the result of careful thought and wholehearted agreement. Eugène's wing would pin Marsin and the Elector to their positions, preventing them from helping Tallard. With the Franco-Bavarian left held in check, Marlborough would be free to defeat Tallard, making best use of his greater numbers of cavalry on ground ideal for their use. However, this meant that there could be no advance until Eugène was ready, and he had a good way to go, across the grain of the country, with numerous streams and ditches that made life especially difficult for his gunners, making extemporised bridges for their pieces.

By ten o'clock Marlborough's infantry, under the overall command of

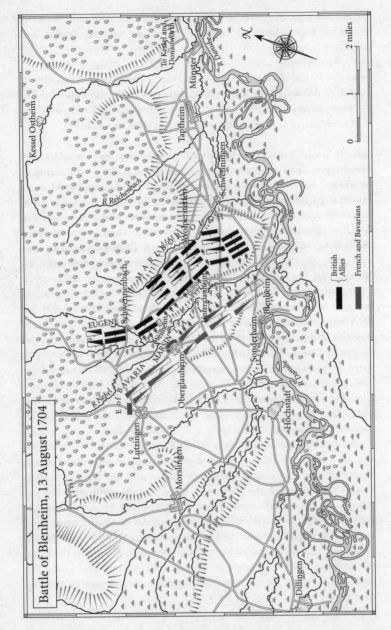

Battle of Blenheim, 13 August 1704

British
Allies
French and Bavarians

Kessel Ostheim

To Kessel and Donauwörth

Münster

Taptheim

Schweningen

R Danube

R Danube

R Reichenbach

Wolperstetten

H O C H S T Ä D T

Schwennenbach

MARLB'GH

EUGENE

Unterglauheim

Weilheim

Blenheim

Sonderheim

Höchstädt

R Nebel

E of BAVARIA

MARSIN

TALLARD

Oberglauheim

Lutzingen

Morslingen

Dillingen

R Danube

his brother Charles, was formed up east of the Nebel facing Blenheim and Unterglauheim. On his extreme left Salamander Cutts, with twenty battalions, faced Blenheim itself, with Major General Wood behind him with fifteen squadrons. Churchill's infantry were interleaved with the Prince of Hesse's horse, with a line of infantry in front, then two lines of cavalry, and then a second line of infantry. This would allow the first line of infantry to cross the Nebel 'and to march as far in advance on the other side as could conveniently be done, and then to form and cover the passage of the horse, leaving intervals in the line of infantry large enough for the horse to pass over and take their post in front'. When the French guns had opened fire at about eight o'clock, Marlborough ordered Blood to reply, and 'visited each battery, and stood by to observe the range of the guns and the effect of their fire'.[81]

The French guns could not engage the full line of the Nebel without being brought well forward of their cavalry, and the high corn obstructed the view on both sides, so they did less damage to Churchill's infantry than we might expect. Mérode-Westerloo recorded that cavalry out in the open certainly suffered from artillery fire. 'I was riding past Forsac's regiment,' he wrote, 'when a shot carried away the head of my horse and killed two troopers.' One roundshot hit the ground at the feet of Marlborough's grey charger, covering horse and rider with dust, but he continued to visit his own gunners, and suggested that the infantry should lie down to avoid the fire and take some cover from what Mérode-Westerloo called 'the brightest imaginable sun'. It was a Sunday, and chaplains conducted service under this desultory bombardment: Robert Parker heard that Marlborough took communion and then mounted, saying: 'This day I conquer or die.'

Marlborough knew that Eugène would have to 'fetch a compass' to get into position, but towards midday he grew impatient and sent off Cadogan to find out what was happening. At about 12.30 one of Eugène's aides de camp arrived to announce that all was ready: Marlborough ordered his brother to cross the Nebel, and sent word to Cutts to attack Blenheim. Pioneers had already done a good deal of work on the Nebel, piling fascines into it, making temporary bridges with wood from ruined houses, and even using some tin pontoons, and the infantry began to cross, forming up, as they had been told, on the far bank, but with enough space between themselves and the water for the cavalry to cross, form up and then move through the infantry.

On the left, Lord Cutts' attack on Blenheim was in the gallant but unsubtle tradition of the famous Salamander, fighting his last battle. Brigadier Rowe, commanding the leading brigade, had told his men not to fire until he had struck the French palisade with his sword, and they stoutly took him at his word. He went down, mortally wounded, and his brigade was thrown back. Ferguson's brigade did no better against the dismounted dragoons holding improvised barricades on the southern edge of the village: Private Deane recalled 'trees, planks, coffers, chests, carts, wagons and palisades'. 1st Foot Guards lost its commanding officer, and the attack was repulsed here too, though only after 'our men fought in and through the fire and pursued others through it, and many on both sides were burnt to death. At length the enemy making all the force they could upon us forced us to retreat and to quit the village.'[82]

As Cutts' first wave fell back, Lieutenant General von Zurlauben, a Swiss professional and one of the few French generals to earn Tallard's approval that day ('He did marvels, both as an officer and a brave man'), led three squadrons of elite *Gens d'Armes*, part of the French Household Troops, into the flank of Rowe's brigade, doing considerable damage before being checked by the Hessians of Wilkes's brigade, now safely across the Nebel and coming on in good order. Although the attack on Blenheim had failed, it persuaded Lieutenant General the marquis de Clérembault, responsible for its defence, to summon more troops from the open country to its north. Tallard complained bitterly that Clérembault eventually denuded the whole of his centre of infantry and then, when the rot set in, 'preferred to get drowned rather than to remain at his post'. By 2 p.m. Cutts' attack on Blenheim was called off for the moment, but Tallard's right had become fatally unbalanced by its defence.

Further north, Churchill's leading infantry scrambled across the Nebel as ordered, and by the time Zurlauben led his *Gens d'Armes* forward as planned, there were already five squadrons of British cavalry on the west bank under Colonel Francis Palmes. The *Gens d'Armes* halted to fire their carbines and were, predictably, roughly handled. Palmes charged them frontally, and ordered his two flanking squadrons to come in at an angle and take them in the flanks: the gallant Zurlauben was mortally wounded. The defeat of this prestigious element of the *Maison du Roi* infuriated Tallard: 'The officers of the gendarmerie are very brave fellows, but the gendarmerie did nothing useful,' he told Chamillart. It also enabled the Elector to engage in a little coalition-bashing, never a useful commodity at a time like this. 'What, the gentlemen of France fleeing?' he said. 'Go, tell them that I am here in person. Rally them and lead them to the charge.'[83]

Palmes's men were soon driven back by a countercharge, but, as the exasperated Tallard observed, they were not broken, and as more Allied squadrons crossed the Nebel the battle slithered out of Tallard's control. He later confessed that 'misfortune . . . came upon us because we did not drive back the enemy in our first charges'.[84] An anonymous French officer affirmed that: 'The general officers were no help to the marshal; they let the enemy pass the marsh and a little brook which was in front of our camp without defending it, and the enemy was across it in three lines before anyone charged.'[85] The line of the Nebel was lost and the French cavalry, their charges described by Tallard as 'useless', were beaten, partly by the disciplined action of the Allied horse, and partly by the steady volleys of the supporting infantry. Mérode-Westerloo grimly recalled one of his charges being broken by fire at thirty paces, after which there was 'a definite but unauthorised movement to the rear'.

The French infantry which might have supported the charges, as Churchill's foot did their own horse, had started the day too far back, and too much of it had now been drawn into Blenheim by that anxious officer the marquis de Clérembault. 'We had too many battalions on our right,' wrote another officer, 'and lacked them in our centre.' Tallard galloped north to ask Marsin for help, but the French and Bavarians on his left, barely holding their own against determined attacks by Eugène, had nothing to spare, and so 'he did not think himself in a state to give me any'.

The baron de Montigny-Languet said that the battle was not simply lost because of French mistakes. Hitherto French armies had been 'every-where victorious', but now they had encountered a new and enterprising foe: 'Nothing was better conducted than the enemy's march. They were superior to us, and apart from their lines which were equal to us in their three attacks, were in column five or six lines deep to support them.' In short, the French and Bavarians were facing an enemy who understood combined arms battle, and it had been madness to offer battle at all: 'It would have been better to have kept the intact forces of the empire together, to have dug in and risked nothing.' Quite how such an option might have been sustained logistically, however, he does not begin to say.[86]

In contrast, Adam de Cardonnel thought that Marlborough threw himself heart and soul into the battle because he knew he had so much to win from a decisive action.

The Duke of Marlborough exposed himself in every place, from one attack to another, beyond what is thought advisable in a general, but

he saw the good effect of his doing so, and no doubt knew the
necessity of a battle better than any of us, for I believe had the
opinion of the majority of us prevailed, we should not have been for
us under our circumstances, in short orders were never better given,
or better executed.[87]

Marlborough was also well served by his generals in an inverse proportion to the way that Tallard was let down by his. John Wilson called
Marlborough and Eugène 'such wise and experienced generals', a
telling tribute from a sergeant to his commander-in-chief.

Communicating in person, or by gallopers and by runners, the latter
wearing jockey caps and carrying staves denoting their function,
Marlborough spent the day riding along his front as the demands of the
battle changed: chaplain Noyes saw how 'he exposed his person the
whole day in a most uncommon manner'. In early afternoon the Dutch
infantry were already in trouble at Oberglauheim, whose defending
Irish infantry fought for King Louis with more courage than some of his
own subjects, when Marsin launched a well-handled cavalry counterattack. Marlborough was on hand to send forward fresh infantry and to
ask Eugène for help. No sooner demanded than delivered: up trotted
Count Fugger with a brigade of Imperial cuirassiers, and the threat
melted away. Soon afterwards, when he felt the battle had reached its
point of balance, Marlborough sent his aide Lord Tonbridge to tell
Eugène that he expected to break the French, but needed Eugène to
continue to hold Marsin and the Elector in play. As always, men noticed
his grace under pressure. When Lord Orkney hurtled in at last to tell him
that the day was his, 'he took my Lord Orkney by the hand, and said
"George, thou art a happy man and a messenger of good tidings. Praised,
therefore, be Almighty God." '[88] Orkney, an experienced professional,
admitted that the victory was 'entirely owing to my Lord Duke, for, I
declare, had it been my opinion, I had been against it, considering the
ground where they were encamped and the strength of their army'.[89]

Before Marlborough was in a position to thank God, however, his
infantry had first to deal with Blenheim, set on fire by its defenders who,
as Mérode-Westerloo wrote, 'were grilled amongst the continually
collapsing roofs and beams of the blazing houses, and thus were burnt
alive amidst the ashes of this smaller Troy of their own making'.[90]
Tallard, seeing that the battle for his left and centre was lost, 'wanted to
go back to the village and make a last effort, in order to fall back with
the infantry: I was followed by a regiment of Hessian dragoons [in fact

Bothmar's Regiment], who surrounded me, the officer having recognised my Order of the Saint-Esprit'. As Tallard was led to the rear, at about 5.30, much of the huge garrison of Blenheim stood fast among the blazing houses, but:

> M de Clérembault, lieutenant general, who commanded the 27 battal-
> ions which were in the village on our right and the 12 squadrons of
> dragoons, did not think of withdrawing with this body; he went and
> drowned himself in the Danube at four in the afternoon, two hours
> before the end of the battle, having lost his head.[91]

Clérembault, dead and in no position to defend himself, was soon to become the French *bête noire*. He had certainly committed a major mistake in packing infantry into Blenheim, but once the battle in the centre was lost his course of action was less than clear. There was then a large bend in the Danube, tipped by the village of Sonderheim, south-west of Blenheim, and the direction of the Allied attack meant that the main Höchstädt road, which might once have enabled the garrison to escape, was already in hostile hands. The suggestion that Clérembault could have formed his men into a huge square and marched them off to safety is absurd: the ground simply did not allow it. Yet again the French found themselves fighting with a river to their back, and yet again they paid the price. Clérembault was wrong to ride for his life and leave his men to their fate: even Tallard had hoped to do something for his still-undefeated whitecoats.

Many officers and men of the broken right wing tried to cross the Danube. There was a single bridge of boats but, says Robert Parker, 'The bridge (as frequently happens in such cases) broke under the crowd that rushed upon it, and down they went.'[92] Many tried to swim their horses or strike out on their own, but the microterrain told against them. Sonderheim is on the outer sweep of a great bend, and the river there, scoured by the current, was far deeper than it was at the far bank. French fugitives, already tired and hot after a day's fighting, entered the Danube well out of their depth. They may have been encouraged to risk it by the sight of a few fortunate comrades scrambling up through the reeds on the far side. Some, shocked by the chill of the river's water, would have died quickly; others would have been dragged down by sodden uniforms or brained by the hooves of flailing horses.

Lieutenant General the marquis de Clérembault cannot have died well in the muddy waters of the Danube; worse, he perished shamed by the courage of better men, most of them with no title or lineage to their name. Nine battalions of newly raised infantry held together well on the open ground north-west of the village, coolly forming square on order and firing steadily till they were overwhelmed. Lord Orkney admiringly wrote that they stood 'in battalion square and in the best order I ever saw, till they were cut to pieces almost in rank and file'.[93] Chaplain Sandby, riding over the field next day, saw the youngsters lying in their ranks as if on parade, apparently asleep, but all were dead.

The best that can be said for the defence of Blenheim is that it forced Marlborough to mask it with part of his infantry, and helped prevent him from rolling up the left wing of the Franco-Bavarian line, which was able to draw off largely intact at the end of the day. The village was surrounded by about seven o'clock, and Churchill's infantry closed for the kill. Colonel de la Silvère tried to extract the regiments of Artois and Provence, but could not break the circle round the village, and there was sustained and heavy fighting as the French fought hard, street by street and house by house, for the village. Tallard, a prisoner in Marlborough's coach, sent the duke a message saying that he would order his men to retire to save further bloodshed, but Marlborough, who had nothing to gain from permitting the escape of the beleaguered garrison, replied: 'Inform Monsieur de Tallard that in the position which he is now in, he has no command.' Eventually Brigadier the marquis de Blanzac asked for terms, but Orkney told him that there were none but to surrender at discretion.

The scenes that followed are not pleasant for a historian with an enduring regard for an army which, in its long history, has scaled the heights as well as plumbed the depths. An ensign of the Régiment du Roi cut a British officer across the arm when he reached out to take his colour, and the Régiment de Navarre, one of the best of the old French line, proud 'Navarre sans peur' to its officers and men, burnt its colours rather than give them up. Officers wept unashamedly in the smoking village, many repeating: 'What will the king say? What will the king say?'

The king would hear that he had lost over 34,000 men, including about 14,000 prisoners, the latter such a millstone round the necks of their captors that Cardonnel was soon complaining to Ellis, 'We know not how to dispose of them . . . if we could get well rid of these gents I hope we might soon make an end of the campaign on this side, for the enemy will hardly make another stand.'[94] Soon afterwards Mrs Davies testified to the abject misery of the captives, most stripped to their shirts and some even 'naked as from the womb'. There were also about a hundred guns, 129 infantry colours and 110 cavalry standards, and a whole mass of impedimenta, not to mention ten general officers. So many senior officers had been taken that normal arrangements for exchanging them on a rank-for-rank basis broke down altogether. Marshal Tallard remained in gentlemanly confinement in Nottingham for the next eight years. He lived in Newdigate House in Castlegate, showed his captors how to make lace and *proper* bread, cultivated celery, hitherto not eaten in England, and, so the Whigs complained, organised shipments of champagne and burgundy for deserving anti-war Tories. When he returned to Versailles, Tallard was well received, though he never commanded again, and remembered the plain of Höchstädt as much for the staggering scale of his defeat as for the fact that his youngest boy, serving on his staff, had been pistolled by one of Bothmar's dragoons.

The Allies had lost 14,000 killed and wounded, 9,000 of them in Marlborough's wing. The Dutch had lost almost the same as the British (2,200 to 2,234), and the Danes, who carried Lutzingen at the day's end, a dreadful 2,400. It was a victory which did not simply change the balance of the war in Germany at a single bloody stroke, but gave Marlborough and his men a cachet which they would retain until the very end of the conflict. The campaign had begun for Marlborough in political and military uncertainty and marital discord. That evening he borrowed a scrap of paper from an aide (it had begun life as a tavern bill, and then done duty for some logistic calculations) and wrote, neither to his queen, nor to his old friend Heinsius, but to the dearest woman in the world. Scarcely was its ink dry than the dashing Colonel Dan Parke galloped off with one of the most famous scribblings in British military history.

> I have not time to say more, but beg you will give my duty to the Queen and let her know her army has had a glorious victory. M Tallard and two other generals are in my coach and I am following the rest. The bearer, my aide de camp Colonel Parke, will give her an account of what has passed. I shall do it in a day or two by another more at large.[95]

6

The Lines of Brabant

Ripples of Victory

It took the hard-riding Dan Parke eight days to reach London, and Sarah immediately sent him on, hot-hoofed, to Windsor. When he arrived the queen and Prince George were playing chequers on the terrace. Anne told Sarah that 'this glorious victory . . . next to God is wholly owing to dear Mr Freeman'.[1] It is, though, noticeable that her letter to Marlborough himself was rather warmer than that to Sarah. The duchess had, over the past year, devoted herself to dislodging the remaining High Tories from government just as surely as her husband had concentrated on beating the French and Bavarians. The Duke of Buckingham, lord privy seal, was, for the moment, her own Schellenberg, though she did not defeat him till the following year. She justified her intransigence by telling Anne that she was simply telling her the truth, but although she seems to have been blissfully unaware of the fact, she was doing serious long-term damage to her relationship with the queen.

Blenheim was almost as much of a shock to the Tories as it was to Louis. They at once did their best to belittle it by equating it to Sir George Rooke's capture of Gibraltar, enabling Sarah, at her vituperative best, to snap that Blenheim was apparently 'an unfortunate accident, and by the visible dissatisfaction of some people on the news of it one would imagine that, instead of beating the French, he had beat the Church'.[2] Marlborough, always nervous about his wife's political views, at first tried to avoid getting involved in her assault on Buckingham, but eventually he fell into step, and told Godolphin that Buckingham should go and be replaced by the Whig Duke of Newcastle. There is, however, good reason to doubt his personal inclination in the matter, for on 20 October 1704 he had told Sarah: 'I am very little concerned what any party thinks of me . . . I will endeavour to leave a good name behind me, in countries that have hardly any blessing but that of not knowing the detested names of Whig and Tory.'[3]

That autumn the political scene was enlivened by an attempt by the Tories to tack an Occasional Conformity Bill onto a Bill modifying the land tax. This was a piece of constitutional sharp practice, for the Lords could not, by well-established precedent, throw out a financial Bill, and the Tories hoped to bring in their favourite measure through the back door.[4] Salamander Cutts, as an Irish peer able to sit in the Commons and, as governor of the Isle of Wight, every bit as able (despite frequent absences to smell gunpowder and deal with perennial money worries) to secure his return for the borough of Newport with its twenty-four electors, regarded the decision as 'of the utmost importance', for the success of this sort of tacking would have produced irreconcilable enmity between the two Houses, forcing the queen to dissolve Parliament and imperilling 'the common cause against France'.

The queen, who attended several sessions of the Lords, sitting 'at first on the throne and after (it being cold) on a bench by the fire', was annoyed by the Tack, as it was known, and her support helped Marlborough and Godolphin come through the session safely. However, with the struggle over the Tack at its height, Sarah had again, in her unyielding way, warned Anne that all Tories were closet Jacobites, and just as characteristically declined to back off when the queen warned her that there was a national unity which went beyond party. Anne warned Godolphin that her relationship with Sarah had now changed fundamentally: 'I can't hope as you do, that she will ever be easy with me again. I quite despair of it now, which is no small mortification to me.'[5]

Publicly the queen could not have been more affable, and it was the apotheosis of the Cockpit circle, now on the verge of breaking up for ever. Marlborough returned home on 14 December, and the following day Parliament recorded its thanks to him for his stunning victory. He brought with him thirty-six senior French officers and the colours and standards captured by his wing of the army, which led to the unlucky Lieutenant General Hompesch being reprimanded by the Estates-General for not retaining those taken by the Dutch. On 3 January 1705 the trophies were marched from the Tower to Westminster Hall, in a display that, as Winston S. Churchill so correctly emphasised, underlined the break with France, 'whom men in middle age could remember as England's disdainful paymaster'. On 17 February the queen told the Commons that she proposed to give Marlborough the royal manor of Woodstock, some 15,000 acres, worth £6,000 a year, and asked the House to vote him sufficient money to build a palace of a scale commensurate with his triumph. Sir John Vanbrugh was appointed the architect, and soon had a scale model to show the queen.

At the beginning of the project Marlborough was passionately enthusiastic about Blenheim Palace, as he named his yet-unbuilt new home, and looked forward to retiring there. In July 1705 he thanked Godolphin for his 'friendship and care' in helping make a start on Blenheim, 'in which place I flatter myself to enjoy your company and some quiet days before I die'.[6] His letters to Sarah are full of detailed instructions, like those in a missive written from the little town of Loos, which would mean something to British soldiers in September 1915:

> When you are most at leisure let me know some particular of what you directed when you were last at Woodstock . . . The two suites of hangings that were made at Brussels at Vanbrugh's measure cost me above eight hundred pounds, so that if possible they should serve for the rooms they were intended for, being sure in England there can be none so good or fine. If Lord Treasurer [Godolphin] and Vanbrugh approve of it, you may keep one of the marble blocks, so that the room where you intend your buffet, may be well done; I remember you were desirous of having one, but if you have taken other measures, or altered your mind, you will say nothing, but take it as I mean it, kindly, as I shall do in the whole course of my life, everything that I think shall be a satisfaction to you.[7]

The exiled Earl of Ailesbury, who sometimes dined with Marlborough in camp, recalled that they once ate 'at his little table, which he loved much, and, being post-day, the meal was not long'. Ailesbury much hoped to be allowed to return to England, but eventually came to realise that he would only receive 'fair obliging words and no performance' from the duke, for Ailesbury's steadfast record of support for James II made him unacceptable to most English politicians. However, Marlborough, with his 'excellent and even temper of mind', encouraged him to believe that he would eventually return home, and showed him a plan of Blenheim, even pointing out a room and saying, 'This is for you when you come to see me there.'[8]

At its beginning, Sarah was dismayed by the Blenheim project, complaining of 'the madness of the whole design [and] I opposed it all that was possible for me to do'.[9] Given Marlborough's evident commitment to the scheme, she did her best to see it through, though she was not in the least temperamentally suited to dealing with folk with egos of their own. Blenheim was designed to be 'monument, castle, citadel and private house, in that order', intended to rival Versailles in the sheer opulence and scale of its Baroque glory.[10] Vanbrugh, its original architect, affirmed that it 'stares us in the face with a pretty impudent countenance', and it was certainly meant to.

The extraordinary expense of the build, which eventually cost around £300,000 (the wonderful Castle Howard, built at the same time, was a mere £40,000), made it every bit as much of a visible symbol of hatred for the Marlboroughs' enemies. Sarah fell out with Vanbrugh as she fell out with so many others. He called her 'the B. B. B. B. the B Duchess of Marlborough', but she had the last laugh, personally banning him from the grounds so that he never saw the finished building. There were endless squabbles with architects and craftsmen. She agreed to pay Sir James Thornhill twenty-five shillings a square yard for his huge allegorical painting on the ceiling of the hall, but when the total bill came to £978 objected that this was 'a higher price than anything of that bigness was ever given for Rubens or Titian'. Payment was made with the worst possible grace, and Thornhill was never asked back.

As Sarah expended her political capital, so building faltered as government money dried up. In October 1710 an Oxford clergyman told Robert Harley that:

> The debt to the workmen at Blenheim that is known is above £60,000. They owe to Strong the mason for his share £10,500. It will go hard with many in this town and the country who have contracted with them. The creditors begin to call on them and can get no money at Blenheim. One poor fellow, who has £600 owing to him for lime and brick, came on Saturday to Tom Rowney [an Oxford MP] to ask for a little money he owes him. Tom paid him immediately. The fellow thanked him with tears, and said that the money for the present would save him from gaol.[11]

Sarah's final break with the queen in 1711 would see her vacate her apartments at St James's, taking all the fixtures and fittings with her, down to fireplaces and doorknobs. In return the queen stopped paying for work at Blenheim, saying that 'She would not build the Duke a house when the Duchess was pulling hers to pieces.'[12] Sarah was undaunted. 'As the building will never be finished at Blenheim,' she wrote, 'it will never be any advantage or pleasure to My Lord Marlborough or his family, but will remain now as a monument of ingratitude instead of what was once intended.'[13]

By 1712 the place was like a huge builders' yard, daubed with anti-Marlborough graffiti, 'a chaos which nobody but God Almighty could finish'. After Marlborough returned from voluntary exile with the accession of George I the Blenheim debt was formally acknowledged, but no more public money was forthcoming, and he resolved to finish the place at his own expense. However, he refused to pay crown rates for the work, and many master-craftsmen, Grinling Gibbons among them, never returned. Marlborough stayed there briefly in 1719 and 1720–21, but the house he so longed for never delighted him as he had hoped: he attended the first party there, in 1719, incapacitated by a stroke, and there is a poignant description of him being helped around the half-completed grounds by Sarah, like a blasted oak in a blighted landscape. All this unhappiness, though, was yet to come, and for the moment there was abundant cause for celebration.

On 15 June 1704, with the battle of Blenheim still unfought, Wratislaw had told Marlborough that the emperor proposed to make him a sovereign prince, with a seat in the Imperial Diet. Marlborough, as we saw in the last chapter, wished to accept the title; not simply because it would be an honour to the queen and himself, but also because it would increase his authority amongst the foreign noblemen who served under his command. He felt, though, that it might actually be easier to take it 'when the business of the war is over'. Sarah, once uneasy about a dukedom, was no more enthusiastic about a principality, and evidently advised against it, though the letter in which she did so is now lost. On 25 August Marlborough told her that 'I shall do what I can to have it delayed since you think that is best.'[14] Anne's consent to the grant was required, for English monarchs were touchy about their subjects' acceptance of foreign honours. Queen Elizabeth I, less than impressed by a young gentleman who swaggered back from the Turkish wars as an Imperial count, immediately locked him up, sharply observing that: 'My dogs shall wear no collars but my own.'

Anne, more generously disposed than her royal predecessor, consented to Marlborough's elevation. On 28 August he heard from the emperor that he had been created a prince of the Empire, but at once wrote to Godolphin to point out that the business had not been done properly: notice should have been given to other princes, and the fief from which his title would derive should have been named. This may, as his opponents were to suggest, have been designed to ensure that there was an estate which would generate some income, or it may simply reflect Marlborough's intention, agreed with Sarah only a few days before, to delay the matter if he could. It was not easy for the emperor, warned by Wratislaw of the new prince's sensitivities on the matter, to find a suitable principality, but eventually a fief 'about fifteen miles square' was carved out of Imperial lands in Swabia to create the principality of Mindelheim: it brought in a welcome £2,000 a year. Marlborough visited it once, in the spring of 1713. 'Stayed but four days at Mindelheim,' he wrote, 'which place I liked much better than expected but not so, as to think of living there.'[15]

It was a remarkable achievement for a man born plain Jack Churchill to become an Imperial prince. It made no difference to his style or title in Britain, and, contrary to the allegations of his opponents, he never expected British officers to call him 'Your Highness', and we may doubt whether men like Orkney and Cutts, who faced down the Régiment de Navarre at Blenheim, would have put up with such fripperies. The Dutch and other allies, however, promptly acknowledged the title, though it was not until 1706 that Heinsius amended his abbreviated honorific from VE (for *Votre Excellence*) to VA (for *Votre Altesse*). When the Allied candidate for the throne of Spain wrote to tell him of the disaster to Stanhope's army at Brihuega, which was in fact to prove fatal to his interests in the Peninsula, it was to 'My Lord Duke and Prince' that the letter was addressed.[16] The happy prince continued to sign himself 'Marlborough' (often, in practice, simply 'M'), but when dealing with foreign dignitaries about important matters he was 'Le Pr et Duc de M', though such formality was rare, and often designed to lend weight to a missive or to show reciprocal respect.

In May 1703 the enormously rich Ralph, Earl of Montagu, who enjoyed what Edward Gregg penetratingly calls 'a singular reputation for profitable dishonour', had suggested that his heir Viscount Monthermer should marry Lady Mary Churchill. Marlborough had objected on the grounds (rather less reasonable then, when child marriages were not uncommon, than they would be now) that both parties were only fourteen, but in 1705 he agreed to the union, and the marriage took place in the Marlboroughs' apartments in St James's Palace on 20 March. The queen not only gave a dowry of £10,000, but on the day of the marriage she created Montagu a duke, and declared that the post of master of the great wardrobe, which he had purchased for life, would revert to his son on Montagu's death. It was indeed the full zenith of royal favour.[17]

The general election that spring was something of a personal triumph for the queen, now committed to maintaining balance between the two parties, for neither gained an absolute majority. She had, however, already made clear her support for Marlborough and Godolphin: on the eve of the election Marlborough personally called on Buckingham to demand the privy seal, like a commander receiving the keys of a captured fortress, and it was duly given to Newcastle. There were significant gains for the Whigs, although they were not able to dispose of all the 'Tackers', and eventually the balance of power was held by the moderate Tories, 'sneakers' to their Tacking friends.

What seemed to offer so much hope for the future, essentially a coalition government under the eye of a queen firmly disposed to rise above faction, was not destined to last, and the ingredients of lethal dissension grew steadily. That spring Godolphin had to threaten to resign to get Lord Sunderland, the Marlboroughs' Whig son-in-law, appointed extraordinary envoy to Vienna, and he repeated the same ploy to get prominent Whig divines made bishops. Tellingly, it took him a week to inform Harley, his closest ministerial colleague, of Sunderland's appointment. These signs of future breakdown would have been invisible to all but the most prescient contemporaries, and we must not give this post-Blenheim election more significance than it warrants. But, like Marlborough's principality and the victory parade through London, it did mark a turning point.

A close observer of the court might have gone further, discerning one of those proverbial clouds, no bigger than a man's hand, which herald a coming tempest. Abigail Hill, appointed bedchamber woman to the queen through Sarah's abundant influence, had begun her slow, self-effacing rise. Over the next three years, as Sarah ranted against the Tories and found new opportunities to exercise her waspish temper, those powerful bonds which had linked her to Anne were gradually dissolved. The quiet, unobtrusive Abigail could never offer her employer a relationship of anything approaching the same intensity, but Anne had grown tired of being hectored. It was not until Abigail married Samuel Masham, a gentleman of the queen's household, in 1707, that Sarah realised that she had been outflanked, and it was by then too late for her to react effectively. After Harley's dismissal from office in 1708 Abigail Masham used her growing influence to drip-feed the queen with Harley's own views, giving the opposition covert access to the monarch. Thus, in the kernel of Marlborough's continuing triumph wriggled the worm of his eventual defeat.

Hark Now the Drums Beat up Again

The campaign of 1705 began under strategic circumstances transformed not only by Blenheim but by Marlborough's brilliant exploitation of his victory. The Elector and Marsin took their survivors back via Ulm to join Villeroi on the Rhine. Marlborough and Eugène, for their part, marched through Württemberg in four large columns to reunite on 5 September at Philipsburg, where they crossed the Rhine, camping on the field of Speyerbach, where Tallard had beaten Prince Louis the year before. It was an inauspicious spot. Marlborough recalled Louis of Baden from Ingolstadt, and the margrave, so Richard Kane tells us, 'could never forgive them for robbing him of a share of the glory in the late victory'.[18] The garrison of the Lines of Stollhofen was brought in to join the army, which now numbered around 130,000 men, and Villeroi had no wish to offer battle, lamely falling back to allow the Allies to besiege Landau.

The siege was entrusted to Prince Louis, anxious for some visible triumph, with Marlborough and Eugène forward on the line of the little River Lauter to cover the operation. The fall of Ulm on 11 September released heavy guns and other siege equipment, strengthening Prince Louis, but Landau still held out till 8 November. It is evident that Marlborough was not happy with the conduct of the operation. On 20 October he warned Godolphin that the business was 'very little advanced', and Louis had just lost five hundred men in a failed attempt to wrest a handhold on the covered way. As late as 7 November Adam de Cardonnel told Ellis that 'Everybody of all sides are dissatisfied with the management and cry out against Prince Louis, if the weather was not favourable, tho' extreme cold, I know not what would become of us.'[19]

With the siege still labouring on, Marlborough himself planned to send a detachment under Colonel Blood to take Trier, and then proposed to go on to besiege Trarbach. Both these attacks succeeded, although the march was through what Marlborough called 'the terriblest country for an army with cannon'. Trier was evacuated as Marlborough approached, and Trarbach fell in mid-December. The campaign ended with the Moselle cleared and the Allies in winter quarters there, 'which I think will give France as much uneasiness as anything that has been done this summer'.[20]

Before returning to England, Marlborough visited Berlin. The King of Prussia was concerned at 'commotions in the north', where those martial titans Charles XII of Sweden and Peter the Great of Russia were in the throes of the Great Northern War, which lurched on, with interruptions, from 1700 till 1720, and ended with the destruction of Sweden as a major power. Marlborough was still able to persuade the king to send a force of 8,000 infantry to join the Allies in north Italy, in return for 200,000 écus from England and 100,000 from Holland, with the Empire providing the bread.[21]

Marlborough was well aware how much the events of that wonderful year owed to the soldiers under his command. After the Schellenberg he ordered the wounded 'to be dressed with all possible care, and sent forthwith to the hospital', and as Eric Gruber von Arni puts it, 'personally supervised many of the talks associated with the work of organising casualty care that would normally have been delegated to a quartermaster or other subordinate officer'.[22] He paid careful attention to the repatriation of wounded soldiers who had fought at the Schellenberg and Blenheim and to dependants of those who had fallen, for at this stage in the army's history many women and children followed their menfolk on campaign. The lyrics of that touching folk song 'High Germany' make the point well.

> O Polly, love, O Polly, the rout has now begun,
> And we must be a-marching to the beating of the drum.
> Go dress yourself all in your best and come along with me,
> I'll take you to the wars, my love, in High Germany.
>
> O Harry love, O Harry, come list what I do say,
> My feet they are so tender, I cannot march away.
> Besides my dearest Harry, I am with child by thee,
> Not fit to go to wars, my love, in High Germany.[23]

Immediately after the storming of the Schellenberg widows were ordered to report to the hospital at Heidenheim, where they were to help as nurses before being given passes and passage money for their journey home. After the campaign the hospital was closed, though not before some 1,710 sick and wounded had passed through it on their way to Flanders, where arrangements were made to hospitalise some men at Ghent and to repatriate others. On 20 March 1705 the commissioners of the Royal Hospital at Chelsea were ordered to give priority to

such of the invalids as being wounded in the last campaign in Germany are in the worst condition and want more than ordinary care to be taken of them. For the remainder of those invalids who, having likewise served in Germany, are entitled to the benefit of the hospital, His Grace does think fit that you appoint a person upon the most reasonable terms to take care of quartering them. And of the due payment of their quarters until vacancies shall happen. If any are found willing to return home and quit their pretensions to the hospital . . . for their encouragement £3 a man is to be paid to them.[24]

A bounty fund of £4,000 was to furnish this money, and also to provide payment for sick and injured NCOs and men on a scale determined by rank and unit, with a corporal of horse receiving one shilling and sixpence per day and a private in the infantry just five pence. Further money was put into the bounty fund so that widows could be paid, and Marlborough personally contributed £600. He also initiated the first ever scheme to give pensions to officers' widows, with part of the capital coming from money paid in by officers on first commissioning or subsequent promotion. Modern research demonstrates conclusively that the historian R.E. Scouller's assertion that Marlborough's medical care was 'remarkable for mismanagement, brutality, inhumanity, and, possibly corruption' is at variance with the facts.[25] Indeed, in his personal recognition that responsibility for the long-term care of his wounded was an inseparable part of the function of command, we see a quality that our own times might envy.

Examples of the battle injuries received by candidates for admission to Chelsea over the course the war make sobering reading. A trooper of Mapper's Horse had been shot in the right arm at Blenheim and in the back at Ramillies, then cut over the head at Oudenarde: he lacked only a wound at Malplaquet to hold every suit. A soldier in Howard's Foot had been shot in the right knee at Blenheim, had his left leg fractured by a mortar bomb and his left arm injured by a halberd. French sergeants, like their British counterparts, carried the halberd, a staff weapon with axe-edge and point: Peter Drake called his fellow sergeants 'the brethren of the halberd'. Halberds could be used to help sergeants dress the ranks, or sometimes, laid across men's shoulders, to hold a wilting rear rank in place by main force. When men came to hand-strokes, shoving with their bayonets or reversing their muskets to lay on with the butt, neither the halberd nor the spontoon, a similar but slimmer weapon carried by infantry officers, was to be despised.[26] A private soldier of Wade's Regiment managed to get shot in the left thigh at Schellenberg and the right knee at Blenheim, while a sergeant of

Harrison's had been wounded in the right groin when he became impaled on a palisade (either while trying to scale it, or having been blown onto it by grenade or mortar bomb). He had also had part of his abdominal lining removed by an operation, and was a fortunate man to get as far as the gates of Chelsea Hospital.[27]

There is no doubt that Marlborough intended to open the campaign of 1705 by advancing up the Moselle while the Imperial army threatened Alsace. He travelled to the Continent to prepare for operations in early April, telling Sarah that a difficult voyage caused him to be 'so very sick at sea, that my blood is as hot as if I were in a fever, which makes my head ache extremely, so that I beg you will make my excuse to my Lord Treasurer, for I can write to nobody but my dear soul, whom I love above my own life'.[28]

These repeated headaches, which were so much a feature of Marlborough's life, deserve further consideration, and all the evidence points to migraine. Full-blown 'classical' migraine starts with an aura, sometimes a visual disturbance, and sometimes with a more severe neurological disturbance such as one-sided tingling or even weakness. This is shortly followed by a severe one-sided headache, accompanied by vomiting, and lasting from six to forty-eight hours. Less severe forms of migraine are common, and the headache may have no preceding aura, may not be unilateral and may not be accompanied by vomiting. These forms are often less incapacitating.

Migraines are not daily events, but tend to come every few weeks or months, sometimes occurring in clusters of great frequency followed by longer periods of freedom. They may be precipitated by substances such as chocolate, cheese and red wine, and often occur after a period of stress rather than during the stressful event itself: typically they often arrive at weekends. Marlborough's symptoms strongly support a diagnosis of migraine. He sometimes distinguishes a 'disorder' in his head, possibly evidence of some kind of aura, from the headaches themselves, and regularly reports headaches after stressful events like difficult voyages, conferences or battles. The headaches did not progress or lead to other problems over the years, so we can safely rule out some serious underlying pathology. However, migraine, especially 'hemiplegic' migraine, is a risk factor for stroke in later life, and Marlborough was to be disabled by strokes.

It is believed that migraines result from the constriction of the cerebral arteries, causing the neurological symptoms, followed by the dilation of the arteries, causing the headache. Marlborough once reported that he felt better after being bled. Theoretically blood-letting should relieve the headache by reducing the pressure in the dilated arteries, but there seems little evidence of this in practice. Marlborough's relief might thus simply have been a placebo effect. These headaches were sometimes totally disabling, although in cases of real emergency, as in the pursuit after Ramillies, Marlborough was able to carry out some of his duties, suggesting a form of migraine that fell short of the most severe. However, these attacks were certainly frequent and damaging, and it is remarkable that he coped as well as he did with the crushing burden of responsibilities and his migraine too.[29]

No sooner had he shaken off this latest headache than Marlborough was confronted with sufficient problems to restore it. The Dutch had not furnished the magazine at Trier, upon which operations in the Moselle depended. German princes, relieved by the disappearance of the direct French threat, were slow in putting their contingents into the field, and even the King of Prussia, far from dispatching his troops to Italy as had been agreed, had still not sent enough to join the Allies in Germany. Eugène was away commanding in Italy, and Marlborough missed his wholehearted collaboration. Prince Louis, suffering from the physical effects of the wound he had received at the Schellenberg (which modern antibiotics would probably have cured in a fortnight) and the chagrin of having missed Blenheim, was not at his best.

There was the usual fast footwork required at the beginning of a campaign. The home front had to be propped up: the Ordnance Board was assured that funds were on their way from Godolphin to meet the 'extraordinary demands' now placed upon it. There was a light gilding of letters to princes along the Moselle. The Elector of Trier was told that Cadogan had already headed south to meet Prince Louis, and was accompanied by a Hamburg merchant who would be responsible for paying the troops on the Moselle. Prince Louis was warned to expect Cadogan, now a brigadier after Blenheim: 'He is briefed on everything, and I beg Your Highness to listen favourably to him, and to send him on as quickly as you can, so that he can join me before I leave Maastricht.'[30] No good evidently came of the visit, for Marlborough himself had to go down to see Prince Louis at Rastatt. He had hoped for a meeting at Creuznach, but the prince was 'incommoded with a swelling in his leg', probably the result of the previous year's wound.

Marlborough soon recognised that without Eugène and with limited German cooperation the original two-army campaign plan would not work. On 27 May he wrote to Secretary Harley from Trier.

I was in good hopes the Prince of Baden would have been enabled to have seconded me in these parts so that we might have acted with two separate armies, but you will be surprised to hear that all he can bring at present does not exceed eleven or twelve battalions and twenty-eight squadrons. These troops were to begin their march about this time, and will be here in ten or twelve days. The Prussians and several others cannot be here sooner, so it will be about the 10th of next month before we are able to move.[31]

Cardonnel radiated similar gloom, telling Ellis that 'the dilatoriness of our friends in joining us is a very great disappointment'.[32] Although Marlborough did manage to move off towards Villars' position at Sierck on 2 June, his army was much smaller than he had hoped, and Villars cunningly declined to offer battle in anything save the most formidable of positions.

While he was lamenting the impossibility of making real progress, Marlborough suddenly learnt the reason for his opponent's clever wagging of the matador's cloak. Up in Brabant, Villeroi was on the move. He snatched the fortress of Huy, and on 16 June opened his trenches before the citadel of Liège. Overkirk, outnumbered two to one, had to fall back on Maastricht. Heinsius had already warned Marlborough that the French planned to take Liège and Limburg, advancing into the bishopric of Cologne so as to block Dutch communications with the Moselle, and Marlborough told Godolphin of the inevitable result of all this.

The post does not go away till tomorrow, but I would ease my head and my heart by letting you know what is resolved. The deputies of the States' army on the Meuse have sent an express to me to desire that 30 battalions of them may be immediately sent to them. This joined with the want of forage, and no hopes of having the horses and carts in less than six weeks for the drawing everything to the siege [of Saarlouis] we have taken the resolution for strengthening Prince Louis' army and leaving a sufficient number of troops at Trier, and to march with the rest to assist them on the Meuse. We shall leave the cannon and all other ammunition at Trarbach and Coblenz, so that if the German princes will enable us to make a siege, we may return after we have put our friends on the Meuse at their ease . . . I have for these last ten days been so troubled by the many disappointments I have had, that I think if it were possible to vex me so for a fortnight longer it would make an end of me. In short, I am weary of my life.[33]

A letter to Sarah, written the same day, told her that he had a thousand things to say to her, but that 'whenever I sit down to write, the business of the army hinders me'. He complained of 'the negligence of princes whose interest is to help us with all they have', and regretted that Hompesch and Overkirk were in such 'great apprehension', for they must know that he could not give them instant succour. 'Adieu, my dearest soul,' he concluded, 'pity me and love me.'[34]

It was normally characteristic of Marlborough to reveal his despair to his wife and his best friend but to nobody else, though now there was a dash of bitters even in a letter to Heinsius sent from Trier on the eighteenth, gently warning that 'I have been so disappointed in every-thing that has been promised me that if I should find a backwardness when I come to the Meuse I shall be discouraged from ever serving another campaign.' Prince Louis, he added, had now decided to go and take the waters.[35] By this time, however, Marlborough had already extracted his army from the defiles of Alsace, made provision for leaving the sick and excess baggage in the villages along his route, and pressed on at such speed under a blazing sun that, as Blackader wrote, 'many fell by weariness and some died'. It was the old story for the infantry, of:

> Marching all day. Uneasy with hot weather. A soldier's life is an unaccountable way of living. One day too much heat, another too cold. Sometimes we want sleep, meat and drink; again, we are surfeited too much. A bad irregular way of living.[36]

Marlborough reached Maastricht on 27 June, but Villeroi did not care to wait for him, raised the siege as soon as he heard that Marlborough was approaching, and was back behind the Lines of Brabant too fast to be caught.

There was a poignant glint of an old mirror. On 11 July Marshal Villeroi sent him, under a flag of truce, two snuffboxes which had been dispatched to Marlborough by well-wishers in France. One was from the comte de Gramont, and was so elegant, as Marlborough assured its donor, that its equal could scarcely have been found in France or elsewhere. The other was 'one of the finest that I have ever seen, and is made inestimable to me by the portrait it bears'. It was from Charles II's old mistress the Duchess of Portsmouth, now living in France and allegedly in straitened circumstances, but not too poor to send a costly gift to the man who had been the lover of her predecessor in Charles's affections, and perhaps a little more.

Marlborough had little enough time to enjoy his presents or to muse on the past. In early July he had been exasperated to hear that Lieutenant General Aubach's force of Palatinate and Westphalian troops left to cover Trier had retired precipitately on the mere appearance of a French detachment. Aubach had at least blown breaches in the city's defences and destroyed much of the equipment it contained, but his behaviour was so 'unaccountable' that Marlborough confessed that it made him 'almost despair'. He ordered Aubach's men to join Prince Louis on the Rhine, where the Prussians were already marching, telling Henry St John that this ought to bring Prince Louis' army up to about 115 squadrons and eighty battalions, making it superior to Villars' force. Meanwhile, he would set about recovering Huy.[37]

Huy's outlying forts were soon taken, and the garrison of 450 men in the citadel surrendered as prisoners of war within two hours of Allied batteries opening fire. Marlborough had already decided that the misfortune at Trier meant that there was no longer any merit in his moving back to the Moselle, and so determined to pierce the Lines of Brabant as soon as the trenches dug before Huy had been filled in and his batteries there levelled. The operation depended on Dutch approval, and Orkney told his brother: 'You cannot believe how much it was opposed by the Dutch.'[38] Sicco van Goslinga, who became a field deputy the following year, acknowledges that all was not well: 'intrigues amongst the generals and even among the deputies, who instead of using their authority to stifle this fire of dissension at birth, encouraged it by choosing sides'.[39]

Marlborough established that the portion of the Lines between Neerhespen and Esmael was poorly guarded, and accordingly told Overkirk to make a diversion, crossing the River Mehaigne and feinting towards the lines north-east of Namur, threatening the very spot that the defenders thought most vulnerable. Villeroi marched at once to the spot. 'As soon as day began to shut in' on 17 July, Marlborough sent off General the comte de Noyelle, Lieutenant General Richard Ingoldsby and Lieutenant General Lumley with an advance guard of twenty-two battalions and twenty squadrons.[40] He brought the rest of his army along in two huge columns two hours later, heading for the Lines, 'three great leagues' from his camp. Overkirk had been sent word, though only that very evening, so as to preserve security, 'that he might likewise march in order and join us'. The advance guard reached the Lines – made up of a ditch and ramparts, protected by the Little Geete – by dawn on the eighteenth, and, as Lieutenant General Lumley reported: 'The too great security of the enemy made them negligent enough to possess with some advanced detachments of foot two of their barriers.'[41] Sergeant Millner was in a party of combined grenadiers under Colonel Godfrey, drawn together from the six British battalions in the advance guard, which was there when the River Geete was forced.

> Notwithstanding they [the enemy] were just on the other side of the river, yet we posted ourselves under cover of a quick set hedge without so much as one shot being fired. Where we continued the space of a quarter of an hour until such time as the pontoons on the carriages came up along a little causeway which led to the river, in order to lay the bridges. At the noise whereof the enemy took the alarum and began firing very sharply on that place where they judged the bridges would be laid. Which galled our workmen so prodigiously that they were not able to stand it. Which Brigadier Blood perceiving, came to Colonel Godfrey desiring three companies of grenadiers from the right to advance to the riverside in order to fire upon the enemy to divert them during the laying of the pontoon bridges. And as the bridges were finished the grenadiers had orders to march over the same; which we accordingly did and beat the enemy from that ground.[42]

Colonel Charles Godfrey was another echo of the past. He had married Marlborough's sister Arabella, very quietly, at some time in the 1680s, and, fecund as ever, she had borne him two daughters and a son. He was 'a sensible and well-liked fellow', a Whig MP and a source of regular support for Marlborough in the House. He was also a brave and determined infantry officer with something of the Salamander's stamp, and Marlborough rewarded him by deploying his interest to see Colonel Godfrey appointed clerk to the Board of Green Cloth and master of the Jewel Office. For all Arabella's early flightiness her marriage to Charles Godfrey was firm and good, although when she died in 1730, after a distressing period of dementia, she was buried in St Paul's with her brother George (who died in 1710), naval officer turned Tory politician and something of a thorn in the Marlburian side. 'I am very sorry that 16 [George Churchill] behaves himself so very ill,' lamented the duke to Sarah. 'I do not flatter myself with having much power over him, but if you please I shall speak to him, for I had much rather he should be unkind and disrespectful to me than to you, whose happiness is dearer to me than my own life.'[43]

Let us return to watch Charles Godfrey at the business he knew best. Neerhespen, on the Allied side of the lines, fell easily, and the château at Wangé, along the river to the south-west, was speedily taken. Three battalions rushed Elixheim, further west still, taking village and bridge; three enemy dragoon regiments encamped nearby did not even try to stem the flood, but fell back on Leau. However, for a time Marlborough's position was excruciatingly vulnerable. Part of the follow-up force had missed its way in the dark, and was still some way back. Marlborough sent a galloper back to Lord Orkney, its commander, urging him to step out. In the meantime, Marlborough pushed Lumley's advance guard cavalry over the obstacle 'without loss of time, though not without difficulty'. Orkney's men, with that turn of speed which the duke's infantry always produced when they knew he really needed them, reached the bridges while the last of the cavalry were still crossing. Orkney reported the bridges so poor that 'hardly above one man could go over abreast though in some places one foot man and a horseman passed over together. However, though the passages were very bad, men scrambled over them strangely.'[44]

Marlborough himself rode forward to join the cavalry, and saw that forty or fifty enemy squadrons were now coming up, with a number of light guns and infantry behind them. Orkney, some way back, saw 'two good lines of the enemy, very well formed, a line of foot following them. We were in a very good position to receive them, and we outwinged [outflanked] them, and still more troops coming over the pass. As I got over to the [1st] foot guards, I saw the shock begin.' Although his infantry was not yet in a position to intervene, many of the enemy cavalry were Bavarian cuirassiers in half-armour, and his own men – British, Hanoverian and Hessian – were 'a good deal mixed up and not in their proper place', Marlborough at once ordered his horse to charge. In the cavalry mêlée, separated from his escort and with only a few staff officers to hand, he was, as Lumley reported, in great peril. Orkney recounts how:

My Lord Marlborough in person was everywhere, and escaped very narrowly, for a squadron, which he was at the head of, gave ground a little, but soon came up again; and a fellow came up to him and thought to have sabred him to the ground, and struck him with that force, and, missing his stroke, he fell off his horse. I asked my Lord if it was so; he said it was absolutely so. See what a happy [e.g. fortunate] man he is.[45]

The battle was really over before the infantry arrived. Blackader wrote that 'our horse had some action with them, and beat them wherever they encountered them. Our foot had nothing to do, for the enemy fled before they came up.'[46] John Marshall Deane of 1st Foot Guards recalled a busier time:

our men were so eager upon the design that they jumped furiously upon the enemy into the trenches, the which they soon quitted, and then our men took the pass it being a pretty big river. Some of our regiments wading through it breast high; and afterwards engaged them with notable valour and broke their army most confusedly, giving the enemy a total rout.[47]

So far, so good. The Lines were pierced on a wide front and the French counterattack was thoroughly beaten. Overkirk was on his way, though about two hours from Marlborough, who felt it rash to follow the retreating French infantry until he arrived. We now know, though Marlborough did not, that Villeroi did not in fact hear of his defeat till nine that morning, by which time Overkirk's men had already started to cross the Geete. Marlborough could have taken the risk of pressing the Bavarian infantry, which had fallen back in good order, without any chance of Villeroi intervening. He did push on to Tirlemont, capturing a battalion there; and some dragoons, pursuing the survivors of the morning's battle, overtook and seized part of Villeroi's baggage train. When Marlborough wrote to Harley from Tirlemont that evening he reported the day's events as a significant victory, and concluded that he hoped to advance on Louvain the following day.

Marlborough announced the capture of two lieutenant generals, the marquis d'Allègre and the comte de Hornes, two major generals, two brigadiers, 'near fourscore other officers, with ten pieces of cannon and a great many standards and colours', as well as over 2,000 men. On the following day his advanced squadrons caught Villeroi's rearguard crossing the Dyle, and took another fifteen hundred prisoners.[48] The captured guns were of an unusual type, designed to provide close support for horse and foot. Private Deane tells how

> each piece having three bores . . . touching the match to one touch hole they fired out each piece 3 balls at once. These very murdering cannon were made the last year at the city of Brussels for the security of the line, but by the providence of God we secured them so that they did our army but little mischief.[49]

Marlborough wrote to Sarah on the evening of the eighteenth. Knowing what we do of his headaches, we will not be surprised to hear that 'my blood is so hot that I can hardly hold my pen, so that you will my dearest life excuse me if I do not say more'. He still paid tribute to the architects of his victory: 'It is impossible to say too much good of the troops that were with me, for never men fought better.' The battle was unquestionably a 'good success' – not Blenheim, to be sure, but a valuable victory in its own right and an earnest of what might come.[50] The ministry, anxious for something to celebrate, proclaimed a day of public thanksgiving for 'having forced the French lines . . . [and obtained] a signal and glorious victory within those lines'. The mellifluous *Gazette* lovingly described the royal procession from St James's to St Paul's Cathedral to hear the Dean of Lincoln preach and join a thundering *Te Deum*.[51]

It may not have been Blenheim, but there was certainly a palpable feeling of unity of purpose linking Marlborough and his men that day. Lieutenant Colonel Cranstoun of the Cameronians wrote:

> Those who know the army and what soldiers are know very well that upon occasions like this where even the common soldier is sensible of the reason of what he has to do, and especially of the joy and success of victory, soldiers with little entreaty will even outdo themselves, and march and fatigue double with cheerfulness what their officers would at other times compel them to do.[52]

Men shouted, 'Now, on to Louvain,' and 'Over the Dyle,' and even the Dutch Lieutenant General Slangenburg, when he came up, told Marlborough: 'This is nothing if we lie here. We should march on Louvain or Parc.'[53] Marlborough was touched by the noisy acclamations he received. He confessed to Sarah that 'the kindness of the troops to me had transported me . . . to make me very kind expressions, even in the heat of the action, which I own to you gives me very great pleasure, and makes me resolve to endure anything for their sakes'.[54]

There was widespread recognition that by marching straight for Louvain on the eighteenth the Allies would have intercepted Villeroi, who had to swing through a quarter-circle to cross the river there. But Overkirk, usually so much in Marlborough's mind, declared (not unreasonably, for they had marched twenty-six miles in thirty-one hours) that his soldiers were exhausted, and camped between Leau and Tirlemont. With the great opportunity missed, a smaller one, of crossing the Dyle to fight Villeroi on the far side, still remained. However, unseasonable rain flooded the water meadows, which the army needed to traverse to reach the river, and then the Dutch Council of War unanimously 'declared the passage of the river to be of too dangerous a consequence'.[55]

Marlborough was furious, but told Godolphin that he dared not show his resentment too much for fear of annoying the Dutch and encouraging the French. He did, however, privately acknowledge that he had not let Overkirk know what his plan really was ('I was forced to cheat them into this action, for they did not believe I would attack the Lines'), which suggests that, for all Marlborough's annoyance at the Dutch decision, his ally's irritation was not without cause.[56] He told both Heinsius and Godolphin of his fear that the decision now gave the campaign 'a very melancholy prospect'. Although he urged secrecy on his correspondents, it is clear that his frustrations were widely aired in Britain, probably because it suited the ministry to blame an ally, rather than its chosen commander, for what now looked very much like a missed opportunity: Blenheim had been such a stunning success that public expectations were unreasonably high.

Most historians believe that Marlborough was right to blame the Dutch, but Ivor Burton sounds a note of caution. There were fundamental differences within the alliance. The Dutch, engaged in a life-or-death struggle against France for the past three decades, never saw battle in the same light as Marlborough. Nor did they welcome his methods, which were, by the standards of the age, secretive. Much later in the war, Goslinga saw how, unusually, 'Milord on his arrival had all the infantry and cavalry generals called to a sort of council of war. I must note that Milord never used these councils: he limited himself to the deputation, or [Dutch] general in chief assisted by the two quartermasters-general, Dopff and Cadogan.' Marlborough went on to tell him: 'I must teach you a general maxim; that is if you find yourself in a delicate situation, or need to decide on a battle or some great and hazardous enterprise, if you are resolved to do it, neither consult your generals, nor call a great council.'[57]

The three centuries since Blenheim emphasise that Marlborough was right to believe that 'It is absolutely necessary that such a power be lodged with the general as may enable him to act as he thinks proper according to the best of his judgement, without being obliged either to communicate what he intends further than he thinks convenient.'[58] Yet it is no less evident that the issue of command goes to the very heart of coalition warfare, and he is a fortunate coalition commander who enjoys the undiluted authority that Marlborough sought.

Of course personal jealousies and ambitions amongst the Dutch generals played their part, just as they had in the squabble between Coehoorn and Slangenburg in 1703. Most of them were *petite noblesse*, gentlemen of ancient lineage but narrow acres, given to high words and long memories. Opdam, who refused to serve under Overkirk, who in turn blocked his promotion, had a remarkable thirty-two quarterings on his coat of arms, and was made a count by the Elector Palatine in 1711. Sicco van Goslinga declined a similar honour from the emperor: being a gentleman of Friesland was quite enough for him.

There were added layers of complexity in 1705. A French deputation was at The Hague, and although Marlborough assured Godolphin that the Dutch would not make a separate peace, there was always a risk that the French might attain, through a diplomatic master-stroke, what they had so far failed to achieve by battle. In the very same letter in which he warned Heinsius of the need for undivided command, Marlborough added an apparently harmless paragraph saying that the captured Lieutenant General d'Allègre, who 'has a very good reputation', had 'pressed me for a pass for two months'. Marlborough was anxious to do this decent fellow 'all the civilities I could', but he just wanted to clear the matter with Heinsius first.

D'Allègre duly received his pass. Then, whether or not with Marlborough's foreknowledge we cannot say, though the implications are obvious, he went straight to Versailles, where Louis XIV told him:

> Until the present moment, the king believed that his honour demanded that he maintain his grandson the King in the possession of all the states which the late King of Spain left him . . . having defended him for five years, without deriving any advantage . . . it is now time that the King puts the interests of France above those of Spain.

Louis gave d'Allègre *plein pouvoir* to negotiate a settlement on his return to Holland, and urged him to get Marlborough firmly on side. The French king could not offer the duke 'more dignities than he already possessed', but a gift of two million livres 'would solidly establish a fortune, always doubtful in England, if it was not supported by great wealth'. D'Allègre was also to pass on to Marlborough 'sentiments full of respect and veneration'.

Marlborough asked d'Allègre to dinner soon after his return to The Hague on the expiry of his leave, but the marquis reported to Louis that: 'As for Marlborough, while affecting a sincere inclination for peace, he claimed to defer entirely to the decisions of his sovereign and above all to the Estates-General.' Nevertheless, they agreed that d'Allègre would 'put himself in the position of being ill' so as not to have to accompany Marlborough to England, so giving himself more time to talk to the Dutch. However, negotiations foundered, and eventually 'nothing was left to d'Allègre but to board the yacht which had been put at his disposal to travel to England'.[59]

It is clear from subsequent correspondence that Marlborough regarded the offer of two million livres as lasting beyond the immediate failure of the d'Allègre mission. Louis later suggested that the offer should be increased to four million if the peace terms were particularly attractive, proposing a menu of rewards related to specific points in any eventual treaty. However, Torcy, the French foreign minister, met Marlborough at The Hague in the spring of 1706, and 'when I mentioned his private interests he blanched and seemed desirous of changing the topic of conversation'. In 1708, when the strategic situation was even more encouraging for the Allies, Marlborough told Berwick: 'You may be sure that I shall be heartily in favour of peace, not doubting that I should find proof of the goodwill which was promised to me two years ago by the Marquis d'Allègre.'[60]

The extant evidence does no more than identify key features, for it was in the nature of such discussions that little entered the written record. However, it is certain that the French 'sweetener' was no mere figment of anti-Marlborough propaganda, and that the duke's desire to make money was so widely known that Louis XIV thought it worth appealing to his cupidity. It is no less clear that, while Marlborough was prepared to grasp the money if he could, he was not willing to let the prospect of such a substantial reward change his view on the conduct of the war. At the very time that he was considering the French *douceur* he was inflicting a series of substantial military defeats on his would-be paymaster, which would be puzzling behaviour from a man who had been bought and sold. Conversely, Marlborough was sometimes accused (not least by Berwick and Goslinga) of prolonging the war for his own financial reward. This is not a view supported by his personal correspondence with Sarah and Godolphin, and it would indeed be an odd line to take given what we now know of his financial interest in *ending* the war.

The campaign of 1705 never really progressed beyond the sharp blow inter-Allied relations received in mid-July. The Allies crossed the Dyle south of Louvain at the end of the month, but Villeroi was there to oppose one of the crossings, and the Dutch demanded that Marlborough should honour an earlier agreement and not force the issue. In August Marlborough outnumbered Villeroi so significantly that Versailles ordered substantial detachments to be sent from the Rhine, where the Imperialists were not fixing the French as Marlborough had hoped, to the Brabant front. But before they could arrive Marlborough carried out a promising manoeuvre round the headwaters of the Dyle, feinting towards Brussels and so persuading Villeroi to move out of Louvain to face him. Marlborough then swung north, advancing upon the outnumbered Villeroi with every prospect of forcing him to fight a major battle on unfavourable terms, near what was to be the 1815 battlefield of Waterloo.

The French position was strong, but Marlborough could see serious flaws in it, and pointed these out to Overkirk, who 'perfectly coincided in his opinion'. The field deputies, however, demanded time to consult their generals, and when Marlborough formally asked his council of war, at about three on the afternoon of 18 August, to support his decision to attack, Slangenburg exclaimed: 'Since I have been led to this place without previous communication of the design, I will give no other opinion than that the passage at Over-Ische is impracticable. However, I am ready to obey the orders which I may receive.' After a lengthy debate the field deputies decided that the suggested attack would not work, but admitted that it might be wise to look elsewhere. 'This survey,' writes Coxe, 'provided a new source of cavils and objections. Every post occupied by the enemy was deemed too strong to be forced; the river was declared not fordable; and the most trifling elevation was declared inaccessible to cavalry.'

Perhaps we should not let a private soldier speak at this council of war, but, interestingly, John Marshall Deane might have voted with the Dutch, for he did not like the look of the French position: 'It appeared impossible for us to pretend to get at the enemy, for their army lay just beyond the pass where it was thought ten thousand men to be sufficient to prevent an army of 100 thousand men from getting over.'[61] Consideration was eventually interrupted by nightfall, and Marlborough observed bitterly: 'I am at this moment *ten* years older than I was four days ago.'

Marlborough, angry before, was now positively furious. On 19 August he told Godolphin:

> You will see by the enclosed to the States that after four days march I found the enemy encamped as I expected, so that I thought we should have had a very glorious day. But as the deputies would not consent without first consulting their generals, who were all against it except Monsieur Overkirk, so that we have been obliged to retire from the enemy, notwithstanding we were at least one third stronger than they, which I take to be very prejudicial to the common cause, and scandalous for the army . . .
>
> The last action of the Dutch generals has given me very great mortification, for the enemy will see very plainly that they have nothing to fear on this side. Nor can I serve with them without losing the little reputation [I have], for in most countries they think I have power in this army to do what I please.
>
> I beg you will give my duty to the Queen, and assure her that if I had the same power I had last year I should have had a greater victory than that of Blenheim in my opinion, for the French were so posted that if we had beaten them they could not have got to Brussels.[62]

A few days later he added that prisoners and deserters all confirmed that Villeroi had been in a hopeless position. It was a missed opportunity of staggering proportions.

Marlborough had been muttering about resigning for much of the year, and now acknowledged that he was finding it almost impossible to put up with the frustration of shackled command. He told Sarah that he had 'a very great desire to have that work of Woodstock finished, and if I can be so happy as to live some years in quietness there with my dear soul, I shall think myself well recompensed for all the vexations and troubles I am now obliged to undergo'.[63] To make matters worse, his eyes were very painful: he thought 'the heat of my blood' was to blame, and hoped to visit a spa when the pressure of campaigning eased.

Marlborough made no effort to conceal his annoyance with the Dutch, which was so serious that, even before this incident, old Portland,

William of Orange's favourite and once a symbol of that Dutch influence Marlborough had so detested, wrote to warn him that leaving the army early would send the worst possible signal.[64] Eugène wrote from Italy to agree that:

> It is extremely cruel that opinions so weak and discordant should have obstructed the progress of your operations, when you had every reason to expect so glorious a result. I speak to you as a sincere friend. You will never be able to perform anything considerable with your army unless you are absolute, and I trust your highness will use your utmost efforts to gain that power in future. I am not less desirous than yourself to be once more united with you in command.[65]

The queen added her own support in a letter which nobly testifies to her ability to set her damaged relationship with Sarah on one side.

> I am very sorry to find, by your letters to the Lord Treasurer, that you are so very much in the spleen. I own all the disagreeable things you have met with this summer are a very just cause for it, and I am very much concerned for the uneasiness you are under; but yet I cannot help hoping, that for the good of your country and the sake of your friends, who cannot support themselves without you, you will be persuaded to banish your melancholy thoughts.[66]

Marlborough's official bulletin noted that the army had been ready to attack, 'but the Deputies of the States, having consulted with their other generals, would not give their assent, and so the proposed attack was countermanded'.[67] The States-General refused to print it, but Marlborough wrote letters condemning the Dutch to Wratislaw and Eugène amongst others, and told Heinsius in the bluntest terms that Slangenburg had deprived them all of a lasting peace. 'I do before God declare to you, that I am persuaded that if Slangenburg had not been in the army, at this day we might have prescribed to France the peace we pleased,' he wrote. Instead of the peace that they might have had, he now looked to a continuation of the war, because the French would not concede what he saw as each of the Allies' minimum aims. For Britain, he suggested, this meant a Spain secured for Charles III, the Hapsburg claimant, and for Holland, a secure frontier with garrisons in Antwerp, Namur and Luxembourg. The Duke of Savoy must be kept secure and, with 'the blessing of God we must do something for the Protestants [in the Cevennes]'.[68]

Marlborough blamed Slangenburg's opposition on personal motives, arguing that as a Roman Catholic it was 'his temper to hinder whatever may be designed', while Robert Parker thought Slangenburg 'so intolerably insolent, that there was no bearing him'.[69] There had certainly been an ill-mannered confrontation on the unfought field of Waterloo. 'Speaking forwardly and harshly to the Duke', says chaplain Hare, he 'was very noisy and cried out that it was sacrificing the army and an impracticable enterprise'.[70] The formal Dutch report suggests that the road to this fatal dissension had been paved by Marlborough's lack of consultation. Marlborough, argued the field deputies, had been authorised by the Estates-General, 'without holding a council of war, to make two or three marches, for the execution of some design formed by his grace'. But he had gone well beyond this. The report concluded: 'We cannot conceal from your high mightinesses that all the generals of our army think it very strange that they should not have the least notice of the said marches.'[71]

Marlborough, now ruefully convinced that all he could do in the remainder of the campaigning season was to take the fortress of Leau and level the Lines where he had overrun them, ordered Slangenburg to besiege Leau with fifteen battalions and fifteen squadrons. Slangenburg demanded twice the force, so Marlborough at once set Lieutenant General van Dedem, another Dutch officer, on to the task, and the place fell easily.[72]

The demolition of the Lines also went well once Marlborough was able to put his army to work on it. The *London Gazette* reported: 'The peasants that were employed in demolishing the enemy's Lines proceeding but slowly, 50 men out of every battalion in both armies were on the 8th Instant ordered for this service, in which this detachment soon made a considerable progress, being relieved every 48 hours.'[73] Private Deane, who saw things from the business end of a shovel, reported that:

> The line was of a most prodigious strength, being 18 foot deep and 16 foot broad. The bastions lying along the middle of it being 8 foot higher than the level or top of the entrenchments, & so thick throughout that 4 men might have walked abreast upon it & fired upon the enemy that should approach it. There were likewise counterscarps one by the side of another to withdraw in if an enemy should have got over. The front of this line being formed triangular, worming and running every way . . . the passage from one side of the line to the other being

all triangle work that a man could not see 6 yards before him, and
barriered with trees very strongly.[74]

While ramparts were being levelled and ditches filled, the English and
Dutch governments worked just as hard to repair the damage done to
their alliance by the recent dissension. Slangenburg might have been a
villain to the British, but he was a hero to some of his own countrymen,
and there was a possibility that the peace party in the United Provinces,
led by Pensionary Buys of Amsterdam, might gain ground on the back
of a disappointing campaign and Slangenburg's resolute opposition to
the high-handed ways of a foreign general. That danger soon passed.
The popular mood so turned against Slangenburg that when
Shrewsbury passed through The Hague that winter he thought that if
Slangenburg had shown himself in the street he would have been
murdered like the de Witt brothers in 1672.

The general, pleading ill-health, retired first to Maastricht and then to
Aachen. Charles Churchill heard that he had spoken 'freely and disre-
spectfully' of his brother, and sent Colonel Palmes to call upon him to
request satisfaction if things were indeed as they had been reported.
Slangenburg promptly denied disrespect, survived unchallenged, but
never again held a command. Robert Parker was among those delighted
to see the last of him, not least because his successor, Lieutenant
General Salisch, was a bird of a very different feather.

> He was born in Switzerland of a family of note, and upon some disgust he
> listed himself with a Dutch officer, who brought him a recruit to Breda,
> in the very regiment he is now colonel of. In this regiment he advanced
> himself by his personal bravery, without any interest or friends, but such
> as his merit had gained him: till from a private sentinel, he became
> colonel of the regiment, Governor of Breda, and General of the Dutch
> infantry; but it was yet more remarkable, that the officer who enlisted
> him, still continued a lieutenant when our regiment was quartered at
> Breda, and it was more than he deserved, for he was an old Geneva sot;
> however, the general, out of pure compassion to him, kept him constantly
> confined, where great care was taken of him, as long as he lived.[75]

The replacement of Slangenburg by Salisch did not end the matter.
Cardonnel had drawn up a report for the *London Gazette* which reflected
Marlborough's view of the missed opportunity. The version that actually
appeared was wholly emasculated:

The 18th the army decamped at three in the morning from Fischermont, and having passed several defiles, came through the wood of Soignies into a spacious plain, with only the Ische between us and the enemy, whom we found, according to expectation, in their former camp . . . In the afternoon the army encamped at Laisne, from when we marched on the 19th to the camp at Basse-Wavre . . . The 22nd the army under His Grace marched from Basse-Wavre to this camp.[76]

Not only was there no mention of the dispute, but the implication that he had deliberately avoided battle irritated Marlborough. He complained to Godolphin that he had been 'used very hardly', enclosing a copy of Cardonnel's original dispatch so that Godolphin could see what had been left out, 'which I think the writer of the Gazette would not have ventured to have done if he had not had orders for it'. He blamed the textual change on a desire not to offend Vryberg, the Dutch ambassador in London, adding that if the Dutch saw the *Gazette* they would have even less reason for yielding to his demands for greater authority. 'I am very sure I must be madder than anybody in Bedlam,' he concluded, 'if I should be desirous of serving, when I am sure that my enemies seek my destruction, and that my friends sacrifice my honour to their wisdom.'[77] Both Hedges and St John maintained that they had had nothing to do with it, blaming the slip on the 'negligence or venality' of the *Gazette*'s editor.

The government decided to send Lord Pembroke to the United Provinces to lodge a complaint, but Marlborough, fearing that the matter was now escalating beyond his control, and confident that Heinsius would achieve the desired result without formal intervention, managed to get the visit cancelled. On 14 September he told Heinsius that 'whatever your deputies and generals shall propose I shall use my utmost endeavours that it may succeed', adding, 'Now that M. Slangenburg is gone if I see anything that I think feasible, I shall make no difficulty of proposing it to them.'[78] Ten days later Marlborough assured Godolphin that although the cancellation of Pembroke's visit might

make some noise in England, I think it is much wiser and honester, to let such as do not mean well to be angry, than to do that which must prejudice the public, as this journey of Lord Pembroke's would certainly do. For Pensionary Buys has confirmed me in my opinion, that the constitution of the States is such, that they can't take away the power that the deputies have had at all times in the army. For in the

King's time they had the same authority, but he took care to choose such men as always agreed what he had a mind to. Now this may, if they please, be put again in practice, but that never can be done by a treaty. I have also underhand assurances that they will never employ Slangenburg in the army where I may be.[79]

The discreet understanding that sympathetic field deputies would be selected henceforth paved the way for a remarkable period of Anglo-Dutch military cooperation. Indeed, almost as if to point the way ahead, the Allies snatched the fortress of Zandvliet, on the Scheldt between Antwerp and Bergen op Zoom, before going into winter quarters.

Throughout the tense summer of 1705 Marlborough had dealt with coalition politics well beyond the borders of Brabant. He ensured that the new emperor, Joseph I, who had just succeeded his father Leopold I, understood the significance of his piercing the Lines, sending a senior aide 'to inform Your Imperial Majesty of the peculiarities of this affair, which I do not doubt will have very advantageous results for the common cause and for the interests of Your Imperial Majesty, for which I will always have a special attention'.[80] He thanked the King of Prussia for his generosity in ensuring that the Prussian contingent destined for the Rhine could now serve in Brabant, though he warned Raby, ambassador in Berlin, that Prince Louis was now in such an awkward mood that he would probably use the non-arrival of these troops as an excuse to do nothing. Yet to read his letters to Prince Louis one would never guess how that gentleman's slow progress exasperated Marlborough, and when the prince at last succeeded in forcing the Lines of Haguenau, 'I could not wait for the arrival of the full details to congratulate you, with all my heart, on such a happy event.'[81]

He commiserated with the Ordnance Board on 'the ill condition of the stores of ordnance', and, alerted to the shortage of saltpetre, an essential ingredient of gunpowder, told the board that there was currently plenty in Holland, where five shiploads had recently arrived. There was interest to be dispensed. Lady Oglethorpe was assured that her son could have his promised ensigncy in the Foot Guards, and 'If you please to send me the young gentleman's Christian name, his commission shall be dispatched immediately.'[82] He was less open-handed to the Earl of Dalhousie, who hoped to succeed a kinsman as colonel of the Scots Guards, saying that he would do his best for him, but gently adding (for he must have guessed that the outcome would not be to the earl's advantage) that in this case the queen would be advised by 'her ministers in Scotland'.

Sarah, pressed by the Earl of Essex's sister, Lady Carlisle, to do something for the cash-strapped earl, asked Marlborough to get him made constable of the Tower of London. Marlborough knew his wife's temper too well to disappoint her, but it created another problem, for Charles Churchill was lieutenant of the Tower, and would thus become Essex's nominal subordinate, which would never do.

> Would it not be barbarous to put my Lord Essex, that is but a major general, over my brother that is Lieutenant of the Tower and General of the Foot? I write to Lady Marlborough to the same purpose by this post, and if this were said to Lord Essex, he would not expect it . . .

Essex was eventually appointed, but only after Charles Churchill had been moved on to be governor of Guernsey, an appointment he coveted: Cadogan replaced him as lieutenant of the Tower, a post which brought income but no duties, and everybody was happy.[83]

There were other family obligations too. When Marlborough heard that Sarah's sister Frances wished to cross the lines to visit Aix, he obtained a pass from the French, and wrote to tell her: 'I have likewise ordered eight dragoons to attend on you on your coming to the Bosch; these will wait on you to Maastricht, where the governor will give you another escort on to Aix. I heartily wish you a good journey, and all the success you can desire with the waters.' He politely recognised her Jacobite title, addressing her as Duchess of Tyrconnell.[84]

Lastly, despite his lack of ministerial office, Marlborough continued to play a central role in government. The issues of fixing the succession and pursuing a union between England and Scotland were uppermost in the minds of Westminster politicians, and that autumn's session of Parliament passed both a Regency Act and legislation authorising the appointment of commissioners to negotiate a Union with Scotland. Godolphin was anxious to continue removing Tories from the ministry, a process which Harley rightly feared would lead to his own replacement and which ran contrary to the queen's desire to have a broadly-based government. She continued to value Marlborough's advice, but even before the summer's exhausting wrangling with the Dutch he expressed a wish to retire at the end of the campaign, and clearly felt that his headaches and associated problems with his vision were the harbingers of something fatal.

> By the vexation and trouble I undergo, I find a daily decay, which may deprive me of the honour of serving Your Majesty any more, which thought makes me take the liberty to beg of Your Majesty, that for your own sake and for the happiness of both kingdoms, you will never suffer anybody to do the Lord Treasurer an ill office. For besides his integrity for your service, his temper and abilities are such, that he is the only man in England capable of giving such advice as may keep you out of the hands of both parties, which may at last make you happy, if quietness can be had in a country where there is so much faction.[85]

Edward Gregg, Anne's distinguished biographer, identifies here 'a maudlin note which was to be repeated later in his correspondence and which the Queen was to find increasingly grating'.[86] Marlborough's correspondence with Sarah and Godolphin testifies to the fact that there was nothing political in his desire to retire: indeed, he rarely mentioned Blenheim Palace save in the context of a place where he might live out his days in peace. Although he had suffered from headaches for many years, their frequency and severity in 1705, together with the appearance of stomach trouble and gout, left him fearing that, as he told Heinsius that autumn, 'I am really ill.'

Despite the closeness of his relationship with Godolphin, Marlborough was often a reluctant participant in the lord treasurer's campaign against the Tories, and was far from sharing his wife's Whig principles. But there was no more escaping his requirement to support Godolphin than his need to keep propping up the alliance. Welded into his myriad of concerns at the close of a difficult year was the need to dissuade the Elector of Hanover from allowing the dowager Electress Sophia, the Tories' preferred candidate to succeed Anne, from settling in England, something that the queen told him 'gives me a great deal of uneasiness'.[87]

The twenty-first century is too often prepared to diagnose stress as a universal illness, but by any reasonable assessment the pressures bearing down upon Marlborough at the close of 1705 were almost intolerable. It was the cruellest of ironies that he was able to sustain them largely because of his relationship with Sarah, but Sarah's own views and attitudes were by now contributing to his burden. His occasional attempts to steer her towards a less confrontational relationship with Anne, or to dissuade her from inciting Godolphin into fresh attacks on the Tories in government, could not be pressed too far without the risk of the sort of marital crisis that had disfigured the early months of 1704. In short, Marlborough could not survive without Sarah, but had come to realise that surviving with her was increasingly hard.

Happy and Glorious: Ramillies

One year tumbled into another. Marlborough spent November and December 1705 visiting Allied capitals. The new emperor urgently needed money to sustain the war in Italy, and Marlborough pressed the bankers of Vienna to supply an immediate 100,000 crowns on Dutch and English security. He undertook to arrange a loan of £250,000, on the security of the silver mines in Silesia, and did so as soon as he returned to England, putting up £10,000 himself: the sum was raised in full by early March 1706. In Berlin he was presented with a diamond-encrusted sword, but found the King of Prussia so irritated by the irregular payment of his troops that he would not, at that time, guarantee to keep them under Prince Louis' command. Finally he went to Hanover, whence he wrote to Godolphin that the Elector 'has commanded me to assure Her Majesty that he will never have any thoughts but what may be agreeable to hers'. He had just heard that the Lords had passed the Regency Act, and later that month the queen gave her assent to an act naturalising the Electress Sophia and her heirs.[88] This bout of diplomacy ended with him prostrate with migraine: 'My head aches to that degree that I can say no more . . .' It was wholly typical of this curmudgeonly year that he did not manage to return to England until late on the evening of Sunday, 29 December.

Marlborough returned to a nation making the greatest military effort of its history so far. In the Iberian Peninsula the Allies had scored significant successes, capturing Gibraltar and Barcelona, overrunning Catalonia, and being poised for an attack on Madrid from Catalonia and Portugal. The threat to the Empire had been blunted at Blenheim, the Duke of Savoy's defection to the Allies had widened the Italian theatre. Marlborough had seventeen British battalions in 1702, and twenty from 1703; maritime enterprises consumed twelve in 1702, eleven in 1703 and six from 1704. The Peninsula gobbled up ten battalions in 1704, fifteen in 1705 and nineteen in the winter of 1705–06. In 1706 the war in Flanders and Brabant cost £1,255,000, and operations in the

Peninsula £829,000 from a military budget of £2,112,000. Even Italy absorbed £334,000 in assorted loans to the emperor, the Duke of Savoy and German princes providing troops.[89] Parliament, now narrowly under Whig control, was prepared to vote unprecedented sums of money for a war which the Allies now seemed to be within measurable distance of winning.

Marlborough was in the unusual position of being Allied commander in a particular theatre of war, captain general of all the queen's land forces, and strategic adviser to a government prosecuting the closest thing to a world war that history had so far seen. Winston S. Churchill maintains that Marlborough merely tolerated the war in the Peninsula as a sop to the Tories, but on the contrary, it is evident that in the winter of 1705–06 he actually recognised that his own theatre of operations was the least important. A drive on Madrid seemed to offer the prospect of winning the war in a single campaign, but conversely failure to reinforce Allied armies in Italy might lead to a crushing French victory there, and reopen the threat to Vienna. And, in just the same way that the French hoped that disaffected Irish or Scots might be used to spearhead an invasion of Britain, so Marlborough believed that Huguenot 'refugee regiments' could be used against France. In March 1706, not long before he left for the Continent, he told Heinsius how he saw the war in the round for the coming campaign.

> I am very sensible that there are very just objections to this project [of refugee regiments], but I can't hinder being of opinion that it ought to be attempted though the success should not be a third part of what is promised; for we should attempt everything that is in our power this campaign, for the troops of France were at no time so divided as they now are. When we shall consider that we have an army in Spain, another in Italy, a third in Germany, and a fourth in Flanders, we may conclude that this is the time, that we ought to do something that they do not expect, and we may be sure, that if they are being surprised, they will find it very difficult to oppose us, their armies being at so great a distance from each other.[90]

This was a wide strategic view from a general capable of lifting his gaze above the Lines of Brabant.

When Marlborough reached The Hague in late April 1706 he first decided on attacks into France, in concert with Prince Louis, by way of the Moselle and Landau. This scheme did not survive early recognition that Prince Louis' army had been too weakened by detachments for Italy to be able to mount a serious offensive. Marlborough then determined to go to Italy himself, where, working in concert with Eugène, he would attack into south-east France, and the Dutch, to his astonishment, agreed to devote troops to the venture. Marlborough had told Heinsius that the French would find it hard to oppose the Allies effectively if they were surprised. However, what applied to one combatant was no less true for the other, and Marlborough was himself surprised by the fact that the French, straining every nerve over the winter, had created a total of eight armies, three of which – under Villars on the Rhine, Villeroi in Brabant, and Marsin on the Moselle – were to attack in unison before the Allies could begin the campaign. Louis had concluded that he was now unable to fulfil his original war aim after Blenheim, but that by mounting a vigorous offensive he could obtain peace on suitable terms.

Marlborough was making preparations for the march to Italy, with the usual problems in getting Allied contingents in on time, when he heard that Villars had attacked Prince Louis and administered what seemed, even from the first unconfirmed reports, to be a considerable defeat. Writing from The Hague, he told Godolphin that:

> we have had news of the Prince of Baden retiring over the Rhine, by which he has not only abandoned his lines, but also Haguenau, and whatever the French shall see fit to attack in lower Alsace. These people here are so very angry with Prince Louis that they will never be brought to let any of their troops be under his command, so that I very much apprehend the campaign on that side.[91]

He was quite right. The Dutch at once deduced that this would enable Villars to send troops to strengthen Villeroi in Brabant, and would allow only 10,000 of their men to go to Italy, and then only if Marlborough himself remained in the north. Worse was to come. Prince Louis was fixed in the Lines of Stollhofen, demanding urgent support. Marsin paused only long enough to ensure that the Allied forces on the Moselle were being sent down to help Louis, and then took most of his troops to join Villeroi. The latter, now far stronger than he had been the previous year, thinned his forces west of Antwerp to a mere eleven battalions, designated sixteen battalions and eight squadrons for the siege of Leau, which, once Marsin's men had come in, he would be able to cover with eighty battalions and 140 squadrons. It was a good plan, capitalising on 'interior lines' which enabled the French to move more quickly than the

Allies. Marlborough would have to let Leau fall, and face subsequent attacks on Huy and Liège, or give battle against a superior force.

There is a hoary old tale of a bear-keeper who, hoping to administer physic to the creature, placed the potion in a piece of rolled-up paper, inserted one end into the bear's mouth and the other into his own, and prepared to blow. The bear, alas, blew first. This is what happened to the unlucky Villeroi. Marlborough, ground down by headaches and Alliance politics during the previous campaign, and now wrong-footed by a development he had not expected, rose at once to the top of his game. His intelligence service, which had given him no warning of Villars' attack on Prince Louis, now focused on the immediate threat, enabling him to track the arrival of reinforcements to Villeroi's army, and making it clear that Villeroi would venture into the field confident in support which might not arrive in time. The editors of the French official account admit that Villeroi was 'determined, by the orders he had received, to act offensively, and by the superiority which he thought he had over the enemy, not to await attack, but to force them to come to an action'.[92]

Although his army was still not ready to march in the first week of May, Marlborough rightly judged that the prospect of Marsin's arrival would tempt the French to take risks, and would 'give them such a superiority as would tempt them to march out of their lines; which, if they do, I will most certainly attack them, not doubting with the blessing of God to beat them'. They could only concentrate to face him by weakening themselves elsewhere, and this was all the more reason why a seaborne 'descent' should be attempted against a suitable spot. He would, come what may, make six regiments of foot and one of dragoons available for it.[93] In short, he was prepared to take a short-term tactical risk to advance towards a wider strategic goal.

By 9 May Marlborough was confident that the balance of forces favoured him, for Marsin's infantry were still some way off.

The English will join the army this day, and the Danes two days hence. We will then be 122 squadrons and 74 battalions. They pretend to be stronger in horse and foot, but with the blessing of God I hope for success, being resolved to venture for as yet they have but 20 squadrons of the Marshal de Marsin's detachment. With my humble duty, assure Her Majesty, that with all my heart and soul I pray to God that I may be able to send her good news, so that her reign may be happy and glorious, and that your faithful friend and servant might have some quiet before he dies.[94]

He was similarly bullish in a letter to Harley, written on 20 May with the army almost complete.

> The enemy having drained all their garrisons, and, depending on their superiority, passed the Dyle yesterday and came and posted themselves at Tirlemont, with the Geet before them, whereupon I have sent orders to the Danish troops . . . to hasten their march. I hope they may be with us on Saturday, and then I design to advance towards the enemy, to oblige them to retire or, with the blessing of God, to bring them to a battle.[95]

At three o'clock on the morning of 23 May, Whit Sunday, the Allies decamped from Corswarem and set off south-westwards, probably in four columns, heading, as Marlborough was to tell Eugène, 'for the gap between the Mehaigne and the Great Geet', passing through a section of the demolished Lines of Brabant near Merdorp. It had been raining heavily for the past few days, but the day dawned dry. As was the normal practice, Cadogan had left camp before the main body with an escort of six squadrons of dragoons, including some of the recently-arrived Danes, ready to mark out that evening's campsite. But as he rode forward through the fog across the plateau of Jandrenouille he met French hussar vedettes, static patrols posted to provide security for the main army. There was a spattering of shots. The hussars fell back westwards, and as the mist lifted Cadogan could see that the broad-shouldered ridge marking his westerly horizon was white with the tents of Villeroi's army.

Villeroi was probably not expecting a battle that day, although he was certainly prepared to fight soon afterwards. Marlborough told Eugène that French prisoners had said that 'their design was not to fight us before Monday, not believing that we would dare to go to them'. The devout Elector of Bavaria, commanding Villeroi's cavalry, was away attending a Pentecost service in Brussels. Both Louis and Chamillart had made it clear to Villeroi that he should fight if a favourable opportunity presented itself, and the gossipy duc de Saint-Simon went further, saying that 'Villeroi had the feeling that the king doubted his courage . . . He resolved to put all at stake to satisfy him, and to prove that he did not deserve such harsh suspicions.'[96] Louis, always given to using a long screwdriver to tinker with his commanders' plans from a distance, warned Villeroi 'to pay special attention to that part of the line which will endure the first shock of the English troops', a process which was to work to Marlborough's advantage.

Although some historians suggest that the French were already drawn up for battle when Cadogan first saw them, this is evidently not the case. John Marshall Deane reckoned that when his regiment arrived the French were 'getting onto the old camping ground on Mount St Andrews'.[97] De la Colonie, whose Bavarian grenadiers were brigaded with the Cologne Regiment on the French right, recalled that when his army finished deploying it was parallel to the Allies, then drawing up in battle array, and already within cannon-shot. There was, however, time for the French to scratch together some field fortifications. Captain Robert Parker recalled that on their right, towards the Mehaigne, they 'had . . . thrown up such an entrenchment as time would permit of', and they had also 'thrown up a trench' on the crest-line just east of Ramillies, with, so Private Deane thought, 'a battery of twelve pieces of treble cannon' in it.[98]

The French had, however, begun to stir before those first shots out on the plateau. The general call to arms was beaten at dawn, and Villeroi's army went through the martial ritual of rising, soldiers tugging on breeches, waistcoats and coats, for men normally slept in their shirts, and falling in with their weapons. Peter Drake, who assures us that he was a cadet (in 'a regimental suit, like those worn by the officers') in an Irish regiment in French service, recalled:

> On Whitsun eve we were all furnished with sixteen charges of powder and ball a man: orders were given out at night for the general to beat at dawn of day; the chaplains to say mass at the head of their prospective regiments; the tents to be struck, the baggage loaded, all sure token there was work cut out for the fighting day.[99]

The French deployed in the simplest way, by forming up in two massive columns, with the artillery between them, and stepping out till the heads of the columns were close to the Mehaigne near Taviers. Successive regiments then wheeled left into line to take up a strong natural position on the western side of the Geete, running from the village of Autreglise, through Offus and Ramillies, down to Taviers, stretching, in a very gentle crescent, for over three miles, and held by about 60,000 men: there were seventy-four battalions, 132 squadrons and seventy guns.

It was big, open country, with more than an echo of Salisbury Plain, and as self-confident as the white-coated infantry who now stood in rank and file upon it. The prosperous, tightly-nucleated villages were marked out from a distance by their church spires. There were few hedges on the plain itself, but the going was more difficult in the trappy terrain of the valleys and amongst the cottage gardens and orchards of the villages. The recent rainy weather and primitive land-drainage system meant that both rivers were far more significant than they seem today. The valley of the Mehaigne was boggy enough to splash a southern edge to the battlefield, and the headwaters of the Geete, which rise just north of Ramillies and are singularly unimpressive today, were then an obstacle to horse and foot, and a very serious barrier to guns. The ground grew more boxy the further north one went, effectively giving Villeroi a secure left flank beyond Autreglise.

A key feature of the terrain, certainly visible to Marlborough when he arrived on the plateau late in the morning, was a long, shallow and undramatic valley running south–north on the eastern side of the Geete, more or less parallel with that river, with its head just east of Ramillies, where the village cemetery now stands. This was to enable him to shift troops from his right to his centre, thus changing the balance of the battle without the transfer being apparent to Villeroi. It was never Marlborough's way to let anyone, except perhaps Cadogan, into his mind, but knowing what we do about his preferences, it is reasonable to assume that he quickly decided on his favourite tactical ploy, persuading his opponent to strengthen one part of his array by drawing troops from another part of the line, thus leaving a weak spot which would then be ripe for attack.

Marlborough turned over the possibilities in his mind when he looked at the French position opposite Ramillies at about eleven o'clock, accompanied only by Overkirk, Daniel Dopff, the Dutch quartermaster general, Cadogan, Goslinga, on his first campaign as field deputy, and a handful of officers. Two of the Dutch officers present had served under the Spaniards in that area, and warned Marlborough that 'The enemy left could not be attacked with any appearance of success: for the hedges, ditches and marshes were a complete barrier to both sides.' This, they thought, would induce the French to mass towards their right, where the ground was better. Marlborough listened politely, but then, to Goslinga's surprise, proceeded to order an equal amount of cavalry to both flanks, giving no hint of his plan. The Dutchman was further dismayed to see how long it took the Allies to get into line, splitting from the four advancing columns into eight for the last phase of the deployment. He thought it 'a very great fault' on the part of the French not to have attacked before the Allies were ready, a criticism which over-looks the fact that Villeroi, having taken up a good position and begun to dig in, could scarcely be expected to leave it and risk a battle in the open.[100]

De la Colonie's description of the French approach march deserves quoting at length, for it gives an insider's view of Villeroi's army and the ground it was to fight on.

The extent of this plain of Ramillies gave us the liberty of marching our army towards the enemy on as broad a front as we desired, and the appearance of our march was as fine a spectacle as one could wish for. The army began to move at about 6 o'clock in the morning. It was composed of two large columns, each marching on the front of a battalion. The artillery formed a third column, marching between the two infantry columns. The cavalry squadrons in battle order occupied an amount of ground equal to the columns, and, on this fine plain, where nothing could hide things, the whole force was seen in such splendid array that one could never hope to view such a striking and brilliant sight as the army made at the beginning of the campaign, before weather and fatigue had dulled its lustre, and nothing inspired as much courage as to see this force in all its splendour. The late M le Marquis de Gondrin, whose company I had the honour to keep during this march, told me that it seemed that France had excelled herself to find such a fine army, and that it was not possible in the coming action for the enemy to break us, and if we were beaten now, we could never dare to present ourselves before them again.

When the heads of the columns had arrived near the marsh which supported our right flank, the first regiments began a quarter-turn to the left, the remaining units in the columns did the same, and in an instant the army was in battle order in two lines facing the enemy, who was now within range of our cannon, and was busy making his dispositions . . . we saw movements to their right and left without being able to guess their intentions . . .[101]

This was just as Marlborough intended, for an obvious massing would have warned Villeroi of his plans. Robert Parker, in contrast, quickly deduced what Marlborough must do.

We drew up in two lines opposite them, having a rising ground on our right, whereon a great part of our British troops were drawn up. From hence the Duke had a fair view of the enemy, and saw evidently that the stress of the battle must be in the plain, where they were drawn up

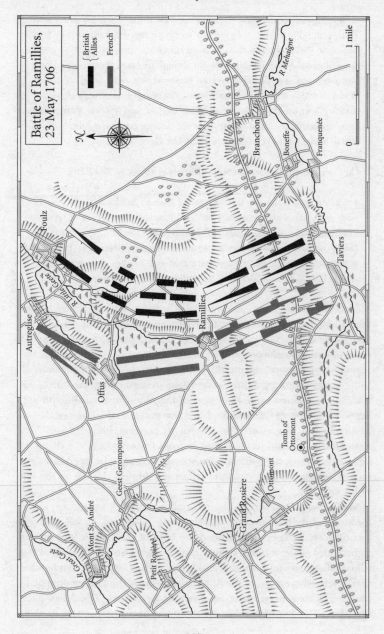

Battle of Ramillies,
23 May 1706

British
Allies }
French

N

1 mile

0

Branchon

R Mehaigne

Boneffe

Franquenée

Foulz

Taviers

R Lune Gecte

Autreglise

Ramillies

Offus

Geest Gerompont

Tomb of
Ottomont

Mont St. André

Grand Rosière

R Great Geete

Petit Rosière

Ottomont

in a formidable manner: he saw also, that things must go hard with him, unless he could oblige them to break the disposition they had made on the plain. On this occasion his Grace showed a genius vastly superior to the French generals; for though he knew the ground along the Geet was not passable, yet he ordered our right wing to march down in great order, with pontoons to lay bridges, as if he designed to attack them on their weak part. The Elector and Villeroi perceiving this, immediately ordered off from the plain a complete line, both of horse and foot, to reinforce those on the Geet.[102]

De la Colonie soon saw that something was amiss on his flank.

I noticed, when passing in front of the *Maison du Roi*, that there were wide gaps between the squadrons, and that the long sector of front it occupied was not held as strongly as the rest of the line. This made me think that the principal attack was not to be made here; that there was some other more dangerous part that the enemy threatened and which had to be supported by a greater number of troops.[103]

Mérode-Westerloo, now an Imperialist officer, having changed sides after Blenheim, gives a thin and partial account of Ramillies, but he too agrees that the *Maison du Roi* was dangerously exposed, arguing that this reflected French overconfidence in its social status, 'believing this formation to be more valiant than Alexander the Great's phalanx'.[104] Villeroi was following Louis' orders and strengthening the left of his line, which seemed to be the target of the nineteen English, Irish and Scots battalions of Marlborough's right under Lord Orkney. It was wholly logical, therefore, for Villeroi to position himself, with Max Emmanuel, who had just galloped in from Brussels, near the village of Offus, to monitor the battle at what seemed certain to be its crucial spot, and to station the powerful four-battalion Régiment du Roi on the left of his line.

Marlborough had seventy-three battalions and 123 squadrons, with a hundred guns and twenty shell-throwing howitzers, in all perhaps 62,000 men. Orkney commanded the bulk of the British foot on the right, with Lumley's horse behind him. In the centre were most of the Allied infantry under Churchill and Schultz, while Overkirk commanded on the left, where most of the Allied cavalry faced the French on a plain that might have been made for charging horsemen. The Allies filled the plateau of Jandrenouille, their straight front, in contrast to their opponents' shallow curve, making them look, to friend and foe alike, more numerous than their enemy. De la Colonie thought that the Allies were in 'four great lines, closed up like walls: while ours were only in three, of which the third was composed of a few squadrons of dragoons'. George Orkney thought that the French had taken up

> a very good post at the head of the Geet, and possessed themselves of several villages on their front, with a marsh ground and a little ruisseau [stream] before them, so that, when we came to attack, it was impossible for us to extend our line, so were drawn up in several lines, one behind another, and indeed even in confusion enough, which I own gave me at first a very ill prospect of things.[105]

While his horse and foot were deploying, Marlborough personally sited his main battery opposite Ramillies. This included some twenty-four-pounders, very heavy guns for use on the battlefield, hauled laboriously into position by teams of oxen. The first shots of the battle proper came as these guns took on the French battery above the village. De la Colonie knew, from long experience, that it was as well to keep his men's minds off what was to come:

> I got the woodwind that followed at the rear of the regiment to strike up some martial flourishes, to divert my people and keep them in a good frame of mind. But the cannon-shots which began to roll out across the battlefield surprised them so much that they disappeared like lightning, without anyone noticing, and went off to raise melodious sounds from their instruments in places where they would not be competing with cannon.[106]

The battle began at about 2.30, with Allied attacks on both Villeroi's flanks. Orkney tells us that his approach was obstructed by

> a morass and a ruisseau before us, which they said was impossible to pass over. But however we tried, and, after some difficulty, got over with ten or twelve battalions; and Mr Lumley brought over some squadrons of horse with very great difficulty; and I endeavoured to possess myself of a village [Autreglise] which the French brought down a good part of their line to take possession of, and they were on one side of the village, and I on the other; but they always retired as we advanced.[107]

Thomas Kitcher, a Hampshire farm labourer serving in Meredith's Regiment, part of Orkney's first wave, told his village curate exactly what a general's 'some difficulty' actually meant for a private soldier. The French commander in Offus, the comte de Guiche, had posted some Walloon infantry on his side of the marsh to make the British pay dearly for their crossing. The front rank of Meredith's was mangled by fire from across the Geete, and Kitcher was tripped by a comrade's entrails.

> They were then commanded to cross the marsh by means of fascines and many were shot and maimed, or killed, which they carried and laid down their foundations. He told me that limbs and bodies, of which it was impossible to ascertain whether or not they were dead, were used to pass the quagmire at some points, and that one redcoat that he knew of raised himself from the supposed dead at the indignity of the treatment and turned upon the pioneers who had thought him one of their bundles of faggots and flayed him with his tongue.[108]

Once the British were across, the Walloons scampered back up the slope towards Offus, with the redcoats close behind them. 'The Frenchies seemed surprised,' recalled Kitcher, 'and showed no mind to fight much. Some of them I saw turned tail and I spiked one of their officers through the throat and another in the arse.'[109]

The fighting here was inconclusive, partly because the ground prevented Orkney from bringing his whole force to bear. John Blackader of the Cameronians had been promoted the previous winter. The death of his colonel seemed likely to trigger a general advancement from which he, as the regiment's senior captain, hoped to profit. He spoke to Marlborough about it, 'got a good answer (for none ever get ill words from him)', and was duly promoted on 15 December. At Ramillies, his first action as a major, his regiment was in the second line, and he found the battle

> not general, but it was hot to those that were engaged. Our regiment was no further engaged but that we were cannonaded for some hours, and had several men killed and wounded. I was not near the Duke, but upon our wing we had a great want of generals and distinct orders.[110]

Robert Parker, too, found that his regiment, at the extreme right of Orkney's first line, had little to do, but 'stood looking on without firing a shot; and as we were posted on an eminence, we had a fair view of the whole battle on the plain'.[111] This is no bad description of what was, had Parker and Blackader but known it, a diversionary attack, where uncommitted troops helped fix French attention on the indecisive flank.

On the Allied left, however, the attack progressed far more swiftly. Here Villars, like many a general before and since, had been drawn forward by the lure of a useful feature to his front. The five Swiss battalions responsible for the small village of Taviers, which marked the right of his line, were ordered to push on and also to hold the tiny Franquenée, another five hundred yards to their front. De la Colonie thought that the villages were embedded in ground so marshy as to be impracticable to cavalry, but their garrisons would be able to fire, from these bastions, on cavalry operating on the southern flank, so they were certainly worth securing. By trying to retain both villages with an inadequate force Villars left himself open to defeat in detail. On Overkirk's orders, Colonel Wertmüller's four battalions of Dutch foot guards, supported by two field guns, manhandled forward by their detachments to breach garden walls and houses, attacked Franquenée first. The Dutch then bundled the Swiss back into Taviers, and took that too after fighting which, so de la Colonie maintained, cost as many lives as the rest of the battle.

The marquis de Guiscard-Magny, commanding Villeroi's right wing, immediately took what should have been textbook steps to recover the lost ground. He ordered three more Swiss battalions to move southwards against Taviers, while fourteen squadrons of dragoons were to dismount near the tumulus called the Tomb of Ottomont, well behind the French right, and attack on foot. De la Colonie's brigade, on the right of the first line of infantry, was then ordered south to support the counter-attack. As the Red Grenadiers marched in front of the *Maison du Roi* they were applauded by the horsemen – partly, thought de la Colonie, because of the reputation his men had earned at the Schellenberg, but also because the gentlemen troopers hoped that the brigade was moving to shield the cavalry's right flank from interference from Allied foot soldiers firing from the marsh.

It was a misplaced hope. The French dragoons dismounted, their strength immediately reduced by the need to detail one man in four to hold horses, and then clumped forward on foot, booted and spurred. They were stoutly received by the Dutch foot and guns in Taviers and then unexpectedly charged by six squadrons of Danish horse which had skirted the two villages, and come on quickly across the southern edge of the plain, first breaking the dragoons and then cutting up the advancing Swiss. De la Colonie's brigade commander, commendably eager to assist, cantered forward but got stuck in the little Vesoul stream which flowed into the Mehaigne. He would never have got out, thought de la Colonie, had the helpful Dutch not rescued him.

Worse was to follow. As the Red Grenadiers neared the marsh they were swamped by a tidal wave of fugitives, Swiss and dragoons alike. Within seconds de la Colonie found himself left with only his regiment's colours and a few officers: 'I yelled in German and French like a madman, I gave all sorts of names to my people, I took the colonel's colour, planted it a certain distance away, and, making many shouts and wild gestures, I attracted the looks and the attentions of many.' He was eventually able to rally the equivalent of four small battalions, but his men were now badly shaken, and one grenadier behind him opined noisily that they were being led to butchery.[112] Although de la Colonie maintained that by holding a crest-line on his army's right, thus giving the impression that there were more infantry behind him, he helped prop up the flank of the *Maison du Roi*, there was no denying the fact that the French right had now been kicked off its hinges.

In the centre, though, the fighting was far more evenly balanced, with squadrons charging, wheeling back and then charging again as French and Allied horsemen, perhaps 25,000 in all, hacked at one another across the green wheatfields south of Ramillies in the biggest cavalry battle of the war. Robert Parker thought that:

In this engagement there was great variety of action; sometimes their squadrons and sometimes ours giving way in different places; and as the fate of the day depended entirely on the behaviour of the troops on the plain, so both sides exerted themselves with the utmost vigour for a long time. The Duke was in all places where his presence was requisite; and in the hurry of the action happened to get unhorsed, and in great danger of his life; but was remounted by Captain Molesworth, one of his aides de camp, the only person of his retinue then near him; who seeing him in manifest danger of falling into the hands of the pursuing enemy, suddenly threw himself from his horse, and helped the Duke to mount him. His Grace, by this means, got off between our lines; the captain being immediately surrounded by the enemy; from which danger (as well as that of our fire) he was, at last, providentially delivered. His Grace, about an hour after, had another narrow escape; when in shifting back from Captain

Molesworth's horse to his own, Colonel Bringfield . . . holding the
stirrup, was killed by a cannon shot from the village of Ramillies.
Notwithstanding which, the Duke immediately rode up to the
head of his troops; and his presence animated them to that degree,
that they pressed home upon the enemy, and made them shrink and
give back.[113]

The Bringfield incident became one of the most commonly recounted
aspects of the battle. Lord Orkney tells how 'My Lord Marlborough was
rid over, but got other squadrons, which he led up again. Major
Bringfield, holding his stirrup to give him another horse, was shot with
a cannon bullet which went through my Lord's legs; in truth there was
no scarcity of 'em.'[114] When helping someone to mount, one often puts
weight on the offside stirrup just as the rider places his left foot in the
nearside stirrup: Orkney's version suggests that Bringfield was decapitated
by a ball which passed under Marlborough's right foot as he swung it
over the horse. Lieutenant Colonel James Bringfield had been commissioned in 1685, was appointed captain in the 1st Troop of Horse Guards
nine years later, and was promoted major in 1702. His death made a
great impression on Marlborough. 'Poor Bringfield is killed,' he told
Godolphin, 'and I am told he leaves his wife and mother in a bad condition.' He said much the same to Sarah: 'Poor Bringfield holding my
stirrup for me, and helping me on horseback, was killed. I am told that
he leaves his wife and mother in a poor condition.' Sarah visited
Mrs Bringfield on 17 May 1706 OS and promised her, on the queen's
behalf, a pension for life.[115] The incident featured as the ten of
diamonds on a set of contemporary playing cards, with Marlborough
firmly in the saddle and Bringfield's corpse standing upright with blood
jetting from its headless trunk.

Marlborough had also been very lucky to escape from the earlier
mêlée. Conspicuous in his red coat and garter star he had led blue-and-
grey-coated Dutch squadrons against the *Maison du Roi*. Lieutenant
Colonel Cranstoun of the Cameronians, not generally one of
Marlborough's admirers, wrote that:

Ten of the Dutch squadrons were repulsed, renversed, and put into
great disorder. The Duke, seeing this, and seeing that things went
pretty well elsewhere, stuck by the weak part to make it up by his
presence, and led up still new squadrons to the charge, till at last

the victory was obtained. It was here when those squadrons were being reversed and in absolute déroute and the French mixed up with them in the pursuit that the Duke, flying with the crowd, in leaping a ditch fell from his horse and some rode over him. Major General Murray, who had his eye there and was so near he could distinguish the Duke in the flight, seeing him fall, marched up in all haste with two Swiss battalions to save him and stop the enemy who were hewing down all in their way. The Duke when he got to his feet again saw Major General Murray coming up and ran directly to get into his battalions. In the meantime Mr Molesworth quitted his horse and got the Duke mounted again, and the French were so hot in the pursuit that some of them before they could stop their horses ran in upon the Swiss bayonets and were killed, but the majority of them, seeing the two battalions, shore off to the right and retired.[116]

Death was no respecter of persons that day, and the young Prince Louis of Hesse-Cassel was cut down.

Just north of this swirl of cavalry, Lieutenant General Schultz, with some twelve Allied battalions, including Churchill's and Mordaunt's, as well as the Duke of Argyll's Scots brigade in Dutch pay, attacked the village of Ramillies. The place was tenaciously defended, but the French were already beginning to give ground by the time Marlborough played his master-stroke. He knew that the re-entrant behind his right wing would enable him to move Orkney's men south without the French seeing them. Indeed, he may very well have been surprised at the progress Orkney had made in attacking the supposedly impregnable French left flank, for it was not his intention for his dogged subordinate to take Autreglise, although Orkney himself had other ideas.

As I was going to take possession [of the village] I had ten aides de camp to tell me to come off, for the horse could not sustain me. We had a good deal of fire at this, both musketry and cannon, and indeed I think I never had more shot about my ears; and I confess it vexed me to retire. However we did it very well and in good order, and whenever the French pressed upon us, with the battalion of Guards and my own, I was able to make them stand and retire. Cadogan came and told me it was impossible I could be sustained by the horse if we went on then, and, since my Lord could not attack everywhere, he would make the grand attack in the centre and try to pierce there.[117]

Robert Parker says that they fell back

> until our rear line had got on the back of the rising ground, out of
> sight of the enemy. But the front line halted on the summit of the hill,
> in full view of them . . . As soon as our rear line had retired out of sight
> of the enemy, they immediately faced to the left, and both horse and
> foot, with a good many squadrons, that slunk out of the front line,
> marched down to the plain, as fast as they could.[118]

This was not a popular move with men like Tom Kitcher, who could see
no reason for it.

> We had the order to give ground and make our way back to the river.
> 'Pray, what's this?' said my Lord Orkney, so his servant told me after.
> He had no mind to give ground when we were giving no quarter, nor
> we hadn't neither, being up to our necks in deadliness and noise. But
> so it was ordered and we went back and back across the river, and
> there we stayed awhile, with the cannon peppering us but not getting
> no success, our cover being good.[119]

Kitcher's comment about cover suggests that even the element of
Orkney's wing that remained behind took some advantage of the reverse
slope on the western edge of the re-entrant, where colour parties and
mounted officers on the crest continued to fix Villeroi's attention.
Although it is almost two miles from Orkney's original position to
Ramillies, his six battalions arrived there, as John Marshall Deane put it,
in 'time enough to beat the enemy quite out of the village & at the same
time charged the rest of their foot that was posted behind the Gheet.
And my Lord Duke ordered the English horse to sustain them.'[120]

It was now approaching six in the evening, and the French cavalry,
weakened by the casualties of the past two hours' fighting, were closing
up to the north, leaving a growing gap between their right wing and
the valley of the Mehaigne. This was first exploited by the Dutch
foot guards who had taken Taviers and Franquenée earlier in the day,
and who now

> pressed home upon the enemy, and made them shrink and give back.
> And this very instant the Duke of Württemberg came up with the
> Danish horse and pressing an opening between the village of
> Franquenay and their main body, fell upon the right flank of their

horse, and with such courage and resolution, that he drove them in upon their centre. This put them into great disorder; and our troops taking this advantage, pressed so close upon them, that they could never recover their order.[121]

Württemberg had in fact taken his squadrons, who had only been in action once that day, right round the southern flank of the French army, brushing aside some of the dragoons who had failed to retake Taviers earlier on, and formed them up in close order near the Tomb of Ottomont. Marlborough and Overkirk both cantered across to join him, and accompanied what was to prove the day's decisive charge. Although Villeroi and the Elector could now see well enough what was coming, they could not deploy their reserve in time to meet it, and in any case the baggage and some unstruck tents, left near Offus when the French deployed that morning, restricted room for manoeuvre.

The Danish charge swept forward at about 6.30, supported from the east by another valiant effort by the sorely tried Dutch horse, now reinforced by fresher cavalry from the right flank. Their combined impact was too much for the bulk of Villeroi's army. 'They indeed behaved themselves shamefully,' complained Peter Drake, probably thinking more of his English-speaking audience than his French-speaking comrades,

and fled with great precipitation, like frightened sheep . . . I saw one of their best, called the King's Regiment, composed of four battalions, lay down their arms like poltroons and surrender themselves prisoners of war. In short they all left the field with infinite disorder, except Lord Clare's which was engaged with a Scotch regiment in Dutch service, between whom there was a great slaughter.

His own regiment, part of Villeroi's reserve, had so far not been engaged, but when it was ordered to turn about and retire,

we had not got fifty yards in our retreat, when, by some means I know not, the usual (*sauve qui peut*) *fly that can* went through the great part, if not the whole army, and put all in confusion. There might be seen whole brigades running in disorder, the enemy pursuing almost close at our heels, and with regularity.[122]

Not all Villeroi's army disintegrated. Count Maffei, whom we last met on the Schellenberg, did his best to keep two steady German battalions together in the road leading out from Ramillies to the plateau of Mont St André, recognising that the village was now the hinge between the static French left wing and the new position of the right, bent back by the impact of the Danish attack. His men were holding up well when he rode over to order some nearby cavalry to join him, but he had failed to spot that they were wearing green sprigs rather than white cockades in their hats. He was duly captured by the Dutch, and his men joined the general flight. Maffei was lucky that his captors were not Danish, for the Danes, infuriated by hearing that their countrymen had been butchered by the French after the Allied defeat at Calcinato in Italy, were not inclined to give quarter. Some of Villeroi's men, indeed, were in no mood to ask for it. Charles O'Brien, Viscount Clare, was mortally wounded at the head of his Wild Geese in Ramillies, and the Régiment de Picardie, proudly the oldest in the French line, fought to a finish in the streets and gardens of the village.[123]

Orkney took his men back across the Geete without Marlborough's orders, for he could read the battle well enough. They were charged by the Bavarian Electoral Guards and the Walloon Horse Grenadiers, but checked them with measured volleys before British cavalry swept the enemy horse from the field. Ross's Irish Dragoons and Lord Stair's Scots Dragoons had been on the extreme right of the Allied right wing, and they charged the Régiment du Roi as it fell back, catching its men just as they were recovering their packs, which they had dropped at the rear of their position earlier in the day. 'Lord John Hay's dragoons and others got in upon the Regiment de Roi,' wrote Orkney with satisfaction, 'which they beat entirely.'

The pursuit was hampered by exhaustion and the onset of darkness, with the added difficulty, for Allied officers unfamiliar with the area, of picking their way over a strange landscape in the dark, through the debris of a broken army. Marlborough was forced to stop for the night near Meldert, over twelve miles beyond the battlefield, having been nineteen hours in the saddle, and then only when his guide admitted that they were lost. Although, as he reported to Sarah the following morning, 'My head aches to that degree that it is very uneasy to me to write,' he was still courtier enough to invite Goslinga to share his cloak, spread out on the ground.

Most first reports underestimated the damage done to Villeroi's army: Orkney, indeed, warned his correspondent that it was not like

Blenheim. 'I own it vexed me to see a great body of 'em going off,' he lamented, 'and not many horse with them; but, for my heart, I could not get up our foot in time; and they dispersed and got into strong ground where it was impossible to follow them.'[124] In fact perhaps as many as 18,000 of Villeroi's men were killed in the battle or captured after it, with 120 colours and standards and fifty-four cannon. Not only were there many desertions in the weeks that followed, but the States-General of Brabant immediately acknowledged the Hapsburg Charles III as king of Spain, which persuaded many Walloon soldiers to change their allegiance. Marlborough had lost 3,600 officers and men killed and wounded, making the balance of casualties even more favourable to the Allies than Blenheim had been.

Amongst the casualties of Ramillies was Mrs Davies, who had sustained a fractured skull near Autreglise.

> Though I suffered great torture by this wound, yet the discovery it caused of my sex, in the fixing of my dressing, by which the surgeons saw my breasts, and by the largeness of my nipples, concluded that I had given suck, was a greater grief to me . . . my Lord [Colonel] John Hay called . . . for my comrade, who had long been my bed-fellow, and examined him closely. The fellow protested, as it was the truth, that he never knew I was a woman, or even suspected it . . . My lord seemed very well entertained with my history, and ordered that I should want for nothing, and that my pay should continue while under care.[125]

Ramillies signalled the wholesale collapse of French fortunes across the whole of Brabant, for Villeroi had bled his garrisons white to raise such a large field army, and many fortress governors felt unable to offer more than a token resistance. As G.M. Trevelyan was to put it, 'The next fortnight witnesses the revolution that secured the sovereignty of Belgium to the House of Austria for three generations.' Charles Churchill entered Brussels unopposed on 28 May, and welcomed his brother into the city the following day. Villars abandoned the Dyle at once, destroying a mountain of stores at Louvain as he did so, and then scrabbled to clutch the line of the Scheldt, but Marlborough was too quick for him and lunged towards Oudenarde and Gavre, threatening his communications with France and forcing him to fall back yet again.

The great cities of Brabant – Louvain, Ghent and Bruges – all opened their gates. Fortresses like Antwerp, Ath, Dendemonde and Ostend, which might normally have delayed Marlborough for months, were swallowed in weeks. John Marshall Deane shared the air of general disbelief. At Antwerp the city fathers formally presented Marlborough with the 'the keys of the town and withall telling him that they had never been delivered to any person since the great Duke of Parma and it was then after a siege of six months'. The siege of Ostend was pressed with such vigour 'that the town surrendered in 3 days time and some odd hours after our batteries began to play upon them; which seems almost incredible if we look back into former relations concerning the siege of the same town having held out and continued many months before it was reduced by a greater army than ours'.[126]

Marlborough was genuinely delighted. On 27 May he complained to Sarah that 'I can't get rid of my headache,' but nonetheless declared that 'we have done in four days, what we should have thought ourselves happy, if we could have been sure of it, in four years'. He foresaw that 'the consequence of this battle is likely to be of greater consequence than that of Blenheim, for I have now the whole summer before me'.[127] At the end of the month he told her: 'So many towns have submitted since the battle, that it really looks more like a dream than truth.' He thought they were likely to achieve more in a single campaign than in the whole of the previous war, 'which is a great pleasure, since it is the likeliest way to bring me to my happiness of ending my days with my dearest soul'.[128] In early October, looking forward to his imminent return to England, he told Godolphin that if only the Dutch could be persuaded 'to go on with the war this next year, we have reason to expect an honourable, safe and lasting peace'.[129]

It is easy to see why he was confident, for the effects of Ramillies were seismic. Louis XIV was so concerned by the direct threat to northern France that his armies on the Rhine and in Italy were immediately hamstrung by being ordered to send men north to help shore up the Flanders frontier. Villeroi wrote a dignified letter to his king, rebutting many of the charges against him but observing glumly that good reasons for being defeated were still no excuse, and concluding that he only expected one more happy day in his life – that of his death. 'I might impute it as a crime, with regard to Your Majesty,' he wrote sadly, 'to be as unlucky as I am.'[130] He was replaced by Vendôme, snatched back from what might have been a winning position in Italy.

His successors first botched their siege of Turin, and were roundly beaten by Eugène's relieving army: Marsin was mortally wounded. Eventually the French concluded a convention with the emperor which allowed them to withdraw their garrisons from Lombardy and Milan: Italy was lost to Louis.

In the Peninsula things looked at first no less promising for the Allies. Galway advanced from Portugal to capture Madrid at the end of June 1706, Peterborough reduced Valencia, and Charles III himself was successful in Aragon. Marlborough, watching from afar with other things on his mind, was probably over-sanguine when he regretted that Charles had not formally entered Madrid as soon as it was taken, for 'His timely appearance there would in all probability put a happy end to the war on that side.'[131] The Allies failed to convert the numerous Iberian successes of 1706 into a wholesale victory which would have secured Spain for Charles III. Matters were not helped by bitter quarrels, for which Peterborough was most culpable, and as winter came on the Allies found themselves, in a manner which foreshadowed French misfortunes in Spain a century later, trying to extract food and fodder from an increasingly hostile population. Although Galway was to take overall command after Peterborough's departure, by the year's close the balance of power in the Peninsula now favoured his opponent, Marlborough's nephew the Duke of Berwick.

With hindsight we can now see that if 1706 was the year that secured Brabant for the Allies, it was also the year that the war in Spain slid quietly from their grasp. Nor was there much comfort from the amphibious 'descent' on the French coast in which Marlborough invested so much confidence. After Ramillies he was busy arranging for the dispatch of British troops, and in June he successfully negotiated with the Dutch for 'three battalions and ten troops of dragoons mounted'. However, in August a first attempt was driven back into Torbay by severe storms, and a second attempt, after as severe a battering, refitted in Lisbon, whence its commander, Lord Rivers, beset by contradictory instructions, was eventually persuaded to join Galway in Seville. Thus a descent which was meant to complicate French decision-making and probably compel the withdrawal of troops from Flanders became the simple reinforcement of what was beginning to look like Allied failure.

The arrival of Lord Rivers complicated the question of command in the Peninsula, an issue which went to the heart of Marlborough's responsibilities as captain general. He warned Godolphin that it was not healthy to have Galway, Peterborough and Rivers all enjoying the status of independent commanders in the same theatre of war. Galway, he feared, was now definitely past his best, and 'continues so very pressing to retire and come home, that I really think it would be too great a barbarity to refuse him'. However, Galway had recommended Peterborough as his successor, a suggestion that Marlborough found amazing.[132] The matter was eventually resolved by persuading Galway to soldier on. In April 1707 Godolphin reported him 'in good heart at the letters he had received from his friends in England, and resolved to stay in the chief command'.[133]

As the campaigning year wound to its breathless close, Marlborough looked forward to returning home. Godolphin told him that the work at Woodstock was coming along well.

> The garden is already very fine and in perfect shape, the turf all laid, and the first coat of the gravel, the greens high and thriving, and all the hedges pretty well grown.
>
> The building is so advanced, as that one may see perfectly how it will be when it is done. The side where you intend to live is the most forward part. My Lady Marlborough is most prying into it, and has really not only found a great many errors, but very well mended such of them, as could not stay for your decision. I am apt to think she has made Mr Vanbrugh a little annoyed.[134]

However, it soon transpired that Godolphin had been at Woodstock with Sarah because the duchess had withdrawn there in a huff after a row with Anne over the queen's determination to govern with an all-party ministry and Sarah's equally strong convictions that Tories were a menace to the public safety and that her son-in-law Sunderland should be appointed to a high office of state. With an unusual flash of diplomacy Sarah begged leave 'to revive the names of Mrs Morley and your faithful Freeman', but the old spells no longer wove their charm.

Marlborough was hauled unwillingly into the dispute, like some great gun required to breach a fortress wall, peppered by a volley of sharp letters from Sarah ('I find when you writ most of them you had very much the spleen . . .') warning him that he was not taking a sufficiently firm line with the queen. While Marlborough genuinely believed that the queen's government could not go on without Godolphin, he was less worried than his great ally about the presence in it of Tories like Harley, and was drawn into the battle with a heavy heart. At the end of this remarkable campaign he found himself mired deep in politics and accused, once more, of weakness by his wife. He wrote glumly that he would never live to see Blenheim Palace finished,

> for I had flattered myself that if the war should happily have ended this next year, that I might the next after have lived in it, for I am resolved on being neither minister nor courtier, not doubting the Queen will allow of it; but these are idle dreams, for while the war lasts I must serve and will do it with all my heart; and if I am at last rewarded with your love and esteem, I shall end my days happily . . . [135]

These were poignant words from a commander at the very height of his powers.

7

The Equipoise of Fortune

Favourites, Bishops and the Union

Over the winter of 1706–07 the Duumvirs – Marlborough and Godolphin – strengthened their position, at last persuading the queen to make Sunderland a secretary of state, having both Tom Wharton and Godolphin himself promoted to earldoms, and getting most of the remaining Tories (save St John, Harley and two others) removed from office. They accomplished this at the expense of the 'unquestioning allegiance' of a queen who resented being exposed to the rapacity of the 'Lords of the Junto', as the Whig grandees were known.[1] There was also a continuing decline in relations between Anne and Sarah. Anne herself was now overweight, dropsical and frequently in pain. Early in 1707 Sir John Clerk of Penicuick, one of the commissioners for the Union with Scotland, described her as

> the most despicable mortal I had seen in any station. The poor Lady, as I saw her twice before, was again under a very severe fit of the gout, ill dressed, blotted in her countenance, and surrounded with plasters, cataplasms, and dirty rags. The extremity of her pain was not then upon her, and it diverted her a little to see company with whom she was not to use ceremonies, otherwise I had not been allowed access to her.
>
> However, I believe she was not displeased to see anybody, for no court attenders ever came near her. All the incense and adoration offered at court were to her ministers, particularly the Earl of Godolphin, her chief minister, and the two secretaries of state [Harley and Sunderland], her palace at Kensington, where she commonly resided, was a perfect solitude . . . I had many occasions to think that few houses in England belonging to persons of quality

were kept in a more private way than the Queen's royal palace of Kensington.[2]

Yet Anne had lost none of her determination, and now, as an experienced monarch, was far less amenable to influence than she had been at the beginning of her reign. With her passionate affection for Sarah 'rapidly decaying into aversion', isolated, in increasing pain, and aware of her husband's declining health, she slipped naturally into a friendship with Abigail Hill. For all sorts of reasons this never equalled her passion for Sarah, which had been as close to a relationship between equals as any friendship between monarch and subject could ever be. When Abigail married Colonel Sam Masham, groom of the bedchamber to Prince George, in Kensington Palace, probably in the early summer of 1707, Sarah was not informed, though she quickly concluded that the £2,000 drawn by the queen from her privy purse, of which she was the custodian, was a dowry. Had Sarah been balanced in her judgements, a virtue no one could ever ascribe to her, she might have reflected that this was the merest trickle of fortune by comparison with the powerful jets of royal favour which had played upon her own family, but she characteristically responded with an outburst of fury at Abigail's ingratitude.

Sarah even ventured a comment on the 'strange and unaccountable' fact of the queen's 'having no inclination for any but of one's own sex', which does something to suggest that her own relationship with Anne had never been physical. It certainly shows that she wholly misjudged Anne's relationship with Abigail, who was always (even after Sam was ennobled) servant, nurse and social inferior. Sarah would spend the rest of her days ranting on about Abigail's 'insolence and anger', and the way she 'spread with malicious zeal all manner of the greatest falsehoods about her'.[3] At about this time Sarah fell under the influence of Arthur Maynwaring, a Whig playwright and pamphleteer who called himself her secretary but was adviser and publicist too. His own contributions to the dispute between the two women were predictably unhelpful, with *A New Ballad to the tune of Fair Rosamond* implying that Abigail's hold on the queen was based on 'Some Dark deeds at Night'.[4]

Yet there is no doubt that Abigail was dangerous to the Marlboroughs and Godolphin, because Robert Harley was her second cousin on her father's side. Anne liked Harley, and used him to help secure a regimental colonelcy for Sam Masham, taking care that the regiment should remain in Ireland so that Sam could stay at court. As the war went on there was increasing concern about regimental colonels who enjoyed life in London while their men were on active service. In June 1706 Godolphin warned Marlborough:

> There's one thing more relating to the army I can't observe to you without some indignation. Here is Major General Harvey and my Lord Mohun, a brigadier, walking in St James's Park and every day in the chocolate house, while both their regiments are serving abroad. Though I instance only these two, I believe there may be a great many others in the same circumstances.[5]

However, with his regiment in Ireland Sam Masham was safe enough.

Abigail was never in fact 'the great and supreme favourite', as Sarah maintained.[6] Harley was quite right to see that her influence with the queen was essentially negative. 'You cannot set anyone up,' he told her, 'you can pull anyone down.'[7] After Harley's resignation in early 1708 Abigail proved invaluable as his eyes and ears at court. He was, though, a skilful politician in his own right, and popular with the queen because, as she thought, he supported her desire to see a broadly-based non-partisan government. Abigail Hill had far less impact upon his eventual political triumph than Sarah Marlborough, well aware of the influence she herself had wielded, ever imagined.

Although Anne resented Godolphin's apparent partiality for the Whigs, neither he nor Marlborough was, strictly speaking, a party man. The death, in November 1706, of Dr Peter Mews, Bishop of Winchester, sometime captain of royalist horse and amateur artillery driver at Sedgemoor, created a minor political storm. Winchester was England's richest diocese, and the Whigs hoped to see the appointment of one of their clerics. Godolphin had, however, promised the post to the Tory Bishop Trelawney of Exeter in return for his electoral help in 1705. The furious Whigs hoped for recompense by the appointment of their friends to Exeter, as well as to the providentially vacated see of Chester and the Regius chair of divinity at Oxford. The queen proceeded to nominate suitable candidates without asking Godolphin's advice, though the Whigs at once blamed minister rather than monarch. Marlborough was involved, as he had his own (now disappointed) candidate for the Oxford chair, and the question of ecclesiastical appointments joined the business of the Board of Ordnance and the captaincy general amongst his papers for the following campaign.

Getting votes for the continuation of the war through Parliament proved easy, thanks to Ramillies and general confidence in the war's successful outcome. The Scots had already ratified the Act of Union, but it was unpopular with High Tories, who resented the fact that the Act established Presbyterianism in Scotland, and who raised their familiar cry that the Church of England was under threat. They could not prevent the Union, which came into being on 1 May 1707, and saw the separate governments of England and Scotland replaced by a reconstituted government of Great Britain.

A Sterile Campaign

The French had much to fear from 1707. Blenheim had dashed their hopes in Bavaria, Ramillies had lost them most of the Spanish Netherlands, and in the early autumn of 1706 Eugène had swept them from northern Italy. While the Alliance, its creaking machinery lubricated by English and Dutch gold, remained intact, France was visibly drained by the cost of a war which had been meant to be short but had already lasted for five years. Yet although Louis might weep bitter tears alone with Madame de Maintenon in her apartment, his public demeanour radiated regal fortitude, and early in the new campaigning season his armies won a victory which went to the very heart of French and Allied war aims.

On 25 April Galway was severely defeated by Berwick at Almanza, in south-east Spain. This was not in itself surprising, for Galway, with 15,000 men, was outnumbered by Berwick, with 25,000, and boldly attacked him after a wearing approach march. The attack was going perhaps better than it deserved when the Portuguese on Galway's right broke, and Galway was badly beaten, losing over 4,000 killed and wounded and perhaps another 12,000 taken prisoner.[8] Major General James Stanhope's elegantly written report, sent to Marlborough from Barcelona, makes melancholy reading:

> I cannot learn that five hundred men are escaped out of the whole body of the foot, which consisted of forty-three battalions, whereof I know not whether sixteen or seventeen were English, nineteen Portuguese, and the remainder Dutch. Of our horse, about three thousand five hundred are come off, but very few English or Dutch . . . My Lord Galway was wounded with a sword over the eye at the beginning of the action, charging with the horse. The accident contributed much to the confusion which followed. Our foot is by everybody said to have done wonders, which makes the loss of it so much the more

sensible. I send this letter by a felucca, which is dispatched by the King to Italy, to ask for succours. I do not know what effect his solicitations will have, nor, indeed, do I know what to wish. If your Grace commanded the armies in Italy, I should not yet think our game desperate; for I should believe it possible for him who marched from Holland to the Danube to save the Empire, to march through Provence and Languedoc to save Spain. I know nothing else that can do it.[9]

Although Almanza did not signal the end of the war in Spain, which may more fairly be dated to Stanhope's own undeserved defeat at Brihuega in December 1710, it was as decisive a blow to Allied aspirations in the Peninsula as Marlborough's victory at Blenheim had been to Louis XIV's hopes for hegemony in Europe. However, 'No victory without Spain' was to become a key plank of the Duumvirs' foreign policy, and Marlborough certainly believed that the best way to Spain was, metaphorically, through France: if Louis XIV was reduced to the last extremity by military defeat elsewhere, then he would relinquish his support for Philip V. This conviction, far more than any desire on Marlborough's part to retain active military employment, helped ensure the continuation of the war until both sides faced exhaustion.

It certainly encouraged Marlborough to support the Allies' strategic grand design of 1707, an attack on the French naval base of Toulon by an army under Victor Amadeus, Duke of Savoy, and Prince Eugène, striking down from Savoy. This had first been bruited in late 1706, primarily as a means of weakening the French position in Spain. In December Marlborough told Heinsius: 'We hope to make such a diversion that France will not be in any condition to send any considerable succours to Spain.' The letter concluded: 'My head aches so that you will excuse my making use of Mr Cardonnel's hand.'[10] Well might Marlborough's affliction trouble him, for he had completed another round of diplomacy designed, among other things, to persuade German princes to contribute to the 28,000 soldiers in British and Dutch pay who were to join the Imperialists for the Toulon project.

He had also been sent on a mission to Charles XII of Sweden, then at war with Russia, and recently victorious over both Saxony and Poland-Lithuania, whose king Augustus II he had deposed, replacing him with his own man, Stanislas Leszczynski. The headstrong and implacable Swedish monarch – he abstained from women and alcohol, but enjoyed wrestling with bears – was in camp at the village of Altranstädt in Saxony, and Marlborough travelled there in April by way of Hanover. Louis' agents had been encouraging Charles to attack the Empire, but his aim of 'securing and supporting the Protestant religion' made him an improbable ally even for Louis. However, he had threatened to intervene on behalf of the Protestants in Silesia, which brought him into conflict with Vienna; and Prussia, fearful of a widening of the Northern War, considered withdrawing from its commitment to the Allies.

Marlborough's undoubted military status, and an opening address so flowery that some historians believed that he could never have brought himself to utter the words (but we must remember what a courtier he was), at once put him on good terms with the king. Charles was content to accept a guarantee from the emperor of freedom of conscience for his Silesian subjects. Marlborough's mission was wholly successful, though it was not without its moments of tension, not least the problem of how to deal with the dethroned Augustus, a staunch supporter of the Allies, without the news of their meeting giving offence to Charles. The Swedish king did not break camp until he heard of the repulse of the Toulon expedition. There have been suggestions that he would not have tolerated an unequal peace treaty being imposed on Louis had the expedition succeeded, and had put pressure on Victor Amadeus to make it fail.[11] In any event, with Toulon secured for the French he turned his back on western Europe and set off on his march into Russia, which ultimately led him to defeat and his army to destruction at Poltava in June 1709.

Marlborough characteristically declined to believe early accounts of Almanza, for they came from the French, and he was wise enough to know that first reports, good or bad, are seldom correct. But by May he was forced to admit that the reverse there 'is greater than what was first reported'. Nevertheless he assured Heinsius that 'if the army in Italy enters France early I no way doubt God Almighty will bless this campaign'.[12] The expedition did indeed force Berwick to send troops from Spain, helping the Allies retain control of Catalonia. However, it accomplished little else. The emperor wanted to seize Naples, and, deaf to Marlborough's assertions that it would fall easily enough once Toulon was taken, duly detached 10,000 men to attack it. Eugène did not work well with his ducal cousin, and in mid-July Marlborough admitted to Godolphin that 'I shall be very uneasy' if the march did not begin soon. Then he began to worry that Victor Amadeus might attack a more convenient but less advantageous spot, like Antibes. When Marlborough did at last hear from Eugène, in a letter written on the thirteenth, it was to be told that the French already outnumbered him, more were on their way, and 'the enterprise is of the most perilous'.[13] Marlborough told Godolphin that he should not be too concerned, as Eugène tended to see problems in principle and to overcome them in practice, 'for it is his way to think everything difficult till he comes to put it into execution. But then he acts with so much vigour that he makes amends for all his desponding.'[14]

In the event, alas, Eugène had good reason for his despondency. Victor Amadeus and Eugène crossed the Var on 11 July and, with Admiral Sir Cloudesley Shovell and a powerful Anglo-Dutch fleet keeping pace with them, marched for Toulon. They took two weeks to accomplish a march that might have been achieved in one, and the British ambassador to Turin later lamented: 'It was the opinion of every officer that if before coming to Toulon, we had not been so dilatory and cautious, we might have done a great deal.'[15] Berwick's reinforcements from Spain arrived to join Marshal Tessé just before the Allies reached Toulon. There were forty-six ships of between fifty and 110 guns in the harbour, with a number of smaller craft, and Louis was so concerned that they might be burnt that he ordered them to be sunk and refloated later: the three-deckers would lie with their upper decks out of the water. When Shovell went ashore to meet Savoy on 28 July he found the duke gloomy: work had not been progressing well, and he awaited Eugène's arrival before deciding whether to press on. Eventually it was decided that heavy guns would be landed from the fleet, as Shovell told Vice-Admiral Byng, 'to make up the whole number between ninety and one hundred'.[16]

Despite the arrival of the guns, the Allies were never strong enough to mount a formal siege, but they did take the commanding heights of Ste-Catherine, just above the harbour, in early August. However, the French recovered them a week later in a sharp action in which the Prince of Saxe-Gotha, who had commanded the Imperialist right wing at Turin the year before, was killed. On 22 August Eugène and Victor Amadeus decided to fall back, having lost about 10,000 men in the enterprise. Eugène, railing against 'cabinets, parliaments, states-general and courtiers', thought that they had simply moved too slowly. 'We ought, as I proposed, to have marched straightway to Toulon after the expulsion of the French from Lombardy,' he wrote. 'Nevertheless, but for the bravery and talents of Tessé, and the unfortunate affair in which my beloved Prince of Gotha fell, we should have been successful.'[17]

Shovell embarked the sick, wounded and artillery in his transports. He was, though, determined to do as much damage as he could before leaving. His battleships first took on the batteries covering the harbour, enabling a flotilla of bomb-ketches (small vessels each armed with a single mortar) to approach within range, and to lob their shells over an intervening spit of land. They spent eighteen hours bombarding the fleet and the dockyard, with its stores full of timber, canvas and cordage, before the fire of repositioned French guns forced them to withdraw. Two French warships were burnt, two more badly damaged, and most were not refloated in time to play a useful part in the war.

The destruction of the French fleet not only gave the Allies control of the Mediterranean, but it effectively saw the French abandon any hope of fighting the British and the Dutch in regular fleet actions, and rely on privateering instead. The episode had one mournful footnote. On its way back home Shovell's squadron missed the entrance to the English Channel (all too easy with the primitive navigation instruments available) and three of his battleships were lost with all their officers and men, including Shovell himself, on the outer rocks of the Scilly Isles. The loss of the popular and competent admiral was a real blow.[18]

However gratifying the damage to the French Mediterranean squadron was, it was no real compensation for failure to take Toulon. Marlborough's early confidence had waned, and even before he heard of the reverse he warned Godolphin that he had received letters from Chetwynd 'and others from the army in Provence, and I am very sorry to tell you that I observe by all of them, that there is not that friendship and reliance between 58 [Savoy] and 48 [Eugène], as should be wished for making such a grand design succeed'.[19] Even from a distance it was evident that the loss of Ste-Catherine was very damaging, and once he had definite news that the Allies had given up the siege he recognised that the strategic consequences of failure would be substantial. Godolphin blamed it on 'the little good understanding between those princes, or rather, in truth, between the Imperial court and the Duke of Savoy'.[20] Marlborough's liaison officer with the expedition, Brigadier Palmes, took an age to return to report: at the end of September he was laid up 'with a violent fit of the gout in the Westerwald'. However, Marlborough thought that Eugène would not serve with Victor Amadeus again, and felt that it would be best if he was sent to Spain in an effort to revive the Allied cause there. Marlborough spent much of the autumn worrying about the next year's campaign, for it seemed certain to him that, with the war in Spain all but won, 'the French will bend their greatest force this way, and I am almost persuaded will offer us battle as soon as they take the field'.[21]

While Victor Amadeus and Eugène had been involved in the Toulon expedition, Marlborough was engaged in an equally unprofitable campaign against Marshal Vendôme on the borders of Brabant. At first he assured Heinsius that he would not risk battle unless he was superior in strength, but privately he told Godolphin that, though he would take any favourable opportunity that presented itself, he had to be less than open with his Allies.

> The true meaning of my letter to the pensioner is to let him see that I am not of the opinion to venture a battle, unless the advantages be on our side. I would have marched yesterday to Nivelle, but the deputies would not consent to it, telling me very plainly, that they feared the consequence of that march might be a battle. So that unless I can convince the pensioner that I am not for hazarding, but when we have an advantage, they will give such orders to the deputies, that I shall not have it in my power of doing good, if an advantage should offer itself . . . I take care not to let the army know that the Dutch are not willing to venture, since that must have an ill effect, and although it is a very unpleasant thing not to have full power at the head of an army, yet I do please myself that I shall do some considerable service this campaign; for I do believe that we shall find that the Elector [of Bavaria] and M. Vendôme grow insolent, by which they will either attack, or give me occasion of attacking them.

He concluded with a prescient warning that the Spanish Netherlands had not taken comfortably to their new ruler. He thought 'the greatest part of this country' was actually more inclined to Philip V than to Charles III, and blamed this on 'the unreasonable behaviour of the Dutch' in their administration of the 'liberated' area.[22] Cadogan was similarly lukewarm about the prospects, warning Lord Raby that 'The Deputies are relapsed into all their former fears and difficulties; which will be harder for my Lord Duke to overcome than to beat the Elector and Marshal Vendôme. I may venture to aver that if in fifteen days or three weeks at furthest we do nothing, you may reckon the campaign lost.'[23]

Part of Marlborough's problem was that he now had to furnish garrisons for the territories conquered after Ramillies, while Vendôme in turn had fewer garrisons to find. Marlborough argued privately that his army was actually better than Vendôme's, but it was probably rather smaller, a fact not calculated to encourage the Dutch to give battle. It was not until Vendôme had detached twenty battalions and eleven squadrons to help relieve Toulon that the balance of advantage passed to Marlborough, but there was little he could do with it. The Allies had the best of some marching and countermarching in filthy weather between the Scheldt and the Dender in late August and early September, and Vendôme's army, outrunning its logistics, lost heavily from desertion, but no telling blows were struck, and by late September Marlborough was thinking about getting into winter quarters, well aware, as we have seen, that Allied failure in Spain and before Toulon would put him at a disadvantage for the 1708 campaign.

Politics and Plans

It was a difficult winter. Marlborough visited Heinsius twice before he returned to England, but they could not agree on a plan for 1708. After his return Marlborough received a long, unusually formal letter from Heinsius warning him that the war was slipping away from them. Spain, he argued, was lost. No good would come out of Italy or Germany, and the French, by concentrating against the British and Dutch in the north, might beat them there and end the war on favourable terms. Only Britain, far more prosperous than Holland, could change this state of affairs, by sending more troops to Flanders, the vital theatre for 1708, and by arranging a descent on the French coast and encouraging an expedition from Italy so as to prevent the French from concentrating. Marlborough told him that he overestimated British economic strength: if Heinsius knew of 'the great scarcity of money in the country and the decay of trade in our sea ports you would not think our condition to differ much from that you represent Holland to be in'.

He regretted 'how little the Emperor and the Empire have done for this war and for their own preservation and how little they seem disposed to exert themselves at present, when all is in a manner at stake'. He hoped that Eugène would be sent to Spain, and urged Heinsius to press Vienna to help ensure this. The emperor should also be reminded that Wratislaw had agreed that 20,000 men should be sent to Italy, for Victor Amadeus might be able to take the offensive if he was properly supported. Finally, a descent on the French coast did indeed have much to recommend it, 'if the ill success we have hitherto had in those expeditions do not give too great a discouragement'. 'I am so tormented with a cold in my head,' concluded Marlborough, 'that I am forced to make use of Mr Cardonnel's hand.'[24] This was not an implied slight, for Marlborough's letter was frank and good-natured. His view of the coming year did not differ substantially from Heinsius's, except for his confidence that Spain could ultimately be saved, but that December he was too over-stretched on the political front to frame a strategy for a war that now seemed to have developed a giddy momentum of its own.

The government was in real trouble soon after the first Parliament of the United Kingdom met. It was really the English Parliament of 1705 with forty-five Scots MPs and sixteen representative Scots peers, and sat for the first time on 23 October 1707. In December both Houses endorsed the official war aim of 'No Peace without Spain'. The queen told the Lords that she would remain committed to an all-party government, and the Duumvirs discussed a scheme of Harley's to get rid of the extreme Whigs and create a centrist ministry – something which the queen applauded. Harley's own position was imperilled when William Greg, a clerk in his office, was found to be in treasonable communication with the French. Greg, apparently offered some mitigation of the grisly due process of law, resolutely refused to implicate his master. While Greg's ghastly fate was still in the balance, Harley privately criticised the management of the war in Spain to the queen, and his associate St John subsequently raised the same issue in Parliament. Fewer than half the British troops designated for Spain had actually been at Almanza, he maintained: had the administration simply done what Parliament expected of it, the Allies would certainly have won.

The Duumvirs were incensed at what they saw as Harley's betrayal. The queen tried hard to broker a compromise, the strain of which gave her 'gout in her stomach', and even said that she was prepared to part with Godolphin. On the evening of 8 February 1708 Godolphin and the Marlboroughs visited the queen to affirm that they would all resign if Harley was not dismissed. Godolphin spoke first, and the queen, 'in respect of his long service', gave him another day to consider his position. Sarah was told briskly that she could 'retire as soon as you desire. I shall then advise you to go to your little house at St Albans and stay there till Blenheim House is ready for your Grace.'

> Then entered the Duke, prepared with his utmost address. He told her that he had ever served her with obedience and fidelity . . . that he must lament he ever came in competition with so vile a creature as H[arley]; that his fidelity and duty should continue as long as his breath. That it was his duty to be speedy in resigning his commands, that she might put the sword into some other hand immediately, and it was also his duty to tell her he feared the Dutch would immediately on the news make a peace very injurious for England.

'And then, my Lord,' says she, 'will you resign me your sword?' 'Let me tell you,' says he, 'your service I have regarded to the utmost of my power.' 'And if you do, my Lord, resign your sword, let me tell you, you will run it through my head.'

She went to council, begging him to follow, he refusing . . .[25]

Harley had broken cover too soon, for he had too little Tory backing in either House. In contrast there was substantial support for the Duumvirs, and Prince George forcefully – and it seems decisively – took their part. Harley resigned: St John, Harcourt and Mansell departed in sympathy, and all were replaced by moderate Whigs. Although Sarah exaggerates Abigail Masham's subsequent contact with the dismissed Harley, they agreed a list of cant names for their correspondence as early as May 1708: the queen was 'Aunt Stephens'. For the moment, though, the connection was of no real political importance. Far more significant was the failure of a French attempt, in early March 1708, to land James II's son, the twenty-year-old James Francis Edward Stuart, in Scotland. From the French viewpoint the expedition was designed at worst to force troop withdrawals from Flanders, and at best to bring the British to the peace table. There was indeed strong anti-Union feeling in Scotland, and a landing might have capitalised on this, but the expedition miscarried, with the capture of one ex-British vessel, the *Salisbury*.

The government capitalised on the failure of the expedition by calling a general election in which the Whigs won a handsome majority. The Whig grandees pressed their advantage by trying to get the queen to take their ally Lord Somers into the cabinet, and Godolphin told her that she should give way. She wrote to Marlborough, by then back on the Continent, to say that she would never consent to the inclusion of Somers, and asking for his support. Marlborough, in view of the February crisis, was now seriously concerned about his own survival, and told the queen that the Dutch were well aware of what had been happening, and would be likely to negotiate with the French if they felt that a threat to its leadership made Britain no longer a reliable ally. He then took up Sarah's familiar line of warning the queen that the Tories were simply closet Jacobites. Her refusal to appoint Somers would, Marlborough warned, be 'a demonstration . . . to everybody, that the Lord Treasurer and I have no credit with your Majesty, but that you are guided by the insinuation of Mr Harley'.[26] The queen replied by assuring Marlborough that she agreed with him that peace could only be made on 'safe and honourable terms', but would not give way on Somers.

Marlborough knew that the crisis had weakened his authority, and he was aware that Anne and Sarah were now hardly on speaking terms. His true feelings towards Harley and Godolphin at this time are very hard to gauge, but it is likely that the real issue for him was whether, if Godolphin fell, his duty would oblige him to serve the queen under any ministry. We know that he had a view of Harley, but he does not deign to tell us what it was. 'I have avoided saying anything to you of Mr Harley,' he told Heinsius, 'when I have the honour of being with you, you shall know my thoughts of him and everything else.'[27] Their correspondence suggests that Marlborough and Godolphin were as close as ever, though it was no thanks to other Churchills. On 19 April Godolphin warned Marlborough that the queen's intransigence 'puts us into all the distraction and uneasiness imaginable. I really believe her humour proceeds more from husband than from herself, and in him it is very much kept up by your brother George, who seemed to me as wrong as is possible.'[28]

George Churchill, one of the first sea officers to offer his services to William of Orange, had commanded battleships at the battles of Beachy Head and Barfleur. He left the service in 1693 but returned after his brother had made his peace with the king, and had a seat on the Board of Admiralty. When Prince George became lord high admiral on Anne's accession George was appointed to his council, and immediately engineered his promotion to admiral of the Blue, flying his flag aboard *Triumph* at Portsmouth for a few days just to make the point. Although Prince George remained in titular charge of the navy, Churchill was responsible for its day-to-day activities, and came in for increasing public and parliamentary criticism as French privateers like Forbin or Dugay-Trouin did much damage to British trade. He was a resolute Tory and steadfastly blocked the promotion of senior officers who were known to be Whigs, playing his part in the politicisation of the navy's upper echelons and lending weight to Shovell's assertion that 'There is no storm as bad as one from the House of Commons.'[29]

By this time Marlborough, who had once encouraged his brother to sail along briskly in his slipstream, now had no time for George, but he could not associate himself with the Whigs' repeated criticism of him, both because of family loyalty (despite his politics George remained one of the MPs for the family borough of St Albans until his death) and because Prince George, whose support was so important to the Duumvirs, disliked having his namesake criticised. The prince ultimately solved the problem of the awkward admiral by dying in October 1708.

George left the Admiralty at once and retired to his house in Windsor Great Park, where he spent the remaining eighteen months of his life adding to his splendid collection of birds. He died without legitimate issue, and his enormous fortune, the fruit of long and assiduous perquisite-pecking (John was certainly no family exception in this regard), went to his natural son.

Not only did political squabbles in London make it unusually difficult for Marlborough to devote himself to strategy for the coming campaign, but he was concerned with a myriad of issues trickling out of the Ordnance Office and flooding from his responsibilities as captain general. He had some responsibility for French prisoners of war in British hands, and he also took the plight of British prisoners in French hands very seriously indeed. The former caused frequent correspondence with Godolphin, because Marlborough was scrupulous in ensuring that nothing he did would cause his colleague political difficulties. Thus, when a lady wrote to him about the comte de Lionne, a colonel taken at Blenheim, Marlborough at once passed the letter on to Godolphin.

> The enclosed is a letter from a young woman of quality that is in love with the Comte de Lionne. He is at Lichfield. I am assured that it is a very virtuous love, and that when they can get their parents' consent they are to be married. As I do from my heart wish that nobody were unhappy, I own to you that this letter has made me wish him in France, so that he might have leave for four months, without prejudice to her Majesty's service, I should be glad of it. But if you think it should not be done, you will then be pleased not to speak to the Queen about it.

Charles-Hughes de Lionne was eventually exchanged with a British officer, and married Marie Sophie Jaeger, daughter of an innkeeper in the delightful town of Wissembourg on the Alsace frontier, in 1709. The marriage was not a success, and seven months later he was striving to have it annulled, a process which took till 1719.[30] Officers allowed back to France on parole sometimes developed serious 'illnesses' in order to extend their stay. In July 1707 Marlborough had warned Godolphin that French officers on leave in France

> have all written as if they were dying, but I have refused them, so that I hope the Queen will not give it to [Brigadier the marquis de] Blanzac, nor any of the others, for they have been long enough, and the others ought to have their turns.[31]

Scouller suggests that prisoners of war 'were, in general, unwelcome. Almost the sole justification for capturing them was to have something to exchange for one's own men in the hands of the enemy.'[32] Marlborough hated having his soldiers captured, and when the Queen's Regiment and Elst's Dutch battalion were forced to surrender after a valiant resistance at Tongres in May 1703 he kept the garrison of Huy, captured later that year, in close confinement until it could be exchanged for the two battalions. Commissioners for Prisoners accompanied armies in the field to oversee the practicalities of escorts, rationing and exchange. Where possible cartels were agreed, specifying the relative exchange values of various ranks: an abortive naval cartel of 1702 specified that a naval captain was worth twenty men. There were always difficulties with such calculations: how did an ensign serving with the fleet rank amongst naval officers, and was a corporal of horse of equivalent rank to a *maréchal de logis*?

Captured senior officers might profit from the attention of their own commander and the courtesy of the enemy's. Cadogan himself had managed to get captured while out looking for forage during the siege of Tournai in 1706. Marlborough at once wrote to Sarah to say that:

> poor Cadogan is taken prisoner or killed, which gives me a great deal of uneasiness, for he loved me, and I could rely on him. I am now sending a trumpet to the Governor of Tournai to know if he be alive; for the horse that beat him came from that garrison. I have ordered the trumpet to return this night, for I shall not be quiet till I know his fate.
>
> I have opened my letter to tell you that Cadogan is a prisoner at Tournai and not wounded.[33]

Cadogan quickly told Raby, who had been riding with him as a volunteer when their patrol was caught, what had happened.

> I was thrust by the crowd. I endeavoured to step into a ditch on the right of the way we passed, with great difficulty I got out of it, and with greater good fortune avoided falling into the Hussars' hands who first came up with me . . . It made us fall to the share of the French Carabiniers, who followed their Hussars and Dragoons, from whom I met with quarter and civility, save their taking my watch and money . . . My Lord Duke has been so kind as to propose exchanging the Marquis de Croissy for me, so I hope my prison will not be of very long continuance.[34]

Initially Marlborough thought that he would have to wait till winter to arrange an exchange, 'which will be very troublesome, having nobody very proper for the execution of his place', but in fact Vendôme sent Cadogan back on parole a few days later, asking for Lieutenant General Baron Pallavicini, a Savoyard captured at Ramillies, in return.[35] Marlborough planned to send Croissy, brother of the French foreign minister, as well, but found that Eugène had already taken steps to exchange him.

In the winter of 1707–08 the French had sought 'a general exchange of prisoners', which Cadogan told Raby was simply 'a total release of all we have of theirs . . . officers and soldiers, by which they would have back four officers for one, and forty-three general officers for five, and your Excellency will easily believe we shall not treat on those terms'. He soon added that 'nothing like a hint of peace' had emerged from the conference to discuss prisoner exchanges, but the French 'threatened extended war and destruction rather than give up any part of the Spanish monarchy'.[36] In an effort to hasten the process Louis 'has given notice to all our officers who are on their parole in England or Holland that they are to return at the expiration of their *congé* to France without hopes of any further prolongations, this extraordinary severity will oblige us to send the like order to all their officers who have the Queen's or the States' leave to be in France'.[37]

The Allied officers and men captured at Almanza were soon counter-balanced by the French taken at Oudenarde, and a general exchange agreement was at last concluded in April 1709. Much of this work was undertaken by Cadogan, who in 1707 had become 'Envoy Extraordinary to the Southern Netherlands' after the death of George Stepney, who had been posted from Vienna to The Hague after falling out with the Imperialists by repeatedly pressing them to come to terms with the Hungarian rebels. This did not simply give him a good deal of purely diplomatic work, but made him one of the two British representatives (Marlborough was the other) on the Anglo-Dutch condominium governing the Spanish Netherlands. He remained Marlborough's quartermaster general, but the workload bearing down on both men was simply colossal. Marlborough was corresponding with Chamillart about the Almanza prisoners, with the usual galaxy of European royalty about troops for the coming campaign, and with the York justices of the peace, up in arms because of some new high-handed act of Lord Peterborough, who, Marlborough assured their worships, had been left in no doubt of the queen's displeasure.

Marlborough stage-managed, from London, the embarkation on the Continent of a suitable force to pursue the Jacobite expedition to Scotland. His letter to Cadogan of 17 January 1708 is a masterpiece of brevity and clear thought. Cadogan, now a major general, was to go to Flanders immediately and, if there was indeed truth in the rumours that a French expedition was being prepared at Dunkirk, to ensure that sufficient British troops were on hand to be embarked 'with all possible speed, either at Ostend or in Zealand'. He was to discuss the allocation of troops with Lieutenant General Lumley, in command there in Marlborough's absence, and to be aware that Overkirk had been copied in on the correspondence and knew what was afoot, although secrecy was essential. Just in case Cadogan had time to spare, he was to note that a copy of the last treaty with the Prussians would arrive by the same post, pay them 56,000 crowns, and sign the treaty governing the terms of service for the Hessian troops, 'leaving out any charge that might accrue by those troops being in Italy'.[38] It was staff work of the slickest and most comprehensive sort.

The Campaign of 1708

In late 1707 Marlborough had suggested that the next campaign would focus on the Spanish Netherlands, and early in 1708 he developed the idea for a campaign there. The French now had little to gain in Germany or Italy, and so would probably concentrate in the north, giving them a numerical superiority which would turn the tide in their favour. Indeed, this is precisely what Louis XIV told Marshal Vendôme in May:

> I cannot see the different orders of battle of my army without asking you the disposition that you intend to make for its first moves; it seems to me so superior to that with which my enemies can oppose you that you must get the Duke of Burgundy to profit from the first movements it will make.

Louis wanted a substantial success, and besieging Huy was simply not good enough. However, he warned Vendôme that he had to watch out for rapid Allied moves designed to tilt the balance of forces in another theatre of war:

> If the English and Dutch strengthen the army of Prince Eugène with a detachment of troops which ought to reinforce their army in

Flanders, in that case, it will be absolutely necessary for the Duke of Berwick to detach a similar proportion and to send a sufficient number of troops to the Elector of Bavaria so that he has nothing to fear from enemy superiority.[39]

Louis had long given instructions like this to his army commanders, which often made them reluctant to act on their own initiative and slowed down their reaction time as contentious issues were referred back to Versailles for resolution, but in this instance the relationship between Vendôme and Burgundy complicated things still further. Burgundy, the king's grandson, was in command of the army, but Louis sent most of his instructions to Vendôme, who was expected to persuade Burgundy to do the right thing.

The events of 1707 had shown that the Allies would be disadvantaged by having to maintain so many garrisons, and Marlborough advocated running the risk of leaving major towns ungarrisoned and maintaining a larger field army which would give him a chance of beating the French. He could persuade the Dutch that this would work only by transferring troops from Germany, and this in turn required him to persuade George, Elector of Hanover (and Marlborough's future king), who was now the new Allied commander on the Rhine, that it would be wise to maintain three armies: the Elector's on the Rhine, Eugène's on the Moselle, and his own on the Flanders frontier. Marlborough always intended to move Eugène up to join him, and so set off to see George in late April with some trepidation. He pulled off his task of deception, telling Godolphin:

After a very great deal of uneasiness, the Elector has consented to the project for three armies; but we have been obliged to leave on the Rhine two more Imperial regiments than we designed, so that Prince Eugène will have 2000 horse less on the Moselle; and as for the joining the two armies, we thought it best not to acquaint the Elector with it, so that when it is put into execution he will be very angry; but since the good of the campaign depends on it, I know no remedy but patience.[40]

The French plan was much as Marlborough had predicted. They hoped that the Jacobite excursion to Scotland would weaken the Allies in Flanders, but that scheme, as we have seen, proved the dampest of squibs. Vendôme and Burgundy were to have 130 battalions and 210 squadrons for the Netherlands, with the Elector of Bavaria and the Duke of Berwick with another seventy-five battalions and 140 squadrons on the Rhine. Despite the failure of the Scottish expedition, the French should have enjoyed a comfortable superiority, and they had another useful card to play.

Marlborough had already warned that the inhabitants of the Spanish Netherlands were not happy under the Anglo-Dutch Condominium. Lord Ailesbury declared that:

> I cannot say that their laws were violated, but their purse paid well, and great sums were laid upon pretence of giving safeguards, and contributions were exacted, and for three years the fields were as bare as the high road by continued foraging for to make the armies subsist . . . And to give them their due they loved the English officers and soldiers, but not the hoarders up of money.[41]

Marlborough's plan to replace the indefensible Brussels as the capital of the Spanish Netherlands by the well-fortified Antwerp, while perfectly sensible from the military viewpoint, was not popular with the two Dutch representatives on the Condominium. One of them, van den Bergh, burgomaster of Leiden, warned Heinsius that the abandonment of Brussels would not simply lead to the loss of Brabant, which was actually well disposed to the Allies, but would put Holland itself at risk. Marlborough, however, was determined to go ahead, and told Heinsius 'to lose no time in sending the necessary orders to your deputies at Brussels for the removing of the archives, it being absolutely necessary for the good success of this campaign'.[42] A Dutch historian, writing in 1945, argued that Marlborough 'intended to leave Brussels and Brabant to the French, after which the waterways of Flanders would have formed his only connection with Holland'. This is history as politics, for it is evident that it was never Marlborough's intention to relinquish Brabant. He believed that in order to defend it he would do better to manoeuvre in open field with as big an army as possible, and was obliged to thin out his garrisons in order to achieve this.[43]

Advised by the pro-French comte de Bergeyck, Burgundy and Vendôme struck before the move could be accomplished. In late May, Vendôme assured Louis that a *coup de main* against Antwerp 'will be put into execution in the first days of the coming month', but it was detected by the Allies in time.[44] An infantry brigade under Major General Murray was posted at Mariekirk, west of Marlborough's main army, then in the Louvain area, to support any threatened garrison. But on the evening of

3 July a party of 2,000 horse and 2,000 foot under brigadiels de Chémerault and de Ruffey, ostensibly foraging around Tubize, crossed the Dender at Ninove and made for Ghent, hub of the Flanders waterways. Led by F.H. de la Faille, formerly grand bailiff of the city, a group of cavalry rushed one of the gates, while others were opened with the connivance of the citizens: the Allied garrison of three hundred men withdrew to the citadel. The main French army, led by Lieutenant General Grimaldi's advance guard, marching at good speed in pouring rain, got past Marlborough's right flank and positioned itself between him and Ghent. The garrison in the citadel agreed to surrender on terms if no help arrived by the eighth. Another small force under the comte de Lamotte, striking up from Comines, went on to take Bruges in much the same way in the early hours of 5 June, again without the Allies being able to intervene.

The French *coups de main* came at a time when both armies had reinforcements on the way. Eugène, as planned, was marching in from the Moselle with thirty-six battalions and seventy squadrons, although he had started later than expected as some of his troops had been slow in joining him, and was not expected at Maastricht till 10 July. As soon as Berwick heard that Eugène was on the move, he sent thirty-four battalions and sixty-five squadrons north, and they were expected to arrive at Namur on the fourteenth. Marlborough's original hope that the arrival of Eugène's detachment would have tilted the balance (and with it the minds of the Dutch deputies) in his favour would probably have been dashed by the arrival of Berwick's men.

There is no doubt that the fall of Ghent and Bruges caught Marlborough badly off-balance, and, probably more than any other single event in his military career, did serious damage to his poise and self-confidence. Goslinga reckoned that it was one of only two occasions when he saw the duke show genuine alarm, and David Chandler, one of his most supportive biographers, acknowledges that 'he was soon plunged into the deepest depression'.[45] Marlborough's letters and dispatches show only his formal response to events, but they depict a swift parry and early recognition that the fortress of Oudenarde, just south of Ghent, would be vital in preventing the French from exploiting their success. At two in the morning on 5 July, long before French intentions were clear, he dashed off a note to Murray, saying that he had just heard that the French had sent 5,000 men towards Ninove, and expected them to follow with their main army. Murray was to send Sir Thomas Prendergast's Regiment to Oudenarde immediately.

Another note assured the governor of Oudenarde that Prendergast's men would march 'without halting' to reinforce him: Marlborough was anxious that he should know that help was at hand.

No sooner was the ink dry on these letters than Marlborough broke camp and headed for Brussels; he was at Anderlecht, south-west of the city, that same afternoon, when he wrote to Henry Boyle, who had become a secretary of state when Harley and his followers left the government. Despite the crisis of the moment, he was the soul of politeness, and began by saying that although he was aware that two issues recently raised by Boyle, the pensions to be given to Swedish ministers, and the response to a letter from the Russian ambassador, were very important,

> I must defer my answer to these particulars till the next post; but having had advice last night that the enemy were decamped, and that they had made a strong detachment some hours before under M. Grimaldi, we have been upon our march since two o'clock in the morning, and having had notice at noon that the [enemy] detachment was advanced as far as Alost, and had broken down the bridges over the Dender, I immediately detached two thousand horse and dragoons, under Major General Bothmar, to pass at Dendemonde and observe them and protect the Pays de Waes. By what we can learn hitherto, their army is advancing as far as Ninove, and we shall continue our march according to their further motions. I have just now an express from Mr Cadogan, whom I sent as far as Maastricht to wait on Prince Eugène, that H[is] H[ighness] arrived there yesterday, and intended to be this evening at Terbanck, so that I expect him tonight or tomorrow morning early.[46]

On the surface it is hard to fault Marlborough's reaction to the crisis. Even before he knew what the French had in mind he had recognised the importance of Oudenarde and taken steps to reinforce it, sent out a strong party to find the French, and established communications with Eugène. However, Goslinga, sketching with an intimacy that sometimes verged on caricature, shows a man who was far less comfortable than his letters suggest. Goslinga arrived at Anderlecht on the evening of the fifth, and

> found him ready to mount his horse. He had received an hour earlier a report from the right that they were in touch with the enemy and that there was a chance of striking at their rearguard . . . . It was upon

receiving this message from the generals of the right that the Duke had risen from his bed, pale, worn out and disconsolate, to go and reconnoitre the enemy's position himself. We had scarcely ridden a couple of miles when he said that there was no use in going further, that it was too late to begin an operation, and thereupon he turned his horse and rode back to his quarters.[47]

Goslinga tells us that he urged Marlborough to attack the French rearguard, but Marlborough replied that the ground was unfavourable. Later that night more information came in which persuaded him to send reinforcements out to his right. At one o'clock on the morning of the sixth Goslinga was awakened by one of Marlborough's aides. 'I dressed in a moment and was at his quarters before two o'clock,' he writes:

I found him at his prayers, and when they were finished he mounted his coach. M. Dopff [the Dutch quartermaster general] and I followed him. It was at the first gleam of dawn that we arrived at the mill of Tombergh [St-Katherina Lombeek, almost midway between Brussels and Ninove]. We there found Bulow with other generals of the right. All were persuaded, against the opinion of Dopff, that we would find an enemy army drawn up ready to fall on us.[48]

The Allied army was 'drawn up in battle; the greater part of the horse and foot having been brought to the right in the night'.[49] When dawn came up there was nobody to be seen, and although a dozen squadrons were sent off all they managed to do was to fall in with part of the French baggage train, and take good booty and some three hundred prisoners. The French had indeed given them the slip. Sergeant Millner thought that their rearguard had been very well handled, and had 'falsified and flourished its colours apace in the scrub in our front as if all their army had there a posting to give our army battle'.[50] Chaplain Hare attributed the confusion to Cadogan's absence. Had he been there, 'he would have known the difference between their coming to us and marching by us, and would have given his Grace better intelligence'.[51]

Back at Marlborough's headquarters, Goslinga pressed him to march south-west towards Menin, and warned him that Oudenarde was very weak, but 'these reasons, solid as they were, made no impression on the Duke, who persisted in wishing to march on Assche [Asse, midway between Brussels and Alost] to wait for the arrival of Prince Eugène and his army'.[52] Marlborough had good reason for doing so. He was still uncertain of the position of the main French army, and it would be potentially fatal to launch an operation until he was sure of it. When he wrote to Bothmar on the sixth he still did not know that the citadel of Ghent had fallen, and the same day he urged the governor of Dendemonde to reinforce it with 250 to three hundred men if he could. Cadogan was away with Eugène, and therefore the heavy burden of staff work fell on Marlborough's own shoulders.

It is clear that he was not at all well, and in addition, the events of the past few days had knocked him off-balance. On the ninth, when the picture had cleared, he told Sarah that 'the perpetual marching I have had, has made me so very uneasy, that I have very little sleep these last three nights, so that I am so hot, that I must beg of you not to answer yours till next post'.[53] Goslinga wrote that on the sixth, when the French rearguard might indeed have been caught, 'instead of pressing the march by his presence' Marlborough dined and then 'went straight to his quarters, as if the enemy was twenty leagues away'. In his view this was 'evident proof that courage and dash without great activity which stands the test of all sorts of fatigue are insufficient to make an accomplished general'.[54]

Marlborough was more than usually pleased to see Eugène on the eighth. The prince tells us that Cadogan had met him at Maastricht to say that the French had surprised Ghent and Bruges 'and that my presence was wanted'. Eugène detoured through Brussels, 'where my interview with my mother, after a separation of twenty-five years, was very tender but very short', and went on, in a post-chaise escorted by Hungarian hussars, to meet Marlborough at Asse. He was four days ahead of his leading cavalry, and his infantry was even further back.

In his memoirs Eugène writes that he asked Marlborough if he intended to give battle. 'I think I ought,' replied the duke, 'and I find with pleasure, but without astonishment, that we have both made this reflection, but without this our communications with Brussels will be cut off. But I should like to have waited for your troops.'[55] Eugène told him not to wait, because the opportunity would not come again. In his private report to the emperor, however, Eugène painted a rather different picture. He admitted that Marlborough was 'pretty consternated', and Ritter von Arneth, one of his biographers, went further, telling us that the prince

> was astonished to see such despondency in a general like Marlborough
> over a relatively unimportant misfortune. They were closeted together

for several hours, and Eugène succeeded in convincing the Duke that his affairs were not in anything like so bad a state as he saw them.[56]

Friedrich Wilhelm von Grumbkow, boyhood friend of the Prussian King Frederick William I and his representative at Marlborough's head-quarters, agreed that all was not well. He told his master:

> The blow which the enemy dealt us did not merely destroy all our plans, but was sufficient to do irreparable harm to the reputation and previous good fortune of My Lord Duke, and he felt this misfortune so keenly that I believed he would succumb to his grief early the day before yesterday, as he was so seized by it that he was afraid of being suffocated.

Just after this interview, while Marlborough was writing a letter, Eugène asked Grumbkow

> exactly what all this meant. The Duke was incomprehensibly exhausted, and talked as though everything was lost, which the Prince did not consider appropriate, for unless he [Marlborough] lost his life we should with God's help obtain satisfaction.
> This morning My Lord Duke had a severe fever and was so ill that he had to be bled. He is very exhausted, and I believe it would do him a great deal of good if your Majesty could write him something consoling and assure him of your continued well-wishing in spite of the losses that he has suffered . . .[57]

Grumbkow's Prussian comrade Lieutenant General Dubislaw von Natzmer agreed that Marlborough was unusually gloomy.

> All Flanders being lost, there was deep depression in the army.
> My Lord Duke was inconsolable over these sad happenings and dis-cussed with me with touching confidence this sudden turn in events which would have become even worse for us had the enemy exploited their advantage with persisting boldness. But our affairs improved through God's support and Prince Eugène's aid, whose timely arrival raised the spirits of the army again and consoled us.

The meeting with Eugène and the reappearance of Cadogan helped Marlborough to rally, and he ordered Brigadier Chanclos, governor of

Ath, to take all the men he could spare to Oudenarde. As soon as he arrived Chanclos made it clear to the citizens of Oudenarde that he would fire the town if there was any sign of the behaviour displayed by the citizens of Bruges and Ghent. The council of war decided that the army should rest for a day or two, send all non-essential baggage to the rear, and then, without waiting for Eugène's men, head for Lessines to succour Oudenarde, and perhaps (for there had so far been no news of its fall) relieve the citadel of Ghent. Having written to Chanclos, however, Marlborough was once more 'indisposed and feverish'. His doctor advised him to go back to Brussels, but he refused to leave camp, although orders for the eighth were issued from old Overkirk's tent. A letter to Major General Murray, sent out that day, was in Cardonnel's hand. 'My Lord Duke being indisposed,' wrote Cardonnel, 'commands me to acknowledge your letter of yesterday, by which his Grace sees that the burghers of Ghent have chiefly contributed to our misfortune in the loss of that place. His Grace approves of the dispositions that you have made for the security of the country, and has no further commands to you at present.'[58]

Marlborough was very much better on the ninth, when the army marched towards Lessines, with Cadogan commanding the advance guard and the Earl of Albemarle 'with all the grenadiers of the army and thirty squadrons' in its rear, in case the French tried to slip past towards Brussels. That day Marlborough admitted to Godolphin that 'the treachery of Ghent, continual marching, and some letters I have received from England, have so vexed me, that I was yesterday in so great a fever that the doctor would have persuaded me to have gone to Brussels, but I thank God I am now better'.[59] In the same post he assured Sarah that 'I can't be at ease till I regain Ghent, or make the enemy pay dear for it. I am with all my heart and soul yours.'[60] On the tenth he sent a brief résumé to Heinsius, concluding, in almost the same words, 'I shall not be at ease till I have regained Ghent or made the enemy pay dearly for it.'[61]

To understand the reasons for Marlborough's determination we must glance at the map. The French now held most of Flanders apart from Ostend, and could defend it by holding the lines of the Scheldt and the Bruges canal. To do so effectively, however, they would first have to deal with the Allied garrison of Oudenarde on the Scheldt, already the subject of Marlborough's interest. Happily for the Allies, the French commanders did not get on well. Vendôme was capable and experienced, but was also brusque, notoriously scruffy and, as a great-grandson of Henri IV, not overly impressed by princes of the blood royal. He was not the ideal foil for the well-bred but less experienced Duke of Burgundy. Vendôme had wanted to march on Oudenarde without delay, while Burgundy favoured besieging Menin. The matter was referred to Versailles, whence Louis XIV wisely observed:

> If Oudenarde had been invested as soon as my army had reached Alost, and if you [Burgundy] had been able to prevent the enemy from sending support there and making a good defence . . . [then] the garrison being weak and the terror great in the first moments, the citizens would have been able to persuade the governor of the fortress to return it to its legitimate sovereign.

He had heard that Eugène was 'marching with incredible speed' to join Marlborough. The capture of Ghent and Bruges was impressive, and Menin 'will fall of its own accord without a siege'. In consequence, he added presciently, 'you must not regard the siege of Oudenarde as your prime objective so that to besiege it you lose your grip on what you are obliged to hold elsewhere'.[62] The two generals agreed that Marlborough was more likely to move against Namur or Charleroi than against them, and so decided, on 9 July, to march on Lessines, whence they could cover the siege of Oudenarde. Vendôme told a fellow general: 'We will make siege by detachments, and the bulk of our army will always defend the river.'[63]

By 9 July Marlborough knew that the French had sent 16,000 men to Oudenarde, and a letter from the robust Chanclos, which reached him at eight o'clock that morning, told him that the town was just about to be invested, and that Chanclos had heard that a siege train was on its laborious way from Tournai. Marlborough hoped that he would be able to reach the crossings of the Dender at Lessines before his enemy, so placing Oudenarde within easy reach and preventing the French from using the line of the Dender to cover their siege. He had stripped down his army to what was, for the age, a very light allowance: generals were permitted a coach and two wagons, and brigadiers simply a coach and a wagon. Chaplain Hare thought that the arrangements were made 'with a greater strictness than has been used on our side this war that we may have nothing to hinder our march'. The heavy baggage had been sent back to Brussels with an escort of four battalions: Marlborough was determined to be able to manoeuvre freely. Nor would he be checked by the need to make bread, for enough had been baked at Asse to last for eight days. The road to Lessines was bad, and that from Lessines to

Oudenarde worse still, so careful attention was paid to sending pioneers forward 'to make ways'.

When the army marched off at two on the morning of the ninth:

> The regulation touching the baggage was exactly observed, and the ways being well made, the army marched with exact order, though with the most extraordinary expedition: the head was past Herselingen, which is six leagues from Ashe, before 1 o'clock, the lines being perfectly closed up without any straggling.

The army made camp on its line of march, 'fronting towards the enemy', and when the retreat was beaten at seven that night tents were struck at once and the march was resumed. Cadogan was well ahead with the advance guard, marching flat-out for Lessines 'like Jehu in his chariot'. By an orderly-room error the letter dated 9 July telling Godolphin of the Allied plan was not actually sent, and Marlborough opened it to assure his old friend that he was a contented man, for Cadogan had reached Lessines before the French, at about midnight on the eighth/ninth, thrown pontoon bridges over the Dender ready for the arrival of the main body, and crossed to secure a camping ground protected by a small tributary. 'I should think myself happy, since I am got into this camp,' concluded Marlborough, 'if they continue with their resolution of carrying on with that siege.'[64] He was similarly confident when he assured Boyle that if the French persisted with the siege 'it may give us an opportunity of coming soon to a battle, wherein I hope God Almighty will bless the justice of our cause'.[65]

The Devil Must have Carried Them: Oudenarde

The French were astonished to find themselves beaten in the race for Lessines. Vendôme was in favour of hurrying on to catch Marlborough before he could cross the Dender in strength, but Burgundy was more cautious, and wanted to get the Scheldt between him and the Allies. Accordingly, the French called off their operations at Oudenarde and sheered away for Gavre (Gavere), six miles below Oudenarde on the Scheldt. When it came within his reach, Chanclos hacked at their rearguard with Wallis's Dragoons. Marlborough realised that if the French were able to bridge the Scheldt at Gavre they could then fall back towards the security of their frontier fortresses, and Berwick's imminent arrival would bring the forces to near-parity. The French might lose

Bruges and Ghent, but any opportunity for bringing them to battle in the open would be lost.

Accordingly, he ordered Cadogan, with eight squadrons, sixteen battalions and thirty-two light 'regimental' guns, the army's pontoon train and a strong party of pioneers – perhaps 10,000 men in all – to make straight for Oudenarde. Once there, he was to supplement its two masonry bridges with five pontoon bridges (two in the town and three downstream), which would enable the main body of the army to cross as fast as possible, and to hold a bridgehead on the far bank to give the newly-arriving troops space to form up. Cadogan was on the move at one on the morning of the eleventh, and about eight hours later he reported that he was in sight of Oudenarde and the French were still at Gavre, east of the river. His five leading battalions were across the river by midday, and the bridges were complete soon afterwards. The French had begun their own rather more leisurely crossing at about ten o'clock on 11 July.

The field of Oudenarde is the most difficult of Marlborough's battle-fields to grasp, for the expansion of the town, especially in the form of light industrial premises and market gardens on the water meadows north of the river, obscures the traveller's vision. The view enjoyed by Cadogan from the high ground at Eename, just above his bridging site north-east of the city, is hard to duplicate today. But for Cadogan, who had something of his master's eye for the ground, the picture was very clear. The Scheldt meandered northwards through Oudenarde, built on both its banks, and then curled out in a great eastward bend south of Gavre. Inside the bend rose a range of low irregular hills, laced by streams – the most substantial of them the Norken, the Diepenbeek and the Marollebeek – which flowed down to the Scheldt. Almost due north of Oudenarde, and a little over four miles from its ramparts, were what some contemporaries called 'the heights of Huyshe', bosky hillocks, one of them crowned, then as now, by a windmill. The Norken flowed across the southern front of this little ridge. The main Ghent road followed the northern bank of the river, while the tree-lined Bruges road ran north-westwards over the wooded ridge of the Boser Couter through the village of Oyke. The area's dark soil was fertile, its villages prosperous. In the short term the heavily-cultivated low ground on the Scheldt's north bank would be crucial, for if Cadogan was to gain Marlborough room for manoeuvre he had first to seize this.

Cadogan kept his first four battalions, all of them Prussian, close to

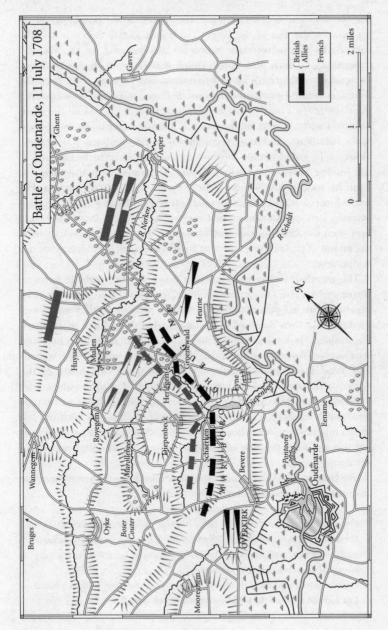

Battle of Oudenarde, 11 July 1708

British
Allies
French

2 miles

1

0

Gavre

Ghent

Asper

R. Norken

R. Scheldt

Heurne

Huysse

Mullen

Groenewald

Royegem

Herlegem

Diepenbeck

Wannegem

Marollebeek

Oyke

Boser Couter

Schaerken

Bevere

Diepenbeck

Pontoons

Eename

Oudenarde

OVERKIRK

MARLBOROUGH

EUGENE

Byrne

Mooregem

the Scheldt to protect the crossing. He formed up the remainder of his infantry on the axis of the Ghent road, with Joseph Sabine's brigade, carrying its Union colours in action for the first time, on the left, and Plattenburg's Dutch and Scotch-Dutch battalions on the right: Major General Josef Rantzau's Hanoverian dragoons were on the left of the foot. Lieutenant General the marquis de Biron, responsible for covering the flank of the French army as it crossed the Scheldt, was on the move towards Cadogan, with two brigades of infantry, comprising seven good Swiss battalions, and one regiment of horse, perhaps 5,000 men. However, he could not see the crossing site, and when he heard shots as the leading Swiss bumped into Rantzau's troopers near the village of Eyne he rode to the windmill there to see what was happening. His second in command, Major General Pfeiffer, in Eyne with the leading brigade, had quickly summoned the second brigade. Biron, who had now seen the crossing site and Cadogan's force, rode back to hasten the arrival of this reserve, and sent a galloper to tell Vendôme what was happening.

The marshal, enjoying an alfresco lunch by the roadside between Gavre and Huysse (Burgundy, tellingly, was some short distance away, lunching with his own entourage), was not pleased. 'If they are there,' he declared, 'then the devil must have carried them. Such marching is impossible.' He looked hard at the southern horizon, where he could see clouds of dust announcing that Marlborough's main army was on its way. Vendôme's decision, although quickly made, was probably the right one. Biron was told to attack the bridgehead as soon as he could: Vendôme himself would take the cavalry of the left wing to support him, and a message was sent urging Burgundy to follow with the left wing's infantry. Vendôme hoped to brush Cadogan away from the crossing site and hold the line of the river before Marlborough was up in strength.

Everyone in the Allied army soon knew that they were running a race against time. Lieutenant General Natzmer wrote:

> On the march we received the cheerful news that Cadogan had thrown bridges over the Scheldt at Eename, near Oudenarde, without any resistance, and also that the enemy, coming up from Alost, were planning to cross the river at Gavre.
>
> This news filled us with joy and in our eagerness we sought out my Lord Duke to allow us to advance at a faster pace.[66]

Even the lowly Private Deane could see what was afoot:

> we marched by break of day, and by 2 in the afternoon we came to
> Oudenarde, which was a good five leagues, where we were drawn up
> on the rampart walls until more of our horse advanced, which they did
> in brave order about 2 in the afternoon. The front of our army passed
> that river and as fast as they came over were drawn up, in brigades, in
> order of battle towards the defiles, as well to sustain Major General
> Cadogan . . .[67]

Eugène was there in person, though his troops were still far behind.
'Towards 12 o'clock the head of our cavalry of the right wing reached the
bridges and crossed by the pontoons at a brisk trot,' he wrote, 'but the
infantry took longer to move, and it was several hours later that they began
to cross.'[68] 'It was no longer a march,' declared Goslinga, 'but a run.' As
successive units breasted the rise at Eename they could see 'the dust of the
enemy's march in the air as far as the Scheldt; a certain sign that the enemy
was trying to cross it before us and dispute the passage'. As this happened,
'the power of emulation was so great that we could not keep the troops
detached to guard our baggage; more than half of them absconded to join
their companies on the march'. Goslinga, overcome by the mood of the
moment, gave ten pistoles to some dragoons to help clear the way for him.
He remained critical of Marlborough, who 'appeared visibly exhausted,
and did not give any positive order for the encouragement of his troops'.[69]
However, this was one of those moments when an army, shocked and
perhaps a little ashamed to have been outwitted, felt strength bubbling
back into its veins, and sensed what was required of it without much need
for orders. Marlborough and Eugène remained, for the moment, at
Cadogan's crossing site, 'the sacred anchor for the whole army', where they
heard the musketry to their right swell from a mutter to a roar.

We cannot be sure quite when Vendôme mounted his horse and rode
down to meet Biron, for in the wake of the French defeat the issue soon
became politicised. Vendôme argued that it was as early as ten in the
morning, and that he could not get Burgundy to move till four in the
afternoon: if only the royal prince had moved when he was asked to do
so, the French would have enjoyed a famous victory. Saint-Simon, in
contrast, suggests that it was not until two o'clock, after Allied cavalry
had begun to cross and the window of opportunity was closing fast, that
Vendôme was sure what was happening. Eugène certainly thought that

the marshals' failure to agree on a joint course of action and carry it out promptly was fatal. 'But for this misunderstanding,' he admitted, 'we should perhaps have been defeated; for our cavalry was engaged a full hour before the infantry could join it.'[70] In contrast, the French Lieutenant General d'Artaignan (sic) maintained that his own infantry was very slow in getting into action in adequate numbers. 'As the army came up,' he wrote, 'we found the enemy had already moved in such strength that we could not oppose the passage of the river, and the business reduced itself to a general action.'[71] The official Allied account reckoned that it was not until five o'clock that there was more infantry than the sixteen battalions that had accompanied Cadogan.

When Vendôme approached Eyne he found that the expected counterattack had not taken place. The Allies facing Biron had grown more and more numerous, and a six-gun battery (sited, had Vendôme but known it, by Marlborough in person) had just come into action behind the village of Schaerken on Cadogan's left. Lieutenant General the marquis de Puységur, Burgundy's chief of staff and a noted military theorist, had arrived to lay out a camp, and warned him that the ground to his front was impassable. Marshal the marquis de Matignon, another staff officer, agreed, and told Biron to stay where he was. Vendôme reluctantly agreed that an attack was indeed impossible, and moved off to the right with his own cavalry. This happened at about three o'clock, thought the author of the official Allied account: 'The French cavalry in the plain before our advance guard began to disappear, taking their ground towards their own right.' The Allies themselves thought that the Diepenbeek in front of Eyne was indeed an obstacle – 'marshy, and hardly passable for horse, though very narrow' – so Puységur's advice was not as foolish as is sometimes suggested.

Cadogan's men had indeed spent some time filling part of the brook with fascines before they were ready to advance, and not long after three o'clock, with his Prussian brigade now summoned up from the crossings, Cadogan attacked. Sabine's brigade, directly opposite the village of Heurne, advanced to the tuck of drum without firing a shot until it was twenty yards from the Swiss, and then began to slam in its platoon volleys. Three of the four battalions in the village surrendered almost at once, and the fourth, making off for Heurne, was caught in the open by Rantzau's horsemen, curling round the northern end of Cadogan's line, and cut to bits. The three battalions of the second brigade, probably on the western edge of Heurne, fell back in disorder.

Rantzau then turned his attention to Biron's twelve squadrons, drawn up across the Ghent road, and charged them too, breaking La Bertoche's regiment and capturing its colonel, standards and kettle-drums. He then assailed the French cavalry drawn up between Royegem and Mullem, but although his initial impact did some damage he was driven off by weight of numbers. 'Here it was that the Electoral Prince of Hanover distinguished himself,' said the Allied account, 'charging with his sword in his hand at the head of a squadron of Bulow's dragoons. His horse was shot under him, and Colonel Loseke that commanded the squadron was killed, fighting bravely by him.'

As Rantzau's men wheeled back they found that Natzmer's twenty squadrons had arrived.

Cadogan himself came to me in great joy at our arrival and my coming up in his support. I crossed the village of Eyne, where the fighting had just ended, and formed up beyond it. Soon afterwards Prince Eugène came and greeted me: 'I find you pretty far ahead.' He then rushed forward to examine the enemy's position for himself. In a little while he returned in great spirits, and exclaimed: 'We have got to get at them hand over fist.'[72]

It was easier said than done. Although 'the troops continued to pass the bridges with great diligence', the Allies were still desperately short of infantry, and the French army, like some great beast aroused from slumber, was at last beginning to grope forward. Burgundy sent Grimaldi with sixteen squadrons to look at the ground on Cadogan's left, but his leading squadrons found the terrain very soft, and he reported that it was poor going for cavalry, so infantry should be used instead. This was certainly not a frivolous objection: Captain Robert Parker thought that the whole of this central area of the battlefield, now richly cultivated, was 'a marshy piece of ground, full of trees and brushwood'. It was only on the western flank that it began to open out to 'a spacious plain . . . here he [the enemy] drew up the greater part of his cavalry. At the end of this plain is the village [of] Oycke, which covered their right flank: here he also posted a good body of foot and dragoons.'[73] Grimaldi rode back to join Burgundy and his entourage at the windmill in Royegem, from which they enjoyed a good view of the field.

Cadogan had now got his infantry into line from Groenewald towards Schaerken, with Natzmer's and Rantzau's horsemen on his right flank. Successive waves of French infantry broke against Cadogan's line, with

Vendôme, in a fighting fury, half-pike in his hand, urging his men on. At perhaps five o'clock he asked Burgundy to throw the whole of the left wing against the cavalry on Cadogan's right. Burgundy, advised by his staff that the ground was impracticable, decided not to attack, and the officer who rode down to give Vendôme these gladsome tidings was shot before he could deliver the message. It is hard not to sympathise with Vendôme, but equally easy to recognise that he would have been in a better position to argue his case had he been with Burgundy at the mill and not 'fighting with a pike, like a private soldier rather than a marshal of France charged with the supreme control of ninety thousand men'.[74]

It was the crisis of the battle. Before Vendôme realised that Burgundy's attack would never materialise, the Duke of Argyll, pounding up from the bridges 'with all possible expedition' with twenty British battalions, came into line on Cadogan's left, just in time to withstand Vendôme's next assault. As the French seemed to be gaining ground, Count Lottum's men, another twenty battalions, swung into action on Argyll's left. Although the French took the inn (in fact a house of ill repute) at Schaerken at about 5.30, and were perhaps half a mile from the crossing site, Overkirk's Dutchmen were now crossing the two stone bridges and two pontoon bridges in Oudenarde itself.

Marlborough and Eugène had ridden forward from Cadogan's crossing site to what seemed the point of main danger, between Groenewald and the Ghent road, early in the afternoon. Now Marlborough sensed that the balance of the battle had changed. At about six o'clock he placed Eugène in command of the whole of his right flank, and galloped across to the centre of Lottum's line, where eighteen Hanoverian and Hessian battalions, forming a second line there, at last gave him an uncommitted reserve. He did not want to commit Overkirk and Tilly, with their twenty-four battalions and twelve squadrons, to a defensive battle on his right or centre if he could avoid it. Marlborough had early on posted Lumley's cavalry to cover his left flank, and Lumley reported that the Boser Couter was still unoccupied by the French. Marlborough accordingly ordered Overkirk and Tilly to make for the Boser Couter in the hope of turning the French right.

Eugène, meanwhile, was under frightful pressure – the French at last carried both Herlegem and Groenewald at about 6.15 – but, typically, did not ask for help. Marlborough, however, sensed that his right was close to collapse, and so ordered Lottum to fall back through the fresh Hanoverian and Hessian battalions and march to Eugène's assistance. Overkirk and Tilly had now made good progress towards Oycke, and

Marlborough ordered them 'to press the French as much as they could on that side'.

In the hour that followed Marlborough, who had begun the battle looking worn-out after a dreadful week, rose to the very height of his powers. He was now shuffling brigades as a seasoned gambler riffles through a pack of cards, his gallopers and runners forming the central nervous system of an army which responded quickly to his touch. Eugène thought that the Allies now attained this battle-winning tempo, just as the French failed to, because of the personalities of their commanders. He and Marlborough 'loved and esteemed one another. Even the Dutch marshal Overkirk, remarkable for his age and services, my old friend and Marlborough's, obeyed us, and fought to admiration.'[75] Grumbkow told his royal master that Marlborough had certainly shaken off his gloom.

> My Lord Duke shone in this battle, giving his orders with the greatest sangfroid, and exposing his person to danger like the commonest soldier. Prince Eugène showed much spirit under the heaviest fire, and was with the Prussians, whom he had specially sought out.[76]

It was Overkirk's last battle, for he was mortally ill, and commanded from his coach. Marlborough had diverted Overkirk's two leading infantry brigades as they marched up, and they nudged into the right flank of the French infantry fighting on the Diepenbeek, turning the battle there. Lottum's men reached Eugène in the very nick of time ('without [them] I should scarcely have been able to keep my ground', confessed the prince), and Herlegem and Groenewald were regained, though the battle continued to be desperate on Eugène's flank.

D'Artaignan reckoned that the firepower of the Allied infantry gave it a decided advantage in the battle of the hedgerows. He thought there had never been a firefight like it, and wrote grimly of 'the terrible fire that the enemy made whenever we appeared'. Even Eugène thought the fighting exceptionally heavy: 'It was one sheet of flame.' With the Dutch and Danish horse in the field Marlborough saw that there was now no need to keep Lumley's troopers on the left, and so he was ordered round to the right, his squadrons trotting behind the battle line to take station behind Natzmer, facing due north against the uncommitted masses of the French left wing.

Lumley's timely arrival enabled Eugène to take some of the pressure off his sorely-tried infantry by ordering Natzmer's Prussian cavalry, intact and drawn up in very good order, to move through a gap made by shifting two battalions, and charge. Natzmer broke the leading French squadrons, crashed into two infantry battalions and broke them too, but then, weary and over-extended, was counterattacked by the *Maison du Roi*. Natzmer himself, cut about the head, jumped a wide ditch to safety, and his survivors rallied behind Eugène's infantry. The presence of Lumley's squadrons deterred the French from exploiting the Prussian repulse. The Allied account paid special tribute to 'the Prussian Gens d'Armes, [who] distinguished themselves very much, and lost nearly half their numbers in this action'.

By now, though, Overkirk was making his presence felt. He had moved up the road, through Bevere and onto the Boser Couter, in column, and when he reached Oycke he swung eastwards and shook out into line, heading for Royegem. Amongst Overkirk's subordinates was the young Prince of Orange and Nassau-Dietz, seeing his first battle at the age of nineteen, but leading the attack with the courage that had always been the hallmark of his house. There was little enough the French, preoccupied with the battle to their front, could now do to stop him. D'Artaignan reported 'our infantry much in disorder . . . without ammunition against an enemy who had plenty of it'. The *Maison du Roi* closed right up behind his foot soldiers 'with a courage and firmness worthy of them', but the infantry itself was played out. As the Dutch began to push eastwards the *Maison du Roi*, again trying to take the weight of the infantry at the close of this awful day, attempted to charge them. Goslinga had earlier galloped across to the Dutch with orders. As the *Maison du Roi* formed up he could see what was coming, and dismounted to fall in with Sturler's Swiss regiment: 'after a little compliment I made them of wishing to fight with such brave fellows . . . Our Swiss were resolved to wait for them with fixed bayonets and not to fire until they were at point-blank range, keeping such a profound silence that I was astonished.' When the volley rolled out, the *Maison du Roi* was stopped in its tracks: Goslinga saw a drum-horse shot down and the kettledrums it bore, scarcely less of a trophy than cavalry standards or infantry colours, taken. The Swiss then advanced against the French infantry, but now it would not stand.

They made only one general discharge ten paces from us, killing four or five soldiers, and made off like worthless creatures. These fell on the others on the right, who we had just cut off from the remainder of

their army, and became the prey of our cavalry almost without firing
a shot . . . Whole regiments gave up to our men: Béarn, Ruphié and
others were of this number.[77]

The Allied account tells how the collapse of the French right wing now
fatally unbalanced the centre, already exhausted by the battle amongst
the hedges north of the Diepenbeek. The French,

> beaten from right to left, were forced back again into the enclosures
> in great disorder, so that at last, when it was growing dark, many
> battalions, and more squadrons, flung themselves out in a desperate
> manner, some of them piercing through others, were cut to pieces,
> some were forced back, some passed through unperceived, and others
> asked to capitulate for their whole regiments.

As it grew dark Marlborough ordered his men to cease fire: it was better
to let some of the enemy escape than lose soldiers to 'friendly' musketry.
Major Blackader, whose regiment had not reached the field till 5 p.m.,
thought that the advent of darkness 'saved them [the French], in all
probability, from as great a defeat as ever they got'.[78] He might have
been surprised to hear that Vendôme agreed with him: 'Had it not been
for the onset of the night, which enabled us to retire, our troops would
have been encircled.'[79] The wily Eugène was determined not to lose any
opportunity to capture more Frenchmen:

> I sent out drummers in different directions, with orders to beat the
> retreat after the French manner, and posted my French refugee
> officers, with directions to shout on all sides – Here Picardy! Here
> Champagne! Here Piedmont! The French soldiers flocked in, and
> I made a good harvest of them: we took in all about seven thousand.[80]

In total, Burgundy and Vendôme lost about 5,000 men killed and
wounded in the battle and 9,000 unwounded prisoners, including
nearly eight hundred officers, with over a hundred standards and
colours and ten pairs of kettledrums. Marlborough, in contrast, lost just
under 3,000 killed and wounded. As was usual with the battles of the
age, the sheer number of wounded imposed a burden that the medical
services could not bear. The Allied army spent the night in the field,
'where the bed of honour was both hard and cold', recalled Blackader,

'but we passed the night as well as the groans of dying men would allow us, being thankful for our own preservation'.[81] 'The battle being over and the field our own,' wrote Private Deane,

> the next morning . . . our two battalions [of 1st Foot Guards] by the Duke's order marched back again to Oudenarde, marching over the same ground where the hottest of the action happened; which was a heart piercing sight for to see. The dead lie in every hole and corner, [and] to hear the cries of the maimed was saddening yet nothing to what was to be expected considering the heat of the service and what vast quantities of ammunition was spent by the enemy in their fierce and continual firing and the extraordinary advantage they had in the ground, that it was as well that we came off as well as we did.[82]

Matthew Bishop, an ex-sailor who had joined Webb's Regiment not long before, had found the victory extraordinary, 'as they had the advantage of the ground, and likewise were superior in numbers, which are two great articles'. However, even the ever-sanguine Bishop thought that 'we were not in a capacity to follow them, but continued there in order to bury our dead on the morrow'.[83]

There had been an ill-tempered interview between Burgundy and a grubby and furious Vendôme on the Ghent road at about ten o'clock on the night of the battle. Vendôme first accused Burgundy of doing nothing to help, and then suggested that the intact left wing of the army should hold its ground around Huysse and give battle the following day. Burgundy replied that it was too scattered and was now short of ammunition, which, given the intensity of the battle on the Diepenbeek, may indeed have been true. Pausing only for a last insult, Vendôme rode off through the drizzle to Ghent, where he gave vent to his feelings by easing his belly in the road outside his quarters, coarse behaviour even for the age. Matignon was left to bring the army off as well as he could, and was well served by some of his subordinates: Lieutenant General St-Hilaire, commanding the artillery (much of it stuck up near Gavre all day), got most of his guns away, and the marquis de Nangis found the cavalry of the left wing calmly awaiting orders that never came and led it off to safety. However, some of the survivors of Oudenarde, making for the nearest French garrison, were pursued by peasantry who had now come to look upon all soldiers as enemies. Others simply deserted.

Marlborough spent the night on the field with his soldiers, and rode into a rainy Oudenarde the following morning, politely doffing his hat to acknowledge the salutes of shoals of captured French officers, who pressed in to see the great man. He immediately wrote to Sarah and Godolphin. 'I have neither spirits nor time to answer your last three letters,' he told Sarah,

> this being to bring the good news of a battle we had yesterday; in which it pleased God to give us at last the advantage. Our foot on both sides having been all engaged has occasioned much blood . . . I do, and you must, give thanks to God for his goodness in protecting and making me the instrument of so much happiness to the Queen and the nation, if she will please to make use of it. Farewell my dear soul.[84]

Godolphin's letter was entrusted to Lord Stair, whose personal knowledge would amplify its single paragraph. Stair, a Scots nobleman, craved a British peerage, and Marlborough hoped (unavailingly, as it happened) that the queen 'might be pleased to distinguish him at this time'. Marlborough said that he had risked battle because he needed a victory, and 'nothing else could make the Queen's business go on well', although he knew that 'If I had miscarried I should have been blamed.' His head ached so badly that he could add no more, and even on the sixteenth complained, 'My head is so very hot that I am obliged to leave off writing.'[85]

At four o'clock on the afternoon of 12 July there was a council of war in the citadel, attended by Marlborough, Eugène, Overkirk, Goslinga and his colleague Gueldermalsen, with the two quartermaster generals, Dopff and Cadogan. Captured standards, colours and kettledrums were brought in as they were talking, and Goslinga remembered 'that good man M. Overkirk, almost moribund, was sitting down fully dressed, in a big armchair at the end of a room surrounded with all these glorious trophies'.[86] The generals were for pressing in against the main fortress line on the French frontier, but Goslinga, with the support of Gueldermalsen, favoured blockading the French army in Bruges and Ghent. It was pointed out to him that such long lines of investment would be vulnerable, and that in an area containing so many civilians, French soldiers would be the last to starve. Eugène was decidedly blunt. 'I proposed the siege of Lille,' he wrote. 'The deputies of the Estates-General thought fit to be of a different opinion. Marlborough was with me, and they were obliged to hold their tongues.'[87] In his memoirs, however, Goslinga attributed being voted down to the fact that Marlborough 'did not wish to see an end to the war, in which his two favourite passions, ambition and avarice, were satisfied and nourished'.[88]

It is, however, clear from Marlborough's letter to Sarah that he saw Oudenarde as a victory which might help obtain a negotiated peace. He gave special parole to the captured Lieutenant General Biron, specifying that he was to return to France without first visiting the French army, hoping that Louis would be told just how much damage had been done to it before evasive reports arrived. Marlborough gave Biron dinner at Oudenarde before he left, and asked for news of 'the Prince of Wales', James II's son, known to the French as the chevalier de St George, who had been with Burgundy during the battle. The company seemed delighted to hear of the young man's character and behaviour, proof, suggests Winston S. Churchill, 'of the latent streak of sentimental Jacobitism that Marlborough and the English army cherished and, oddly enough, felt able to indulge more particularly in their hours of triumph over French supporters of the Jacobite cause'.[89] Biron told Saint-Simon that:

> He was struck by an almost royal magnificence at Prince Eugène's quarters and a shameful parsimony at those of the Duke of Marlborough, who ate the more often at the tables of others; a perfect agreement between the two captains for the conduct of affairs, of which the details fell much more on Eugène; the profound respect of all the generals for the two chiefs, but a tacit preference on the whole for Prince Eugène, without the Duke of Marlborough being at all jealous.[90]

The day after the battle Eugène 'was sure that Marlborough would make no arrangements but what were excellent', and went off to see his mother in Brussels. 'She was glad to see the King humbled who had left her for another woman in her youth, and exiled her in her old age,' wrote Eugène, who had certainly played his own implacable part in the humbling.[91]

In the Galley

There was always a good chance that the victorious Allies would turn their attention to the powerful fortress of Lille, known, not for nothing, as 'Vauban's masterpiece'. The capital of the old county of Flanders, Lille had been taken by Louis after a short siege in 1667 and then fortified by Vauban in 1668–74. Much of the town's fortifications has now gone, but some of the old gates remain. The Paris Gate, built by Simon Vollant, survives, proudly embellished with the arms of France and Lille, crowned by an image of that Victory which seemed so elusive in 1708. The citadel, still sitting like a huge starfish on the north-west edge of the city, covered an area of ninety acres (thirty-six hectares), and its six huge bastions, each protected by a ravelin, had wolfed down sixty million bricks. Its broad ditches were fed from the nearby River Deule. Taking the place would weaken France's administrative grasp on the whole region, significantly reduce the threat from the Dunkirk privateers, many of whom were financed by its merchants, and provide an invaluable bargaining counter for peace negotiations. But not only was Lille formidable in its own right: it was the spider in a web of French fortresses – Ypres, Douai, St-Venant, Tournai and Béthune – and a besieger's lines of communication, along which heavy guns and ammunition must pass, lay within reach of other French garrisons.

The Duke of Berwick reached Givet on the Meuse the day Oudenarde was fought, and soon learnt of the magnitude of the French defeat. He assembled some 9,000 stragglers who had made off southwards, and, recognising that they were too badly shaken to stand in open field, parcelled them up amongst the garrisons. Leaving his army to concentrate at Douai, he went forward to Lille, and did what he could to prepare it for the attack he thought likely. Marlborough, meanwhile, had sent Lottum with thirty battalions and forty squadrons to break the line of French fortifications between Warneton and Comines, not far from the small fortress of Ypres, whose name would be seared onto British history two centuries later. Lottum arrived before Berwick could reach the lines, and set his infantry on to levelling the ramparts. Amongst the foot was Matthew Bishop.

> We slung our firelocks and every man had a shovel in his hand; and when we got to the place appointed, we ran up their works. It was like running up the side of a house. When we got to the top we began to throw [the rampart] down as quickly as possible in order to make way for the army.[92]

Penetrating the lines put Lille within Marlborough's reach, but it did not end his problems. Louis, now conspicuously writing to Burgundy rather than Vendôme, warned that the Allies would probably besiege Lille, but urged him to retain Bruges and Ghent if he could. This would both complicate Marlborough's logistics and leave the French something from the wreckage of Oudenarde. Another pitched battle, though, was out of the question. Vendôme, for his part, doubted if it could be done. He warned the king that pessimistic officers 'have thrown doubt into the spirit of M the Duke of Burgundy . . . From the brigadier to the soldier, good will is equal to all trials, but amongst the general officers it is not the same.'[93] Marlborough recognised that 'their possessing of Ghent, will be a great obstruction to the bringing up of heavy cannon and artillery, so that I fear we shall be obliged to retake that place before we can make any progress'.[94]

His first solution was a daring amphibious enterprise. His army would march to the coast and then follow the Channel as far as the mouth of the Seine, leaving the fortresses on the frontier grinning away at nothing. Major General Thomas Earle, at that moment off the Isle of Wight with eleven embarked battalions, would seize Abbeville as a forward base. The scheme was bound to be too much for the Dutch, and even Eugène, his fingers burnt at Toulon, would not countenance it. The project had foundered by the end of July, when Marlborough was bending every nerve to assembling resources for the siege of Lille.

Just as Cadogan had been the right man to command the advance guard on the sprint to Oudenarde, so now he was the right man to supervise bringing up the battering train which was to concentrate at Brussels, most of the guns coming by water from Antwerp. The eighty siege guns in the Great Convoy required twenty horses apiece and the twenty heavy mortars sixteen, and there were 3,000 four-horse ammunition wagons. 'I received this afternoon yours of yesterday evening,' wrote Marlborough on 31 July, 'and am glad to see you have found means to get the whole number of wagons from the province of Brabant.' Later the same day he told Cadogan that he had just held a meeting with Eugène and the deputies, and that it was imperative to get the whole train up just as soon as he could. He followed this, the very next day, with a warning that he had heard that some horses bringing guns in from Mechelen had 'failed by the way'. Cadogan must not on any account yield up any of his spare horses: 'They must wait with the train to supply any like accidents that may happen.'[95]

On 2 August Marlborough told Secretary of State Boyle that almost all the siege train had now reached Brussels, though he was still very concerned that it might be intercepted on its journey thence. A letter to Cadogan of the same date, in a clerkly hand, bears a concerned postscript in the duke's: 'For God's sake be sure you do not risk the cannon, for I had rather come with the whole army than receive an affront.'[96] Eugène's army covered the first phase of the move from its base near Soignies, and the responsibility then passed to Marlborough's men at

Helchin, as Eugène marched down to begin the investiture of Lille. The convoy was accompanied throughout its journey by the Prince of Hesse-Cassel, commanding an escort of sixteen squadrons and six battalions, and for the first day of its march from Brussels another six squadrons, based in the city, accompanied it. On 3 August Marlborough formally told Boyle that 'the siege of Lille has been thought preferable to any other operation' by unanimous vote of his council of war. The train, toiling along in two columns, covering thirty miles of road space between them, had crossed the Dender at Ath by the ninth, and was at Menin on the thirteenth, the very day that Eugène completed the encirclement of Lille.

Berwick had guessed that the convoy was actually heading for Mons, and so failed to intercept it, but as soon as he realised what was afoot he rushed a final reinforcement into the threatened city, bringing its garrison up to a total of twenty battalions, seven squadrons of dragoons and two hundred spare horses, all under the command of the squat and energetic Marshal Boufflers, hero of the defence of Namur in 1695: there were few more resolute or resourceful defenders. At his elbow was the engineer du Puy Vauban, whose distinguished uncle had built the place. Eugène was to conduct the siege with fifty battalions and ninety squadrons, most of them Dutch and Imperialist, though including one British brigade. Marlborough, with sixty-nine battalions and 140 squadrons, would cover the operation from Helchin, about twenty miles north-east of the city, against interference by French field armies. It seemed a textbook plan.

Careful reading of the documents shows, however, that the capture of Lille was not Marlborough's immediate object. He hoped that the threat to this jewel in the crown of French fortification would force his opponents to offer battle, and on 16 August he outlined his plan in a letter to Eugène.

If the enemy comes into Brabant, as I believe they will, I must go at them head down. I hold myself ready to march to Ath, and as, without doubt, the Duke of Berwick will act in concert with them, and may even join them, I beg Your Highness to hold himself in readiness to execute what we are agreed upon. As soon as we march, four or five days will decide this whole affair by a battle.[97]

Ironically, it was Marlborough's own nephew who warned a truculent Versailles not to rise to the bait and risk a battle which the French would inevitably lose. 'It is sad to see Lille taken,' he told Chamillart, 'but it is sadder still to lose the one army left to us, which can stop the enemy after the loss of Lille.'[98] Uncle and nephew both recognised that a major French defeat would compromise the whole of the Flanders frontier. Without a surviving field army to protect them, the fortresses of the north must inevitably fall one after another, but the loss of Lille need not prove fatal in itself. Modern apostles of manoeuvre warfare argue that a general must 'focus on the enemy, not on the ground', and this is precisely what Marlborough did in the summer of 1708. It was his misfortune that the astute Berwick did precisely the same, and, despite Versailles' urging the marshals to attack, Marlborough never got his battle. He later lamented to Godolphin: 'We shall endeavour all we can to bring the French to a general engagement, but as that is what we shall desire, I take it for granted that is what they will avoid.'[99] So the scene was set, not for the decisive battle that Marlborough sought, but for the most bloody and protracted siege of his career.

As Shakespeare's Richard III cynically observed, short summers lightly have a forward spring. The siege seemed to begin well enough, with Eugène's men breaking ground for their first parallel before the gates of Ste-Marie Madeleine and St-André on Lille's northern front on 22 August. Marlborough told Boyle that this had been accomplished 'with good success', but he was anxious to hear what had become of Major General Earle's embarked force, now that it was no longer making for Abbeville: it was imperative 'to give the enemy a diversion and oblige them to detach that way'.[100] Two weeks later he was vexed 'to see so little prospect of success from our sea-expedition', whose commanders, in another of those hand-wringing councils of war, had decided against a landing in the bay of La Hogue. However, he told Boyle that he had just visited Lille and had ridden out with Eugène to 'mark the place for the field of battle, in case the enemy should . . . attempt to succour the town'. Even if he did not get the battle he hoped for, 'Our siege is so far advanced that the engineers intend tomorrow in the afternoon to attack the counterscarp, wherein if we succeed the town must soon surrender.'[101]

Marlborough was quite wrong, and over the next few weeks the siege went badly. On the evening of 7 September the Allies exploded four mines under the counterscarp, and seized four of the salient angles of the covered way at the cost of 3,000 men, perhaps more than had fallen at Oudenarde and, in the awful way of sieges (the trench warfare of the eighteenth century), with a high proportion of killed to wounded.

Marlborough admitted to Galway that he had hoped that they would either have taken the town by this time, or fought a battle outside it. 'We offered them battle twice but they declined it,' he wrote, 'and their design seems now chiefly to be to distress us for want of provisions, being at a great distance from our magazines . . . but I hope with the blessing of God we shall succeed.'[102] He had assured Sarah that he had chosen such good positions that he was wholly confident of beating the French if they attacked, 'Which makes me think they must be mad if they venture it,' and added that although the enemy probably had more battalions than he did, his were better manned.

In early September the French did indeed conclude that they had no chance of raising the siege without risking a major battle, and thereupon occupied all the crossings of the Scheldt and attempted to make the siege logistically unsustainable, for their possession of Bruges and Ghent already prevented supplies coming in from the west. This, had they but known it, was Marlborough's worst fear. On 17 September he assured Sarah:

> I am so well entrenched that I no way fear their forcing us. But the siege goes on so very slowly, that I am in perpetual fear that it may continue so long, and consequently consume so much stores, that we may at last not have the wherewithal to finish, which would be very cruel. These are my fears, but I desire you will let nobody know them. I long extremely to have this campaign well ended, for of all the campaigns I have made, this has been the most painful. But I am in the galley, and must row as long as the war lasts.[103]

A second assault on the counterscarp was made on 12 September, and the Godfearing Major Blackader, detailed to command four hundred grenadiers, recorded his adventures in characteristic form.

> I was easy and calm, committing myself to God . . . I take the order from him, and not the Brigade-Major . . . I went up and down to see where our attack was to be. Prince Alexander of Württemberg came in about four [p.m.], made the dispositions, and gave us our orders. When he posted me, he bade me speak to the grenadiers and tell them that the Duke of Marlborough and Prince Eugène expected that they would do as they had always done – chase the French, and that it was better to die than to make a false step. I answered 'I hope we shall all do our duty'; so he shook hands with me, and went away.

Near seven, the signals being given by all our cannon and bombs going off together, I gave the word upon the right, '*Grenadiers, in the name of God attack!*' Immediately they sprung over the trenches, and threw their grenades into the counterscarp, but they fell into some confusion. I then ordered out fifty more to sustain them, and went out myself, and in a little time got shot in the arm. I felt that the bone was not broken; and all the other officers being wounded, I thought it my duty to stay a while, and encourage the grenadiers to keep their warm post. About a quarter of an hour afterwards, the fire continuing very hot, I got another shot in the head. I then thought it time to come off . . . I had a great deal of trouble to get out of the trenches in three hours space . . . [104]

On 21 September a major assault by 15,000 men captured most of the ravelin between Bastions II and III, but Eugène himself, snicked above the left eye by a musketball, was among the 1,000 casualties. Marlborough had already confessed to Godolphin:

It is impossible for me to confess the uneasiness I suffer at the ill conduct of our engineers at the siege, where I think everything goes wrong. It would be a cruel thing if we have obliged the enemy to quit all thought of relieving the place by force, which they have done by repassing the Scheldt, we should fail to take it by the ignorance of our engineers, and the want of stores; for we have fired very nearly as much [ammunition] as was demanded for the taking [of] the town and the citadel, and as yet we are not entire masters of the counterscarp; so that to you I may own my despair of ending the campaign, so as in reason we might have expected. [105]

With Eugène wounded, Marlborough needed to attend the siege every day, 'which with the vexation of it going so ill, I am almost dead'. To make matters worse, the Dutch commissaries had now formally told the deputies 'that they have not sufficient stores for the taking of the town'. [106] A letter to Heinsius, written the same day, ended crossly: 'I have the spleen and say no more.' [107]

There was now a chance that Earle's embarked force, unable to create a diversion by being landed on the Normandy coast, could help unlock the main theatre of operations, and on 10 September Marlborough told Boyle that he hoped it would be sent to Ostend. On 21 September Marlborough informed Earle that he knew he had now been ordered to

Ostend, and sent the letter by hand of a well-briefed staff officer, including some detailed instructions from Cadogan. These were amplified three days later, when Earle, now with around 7,000 men, was told to threaten Bruges as strongly as he could, and to 'leave nothing unattempted that is possible to possess yourself of Plassendale'.[108] The French cut the Nieuport canal in several places and flooded much of the surrounding countryside, and then, in the way of that curmudgeonly autumn, Earle was afflicted by gout. Marlborough, having told him what he hoped might be achieved, assured him, 'You will be the best judge upon the spot of what can be effected,' and wished him a speedy recovery.[109]

If the Allies were running short of ammunition outside Lille, Boufflers' men, within its walls, were no better off. On the night of 28 August the chevalier de Luxembourg left Douai with 550 grenadiers and 2,000 troopers, each carrying fifty pounds of gunpowder. A few men were blown up in accidents on the way, but thanks to their Allied field-signs and some Dutch-speaking officers at the head of the column, the Frenchmen bluffed their way through the checkpoint of the Allied lines of circumvallation near Pont-à-Tressin. At that point an officer in the middle of the column unwisely ordered his men to close up in French – '*Serre, serre!*' – and the guard, duly alerted, turned out and opened fire. There were more explosions, but Luxembourg reckoned that he got 40,000 pounds of much-needed powder through to Boufflers.[110]

The presence of Earle's British battalions at Ostend encouraged Marlborough to try a similar venture on a far larger scale. Earle, undaunted by his gout, had managed to drain some of the inundations, bridge the canal at Leffinghe, and assemble a huge convoy of munitions which would go to Lille via Thourout and Roulers. Marlborough sent Cadogan with twenty-six squadrons and twelve battalions to meet him, 'for should this not come safe, I am afraid that we must not flatter ourselves of hoping to get any other'.[111] Hearing that Lamotte was being sent from Bruges to intercept the convoy, Marlborough quickly dispatched another eight battalions and some extra cavalry, but when Lamotte caught the convoy on the wooded heath at Wynendaele, just outside Thourout, on the morning of 28 September he outnumbered its escort by at least two to one. Cadogan had still not come up, and Major General John Webb, a vain and loquacious Tory MP but a brave and seasoned soldier, was in command.

Lamotte had been briefed by Vendôme that the capture of the convoy was absolutely critical to French fortunes, and that he was to 'march on the enemy, strong or weak, and to attack them'. He drew up his infantry in the space of perhaps 1,000 yards between two woods, facing the main road near Wynendaele château, and could clearly see the convoy making off behind Webb's infantry, formed up in three lines ready to receive him. A long cannonade went well enough, although Webb wisely made his men lie down, so lost fewer men than he might. When Lamotte at last thrust forwards, his infantry promptly splintered in his hands. Most of his regiments were French-speaking Netherlanders who were now not sure where their real interests lay, and the repeated thump of the platoon volleys all along Webb's line was too much for them.

Lamotte complained that they 'behaved badly. Instead of charging with the bayonet as they had been ordered, they shot, and shot too soon.' Then, 'at the first discharge they made, our infantry began to fold by the left and fall back to the right, and all the lines were mixed up without it being possible to rally them for the whole of the action'. Lamotte paid handsome tribute to the fact that 'I did the impossible to rally our infantry,' and he was sure that 'the enemy lost more men than us'.[112] In fact Webb had lost about 1,000, most from the bombardment which preceded the attack, but perhaps 2,000 Frenchmen had been hit, and the convoy creaked its way to the safety of the besiegers' camp. It is not too much to say that this encounter sealed the fate of Lille.

Cadogan rode up with his cavalry after the battle was won, asked Webb whether he should charge the French, and was wisely advised not to. When he told Godolphin of the victory on 1 October Marlborough reported that: 'Webb and Cadogan have on this occasion, as they will always do, behaved themselves extremely well.' However, the Prince of Hesse-Cassel, stationed the other side of Lille and with no personal knowledge of the battle, told the States-General of 'the advantage which the troops, lately arrived from England, sustained by those of Mons. Cadogan . . . have obtained over . . . the troops which attacked them'. Winston S. Churchill suggests that it was this report which reached London first, and gave rise to the *Gazette*'s brief description of the action.[113] The story is improbable, for the *Gazette* entry is fuller than Hesse-Cassel's account. It is more likely that Cardonnel had dashed off a first report before the information was complete and, given that Cadogan had been meant to command the force, assumed that he had arrived in time to do so. The next *Gazette* corrected the error, and Marlborough had already congratulated Webb, attributing the victory 'chiefly to your good conduct and resolution', and promising to 'do you justice at home'.[114] He told Godolphin that he would nominate some generals for promotion at the end of the campaign, 'which will be a mark of her favour and their merit'.[115] Webb, he was sure, certainly deserved to be made a lieutenant general.

Webb, however, was annoyed at the earlier implied slight, and his political backers prolonged a row that might easily have blown over. Although he was received by the queen 'very kindly, and with a great deal of distinction', he refused to return to the Continent without his promotion. The government thought about increasing the scale of the promised reward by giving him a governorship, as well as the lieutenant generalcy which would materialise in a general promotion at the New Year, but nothing suitable was available at the moment. The Tories would not leave the matter alone, and set about getting the Commons to pass a vote of thanks to Webb, 'Which was brought on,' grumbled Godolphin, 'not so much out of any real kindness to him, but that one of their leaders might have that handle to show as much malice as they could to 39 [Marlborough] and to Mr Montgomery [Godolphin].'[116] Nor was it Webb's nature to forgive and forget. He was soon very much the Professional Veteran, steering every conversation unerringly round to Wynendaele, causing even the Duke of Argyll, his political ally, to lament, after Webb was wounded at Malplaquet the following year, that he had not been hit in the tongue, which would have done everyone a service. Richard Kane probably spoke for many when he maintained that 'a great deal was owing to Lamotte's ill conduct; and Webb spoiled all, by boasting too much of it'.[117]

The siege of Lille, meanwhile, lumbered on as creakily as the wagons of Webb's convoy. Maintaining communication with his logistic base at Ostend, now periodically isolated behind floodwaters which enabled French gunboats to dart in to shoot at ammunition wagons, was the key to Marlborough's success. Vendôme had sworn to Louis that he would cut the narrow lifeline between Lille and Ostend, and in early October Marlborough took the army out to Wynendaele to see him off. There is no doubt that Eugène had been ill served by his engineers, the Huguenots du Muy and Le Vasseur des Roques, but equally, there is no doubt that these gentlemen learnt from their mistakes. The Saxon general Schulenberg tells us that:

> Six weeks after the opening of the trenches the engineers appreciated that they had opened the attack on too broad a front, and tried to breach the fortifications at too many points, namely twelve. It would have been better to confine the breaching fire to the two main bastions and the intervening curtain.[118]

On the eighteenth Marlborough told Sunderland that they had at long last established breaching batteries atop the counterscarp – 'nearly fifty pieces of cannon . . . beside a battery of mortars' – and hoped to start work on breaching the main walls the following day. Sadly, that brave old warrior Overkirk would not live to see the ramparts of Lille crumble under Allied fire: he 'died here yesterday', wrote Marlborough, 'and is very much lamented as well in the army as by all that knew him'.[119] On 22 October, after a day's battering, the troops were at their stations to mount the final assault, which Marlborough knew 'will cost a good many lives', when they heard Boufflers' drummers beating the chamade, the request for a parley. Boufflers agreed to give up the town if allowed two days to retire into the citadel with his surviving troops, some 4,500 men, and to send his sick and wounded to Douai.

The fall of the city enabled the defenders to hold a much smaller area, but the attackers, too, could draw in their lines, freeing more troops to guard against attempts at relief. The war did not stop elsewhere simply because the cannon still thundered before Lille. Marlborough was aware that French agents were at work in Brussels, and warned the governor, Colonel Pascal, to be on his guard and, above all, to keep sending his cavalry deep into the countryside: 'Make them go out all the time, I beg you, without relaxing.' It is an index of Marlborough's responsibilities that the same letter confirmed his pardon of Private John Donia of Sarrablanca's Regiment, who was to have been shot, and instructions that a German nobleman with a French commission was to be arrested 'without fuss' if he reappeared in Malines.[120] The Elector of Bavaria had appeared before Brussels, but Pascal, confident that he had neither the troops nor the time to mount a proper siege, sent a courteous reply to his summons to surrender, and sat tight to await help.

Despite 'the backwardness in the siege of the citadel of Lille', Marlborough knew that because of the threat to Brussels he was now 'obliged to attempt to force our passage over the Scheldt', even at the risk of reducing the forces before Lille to a bare minimum.[121] On the morning of 26 October, after a night march, he staged a slickly handled attack on the crossings of the Scheldt from Gavre in the north to Hauterive in the south. He had first sent his quartermasters to Courtrai with very public orders to arrange accommodation for himself and his generals so that they could pause before the next phase of the campaign, a thrust westwards against Bruges and Ghent. 'This farce was so well managed,' observed his aide de camp Colonel Molesworth, 'that our whole army was imposed upon by it, and I'm confident that all our generals except those few whom it was necessary to admit into the bottom of our design, really thought it was intended (as was given out) to canton and refresh the army for a while.'[122] Lieutenant General de Hautefort, commanding thirty-two battalions and thirty squadrons, decided that he could not hold his entrenchments outside Oudenarde with the Allies over the river in strength, but as the French fell back Marlborough's cavalry caught up with their baggage train and took 1,000 prisoners. At Brussels the Elector did not stand on ceremony. Leaving twelve cannon and two mortars, as well as eight hundred immobile wounded, he made off to Mons.

Keeping the army in the field long after it would normally have dispersed into winter quarters meant that there was no let-up in its remorseless appetite for food and fodder. On 10 November Marlborough warned the Earl of Stair that he had had complaints of

> the great looseness and disorderly conduct of the troops that are with you, particularly the horse, in plundering the churches, and all the whole country round about, I cannot forbear sending this to you to desire that all possible care may be taken to prevent it, and that some examples may immediately be made by execution, and that public notice of it given to the country that they shall be indemnified, otherwise I fear we may in great measure be disappointed of the hopes we had of a good quantity of corn from your parts. I believe that it would likewise be necessary that a guard be posted at the bridge with a careful, severe officer to search the troopers and others, and to take from them whatever they have plundered in the country, in order to its being restored to the owners.

As was often his habit, Marlborough summarised the letter in a short postscript in his own hand, transmitting what we would now call 'commander's intent'. 'All our happiness,' he wrote, 'depends upon your getting a good quantity of corn.'[123]

The reduction of the citadel of Lille proceeded remorselessly, and on 9 December the gallant Boufflers at last came to terms. Marlborough had generously declared that he would allow him to propose any reasonable conditions, and so the garrison was to march out with the honours of war 'on the 13th of the present month, at nine in the morning, by way of the Porte Dauphin, with arms and baggage and horses, drums beating, musket-balls in mouth, matches burning at both ends, enough ammunition for 20 rounds per man, flags flying . . .' Six cannon, three twelve-pounders and three eight-pounders, were to accompany the garrison, and the Allies were to provide it with safe conduct, by the shortest route, to the nearest French fortress. This was more than gentlemanly flummery. It was worth giving Boufflers good terms to get him out of the citadel, for there was still work to be done elsewhere. And, while Marlborough was happy to be generous, the conditions affirmed that the French were to pay all debts, public and private, incurred during the siege, and were to leave three officers in Allied hands till these had been discharged.[124] Goslinga, who had clashed with Marlborough on the advance to the Scheldt, did not share the general delight. The defence of the citadel 'was not remarkable for any vigorous action, that one might have expected from such a large garrison . . . There must have been secret reasons, and a lack of necessary things, which contributed to this prompt capitulation.'[125]

The fall of Lille did not end the campaign. Although Goslinga assures us that he sowed the idea of retaking Bruges and Ghent in Marlborough's mind, it is certain that Marlborough had always regarded the recapture of these cities as essential, and on 6 November he assured Godolphin that he still hoped for 'further success' after the citadel fell, although he feared that it was very late in the year. However, 'the disagreeableness of the French having it in their powers to see all our letters' made him a cautious correspondent.[126] But even before the citadel had surrendered he reminded Godolphin that 'I have formerly told you that we must end this campaign with the retaking of Ghent, if possible.'[127] He was even more positive three days later: 'Yet I think we must have Ghent and Bruges, cost what it will.'[128] Winston S. Churchill (though as *parti pris* as those historians who take their cue from Goslinga) is right to suggest that Marlborough encouraged Goslinga to think of the idea as his own so as to increase its attractiveness to the Dutch.

Scarcely was the ink dry on Boufflers' capitulation than Marlborough moved against Ghent, held by Lamotte with thirty-four battalions and nineteen squadrons, but now with a worried population which sent a delegation of 'clergy, nobility and citizens' to plead that he would not bombard the place. He told Sarah, 'with all my heart I wish it could be taken without doing hurt, but in kindness to our own soldiers we must use all means for the reducing in the shortest possible time'.[129] At last fortune, scowling for so much of the autumn, beamed on him: a sudden thaw enabled him to move his siege train by water, and on Christmas Eve he opened his trenches before Ghent.

Mrs Christian Davies had laid aside her dragoon's coat after Ramillies and become a sutler. Riding her little mare with its provision bags, she had a narrow escape from a dreadful fate when Colonel Cholmondley's black stallion (small but perfectly formed) had, 'like a brute as he was, began to be very rude with my poor beast, and in his rough courtship broke me four bottles of wine'. Her husband Richard was sent forward with the party that first night, 'ordered to lay the [marker] ropes and direct the cutting of the trenches'. She tells us that she 'always accompanied my husband, however dangerous it was', but was stopped by his commanding officer until the trench-line was laid out, and

> he with his companions were retired into a turnip field, and lay flat on their bellies, expecting the trench, which the workmen were throwing up, to cover them. Major Irwin told me where he was, and both the major and Lieutenant Stretton begged hard of me for some beer; but as I had but three flasks, and feared my husband might want, I had no pity for anyone else: as the night was very cold, and the ground wet, I had also provided myself with a bottle of brandy, and another of gin, for my dear Richard's refreshment.[130]

Her husband's comrades were fortunate, for Private Deane recalled that 'the enemy fired both cannon and small shot all night'. In 1st Foot Guards the fire killed the veteran Colonel Charles Gorsuch, commanding its two battalions, Captain Nicholas Hearne and a private soldier. It was, though, small loss for having 'entrenched ourselves to admiration, and very near their palisades too'.[131]

On 27 December the Allies took Fort Rouge, on the northern side of the city, and planted their batteries. Lamotte, perhaps fearing that his infantry, which had performed so poorly at Wynendaele, would not stand a storm, at once asked for terms, agreeing to march out unless relieved within a week. Louis, furious at this 'premature' capitulation, had him court-martialled. As Marlborough had predicted, 'I believe Monsieur de Lamotte will not be able to give good reason for what he has done,' and he never served again. On 3 January 1709 Marlborough mused on the way his luck had changed.

> I was yesterday from ten in the morning till six at night seeing the garrison of Ghent, and all that belonged to them, march by me. It is

astonishing to see so great numbers of good men look on, and suffer a place of this consequence to be taken at this season with so little a loss. As soon as they knew I had possession of the gates of the town they took the resolution of abandoning Bruges [and retiring right along the coast as far as Dunkirk]. The campaign is now ended to my heart's own desire, and as the hand of God is so visible in this whole matter, I hope her Majesty will think it due to him to return public thanks, and at the same time to implore his blessing on the next campaign.[132]

8

Decline, Fall and Resurrection

Failed Peace, Thwarted Ambition

While Marlborough was racing for Oudenarde and battering at Lille, the Duumvirs were inexorably losing their grasp on government. A biographer who sought to present his readers with Marlborough's political and military identities in parallel would be forced to intersperse correspondence on strategic policy, tactical detail, administrative minutiae, cabinet reshuffles, borough-mongering and monarch-management. The fact that no reference has been made here to Marlborough's political tribulations does not, however, mean that they were not both real and present. A psychologist considering his behaviour after he received news of the loss of Ghent and Bruges might opine that those events were simply the trigger for the breakdown that followed, and that Marlborough had simply been doing too much for too long to tolerate the sudden and unexpected appearance of a new crisis. This, indeed, is why his well-wishers, like Natzmer and Grumbkow, found it hard to link the crisis itself to what seemed to them an extreme response.

Relations between Sarah and the queen went from bad to worse, and, with more unwise insinuations of lesbianism from the prurient pen of Arthur Maynwaring, from worse to impossible. The final breakdown came on 19 August 1708, the day of thanksgiving for the victory of Oudenarde. Prince George, beset by chronic asthma, was in slow decline, and the queen had been at Windsor nursing him. It was a hot day, and when she changed her clothes at St James's Palace, Anne took exception to the heavy jewels that Sarah, as groom of the stole, had laid out for her. Sarah interpreted her refusal to wear the jewels as evidence of Abigail Masham's influence, and the two women had a blazing row in the royal coach on their way to St Paul's Cathedral. It apparently ended with Sarah telling the queen to 'be quiet' as they reached their destination, so that they would not be overheard by the onlookers. Sarah later tried to make

407

amends, ending what came close to a letter of apology with the assertion that 'I shall never forget that I am your subject, nor ever cease to be a faithful one'; but the damage was done.[1]

Anne recognised that at the same time that her relationship with Sarah – groom of the stole, first lady of the bedchamber, and keeper of the privy purse – had collapsed, she needed to retain Marlborough's services. Yet he had made it clear to her that the continuing pressures of command were imposing a burden that he found all but intolerable. If she dismissed Sarah, then Marlborough might simply retire. Things were not helped by the fact that Sarah was now hard at work on the construction of Marlborough House, on Pall Mall just to the east of St James's Palace. She wanted it (in contrast to the infinitely grander Blenheim) to be 'strong, plain and convenient', and Christopher Wren and his son responded with a two-storeyed house in brick with rusticated stone quoins. In order to pay for it, Sarah, with the queen's knowledge, borrowed money from the privy purse, probably a total of £20,800, for which, as Anne's biographer politely observes, 'No repayments are shown in the extant records.'[2]

Although the political nation paused to watch the progress of the siege of Lille, recorded in detail in the *London Gazette*, the grim reaper did not check his stride. In early October Prince George was so ill that the queen could not attend the christening of Abigail Masham's daughter, and on 25 October Godolphin warned Sarah that: 'The Prince seems to be in no good way at all (in my opinion) as to his health, and I think the Queen herself now seems much more apprehensive of his condition, than I have formerly remembered upon the same occasion.' It is a reflection on the state of Sarah's relationship with the queen that she heard this from Godolphin, who had earlier told her that the leading Whig Tom Wharton 'seemed very much to wish that Mrs Freeman would come to town. All my answer was, that I wished it at least as much.'[3] On the twenty-sixth Godolphin complained to Marlborough that he was not writing often enough ('how disagreeable it is to see 3 Holland mails come in successively without one letter from you'), and concluded that Prince George

> has such a general weakness and decay of nature upon him, that very few people that see him have any hopes of his recovery. The Queen herself . . . begins to think 'tis hardly possible for him to hold out long. I pray God her own health may not suffer by her perpetual watching and attendance upon him.[4]

George died early on the afternoon of 28 October. The queen, 'who continued kissing him until the very moment the breath went out of his body', had to be helped away by Sarah. Godolphin warned Marlborough that the queen's grief created 'a new additional affliction which our circumstances did not need', and said that unless he could return to England without delay 'it will be next to impossible to prevent ruin'.[5] For Marlborough the blow was as much personal as political. He had known Prince George since 1683, and the two men had always got on very well. Moreover, the Danes had provided one of the most reliable of the Allied contingents, and George had helped ensure that it stayed in the field. In May 1706, for instance, he told Marlborough:

> I am very glad the Danish troops have been assisting to you, and hope that they will always do their duty however others behave themselves, nothing shall be wanting on my part to persuade their master to follow the interest of England in everything.[6]

The duke confessed that the news of the prince's death 'made such an impression on me that I have not been well for several days, insomuch that I was obliged to march last night in a litter, but have been all this day on horseback. I pray God to enable HM to support this great afflic-tion.'[7] Sarah, however, was little help to her mistress in the hour of her need. She declined the queen's order to fetch Abigail Masham, and as they were leaving St James's arm in arm, noted disparagingly that Anne 'found she had the strength to bend down towards Mrs Masham like a sail'. The fact that the new widow 'ate a very good dinner' surprised her, and she 'could not help smiling' when the queen, addressing her as 'dear Mrs Freeman' for the last time, wrote to say that she had ordered 'a great many Yeomen of the Guard to carry the Prince's dear body that it may not be let fall, the Great Stairs being very steep and slippery'.[8] There is no doubt that Sarah's 'unsympathetic analysis of the Queen's grief is contradicted by every contemporary authority'.[9]

The queen was at first too prostrated by grief to oppose further Whig advances, but as the year went on she had recovered sufficient strength to fight a valiant rearguard action against the replacement of the moderate Earl of Pembroke, who had taken over as head of the Admiralty Commission not long after Prince George's death, by the Whig grandee the Earl of Orford. The parliamentary session of 1708–09, whose first half was missed by Marlborough, did little but define Britain's minimum terms for peace: Louis XIV should recognise Anne's royal title and the

Protestant succession, order Philip V back from Spain, expel the Old Pretender and demolish the harbour and defences of Dunkirk. The French king was in such financial difficulties that he had had the silver furniture at Versailles melted down, and there was widespread belief that he would be forced to accept a humiliating peace.

French and Allied delegates met at The Hague in April 1709. The Allies had agreed a list of forty terms which, in summary, would indeed have embodied a wholesale defeat for Louis. Marlborough, one of the British delegates, was sure that the French would accept, although he noted with irritation that Torcy, the French foreign minister, had been heartened by news of yet another Allied defeat in Portugal, which, he told Sarah, 'makes our negotiation move slowly'.[10] Overall, though, he assured her that:

> there is not doubt of it ending in a good peace, but for some little time it must not be spoke of. You must have in readiness the sideboard of plate, and you must let Lord Treasurer know that since the Queen came to the crown I have not had neither a canopy and chair of state, which now of necessity I must have, so the Wardrobe should immediately have orders; and I beg you will take care to have it made so it may serve as part of a bed when I have done with it here, which I hope will be the end of this summer, so that I may enjoy your dear company in quiet, which is the greatest satisfaction I am capable of having. I have so great a head that you will excuse my saying no more by this post.[11]

Marlborough's hopes of cutting a fine figure at the formal signing of the peace treaty were to be dashed. Torcy, 'not having powers sufficient to agree all we insist upon', sent the preliminary articles to Louis for his consideration.

The king was at his lowest ebb, well aware of the damage done by the war, a particularly harsh winter, and failed harvests. The frost killed vines in Provence, wine froze in its glasses at Versailles, and Mrs Christian Davies recalled that, not long after the capture of Ghent, 'two of our sentinels were found frozen to death'. As Torcy tells us: 'Sensibly affected by the distress of his people', Louis 'thought that he could not purchase peace for them too dearly'. Yet the Allies, notably by their insistence on 'No Peace without Spain', had pitched that price too high. Conditions 4 and 37 of the articles bound Louis to hand over Spain within two months or face a renewal of the war. He could not in honour order Philip to vacate his throne, and would not consent to using French armies to expel him from it. After intense soul-searching, in early June he rejected the Allied terms, and summoned his people to make a final effort to win peace with honour. It was a phenomenal achievement: one of his biographers is right to maintain that 'The Revolutionaries of 1792–93 did not do much better.' 'I have conducted this war with hauteur and pride worthy of this kingdom,' he told his people.

> With the valour of my nobility and the zeal of my subjects, I have suc-ceeded in the enterprises I have undertaken for the good of the state . . . I have considered proposals for peace and no one has done more than I to secure it . . . I can no longer see any alternative to take, other than to prepare to defend ourselves. To make them see that a united France is greater than all the powers assembled by force and artifice to overwhelm it, at this hour I have put into effect the most extraordinary measures that we have used on similar occasions to procure the money indispensable for the glory and security of the state . . . I come to ask for your counsels and your aid in this encounter that involves your safety. By the efforts that we shall make together, our foes will understand that we are not to be put upon. The aid that I ask of you will oblige them to make a peace honourable for us, lasting . . . and satisfactory for the princes of Europe.[12]

These were high words, not all of them honest, but they helped inspire genuine sympathy for a monarch who had confronted so much personal misfortune – and who was soon to lose both his son and his eldest grandson. There are moments in French history when military defeat has summoned up an unexpected reserve of national strength. The threadbare citizen armies of the new Republic were to trounce the pipe-clayed warriors of old Europe at the century's close; in 1870–71 the Armies of National Defence fought with a determination that often astonished their opponents; and in 1916 the defence of Verdun tapped a vein of resolve and self-sacrifice whose outpouring bleached France for another generation. In 1709 the process was neither instant nor comprehensive, and Cadogan was to write at the year's close that:

> Great numbers of deserters come in daily, they are half starved and quite naked, and give such an account of the misery the French troops are in as could not be believed were it not confirmed by the reports and letters from all their garrison towns on the frontier.[13]

Yet a fresh spirit began to animate the French army, associated with its new commander in Flanders, Marlborough's old comrade in arms, Claude Louis Hector, duc de Villars. Like many great generals before and since, Marshal Villars was not a comfortable fellow. His willingness to seek battle had often vexed a more cautious Versailles; an irascible man, he was hard on his subordinates, though he never asked more of them than he would freely give himself; and, no less to the point, he got on so badly with Max Emmanuel of Bavaria that he could not be used in Flanders as long as the Elector was there. With Vendôme out of favour, Burgundy a broken reed, Boufflers ill and Max Emmanuel tainted by failure at Brussels, Villars was simply too competent for his boldness or his hot temper to exclude him from command in France's hour of need. 'All I have left is my confidence in God and in you, my outspoken friend,' said Louis, and his confidence was not misplaced.[14] Nor was this all. On 10 June Louis sacked his billiards partner Chamillart, and replaced him as war minister with the capable and energetic Voisin.

The collapse of peace negotiations saddened Marlborough, who assured Sarah, even as he was on his way to the army to begin a campaign he had hoped never to fight, that:

> I can't but think that some way will be found before the end of this month for our agreeing, everybody having approved of the pleasuring thoughts of peace . . . I confess I thought it sure, believing it very much in the interest of France to have agreed with us; but since they seem to think otherwise, I hope God has a further blessing in store. I was in hopes to have had the happiness of being with you before the winter; I wish I could still flatter myself with these thoughts. I do wish you all happiness and speed with your building at London, but beg that may not hinder you from pressing forward the building at Blenheim, for we are not so much master of that as of the other.[15]

Marlborough's concerns about Blenheim, whose completion depended on the grant of public money, reflected a deeper worry about the future. The Whigs were at the height of their ascendancy, but the Duumvirs knew that they had prejudiced their relationship with the queen, who still craved a balanced administration, by packing the government with Whigs. The death of Prince George and the increasing alienation of Sarah worsened matters, and although the Harley–Masham back door into the queen's closet was not yet fully open, it was evidently ajar.

In the spring of 1709 Marlborough tried to tighten his grip on royal favour and gain public affirmation of his status as military leader of the Grand Alliance by persuading the queen to appoint him captain general for life. Unusually, he does not seem to have consulted Godolphin, his closest political associate; possibly because he knew that Godolphin's own hold on power was weakening, and that securing the captain generalcy might enable him to swim while Godolphin sank. Neither did he speak to Sarah, probably because he deduced that any interventions she might make would be counterproductive. He weeded his own papers of most of the references which might have helped historians, but the painstaking forensic work of Henry L. Snyder, doyen of Marlburian scholars, now enables us to go well beyond the surmises of Marlborough's early biographers.

Marlborough had always disliked party politics, but the Harley affair of early 1708 had, in the view of Arthur Maynwaring, shown him that 'it will not be enough hereafter, to make no enemies. Something more of warmth and zeal will be requisite towards those men that will always applaud his actions and who, I verily believe, though they are sometimes a little forward and angry, do yet really love his person.'[16] In short, urged Maynwaring, Marlborough should recognise his true friends and give more support to the Whigs, and he did indeed make a special trip to England to get Anne to include Lords Somers and Wharton in her cabinet. That autumn, stuck fast at Lille, Marlborough could only see, as Professor Snyder relates, 'dismal prospects for the future. His support of the Whigs had placed him in a more vulnerable position, and he knew that if the Queen and her secret counsellors ever found the strength to turn out the ministry he too would suffer the loss of his places.'[17]

The Tories had used their parliamentary congratulation of Major General Webb to disparage the duke, and Maynwaring suggested that Marlborough's supporters should riposte with some 'Addition of honour . . . and not of wealth'. The somewhat sketchy evidence suggests that Marlborough made his first request for the captain generalcy for life when he was in England in early 1709, and, after the queen's temporising response, for there was no precedent for the grant, repeated it later that year. Of the four letters he wrote to Anne on the subject only one, of 10 October NS, has survived.

> God Almighty knows with what zeal and duty I have served you for all this many years, and all Europe as well as yourself are witnesses how far God has blessed my endeavours ever since your accession to the Crown.

I have for some time with the greatest mortification imaginable observed your Majesty's change from Lady Marlborough to Mrs Masham, and the several indignities Mrs Masham has made her suffer, of which I am much more sensible than of any misfortune that could have befallen myself, which has made me to take the resolution of retiring as soon as this war shall be ended. I was assured last winter of what I am convinced is true, that Mrs Masham has assured Mr Harley and some of his wretches that let my services or success be whatever they would, from thenceforward I should receive no encouragement from your Majesty . . . In order to know how far your Majesty's intentions went in this project, I acquainted you of the desire I had of having that mark of your favour that my commission might be for life. You were pleased to judge it not proper.[18]

The queen replied on 25 October OS by telling Marlborough that she was not surprised to see him 'so incensed against poor Masham since the Duchess of Marlborough is so'. She thought she had told him, in a previous letter, why she had refused his request, but concluded by saying that if he was of the same mind when he returned to England at the campaign's close, 'I will comply with your desires.'[19]

By the time he returned, however, the Junto peer Lord Orford had been forced upon the queen, and the influential clergyman Dr Henry Sacheverell had preached two inflammatory sermons attacking the government, the 1688 settlement and 'by implication the Hanoverian succession'.[20] The government duly impeached Sacheverell, and although he was found guilty after a divisive trial, his punishment was nominal, and it was in effect a defeat for the Whigs. When Godolphin told Marlborough that Sacheverell had been 'found guilty of high crimes and misdemeanours' by a mere seventeen votes in the Lords, he added that the Duke of Somerset, a great lord of the middle party, always high in the queen's esteem since he had loaned her Syon House half a lifetime ago, had not voted. Somerset had claimed to be sick, said Godolphin, 'but I fancy 'twas only profound wisdom kept him away from the House'. 'So all this bustle and fatigue,' he lamented, 'ends in no more but a suspension for 3 years from the pulpit, and the burning of his sermons at the old Exchange.'[21]

By the time of the Sacheverell verdict worse was already afoot. Early in 1710, when the Earl of Essex died, the queen gave his post of constable of the Tower to Lord Rivers, and his colonelcy of a regiment of dragoons to Abigail's brother Jack Hill, without consulting Marlborough, her captain general. After a period of intense political crisis the queen gave way over Jack Hill, encouraging Marlborough to set the seal on his victory by again requesting the captain generalcy for life, this time demanding both the appointment and Abigail Masham's removal from court by means of a parliamentary address. The scheme misfired grotesquely. The Tories in both Houses opposed the measure on principle, and many moderates were swayed by strong personal loyalty to the monarch. The Duke of Argyll, Marlborough's political opponent and personal rival (though also a general serving under his command), declared that 'her Majesty need not be in pain; for he would undertake, whenever she commanded, to seize the Duke at the head of his troops, and bring him away either dead or alive'.[22] Marlborough did his best to pretend that he had never supported the measure, but was forced to leave for the 1710 campaign in February, unusually early, to spare himself further humiliation.

There was more to the queen's repeated refusal to grant Marlborough the captain generalcy for life than her antipathy towards Sarah or her desire not to be bullied. She believed that any grant would be unconstitutional unless ratified by Parliament, and thought that the creation of a permanent captain general by a Whig-dominated Parliament was a most dangerous precedent. Even the Whig leader Lord Somers, lord president of the council and a distinguished lawyer, warned the queen of the danger she ran if Marlborough's friends managed to force their way by parliamentary address. The Tories, with their traditional antipathy to a standing army and readiness to see their own times in the light of the 1640s, began to snipe at Marlborough as 'Oliver' or 'King John'. The ensuing propaganda war did Marlborough significant damage, though there is not a jot of evidence to suggest that his ambitions went beyond the captain generalcy.

Although the squabble went on from early 1709 till the beginning of 1710, even in its early stages the queen began to flex her muscles and to take a personal hand in senior army appointments. Early in 1709 the experienced Major General George Macartney, one of Marlborough's favourite commanders, was appointed governor of Jamaica and selected to command an expedition to Newfoundland, part of which had been taken by the French. In May, however, he was accused of raping his housekeeper, a clergyman's widow. Rape was then a capital offence, and although Macartney escaped the full penalty of the law, the queen, who took the advice of the Bishop of London, saw that he was cashiered for 'disgraceful conduct', though he was allowed to sell his regiment. Marlborough made his own feelings in the matter clear by letting

Macartney stay with the army as a volunteer, and he fought so valiantly at Malplaquet with Sir Thomas Prendergast's Regiment that the queen forgave him, giving him the colonelcy made vacant by Prendergast's death in the battle. He did not stay forgiven for long, for he was one of the three senior officers dismissed for drinking damnation to the new ministry in November 1710. 'The orders for their stripping were passed through Marlborough,' writes Scouller, 'who had to deliver them unopened.'[23] So far had the mighty fallen.

In mid-1709 Marlborough felt that his powers as captain general were not what they had been. From his camp before Tournai he wrote to Robert Walpole, the Secretary at War, enclosing

> a memorial delivered to me by Captain Chudleigh of Colonel Bretton's regiment, complaining of the great hardship he lies under by a much younger officer being made major over his head during his absence in France.
>
> You have likewise a memorial of Major Wedderburn of Colonel Sutton's regiment. There are so many more instances of the like nature, which deserve to be considered and redressed, that I know not what to advise on it: but I hope that when I come home in the winter, H.M. will think it fit to refer all these matters to the general officers, that proper measures may be taken to relieve those that are prejudiced, and make the officers of the army more easy in the service.[24]

A Very Murdering Battle: Malplaquet

Even without the painful recognition that his hold on the queen's affections had been loosened, Marlborough would have begun the campaign of 1709 at a disadvantage, because he had genuinely believed that the French would accept the Allied peace terms. Yet the early spring was not wasted, and Cadogan was ready to put the army into the field, whether to fight or to occupy territory given up by the French under the terms of the peace. On 22 April he cheerfully reported that he could 'assemble the army at the time your Grace is pleased to direct it . . . Fine weather has forwarded everything, and a great deal of the corn which was thought dead begins to spring out again, so that suffering the assembly of the army for eight or ten days is as long as any may require.'[25] On the following day Marlborough told Major General Palmes, then at Vienna, to meet the Duke of Savoy and 'press H.R.H. in his preparations to take the field', for if the French did not make peace, then 'if we neglect the opportunity of this campaign, while the enemy's circumstances are reduced to so low an ebb, it is to be doubted whether we may ever have the like again of reducing them to reason'.[26] He was doomed, yet again, to be disappointed in the Duke of Savoy, who took so long to agree arrangements with the Imperialists that French troops were able to redeploy from Spain to Dauphiné to parry his thrust.

By the time the Allied army did actually need to assemble, though, both time and weather had worked in favour of the French. 'We have rain every day,' Marlborough told Godolphin, 'which gives us the spleen, and is of great advantage to Marshal Villars, since it gives him time to finish his lines, which he is working at the head of his army.' Villars was closer to his soldiers than his illustrious predecessors, and knew just how near to starvation they were. 'I am humble,' he told Louis' wife Madame de Maintenon, 'when I see the backbreaking labour men perform without food.'[27]

When Marlborough took the field in June, Villars had already been hard at work. He had some 128 battalions and 247 squadrons arrayed in a strong line of field defences between the fortresses of Douai on the Scarpe and St-Venant on the Lys. Much of his infantry was in a strong fortified camp at La Bassée, with most of his cavalry drawn up behind it and a strong detachment thrown out to watch his right flank. 'He has La Bassée on his front leaving Lens to his rear,' Marlborough wrote to Godolphin.

> His flanks are covered by two little rivers which have marshy grounds to them. By this situation you will see that he has no mind to offer battle but on very advantageous terms . . . Their people are in great misery, but by what we hear from Paris all the money they have will be employed for the subsisting of their armies. And I think it is plain by the entrenching of Monsieur de Villars' army that they will be upon the defensive, which they would not do, were they not sure of subsistence. If we should be so fortunate as to have an occasion of beating them, we could not, for want of forage and provisions enter into France, but by the sea coast, and then we should be in want of your assistance.[28]

Godolphin assured him that he could indeed help with supplies. If Marlborough took his army to the coast it could be supplied with bread for 40–50,000 men with little notice, and agreed that a move along the Channel coast offered better prospects than a thrust into Artois, 'where the enemy has eaten or destroyed the greatest part of it'.[29]

In late June Marlborough had 164 battalions and 271 squadrons in the plain of Lens, outnumbering Villars by 110,000 men to about 90,000, and far better sustained. The general dearth, however, made life uncomfortable even for the Allies. Although the weather had now improved, 'there is no straw in this country, so that the poor men have been obliged to lie on the wet ground'.[30] On 24 June Marlborough and Eugène looked at the French position, and their conclusions, as he admitted to Sarah, were unsurprising. 'If it had been reasonable,' he wrote,

> this letter would have brought you the news of a battle, but Prince Eugène, myself and all the generals did not think it advisable to run so great a hazard, considering their camp, as well as their having strengthened it so by their entrenchments, so that we have resolved on the siege of Tournai, and accordingly marched last night, and have invested it when they expected our going to another place, [so] that they have not half the troops in the town that they should have to defend themselves well, which makes us hope it will not cost us dear. I am so sleepy that I can say no more but that [I] am entirely yours.[31]

Goslinga maintains that Marlborough would have preferred to besiege Ypres, but Eugène and the rest of the council of war preferred Tournai. Jinking swiftly to invest Tournai was certainly a tactical masterstroke, achieved by striking camp at tattoo on the evening of 15 June and marching all night. 'Nay, he had done it so privately,' wrote an admiring Private Deane, 'that the inhabitants of the town nor soldiers in the garrison knew nothing of it till next day at 3 o'clock in the morning – and then was discovered by a convoy of bread wagons coming innocently out of town laden with provisions for their army'.[32] Even Goslinga admitted that it had gone surprisingly well, and that 'M de Villars was caught head down in the basket'.[33]

The move may, however, have made less strategic sense. Marlborough had recently asserted that the French, at their last gasp, should be pressed as hard as possible, and sieges, no matter how successful, were unlikely to cause their collapse. Although the written record is silent on the subject, we may doubt whether a thrust along the Channel coast, sustained by seaborne logistics, would have appealed to either Eugène or the Dutch. One of Marlborough's most astute biographers argues that the abandonment of an offensive reflected Eugène's influence, 'which consistently worked towards a conservative policy and by which, almost uniquely, Marlborough would allow himself to be guided when it contradicted his own opinion'.[34]

Perhaps there may be more to it than that. Marlborough's correspondence consistently reflects astonishment at the blighted state of France, and a conviction that the French could not continue the war. Louis was indeed in dire straits: early in July he told Villars that he could spend two or three thousand louis d'or on the fortification of Béthune and St Venant, though it was 'a sum difficult to assemble in the present state of affairs'.[35] Early in July Marlborough warned Heinsius that he did not expect better terms at the end of the campaign than had been embodied in the rejected preliminaries. He was wholly correct in emphasising that the Spanish clause had proved fatal: 'Were I in the place of the King of France, I should venture the loss of my country much sooner than be obliged to join my troops for the forcing [of] my grandson.'[36] Yet he still expected that the French would agree terms close to those suggested that spring, and on 22 July suggested that: 'The account of the misery and disturbances in France are such, that if it continues they must be ruined.'[37] Perhaps the whole rotten structure was about to tumble down, and a brisk kick at Tournai might just prove the last straw. He had a well-placed agent at Versailles whose reports told of people struggling to tear fragments from a dead horse on the Pont Neuf, crowds of unemployed workmen seeking jobs, aristocrats preparing to leave the country, and the king's guards sleeping booted and spurred in case of insurrection. 'Certainly,' he told Godolphin, 'the misery of France increases, which must bring us to a peace.'[38]

There was, alas, to be nothing brisk about the siege of Tournai. It was defended by the marquis de Surville-Hautefort with a garrison of some 7,700 men. Surville lacked the troops to defend the town itself, and on 28 July agreed to give it up after some of his outworks had been taken by storm. Marlborough promptly informed the queen of this success, hoping that it might 'oblige the enemy to submit to such terms as may conduce to a happy and lasting peace'.[39] Surville retired into Tournai's citadel, which, as Private Deane reported, 'is an invincible strong place for mines'.[40] Richard Kane agreed that it was 'one of the best fortified places by art that is in the world, there being more works a great deal under ground, than above, which made our approach very difficult'.[41] Marlborough took direction of the siege while Eugène commanded the field army, but 'bloody work at the siege' meant that some regiments had to be relieved from the trenches and replaced by fresh units. The defenders' use of mines lent a particular horror to operations, and Sergeant John Wilson thought that

> of all the horrid schemes of war, this bringing of mines and sapping to find out the same was the most dreadful, for it was with great reluctance that even the boldest men in the army then on this service have turned their backs and given way. Nay, even those who had seen death in all its shapes above ground was struck with horror to stand (as he supposed) on the top of a mine in danger of being blown up every minute. And those who went under ground into the saps had a co-equal reluctance, if not more, they being in danger every minute either of being suffocated or buried in the rubbish in the like nature.[42]

Villars, meanwhile, extended his lines to the Scheldt above Condé, and swung his army up behind them between Douai and Valenciennes. On 8 August Marlborough assured Godolphin that Villars was too weak to cover the lines at La Bassée and to prevent the Allies from moving against Valenciennes if they wished to do so. He watched from a distance the slow unrolling of Allied plans for the invasion of south-east France, spoiled first by its slow development, and then checked fatally by the defeat of the Elector of Hanover's advance guard at Rummersheim in late August. Perhaps, by any reasonable standards, France might be dead, but her corpse was still twitching to some purpose. Marlborough was convinced that the French would come to terms if only the Allies would moderate their demands, and Spain was still the sticking point. He assured Heinsius that 'the French ministers have it not in their powers to recall the Duke of Anjou', and declared that 'the insisting on the [surrender of] three towns in Spain' made it impossible for the French to come to terms. 'I call to God to witness that I think it is not in the power of the King of France . . . it is in my opinion declaring the continuation of the war.'[43]

Goslinga thought precisely the same, and warned Marlborough that he could not see how 'by the terms of this treaty we could enter, without firing a shot, into possession of these fortresses which we could never . . . take by force of arms in four campaigns'. Marlborough, he complains, could give him no satisfactory answer, and attributes this to the fact that he 'wished for the war to continue because of resentment at his rejection as Governor of the Low Countries, by ambition and desire for money'.[44] As we can now see from Marlborough's correspondence, the accusation that he was anxious for the war to continue was

François de Neufville, duc de Villeroi, had been governor of the young Louis XIV and was appointed marshal of France before winning any notable victories. Beaten by Eugène at Chiari in 1701, he was roundly defeated by Marlborough at Ramillies in 1706.

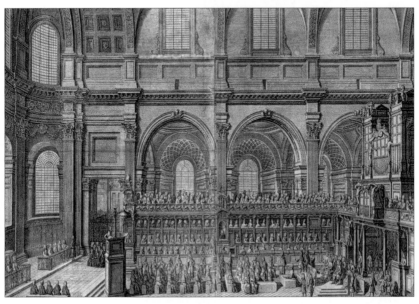

The queen and members of both Houses of Parliament attended the thanksgiving service in St Paul's Cathedral for the victory of Ramillies.

The great siege of Lille, 1708. This engraving shows the geometrical profiles of both defence works and attackers' trenches. Siege guns batter at the walls, and mortars lob their bombs into the body of the town.

The main gate of 'Vauban's masterpiece', the citadel of Lille, now named in honour of Marshal Boufflers who held it so well in 1708.

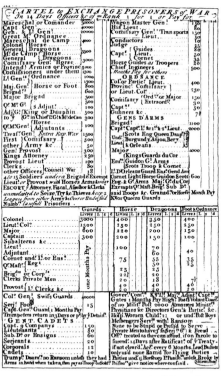

A draft cartel for the exchange of prisoners of war, which tries to establish relative values of prisoners. It notes that no ransom is payable for drummers and trumpeters, traditionally used to accompany negotiators, 'unless they had arms in hand when taken, then pay as troopers or soldiers'.

Looking southwards along the eastern edge of Sars Wood at Malplaquet. The trees which stood here had been felled to form an abbatis, and Marlborough's infantry attacked from the left in the teeth of heavy fire.

Dutch infantry of the late seventeenth century. The figure on the left seems to be wearing an early form of what became the grenadier's mitre cap.

Dragoon regiments carried swallow-tailed standards rather than the large rectangular colours of the infantry. This is the standard of the Royal Dragoons, and bears the cipher of Edward Hyde, Lord Cornbury (later 2nd Earl of Clarendon), who succeeded John Churchill as the regiment's colonel in 1685. He was amongst the first to desert to William of Orange in November 1688.

These plates of a grenadier of 1st Foot Guards at drill narrowly post-date Marlborough, though uniform had changed little since his day. The first shows the grenadier slinging his musket, which caused him to wear the mitre cap, for the standard tricorn hat would have obstructed the sling. In the second he blows on his match (a length of smouldering saltpetre-impregnated cord), and in the third he applies match to grenade before throwing it.

Queen Anne in the House of Lords by Peter Tillemans (circa 1708–14). The queen did not simply attend state openings of Parliament, but sat in the House to listen to important debates.

High Lodge, Blenheim Park, where the Marlboroughs sometimes stayed while the palace was under construction.

Above John, 2nd Duke of Montagu, with his wife, formerly Lady Mary Churchill, and their daughter Lady Mary Montagu. Sarah characteristically fell out with Mary, her youngest daughter, and was never reconciled with her.

Henrietta Churchill (left) was married to Francis, son of Marlborough's ally Sidney Godolphin, and was Countess of Godolphin until she succeeded as Duchess of Marlborough in her own right in 1722. Her son William ('Willigo'), Marquess of Blandford, predeceased her and left no issue. The dukedom then passed through Anne Churchill, Countess of Sunderland (right), to her son Charles Spencer, who became 3rd Duke of Marlborough.

Grandchildren. Left to right: Charles Spencer, later 4th Earl of Sunderland and 3rd Duke of Marlborough; the Hon. John Spencer, from whom the Earls Spencer descend; and Lady Diana Spencer, later Duchess of Bedford. Diana was Sarah Marlborough's favourite grandchild, and spent much of her early life living with her in Windsor.

James FitzJames, Duke of Berwick, the eldest of James II's illegitimate sons by Arabella Churchill, and thus Marlborough's nephew. The most capable of the later Stuarts and one of the best French commanders of his generation, he was killed by a chance shot at the siege of Philippsburg in 1734.

In his declining years Marlborough loved to sit by the bridge (bottom left) and watch work on Blenheim Palace proceeding towards completion.

A modern aerial view of Blenheim Palace. The present Duke of Marlborough's private apartments are, like the 1st duke's, in the wing adjacent to the formal garden nearest to the camera.

patently untrue: he was now heartily sick of it, and longed to live out his days at Blenheim, albeit with the captain generalcy as a souvenir of his great and glorious days. In 1706 the emperor, on behalf of Charles III, had offered to make Marlborough governor of the Spanish Netherlands. Godolphin had assured him that the queen 'likes the thing very well and leaves it to you to do, as you shall judge best for her service and the common cause'.[45] Marlborough quickly recognised that 'it would create a great jealousy, which might prejudice the common cause', and turned it down.[46] It is hard to see how Goslinga could have read Marlborough more incorrectly.

The citadel of Tournai capitulated at last on 3 September, having cost the Allies over 5,000 killed and wounded. Its garrison was allowed to go to France on parole, to await formal exchange with the Allied garrison of Warneton, taken by Le Blanc, the 'lively, bold and enterprising' *Intendant* of Ypres. Marlborough at once darted south-east to besiege Mons, moving his siege train by water to Brussels and then down to Mons by road. On 7 September he told Godolphin that although he could not begin serious battering till the train arrived, probably towards the twentieth of the month, he hoped to take the little fort of St Ghislain with the guns he had with him, and complete his lines of circumvallation around Mons. Villars had just managed to reinforce its garrison before the iron fist closed around Mons, but there could be little doubt that, once the heavy guns started gnawing at its walls, Mons would go the same way as Tournai.

Louis had hitherto been reluctant to allow Villars to risk battle, arguing that a lost battle would leave France open to invasion, while a victory could not be exploited. That summer Villars was given heavily-qualified permission to fight, and on 6 September Marlborough's agent at Versailles warned him that Villars now planned to give battle as soon as Tournai surrendered. Moreover, claimed the agent, Boufflers, who had been at Versailles, had now departed for the frontier with his cuirass and weapons.[47] The marquis de Cheldon, captured in an outpost action near Mons, was happy to assure his captors that Villars intended to fight, and Lord Orkney told his brother that 'we had intelligence of Boufflers being come up to their camp with orders to risk all and venture a battle'.[48] On 10 September, in his last letter written before Malplaquet, Marlborough told Sarah that a battle might not be far off.

I have received intelligence that the French were on their march to attack us. We immediately got ourselves ready and marched to a post some distance from our camp. We came in presence between two and three o'clock yesterday in the afternoon, but as there was several defiles between us, we only cannonaded each other. They have last night entrenched their camp, by which they show plainly that they have changed their mind and will not attack us, so we must take our measures in seeing which way we can be most troublesome to them.[49]

Marlborough had swept down from the north-west to beleaguer Mons, crossing the little River Haine not far from the town. Villars, in turn, had crossed the headwaters of the Scheldt and marched north-eastwards, with the Sambre away to his right. The town of Bavay was the hub of the local road-system, with Roman roads spreading out from it like the spokes of a wheel. Between the two armies lay a series of big, broad-leaved woods. The most northerly, jutting up towards the Haine, and today dismally curtailed by the post-industrial sprawl of towns like Frameries, Paturages and Boussu (for this was once mining country), was then called Sars Wood, named for the village of Sars-la-Bruyère. Then came the small round copse of Thiery Wood. Finally, Lanière Wood, astride the Roman road from Bavay to Givry, closed the southern front of the battlefield, with a bosky finger poking down towards the Sambre near Hautmont. The woods have changed their size and shape somewhat with the passage of two centuries, and, confusingly, the nomenclature of modern maps bears limited relation to that in contemporary accounts. To any traveller making his way from Mons to Malplaquet, and passing the deserted checkpoint that marks the Franco-Belgian border and the stone obelisk that commemorates the battle, the message is clear. This is close country, made for defence, that denies even the most capable general any room for manoeuvre.

There were three militarily-practicable gaps between the woods: the *trouée de Boussu* north of Sars Wood, then the *trouée de la Louvière* north of Thiery Wood, and the Aulnois gap to its south. The ground was generally flat and often marshy, but there was enough microterrain to make a difference to those who must live and die by it. The road from Mons to Bavay forks just north of Sars, and its eastern extension climbs the gentlest of gradients as it traverses the Aulnois gap towards the village of Malplaquet, then as now a few houses strewn along both sides of the road. The solidly-built farm complex of Bléron stood beside a brook just west of Thiery Wood, and, with it, separated the Louvière from the Aulnois gap as the cutwater of a bridge divides the current.

Neither army could get at the other without passing through one of the gaps, and with alert cavalry on both sides it was impossible to 'steal a march' and pass a gap without the enemy being able to react. On 8 September, after jockeying around the Boussu gap, the two armies moved up to either end of the Louvière and Aulnois gaps. Marlborough had to leave forces to invest St Ghislain and Mons, and Lieutenant General Henry Withers, with nineteen battalions and ten squadrons, was still on his way down from Tournai. On the eighth Villars told Louis:

> I have the honour to inform your Majesty of the resolution taken to assemble the army and give battle to the enemy . . . I have the honour to tell your Majesty that I am delighted that M le Maréchal Boufflers is here; if we attack, he will bear witness that it is with good reason; if we do nothing, I will be pleased that such a brave man will bear witness that we could not have done better.[50]

Early on the ninth Marlborough rode forward to reconnoitre, and saw Villars' army coming up in four large columns. For a moment it seemed as if he might simply push on through one of the gaps beside Thiery Wood, which would have caused some consternation as Eugène was away covering the Boussu gap, but by midday it was evident that he was entrenching a position including Sars Wood on its left and Lanière Wood on its right.

Marlborough was in no position to attack on the ninth. His army was spread out watching the gaps, and what Orkney called 'a prodigious dusty rain' caused much confusion. It was only towards mid-afternoon that he had enough guns available to bombard the French, by which time they had 'began and cannonaded us pretty briskly, particularly where our English foot were, and killed us a good many men'.[51] Surprisingly, the Allied commanders decided not to attack on the tenth either. Neither Withers' men, who would be freed by the fall of St Ghislain on the tenth, nor four German battalions ordered down from Mons, had yet arrived, but Marlborough and Eugène were already stronger than Villars, and the French position grew more formidable by the minute. Failure to attack on the tenth was indeed a serious mistake. 'Either the battle should have taken place on the 10th or not at all,' declares Ivor Burton.[52] Marlborough, however, was anxious not to miss the chance of what he hoped would be a decisive contest, and trusted to his own skill and his army's courage to win it.

'The Allies could not attack the day we arrived,' recalled de la Colonie, who was to command a Bavarian brigade in the French centre, 'nor the day afterwards.'[53] He watched the Allies preparing a great battery of about thirty heavy guns, facing his position, but at the same time the soldiers of his own army were working with passionate energy on their own position. Five arrowhead-shaped redoubts, their parapets thick enough to be cannon-proof, were thrown up on the open ground between Sars Wood and Bléron Farm, with a gentle slope between them and the Allies. A battery of thirty guns was tucked carefully into a re-entrant near Thiery Wood, while the trees on the forward edges of the French-held woods were felled with their tips facing the expected direction of assault. Where possible leaves were stripped and branches sharpened, but even without these refinements an *abatis* of felled timber presented a cruel obstacle to attacking infantry. Entrenchments for infantry and guns alike creased the landscape, dug by famished men who now rose supremely to their task. Not long before they had grumbled when Villars had come to speak to them, intoning, with mock piety, 'Give us this day our daily bread.' Now they roared '*Vive le Roi*' and '*Vive le Maréchal Villars*' as he rode amongst them. Old Boufflers, born in 1644, was senior to Villars as a marshal of France, but freely agreed to serve under his command, and the sight of this stubby warrior reminded men that he was a doughty defensive fighter, and there were cheers for him too.

Villars gave Boufflers command of his right wing, with forty-six battalions in Lanière Wood under d'Artaignan and de Guiche. The twenty-gun battery swept the ground to their left front, and eighteen battalions, including the Swiss and French Guard, were entrenched opposite Bléron Farm. A nearby memorial now makes the tragic point that there were Swiss in both armies, and that they met in battle here. There were thirteen battalions, some of them Bavarian and Irish, manning the redoubts, with four in close support, and the bulk of the French artillery, some sixty guns, was sited to beat the open ground in front of them. Lieutenant General Albergotti commanded twenty-one battalions securing the angle where the line of the redoubts swung north to the edge of Sars Wood, and Lieutenant General de Goësbriand, in overall command of the left, had seventeen battalions near La Folie Farm. Most of the cavalry was drawn up just behind the redoubts, close enough to support the infantry if required, and to take advantage of any disorder produced by the repulse of an Allied attack, but not so close as to get caught up in the infantry battle. The gentle rise of the ground meant, though, that British cannonballs that skimmed above the low

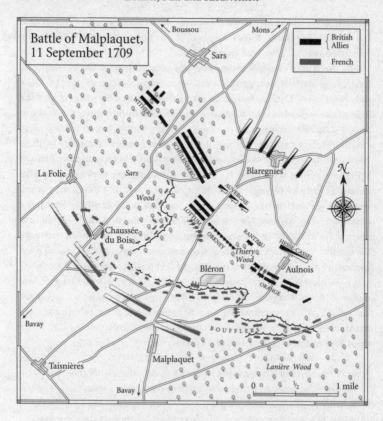

Battle of Malplaquet,
11 September 1709

British
Allies

French

crest defended by the redoubts went on to hit the cavalry behind. Villars'
units were under-strength, but he had some 85,000 men and eighty
guns, posted to take best advantage of the ground.

Marlborough proposed to attack the French army in much the same
way that he had at Blenheim and Ramillies, first unbalancing it, and
then administering the knockout blow. In this case he would attack the
French flanks, thereby inducing Villars to reinforce them from his
centre, which would then be broken by direct assault. He had about
110,000 men and a hundred cannon. Though Withers' men were not to
arrive in time to form part of the attack on the left, as was first intended, he decided to commit them to his right, the closest part of the line
to their direction of arrival, hoping that they might be able to crash their

way through the ungarrisoned portion of Sars Wood and hook round the French left flank. Prince Eugène, in overall command on the right, recorded this as 'a special attack'.

On the Allied right, Schulenberg was to assault Sars Wood with forty battalions, with d'Auvergne's forty squadrons of Dutch cavalry close behind. Count Lottum would attack at the angle of Sars Wood and the line of the redoubts with twenty-two battalions, among them the Duke of Argyll's British infantry. In the centre Orkney commanded fifteen battalions, eleven of them British, with 179 squadrons of cavalry to their rear – a sure sign that Marlborough intended to pass his cavalry through a French centre weakened by making detachments to the flanks. The young Prince of Orange, who had done so well at Oudenarde, commanded the left flank. Although he was not reinforced, as had been expected, by Withers, he nonetheless had thirty Dutch battalions, among them the Blue Guards and the Scots brigade, troops of the highest quality. The attack would begin at daybreak, signalled by a salvo from the entire British artillery, immediately taken up by the Dutch cannon.

11 September 1709 dawned foggy, and both Lord Orkney and Colonel de la Colonie, perhaps a thousand yards apart at the time, thought that this was advantageous for the Allies, letting them form up without interference from French guns. 'It was hardly 7'oclock when we marched to the attack,' observed Orkney,

> and it really was a noble sight to see so many different bodies marching over the plain to a thick wood where you could see no man, as all Schulenberg's, Lottum's, Argyll's and Webb's foot marched and fronted to the wood to attack. I fronted quite another way, to the high ground where the mouth of the defile was, so that we made a crocket [a protrusion in the main line]. My orders were to bring my right into the wood, cross the plain, and advance my line up to their entrenchments. As the others beat them from their retrenchments, such a fire of musketry and cannon I believe no man alive ever heard, and great execution was done on both sides with our artillery.[54]

De la Colonie found himself facing Orkney in the very centre of the field. A fourteen-gun battery came into action on the right of his regiment, almost touching the *Gardes Français*, the next unit along.

> I noticed the officer commanding the artillery in front of our brigade, who was not terribly young, but so active in his task that he lost no

opportunity to hasten the fire of his battery: I was able to see the balls plunge deep into the depth of the enemy column. But as soon as a breach was made, it was at the same instant filled up, and the enemy marched, meanwhile, at a normal pace.

As the Allied infantry advanced, they made a quarter-turn to the right, and disappeared into Sars Wood, 'in the place where their battery had made a breach'. 'The head of this column soaked up all the fire of our infantry which was entrenched before it,' said de la Colonie, 'and which did it terrible damage, but it did not slacken in its stubbornness.' As the column vanished into the smoke and confusion of the wood, an Irish brigade was ordered to leave the central entrenchments and move into the wood, and de la Colonie's brigade was told to replace it. Later his own brigade was ordered to follow the Irish.

> The first order which was brought to us, addressed to the brigade major, we refused to obey because of the importance of retaining the post we then held, and the danger of abandoning it; but a lieutenant general came a second time to order us, with great passion, to march.[55]

De la Colonie's memory has compressed the events of several hours into a single narrative, and the vision-narrowing effects of stress, combined with the obscuration caused by the grey-white powder smoke, meant that he could never see what went on to his flanks. The fighting in Sars Wood was a bitter close-quarter struggle, with successive Allied attacks being checked and fresh battalions committed to replace broken ones. Sergeant John Wilson wrote of

> an obstinate engagement for the space of two hours in which there was a great effusion of blood on both sides, the armies firing at each other bayonet to bayonet. And after they came to stab each other with their bayonets and several came so close that they knocked one another's brains out with the butt end of their firelocks.

Having taken the first part of the wood, the attackers found more trees and earthworks before them.

> This action continued both desperate and bloody which continued for the space of five hours with incredible fury and resolution on both sides. And all this while doubtful of success because the enemy rallied

and regained, with extraordinary valour, the entrenchments from which we had beaten them.[56]

Allied progress was agonisingly slow and costly, and, as senior officer casualties were to show, death was often the price of superfine cloth and gold lace. Eugène was hit in the neck but refused to have his wound dressed: if the Allies won, he said, there would be time enough later, and if they lost it would not matter. John Marshall Deane, whose 1st Foot Guards saw some very hard fighting, regretted that

> abundance of men was lost in our side at these bold attacks, and amongst the rest a great many of our commanding officers as generals, brigadiers, colonels, lieutenant colonels, majors and officers of all ranks, likewise several gentleman officers and engineers belonging to the two trains of artillery, and abundance of good old experienced soldiers.[57]

The Duke of Argyll, whacked three times by spent musketballs, heard his soldiers mutter that he must be wearing a breastplate, and ripped open his waistcoat and shirt to show them that he was not. 'The Duke of Argyll went open-breasted amongst the men to encourage them to behave as became Englishmen,' wrote Mrs Davies. 'You see, brothers, he said, I have no concealed armour, I am equally exposed with you.' She went forward into the wood to take her husband some beer, but her dog began to howl, leading her to fear the worst. 'I ran amongst the dead,' she wrote, 'and turned over near two hundred, amongst whom I found Brigadier Lalo, Sir Thomas Prendergast, and a great number more of my best friends, before I found my husband's body which a man was stripping. At my approach he went off, and left his booty.'[58]

The Royal Regiment of Ireland was the last to come in from Tournai, where it had been levelling the siege works, and it is impossible for us to be certain whether it actually formed up on the right of Withers' detachment, which is where it should have gone, or was a good deal further to the east, and engaged in the fighting for Sars Wood, as David Chandler suggests. In any event, as Captain Parker recalled:

> We continued marching slowly on, till we came to an opening in the wood. It was a small plain, on the opposite side of which we perceived a battalion of the enemy drawn up, a skirt of the wood being in the rear of them. Upon this Colonel [Richard] Kane, who was then at the

head of the regiment, having drawn us up, and formed our platoons, gently advanced towards them, with the six platoons of our first fire made ready. When we had advanced within a hundred paces of them, they gave us a fire of one of their ranks: whereupon we halted, and returned the fire of our six platoons at once; and immediately made ready the six platoons of our second fire, and advanced upon them again. They then gave us the fire of another rank, and we returned them a second fire, which made them shrink; however, they then gave us the fire of a third rank after a scattering manner, and retired into the wood in great disorder; on which we sent our third fire after them, and saw them no more.[59]

Parker's comrades found, amongst the forty dead and wounded marking the enemy's line, the wounded Lieutenant O'Sullivan, who told them that they had beaten the Jacobite Royal Regiment of Ireland. Parker's regiment had only four killed and six wounded.

On the Allied left the Dutch attack fared much worse. At their first attempt the Dutch on the extreme left actually got into the entrenchments in Lanière Wood, but were dislodged by a counterattack by the Régiment de Navarre, 'which happened at that time to be composed of very short men, nearly in rags'. The Dutch Blue Guards, further to the right, were raked by the concealed French battery and fell in their hundreds. As the Dutch tide ebbed the Prince of Hesse-Cassel brought his cavalry forward to discourage a counterattack. The Dutch, Scots and Danish battalions rallied and attacked again, only to be scythed down in their windrows by French musketry and cannon fire: Generals Fagel, Spaar and Oxenstiern were among the dead. 'The Hollands army suffering very much,' wrote Private Deane. 'The 2nd and 3rd battalions of Blue Guards being bloodily smashed and broke, insomuch that the three battalions altogether cannot make above 800 men . . . And a great many other regiments in the Hollands service being very much broke and shattered.'[60]

At a little before eleven o'clock Goslinga galloped over to Marlborough, who was preoccupied with the battle for Sars Wood, and urged him to support the Dutch attack. Marlborough rode across to his left, congratulated Orange on the valour of his men, and told him to make no more assaults for the moment, but simply to keep the French right fixed and unable to move. Commentators have not been slow to blame the Prince of Orange for what was, by any standards, a disaster. The redoubtable C.T. Atkinson suggests that Orange was simply meant to 'demonstrate' against the wood, but 'suddenly converted his demonstration into real attack', though he gives no evidence to support this interesting deduction.[61] Marlborough was perhaps a mile away from the Dutch attack, and we cannot suppose that he would have mistaken, over a period of several hours, the noise of a real attack as opposed to a feint. Nor is it really credible to suggest that Orange was so piqued at the absence of Withers' detachment that he decided to risk his own life repeatedly, and to persist in a course of action that killed most of the generals to whose care he had been entrusted, not to mention thousands of his rank and file. The suggestion that he lost direction in the smoke and thus attacked the wrong wood is not wholly incredible, but does raise the issue of what wood he was meant to attack, and, again, why Marlborough, probably just within sight and certainly within earshot, did not intervene.

Marlborough never blamed Orange, even at a time when a scapegoat would have been useful. Indeed, he told Godolphin: 'Our left was Dutch troops only, who behaved themselves extremely well but could not force the enemy's retrenchments, so that their foot has suffered more than any other nation.'[62] It is more likely that, just as Marlborough did not tell Orkney that his role at Ramillies was essentially diversionary, preferring to keep his options open until he could see how the battle was shaping, so at Malplaquet he did indeed order Orange to attack Lanière Wood. What surprised him, and most Allied commentators, was how very well the French fought. There were those who, like Sergeant Wilson, maintained that French soldiers could only fight from behind entrenchments and barricades, but the fact remains that at Malplaquet, Villars' men withstood a shock that had broken their comrades at Blenheim, Ramillies and Oudenarde, and Marlborough had underestimated their staying power: perhaps the French had underestimated it themselves. In sum, it is hard to disagree with David Chandler's judgement that 'the fact that Marlborough unquestioningly shouldered the responsibility for Orange's attacks should at least dispose of allegations of misconduct or blatant error on the part of the Prince of Orange'.[63]

At about midday Villars was strengthening his failing left wing by leaching troops from his centre, the Irish brigade first, with de la Colonie's Bavarians to follow, hoping to attack Schulenberg's men when they emerged from the wood. In the process, as Boufflers was to tell Louis, 'our centre was deprived of infantry by the necessity to send it to the left'.[64] Marlborough, prompted by Schulenberg, told Orkney to press on into them, and ordered d'Auvergne and Hesse-Cassel to prepare to follow him with their cavalry. 'It was about one o'clock that my 13 battalions got up to the retrenchments,' wrote Orkney, 'which we got very easily, for as we advanced they quitted them and inclined to their right.'[65]

Villars might yet have reaped a dividend from weakening his centre, for he had by now assembled some fifty battalions ready to counterattack the Allies as they emerged from Sars Wood. He had just been told that the redoubts had been lost when he was hit in the knee by a musketball: he tried to retain command, but fainted, and was carried off in a sedan chair. At the same moment another general was killed and Albergotti himself was seriously wounded. Command of the French left wing now passed to Puységur, but he failed to launch the quick counterattack that might have jarred the Allies. However, when Miklau's ten squadrons of cavalry, which had accompanied Withers' outflanking force, appeared near La Folie well ahead of the infantry which might have supported it, it was roundly charged by ten squadrons of *carabiniers* and scattered.

In the centre, though, the battle was now turning decisively against the French. The Allied cavalry began to pass through Orkney's battalions, 'and formed up', as he tells us,

under [e.g. covered by] my fire. The enemy were in two lines on the other side of the retrenchment, and there was Boufflers at the head of the Maison du Roi and the gens d'armes. I took care not to fire even when they came pretty near – only some platoons to make them pay us respect, and to give us opportunity to form our horse on the other side of the retrenchments. But, as our horse got on the other side their horse came very near ours. Before we got 80 squadrons out they came down and attacked; and there was such pelting at each other that I really never saw the like. The French fired a little, but ours not at the first. We broke through them, particularly four squadrons of English. Jemmy Campbell, at the head of the grey dragoons, behaved like an angel, and broke through both lines. So did Panton, with little Lord Lumley, at the head of one [squadron] of Lumley's and one of Wood's. At first we pushed them, but it did not last long, for they pushed back our horse again so that many of them ran through our retrenchments . . . However, more squadrons went out, and sometimes they gained a little ground, and were as fast beat back again. I could see however it go better in other places . . . While the horse were engaged, I had little to do but encourage them, in which I was not idle, but oftentimes to little purpose.[66]

That genial soldier of fortune Peter Drake, now serving with the *Maison du Roi*, was shot in the calf and received two sword-cuts in the unavailing struggle to hold back the Allied horse. Drake believed that the second Allied cavalry attack worked because cannon had been hauled forward to support it. 'The success of this last attack was greatly owing to a large number of cannon, and small mortars continually firing and throwing their shells into the woods, which tore down whole trees,' he affirmed. He tried to surrender to a cavalry officer, but took the wise precaution of keeping his carbine cocked and handy. The officer aimed a pistol at him, and 'his shot and mine went off instantaneously, I shot the upper part of his head, and he tumbled forward; his ball only gouged my shoulder, and tore the flesh a little'. An officer in the same regiment later accepted Drake's surrender.[67]

De la Colonie thought that the first shock of cavalry was violent but indecisive, but that the Allies had the edge after they had rallied and passed through the redoubts again. He admitted that those grey-horsed dragoons – he called them 'the Scots Guards of the Queen' – were very good indeed. He reckoned that Villars was wounded during the second phase of the cavalry battle, and argued that if Boufflers had not ordered a retreat the battle might yet have been won, for there were fresh cavalry further back to support the *Maison du Roi*. All the evidence suggests that he was too sanguine, for the French infantry on both flanks had now begun to give way. Puységur's men had at last been taken in the flank by Withers' detachment, and the dogged Schulenberg had hauled seven twelve-pounder guns through the wood and begun to gall the French from its southern edge. Puységur knew that it was time to go, and ordered a retreat on Quiévrain. On the French right, d'Artaignan, who had taken command when Boufflers rode to the centre to assume command of the whole army, fell back on Bavay. Some historians suggest that he was forced from his entrenchments by another Dutch assault, but Marlborough admitted that 'we were afraid to make them advance, having been twice repulsed'. De la Colonie was right to say that this was not broken infantry, seeking safety in flight, but formed brigades coming off, badly mauled but in good order. The Allied cavalry followed the French rearguard to the banks of the little Hogneau, but the chevalier de Luxembourg's well-handled rearguard kept them at bay, and there was nothing approaching collapse and pursuit. Sensitive to French accusations of 'our not pressing them in their retreat', Marlborough told Sarah that 'we had not foot' to support the cavalry, as the infantry on his right were too far away and the Dutch on his left were too badly knocked about.[68]

Most combatants recognised at once that there was something wholly shocking about Malplaquet. The Allies probably lost just over 20,000 killed and wounded, with the burden falling disproportionately on the Dutch, with 8,462 casualties, and the French perhaps 12,000. Later that month Boufflers told Louis that 6,000 of his soldiers were still receiving treatment, and this takes no account of those killed on the spot or who died of wounds in the days after the battle. His official list gave 240 officers killed and 593 wounded, but only seventeen prisoners. Lord Orkney, who had seen many a stricken field, told his brother:

> As to the dead and wounded, I leave you to the public letters: but depend on it, no two battles this war could furnish the like number. You will see great lists of generals and officers. I can liken this battle to nothing so much as an attack of a counterscarp from right to left; and I am sure you would have thought so, if you had seen the field as I did the day after. In many places they lie as thick as ever you saw a flock of sheep; and, where our poor nephew [Colonel Lord] Tullibardine was, it was prodigious. I really think I never saw the like; particularly where the Dutch guards attacked, it is a miracle. I hope in God it may be the last battle I may ever see . . . The French are very proud they have done so well. I doubt it is with us as it was with the French at the battle of Landen . . .
>
> There is hardly any general that either is not shot in his clothes or his horse . . . many had 3, 4 and 5 horses shot under them. None alive ever saw such a battle.[69]

Major Blackader was soon to become Lieutenant Colonel Blackader, for his commanding officer, Colonel Cranston, had been 'killed by a cannon-ball . . . shot in at the left breast and out at the back: he spoke not a word'. The morning after:

> I went to view the field of battle . . . in all my life, I have not seen the dead bodies lie so thick as they were in some places among the retrenchments, particularly at the battery the Dutch guards attacked. For a good while I could not go among them, lest my horse should tread on the carcasses that were lying, as it were, heaped on one another . . . The Dutch have suffered most in this battle of any. Their infantry is quite shattered; so that it is a dear victory.[70]

Corporal Matthew Bishop and some comrades had hoped, 'having no tents to fix', that they could spend the night in a convenient house, but found it 'full of miserable objects, that were disabled and wounded in such a manner that I thought them past all recovery'. They looked elsewhere, but 'all the hedges and ditches were lined with disabled men . . . the horrible cries and groans of the wounded terrified my soul, so that I was in tortures and fancied I felt their sufferings'.[71]

Marlborough himself thought that 'There never was a battle in which there has been so many killed and wounded as this, for there are very few prisoners, considering the greatness of the action.'[72] He told Boyle that this was because 'in the heat of the battle there was little quarter given on either side . . . Most of the officers we have taken are wounded.'[73] On 13 September he wrote to Villars, lying wounded at Le Quesnoy, to wish him well after 'the accident which you suffered in the battle', and to propose measures 'for the succour of officers and others of your army who have been left on the field of battle, or who have dragged themselves into neighbouring houses'. If Villars was to dispatch wagons to Bavay, the wounded would be collected and could then be sent, on parole, wherever Villars wished. Marlborough intended to send Cadogan there on the fourteenth, at whatever hour Villars thought suitable, to supervise 'prompt succour and transport'. In case Villars was 'no longer with the army', he copied the letter to Boufflers.[74]

Failed Peace and Falling Government

Publicly Marlborough claimed a victory. Strictly speaking he was entitled to do so, for he had forced the French from a well-chosen position, though at appalling cost, and Boufflers himself opened his report to Louis with the words: 'I am much afflicted, sire, that misfortune compels me to announce the loss of another battle, but I can assure your Majesty that misfortune has never been accompanied by greater glory.'[75] On the afternoon of the action Marlborough told Godolphin that 'we have had this day a very murdering battle . . . If 110 [Holland] pleases it is now in our power to have what peace we please, and I have the happiness of being pretty well assured that this is the last battle I shall be in.'[76] He took the same line with Sarah, telling her: 'I have every minute the account of the killed and wounded, which grieves my heart, the numbers being considerable, for in this battle the French were more opinaitre [Fr: stubborn, obstinate] than in any other of this war. I hope and believe it will be the last I shall see, for I think it impossible for the French to continue the war.'[77]

With the French field army beaten, the Allies went on to besiege and capture Mons, which was no mean prize, although Cadogan was hit in the neck by a musketball on the night of 26 September when the besiegers opened their trenches before the fortress. 'I hope he will do well,' wrote Marlborough,

> but till he recovers it will oblige me to do many things, by which I shall have very little rest. I was with him this morning when they dressed his wound. As he is very fat their greatest apprehension is growing feverish. We must have patience for two or three dressings before the surgeons can give their judgement. I hope in God he will do well, for I can entirely depend upon him.[78]

The real results of Malplaquet were political rather than military. As Marlborough hoped, it did bring Louis back to the conference table, although as he had feared, the Allies still pitched their terms too high. An Anglo-Dutch agreement, the first Barrier Treaty, signed that October, bound the Dutch to support the British demand for 'No Peace without Spain', and in return Britain supported Dutch territorial claims in the Netherlands, agreed to relinquish trading concessions secured by a secret treaty with Charles III, and to give up Minorca. Godolphin backed the treaty, but Marlborough, correctly recognising that it would cause trouble in Parliament because of the damage that the Tories feared it would do to British economic interests, refused to sign it.

The negotiations, carried on at Gertruydenberg in the spring of 1710, eventually hit the same sticking point as the peace talks of 1709: the future of Spain. Louis would not use troops to force Philip off his throne, and attempts to procure his voluntary withdrawal in return for compensation elsewhere, which might have moved him, failed because Charles would not make concessions. Marlborough, well aware that Spain had wrecked the 1709 talks, had no doubt that it would ruin those of 1710 too. Although publicly he toed the government line, privately he warned Heinsius:

> I think it very unreasonable to press France to do so treacherous a thing as to deliver three towns in Spain, I think that they should deposit the three towns formerly mentioned: Thionville, Valenciennes and Cambrai, and that for the rest the preliminaries should continue as they are except the 37th article ... If I could flatter myself that Holland were willing and able to continue for three years longer the war, you might then reject what is now proposed, and be assured that in that time and with the blessing of the Almighty you might impose

what conditions you should see fit; but if the war can't be continued,
then this is a properer time [to make peace] than the [next] winter.[79]

The fact that Malplaquet eventually emerged as an empty victory was not
Marlborough's fault, and he took the field in the spring of 1710 with a
heavy heart. By now the political balance at home was tilting against
him, and he asked Sarah, 'Am not I to be pitied that am every day in danger of exposing my life, for the good of those who are seeking my ruin?'
A few days later, recognising that negotiations at Gertruydenberg would
indeed founder, he confessed unhappily: 'I never in my life wished for
peace more than I do now, being extremely dissatisfied with everything
that is doing.'[80]

Some of Marlborough's gloom stemmed from the fact that Sarah had
now had her final meeting with the queen. Anne increasingly flouted
Sarah's traditional prerogatives over household appointments, and
there was a major row in August 1709 over the appointment to the bedchamber of one Belle Danvers, who, Sarah maintained waspishly, 'did
not look like a human creature'. The queen's dispute with Sarah
became inextricably entwined with Marlborough's continuing attempt
to obtain the captain generalcy for life. Having made predictably poor
progress in her efforts to secure proper respect from Sarah, the queen
pointedly told Marlborough:

> You seem to be dissatisfied with my behaviour to the Duchess of
> Marlborough. I do not love complaining, but it is impossible to help
> saying on this occasion, I believe nobody was ever so used by a friend
> as I have been ever since my coming to the crown. I desire nothing but
> that she would leave off teasing & tormenting me & behave herself
> with the decency she ought both to her friend and her Queen & this
> I hope you will make her do, & is what I am sure no reasonable body
> can wonder I should desire of you, whatever her behaviour is to me,
> mine to her shall be always as becomes me.[81]

Another royal trespass on her prerogative provoked Sarah into sending
Anne a long and tendentious 'Narrative' of her relationship with the
queen, complaining again of Abigail Masham's influence. She followed it
shortly with a fresh tirade which reflected some material from one of
Maynwaring's tasteless insinuations about 'passions between women'. To
show how shamefully her enemies were treating her, she included large
chunks of the even more tasteless *Secret Memoirs and Manners . . . from the*

New Atlantis, the work of Mrs Mary de la Rivière Manley, a catspaw of Harley's, which defamed both of the Marlboroughs in a barely concealed and often quasi-pornographic way. Upon whom can Mrs Manley have modelled 'Stauvatius the Thracian'?

> A man who at present, and for some time past, has seen himself as the greatest subject upon earth, who never undertook any adventure that he did not perform to his satisfaction; whether it were to subdue a mistress, to win a battle, to take a town, or to secure himself such and such heaps of money, employment, grant or contribution . . . could one repeat the individual distresses of so many brave officers and soldiers, upon whose shoulders he has mounted to victory, through whose blood he has so often waded to conquest, one would detest, despise and loathe that abominable, sordid, despicable vice, which makes him more the hated of his own army, than their bravery has made him the dread of his enemies.[82]

Mrs Manley was prosecuted for seditious libel, but the case against her was not pressed, and as soon as the Tories were in power she was one of the most notable anti-Marlborough pamphleteers, accusing him of prolonging the war for his own profit.

In the autumn of 1709, before he returned to England after the fall of Mons, Marlborough made it clear to Sarah that he sided with her against Anne, who was 'set so entirely wrong'. He thanked her for the draft of the letter he was to send the queen, assuring her that 'I shall be careful in making the alterations as they are marked.' This was the basis of his letter of 10 October in which he again demanded the captain generalcy for life and begged the queen 'to be sensible of the long and faithful services of Lady Marlborough'. But he went on to warn Sarah that he had had quite enough of politics, and that

> all the honours and riches in the world could not tempt me to take any other part in Ministry than what belongs to my employments, which in time of peace is very little. As I hope you will approve of this resolution and that no consideration will make me depart from it. I would not have my friends deceived by taking other measures for me.[83]

When he returned home in November the Whigs, who were perforce his supporters, though not his friends, seemed at the very zenith of their power. They had at last forced the queen to accept Orford at the

Admiralty, and her speech at the formal opening of Parliament on 15 November described Malplaquet as 'a most remarkable victory, and with such other great and important successes, both before and after it, that France is thereby become much more exposed and open to the impression of our arms, and consequently more in need of a peace, than it was at the beginning of this campaign'.[84] However, Arthur Maynwaring told Sarah that the queen's voice was fainter, and her manner 'more careless and less moving' than it had been on previous occasions.[85]

Dr Henry Sacheverell had preached his inflammatory sermon, 'The Perils of False Brethren in both Church and State', on 5 November, and the events of the next four months went on against the backcloth of his trial. During this period Harley capitalised on the fierce passions raised by the trial, used Abigail Masham to give him secret access to the queen, and worked hard at the creation of an opposition party founded, as Edward Gregg tells us, on two principles: 'The queen should be liberated from the tyranny of the Marlborough family and England should be given a respite from the war.' Both planks of his policy attracted widespread and increasing support for many reasons.

First, it was and remains the nature of British politics for tall poppies to excite the malice of small boys with big sticks, and there were no fairer flowers than John and Sarah. Marlborough's thirst for wealth was remarkable even by the standards of the age, and those who felt inclined to forgive a successful commander were less inclined to tolerate the frequency with which Cadogan's plump fingers also slid into the till. Some of their perquisites, although wholly unjustifiable to us, were tolerated then. Other sources of income were far more suspect, and Cadogan's conduct aroused particular indignation. Van den Bergh, who served alongside him on the Anglo-Dutch condominium, called him 'the greatest thief in the whole army', and Giulio Alberoni, Vendôme's secretary during the period in question, maintained that Cadogan had 'carried off more than 200,000 pistoles from Flanders, quite apart from other unknown thefts'.[86]

However, what qualified as theft to a French marshal's secretary could easily seem legitimate to the recipients of its proceeds. In December 1706 Marlborough told Stepney that the *règlement* for the governance of Netherlands

was made with a great deal of deliberation and, as the Deputies assured me, contained nothing contrary to the known laws of the country. However, our chief aim ought to be to satisfy the people, and to make them easy under the present administration, so that the collecting at present a little money more or less ought not . . . to come into competition in a matter of this moment, especially considering that when we take the field we shall be able to leave but small garrisons in the great towns, and must depend in some measure on the faithfulness of the inhabitants. I believe the states will readily agree with me in this point, and authorise their Deputies to concur with you in leaving the Council of Sate to do what might be most advisable for quieting the minds of the people, and putting them to good humour.[87]

The selective quotation of the middle part of this letter has been used to imply that Marlborough had a personal interest in extracting money from the Netherlands, but the whole document makes it clear that the issue was one of legitimate taxation, and that Marlborough was primarily concerned with alleviating its burden so as to encourage citizens to remain loyal. Indeed, had more attention been paid to his concerns, then Ghent and Bruges might have remained loyal.

Huge sums of money passed through Marlborough's hands for the pay of British and British-funded foreign troops as well as for provision contracts. In June 1710, for instance, Cadogan told Marlborough: 'The present wants of the contractors are supplied with an advance of five hundred and fifty thousand guilders.'[88] The money often arrived long before it was required, and Cadogan generally invested it wisely and remitted the interest to Marlborough. The combination of legitimate perquisites, interest on government money and what his enemies alleged were simply bribes or extortions, produced very large sums. In the spring of 1709 van den Bergh told Heinsius that Marlborough had had 'six hundred thousand rixdollars or 15 tons of gold transferred to England by Antwerp bankers; so that the safeguards, the marches, the orders for winter quarters, and more things of that kind no doubt bring in nice profits'.[89]

Cadogan was an inveterate gambler: in 1707 James Brydges wrote to congratulate him 'on two pieces of good news the town is full of: one that you have won six thousand pistoles at play, the other that you are to reside at the Hague or Brussels in the room of Mr Stepney'. Usually his deals worked well, and the fact that Brydges was paymaster general to the army overseas put them both in a good position to slice off percentages here and there. In the spring of 1707 the two men agreed a complex scheme of shuffling government money between currencies with different agents. 'I am persuaded this method is so settled,' wrote

Cadogan, 'that we shall turn £15,000 or £16,000 a month at 100 per cent clear of all charges.'[90] Cadogan's friendship with Lord Raby meant that he enjoyed some of the benefits of what we might now call insider trading. In July 1707 he confessed to Raby: 'We are in mighty pain about the King of Sweden. If that storm should break on the Hereditary Countries [of the Hapsburg crown] the affairs of the Allies would be in worse condition than ever. I that am a thousand deep in the Silesia loan, have some reason to enquire about it, for upon any hint from your Lordship I could dispose of it in time.' Raby reassured him, correctly predicting 'an accommodation between the Emperor and the King of Sweden'.[91]

However, Cadogan was not always fortunate, and shortly before Marlborough's death Sarah pursued him in court for having placed £50,000, given him for investment in Holland, in Austria instead, where the rates seemed better: a sudden fall in Austrian rates left the Marlboroughs out of pocket. With a determination untroubled by Cadogan's long personal loyalty to the duke, Sarah hounded him to what she regarded as a satisfactory conclusion even after her husband had died. She was so concerned that Marlborough, close to death, would wreck her suit by changing his will in Cadogan's favour, that 'I ordered his gentlemen that they should be sure to let me know when Lord Cadogan came to see him . . . I was so fearful of his altering his will that I locked up all the pens and ink.'[92]

If Cadogan's evident rapacity helped prejudice people against Marlborough, the duke's own 'close accounting' helped convey the impression that he was not only very rich but a skinflint into the bargain. In June 1709, with many other things on his mind, he drew Sarah's attention to the fact that Lord Feversham, who had just died, had fallen into arrears with a mortgage he owed Marlborough, and that she might thus purchase his property at advantageous terms.

> I think Lord Feversham owed three years last Christmas, but if you send for the steward he will show you the last acquittance. As for his estate, when I was about it two years ago, everyone thought him unreasonable in his demand, but if you can have it a penny worth you will do well by it. I remember one objection was that he had ploughed up the meadow ground so that some years hence it would not yield the same rent.[93]

What was in fact financial astuteness was easily misrepresented by Marlborough's enemies, who claimed that he chivvied the dying and impoverished Feversham for payment, telling him that he could not invest his money on such good terms elsewhere. The fact that the mortgage was so long overdue is actually proof of the latitude he allowed his old commander. Moreover, as Philip Rambaut's recent work demonstrates, Feversham died 'a man of considerable means', having an estimated income of £8,000 a year.[94]

It was not hard for folk to compare the Marlboroughs' all too evident wealth with the financial state of the country. Over the duration of the war public expenditure had risen from £3 million to £13 million a year, and the national debt eventually rose from £10 million to £50 million during Anne's reign. The hard winter of 1708–09, which had caused such suffering in France, also caused great hardship in Britain, and in January 1710 the price of grain in London was higher than ever before. There was an influx of some 10,000 Protestant refugees from the Palatinate, some of them hard-working but others (and where have we heard this before?) 'inactive and mutinous'. 'Charity begins at home,' was the cry among the labouring poor, 'and these foreigners are a plague to us.'[95]

Country gentlemen of a Tory persuasion met to quaff their bumpers, thump the table and damn the government and its land tax. City merchants complained of the damage done to trade by French privateers – the contemporary claim that 3,600 merchantmen were lost during the war is, thinks N.A.M. Rodger, 'not much exaggerated'.[96] G.M. Trevelyan was quite right to observe that Malplaquet might have once been regarded as a victory, but that under the shadow of the failed peace talks only a decisive battle and a march on Paris would have sufficed. Terrible though the slaughter had been, the British contingent of 14,000 had lost fewer than six hundred killed and under 1,300 wounded. Tories and Jacobite sympathisers, though, were not slow to magnify these figures. The Oxford diarist Thomas Hearne had been unmoved by Blenheim, Ramillies and Oudenarde, but now described

> the most direful battle to England that has yet happened, and there is not, in the opinion of honest men, the least reason for bragging. Private letters frequently come which give the most impartial accounts, and we are well assured from the greatest to the meanest officer hardly one escaped but was either slain or very much wounded.[97]

Lastly, 'No Peace without Spain' was evidently what had wrecked the talks, and that was a key plank of Whig policy. This was an administration in deep trouble, now faced, in the shape of Robert Harley, with a politician with the skill to bring it down, and a monarch with slights to avenge.

The tale is quickly told. Harley succeeded in converting the Dukes of Shrewsbury, Somerset and Argyll to his cause. All were Whiggish by sympathy but were distinct from those 'Lords of the Junto' so detested by Anne, and were invaluable allies for Harley. Marlborough's own position had been very seriously damaged, as we have already seen, by his failure to make the queen part with Abigail Masham in early 1710, and was later dented again by a row with the queen over promotions, in which he tried, ultimately without success, to avoid promoting Abigail's brother Jack and her husband Sam. The narrow majority which convicted Sacheverell, and the very moderate penalty imposed on him, weakened the government's authority. And then, on Thursday, 6 April 1710, there was a final, fulminating interview between Sarah and the queen. There is no impartial account, for Lord Dartmouth, who tells us the story, was a political opponent of the Marlboroughs, and the tale comes second-hand via Mrs Danvers, who was in waiting at the time. She told Dartmouth that:

> The Duchess reproached her [the queen] for above an hour with her family's services in so loud and shrill a voice, that the footman at the bottom of the back stairs could hear it . . . The Queen, seeing her so outrageous, got up, to have gone out of the room: the Duchess clapped her back against the door, and told her that she must hear her out, for that was the least favour she could do her, for having set and kept the crown upon her head. As soon as she had done raging, she flounced out of the room and said, she did not care if she never saw her more; to which the Queen replied, very calmly, that she thought the seldomer the better.[98]

In mid-April, without consulting the Duumvirs, the queen made Shrewsbury her lord chamberlain, not in itself a fatal blow but a dangerous sign of the way the wind was now blowing. She toyed with the idea of dismissing Sunderland, the Marlboroughs' Whig son-in-law, as secretary of state, and her determination to do so was strengthened rather than diminished by Sarah's clumsy threat to make public some of the royal correspondence. Godolphin warned Anne that Marlborough would resign if she did indeed sack Sunderland, and the queen sweetly replied that she had no intention of replacing Marlborough, and that if he did 'desert my service' at what she called 'this critical juncture' then the blame would be Godolphin's alone. On the same day, 14 June, Godolphin joined seven leading members of the government in urging Marlborough not to resign because of Sunderland's dismissal. The duke, then besieging Douai, told Sarah:

> I am only thinking how I may soonest get out of all business. All my friends write me that I must not retire, and I myself think it would do great mischief if I should quit before the end of this campaign. But after the contemptible usage I meet with, how is it possible to act as I ought to do? . . . I hope tomorrow we may sign the capitulation of this town, which would give me pleasure, were I not so extremely mortified with what you are doing in England.[99]

On the following day he informed Godolphin that Douai had indeed surrendered, but that 'My spirits and zest are quite gone.' He feared that 'the expectation of disorders in England' could only hearten the French, and was afraid that he would simply 'drudge on for four or five months longer, and venture his life for those who do not deserve it from him'.[100]

By now Harley and his associates were applying increasing pressure to the queen to make her part with Godolphin, and he, tired and isolated, responded with a sourness that did not help his cause. An attempt by the Whigs to hold their ground backfired. The Dutch, Imperial and Hanoverian envoys were persuaded to ask the queen neither to change her ministry nor dissolve her Whig-dominated Parliament until the war was over. Harley was easily able to persuade Anne that this was foreign interference in her affairs, and both Godolphin and Marlborough were associated, probably rightly, with the appeal. On 8 August the queen sent a letter dismissing Godolphin with a pension of four thousand a year. She thought that it would be easier for them both if he broke his staff of office rather than, as was the custom, returning it to her personally. Anne probably felt genuine pain at parting with Godolphin, but what was meant to be a courteous dismissal turned into brusqueness.

The letter which effectively ended Godolphin's distinguished political career was delivered to him by one of the Duke of Somerset's grooms. John Smith, chancellor of the exchequer, called on him shortly afterwards, and saw Godolphin break his staff and fling the pieces into the fireplace, telling him 'to witness that he had obeyed the Queen's commands'.[101] His pension was never paid, although the fact that he inherited the bulk of the family fortune when his elder brother died soon afterwards meant that he was able to survive without it. Arthur Maynwaring, writing before Godolphin had inherited, warned Sarah that Godolphin 'will not be able to keep his family, unless 39 [Marlborough] assists him, which I really think he should do'.[102] Godolphin continued to attend Parliament and to associate with what had become the Whig opposition, but his health failed fast, and he died at the Marlboroughs' house in 1712. Sarah wrote on the flyleaf of her Bible: 'The 15th of September at two in the morning the Earl of Godolphin died at the Duke of Marlborough's house at St Albans, who was the best man that ever lived.'[103]

On 8 August Godolphin wrote to tell Marlborough that 'The Queen has this morning been pleased to dismiss me from her service.'[104] On the same date Anne herself told Marlborough what had happened, so 'that you may receive this news first from me & I do assure you I shall take care that the army shall want for nothing'.[105] On the ninth, when his initial pain had begun to subside, Godolphin assured Marlborough that although his 'circumstances are at present a little discouraging' he would do his best to ensure that Marlborough was 'effectually supported to the end of this campaign, in the post where he now is', and emphasised that it was essential to keep the Alliance together.[106]

At a meeting of the Privy Council on 20 September the queen ordered a proclamation dissolving Parliament to be read out – the clerk did it so eloquently that it was clear he had been practising. Most of the Whig ministers resigned the following day. The queen bade farewell to the Whig leader Somers and the lord keeper, Lord Cowper, with evident regret, in Cowper's case probably because Harley had no one in mind to replace him. Some of the new ministers, notably Harcourt, who became lord chancellor, and St John, lord keeper, sympathised with Marlborough. St John, who kept in touch with the captain general through his confidential man of affairs, James Craggs the elder, did much to prevent a war office committee established by Harley from wresting political control of the army from Marlborough's hands.[107]

Craggs, born in 1657, had entered the Duchess of Marlborough's service and, through her interest, became MP for the Cornish borough of Grampound in 1702, retaining the seat till 1714. He served as clerk of the deliveries of the Ordnance from 1702 to 1711 and again in 1714–15. He died, possibly by his own hand, enormously wealthy but in disgrace over his involvement in the South Sea Bubble, in 1721. All the property he had acquired since December 1719 was subsequently confiscated by Act of Parliament. His correspondence with Marlborough seems not to have survived, but he flits through extant documents like a rather substantial wraith. By 1710 he was coded as '185' in letters between Marlborough and Godolphin, and the latter told Marlborough: 'I have spoken to him as fully as I can upon the posture of our affairs here, and I think nobody understands them as fully as he does.'[108] In August that year Marlborough asked Villars for a passport for 'Mr Craggs the elder, an English gentleman returning from Italy, who wishes to pass through here on his way back to England'.[109] A year later, rightly foreseeing worsening problems over getting the Treasury to pay for Blenheim Palace, Marlborough wanted Craggs to work on the accounts, as it was clear that Harley, now Earl of Oxford, was anxious to avoid any official recognition that the queen was obliged to pay for the place.[110]

Although Cragg's shuttle diplomacy ensured that the captain general was in close contact with sympathetic members of the new government, the fall of Godolphin and the rise of Harley and his associates left him increasingly isolated. The election of 1710, which resulted in a Tory majority of 151 in the Commons, further strengthened his enemies. Marlborough had initially hoped that the Tory majority would not be so overwhelming, and told Heinsius of his distaste at seeing 'a great many honest people turned out to make room for the Earl of Rochester and the Duke of Buckingham and such like men. God knows where this can end . . .'[111] Although Sarah and the queen had met for the last time in April 1710 they still corresponded – or, more accurately, Sarah wrote to the queen through the agreed medium of Sir David Hamilton, a Whig doctor – but now her further insinuations of a lesbian relationship between Anne and Abigail Masham determined the queen to be rid of her at last. Anne did her best to prevent Sarah from travelling to the coast to meet Marlborough when he returned home on 11 December, and hoped that he would be 'calm and submissive' and would not be inflamed by his wife.

It was very hard for him to remain calm, for he had already been publicly humiliated. In September Harley had engineered the dismissal of Marlborough's private secretary Adam de Cardonnel, the newly appointed secretary at war, and his replacement by George Granville, later Lord Lansdowne, a personal enemy of Marlborough's. In November generals Meredith, Macartney and Honeywood were dismissed from the army for drinking damnation to the new ministry. All three were Marlborough's men, and he had only recently pressed to have Honeywood (the least culpable of the three, and the only one to have a notable military career after reinstatement in 1714) made a brigadier general.

Not only was Marlborough commanding the Allied army on a busy and successful campaign while all this was going on, but he remained determined to keep the British army under tight administrative control as long as he remained captain general. He promoted officers by seniority where this was appropriate, but always tried to give an advantage to those on active service. On 11 September he informed a Mr Pulteney that, despite 'having just reason to be satisfied with his services', he could not make his brother a captain, for there were several officers in the Guards who were senior to him. In a similarly conciliatory vein, he told another correspondent that while 'I am very sorry the death of Captain Hearne should occasion you any loss than that of a brother', his captaincy had already been given to an officer 'to whom I could not refuse it without doing a piece of injustice'.[112] Some correspondents railed against what they saw as such injustices. A lady describing herself as 'an officer's wife that was killed under your command' bewailed 'the loss of twenty thousand pounds a year to his family'. She felt that 'the quality and estates of my near relations' entitled her to 'the same favours others receive from your Grace or my Lady Duchess', but her late husband's regimental agent was unable to produce the money. 'May God send your Grace a happy conscience,' she concluded.[113]

The process inevitably had political overtones. Regimental colonelcies were potentially lucrative appointments, coveted by the government's friends, real or imagined. When Lord Essex's death left the colonelcy of his dragoon regiment vacant, Marlborough hoped to fill it with Lord Hertford, son of the Duke of Somerset, who the ministry was eager to please. Jack Hill, the queen's candidate for the post, was actually far better qualified from a purely military point of view. Because generals did not receive pay for the rank they held, but only for the post they filled, command appointments were also useful ways of rewarding the government's supporters and punishing its opponents. Marlborough was certainly not immune to personal or political favouritism. There were some officers, like his brother Charles or the capable Philip Honeywood, whose interests he looked after, and others, like Jack Hill and Sam Masham, who were elevated despite his attempt to rig the lists for a periodic promotion so that the elevation of brigadiers stopped just short of Hill and that of new colonels just short of Masham. Marlborough professed friendship for Lord Raby, a major general and colonel of a dragoon regiment, whose old schoolfriend Cadogan assured him: 'I hope that I shall soon wish your Lordship the joy of being lieutenant general.'[114] Marlborough, however, had no intention of making somebody he regarded as a Harley supporter a lieutenant general, and was anxious that Raby should not join him and Lord Townshend as a plenipotentiary in the 1710 peace talks. Once Harley gained control of the government he did his best, not wholly successfully, to deprive the captain general of his patronage by setting up a board under Ormonde, later Marlborough's successor, which began its work by dismissing all the captain general's brigadiers.

Brevet promotion, which gave its holder rank in the army but not in his regiment (and thus conferred status but not necessarily employment consistent with that rank) was a cheap and widely used way in which, in an age where decorations were not available, commanders-in-chief could reward the successful or the favoured. It inevitably produced confusion, which Marlborough did his best to mitigate. 'Besides Colonel Hollins having a commission of brigadier,' wrote Marlborough, 'does nowise exempt him from his duty as major, there are older captains in the first regiment to whom it would be a prejudice when they come to roll together.'[115] However, attempts to sort out the rank structure created almost as many problems as they solved, and officers who were passed over often responded by blaming political interference.

Ormonde's board of general officers produced a set of regulations intended to govern officer appointments and promotions. No officer who had retired by selling his commission could serve again; sales of commissions could take place only with the crown's consent; officers could normally sell after twenty years' service, disablement, or 'on some extraordinary occasion', and twelve pence in the pound would be payable, by both buyer and seller alike, to help run the Royal Hospital. Although the work of the board inpinged (as Harley had intended) on what might have been regarded as his legitimate interest, Marlborough at once told St John that he would ensure that the new regulations would 'be duly observed by those under his command', although he had some suggestions for minor modifications. First, it would be wiser to allow subalterns to sell out without the need to obtain prior royal approval, as many 'by misfortune in their recruits or otherwise, have run themselves so far behindhand as not to be able to continue the service, so that, unless they have the liberty to dispose of their commissions, the debt must fall on the regiment'. Next, officers who died in service often had 'great families in a starving condition' who deserved the sale price of their relative's commission. Finally, regimental colonels should be able 'to have officers out of other regiments whom they judge better qualified than those in the next rank in their own', and in a distant theatre of war it was simply impractical to await what would inevitably be a lengthy process of approval for cross-posting between regiments. Marlborough's suggestions were practical and humane.[116]

Not all Marlborough's work consisted of promoting the few and apologising to the many. There were lists to be furnished of French officers on parole, Scots recruiting officers to be transported from Ostend to Leith, Lieutenant General Ross's regiment of dragoons to have 720 guilders charged to its account and payment of the same sum made to the inhabitants of Steesch, near Bois-le-Duc, who had complained of 'exactions committed . . . in their march to winter quarters'.[117]

Marlborough assured Lord Halifax that he was determined that his recent misfortunes should not 'lessen my zeal for the public, nor my endeavours to carry on this war with all possible vigour while I have the honour to command the army'.[118] He corresponded with the new ministers with all the energy he had shown in his dealings with the old, and told Heinsius that an augmentation of the British contingent by ten squadrons was a new mark of the queen's enthusiasm for the common cause. He certainly considered resignation, but decided against it, partly because of pressure from leading Whigs and the Elector of Hanover. He told Baron Bothmar, who was shortly to become the Elector's envoy to London, that 'I will never be able to applaud and recognise sufficiently the manner with which Monseigneur the Elector has used me on this occasion.'[119] The end of the campaign found him 'a sick man, desirous and believing still to find ease in another place', but determined above all 'to act as becomes an honest Englishman'.[120]

No sooner had Marlborough returned to England in December 1710 than the humiliation began afresh. Before she met him, the queen had a long conversation with Hamilton, making it clear that not only must Sarah be dismissed from all her offices, but her daughters must go too, for none was suitable to be at court. Anne Sunderland was 'cunning and dangerous', and the 'silly and imprudent' Henrietta Godolphin had 'lost her reputation', a process she was to continue with a relationship with the poet William Congreve, who was probably the father of Lady Mary Godolphin – thanks, some said, to the waters of Bath, which had 'a wonderful influence on barren ladies, who often prove with child, even in their husbands' absence'.[121] Mary Montagu was worst of all, for 'she was just like her mother'.[122]

In one sense Anne was perfectly correct. Just as Sarah's character was heavily influenced by her own difficult relationship with her mother, so too her daughters were marked by their stormy relationship with Sarah.

She even fell out with Henrietta's son, the odious Willigo, who became Marquess of Blandford, despite the fact that Willigo's 'drunken habits and partiality for low company put him on bad terms with his mother, which in itself was probably sufficient to commend him to his grand-mother'. When in 1731 Willigo died 'of a drunken fit or fever' in the wholly apt surroundings of Oxford, Lord Hervey

> could not help reflecting how peculiar it was, that the only remaining branch of such a family as the Lord Treasurer Godolphin, and the head of such a family as the late Duke of Marlborough's, should go off so universally unregretted, especially when nobody ever pretended to say that he had not sense, good nature and honesty.[123]

On 28 December 1710, when Marlborough had his first meeting with the queen, she told him that he must not expect the thanks of Parliament for the year's not inconsiderable achievements, and he took the news calmly. Hamilton passed the queen's message to the duke on the twenty-ninth, and on the following day reported that Marlborough had offered his 'duty and submission', adding that 'he longed to have his wife quiet'. This encouraged Hamilton, who should have known better, to suggest a three-phase reconciliation, first between Marlborough and Harley, then between Sarah and the queen, and finally and most ludicrously, between Sarah and Abigail. The queen recognised that this would never work, and was determined to sack Sarah, though she would not risk a meeting because of the display of bad temper that would inevitably ensue.

On the evening of 5 January 1711 Hamilton discussed the matter with Marlborough and Godolphin. This was apparently the first time that Marlborough was made aware of the full details of Sarah's correspon-dence with the queen, and Hamilton told Anne 'how angry my Lord Duke was to hear that the Duchess had spoke so to her Majesty', adding unsurprisingly that Anne was 'extremely pleased' to hear this.[124] In one of his addenda to Burnet's *History*, Lord Dartmouth maintained that Marlborough had 'complained of his wife who, he said, acted strangely, but there was no help for that, and a man must bear with a good deal, to be quiet at home'.[125] Lord Cowper, who had heard Sarah 'railing in the most extravagant manner against the Queen, and said she had always hated and despised her', was assured by the duke that 'he should not mind what she said, for she was used to talk at that rate when she was in a passion, which was a thing she was very apt to fall into, and there was no way to help it'.[126]

We cannot be sure whether Marlborough's astonishment at hearing just how bad things had become was real or feigned, for he remained, even now, a consummate courtier. Over the next few days, however, it became clear that Sarah would have to go. At first she blustered, announcing that 'such things are in my power, that if known by a man that would apprehend, and was a right politician, would lose a crown'.[127] Bothmar, now the Hanoverian envoy, was assured by Shrewsbury and St John that Sarah's departure was the price of Marlborough's remaining in command. He passed the news on to Sarah, who agreed to submit. She made a last attempt to save herself by writing a letter of apology to the queen, but when Marlborough tried to deliver it, Anne would not receive it. Instead, she told Marlborough that he had two weeks in which to procure Sarah's resignation.

The only surviving account of Sarah's giving up the golden key of office as keeper of the privy purse is Dartmouth's, and so must be treated with caution, though it is wholly in character. 'When the Duke of Marlborough told her the Queen expected the gold key,' he wrote, 'she took it from her side, and threw it into the middle of the room, and bid him take it up, and carry it to whom he pleased.'[128] Marlborough returned it to the queen the next morning. Sarah later maintained that she had agreed not to publish the queen's letters in return for retrospectively accepting the 1704 offer of a pension of £2,000 a year, deducting the resultant £18,000 from the money she owed the privy purse.[129] In the absence of proper accounts it is impossible to be sure quite how Sarah left the privy purse, though Edward Gregg suggests that in all 'Sarah gained £32,800 above her normal salary and prerequisites [sic].'[130] There was a last undignified spat when Sarah asked to store her furniture at St James's Palace until Marlborough House was finished, and the queen retorted that she would charge her ten shillings a week for the privilege. Sarah responded by having all fixtures and fittings, including the fireplaces, removed from her apartments, and Anne duly ceased paying for work at Blenheim. It was a dreadful end to a remarkable friendship.

Last Campaigns

While he faltered at home, Marlborough remained reasonably successful abroad. In 1710 he began well by taking the field before Villars, forcing the French to withdraw from the line of the River Scarpe and besieging Douai. Villars held a council of war which promptly decided against offering battle (the bellicose marshal was outvoted by all his generals), and Marlborough's intelligence service produced a copy of its deliberations only two days after the document was sent to Paris. Douai, without support from the French field army, surrendered on 29 June. Immediately afterwards Marlborough was still confident that 'the intention of Monsieur de Villars is not to risk a battle', so the best the Allies could do was to 'put all the country on both sides of the Somme, and home to the sea, under contribution, and make such sieges as the Dutch may think worth the expense they must make'.[131] When he moved on to besiege Béthune he again believed that 'they do not intend venturing a battle', and he was right: the governor duly beat the chamade on 28 August and capitulated on the twenty-ninth. Marlborough then besieged St-Venant and Aire-sur-la-Lys simultaneously, taking the former on 30 September but the latter not till 9 November.

Both sieges had been held up by a successful French attack on an ammunition convoy at St-Eloois-Vijve, on the Lys just upstream of Ghent, on 18 September. The escort blew up the powder and sank the store-boats to prevent their capture, but Marlborough sent Walter Colyear, a Scots lieutenant general in Dutch service, to the scene of the action, and he managed to recover many of the unfilled mortar bombs.[132] Pioneers had to raise the sunken craft and dredge the river before it could be reopened to traffic. Marlborough had clearly hoped that he would be able to move on to attack Calais, which might indeed have unravelled the French defence of the northern frontier: 'I never was more fond of any project since this war,' he announced.[133] However, the protracted defence of Aire was aided by 'the continual rains . . . Our poor men are up to their knees in mud and water, which is a most grievous sight, and will occasion great sickness.'[134] It was now obvious that nothing else could be accomplished before the troops went into winter quarters, for they had 'suffered much by the late ill season'.[135]

By the time Marlborough returned to the Continent in March 1711 the political landscape of Britain had, as we have seen, been transformed. He was now so concerned about the interception of his mail by agents of the new government that he urged Sarah to 'be careful in your discourse as well as in your letters'. Marlborough was always sensitive to press criticism, and now lamented that 'the villainous way of printing . . . stabs me to the heart'.[136] He was also unwell, with what might have been a recurrence of the familiar migraine, or something more akin to labyrinthitis, a disease of the inner ear. 'I found myself in the night so out of order,' he told Sarah, 'that I have been obliged for some days [to] keep at home . . . I let you know this fearing you might hear it from others, and think it worse than it is. My illness was giddiness and swimmings in my head, which gave me often sickness in my stomach.'[137]

The Emperor Joseph I died of smallpox in April and was succeeded by his brother, Charles III of Spain. Villars cheerfully assured a trumpeter of Marlborough's that this would 'occasion great disorders amongst the Allies', and he was perfectly right, for to press on with 'No Peace without Spain' would now risk creating a Hapsburg super-state of Spain linked with the Holy Roman Empire, and it was precisely the fear of a French super-state being created that had drawn Britain into the war in the first place.[138] Whatever his political concerns, though, Marlborough noted that Villars was doing all he could to strengthen his position along the Rivers Scarpe and Sensée and, for all his gasconading, was again unlikely to offer battle. However little he liked the new ministry, Marlborough had come to terms with it, and, fighting the last campaign of his career, he rose to the very peak of his form.

For the 1711 campaign the Allies made their major effort in Flanders, where the captures of 1710 had left them with only the rearmost belt of Vauban's *pré carré* between themselves and Paris. Eugène's Imperialists brought Marlborough's field army up to 142 battalions and 269 squadrons. The death of Joseph I, however, produced a change in strategy. The French sought to use it as an opportunity to intervene in Germany once more, and Vienna decided to switch Eugène's command from Flanders to the Rhine to parry any thrust. Marlborough feared that this would lead to the Allies failing to concentrate on what he saw as the war's decisive theatre. He did all he could to prevent it, and enlisted the help of Heinsius:

> We are assured the King of France is coming to a resolution of sending troops from hence for the reinforcing of his army on the Rhine. What I fear is, that he may send a detachment thither which may occasion Prince Eugène's marching there with the Imperial and Palatine troops, by which we shall lose so great a body of horse as may give Marshal Villars the superiority in the horse as well as in the foot.[139]

Two weeks later he told Heinsius that the French had already sent a detachment to the Rhine, and that he expected the whole of the Bavarian contingent to follow soon. But Eugène had also gone with his own Imperial and Palatine troops, and he had just heard from the Prince of Anhalt, commander of the Prussian contingent, that his king, who had a territorial claim against the Prince of Orange, would recall them unless he obtained satisfaction during his current visit to The Hague. Marlborough urged Heinsius not to say anything 'that may hurt the Prince of Anhalt', but it was essential not to let the King of Prussia depart without an agreement which would leave his troops in Flanders 'for at least this campaign'.[140] The Prince of Orange's untimely death while crossing the Rhine estuary on his way to The Hague to discuss the issue did indeed produce a settlement in favour of the Prussians, who took part in the campaign.

Marlborough's relationship with Anhalt, which had given him early warning of the danger of Prussian withdrawal, testifies to his skill as an alliance manager. On one occasion Anhalt decided that the duke had offended him, and set off for Marlborough's quarters to expostulate.

> Upon his admittance, his eyes darting fire, the Duke received him with open arms, and, embracing him, said, 'My dear Prince, you have prevented me. I was just sending to beg the favour of your company in order to have your opinions upon a design I have formed for attacking the enemy, which I cannot undertake without your approbation, and assistance in the execution, for there are no troops I depend upon like those you command, nor any general in the army but yourself whose head and heart I can trust so in the conduct of an enterprise of such importance. If your Highness will be pleased to sit down, I will inform you of the particulars of my scheme . . .' When the Prince returned, he said to his friends, whom he had informed of his intentions to insult the Duke of Marlborough, 'The ascendancy of that man is inconceivable. I was unable to utter an angry word; he totally disarmed me in an instant.'[141]

With Eugène gone but the Prussians under his command, Marlborough had some 90,000 men in the Douai plain, confronting a French army perhaps 30,000 men stronger. Villars had thrown up the lines of *Ne Plus Ultra*, 'No Further Back' – or perhaps, if we accept Winston S. Churchill's suggestion that Villars had borrowed the phrase from a tailor's description of Marlborough's latest red coat, 'The Last Word'.[142] The lines were a thick belt of field fortifications, woven into inundations, running from Bouchain on the River Scheldt, along the southern bank of the Sensée, and then following the Scarpe to Arras. Their left flank was secured by field fortifications on the River Canche and the fortresses of Frévent, Hesdin and Montreuil, and their right by Valenciennes, Le Quesnoy,

Maubeuge, Charleroi and Namur. Ypres and St Omer, outside the lines, were both strongly garrisoned, and although Marlborough might take them, he would waste the campaign doing so. There were two causeways through the central part of the lines, at Arleux and Aubenchel le Sec.

Before deciding what to do in 1711, Marlborough sent Lord Stair to England in an effort to persuade Harley (now Earl of Oxford) to provide sufficient extra money to enable the Allies to remain in the field all winter, imposing a pressure that the French would be unable to bear. The idea was shelved, however, because it was not Oxford's intention to continue the war on the same basis through 1712. This left Marlborough with the pressing need to do something about Villars and his pestilential lines. He began on 6 June by snatching the little fort of Arleux, which guarded the northern end of one of the causeways over the Sensée, and began to refortify it on a larger scale. The operation was covered by Hompesch, with a strong force camped just outside Douai, and when Villars mounted a surprise attack Hompesch's force was badly cut about, although Arleux held out. Marlborough was visibly irritated, as well he might be, for as Richard Kane tells us, 'this was the only affront the Duke of Marlborough received during the whole war'.[143] However, he then proceeded to leave Arleux so thinly garrisoned that Villars was able to take it on 22 July.

It is widely agreed that Marlborough's action was deliberate. Cadogan was sent to relieve the place, but 'took not as much haste as the occasion seemed to require'. Having captured Arleux, Villars demolished its fortifications, thereby leaving the northern end of the causeway undefended, and, encouraged by his success, sent a strong detachment to Maubeuge, whence he might be able to raid into Brabant. Marlborough's correspondence, admittedly an inexact guide to his thoughts, for he was always concerned about the danger of his letters being captured, gives no hint of his detailed intentions. On the twenty-seventh he told Godolphin that he had been 'so out of humour' that he had not written by the last post, though whether this irritation was caused by the simple fact of Arleux's capture or because the captured garrison had been 'stripped naked' it is impossible to say.[144] Sometimes the smallest of things can make a difference. In August Marlborough received a letter from his eleven-year-old grandson William Godolphin (eventually to earn notoriety as Willigo, Marquess of Blandford), who had visited Queen Anne to present the standard, due on 13 August each year as the 'peppercorn' rent for Blenheim. The boy reported that he had been 'received but coldly', a sure sign that the family was out of favour.[145]

Richard Kane thought that Marlborough 'seemed very much chagrined' by all this, and, unusually, 'seemed very peevish, and would see but little company, and seemed resolved upon attacking Villars'.[146] On 30 July Marlborough informed Godolphin: 'I shall march the army on Saturday [1 August], and if I can see any hope of success, I shall attack them.'[147]

Marlborough now had much of his army concentrated opposite the lines just west of Arras. He reconnoitred Villars' position with an escort of 2,000 horse, and discussed his intention to attack with the Dutch general Count Tilly, whose wife, present on the campaign, was at best talkative and at worst, if Goslinga is to be believed, in communication with the French. Villars deduced, not unreasonably, that the attack would be delivered in the area between Vimy Ridge and Avesnes le Comte, and concentrated to meet it. Although Marlborough had apparently placed all his weight on his right foot, he had begun, imperceptibly, to shift it to his left. Albemarle had been sent to Béthune, a little to his left, with twelve battalions and twenty-four squadrons, and in the general clutter of his move the army's heavy guns and baggage were slipped further eastwards behind Vimy Ridge. Marlborough stripped the garrisons of Lille, Tournai and St Amand to bring Hompesch's force at Douai up to twenty-three battalions and seventeen squadrons, and, a key intelligence indicator had Villars only known of it, now had all his pontoons at Douai.

Captain Robert Parker, who knew the duke's methods well, thought that there was 'something extraordinary' in his reconnaissance of the French position, and saw how 'his countenance was now cleared up, and with an air of assurance, as if he was confident of success, he pointed out to the General Officers, the manner in which the army was to be drawn up, the places that were to be attacked, and how sustained'. Parker saw Cadogan break away from the group with only a single servant, but thought nothing of it at the time.[148] Having fluttered the matador's cloak, Marlborough lunged with the sword. On the evening of 4 July,

on our beating Tattoo, to our great joy, orders came along both lines, to strike our tents, and form our regiments with all dispatch imaginable; and in less than an hour, the whole army was on a full march away to the left. This was no small surprise to us; nor could we yet conceive what he meant by it. We continued marching all night, being favoured by the light of a bright full moon, and fine calm weather. A little before day [at about 3 a.m. on the fifth], the Duke being at the head of the march, an express arrived from General Cadogan, signifying that he and General Hompesch had passed the causeway of Arleux without opposition . . . and that they were in possession of the enemy's lines. Upon this the Duke rode off with all the left wing of horse; at the same time he sent an account of it to every particular regiment of foot, with orders to continue their march with all the expedition they possibly could.[149]

It was the apotheosis of Marlborough's infantry. With the French sometimes in sight in the moonlight on the other side of the Scarpe, and with the men lengthening their stride, the word was passed back, for the last time, that 'My Lord Duke desires the foot to step it out.' Private Deane remembered how 'we accordingly marched . . . at a very sharp rate all the night long, leaving Arras on the right hand . . . and got to Arleux and marched through it at about 4 or 5 o'clock in the morning'. He could see that the French cavalry had already come up, but that they dared not attack without infantry, which was still strung out along the line of march. 'And by this means and nobly thought and notable stratagem,' exulted Deane, 'was this noted admirable pass taken and nearly tricked from the enemy by the noble conduct and the profound judgement of a wise, prudent general.'[150]

Villars' army was complete in the area of Bourlon Wood, just west of Cambrai, and Marlborough debated attacking it. Goslinga, our main source for the discussion, records his despair at Marlborough's eventual decision, backed by the majority of his council of war, not to attack. Goslinga complained that suggestions that the ground was ill-suited to an attack were merely temporising, but Villars had already begun making *abatis* on the northern edge of Bourlon Wood, and the shadow of Malplaquet fell across the debate. Marlborough's decision aroused criticism, some of it from the same folk who had blamed him for attacking at Malplaquet, and on 13 August he told Heinsius:

I cannot help unburdening myself to you, that I think I lie under great hardships and discouragement on this occasion by some letters I have seen in Holland, which seem to reflect on my note making the best use of our advantage by giving the enemy battle as soon as we had passed the lines. I own that had it been practicable there is no comparison between the advantage of a battle and what we can reap from a siege, but there is not one general or other officer that have the least judgement in these matters but must allow it was altogether impossible to attack the enemy with any probable hopes of success. I cannot but think it is very hard, when I do my best, to be liable to such censures.[151]

Instead, Marlborough swung north-east to besiege Bouchain. He could not begin the siege proper until he had dislodged Albergotti from a strong intermediate position, and on the morning of the ninth Robert Parker, waiting in a wheatfield with the grenadiers of the British contingent, saw how

> the Duke of Marlborough (ever watchful, ever right) rode up quite unattended and alone, and posted himself a little on the right of my company of grenadiers, from whence he had a fair view of the greater part of the enemy's works. It is quite impossible for me to express the joy which the sight of this man gave me at this very critical moment. I was now well satisfied that he would not push the thing, unless he saw a strong possibility of success; nor was this my notion alone: it was the sense of the whole army, both officer and soldier, British and foreigner . . . He stayed only three or four minutes, and then rode back. We were in pain for him while he stayed, lest the enemy discovered him, and fired upon him; in which case they could not very well have missed him.[152]

Marlborough cancelled the assault, and when the French followed up his withdrawal, savaged their advance guard.

In order to press the siege of Bouchain while Villars was on hand with an army roughly the size of his own, Marlborough constructed elaborate lines of circumvallation, fortified his camp, and entrenched a corridor up to the Scarpe at Marchiennes to protect the arrival of his supplies. In mid-August the besiegers cut the 'Cow Path' linking Albergotti's position outside the town to the fortress itself, and on the twentieth Marlborough happily reported to Godolphin that 'They are now shut up on all sides.' On 14 September he told his old friend: 'I am sure you will be very well pleased with the good news I now send . . . of our being masters of Bouchain, and that Marshal Villars has done us the honour of being witness of the garrison being made prisoners of war. They consist of eight battalions and 500 Swiss.'[153]

Marlborough rated highly his achievement in breaking the *Ne Plus Ultra* lines and capturing Bouchain, and three of the great tapestries in Blenheim Palace were to be devoted to these episodes. However, with Maynwaring and other Whig pamphleteers assailing the ministry, Tory propagandists struck back, belittling the captain general's achievements, and Marlborough looked vainly to his political masters for some support. But, unknown to him, as early as August 1710 Harley had opened secret negotiations with Torcy, the French foreign minister, based on the recognition that Philip V was never going to be expelled from Spain. The negotiations became formal in April 1711, and were placed in the hands of St John, who became Viscount Bolingbroke in 1712, though with a very bad grace, for he had hoped to be an earl. 'I was dragged into the House of Lords,' he complained, 'in such a manner as to make my promotion a punishment, not a reward.'[154] Bolingbroke sought to get the best peace he could for Britain, even though this involved forcing her allies to accept worse terms than those which had so nearly been achieved in previous negotiations. Preliminaries were signed in October 1711, although they did not end the war, and a conference was to assemble at Utrecht in January 1712 to discuss definitive terms. The ministry used Jonathan Swift to support its case for peace in a brilliant pamphlet called *The Conduct of the Allies in the late War*, in which he argued that the conquest of Spain had never been in Britain's interest, and that had it not been for the Whigs' rash insistence upon it the war could have been ended in 1709.

The peace signed at Utrecht in early 1713 embodied a number of individual treaties between the belligerents. The Duke of Anjou was recognised as Philip V of Spain, but he renounced, for himself and his descendants, all claims to the throne of France, while various French princes relinquished their own possible claims to the Spanish throne. The Pyrenees had been rebuilt. Archduke Charles, the Hapsburg claimant to Spain, could survive well enough without his pretended throne, for he had in fact succeeded his brother Joseph as Holy Roman Emperor in 1711. At Utrecht he received the Spanish Netherlands, the Kingdom of Naples, Sardinia, and most of the Duchy of Milan. Victor Amadeus of Savoy was rewarded for his adherence to the Allies by gaining the remainder of Milan and the whole of Sicily.

Spain ceded both Gibraltar and Minorca to Britain, enabling Richard Kane of the Royal Irish to set off for the latter as its new governor, and to pen his own account of the war in its pleasant climate. Spain also granted Britain the *asiento de negros*, a thirty-year agreement to sell slaves and five hundred tons of merchandise annually in Spanish colonies. This allowed legitimate traders into the hitherto closed markets of Central and South America, and smugglers immediately followed: disputes, and the alleged mutilation of a British sea captain, led to the War of Jenkins' Ear in 1739.

France made extensive concessions in North America, renouncing its claims in Newfoundland, the huge territory of Rupert's Land (named for the cavalier Prince Rupert) around Hudson's Bay, and the coastal region of Acadia. Both Île St-Jean (Prince Edward Island) and Île Royale (Cape Breton Island) remained in French hands, and work soon began on building the Vauban-style fortress of Louisbourg on the latter. War between France and the Empire formally lurched on until it was ended by the Treaties of Rastatt and Baden in 1714. In the following year the Treaty of Madrid closed the struggle between Spain and Portugal, although a state of war between Spain and the Empire officially existed till 1720.

There was widespread indignation amongst the Whigs that the French had escaped too lightly, especially in view of the fact that the terms agreed at Utrecht fell well short of those the French had earlier seemed so close to accepting. The Whig politician John Wilkes later said that, like 'the Peace of God, the treaty passeth all understanding'. The Tories argued that the treaty served British interests well, though there was no denying that the Dutch, who had played such a resolute part in the struggle and then hosted the negotiation that ended it, had gained little. '*De vous, chez vous, sans vous*' ('About you, at home with you, but without you'), quipped bitter Dutchmen. However, although many of the fortresses captured by the Allies in the last three years of the war were, like the mighty Lille, restored to the French, there was no realistic threat to Dutch sovereignty for the next two generations.

What was undeniably true, though, was that the treaty had removed the danger of a huge Bourbon super-state, comprising not only France and Spain but all the latter's overseas colonies, whose existence could only have been inimical to British interests. The lesser risk of a Hapsburg super-state had also been averted, and the Tories could claim, with some justice, that the agreement created a European balance of power which it would be hard for a single nation to disrupt.

Dismissed the Service

Marlborough's position was exceptionally difficult. He had long had reservations about the Whigs' policy of 'No Peace without Spain', but as what Winston S. Churchill calls 'the soul of the Grand Alliance', he disliked the notion of abandoning the allies upon whose troops he had relied. He had especially close relations with Hanover, whose Elector, likely to become king of Great Britain in the foreseeable future, was firmly opposed to the preliminaries. However, he was more Tory than Whig by personal persuasion, and had worked well enough with members of the present ministry, most notably Bolingbroke.

He was certainly convinced that the war could not go on, though he was less sure what constituted reasonable peace terms. In October 1711 he told Oxford that 'there is nothing upon earth I wish more than an end of the war . . . I am perfectly convinced that it brings the draining of our nation both of men and money, almost to the last extremity. Our Allies by degrees so shift the burthen of the war upon us, that at the rate they go on, the whole charge must at last fall on England.'[155]

It would have been hard for Marlborough to keep his head below the political parapet, although the signs are that, tired and beset by an increasing number of headaches, he might well have wished to. In December 1711 the House of Lords debated a Whig amendment to the queen's speech. It affirmed that 'No Peace could be safe or honourable to Great Britain or Europe if Spain and the West Indies were allotted to any branch of the House of Bourbon.' Marlborough supported the amendment, and sealed his fate: the Lords took the same view and sealed their own. Twelve Tory peers were to be created so as to ensure the passage through the Lords of the eventual peace, and the ministry unleashed the commissioners of public accounts, already digging deeply into the parlous state of the nation's finances, upon Marlborough.

Two of the many irregularities that the commissioners discovered in army accounts affected Marlborough personally. The first was that he had accepted a total of £60,000 in gifts from Antonio Machado and Sir Solomon de Medina, contractors for bread and bread wagons. Medina, testifying in London, agreed that he had indeed given Mr Sweet, the deputy paymaster at Amsterdam, 1 per cent of all the monies he had received for the contracts, and had also paid Cardonnel five hundred ducats a year. As soon as Medina had given his evidence, Marlborough assured the commissioners that 'this is no more than what has been allowed as a perquisite to the general, or commander-in-chief of the army in the Low Countries, even before the Revolution'. He told them that he had not accepted the money on his own behalf, but that it had been 'constantly employed for the service of the public, in keeping secret correspondence, and getting intelligence of the enemy's motions and designs'.[156] Cadogan, who produced the papers to assist Marlborough in his defence, went back so far in the accounts that he was sure it was 'undeniably evident, that for these five and thirty years past it was the established custom to present the grand commander-in-chief with a considerable annual gratification in proportion to the number of troops of the army'.[157]

The second accusation against Marlborough was that he had received 2½ per cent of the money paid to foreign troops in British pay. He replied that this was the traditional way in which a commander-in-chief financed his secret intelligence, and added that he had himself negotiated the agreement in the time of William III, and also held a warrant from Queen Anne, dated 6 July 1702, authorising the practice. His defence was not wholly persuasive. William had instituted the scheme to get round Parliament's tight control over military expenditure during his reign, and the 1702 warrant had lapsed and its existence was not known to the paymaster general or to the exchequer. While Marlborough had undoubtedly spent some of the money on that intelligence service which had served him so well, Ivor Burton is surely right to suggest that 'nothing like 2½ per cent of the entire cost of 30,000 auxiliary troops could possibly have been needed for this purpose'.[158] Nevertheless, the fact that Marlborough's successor enjoyed the same perquisites emphasises that his conduct was not wholly unreasonable.

The findings of the inquiry were enough for Harley to persuade the queen to dismiss Marlborough from all his military offices on 31 December 1711. The *London Gazette* on New Year's Day 1712 duly recorded Marlborough's dismissal. The Duke of Ormonde succeeded him as commander-in-chief and colonel of 1st Foot Guards, and Lord Rivers became master general of the ordnance. The same *Gazette* announced the promotion of the twelve new Tory peers.

Marlborough took his downfall with remarkable equanimity, writing to assure his well-wishers that he sought only 'a quiet retirement . . . [which is] what I have long wished for, I shall be easy in my relation to my own destiny, and shall always add my good wishes for the continued success and prosperity of the public'.[159] Amongst the dozens of replies to foreign monarchs, soldiers and diplomats who had sent their commiserations was a note to Sir Thomas Wheate, who lived at Glympton, near Woodstock. 'I am very much obliged to you for being mindful of my want of beagles,' Marlborough wrote, 'though I am yet at a loss where to keep them; however I should be glad to know where they are, and if the huntsman will undertake to keep them till I have a proper place, and upon what terms, to which I shall pray your answer at your leisure.'[160] It seemed that he might, at long last, be able to live in retirement as a country gentleman, albeit in a rather big house.

Marlborough had little to do with the Treaty of Utrecht, though he can have taken little comfort in the events leading up to it. Bolingbroke's plans received a serious jolt when in 1713 the Duke of Burgundy and his eldest son both died, leaving only one infant prince, the future Louis XV, between Philip of Spain and the French throne. Bolingbroke and Oxford decided that Philip could either keep Spain but renounce France, or leave Spain to the Duke of Savoy and take the latter's territories and Sicily instead. Neither the Imperialists nor the Dutch would accept this, and resolved to fight on. To prevent the Allies from gaining a victory which might have upset their plans, the ministry imposed 'restraining orders' on Marlborough's successor. Ormonde was secretly forbidden to engage the French, leading to letters like this, from Ormonde to Villars:

> It is true, Sir, that for the siege of Quesnoy, which it was not in my power to prevent, I was obliged to contribute some troops in the pay of the Estates-General, but not a single man in the Queen's pay; it seems to me that, as we had not even opened our trenches, that the siege could in no way break the measures agreed by our sovereigns.[161]

'Whether the Duke of Ormonde was really concerned at receiving these orders, I shall not take it upon me to say,' wrote Robert Parker; 'but however that was, most certain it is, that he was extremely punctual in observing them.'[162] Corporal Bishop thought that with Marlborough's departure, 'the neck of the war was broke, and that I should be disappointed of the pleasure of seeing Paris next year'.[163] Richard Kane was even more critical. Ormonde, he thought, was 'a good natured, but a weak and ambitious man, fit to be made tool of by a crafty set of knaves'.[164] Without British help, the Allies took Quesnoy but lost it again almost immediately, and Eugène, who had taken over as Allied commander-in-chief, was beaten by Villars at Denain. Villars finished up with Marchines, Bouchain and Douai in his hands, having undone much of the work of Marlborough's last two campaigns.

The treaty was not signed till 1713, and it took the Empire another year to agree to it. The terms were approved by Parliament, passing the Lords by eighty-one to thirty-six votes. Twenty-four peers, Marlborough and Godolphin among them, recorded their formal protest, but the majority ordered this to be struck from the records of the House. When the protest was printed for circulation, the ministry prosecuted its printers and publishers.

By this time Marlborough's own position had deteriorated. Parliament concluded, by a substantial majority, that 'the taking of several sums of money annually by the Duke of Marlborough from the contractor for foraging the bread and wagons in the Low Countries was unwarrantable and illegal', and that the 2½ per cent deducted from the pay of foreign troops 'is public money, and ought to be accounted for'.[165] The House of Commons took vengeance on Cardonnel, one of the MPs for Southampton, and duly expelled him for having accepted bribes from Medina. The government press enjoyed open season on Marlborough, that man who had 'once perhaps been fortunate'. Captain Parker was shocked to see that the *Examiner*, one of the ministry's news-sheets, described the former captain general as 'naturally a very great coward . . . all the victories and successes that attended him, were owing to mere chance, and to those about him'. 'Had I not read those words,' Parker wrote, 'I should never have believed that any man could have the face to publish so notorious a falsehood.'[166]

Exile and Return

Falsehood or not, it was clear to Marlborough and his supporters that he was in real trouble. The ministry's lawyers had it in mind to make him repay the cash he had acquired from Medina and his percentage of the pay of foreign troops, and the crown was likely to demand the return of part of the money expended on Blenheim Palace, still far from completion. The repeated attacks on his reputation made it dangerous for him to remain in England, and with Anne's health visibly failing, the prospect of a Hanoverian succession might provoke factional violence or, as many Whigs feared (with good reason, as we shall see), a Jacobite invasion. He had other reasons for wishing to go to the Continent. It seemed probable that peace negotiations would result in his principality of Mindelheim being given to Bavaria, and he hoped to prevent this. Marlborough also hoped that he might persuade the Elector of Hanover and other Allied sovereigns to send an expedition to Britain to forestall the expected Jacobite attack. In short, he had much to risk and little to gain by staying at Holywell. 'In England,' writes Winston S. Churchill, 'he was a prey. In Europe he was a prince.'[167]

The queen, who retained great personal attachment to Marlborough, told Dr Hamilton that 'it was prudent of him' to depart, and signed his passport on 30 October. Bolingbroke maintained that there had been 'a good deal of contest' within the cabinet about allowing him to go, though the passport bears his countersignature. There have been suggestions that Oxford was so anxious to get Marlborough out of the country that he threatened to make public details of his dealings with the French over the money promised him for helping bring about peace. There is no doubt that Marlborough met Oxford that autumn, but the best we can say of the 'blackmail' assertion is that, even if it were true, Oxford was 'forcing at an open door with a battering ram', for Marlborough had many other reasons to depart.[168] However, one of Oxford's letters to Maynwaring, Marlborough's intermediary in his application for a pass-port, tells him that 'You will . . . assure your friend that there have been endeavours from both sides to obstruct granting the pass desired, yet I shall have the honour to put it into his hands.'[169] This would be odd lan-guage had the idea of exile been Oxford's in the first place. Marlborough passed much of his money to his sons-in-law, and transferred £50,000 to Cadogan, then serving as envoy extraordinary and minister plenipoten-tiary at The Hague, in case, as Sarah put it, 'the Stuart line were restored': Cadogan's error in investing this money in Austria rather than Holland, losing interest in the process, was to attract Sarah's wrath.

Marlborough at least had the opportunity of seeing Sidney Godolphin to his grave before going into exile. Godolphin died at Holywell, and it took three weeks to get sufficient Whig Knights of the Garter to act as his pallbearers, 'for they don't find the Tory knights so ready to come to town a purpose'. He was buried in Westminster Abbey on 7 October with the Dukes of Marlborough, Devonshire, Richmond and Schomberg bearing his pall. Sarah recognised in their old friend a virtue she admired, even if she could not share it: 'He was a man of wonderful fru-gality in the public concerns but of no great money above his paternal estate. What he left at his death showed that he had indeed been the nation's treasurer and not his own.'[170]

Marlborough drove to Dover on 24 November 1712 with just a few servants, but, held up by contrary winds, could not get a packet boat till the end of the month, and arrived in Ostend on 1 December. He was received there with enthusiasm, and went on to Antwerp, where his welcome was so spectacular, with shipping in the harbour firing salutes, that he made the next stage of his journey, to Maastricht, in Dutch ter-ritory, by a circuitous route to avoid stirring up public excitement that might affront the British government. Now accompanied by both Cadogan and the Dutch General Dopff, he was greeted by a guard of honour and yet more demonstrations of public regard when he reached Aachen on 21 January 1713.

That day he told Sarah that he had received no letters from her since 20 December, and was not sure where she now was. He advised her that because of a sudden thaw 'you will find the ways extremely bad, and as this place is extremely dirty I have resolved to go to Maastricht at the beginning of the week, and there to expect you. I send this letter to Ostend in hopes it may meet you there.'[171] By early February he was palpably concerned at not having heard from her. 'If you have observed by my letters that I thought you would have left England sooner than you have been able to do,' he wrote,

> I hope you will be so kind and just to me, to impute it to the great desire I had of having the satisfaction of your company. For I am extremely sensible of the obligation I have to you, for the resolution you have taken of leaving your friends and country for my sake. I am very sure, if there be anything in my power that may make it easy to you, I should do it with all imaginable pleasure. In this place you will have little conveniences; so that we must get to Frankfurt as soon as we can. I wish we may be better there; but I fear you will not be easy till we get to some place where we may settle for some time; so that we may be in a method and orderly way of living; and if you are then contented, I shall have nothing to trouble me.[172]

Sarah applied for her passport on 29 January. It was granted without delay, and she set off to join her husband. But while he had travelled light, she took with her a substantial wardrobe, which included forty cloaks and petticoats and several leopard-skin muffs, as well as a chocolate pot and a five-pint kettle. Her little retinue included a Protestant chaplain with the improbable name of Whadcock Priest. What she saw soon convinced her of 'the sad effects of Popery and arbitrary power', though she was delighted by her reception by the nuns of Aachen.

> If our enemies do prevail to our utter ruin, I think I had best go into a monastery. There are several of them in this town, and tis all the entertainment I have to vist [them]. I supped with about twenty [nuns] the other night but twas a very slight [meal] nothing but brown bread and butter . . . They were as fond of me as if I had not been a heretic.[173]

They reached Frankfurt in the middle of May, and Sarah was delighted to see that the troops, under Eugène's command, paid her lord 'all the respects as if he had been in his old post'.

To see so may brave men marching by was a fine sight. It gave me melancholy reflections, and made me weep; but at the same time I was so much animated that I wished I had been a man that I might have ventured my life a thousand times in the glorious cause of liberty . . .

When I had written so far I was called to receive the honour of a visit from the Elector of Mainz. I fancy he came to this place chiefly to see the Duke of Marlborough. His chap [cheek] is, like my own, a little of the fattest, but in my life I never saw a face that expressed so much openness, honesty and good nature . . . I can't help repeating part of his compliment to the Duke of Marlborough, that he wished any Prince of the Empire might be severely punished if they forgot his merit. It would fill a book to give you an account of all the honours done the Duke of Marlborough in all the towns . . . as if he had been king of them.[174]

She could not but contrast the civility with which they were received on the Continent with the way they had been cold-shouldered in England.

'Tother day we were walking upon the road, and a gentleman and a lady went past us in their chariot who we had never seen before, and after passing with us the usual civilities, in half a quarter of an hour or less they bethought themselves and turned back, came out of their coach to us, and desired that we would go into their garden, which was very near that place, and which they think, I believe, is a very fine thing, desiring us to accept of a key. This is only a little taste of the civility of people abroad, and I could not help thinking that we might have walked in England as far as our feet would have carried us before anybody that we had never seen before would have lighted out of their coach to have entertained us.[175]

Marlborough visited his principality of Mindelheim, where he was received with royal honours. He already suspected that its location meant that it would go to Bavaria when peace was concluded, and this is indeed what happened. The emperor promised to 'give his highness an equivalent principality out of his own hereditary dominions', and eventually created a new principality from the county of Mellenburg, in Upper Austria. Archdeacon Coxe doubted if this had actually happened, grumbling that 'The most eminent services are but too often ill requited, when they cease to be necessary or useful,' but the best evidence suggests that the exchange was indeed made.[176]

Marlborough was in very close contact with the Electoral court at Hanover, and worked hard, with Cadogan and Robethon, to ensure that the Elector would succeed bloodlessly to the throne on Anne's death, although the Elector made it clear that he had no intention of sending an expedition to Britain before he had formally succeeded to the throne. They concluded that most of the British troops on the Continent at the time of her death 'would readily obey a man so agreeable to them as the Duke of Marlborough', and both the Duke and Cadogan received provisional commissions from the Elector authorising them to take command of these troops when the queen died. Marlborough moved from Frankfurt to Antwerp, to be as close as possible to England when the moment came. In Britain, meanwhile, the ministry purged the army not simply of outright Whigs, but of men like Argyll and Stair, many of whom joined armed associations ready to support the Protestant succession when Anne died.

At precisely the same time that he was working so eagerly for a Hanoverian succession, Marlborough was corresponding with the Jacobites. Indeed, the German historian Onno Klopp argued, in *Der Fall des Hauses Stuart*, that 'Marlborough succeeded in an astonishing way in not losing the confidence of Saint-Germain, while at the same time preserving that of Hanover.' Winston S. Churchill maintains that his contact with the Jacobite court gave him 'a window of indispensable intelligence', and that this is the only motive for his behaviour that 'fits all the facts of twenty years'.[177] It is hard to share this confidence. We have already seen that Marlborough had shifted £50,000 to the Continent in case of a Stuart restoration, and we shall soon note that he remained on good terms with the Jacobites when he was close to death and had no official responsibilities or personal ambitions. The truth is probably that, as Sarah observed on 17 October 1713, it was impossible to be sure of anything, and dangerous to burn any bridges. 'This is a world that is subject to frequent revolutions,' she wrote, 'and though one wishes to leave one's posterity secure, there is so few that makes a suitable return even upon that account.'[178]

Moreover, the spirit of the age saw little wrong in Marlborough's continuing friendship with James II's illegitimate son the Duke of Berwick, who was his nephew long before he became a Marshal of France. As Berwick pointed out, when asking Marlborough leave for an equerry to visit the Allied army 'to buy some English horses', there were contacts 'so indifferent to the public cause' as not to excite reasonable criticism. Berwick concluded: 'pray [give] my compliments to Mr Godfrey,' the

English officer now married to his mother.[179] When they were in exile Sarah feared that her husband's old fire had left him. She thought he had grown 'intolerably lazy', and one early biographer recorded a comment made at the time: 'The only things the Duke has forgotten are his deeds. The only things he remembers are the misfortunes of others.'[180] In early 1714 his favourite daughter Elizabeth, Countess of Bridgewater, died of smallpox. He received the dreadful news in his house at Antwerp, where he was leaning on a marble mantelpiece: it was said that his head slammed against the marble so hard that he fell to the floor unconscious.

Queen Anne had been very ill over the winter of 1713–14, but had recovered sufficiently to open Parliament in person on 15 February. However, it was 'universally recognised that her days were numbered', and on 5 January Oxford's cousin Thomas Harley was sent to Hanover to assure the Electoral court that Anne was determined to adhere to the Act of Settlement that enshrined the Hanoverian succession.[181] Just as Marlborough kept a foot in both camps, so Oxford also negotiated with the Jacobites, though there can be no doubt that his overtures to St Germain were perfectly sincere. He used an intermediary to ask James, the Old Pretender, to change or at least conceal his religion, and Bolingbroke assured the French envoy in London that unless he did so there was no chance of his succeeding, for 'people would rather have a Turk than a catholic'. Happily for the Protestant succession, James declined to temporise.

On about 9 June Marlborough told Viscount Molyneux of yet another twist: there would be no Queen Sophie. He had arrived at Herrenhausen, the country retreat of the Electoral court,

> And there the first thing I heard was that the good old electress was dying in one of the public walks. I ran up there, and found her just expiring in the arms of the poor electoral princess, and amidst the tears of a great many of her servants, who endeavoured in vain to help her . . . No princess ever died more regretted, and I infinitely pity those servants that have known her a long time, when I, that have had the honour to know her but a month, can scarce refrain from tears in relating this.[182]

Marlborough thought that the electress's death had been brought on by receiving letters from Oxford saying that, despite her hope that her grandson would be summoned to Parliament by virtue of his British dukedom, so as to be on hand when Anne died, no member of her family would be allowed to enter the kingdom while the queen still lived. Anne at once ordered that 'The Princess Sophia' should be replaced by 'the Elector of Hanover' in the appropriate part of *The Book of Common Prayer*. The Elector, now heir apparent to the throne of Great Britain, repeated his request for a senior member of his family to reside in England, and replaced his envoy there with Baron von Bothmar, not only his close confidant but an enemy of Oxford's.

On 9 July Marlborough, writing from Antwerp, told Robethon that 'the arrival of Mons Bothmar may be of great use'. He added that he would not leave for England till the end of the month, and was confident that the British troops at Dunkirk 'are all well inclined apart from the two battalions of Orkney's [Regiment]'.

Although Winston S. Churchill argues that Marlborough's determination to return home was a bold personal decision, we now know that he had written to the queen through the medium of his daughter and her godchild Lady Sunderland. Although the contents of the letter are unknown, it is possible that the queen may have summoned him home, using Cadogan as her point of contact. In any event, Bolingbroke had been in touch with James Craggs, Marlborough's man of affairs, and it seems to have been agreed that Marlborough would be reinstated in his former offices, with Ormonde becoming viceroy of Ireland by way of compensation. Adverse winds delayed Marlborough's arrival in London, where he had been expected on 21 July, and this probably thwarted Anne's hope that Marlborough and Bolingbroke between them would assume the reins of government, ensuring a smooth succession on her death.

On 7 July Anne dismissed Oxford, leaving Bolingbroke, directionless at the moment of supreme crisis, in effective charge of the ministry. On the thirtieth, barely conscious, she passed the lord treasurer's white staff to the Duke of Shrewsbury, one of the middle party who had brought Oxford to power in 1710, and she died at 7.45 on the morning of Sunday, 1 August. She was forty-nine years old. The Elector of Hanover was proclaimed King George I at St James's Palace at four o'clock that afternoon, and the Marlboroughs reached Dover on the following morning. The *Flying Post* reported from Rochester that:

> The Duke and Duchess of Marlborough passed through this city; they were received with great expressions of joy from the people, especially those at Chatham, who strewed their way with flowers, as they adorned

their houses with green boughs, and welcomed them with repeated shouts and acclamations.[183]

They arrived in London later that day, and rode through the streets of the city in their coach, escorted by a great body of gentlemen on horseback, the civic authorities and a detachment of grenadiers, to the accompaniment of cheers leavened with the occasional boo. Marlborough was irritated to discover that his name was not on the list of regents kept by Bothmar, but as he was abroad when the list was made out his absence from it is not surprising. George had decreed that he wished Anne's funeral to have taken place before he arrived, and she was buried in Westminster Abbey, in the presence, amongst others, of both Henrietta Godolphin and Mary Montagu.

King George arrived in London on 18 September. He had already dismissed Bolingbroke and ordered the seizure of his papers, and received Oxford 'with a most distinguishing contempt'. Now the Tories were out and the Whigs were in, and when a parliamentary committee investigated the Utrecht negotiations Bolingbroke fled to France, and though he was eventually allowed to return to England he never again held office. Oxford was impeached and lodged in the Tower, but although the case against him was dropped he too never again held office. Marlborough, in contrast, was received by the new king with the greatest cordiality. 'My Lord Duke,' he said, 'I hope your troubles are now all over.'[184] The first warrant signed by George I reinstated Marlborough as captain general, master general of the ordnance, and colonel of 1st Foot Guards. The first knighthood of the new reign was bestowed on the king's physician, Dr Samuel Garth. He asked to have the ceremony performed with Marlborough's sword, and the king was happy to agree. A Whig majority was returned at the new election: the Tories were to be out of power for almost forty years.

Marlborough's natural good nature had been somewhat bruised by the treatment he had received, and when, with the aid of Cadogan and Argyll, he remodelled the army in 1714–15 he reinstated his friends and evicted many of his enemies. During the Jacobite rebellion of 1715 Argyll and Cadogan commanded the army in the field, and Marlborough presided over the campaign from London. Documents in the Cadogan papers show that there was nothing nominal in his exercise of authority. He helped ensure that the Dutch sent a lieutenant general and six battalions, six Flemish and six Swiss, to help government forces, and Cadogan relied on him to get the exchequer to open its stopcock.

'I beg your Grace to press the giving orders for the payment of my bills,' begged Cadogan; 'the least failure in that point would ruin my credit entirely.'[185]

Like so many Jacobite attempts on the throne, the 'Fifteen suffered from abysmal leadership. The proverbial unsteadiness of the Earl of Mar, James Stuart's chosen instrument in Scotland, had already gained him the nickname 'Bobbin' John', and although he raised around 8,000 men and seized Perth, he failed to take swift and potentially decisive action. He sent a detachment to join other Jacobites in the Lowlands, and although this little army got as far as Preston it was overwhelmed in November. His main force, over twice the size of the government army, had the better of a battle against Argyll at Sheriffmuir near Perth on 13 November, but did little to exploit this success. When James landed in Scotland and established himself at Scone he did no better, consumed by melancholy and bouts of fever which were an ominous echo of his father's misfortunes in 1688. He departed for France early in 1716, advising his followers to shift for themselves. Three years later a small Spanish fleet was providentially scattered by storms before it could land the troops it carried, and the handful who reached Scotland found little local support and soon surrendered. In 1715 intended risings in Wales and the West Country had been quickly snuffed out by the arrests of their leaders.

The government sought to strengthen its grip on Scotland by passing the Disarming Acts, building forts and barracks linked by military roads, and, in 1725, raising local independent companies soon known, from the dark hue of their plaids, as the Black Watch. However, it would have taken an unusually prescient man to write off Jacobitism, for the 'Forty-Five rebellion, which was to end in drizzle, blood and powder smoke at Culloden, got as far as Derby, just 125 miles from London, and enjoyed a tantalising prospect of success. As long as Marlborough lived a Jacobite restoration could not be ruled out, and he continued to entertain Jacobite agents until shortly before his death.

That 'ease and quiet' which had been the subject of so many wistful letters was denied Marlborough. He had already lost Elizabeth Bridgewater during his exile, and in April 1716 Anne Sunderland died of 'pleuritic fever' – probably septicaemia after blood-letting. Sarah complained that the doctor 'did as certainly murder my dear Lady Sunderland as surely as if he had shot her through the head'.[186]

Soon afterwards, at Holywell on 28 May 1716, Marlborough suffered the first of his strokes, losing the power of both speech and movement. Thanks to (or perhaps despite) the efforts of his physician Samuel Garth he improved sufficiently to go to Bath in mid-July, where Sarah thought him 'vastly better in his head and his speech', although 'he can't come upstairs without uneasiness'. Sometimes he felt well enough for a hand or two of ombre, but he was often gloomy about his health, and complained that his belly had grown hard: Sarah agreed that his coat, roomy when they went down to Bath, no longer buttoned easily. She had him fed vipers boiled in broth, and the Duchess of Shrewsbury assured her that the best viper broth came from Montpellier. Although Sarah hoped that the vipers might 'mend his blood and take off the lowness of his spirits', she soon decided that hartshorn and calvesfoot jelly would be much better.

In November, while staying in a house on the Blenheim estate, Marlborough had another, more severe stroke. The diarist Dudley Ryder was shocked by what he saw.

> The Duke of Marlborough is very ill and has lost much of his senses that he often falls into fits of crying. Methinks the frailty and mortality of human nature never appeared in a more moving and affecting light than in him. To see a man that was but just now the glory and pride of a nation, the hero of the world, of such vast abilities and knowledge and consequence sink almost below a rational creature, all his fine qualities disappear and fall away.[187]

Marlborough recovered well enough to ride again, and his mind was as sharp as ever, but his speech remained impaired, and his inability to manage certain words kept him increasingly confined within the family circle, though he attended the Lords to vote for Oxford's impeachment, and wept with frustration when he escaped without punishment.

Building at Blenheim, which had stopped in 1712, began again in 1716. Many of the craftsmen who had previously worked there were reluctant to return, fearing that the lumbering venture would stall yet again. Left to her own devices Sarah would not have pressed on with it. She thought that it had already cost a quarter of a million pounds, and that the whole business was 'a ridiculous madness'. Vanbrugh did his best to persuade her that the expense would be justified by its result, but she was not in the least convinced, and had a final row with him just before Marlborough suffered his second stroke.

With death now almost audibly falling into step behind him,

Marlborough was more determined than ever to see Blenheim finished. Sarah's biographer Frances Harris argues cogently that 'Nothing demonstrates the limitation of her influence with him . . . more clearly than the continued slow rise of his baroque palace in the Oxfordshire countryside, in spite of all she could do or say to hinder it.'[188] Now the project became an obligation laid upon Sarah by her husband's burning desire to see the palace completed at last. They spent part of their time at Holywell, part in the Lodge at Windsor Great Park, and part on the Blenheim estate. Marlborough often rode out to watch the workmen, or sat by Vanbrugh's ornamental bridge (a particular dislike of Sarah's) to see work on house and estate proceed. The Marlboroughs moved into rooms in the east wing in the summer of 1719. The duke was delighted, although many contemporaries agreed with the waspish Alexander Pope that it could be no fun actually to live in the place: 'I find, by all you have been telling,/That 'tis a house, but not a dwelling.'

Marlborough enjoyed playing cards with his grandchildren: whist was his favourite, but he liked basset, ombre and piquet too. He took particular pleasure in watching Lady Anne and Lady Diana Spencer act in John Dryden's *All for Love* (the story of Antony and Cleopatra, thoughtfully censored by Sarah) at Blenheim, and walked with difficulty through the house and the park, once stopping to gaze up at his portrait by Kneller and murmuring wistfully: 'That was once a man.'

Storms flashed and flickered over his head. Sarah fell out with Sunderland, who she thought had remarried beneath him. His new wife, Judith Tichborne, was an Irish heiress. She was 'about fifteen', complained Sarah, with 'a squinty look' to boot, a wholly unsuitable match for a man of forty-two. It was like 'marrying a kitten', and he would doubtless be persuaded 'to come out of his library to play with puss'. Although Sunderland's new wife's character was unblemished, Sarah doubted if it would remain so for long, and she feared that his second litter would be 'beggars with the titles of lords and ladies', who could only be provided for at the expense of his first children.[189] She invested in the South Sea Bubble but, with what Winston S. Churchill called 'her almost repellent common sense', got her money out well before the bubble popped, made £100,000 and then proceeded to lambast the stupidity of those who had not realised that 'the project must burst in a little while and fall to nothing'.

Sarah not only fell out with James Craggs (she thought him 'wicked enough to do anything'), but with his flamboyant son, James Craggs Junior. She might have forgiven him for misconduct with a servant at

Holywell, but he went too far when, on his way to a masquerade disguised as a friar, he cautioned her against issuing a general invitation to other folk in disguise because her enemies might arrive pretending to be her friends, and 'the Duchess of Montagu or my Lady Godolphin may come, and . . . you may give them a cup of tea or a dish of coffee'.[190] Sarah did not care to have it known that she had quarrelled with her daughters, Henrietta Godolphin and Mary Montagu, but it was all too true. Winston S. Churchill suggests that the fault was theirs, but it is fairer to say that there was blame on both sides, and Sarah, like her mother before her, had never been one to kiss and make up. Both daughters would come to visit their father, not in the morning, when they might have seen him alone, 'but at the hours when company was there'. They would, complained Sarah, go straight to him without paying any attention to her, 'as if they had a pleasure in showing everybody that they insulted me'.[191] Marlborough was offended by their behaviour, and told Mary: 'I observe that you take no manner of notice of your mother; and certainly when you consider of that, you can't imagine that any company can be very agreeable to me, who have not a right behaviour to her.' Early in 1721 he wrote, in a faltering hand, to lament: 'I am the worse to see my children live so ill with a mother for whom I must have the greatest tenderness and regard.'[192]

Even now Marlborough still dallied with the Jacobites. In June 1718 the Jacobite agent James Hamilton reported to the Earl of Mar:

> *Lord Portmore* was last Saturday with *Marlborough*. After several things passing the latter advised him to draw all his effects out of the stocks, which he did that day. *Marlborough* entertained him with railing against *Cadogan* and the measures of his directors, notwithstanding few doubt of *Marlborough* being the mainspring of the club, though he still affects the reverse. *Lord Portmore* looks on his head to be as sound as he has known it for some years . . . [193]

In mid-June 1722 Sarah was warned that Marlborough, in the Lodge at Windsor, was dying. She summoned her children and grandchildren to his sickbed, but there was the usual row. Sarah tells us:

> I am sure it is impossible for any tongue to express what I felt at the time, but I believe anybody that ever loved another so tenderly as I did the Duke of Marlborough may have some feeling of what it was to have one's children come in, in those last hours, who I knew did it not to

comfort me, but like enemies that would report to others whatever I did in a wrong way.

Eventually Sarah asked her daughters and granddaughter Harriot to leave the room so that she could lie down beside her husband. Mary Montagu replied:

> Will our being here hinder you from lying down? Then I sent Grace [Ridley, her servant] to ask again, to ask if she had such an affliction & was in my condition, whether she would like to have me with her? She said no, but did not go out until I sent her a third time.

With his wife lying beside him, John Churchill slipped away at four o'clock in the morning of 16 June 1722, at the very hour that his armies in Flanders and Brabant had been accustomed to hear the general call to arms rouse them from their tents for a day's march. Sarah said that she felt the soul tearing from her body as he died.

They buried him, with 'solemn splendour and martial pomp', in the vault at the east end of Henry VII's chapel in Westminster Abbey. Montagu was chief mourner, and eight dukes who were also Knights of the Garter followed him. Cadogan, who had succeeded Marlborough as commander-in-chief, walked in the procession behind the coffin, but was criticised for being ill-dressed and bumptious. Sarah was determined to pay for the funeral herself, to avoid being criticised for imposing a charge on the public purse when the family was so rich, but was horrified to discover that it had cost over £5,000. She went over the accounts carefully, discovering that she had been charged twice for the horses' black plumes, and complaining that the forty-eight yards of black cloth for the mourning coach would have been enough to cover her garden.[194]

Sarah lived on for another twenty-two years. Scarcely was Marlborough cold in his grave than she found herself courted. At sixty-two she was still attractive, although, in the way of ladies of a certain age, she thought herself rather overweight. Lady Mary Wortley Montagu said that she had 'the finest hair imaginable, the colour of which she had preserved by the constant use of honey water'.[195] She brushed Lord Coningsby aside, and also rejected the proud and wealthy Duke of Somerset, telling him that 'I would not marry the Emperor of the world though I were but thirty years old.' When he persisted, she silenced him by saying, 'If I were young and handsome as I was, instead of old and faded as I am, and you could lay the empire of the world at my feet, you should never share the heart and hand that once belonged to John Duke of Marlborough.'[196]

Marlborough's death did not bring about a family reconciliation. As he had died without male heirs, Henrietta Godolphin became Duchess of Marlborough in her own right. Her relationship with her mother was improved neither by the fact that she produced a child in 1723, after visiting Bath with the dramatist Congreve, nor by her friendship with Marlborough's sister Arabella, of whom Sarah had always disapproved. Henrietta died in 1733, and was succeeded by her nephew Charles Spencer, second son of her sister Anne and Charles Spencer, 3rd Earl of Sunderland: Charles had already inherited the Sunderland title from his elder brother (his death deeply regretted by Sarah) in 1729. Thereafter the dukedom passed steadily along the male line of the Spencers, and George Spencer, 5th Duke of Marlborough, obtained royal licence to assume the name and arms of Churchill, with the family name formally becoming Spencer-Churchill. Britain's Second World War leader Winston S. Churchill was a grandson of the 7th Duke, and was, rather unexpectedly, born at Blenheim in November 1874. His arrival was not anticipated for some weeks, but his mother fell while accompanying a shooting party, was rushed back to the palace in a donkey cart, and gave birth in a ground-floor room. His first name was that of John Churchill's father, and he always had a particular affection for the ancestor he loved to call 'Duke John'. He was fond of Blenheim too, and in 1908 proposed to Clementine Hozier, who was to become his long-suffering wife, in the Greek temple in its garden.

When Henrietta died Sarah was far more unhappy than she had ever expected, and told a goddaughter that Henrietta had begun by being sweet-natured, but 'wretched' friends like Congreve and John Gay were responsible for corrupting her. 'But,' she added perceptively, 'families seldom agree to live easily together.'[197] In contrast, she could not find a good word for Mary Montagu, and returned all her letters unopened. When the Duke of Montagu wrote to Sarah to complain 'upon her daughter's F[ucking] with M. Craggs', Sarah promptly replied: 'Milord, I have received your gracious letter. I am sorry you are a cuckold, my daughter a whore . . . and my niece such a bawd: I am your Grace's etc.'[198]

Sarah spent her last two decades supervising accounts of her husband's life, drawing up twenty-six drafts of her will, and working, with the assistance of various ghosts, on successive versions of her own political role. She lived so long that somehow people forgot how exasperating she had been. As the historian Christopher Hibbert put it, by the time of George II's coronation, when, exhausted by trudging to Westminster Abbey in her robes, she sat on a drum to recover herself, 'she had long been accepted as a kind of national institution'.[199]

She died in 1744, 'immensely rich', wrote Tobias Smollett, 'and very little regretted by either her own family or by the world in general'.[200] Frances Harris's luminous prose tells us that 'she went into the unknown not hoping or fearing very much; only trusting, in spite of everything, that the sincerity on which she had so long prided herself would be her saving grace if any were needed'.[201] She had long finished Blenheim, first jettisoning Vanbrugh, and then taking little notice of his successor Hawksmoor, but dealing direct with several of the master craftsmen working there. Economy and simplicity coloured much of what she did, but she spent £2,200 on a tomb in the chapel, designed by William Kent and carved by William Rysbrack. She had left instructions that Marlborough should be exhumed from Westminster Abbey to join her at Blenheim, and on 1 November 1744 their bodies were laid side by side in the vault beneath the chapel.

Sarah had never much liked the place, and John had not lived to see it completed. Yet there is good reason for him to rest in that overstated pile for eternity. It had been built to commemorate a battle that changed the fate of Europe. No reasonable observer, glancing at the Continent in 1700, could have predicted anything other than its domination by the French. And yet the same observer, looking at the world in 1722, the year Marlborough died, could not have ignored the rise of Great Britain to European stature and the beginnings of world power.

The process owed a good deal to men in dirty shirts and powder-burnt red coats, too often reviled by their countrymen and cast aside once the need for them had passed. The British army came of age under Marlborough's tutelage. The *Dictionary of National Biography* entry on that stormy petrel George Macartney, who rose, fell, rose, fell and rose again, makes the point perfectly. Macartney 'was a man of no great note on his own account, but he belonged to a band of fighting-men who built an army that . . . altered the course of European history'.[202] Some of them have tramped across these pages: Salamander Cutts and Charles Churchill, little Lord Lumley and Jemmy Campbell, the Duke of Argyll ('Red John of the battles'), Sergeant Millner, Corporal Bishop and Private Deane, drinking more than was good for them and not doing all their fighting against the Queen's enemies, but standing steady in rank and file when the drums beat up and their colours gleamed through the smoke. It was an army whose tactics leaned forward to Wellington rather than back to Oliver Cromwell and Prince Rupert, and whose regimental identity still strikes a chord (its tone, sadly, more muted than it once was) with the British army of the early twenty-first century.

Marlborough firmly grasped the essentials of his three combat arms. His infantry achieved its effect primarily by fire and his cavalry by shock. He recognised that artillery had the power to shape battle: at Blenheim, pushing his cannon across the Nebel helped tilt the balance in his favour; at Ramillies the French lamented the damage done to their battalions around the village by the Allied guns; and even at Malplaquet, where so much went wrong, the massed guns in his centre helped pave the way for the decisive stroke.

Marlborough knew that effectiveness on the battlefield depended on solid training, and that this could not simply be left to regimental commanders: standardisation was required. In December 1706 Lieutenant General Richard Ingoldsby wrote from Ghent:

> My Lord, I have begun to exercise all the adjutants, sergeants and corporals, who are already pretty perfect, and [am] mightily pleased that your Grace has thought fit to put them upon exercise.
>
> It is impossible to tell your Grace the disorder they were in, no two regiments exercising alike, nor any one company of grenadiers able to exercise with the battalion [from which it came] so that if your Lordship had a mind to see the Line exercise, all the grenadiers of the army must have stood still.
>
> I must not forget to tell your Grace that the Duke of Argyll's Regiment never had any pouches, or slings, but are trusting to a little cartouche-box which will not contain half the ammunition necessary for a day of action . . . [203]

It speaks volumes for Marlborough that he could attend to the detail of grenade drill and cartridge boxes while commanding the biggest army that Britain had ever put into the field and presiding over a large and complex coalition.

Marlborough's soldiers knew that they owed much to the man they liked to call 'Corporal John'. He bore a greater burden, military and political, than any British commander before or since, and of him alone could it be said that he never besieged a town he did not take, or fought a battle he did not win. In some respects Marlborough was a child of his times. He tried to give his men a day's rest on Sunday if the tempo of operations allowed it (though both Blenheim and Ramillies were fought on the Lord's day), and his courteous behaviour to his opponents betokened an age which strove, not altogether successfully, to introduce something of the first stirrings of the Enlightenment into war.

The German military thinker Carl von Clausewitz, who lived a century later, told his readers that in a coalition war the very cohesion of the coalition was of fundamental importance, and Marlborough was, first to last, a coalition general, supremely skilled at holding the Grand Alliance together, and at devising what a recent commentator calls 'agreed "systems" of orders, staffwork and movement'.[204] He was always keen to attack the cohesion of his enemies while at the same time protecting his own, and recognised that wars were not won by resolute defence, but by offensive action against the enemy's army in the field. If that was beaten, then territory could be taken and fortresses must inevitably fall. Of his contemporaries only Charles XII of Sweden grasped the importance of offensive action to the same degree, but he lacked Marlborough's sense of judgement, and owed his decisive defeat at Poltava to launching his marvellous infantry against a position which even they could never hope to take.

On the battlefield, Marlborough's methods embodied all the ingredients of the best modern military doctrine. The acquisition and analysis of intelligence underlay everything he did. He had a remarkable eye for the ground, quickly identifying the potential it offered. At Blenheim, he knew that his infantry could form up on the Nebel in relative safety, because the French guns could not hit them if they lay down, and at Ramillies he spotted the covered route that enabled him to shift his weight from right to centre. Once battle was joined, he attacked on one part of the front to pin his opponent to the ground, before jinking elsewhere to strike an enemy who had now lost his balance, like a skilled *judoka* who uses his opponent's weight to throw him all the more heavily.

Marlborough was essentially manoeuvrist, always trying to apply his own strength to an enemy's weakness. There were, though, times when, by accident or design, attrition trumped manoeuvre. He launched a doggedly attritional frontal assault on the Schellenberg because he had no time for subtlety (one needs both time and space to manoeuvre), and knew that a speedy victory, even if dearly bought, must tilt the balance of the campaign in his favour. At Malplaquet he badly misjudged the strength of French resistance, and although his customary technique of unbalancing his opponent in order to create a fatal weakness ultimately worked, it did so at appalling cost. Though it might have helped him politically, he made no attempt to shift the blame, but his biographers have not always been as generous. He had a gentle streak: he begged Queen Anne that a man convicted of libelling him should be remitted the prescribed period in the pillory. The prospect of men lying out on wet straw upset him, but he did not hesitate to send the same men into the cannon's mouth if he had to. Soldiers know that their trade requires them to risk death. They often mind this far less than civilians imagine: what they resent is the risk of pointless death, of purposeless sacrifice. Marlborough was never vindictive towards his opponents: the harrying of Bavaria before Blenheim was the cruellest of necessities, intended to bring about a decisive confrontation, and it is evident from his letters that he hated it.

Officers and men loved him in part because of the care he took in ensuring their well-being. Yet this did not spring simply from his good nature. Like Wellington, he knew that one penalty of logistic failure was the collapse of discipline and the pillaging that inevitably ensued. This not only exasperated friendly rulers but alienated their populations, demanding ever-greater protection for foraging parties and couriers, and making it harder to glean intelligence. Marlborough's subordinates sensed that he was a natural winner, who set his army on that virtuous spiral of success breeding success, consigning his opponents to the vicious circle of defeat reinforcing defeat. There is a shamanistic quality to great generals which goes beyond wise strategy, solid logistics and successful tactics, enabling them to get straight to the hearts of the soldiers they command. It is one of the intangibles of generalship, what T.E. Lawrence saw as its elusive 10 per cent, like a kingfisher flashing across a pool, and Marlborough had it in abundance. Captain Robert Parker tells us:

It may perhaps be thought that . . . I am too sanguine in favour of the Duke of Marlborough, and that my attachment to him may be occasioned by favour received from him. But for my part, I never lay under any private or personal obligation to his Grace; on the contrary he once did me the injustice of putting a captain over my head. This however I knew he could not well avoid doing sometimes, for men in power are not to be disobliged. My zeal for the man is founded on his merit and service, and I do him no more than bare justice. I have been an eyewitness of many of his great actions. I knew that he never slipped an opportunity of fighting the enemy whenever he could come at them; that to the last moment he pushed on the war, with a sincere desire of reducing France within her proper bounds . . . [205]

Marlborough was unquestionably avaricious in an avaricious age, though even here we must be cautious, for his reputation for tight-fistedness was first earned when he was a young man, simply because he did not share the spendthrift habits of the bewigged gallants at Charles II's court. He never forgot what it was like to be poor and friendless. Men who rose high often fell hard, and his own career faltered twice, with imprisonment on the first occasion and exile on the second. Despite his material rewards – huge wealth, a dukedom and an Imperial principality – he was often unhappy, a martyr to migraine, and worn to a frazzle by endless scrabbling in the busy ant-heap of coalition warfare. His urge to stay near the top of the greasy pole of British politics was tempered by a deep desire to be rid of it all, and to live quietly in the country with wife, horses and dogs. Far from prolonging the war for his own interest, he became heartily sick of it, and saw, far better than many of his countrymen, that there was much to be lost by pushing France to the last extremity. If, on the one hand, he genuinely feared the expansionist ambitions of Louis XIV, on the other he sought to constrain France, not to cripple her. If there is indeed a tragedy to Marlborough, it is that his retirement was short and racked by ill health, by the loss of two of his daughters and by repeated bickering between Sarah and her surviving offspring.

We cannot say with any certainty what John Churchill would have been like without Sarah Jennings, though perhaps the indolence observed by that shrewd judge Charles II might have become his dominant trait. He might have reverted to bucolic type, sitting for a pocket borough in the Tory interest, worrying about his hunters and his partridges, riding into town for the quarter sessions, and earning the admiration of the *Spectator* for kicking Bully Dawson down St James's Street. Sarah not only helped give him dynastic ambitions (so cruelly blighted by young Blandford's untimely death), but also produced the contacts that helped realise them. There were occasional tales of his infidelity – with Lady Southwell in early 1705, and later with the dancer Hester Santlow – but there is no surviving evidence. Marlborough's early conduct at court, mud-slinging by his detractors and Sarah's own constant jealousy (she admitted that she was 'tormented by fears of losing him') all helped generate smoke where there was, at least as far as a historian can tell, no fire.[206] There comes a time when a biographer can make as much of a judgement about his subject as he might about a close friend, and the Marlboroughs' marriage seems a shining example of a love-match (interspersed, let it be said, with the crashes and bangs from which even the happiest of marriages are not immune), not only across the political divide, for she was always a firm Whig and he an instinctive Tory, but between different personalities. John was affable and courtly but always guarded, and Sarah passionate and intense, her opinions never understated, her sincerity at once her greatest virtue and her most striking liability.

Even Marlborough's enemies could not deny that there was something very special about the man. When his old adversary Bolingbroke was in exile in France, some of his friends began to criticise Marlborough's tight-fistedness, hoping to please him. 'I am the last person in the world to be told this,' Bolingbroke replied. 'I knew the Duke of Marlborough better than any of you; and he was so great a man that I have entirely forgotten any of his failings.' In his *Letters on the Study of History*, published in 1752, after his death, Bolingbroke declared: 'I take with pleasure this opportunity of doing justice to that great man, whose faults I knew, whose virtues I admired, and whose memory, as the greatest general, and as the greatest minister that our country, or perhaps any other has produced, I honour.'[207]

NOTES

AUTHOR'S NOTE

1 *Amiable Renegade: The Memoirs of Captain Peter Drake* (Stanford, California 1960) p.58.
2 *The Private Papers of William First Earl Cowper* (Eton 1833) pp.1, 3, 59.
3 *Continuation of the review of a late treatise . . .* (London 1742) bound in with Marlborough *Account* pp.67–8.
4 'Gregory King's Tables 1688' in Charles Davenant *Works* (London 1771) II p.184.
5 G.M. Trevelyan *English Social History* (London 1948) pp.312–13.
6 Drake *Amiable Renegade* pp.136, 141.
7 'Account Book of Isabella, Duchess of Grafton' in *The Correspondence of Sir Thomas Hanmer Bart* (London 1838).
8 Major R.E. Scouller *The Armies of Queen Anne* (Oxford 1966) pp.131–2.
9 Drake *Amiable Renegade* p.312.
10 B.R. Mitchell *Abstract of British Historical Statistics* (Cambridge 1962) p.468.
11 Maureen Waller *1700: Scenes from London Life* (London 2000) p.253.
12 Sir William Beveridge et al. *Prices and Wages in England from the Twelfth to the Nineteenth Century* (London 1939) pp.199, 292, 313.
13 Robert Latham (ed.) *The Shorter Pepys* (London 1985) p.923.
14 *The Wentworth Papers* (London 1883) pp.47, 64, 147.
15 Frederick Shobel (ed.) *Memoirs of Prince Eugène of Savoy Written by Himself* (London 1811) p.xl.

INTRODUCTION:
Portrait of an Age

1 John Keegan and Andrew Wheatcroft *Who's Who in Military History* (London 1976) pp.216–17.
2 Winston S. Churchill *Marlborough: His Life and Times* (6 vols, New York 1938) VI p.652. I use this author's middle initial (as he himself preferred to do) to avoid confusion with Winston Churchill, my subject's father.
3 H.J. and E.A. Edwards *A Short Life of Marlborough* (London 1926) pp.299–300.
4 W.A. Coxe *Memoirs of the Duke of Marlborough* (3 vols, London 1896) III p.437.
5 J.W. Fortescue *A History of the British Army* (20 vols, London 1910) I p.590.
6 Ibid. p.591.
7 Sir John Fortescue 'A Junior Officer of Marlborough's Staff' in *Historical and Military Essays* (London 1928) p.184.
8 Fortescue *History* I p.590.
9 Charles Spencer *Blenheim: Battle for Europe* (London 2004) p.341.
10 G.K. Chesterton *A Short History of England* (London 1917) p.189.

11 Sir Tresham Lever *Godolphin, His Life and Times* (London 1952) p.127.

12 G.M. Trevelyan *England Under Queen Anne: Blenheim* (London 1946) p.182.

13 Ibid. p.178.

14 Thomas Babington Macaulay *History of England* (8 vols, London 1858) Vol. II *passim.*

15 John Paget *The New 'Examen'* (London 1934) p.31.

16 I would not wish to seem churlish to my old mentor, who wrote in a 'military commanders' series. But the notion is still a preposterous one.

17 Sarah, Duchess of Marlborough *Private Correspondence of the Duchess of Marlborough* (2 vols, London 1838) II pp.119–20.

18 David Chandler and Christopher L. Scott (eds) 'The Journal of John Wilson . . .' in David Chandler et al. (eds) *Military Miscellany II* (Stroud, Gloucestershire 2005) p.43.

19 David Chandler (ed.) *A Journal of Marlborough's Campaigns . . . by John Marshall Deane, Private Sentinel in Queen Anne's First Regiment of Foot Guards* (London 1984) p.7.

20 Frances Harris 'The Authorship of the Manuscript Blenheim Journal' in *Bulletin of the Institute of Historical Research* LV 1982.

21 Tallard to Chamillart 4 September 1704 in G.M. Trevelyan (ed.) *Select Documents from Queen Anne's Reign Down to the Union with Scotland* (Cambridge 1929) pp.120, 122.

22 Baron de Montigny-Languet ibid. p.133.

23 Sicco van Goslinga *Mémoires relatifs à la Guerre de Succession de 1706–1709 et 1711* (Leeuwarden 1857) p.44.

24 Edwin Chappell (ed.) *The Tangier Papers of Samuel Pepys* (London 1935) p.311.

25 William Bray (ed.) *The Diary of John Evelyn Esq FRS from 1641 to 1705–6* (London 1890) p.586.

26 Ibid. p.598.

27 Margaret Whinney and Oliver Millar *English Art 1625–1714* (Oxford 1957) p.174.

28 Donald Adamson (ed.) *Rides Round Britain: John Byng, Viscount Torrington* (London 1996) p.161.

29 Arthur Symonds (ed.) *Sir Roger de Coverly and other essays from The Spectator* (London 1905) p.vii.

30 John Tincey *Sedgemoor 1685: Marlborough's First Victory* (Barnsley 2005) p.110.

31 Evelyn *Diary* p.268.

32 *Bishop Burnet's History of His Own Times* (6 vols, Oxford 1833) III p.62.

33 Symonds *Sir Roger de Coverly* p.7.

34 *The Spectator* 13 July 1711.

35 Drake *Amiable Renegade* p.319.

36 Ibid. p.49.

37 Ibid. p.83.

38 John Childs *The British Army of William III* (Manchester 1979) pp.45–6.

39 *Journal of the Society for Army Historical Research* Vol. 4 1925 pp.11–12.

40 Sir George Murray (ed.) *Letters and Dispatches of John Churchill . . .* (5 vols, London 1845) IV p.499. See, in contrast, some desperate Marlburian stonewalling in his letter to Sir John Shaw of 16 December 1708 in Murray V p.359. There is no doubt where the duke's sympathies lay, and one wonders how Sinclair

'found means to get away'. He later received a royal pardon, but joined the Jacobite rebellion in 1715, was attainted and never succeeded to the peerage.

41 Evelyn *Diary* p.52.

42 *The Craftsman* Collected Edition (London 1737) Vol XI p.16.

43 Whinney and Millar *English Art* p.331.

44 Sarah, Duchess of Marlborough *An Account of the Conduct of the Dowager Duchess of Marlborough from her first coming to court to the year 1710* (London 1742) pp.180–1.

45 Sarah Duchess of Marlborough *Private Correspondence* II p.81.

46 *Wentworth Papers* p.197.

47 Ibid. p.121.

48 Ibid. p.165.

49 Ibid. pp.198–9.

50 *Memoirs of Thomas, Earl of Ailesbury* (2 vols, London 1890) I p.23.

51 The Earl of Dumbarton's Regiment, lineal ancestor of the 1st of Foot, the Royal Scots.

52 *Ailesbury* I p.20.

53 Ibid. p.87.

54 Pepys *Diary* p.847.

55 This unlovely cul de sac culminates in the back entrance to my club, and often eludes even those knowledgeable folk of the London licensed cab trade.

56 *Ailesbury* I p.215.

57 Marlborough *Account of the Conduct* p.110.

58 Peerages of Great Britain appeared after the Union with Scotland.

59 Oxford was restored to his offices after the fall of James. He died without male heirs, leaving his ancient title extinct, but his daughter Diana married Charles Beauclerk, Earl of Burford and Duke of St Albans.

60 *Ailesbury* I p.286.

61 Mark Bence-Jones and Hugh Montgomery-Massingberd *The British Aristocracy* (London 1979) p.22. In 1799 Richard, Earl of Mornington, the future Duke of Wellington's elder brother, was created Marquess Wellesley for his services as governor-general of India. It was an Irish peerage, and he referred to it scornfully as 'my double-gilt potato'. But his earldom was Irish, so the promotion was not wholly unreasonable.

62 John Laffin *Brassey's Battles* (London 1986) p.42.

63 G.M. Trevelyan *England Under Queen Anne: The Peace and the Protestant Succession* (London 1946) pp.197–8.

64 Lever *Godolphin* p.269.

65 A member of the great ducal house of Northumberland, and thus very much a lady in her own right.

66 Lt Gen the Hon Sir James Campbell of Lawes 'A Scots Fusilier and Dragoon under Marlborough' *Journal of the Society for Army Historical Research* No. 58 (summer 1936).

67 Cadogan to Marlborough 23 February 1716, Cadogan Papers.

68 Letters Patent in the Cadogan Papers.

69 Historical Manuscripts Commission *MSS of the Duke of Somerset, the Marquess of Ailesbury* . . . (London 1888) p.188.

70 HMC Somerset pp.191, 195–6, 204.

71 Ibid. p.105.

72 Quoted in Trevelyan *Blenheim* pp.195–6.

73 *Private Correspondence* I p.xix.

74 Trevelyan *Blenheim* p.190.

75 Trevelyan, with scrupulous fairness, initially suspected that the accusation that Wharton had 'indecently profaned a church' was the work of Tory pamphleteers. He later concluded that the story – based on an incident when Wharton led a group of late-night revellers into Barrington church, Gloucestershire – was in fact true.

76 Tim Harris *Revolution: The Great Crisis of the British Monarchy, 1685–1720* (London 2006) p.16.

77 *The Spectator* 20 July 1711.

CHAPTER 1: Young Cavalier

1 For Churchill genealogy see Kate Fleming *The Churchills* (London 1975) and G. Cokayne et al. (eds) *The Complete Peerage of England, Scotland, Ireland, Great Britain and the United Kingdom . . .* (13 vols, London 1910–59) VII p.491.

2 Peter Young (ed.) 'The Vindication of Richard Atkyns' in *Military Memoirs: The Civil War* (London 1967) p.23.

3 Churchill *Marlborough* I p.22.

4 A.L. Rowse *The Early Churchills* (London 1956) p.11.

5 See http:www.stirnet.com/ HTML/genie/british/dd/drake 01/htm. This suggests that an Elizabeth Drake married Winston Churchill: elsewhere her name is given as Ellen, Elinor and Helen. In the contemporary way, her mother's maiden name is sometimes spelt Butler.

6 Churchill *Marlborough* I p.17.

7 Ibid. p.27 and Louisa Stoughton Drake *The Drake Family in England and America 1360–1895* (Boston 1896) and Coxe *Marlborough* I p.1 are among those favouring Ashe House. For a contrary view see W.G. Hoskins *Devon* (London 1954), currently supported by the Devon Libraries Local Studies Service.

8 Churchill *Marlborough* I p.26 suggests that there were twelve children in all; my figure is from *Burke's Peerage* and http://www. thepeerage.com/p100559.htm

9 Anon. *The Lives of the Two Illustrious Generals* (London 1713) p.18.

10 Ophelia Field *The Favourite: Sarah Duchess of Marlborough* (London 2002) p.6

11 Lady Drake's sister was married to James Leigh (or Ley), 1st Earl of Marlborough of the first creation: James, the royalist admiral, was the 3rd Earl, and William, who died in 1679, the last of that creation.

12 'The Declaration of Breda' in S.R. Gardiner (ed.) *Constitutional Documents of the Puritan Revolution 1625–1660* (Oxford 1962) pp.465–7.

13 Pepys *Diary* pp.52–3.

14 Evelyn *Diary* p.165.

15 Gardiner *Constitutional Documents* p.lxiii.

16 Churchill *Marlborough* I p.44.

17 'Flavius Vegetius' in Gérard Chaliand (ed.) *The Art of War in World History* (Berkeley, California 1994) p.217. Flavius Vegetius Renatus probably lived in Constantinople in the late

fourth century AD, and dedicated his *Epitoma rei militaris* (its proper title) to the Emperor Theodosius.

18 Pepys *Diary* pp.476, 556, 1006–7.

19 Catharine MacLeod and Julia Marciari (eds) *Painted Ladies: Women at the Court of King Charles II* (London 2001).

20 Burnet *History* I p.273.

21 Pepys *Diary* p.320.

22 Henry Hanning *The British Grenadiers* (London 2006) p.13.

23 John Childs *The Army of Charles II* (London 1976) p.196.

24 In practice the cabal was not a unified ministry, for its members, though loyal servants of the king, rarely agreed with one another.

25 'The English Brigade in French Service 1672–8' Appendix D to Childs *Army of Charles II.*

26 *The Diary of Dr Edward Lake* (London 1846) p.vi. Charles was actually being even more bawdy than we might think. In contemporary parlance 'to ride the St George' was the precise opposite of the missionary position, and Charles may have believed that the weedy-looking William would be well advised to surrender himself to the rather sturdier Mary.

27 Norman Tucker (ed.) 'The Military Memoirs of John Gwyn' in *Military Memoirs: The Civil War* (London 1967) pp.99–100.

28 Anthony Bruce *The Purchase System in the British Army 1660–1871* (London 1980) p.6.

29 Ibid. p.20. Officer ranks began with ensign in the infantry and cornet in the cavalry: these gentlemen, with the lieutenants, who took seniority immediately

above them, were, then as now, termed subalterns. Captains, the next rank up, commanded troops in the cavalry or companies in the infantry: thus 'to buy a company' meant to purchase the rank of captain. During and after the Civil War the next rank up was formally styled sergeant major, and its holder was the regiment's principal drillmaster. A Devon militia commission of 1677, for instance, appointed 'Edward Greenwood, gentleman, ensign of the militia, in the company of foot of which Arthur Tremayne, sergeant major, is captain, and of which Sir Edward Seymour, Bart, is colonel'. The rank was more generally known as major *tout court*, and a generation later the sergeant major emerged as the senior non-commissioned member of the regiment. The lieutenant colonel deputised for the colonel, who might have weighty duties elsewhere which kept him away from the practical exercise of regimental command, or who might (like the Duke of Grafton with 1st Foot Guards) not really know much of what he was about. In the British service at this time most regiments had a single battalion, and battalions might be combined into brigades commanded by the senior colonel, sometimes styled brigadier by courtesy, or given a formal commission as brigadier general.

Major generals confusingly ranked beneath lieutenant generals: the latter were, as the title of their rank suggests, expected to stand in for their general, just as lieutenants could take their captain's place and lieutenant colonels deputised for colonels. The rank of field marshal did not then exist in the British service, but the army's overall commander enjoyed the title of captain general. This being the British army, there were numerous exceptions and variations, notably in the Life Guards, to understand whose rank system one must consult Barney White-Spunner's majestically produced *Horse Guards* (London 2006).

All of the above held a commission signed by the monarch, the captain general, or (for militia officers) the lord lieutenant of their county, and at the time were styled 'commission officers'. Non-commissioned officers were corporals and sergeants, appointed by their colonels.

30 Liza Picard *Restoration London* (London 1997) p.3.
31 Lever *Godolphin* p.45.
32 Evelyn *Diary* p.465.
33 Ibid.
34 Burnet *History* II p.482.
35 Whinney and Millar *English Art* pp.322–3.
36 Churchill *Marlborough* I p.52.
37 See *The Oxford Dictionary of Quotations* (Oxford 1996) p.446. There are many versions of this quotation, but there will be few soldiers reading these lines who do not understand precisely what the lady meant.
38 Coxe *Marlborough* I p.3.
39 Pepys *Tangier Papers* p.90.
40 Ibid. p.93.
41 Ibid. p.96.
42 Childs *Army of Charles II* p.142.
43 Churchill *Marlborough* I p.56. Roger Palmer was created Baron Limerick and Earl of Castlemaine in December 1661, with a remainder limited to his heirs male by Barbara, 'the reason whereof everybody knows', muttered Pepys.
44 Ibid. p.57.
45 For contrasting views see Childs *Army of Charles II* p.72 and N.A.M. Rodger *The Command of the Ocean* (London 2004) p.129.
46 Sir Charles Lyttelton to Christopher Hatton 21 August 1671, in E.M. Thompson (ed.) *Correspondence of the Family of Hatton . . .* (2 vols, London 1878) I p.66.
47 S. Wynne 'The Mistresses of Charles II and Restoration Court Politics, 1660–1685' (unpublished PhD thesis, University of Cambridge 1997) p.32.
48 Pepys *Diary* pp.353–4.
49 Maurice Ashley *Charles II* (London 1973) p.150.
50 S.M. Wynne 'Palmer, Barbara' in *The New Dictionary of National Biography*.
51 Rowse *Early Churchills* p.144.
52 Philip Dormer Stanhope, Earl of Chesterfield, *Letters* (5 vols, London 1892) I p.232.
53 Ashley *Charles II* p.161, Churchill *Marlborough* I p.61, Bryan Bevan *Marlborough the Man* (London 1975) pp.26–7.
54 Philip W. Sergeant *My Lady Castlemaine* (London 1912) pp.207, 214, 271.
55 John B. Wolf *Louis XIV* (New York 1968) pp.218–19.
56 For a scintillating glimpse of Louis and his ladies see Antonia

Fraser *Love and Louis XIV* (London 2006).

57 Wolf *Louis XIV* pp.213–15.

58 Evelyn *Diary* p.210.

59 The best account is Anne Somerset *The Affair of the Poisons* (London 2003).

60 Nancy Mitford *The Sun King* (London 1966) p.72.

61 Fraser *Love and Louis XIV* p.259.

62 Rodger *Command* pp.82–3.

63 Churchill to Richmond 15 October 1692, BL Add Mss 21948.

64 David Chandler *The Art of Warfare in the Age of Marlborough* (London 1976) p.234.

65 Captain George Carleton *Military Memoirs* (London 1929) p.49.

66 Ian A. Morrison 'Survival Skills: An Enterprising Highlander in the Low Countries with Marlborough' in Grant G. Simpson (ed.) *The Scottish Soldier Abroad* (Edinburgh 1992) p.93.

67 Carleton *Memoirs* p.50.

68 'That's ripe, that's nice and ripe.'

69 Chandler *Art of Warfare* pp.245–6.

70 Richard Kane *Campaigns of King William and Queen Anne . . .* (London 1745) pp.26–8. For the Danish account see J.H.F. Jahn *De danske Auxiliairtropper* (2 vols, Copenhagen 1840) II pp.29, 150ff. I am indebted to Dr Kjeld Galster for this reference.

71 Alington to Arlington SP 78/137 f.142. As if the names of the writer and the addressee are not perplexing enough, in the original Villiers is spelt 'Villars', which often gives rise to confusion. He was probably the Hon. Edward Villiers, Lord Grandison's son, and so Barbara Castlemaine's brother: he died as a brigadier in 1690. The fact that his family name was easily mistaken for that of Louis Hector de Villars (also present at the siege as a French officer, and later commander of the army that Marlborough beat at Malplaquet) meant that it is probably Edward's brother who was nicknamed 'the marshal'. D'Artagnan was the real-life model for the hero of Alexandre Dumas' *The Three Musketeers*.

72 Christopher Duffy *The Fortress in the Age of Vauban and Frederick the Great* (London 1985) p.10.

73 Burnet *History* III p.55.

74 Childs *Army of Charles II* p.246. Churchill's amalgamated regiment was apparently given seniority over the existing Royal English Regiment, which had Monmouth as its colonel in chief and Robert Scott as its commanding officer, because many of its recruits had been drafted in from Guards regiments. However, more work needs to be done on these British regiments in French service.

75 Historical Manuscripts Commission *Le Fleming Papers* (London 1890) p.108.

76 Field Marshal Viscount Wolseley *The Life of John Churchill, Duke of Marlborough . . .* (2 vols, London 1894) I p.146.

77 J. Laperelle *Marshal Turenne* (London 1907) pp.318–19.

78 Ibid. p.331.

79 Raguenet *Vie de Turenne* pp.259, 268.

80 C.T. Atkinson *Marlborough and the Rise of the British Army* (New York 1921) p.53, Churchill *Marlborough* I pp.108–9. For a French view see Capt. J. Revol *Turenne: Essai de Psychologie militaire* (Paris 1910) pp.319–22.

81 Atkinson *Marlborough* pp.57–8.

82 Troops of horse, the equivalents of companies of infantry, continued to carry their own standards long after infantry companies had ceased to have their own colours. In this passage Churchill actually calls the standards 'colours', an easy enough slip for an infantry officer to make.

83 Laperelle *Turenne* p.340.

84 Coxe *Marlborough* I p.8. As Winston S. Churchill points out, the dates do not quite add up: the widow thanks Churchill for his kindness 'thirty-four years ago', whereas Turenne's devastation actually took place thirty-seven years before.

CHAPTER 2:
From Court to Coup

1 Sarah and some of her contemporaries actually spelt her surname 'Jenyns', which is probably how they pronounced it.

2 Churchill *Marlborough* I p.116.

3 Ibid. p.118.

4 Colonel John Churchill to Sarah Jennings, undated, BL Add Mss 61427 f.13.

5 Colonel John Churchill to Sarah Jennings, undated, BL Add Mss 61427 f.33.

6 Colonel John Churchill to Sarah Jennings, undated, BL Add Mss 61427 f.10.

7 John Childs lists Churchill as the lieutenant colonel commanding his regiment. Monmouth was colonel in chief of his own regiment, and its commander was styled (in a direct read-across from French practice) the colonel lieutenant. The post that Churchill was being canvassed for was that of colonel lieutenant of Monmouth's Royal English, in place of the rapacious Robert Scott, Churchill's own regiment having apparently been amalgamated with Monmouth's in May 1775. The job in fact went to Justin MacCarthy, later Lord Mountcashel, who had served with Churchill at the siege of Maastricht. Churchill does not seem to have served with the French army after the winter of 1674–75. He was in Paris, probably on a diplomatic mission, in August 1675, and in September the following year sat on the court-martial which tried Lieutenant Morris for assaulting the governor of Plymouth.

8 Churchill *Marlborough* I p.126. Mary, as James II's daughter, had opposed him in 1688 and accepted the throne jointly with her husband William. This fell some way short of honouring her father.

9 Sarah Jennings to Colonel John Churchill, undated, BL Add Mss 61427 f.12.

10 Sarah Jennings to Colonel John Churchill, undated, BL Add Mss 61427 f.21.

11 Colonel John Churchill to Mrs Elizabeth Mowdie, undated, BL Add Mss 61427 f.25.

12 Sarah Jennings to Colonel John Churchill, undated, BL Add Mss 61427 f.38.

13 Colonel John Churchill to Sarah Churchill 3 September 1678, BL Add Mss 61427 ff.75–6.

14 Keith Feiling *A History of England* (London 1959) p.555.

15 *Ailesbury* I p.20.

16 Richard Talbot was eventually created Duke of Tyrconnell by the exiled James, but the promotion had no legal validity in the Irish peerage.

17 Colonel John Churchill to Sarah Churchill January 1680, BL Add Mss 61427 f.105. This is the first reference I have encountered to Churchill's headaches, discussed at length on pp. 308–9

18 Letter 6 October 1744 in Churchill *Marlborough* I p.172.

19 Laurence Hyde was second son of Edward Hyde, Earl of Clarendon, and brother of James's late wife Anne Hyde.

20 HMC Dartmouth XI Appendix V pp.67–8.

21 Sir John Werden to Churchill 22 December 1681 in Churchill *Marlborough* I p.174.

22 Brian Miller *James II: A Study in Kingship* (London 1978) p.240.

23 *Ailesbury* I pp.96, 131.

24 Miller *James II* p.241.

25 Churchill *Marlborough* I p.191.

26 Burnet *History* II p.324.

27 *Ailesbury* I p.67.

28 Churchill *Marlborough* I pp.176–7.

29 Arthur Bryant *Samuel Pepys: The Years of Peril* (Cambridge 1935) p.378.

30 Ibid. p.379.

31 Barons in this context were county Members of Parliament, selected by the crown's tenants in chief in their constituencies. Churchill's title of baron, however, was the junior step in the peerage, ranking him with the nobles.

32 John Churchill to Sarah Churchill 23 April 1703 in Henry L. Snyder (ed.) *The Marlborough–Godolphin Correspondence* (3 vols, Oxford 1975) I p.170.

33 Sidney was the third son, and in 1667 the family baronetcy passed to his eldest brother. Sir Francis Godolphin's second daughter married Edward Boscawen, and was the mother of the 1st Viscount Falmouth, and of two daughters, the younger of whom married Sir John Evelyn, grandson of the diarist.

34 Evelyn *Diary* p.403.

35 Snyder *Marlborough–Godolphin* I p.xxi.

36 Ibid. p.xxiii.

37 We are often told that the Whig leader Sir Robert Walpole (1676–1745) was the first prime minister, but the expression was occasionally used in Godolphin's time and he was, while he held power, rather better than first among equals.

38 See C.H. Firth *Cromwell's Army* (London 1962) pp.124–8.

39 *A Military Dictionary . . . by an Officer who served several years abroad* (London 1702) p.28.

40 Churchill *Marlborough* I p.183.

41 Edward Gregg *Queen Anne* (London 1980) p.27.

42 Lever *Godolphin* p.42.

43 Field *Favourite* p.35.

44 Ibid. p.37.

45 Ibid. p.34.

46 Sarah Duchess of Marlborough
    An Account p.6.
47 Ibid. p.10.
48 Ibid. p.14.
49 Sarah Duchess of Marlborough
    (attrib.) *A Faithful Account of
    Many Things*, BL Add Mss.
50 Sarah Duchess of Marlborough
    Correspondence II pp.121, 119.
51 Evelyn *Diary* p.447.
52 James Brydges to William
    Cadogan 29 October 1708,
    Cadogan Papers.
53 Field *Favourite* p.42.
54 Gregg *Queen Anne* p.36.
55 Lord Churchill to Lady
    Churchill, undated but probably
    1682–83, BL Add Mss 61427
    f.114.
56 *Ailesbury* I pp.88–90. Strictly
    speaking Ailesbury was Lord
    Bruce at this time.
57 Evelyn *Diary* p.466.
58 Burnet *History* III p.269.
59 Sarah Duchess of Marlborough
    An Account p.14.
60 Churchill *Marlborough* I p.205.
61 'Mr Wade's further information'
    in Philip Yorke, Earl of
    Hardwicke *Miscellaneous State
    Papers from 1501 to 1726* (2 vols,
    London 1778) I pp.319–20.
62 Tincey *Sedgemoor* p.57.
63 HMC Northumberland III p.99.
64 Tincey *Sedgemoor* p.26.
65 National Archives WO 5/1 f.56
    15 June 1685.
66 HMC Northumberland III p.97.
67 Churchill *Marlborough* I
    pp.211–12, and for the sillier
    assertion http:/en.wikipedia.
    org/wiki/John _Churchill . . .
    Atkinson (*Marlborough* p.77)
    cites as evidence of this
    resentment Churchill's letter of
    4 July 1688 to the Earl of
    Clarendon. This testifies to

difficult relations with
Feversham and suspicion of
Oglethorpe, rather than to
general dissatisfaction at his
supersession.
68 HMC Northumberland III p.98.
69 Ibid. p.96. Theoretically
    Somerset should have used 'your
    Grace', not 'your Lordship', had
    he been writing to Albemarle,
    although at the time such strict
    form was very often ignored. But
    the preremptory tone – 'I do
    desire' – would have been strong
    language from one ducal lord
    lieutenant to another. Churchill
    was certainly in a position to
    march to Somerton, but only by
    moving north-east and losing
    contact with Monmouth's main
    body in the process. This was a
    missive best confined to an
    inside pocket and forgotten.
70 Tincey *Sedgemoor* p.63.
71 Wolseley *Marlborough* I p.306.
    Winston S. Churchill
    (*Marlborough* I p.216) quotes the
    same letter very selectively.
72 This messenger was illegitimate,
    and is sometimes called, from
    his mother's surname, Benjamin
    Newton, or even Richard
    Godfrey: Tincey *Sedgemoor* p.88.
73 Ibid. p.92.
74 Armies of the period generally
    formed up with the most senior
    regiment on the right, the next
    most senior on the left and so
    on, so that the most junior
    finished up in the centre of the
    line. However, at Sedgemoor the
    infantry deployment seems to
    have been, from the right,
    Dumbarton's, 1/1st Foot
    Guards, 2/1st Foot Guards,
    Coldstream Guards, Trelawney's
    and Kirke's.

75 White-Spunner *Horse Guards* p.90.

76 Not all Grey's horse was hopeless. Captain John Jones, sometime of the New Model Army, kept a sizeable handful together, found the northern plungeon and tried hard to cross it in the face of resistance from Compton's men, now under Captain Sandys. Jones earned the respect of his adversaries, and shows what a trained and determined man might accomplish even amidst the wreckage of Monmouth's fortunes.

77 James II to William of Orange 13 July 1688 in Tincey *Sedgemoor* p.138.

78 Stephen Saunders Webb *Lord Churchill's Coup* (New York 1995) p.97.

79 Buckingham *Works* (London 1775) II pp.117–24.

80 Churchill *Marlborough* I p.223.

81 Tincey *Sedgemoor* p.158.

82 J.S. Clarke (ed.) *The Life of James II* (2 vols, London 1816) II p.278.

83 Evelyn *Diary* p.492.

84 Ibid. pp.499–500.

85 Waller *1700* pp.266–7.

86 Burnet *History* III p.88.

87 Matthew Glozier *The Huguenot Soldiers of William of Orange and the Glorious Revolution of 1688* (Brighton 2002) pp.41, 55.

88 Walter C.T. Utt and Bryan E. Straymer *The Bellicose Dove: Claude Broussan and Protestant Resistance to Louis XIV 1647–1698* (Brighton 2003) pp.28–9.

89 *Memoirs of the Marshal Duke of Berwick, Written by Himself . . .* (2 vols, London 1774) I p.256.

90 Harris *Revolution* p.236.

91 John Childs *The Army, James II and the Glorious Revolution* (Manchester 1980) p.5.

92 Ibid. p.49.

93 Ibid. p.58.

94 David Chandler (ed.) *Military Memoirs: Robert Parker and the Comte de Mérode-Westerloo* (London 1968) pp.5–6.

95 *London Gazette* 11–14 March 1688.

96 Evelyn *Diary* p.500.

97 Childs *The Army and the Glorious Revolution* pp.110–11.

98 Webb *Lord Churchill's Coup* pp.118–23.

99 Burnet *History* III p.262.

100 *Ailesbury* I pp.184–5.

101 Webb *Lord Churchill's Coup* pp.132–3.

102 *The Lives of the Two Illustrious Generals* p.22.

103 Sir John Dalrymple *Memoirs of Great Britain and Ireland* (3 vols, London 1790) II pp.107–10.

104 White-Spunner *Horse Guards* p.111.

105 Evelyn *Diary* p.518.

106 Ibid. p.521.

107 *The Lives of the Two Illustrious Generals* pp.19–21, put into direct speech by Churchill in *Marlborough* I pp.242–3. This is hearsay evidence, but certainly reflects what Churchill later told James were the reasons for his betrayal in 1688.

108 Lady Churchill to Mary of Orange 29 December 1687 (OS) in Atkinson *Marlborough* p.89.

109 Childs *The Army and the Glorious Revolution* p.149.

110 Princess Anne to Mary of Orange 29 April 1686 in Beatrice Curtis Brown *Letters and*

Diplomatic Instructions of Queen
Anne (London 1968) p.16.

111 Princess Anne to Mary of
Orange 9 May 1687 ibid. p.31.

112 Gregg *Queen Anne* p.51.

113 Anne to Mary of Orange 9 July
1688 in Brown *Letters* p.39.

114 Sarah Duchess of Marlborough
Conduct p.18.

115 Major General Lord Churchill to
William of Orange in Churchill
Marlborough I p.272.

116 Evelyn *Diary* pp.520–1.

CHAPTER 3:
The Protestant Wind

1 Rodger *Command* pp.138–9.

2 Ibid. p.139.

3 Churchill *Marlborough* I p.301.

4 George Hilton Jones *Convergent
Forces: Immediate Causes of the
Revolution of 1688 in England*
(Ames, Iowa 1990) p.172.

5 Diane W. Ressinger (ed.)
*Memoirs of Isaac Dumont de
Bostaquet, a Gentleman of
Normandy* (London 2005)
pp.169, 189–92.

6 Berwick *Memoirs* I p.29. There
were in fact three regiments: the
Blues, the Royal Dragoons and
St Albans' Horse.

7 Burnet *History* III p.245.

8 Ibid. p.337.

9 *Ailesbury* I p.194.

10 Princess Anne to William of
Orange 18 November 1688
in Dalrymple *Memoirs* II
pp.249–50.

11 Miller *James II* pp.202–3.

12 John Childs *The British Army of
William III 1698–1702*
(Manchester 1987) p.6.

13 Berwick *Memoirs* III p.31.

14 S.W. Singer (ed.) *The
Correspondence of Henry Hyde,*

Earl of Clarendon (2 vols, London
1828) II pp.211, 214.

15 Lord Churchill to James II,
undated, in Churchill
Marlborough I pp.299–300.

16 G.K. Chesterton *A Short History of
England* (London 1917) p.189.

17 Glozier *Huguenot Soldiers* p.99.

18 Childs *Army of William III* p.14.

19 John Menzies to the Earl of Mar
4 February 1716, HMC Stuart
I p.507. We must be cautious
about the reports of Jacobite
agents, for it was not their way to
acknowledge wholesale failure.
I follow *DNB* in styling this agent
Lloyd: he is sometimes known as
Floyd.

20 The Duke of Berwick to the
Duke of Mar (his Jacobite title)
4 May 1716, HMC Stuart II.

21 Sarah's version of the escape is
in *An Account* pp.16–18.

22 H.C. Foxcroft (ed.) *The Life and
Letters of Sir George Savile, First
Marquess of Halifax* (2 vols,
London 1898) II pp.202–3.

23 Sarah Duchess of Marlborough
A Faithful Account BL Add Mss.

24 *Ailesbury* I p.310.

25 Ibid. pp.244–5.

26 Childs *Army of William III* p.25.

27 *Ailesbury* I p.245.

28 Ibid.

29 Churchill *Marlborough* II p.15.

30 Chandler *Art of Warfare* p.113.

31 Waldeck's report to the
States-General is in *London
Gazette* 22–26 August 1689.

32 Gregg *Queen Anne* p.75.

33 Sarah Duchess of Marlborough
Conduct p.25.

34 Gregg *Queen Anne* p.78.

35 Ibid. p.79.

36 Ibid. p.82.

37 Lever *Godolphin* p.87.

38 Clarke *James II* II p.446.

39 Brown *Letters* pp.52–3.

40 Quotations from my own brief account of the Boyne in *War Walks* 2 (London 1997) pp.120–51.

41 Churchill *Marlborough* II p.25.

42 Dalrymple III Part 5 p.128.

43 Glozier *Huguenot Soldiers* p.130.

44 A masterly short account of Aughrim is in Richard Brooks *Cassell's Battlefields of England and Ireland* (London 2005) pp.583–5.

45 Atkinson *Marlborough* pp.120–1.

46 Churchill *Marlborough* II p.47.

47 Dalrymple III Part 2 p.247.

48 *Lives of the Two Illustrious Generals* p.30.

49 H.C. Foxcroft *A Supplement to Burnet's History of My Own Time . . .* (Oxford 1902) pp.373–4.

50 Wolseley *Marlborough* II p.263.

51 Webb *Lord Churchill's Coup* p.248.

52 'Review of a late Treatise entitled an Account of the Conduct of the Dowager D____ of M____' (London 1742) pp.36–7.

53 Burnet *History* IV p.161.

54 David Green *Sarah Duchess of Marlborough* (London 1967) pp.62–3.

55 Princess Anne to Countess of Marlborough 'Wednesday three o'clock' 27 April 1693 in Gregg *Queen Anne* p.85.

56 Ibid. p.86.

57 Sarah Duchess of Marlborough *Account of the Conduct* pp.30–1, 41.

58 Anne to Sarah undated March 1693 in Gregg *Queen Anne* p.88.

59 Ibid. p.89.

60 *Ailesbury* II p.200.

61 Ibid. p.383.

62 Brown *Letters* p.58.

63 Wolseley *Marlborough* II pp.273–4, 283.

64 Sarah Duchess of Marlborough *Account of the Conduct* pp.98–9.

65 Ibid. p.81.

66 Dalrymple III Part 2 p.20.

67 Goslinga *Mémoires* p.35.

68 Rodger *Command* p.156.

69 To understand the contribution made by the Tollemaches to more than five hundred years of English history one must visit this delightful church. One memorial commemorates an eighteen-year-old who died before Valenciennes, his father shot in a New York duel and two uncles lost at sea. Four Tollemache boys died in the First World War. We should not, I suppose, be surprised that Thomas Tollemache went ashore with his first wave, for this was never a brood given to hanging back.

70 William Coxe (ed.) *Private and Original Correspondence of Charles Talbot, Duke of Shrewsbury* (London 1821) pp.44–6.

71 Paget *New 'Examen'* p.28.

72 Atkinson *Marlborough* p.147.

73 Webb *Lord Churchill's Coup* p.253.

74 Lever *Godolphin* p.99.

75 Coxe *Shrewsbury Correspondence* p.47.

76 Ibid. p.220.

77 *True Conduct* BL Add Mss.

78 Berwick *Memoirs* p.131.

79 *Ailesbury* I p.383.

80 Coxe *Shrewsbury Correspondence* p.438.

81 J.S. Bromley (ed.) *The New Cambridge Modern History: Vol VI The Rise of Great Britain and*

Russia 1688–1715/25
(Cambridge 1970) p.253.

82 Rodger *Command* p.198.

83 Gregg *Queen Anne* p.121.

84 John Callow *King in Exile*
(Stroud 2004) pp.300, 308.

CHAPTER 4:
A Full Gale of Favour

1 Account of Baron de
Montigny-Languet, 25 August
1704, in Trevelyan *Select
Documents* pp.131–2, based on
originals in François Eugène de
Vault and Jean Jacques Germain,
baron Pelet *Mémoires relatifs à la
succession d'Espagne . . .* (11 vols,
Paris 1835–62). Each of these
volumes contains a narrative of
the year's campaigning, divided
up by theatre, and then a digest
of appropriate documents
relevant to each section. They
are indispensable for
understanding the French side
of the war, and have no British
equivalent.

2 BL Add Mss 61428 f.32.

3 Not everything was unreasonable
in Louis XIV's France:
Bostaquet's eighty-year-old
mother was pardoned on
account of her age.

4 Kane *Campaigns* p.33.

5 Murray *Dispatches* I p.11.

6 Snyder *Marlborough–Godolphin*
p.103.

7 Trevelyan *Select Documents* p.11.

8 Marlborough to Thungen 26
August 1704 in Murray
Dispatches I p.433.

9 Marlborough to Heinsius 17
December 1706 ibid. III p.254.

10 Marlborough to the Ordnance
Board 13 July 1703 ibid. I
pp.11–12.

11 Marlborough to the Ordnance
Board 25 August 1707 ibid. III
p.529.

12 Drake *Amiable Renegade* p.51.

13 Earl of Portmore to Duke of
Somerset 9 February 1704 in
HMC Somerset p.118.

14 Kane *Campaigns* p.110.

15 C.T. Atkinson (ed.) 'A Royal
Dragoon in the Spanish
Succession War' *Journal of the
Society for Army Historical Research*
No. 60 1938 p.20.

16 Marlborough to Hedges 6 April
1704 in Murray *Dispatches* I p.248.

17 Marlborough to Blathwayt 8
April 1704 ibid. p.248.

18 Marlborough to Somerset 30
September 1709 ibid. IV p.607.

19 Marlborough to Pennefather 30
September 1709 ibid. p.609.

20 Marlborough to Halifax 30
September 1709 ibid. p.608.

21 Marlborough to Mar 31 May
1708 and Marlborough to the
king of Portugal 25 February
1709 ibid. pp.44, 459.

22 Lever *Godolphin* p.251.

23 Marlborough to Godolphin 19
October 1703 in Snyder
Marlborough–Godolphin I p.255.

24 *Life of the Duchess of Marlborough* I
p.137.

25 Colin Ballard *The Great Earl of
Peterborough* (London 1929)
p.150.

26 Patricia Dickson unpublished
typescript 'William, 1st Earl
Cadogan' p.4, Cadogan Papers.

27 J.N.P. Watson *Marlborough's
Shadow* (London 2003) p.163.

28 HMC Portland V p.257.

29 Cadogan to Marlborough 23
February 1716, Cadogan Papers

30 Letters Patent of 1718, Cadogan
Papers. Although the patent
styles the earldom 'of' Cadogan,

William and his descendants, earls of the second creation, always used the style 'Earl Cadogan'. The barony of Oakley was indeed allowed to revert to Cadogan's brother Charles, an infantry officer who fought at Oudenarde and Malplaquet and eventually reached the rank of general. Charles inherited numerous debts with the title, but maintained a substantial estate in Chelsea, and his son, Charles Sloane Cadogan, was created Earl Cadogan and Viscount Chelsea in 1800. The 2nd Earl of the new creation married Mary Churchill, a cousin of the then Duke of Marlborough, but she ran off with a clergyman. The present Earl Cadogan, the 8th of his line, has delegated the running of his London estate to his heir Edward, Viscount Chelsea, to whose kindness I owe my access to the family papers.

31 Dickson 'Cadogan' p.39.
32 Ibid. p.40.
33 Snyder *Marlborough–Godolphin* I p.237.
34 Cadogan to Marlborough 22 April 1709, Cadogan Papers.
35 Cadogan to Marlborough 10 April 1710, Cadogan Papers.
36 Cadogan to Marlborough 15 February 1711, Cadogan Papers.
37 Cadogan to unknown correspondent 12 August 1710, Cadogan Papers.
38 Patricia Dickson 'Lieutenant General William Cadogan's Intelligence Service, Part I 1706–1715', offprint of unknown source, Cadogan Papers p.1.
39 Ibid. p.3.
40 Ibid. p.2.
41 Ibid. p.17.
42 Cadogan to Raby 16 June 1710 in BL Add Mss 22196 f.79.
43 Unsigned note in BL Add Mss 4747 f.25.
44 Sir John Fortescue 'A Junior Officer of Marlborough's Staff' in *Historical and Military Essays* (London 1928) pp.180–1, 184, 186.
45 Cadogan to Marlborough 28 February 1716, Cadogan Papers.
46 Cadogan to Marlborough 26 June 1710, Cadogan Papers.
47 Cardonnel to Ellis 30 July 1703, BL Add Mss 28918 f.194.
48 Cardonnel to Stepney 25 May 1706, BL Add Mss 7063 f.199.
49 *London Gazette* 8–11 March 1711.
50 *London Gazette* 27–29 November 1711.
51 *London Gazette* 12–15 January 1711.
52 *London Gazette* 9–12 October 1704.
53 Marlborough to Lady Marlborough May 1702, BL Add Mss 61427 f.134.
54 Marlborough to Lady Marlborough 10 July 1703 in Snyder *Marlborough–Godolphin* I p.221.
55 Lady Marlborough to Marlborough, undated (1701–02), BL Add Mss 61427 f.134.
56 Marlborough to Duchess of Marlborough 16 August 1710 in *Life of the Duchess of Marlborough* I p.363.
57 Marlborough to Godolphin 16 August 1702 in Snyder *Marlborough–Godolphin* I p.104.
58 Marlborough to Godolphin 2 July 1702 ibid. p.80.
59 Marlborough to Heinsius 20 July 1702 in B. van 'T Hoff *The*

Correspondence 1701–1711 of John Churchill and Anthonie Heinsius (The Hague 1951) p.19.

60 David Chandler and Christopher L. Scott (eds) 'The Journal of John Wilson, an "Old Flanderkin Sergeant" of the 15th Regiment . . .' in David Chandler et al. (eds) *Military Miscellany II* (Stroud 2005) p.35.

61 Ibid.

62 Ibid. p.36.

63 Chandler *Robert Parker* p.20.

64 Marlborough to Godolphin 19 July 1702 in Snyder *Marlborough–Godolphin* I p.90.

65 16 August Old Style, for Marlborough and Godolphin were then corresponding by the English calendar. In Continental New Style the missed opportunity was on 26 August 1702. During the Blenheim campaign Marlborough took to dating his letters 'according to the custom of the country'.

66 Marlborough to Heinsius 4 September 1702 in *Marlborough–Heinsius* p.28.

67 Chandler *Robert Parker* p.22.

68 HMC Coke III p.16.

69 Marlborough to Godolphin 14 September 1702 in Snyder *Marlborough–Godolphin* I p.115.

70 Chandler *Robert Parker* p.25.

71 Marlborough to Nottingham 23 October 1702 in Murray *Dispatches* I p.47.

72 Chandler *Robert Parker* p.25.

73 De Vault and Pelet II p.613,

74 Berwick *Memoirs* I p.181.

75 Chandler *Robert Parker* p.25.

76 *Ailesbury* II p.542.

77 Murray *Dispatches* V p.580.

78 Queen Anne to Lady Marlborough 22 October 1702 in Brown *Letters* p.97.

79 Sarah Duchess of Marlborough *Conduct* p.304.

80 Marlborough to Lady Marlborough 4 November 1702 in Snyder *Marlborough–Godolphin* I p.142.

81 Marlborough to Lady Marlborough 6 November 1702 ibid. p.143.

82 Gregg *Queen Anne* p.165.

83 Coxe *Marlborough* I p.106.

84 Marlborough to Duchess of Marlborough 18 February 1703 in Snyder *Marlborough–Godolphin* I p.150.

85 Marlborough to Duchess of Marlborough 18 February 1703 ibid. p.151.

86 Cardonnel to Heinsius 23 February 1703 in *Marlborough–Heinsius* p.58.

87 *Ailesbury* II p.558.

88 Marlborough to Godolphin 9 April 1703 in Snyder *Marlborough–Godolphin* I p.165.

89 Marlborough to Duchess of Marlborough 9 March 1703 ibid. p.253.

90 Queen Anne to Duchess of Marlborough 18 and 19 February 1703 in Gregg *Queen Anne* pp.168–9.

91 Ibid. p.169.

92 Marlborough to Duchess of Marlborough 9 March 1703 in Snyder *Marlborough–Godolphin* I p.200.

93 Marlborough to Duchess of Marlborough 17 May 1703 ibid. p.186.

94 I owe this insight to Ophelia Field in *The Favourite.*

95 Queen Anne to Duchess of Marlborough 22 May 1703 in Brown *Letters* p.125.

96 Chandler *Mérode-Westerloo* p.147.

97 Marlborough to Heinsius
5 January 1703 in
Marlborough–Heinsius p.46.
98 Marlborough to Heinsius
21 April 1703 ibid. p.61.
99 Marlborough to Godolphin
9 April 1703 in Snyder
Marlborough–Godolphin I
p.165.
100 Marlborough to Heinsius
27 April 1703 in
Marlborough–Heinsius p.63.
101 Overkirk (1640–1708) came
from an illegitimate line of the
Orange-Nassau family, and had
saved William of Orange's life at
the siege of Mons in 1678.
Promoted general in 1701, he
replaced Athlone as the Estates-
General's field marshal when
the latter died in February 1703.
102 Chandler *Robert Parker* p.26.
103 Marlborough to Opdam 19 May
1703 in Murray *Dispatches* I
p.102.
104 Marlborough to Coehoorn
23 May 1703 ibid. p.105.
105 Marlborough to Godolphin
31 May 1703 NS in Snyder
Marlborough–Godolphin I p.188.
106 J.W. Sypesteyn (ed.) *Het leven
van Menno baron van Coehoorn*
(Leeuwarden 1860) p.209.
107 Marlborough to Heinsius
17 June 1703 in
Marlborough–Heinsius p.75.
108 Marlborough to Heinsius
22 June 1703 ibid. p.76.
109 Marlborough to Opdam 28 June
1703 in Murray *Dispatches* I p.125.
110 Marlborough to Heinsius 2 July
1703 in *Marlborough–Heinsius*
p.78.
111 Marlborough to Godolphin
2 July 1703 NS in Snyder
Marlborough–Godolphin I
p.209.

112 Hop to the Estates-General
1 July 1703 in Murray *Dispatches*
I p.129.
113 Chandler *Mérode-Westerloo* p.152.
114 Marlborough to Godolphin
5 July 1703 NS in Snyder
Marlborough–Godolphin I p.211.
115 Marlborough to Heinsius 21 July
1703 in *Marlborough–Heinsius*
p.83.
116 Marlborough to Duchess of
Marlborough 4 July 1703 NS in
Snyder *Marlborough–Godolphin*
I p.212.
117 Marlborough to Godolphin
30 July 1703 NS ibid. p.223.
118 Notes on the Council of War
24 August 1703 in Murray
Dispatches I pp.165–6.
119 Marlborough to Godolphin
27 August 1703 in Snyder
Marlborough–Godolphin I p.235.
120 Marlborough to Godolphin
6 September 1703 ibid. p.239.
121 Marlborough to Heinsius
26 August 1703 in
Marlborough–Heinsius p.89.
122 Marlborough to Heinsius
11 October 1703 ibid. p.95.
123 Marlborough to Berwick
23 October 1703 in Murray
Dispatches I p.203.

CHAPTER 5: High Germany

1 Marlborough to Heinsius 8 June
1704 in *Marlborough–Heinsius*
p.109.
2 Eugène *Memoirs* p.34.
3 Marlborough to Duchess of
Marlborough 18 January 1704
in Snyder *Marlborough–Godolphin*
I pp.260–1.
4 Churchill *Marlborough* III p.283.
5 Marlborough to Godolphin
8 February 1704 in Snyder
Marlborough–Godolphin I p.269.

6 Marlborough to Duchess of
   Marlborough 4 February 1704
   ibid. p.268.
7 Marlborough to Hedges
   12 January 1704 in Murray
   Dispatches I p.234.
8 Cadogan to Raby 17 February
   1704, Cadogan Papers.
9 Marlborough to Heinsius
   7 and 14 March 2004 in
   Marlborough–Heinsius pp.101–2.
10 Eugène *Memoirs* p.82.
11 Marlborough to Godolphin
   14 April 1704 OS in Snyder
   Marlborough–Godolphin I p.277.
12 Marlborough to Godolphin
   18 April 1704 ibid. p.279.
13 Cadogan to Raby 5 May 1705 NS
   in BL Add Mss 22196 f.17r.
14 Marlborough to Heinsius from
   Kuhlseggen, just west of Bonn,
   21 May 1704 in *Marlborough–
   Heinsius* p.105.
15 Marlborough to Duchess of
   Marlborough, two undated
   letters of April 1704 in Snyder
   Marlborough–Godolphin I p.273.
16 Marlborough to Duchess of
   Marlborough 11 April 1704 OS?
   ibid. p.276.
17 Marlborough to Duchess of
   Marlborough 24 April 1704
   ibid. pp.286–7.
18 J.M. Brereton *History of the
   4th/7th Dragoon Guards*
   (Catterick 1982) p.57.
19 Marlborough to St John in
   Murray *Dispatches* I pp.260–1.
20 Kane *Campaigns* p.45. The
   regiment of the Electoral Prince
   of Hesse was, as Marlborough
   made clear to the Estates-
   General on 27 May (Murray
   Dispatches I p.282), in the
   king of Prussia's service,
   though paid for by
   English gold.
21 Cadogan to Raby 27 August
   1703, Cadogan Papers.
22 Cardonnel to Ellis 14 May 1704,
   BL Add Mss 28918 f.271.
23 De Vault and Pelet IV pp.18–23.
24 Ibid. p.420.
25 Cardonnel to Robethon 19 and
   26 June 1704, BL Stowe Mss 222
   ff.243, 248.
26 J.F. Dutems *Histoire du Jean
   Churchill . . .* (3 vols, Paris 1808)
   II p.293.
27 Churchill *Marlborough* III
   pp.337–8.
28 Marlborough to the Elector of
   Mainz 26 May 1704 in Murray
   Dispatches I p.282.
29 Chandler *Robert Parker* p.31.
30 Wilson *Journal* p.40.
31 Marlborough to Godolphin
   24 May/4 June 1704 in Snyder
   Marlborough–Godolphin
   I pp.310–12.
32 *The Life and Diary of Lieut. Col.
   J. Blackader of the Cameronian
   Regiment . . .* (Edinburgh 1724)
   p.197. Blackader spelt his name
   thus, and I follow his good
   example.
33 *The Memoirs of Captain George
   Carleton and the Life and
   Adventures of Mrs Christian Davies,
   commonly called Mother Ross . . .*
   (London 1840) p.288.
34 Chandler *Journal of
   Marlborough's Campaigns . . .
   by John Marshall Deane* p.5.
35 Marlborough to Charles
   Churchill 22 June 1704 in
   Murray *Dispatches* I p.321.
36 Derek McKay *Prince Eugène of
   Savoy* (London 1977) p.206.
37 *Journal of the Society for Army
   Historical Research* No. 36 1958
   Vol IV p.162.
38 Nicholas Henderson *Prince Eugène
   of Savoy* (London 1964) p.71.

39 Ibid. p.xii.

40 Churchill *Marlborough* III p.354.

41 Sandby Journal in BL Add Mss 9114.

42 Marlborough to the Prince of Hesse 10 June 1704 in Murray *Dispatches* I p.303.

43 Marlborough to Hedges 15 June 1704 ibid. p.309.

44 Marlborough to Duchess of Marlborough 29 June 1704 NS in Snyder *Marlborough–Godolphin* I p.326.

45 HMC Coke III p.38.

46 Anne-Marie Cocula (ed.) *Mémoires de Monsieur de la Colonie, Maréchal de Camp des Armées de l'Electeur de Bavière* (Paris 1992) p.258.

47 Marlborough to Godolphin 3 July 1704 NS in Snyder *Marlborough–Godolphin* I p.327.

48 De la Colonie *Mémoires* p.264.

49 Wilson *Journal* p.43.

50 De la Colonie *Mémoires* p.264.

51 'The Letters of Samuel Noyes, Chaplain of the Royal Scots 1703–4' in *Journal of the Society for Army Historical Research* No. 37 1959 pp.130–1.

52 Marlborough to Duchess of Marlborough 3 July 1704 in Snyder *Marlborough–Godolphin* I p.327.

53 Deane *Journal* pp.7–8.

54 Noyes *Letters* p.131.

55 Marlborough to Harley 4 July 1704 in Murray *Dispatches* I p.341.

56 Deane *Journal* p.7 fn 10.

57 Marlborough to Duchess of Marlborough 23 July 1704 in Snyder *Marlborough–Godolphin* I p.342.

58 Marlborough to Duchess of Marlborough 30 July 1704 ibid. p.344.

59 De la Colonie *Mémoires* pp.288–9.

60 Wilson *Journal* p.47.

61 Davies *Life and Adventures* p.294.

62 Trevelyan *Blenheim* p.369.

63 James Falkner *Great and Glorious Days: Marlborough's Battles 1704–9* (London 2002) p.53.

64 Marlborough to Heinsius 31 July 1704 in *Marlborough–Heinsius* p.121.

65 Marlborough to Duchess of Marlborough 10 August 1704 in Snyder *Marlborough–Godolphin* I p.348.

66 Marlborough to Heinsius 10 August 1704 in *Marlborough–Heinsius* p.124.

67 Marlborough to Harley 10 August 1704 in Murray *Dispatches* I p.387.

68 Marlborough to Duchess of Marlborough 13 July 1704 in Snyder *Marlborough–Godolphin* I p.336.

69 Marlborough to Harley 14 August 1704 in Murray *Dispatches* I p.391.

70 Montingy-Languet in Trevelyan *Select Documents* p.130.

71 Tallard to Chamillart 4 September 2004 ibid. pp.118–24.

72 For a useful discussion of relative strengths see Ivor F. Burton *The Captain-General* (London 1968) p.67.

73 Kane *Campaigns* pp.111–12.

74 J.A. Houlding *Fit for Service: The Training of the British Army 1715–1795* (Oxford 1981) p.174.

75 For infantry tactics of the age see David Chandler at his best in *Art of Warfare* pp.114–24.

76 Michael Orr *Dettingen 1743* (London 1972) p.65.

77 Ibid. p.64.
78 Mérode-Westerloo p.164.
79 Sandby *Journal* in BL Add
    Mss 9114.
80 Tallard to Chamillart
    4 September 1704 in Trevelyan
    Select Documents p.122.
81 Sandby *Journal* in BL Add
    Mss 9114.
82 Deane *Journal* p.11.
83 Falkner *Great and Glorious* p.69.
84 Tallard to Chamillart
    3 December 1704 in Trevelyan
    Select Documents p.126.
85 Unnamed French officer to
    Chamillart ibid. p.128.
86 Baron de Montigny-Languet
    24 August 1704 ibid. p.133.
87 Cardonnel Mss circular
    describing Blenheim in BL Add
    Mss 28918 f.288.
88 Millner *Journal* p.55.
89 H.H.E. Craster (ed.) 'Letters of
    the First Lord Orkney' in
    English Historical Review XIX
    1904 p.311
90 Mérode-Westerloo p.169.
91 Anonymous officer in
    Trevelyan *Select Documents*
    p.128.
92 Chandler *Robert Parker* p.42.
93 Trevelyan *Blenheim* p.387.
94 Cardonnel to Ellis 17 August
    1704, BL Add Mss 28918
    f.294.
95 Marlborough to Duchess of
    Marlborough 13 August 1704 in
    Marlborough–Godolphin I p.349.
    Virginia-born Dan Parke was
    rewarded with a diamond-set
    picture of the queen and a
    thousand guineas. He was
    appointed governor of the
    Leeward Islands the following
    year, and murdered there by
    rebels in 1710: there is no
    armour against fate.

CHAPTER 6:
The Lines of Brabant

1 Queen Anne to Duchess of
   Marlborough 10 August 1704
   OS in Coxe *Marlborough*
   II p.38.
2 Sarah Duchess of Marlborough
   Account of the Conduct p.146.
3 Marlborough to Duchess of
   Marlborough 20 October 1704
   in Snyder *Marlborough–Godolphin*
   I p.385.
4 Gregg *Queen Anne* p.193.
5 Ibid.
6 Marlborough to Godolphin
   9 July 1705 in Snyder
   Marlborough–Godolphin I p.455.
7 Sarah Duchess of Marlborough
   Private Correspondence I p.181.
8 *Ailesbury* II pp.523, 586.
9 Gregg *Queen Anne* p.195.
10 *Blenheim Palace* (Norwich
   2006) p.5.
11 Marian Fowler *Blenheim:
   Biography of a Palace* (London
   1989) p.59.
12 Gregg *Queen Anne* p.329.
13 Fowler *Blenheim* p.60.
14 Marlborough to Duchess of
   Marlborough 25 August 1702 in
   Snyder *Marlborough–Godolphin*
   I p.358.
15 Marlborough was formally
   invested with the principality on
   24 May 1706, and in 1713
   Mindelheim was exchanged for
   the county of Mellenburg (then
   created a principality) in Upper
   Austria.
16 Murray *Dispatches* V p.154.
17 Gregg *Queen Anne* pp.195–6.
18 Kane *Memoirs* p.57.
19 Cardonnel to Ellis 7 November
   1704, BL Add Mss 28918 f.323.
20 Marlborough to Godolphin
   3 November 1704 in

Snyder *Marlborough–Godolphin* I p.391.

21 Marlborough to Harley 28 November 1704 and attached *Mémoire de My Lord le Duc de Marlborough* in Murray *Dispatches* I pp.545–6.

22 Eric Gruber von Arni *Hospital Care and the British Standing Army 1660–1714* (Aldershot 2006) pp.126–7.

23 These are the words I learnt as a boy, though there are many versions, some of which call the soldier 'Billy' or 'Willie'. Polly decides not to follow her man, but curses the events that 'pressed my Harry from me, and all my brothers three/And sent them to the cruel war in High Germany'. The date of the song is conjectural, though it is certainly eighteenth-century, and the title suggests an early date, for 'Low Germany' was a more usual stamping ground for the redcoat later in the century.

24 Gruber von Arni *Hospital Care* p.131.

25 Scouller *Armies of Queen Anne* p.235.

26 British officers and sergeants carried staff weapons and swords for the rest of the century, though the demands of soldiering in North America told against the practice. Nevertheless, on either side of the Grand Entrance to Old College at RMA Sandhurst are racks designed to hold the sergeant's half-pike that replaced the halberd at the end of the century and did not itself disappear till the 1830s.

27 Gruber von Arni *Hospital Care* pp.209–10.

28 Marlborough to Duchess of Marlborough 14 April 1705 in Snyder *Marlborough–Godolphin* I p.415.

29 I am grateful to Dr Christopher Everett and Dr Hugh Bethell for their long-range diagnosis of Marlborough. The former also deserves my thanks for having preserved me from the terminal hypochondria which threatened my early career.

30 Marlborough to the Margrave of Baden 25 April 1705 in Murray *Dispatches* II p.23.

31 Marlborough to Harley ibid. p.55.

32 Cardonnel to Ellis 2 June 1704, BL Add Mss 28918 f.355.

33 Marlborough to Godolphin 16 June 1705 in Snyder *Marlborough–Godolphin* I pp.442–3.

34 Marlborough to Duchess of Marlborough 16 June 1705 ibid. pp.443–4.

35 Marlborough to Heinsius 18 June 1705 in *Marlborough–Heinsius* pp.184–5.

36 Blackader *Life and Diary* p.247.

37 Marlborough to St John 9 July 1704 in Murray *Dispatches* II p.159.

38 'Letters of the First Lord Orkney' in *English Historical Review* April 1904 p.311.

39 Goslinga *Mémoires* pp.1–2.

40 Jacques Louis, comte de Noyelle en Falaise, was French-born but had entered Dutch service in 1674, commanded an infantry regiment and was promoted general in 1704. Marlborough had a high regard for him, and would have liked to see him command in Spain, where he

died as adviser to the Hapsburg claimant to the throne.

41 Atkinson *Marlborough* p.259.

42 Millner *Journal* p.59.

43 Marlborough to Duchess of Marlborough 19 October 1703 in Snyder *Marlborough–Godolphin* I p.256.

44 Orkney 'Letters' in *English Historical Review* April 1904 p.313.

45 Ibid.

46 Blackader *Life and Diary* p.249.

47 Deane *Journal* p.26.

48 Marlborough to Galway 21 July 1705 in Murray *Dispatches* II p.183. There is some doubt about the number of guns: Deane says that they took ten, but Chandler's note to Deane *Journal* p.27 suggests eighteen.

49 Deane *Journal* p.27.

50 Marlborough to Duchess of Marlborough 18 July 1705 in Snyder *Marlborough–Godolphin* I p.459.

51 *London Gazette* 23–27 August 1705.

52 HMC Portland IV p.253.

53 Churchill *Marlborough* IV p.215.

54 Marlborough to Duchess of Marlborough 20 July 1705 in Snyder *Marlborough–Godolphin* I p.460.

55 Marlborough to Godolphin 27 July 1705 ibid. p.462.

56 Marlborough to Godolphin 20 July 1705 ibid. p.458.

57 Goslinga *Mémoires* pp.136–8.

58 Marlborough to Heinsius 2 August 1705 in *Marlborough–Heinsius* p.199. Normally Marlborough seems to have kept no copies of his correspondence with Heinsius, but the fact that this appears in Murray *Dispatches* II p.197 demonstrates that

copies were kept, suggesting that the issue of command had now become a live political matter.

59 The issue is dealt with at length in A. Legrelle *La Diplomatie Française et la Succession d'Espagne* (6 vols, Paris 1892) IV pp.364–75.

60 Marlborough to Berwick 30 October 1708 in Trevelyan *Select Documents* p.397.

61 Deane *Journal* p.28.

62 Marlborough to Godolphin 19 August 1705 in Snyder *Marlborough–Godolphin* I pp.473–4.

63 Marlborough to Duchess of Marlborough 24 August 1705 ibid. p.476.

64 Portland to Marlborough 1 August 1705 OS, BL Add Mss 61153 f.218.

65 Eugène to Marlborough 13 September 1705 in Coxe *Marlborough* I p.322.

66 Queen Anne to Marlborough 6 September 1705 ibid. p.321.

67 Bulletin of 19 August 1705 in Murray *Dispatches* II p.224.

68 Marlborough to Heinsius 19 August 1705 in *Marlborough–Heinsius* p.203.

69 Chandler *Robert Parker* p.56.

70 Hare Journal in BL Add Mss 9114.

71 Coxe *Marlborough* I p.313.

72 An alternative has him refuse the duty on the grounds that the place was beneath his dignity: in either case his refusal left him wrong-footed.

73 *London Gazette* 6–10 September 1705.

74 Deane *Journal* p.30.

75 Chandler *Robert Parker* p.57.

76 *London Gazette* 16–20 August 1705.

77 Marlborough to Godolphin
    9 September 1705 in Coxe
    Marlborough I p.320.
78 Marlborough to Heinsius
    14 September 1705 in
    Marlborough–Heinsius pp.211–12.
79 Marlborough to Godolphin
    24 September 1705 in Snyder
    Marlborough–Godolphin I p.496.
80 Marlborough to the emperor
    19 July 1705 in Murray
    Dispatches II pp.178–9.
81 Marlborough to Louis of Baden
    3 September 1705 ibid. p.251.
82 Marlborough to Lady
    Oglethorpe 17 September 1705
    ibid. p.268.
83 Marlborough to Godolphin
    6 July 1705 in Snyder
    Marlborough–Godolphin I p.454.
84 Marlborough to Duchess of
    Tyrconnell 5 September 1705 in
    Murray *Dispatches* II p.254.
85 Marlborough to the queen 6
    July 1707 in Coxe *Marlborough* II
    pp.131–2.
86 Gregg *Queen Anne* p.203.
87 Queen Anne to Marlborough
    13 November 1705, BL Add Mss
    61101 f.89.
88 Marlborough to Godolphin 8
    December 1705 in Snyder
    Marlborough–Godolphin I p.511.
89 Burton *Captain-General* pp.94–5.
90 Marlborough to Heinsius
    26 March 1706 in *Marlborough–
    Heinsius* pp.229–30.
91 Marlborough to Godolphin
    9 May 1706 in Snyder
    Marlborough–Godolphin I
    pp.532–3.
92 De Vault and Pelet VI pp.30–1.
93 Marlborough to Godolphin
    15 May 1706 in Snyder
    Marlborough–Godolphin I
    pp.535–6.
94 Marlborough to Godolphin

        9 May 1706 ibid. p.542.
95 Marlborough to Harley 20 May
    1706 in Murray *Dispatches* II
    p.518.
96 Coxe *Marlborough* I p.375.
97 Deane *Journal* p.34.
98 Chandler *Robert Parker* p.59,
    Deane *Journal* p.34.
99 Drake *Amiable Renegade* p.78. It
    seems likely that not all tents
    were struck: David Chandler, too
    good a Marlburian scholar to be
    brushed aside, suggests that
    reserves later became 'entangled
    amidst the unstruck tents of the
    French camp behind Ramillies'
    (Deane *Journal* p.36 fn 223).
100 Goslinga *Mémoires* pp.12–13.
101 De la Colonie *Mémoires*
    pp.393–4.
102 Chandler *Robert Parker* p.60.
103 De la Colonie *Mémoires* p.397.
104 Mérode-Westerloo p.197.
105 Letter 24 May 1706 in *English
    Historical Review* April 1704
    p.315. The formal 'Ramillies
    Order of Battle' reproduced as
    Plate XII in Kane's *Campaigns*
    follows representational
    convention rather than tactical
    fact by placing all the Allied
    horse on the flanks of the foot:
    we know, for instance,
    that Lumley's horse were
    actually behind Orkney's foot,
    not on their flank as the
    map suggests.
106 De la Colonie *Mémoires* p.395.
107 Orkney in *English Historical
    Review* April 1904 p.315.
108 A. Wykes *The Royal Hampshire
    Regiment* (London 1968) p.29.
109 Ibid. p.30.
110 Blackader *Life and Diary* p.280.
111 Chandler *Robert Parker* p.61.
112 De la Colonie *Mémoires* p.399.
113 Chandler *Robert Parker* pp.60–1.

114 Orkney in *English Historical Review* April 1904 p.315.

115 Marlborough to Godolphin 24 May 1704 and Marlborough to Duchess of Marlborough 24 May 1704 in Snyder *Marlborough–Godolphin* I pp.545–6.

116 HMC Portland IV p.309.

117 Orkney in *English Historical Review* April 1904 p.315.

118 Chandler *Robert Parker* p.60.

119 Wykes *Royal Hampshire Regiment* p.29.

120 Deane *Journal* p.35.

121 Chandler *Robert Parker* p.61.

122 Drake *Amiable Renegade* p.79.

123 There was a long-running feud between Picardie and the Royal Scots, senior regiment of the British line and 'Pontius Pilate's bodyguard' by nickname. Had *they* been on duty that first Easter, maintained some of the Scotsmen, there would have been no sleeping sentries and no Resurrection.

124 Orkney in *English Historical Review* April 1904 p.316.

125 Davies *Life and Adventures* pp.311–12.

126 Deane *Journal* pp.39, 41.

127 Marlborough to Duchess of Marlborough 27 May 1706 in Snyder *Marlborough–Godolphin* I p.553.

128 Marlborough to Duchess of Marlborough 31 May 1706 ibid. pp.555–6.

129 Marlborough to Godolphin 4 October 1706 ibid. II p.693.

130 Villeroi to Louis XIV 3 June 1706 in De Vault and Pelet VI p.41.

131 Marlborough to Harley 12 August 1706 in Murray *Dispatches* III p.78.

132 Marlborough to Godolphin 1 November 1706 in Snyder *Marlborough–Godolphin* II p.727.

133 Godolphin to Marlborough 8 April 1707 ibid. p.746.

134 Godolphin to Marlborough 25 September 1706 ibid. p.694.

135 Marlborough to Duchess of Marlborough 7 October 1706 ibid. p.695.

CHAPTER 7:
The Equipoise of Fortune

1 Gregg *Queen Anne* p.231.

2 Ibid. pp.232–3.

3 Sarah Duchess of Marlborough *Life* I p.415, II p.131.

4 Gregg *Queen Anne* p.275.

5 Godolphin to Marlborough 5 June 1706 in Snyder *Marlborough–Godolphin* I p.576. Charles, Lord Mohun, Whig, rake and duellist, was to kill (and be killed by) George, Duke of Hamilton (father of Marlborough's unacknowledged grandson by Lady Barbara Palmer) in 1712.

6 Sarah Duchess of Marlborough *Life* II p.140.

7 Gregg *Queen Anne* p.237.

8 There is still no readily available account of this battle in English: I rely here on Fortescue *History* I pp.487–9.

9 Stanhope to Marlborough 3 May 1707 in Murray *Dispatches* III pp.352–3.

10 Marlborough to Heinsius 17 December 1706 in *Marlborough–Heinsius* pp.286–7.

11 See Bromley *New Cambridge Modern History* VI p.432 and R.M. Hatton *Charles XII of Sweden* (London 1968) p.232.

12 Marlborough to Heinsius
    15 May 1707 in *Marlborough–
    Heinsius* p.310.

13 Eugène to Marlborough 13 July
    1707 in Murray *Dispatches* III
    p.483.

14 Marlborough to Godolphin
    27 July 1707 in Snyder
    Marlborough–Godolphin II
    pp.850–1.

15 Chetwynd to Marlborough
    14 August 1707 in Churchill
    Marlborough V p.283.

16 Simon Harris *Sir Cloudesley
    Shovell: Stuart Admiral*
    (Staplehurst, Kent 2001) p.325.

17 Eugène *Memoirs* pp.105–6.

18 Rodger *Command* pp.171–2.

19 Marlborough to Godolphin
    25 August 1707 in Snyder
    Marlborough–Godolphin II p.880.

20 Godolphin to Marlborough
    9 September 1709 ibid. p.908.

21 Marlborough to Heinsius
    17 September 1707 in
    Marlborough–Heinsius p.345.

22 Marlborough to Godolphin
    30 May 1707 in Snyder
    Marlborough–Godolphin II
    pp.785–6.

23 Cadogan to Raby 16 June 1707,
    Cadogan Papers.

24 Marlborough to Heinsius
    5 December 1707 in
    Marlborough–Heinsius pp.355–6.

25 Sir John Cropley to the Earl of
    Shaftesbury n.d. [19 February
    1708] in Geoffrey Holmes and
    William Speck 'The Fall of
    Harley in 1708 Reconsidered' in
    English Historical Review LXVI
    1965 pp.695–6.

26 Gregg *Queen Anne* p.264.

27 Marlborough to Heinsius
    27 February 1708 in
    Marlborough–Heinsius p.374.

28 Godolphin to Marlborough

19 April 1708 in Snyder
    Marlborough–Godolphin II p.957.

29 Rodger *Command* p.201.

30 Marlborough to Godolphin
    10 September 1705 in Snyder
    Marlborough–Godolphin I p.487.

31 Marlborough to Godolphin
    11 July 1707 ibid. II p.837.

32 Scouller *Armies of Queen Anne*
    p.310.

33 Marlborough to Duchess of
    Marlborough 16 August 1706 in
    Snyder *Marlborough–Godolphin* II
    p.645.

34 Cadogan to Raby 18 August
    1706, BL Add Mss 22196 f.33.

35 Marlborough to Godolphin in
    Snyder *Marlborough–Godolphin* II
    p.645 and fn 2.

36 Cadogan to Raby 29 December
    1707 and 19 January 1708,
    Cadogan Papers.

37 Cadogan to Raby 19 January
    1708, Cadogan Papers.

38 Marlborough to Cadogan
    17 February 1708 in Murray
    Dispatches III pp.680–1.

39 Louis XIV to Vendôme 20 and
    21 May 1708 in De Vault and
    Pelet VIII pp.9, 17.

40 Marlborough to Godolphin
    3 May 1708 in Snyder
    Marlborough–Godolphin II p.960.

41 *Ailesbury* II p.602.

42 Marlborough to Heinsius
    22 April 1708 in *Marlborough–
    Heinsius* p.382. The admirable
    Major J.N.P. Watson is wrong to
    suggest that 'no British writer'
    has mentioned this 'plot'. It is
    referred to in both *The
    Cambridge Modern History* and
    Ivor Burton's *Captain-General.*

43 A.J. Veenendaal *Het Engels-
    Nederlands Condominium in de
    Zuidelike Nederlanden . . .*
    (Utrecht 1945) pp.187–8.

44 De Vault and Pelet VIII p.11.
45 Chandler *Marlborough* p.213.
46 Marlborough to Boyle 5 July 1708 in Murray *Dispatches* IV p.96.
47 Goslinga *Mémoires* p.45.
48 Ibid.
49 'Journal of March of the Confederate Army . . .' in *London Gazette* 8–12 July 1708.
50 Sergeant John Millner *A Compendious Journal* (London 1733) p.212.
51 Hare Journal in BL Add Mss 9114.
52 Goslinga *Mémoires* p.49.
53 Marlborough to Duchess of Marlborough 9 July 1708 in Snyder *Marlborough–Godolphin* II p.1023.
54 Goslinga *Mémoires* p.50.
55 Eugène *Memoirs* p.14.
56 Churchill *Marlborough* V p.397.
57 Grumbkow to Frederick William I, 9? July 1708 in K.W. von Schöning (ed.) *Das General-Feldmarschalls Dubsilaw Gneomar von Natzmer Leben und Kriegshaten* (Berlin 1838) p.286.
58 Marlborough to Murray 8 July 1708 in Murray *Dispatches* IV p.101.
59 Marlborough to Godolphin 9 July 1708 in Snyder *Marlborough–Godolphin* II p.1022.
60 Marlborough to Duchess of Marlborough 9 July 1708 ibid. p.1023.
61 Marlborough to Heinsius 10 July 1708 in *Marlborough–Heinsius* p.390.
62 Louis XIV to Burgundy 11 July 1708 in De Vault and Pelet VIII pp.30–1.
63 Vendôme to Saint-Frémont 10 July 1708 ibid. p.33.
64 Marlborough to Godolphin 9 July 1708 in Snyder *Marlborough–Godolphin* II p.1023.
65 Marlborough to Boyle 9 July 1708 in Murray *Dispatches* IV p.102.
66 Schöning *Natzmer* p.288.
67 Deane *Journal* p.59.
68 Churchill *Marlborough* V p.407.
69 Goslinga *Mémoires* pp.53–4.
70 Eugène *Memoirs* p.113.
71 D'Artaignan's account in De Vault and Pelet VIII p.386.
72 Schöning *Natzmer* p.289.
73 Chandler *Robert Parker* p.73.
74 Churchill *Marlborough* V p.418.
75 Eugène *Memoirs* p.114.
76 Schöning *Natzmer* p.293.
77 Goslinga *Mémoires* p.59.
78 Blackader *Life and Diary* p.318.
79 Vendôme to Louis XIV 19 July 1708 in De Vault and Pelet VIII p.391.
80 Eugène *Memoirs* p.116.
81 Blackader *Life and Diary* p.320.
82 Deane *Journal* p.62.
83 Matthew Bishop *The Life and Adventures of Matthew Bishop of Deddington in Oxfordshire* (London 1744) p.160.
84 Marlborough to Duchess of Marlborough 12 July 1708 in Snyder *Marlborough–Godolphin* II p.1024.
85 Marlborough to Godolphin 12 and 16 June 1708 ibid. pp.1025, 1026.
86 Goslinga *Mémoires* p.72.
87 Eugène *Memoirs* p.118.
88 Goslinga *Mémoires* p.68.
89 Churchill *Marlborough* V p.442.
90 Saint-Simon V p.64.
91 Eugène *Memoirs* p.117.
92 Bishop *Life and Adventures* p.162.
93 De Vault and Pelet VIII p.89.
94 Marlborough to the Earl of Manchester 15 July 1708 in Murray *Dispatches* IV p.109.

95 Marlborough to Cadogan
31 July (twice) and 1 August
1708 ibid. pp.139–41.

96 Marlborough to Cadogan
2 August 1708 ibid. p.144.

97 Marlborough to Eugène
16 August 1708 ibid. p.173.

98 De Vault and Pelet VIII p.91.

99 Marlborough to Godolphin
20 September 1709 in Snyder
Marlborough–Godolphin II p.1100.

100 Marlborough to Boyle 23 August
1708 in Murray *Dispatches* IV
p.184.

101 Marlborough to Boyle
3 September 1708 ibid. pp.203–4.

102 Marlborough to Galway 10
September 1708 ibid.
pp.218–19.

103 Marlborough to Duchess of
Marlborough 17 September
1708 in Snyder *Marlborough–
Godolphin* II p.1097.

104 Blackader *Life and Diary*
pp.327–8.

105 Marlborough to Godolphin
20 September 1708 in Snyder
Marlborough–Godolphin II p.1099.

106 Marlborough to Godolphin
24 September 1708 ibid. p.1100.

107 Marlborough to Heinsius
24 September 1708 in
Marlborough–Heinsius p.402.

108 Marlborough to Earle
24 September 1708 in Murray
Dispatches IV p.236.

109 Marlborough to Earle
24 September 1708 ibid. p.240.

110 This is the French version from
'Projet pour secourir Lille' in De
Vault and Pelet VIII pp.454–6.
See also Churchill *Marlborough* V
p.506.

111 Marlborough to Godolphin
27 September 1708 in Snyder
Marlborough–Godolphin II
p.1104.

112 Lamotte 'Détail du combat de
Wynendaele' in De Vault and
Pelet VIII pp.444–9.

113 *London Gazette* 20–23 September
1708.

114 Marlborough to Webb
29 September 1708 in Murray
Dispatches IV p.242.

115 Marlborough to Godolphin
1 October 1708 in Snyder
Marlborough–Godolphin II p.1107.

116 Godolphin to Marlborough
14 December 1708 in Snyder
Marlborough–Godolphin II p.1175.

117 Kane *Campaigns* p.79.

118 Duffy *The Fortress* p.38.

119 Marlborough to Sunderland
19 October 1708 in Murray
Dispatches IV p.269.

120 Marlborough to Pascal
7 November 1708 ibid. p.293.

121 Marlborough to Boyle 27
November 1708 ibid. p.323.

122 Churchill *Marlborough* V p.523.

123 Marlborough to Stair
10 November 1708 in Murray
Dispatches IV pp.298–9.

124 'Articles pour la citadelle de
Lille' 9 December 1708 in
De Vault and Pelet VIII p.661.
There were minor modifications
to these terms: for instance, the
Allies thought that ten rounds
per man was quite enough. The
inclusion of the 'matches
burning' condition implies that
there were still matchlocks in
use by the French army,
though equally it may
simply be a formal survival
from an even more
smoky age.

125 Goslinga *Mémoires* p.96.

126 Marlborough to Godolphin
6 and 28 November 1708 in
Snyder *Marlborough–Godolphin* II
pp.1141, 1151.

127 Marlborough to Godolphin
3 December 1708 ibid.
p.1155.

128 Marlborough to Godolphin
6 December 1708 ibid.
p.1159.

129 Marlborough to Duchess of
Marlborough 17 December
1708 ibid. p.1171.

130 Davies *Life and Adventures*
pp.329, 340–1.

131 Deane *Journal* p.74.

132 Marlborough to Godolphin
3 January 1709 in Snyder
Marlborough–Godolphin II p.1184.

CHAPTER 8:
Decline, Fall and
Resurrection

1 Gregg *Queen Anne* p.277.

2 Ibid. p.279.

3 Godolphin to Duchess of
Marlborough 25 and 22
October 1708 in Snyder
Marlborough–Godolphin II
pp.1139, 1137.

4 Godolphin to Marlborough
26 October 1708 ibid.
pp.1139–40.

5 Godolphin to Marlborough
29 October 1708 ibid. p.1142.

6 Prince George to Marlborough
28 May 1706 in BL Add Mss
61001 f.94.

7 Marlborough to Boyle
27 November 1708 in Murray
Dispatches IV p.323.

8 Sarah Duchess of Marlborough
Private Correspondence II
pp.412–13; Brown *Letters*
p.263.

9 Gregg *Queen Anne* pp.282–3.

10 Marlborough to Duchess of
Marlborough 25 May 1709 in
Snyder *Marlborough–Godolphin* III
p.1255.

11 Marlborough to Duchess of
Marlborough 19 May 1709 ibid.
pp.1250–1.

12 Wolf *Louis XIV* p.565.

13 Cadogan to Marlborough
6 December 1709, Cadogan
Papers.

14 C. Sturgill *Marshal Villars and the
War of the Spanish Succession*
(London 1965) p.85.

15 Marlborough to Duchess of
Marlborough 9 June 1709 in
Snyder *Marlborough–Godolphin* III
pp.1268–9.

16 Sarah Duchess of Marlborough
Private Correspondence I p.120.

17 Henry L. Snyder 'The Duke of
Marlborough's Request of his
Captain-Generalcy for Life: A
Re-examination' in *Journal of the
Society for Army Historical Research*
Vol. 45 1967 p.69.

18 Marlborough to Queen Anne
10 October 1709 ibid.
pp.73–4.

19 Queen Anne to Marlborough
25 October 1704 in BL Add Mss
61101 f.163.

20 Gregg *Queen Anne* p.297.

21 Godolphin to Marlborough
20 and 21 March 1710 in
Snyder *Marlborough–Godolphin* III
p.1440.

22 Snyder 'Duke of Marlborough's
Request' p.80.

23 Scouller *Armies of Queen Anne*
p.272.

24 Marlborough to Walpole 25 July
1709 in Murray *Dispatches* IV
p.551.

25 Cadogan to Marlborough
22 April 1709, Cadogan
Papers.

26 Marlborough to Major General
Palmes 23 April 1709 in Murray
Dispatches IV p.485.

27 Wolf *Louis XIV* p.565.

28 Marlborough to Godolphin
20 June 1709 in Snyder
Marlborough–Godolphin III
p.1280.

29 Godolphin to Marlborough
10 June 1709 ibid. p.1281.

30 Marlborough to Godolphin
24 June 1709 ibid. p.1283.

31 Marlborough to Duchess of
Marlborough 27 June 1709 ibid.
p.1286.

32 Deane *Journal* p.81.

33 Goslinga *Mémoires* p.105.

34 Burton *Captain-General* p.146.

35 Louis to Villars 2 July 1709 in
De Vault and Pelet IX p.49.

36 Marlborough to Heinsius 10 July
1709 in *Marlborough–Heinsius*
p.444.

37 Marlborough to Heinsius 24 July
1709 ibid. p.448.

38 Marlborough to Godolphin
30 July 1709 in Snyder
Marlborough–Godolphin III
p.1317.

39 Marlborough to Queen Anne
29 July 1709 in Murray
Dispatches IV p.556.

40 Deane *Journal* p.84.

41 Kane *Campaigns* p.83.

42 Wilson *Journal* p.75.

43 Marlborough to Heinsius
2 September 1709 in
Marlborough–Heinsius p.462.

44 Goslinga *Mémoires* p.100.

45 Godolphin to Marlborough
25 June 1706 in Snyder
Marlborough–Godolphin II
pp.598–9.

46 Marlborough to Godolphin
6 July 1706 ibid. p.600.

47 Churchill *Marlborough* VI
p.132.

48 Orkney in *English Historical
Review* April 1904 p.317.

49 Marlborough to Duchess of
Marlborough 10 September

1709 in Snyder
Marlborough–Godolphin III
p.1359.

50 De Vault and Pelet IX p.343.

51 Orkney in *English Historical
Review* April 1904 p.317.

52 Burton *Captain-General* p.159.

53 De la Colonie *Mémoires* p.442.

54 Orkney in *English Historical
Review* April 1904 p.319.

55 De la Colonie *Mémoires*
pp.443–5.

56 Wilson *Journal* p.78.

57 Deane *Journal* p.94.

58 Davies *Life and Adventures*
pp.364–6.

59 Chandler *Robert Parker* pp.88–9.

60 Deane *Journal* p.94.

61 Atkinson *Marlborough* p.402.

62 Marlborough to Godolphin
13 September 1709 in Snyder
Marlborough–Godolphin III
p.1363.

63 Chandler *Marlborough* p.261.

64 Boufflers to Louis 11 September
1709 in De Vault and Pelet IX
p.45.

65 Orkney in *English Historical
Review* April 1904 p.319.

66 Ibid. p.320.

67 Drake *Amiable Renegade* p.167.

68 Marlborough to Duchess of
Marlborough 26 September
1709 in Snyder *Marlborough–
Godolphin* III p.1377.

69 Orkney in *English Historical
Review* April 1904 pp.320–1.

70 Blackader *Life and Diary*
pp.351–2.

71 Bishop *Life and Adventures* p.214.

72 Marlborough to Godolphin
13 September 1709 in Snyder
Marlborough–Godolphin III
p.1365.

73 Marlborough to Boyle
13 September 1709 in Murray
Dispatches IV p.597.

74 Marlborough to Villars
13 September 1709 ibid. p.596.

75 Boufflers to Louis 11 September
1709 in De Vault and Pelet IX
p.44.

76 Marlborough to Godolphin
11 September 1709 in Snyder
Marlborough–Godolphin III
p.1360.

77 Marlborough to Duchess of
Marlborough 13 September
1709 ibid. p.1364.

78 Marlborough to Duchess of
Marlborough 26 September
1709 ibid. pp.1377–8.

79 Marlborough to Heinsius
12 December 1709 OS in
Marlborough–Heinsius pp.475–6.

80 Marlborough to Duchess of
Marlborough 2 and 5 June 1710
in Snyder *Marlborough–Godolphin*
III pp.1505, 1507.

81 Queen Anne to Marlborough
25 October 1709 in Gregg
Queen Anne p.294.

82 M. de la R. Manley *Secret Memoirs
and Manners of Several Persons of
Quality of both sexes from the New
Atlantis, an Island in the
Mediterranean* Vol IV (London
1741) pp.30–2.

83 Marlborough to Duchess of
Marlborough 7 October 1709 in
Snyder *Marlborough–Godolphin* III
p.1387.

84 *London Gazette* 15–17 November
1709.

85 Maynwaring to Duchess of
Marlborough 18 November
1709 in Sarah Duchess of
Marlborough *Private
Correspondence* I p.270.

86 Watson *Marlborough's Shadow*
p.105.

87 Marlborough to Stepney
6 December 1706 in Murray
Dispatches III p.245.

88 Cadogan to Marlborough
26 June 1710, Cadogan Papers.

89 A.J. Veenendaal 'The opening
phase of Marlborough's
campaign of 1708 in the
Netherlands' in *History* February
1950 p.45.

90 Cadogan to Brydges 28 April
1707 in Dickson *Cadogan* p.34.

91 Cadogan to Raby 7 July 1707
ibid. p.38.

92 Ibid. p.154.

93 Marlborough to Duchess of
Marlborough 24 June 1709 in
Snyder *Marlborough–Godolphin* III
p.1283.

94 Philip Rambaut 'A study in
misplaced loyalty: Louis de
Duffort-Duras, Earl of Feversham'
in M. Glozier and D. Onnekink
(eds) *War, Religion and Service*
(Aldershot 2007) p.57.

95 Trevelyan *The Peace and the
Protestant Succession* p.37.

96 Rodger *Command* p.177.

97 Trevelyan *The Peace and the
Protestant Succession* p.20.

98 Burnet *History* V p.454.

99 Marlborough to Duchess of
Marlborough 26 June 1710 in
Snyder *Marlborough–Godolphin* III
pp.1530–1.

100 Marlborough to Godolphin
27 June 1710 and Marlborough
to Duchess of Marlborough
29 June 1710 ibid. pp.1533,
1535.

101 Lever *Godolphin* p.241.

102 Maynwaring to Duchess of
Marlborough September or
October 1710 in Sarah Duchess
of Marlborough *Private
Correspondence* I p.395.

103 Lever *Godolphin* p.251.

104 Godolphin to Marlborough
8 August 1710 in Snyder
Marlborough–Godolphin III p.1596.

105 Queen Anne to Marlborough
8 August 1710 in Gregg *Queen
Anne* p.320.
106 Godolphin to Marlborough
9 August 1710 in Snyder
Marlborough–Godolphin III
pp.1597–8.
107 Gregg *Queen Anne* p.323.
108 Godolphin to Marlborough
30 June 1710 in Snyder
Marlborough–Godolphin III
p.1552.
109 Marlborough to Villars
31 August 1710 in Murray
Dispatches V p.122.
110 Marlborough to Godolphin
14 September 1711 in Snyder
Marlborough–Godolphin III
p.1679.
111 Marlborough to Heinsius
13 October 1710 in
Marlborough–Heinsius p.527.
112 Marlborough to Pulteney
and Marlborough to Hern
11 September 1710 in Murray
Dispatches V p.136.
113 B. Cadogan to Marlborough
15 February 1711, Cadogan
Papers. The tone of this barely
legible letter suggests that it was
written by the widow of a
regimental colonel killed at
Malplaquet, and its content,
author's name and present
location suggest a Cadogan
family connection. I have,
however, been unable to
discover the lady's identity.
114 Cadogan to Raby 5 December
1707, Cadogan Papers.
115 Scouller *Armies of Queen
Anne* p.75.
116 Marlborough to St John 16 July
1711 in Murray *Dispatches* V
pp.412–13.
117 Marlborough to Sweet
20 December 1710 ibid. p.245.
118 Marlborough to Halifax
13 September 1710 ibid. p.139.
119 Marlborough to Bothmar
17 September 1710 ibid. p.143.
120 Marlborough to Duchess of
Marlborough 10 November
1710 in Snyder *Marlborough–
Godolphin* III p.1654.
121 Lever *Godolphin* p.257.
122 Philip Roberts (ed.) *The Diary of
Sir David Hamilton 1709–14*
(Oxford 1975) pp.22–3.
123 Lever *Godolphin* pp.259, 261–2.
124 *Hamilton Diary* p.25.
125 Burnet *History* VI p.33.
126 Ibid. p.34.
127 *Hamilton Diary* p.27.
128 Burnet *History* VI p.33.
129 Sarah Duchess of Marlborough
Conduct p.279.
130 Gregg *Queen Anne* p.329.
131 Marlborough to Godolphin
5 July 1710 in Snyder
Marlborough–Godolphin III
p.1543.
132 Colyear had joined his father's
regiment in Dutch service in
1675, and risen to command it:
his English was now so rusty that
Marlborough wrote to him in
French.
133 Marlborough to Godolphin
9 November 1710 in Snyder
Marlborough–Godolphin III
p.1652.
134 Marlborough to Godolphin
27 October 1710 ibid. p.1648.
135 Marlborough to Raby 10
November 1710 in Murray
Dispatches V p.218.
136 Marlborough to Duchess of
Marlborough 16 April 1711 in
Snyder *Marlborough–Godolphin* III
p.1662.
137 Marlborough to Duchess of
Marlborough 18 May 1711 ibid.
pp.1666–7.

138 Burton *Captain-General* p.180.
139 Marlborough to Heinsius
     11 June 1711 in *Marlborough–
     Heinsius* p.547.
140 Marlborough to Heinsius
     25 June 1711 ibid. p.550.
141 Churchill *Marlborough* VI
     pp.410–11.
142 Ibid. p.418.
143 Kane *Memoirs* p.90.
144 Marlborough to Godolphin
     27 July 1711 in Snyder
     Marlborough–Godolphin III
     p.1673.
145 William, Viscount Rialton to
     Marlborough 9 August 1711 in
     BL Add Mss 61368 f.41.
146 Kane *Memoirs* pp.91–2.
147 Marlborough to Godolphin
     30 July 1711 in Snyder
     Marlborough–Godolphin III
     p.1674.
148 Chandler *Robert Parker* pp.100–1.
149 Ibid. pp.101–3.
150 Deane *Journal* p.133.
151 Marlborough to Heinsius
     13 August 1711 in *Marlborough–
     Heinsius* p.558.
152 Chandler *Robert Parker* p.108.
153 Marlborough to Godolphin
     14 September 1711 in Snyder
     Marlborough–Godolphin III
     p.1679.
154 Trevelyan *The Peace and the
     Protestant Succession* p.207.
155 Marlborough to Oxford 8
     October 1711 in BL Add Mss
     61125 f.129.
156 Churchill *Marlborough* VI p.483.
157 Cadogan to Marlborough
     20 January 1712, Cadogan
     Papers.
158 Burton *Captain-General* p.188.
159 Marlborough to Albemarle
     28 January 1712 in Murray
     Dispatches VI p.574.
160 Marlborough to Wheate
     4 March 1712 ibid. p.579.
161 De Vault and Pelet XI p.463.
162 Chandler *Robert Parker*
     pp.119–20.
163 Bishop *Life and Adventures*
     p.235.
164 Kane *Memoirs* p.102.
165 Churchill *Marlborough* VI p.530.
166 Ibid. p.569.
167 Ibid. p.571.
168 Ibid. p.575.
169 Oxford to Maynwaring
     31 October 1712 in Coxe
     Memoirs III p.325.
170 Churchill *Marlborough* VI p.575.
171 Marlborough to Duchess of
     Marlborough 21 January 1713
     ibid. pp.579–80.
172 Marlborough to Duchess of
     Marlborough 5 February 1713
     ibid. p.580.
173 Quoted in Frances Harris *A
     Passion for Government: The
     Life of Sarah Duchess of
     Marlborough* (Oxford 1991)
     p.193.
174 Sarah Duchess of Marlborough
     *Letters . . . from the originals at
     Madresfield Court* (London 1875)
     pp.32–3.
175 HMC Bath I pp.37–8.
176 Coxe *Memoirs* III pp.341–3. For
     confirmation of the exchange
     see Cokayne et al. *The Complete
     Peerage* (13 vols, London
     1910–59) VIII p.493.
177 Churchill *Marlborough* VI
     p.589.
178 Ibid. p.584.
179 Duke of Berwick to
     Marlborough 8 September 1703
     in BL Add Mss 61270 f.1.
180 Sir Archibald Alison *Life of John,
     Duke of Marlborough* (2 vols,
     London 1852) II p.247.

181 Gregg *Queen Anne* p.375.

182 Marlborough to Maynwaring 9? June 1714 in Coxe *Memoirs* III pp.360–1.

183 Marlborough to Robethon 9 July 1714 in Macpherson *Original Papers* II p.632.

184 Churchill *Marlborough* VI p.623.

185 Cadogan to Marlborough 30 October 1715, Cadogan Papers.

186 Harris *Passion for Government* p.210.

187 William Matthews (ed.) *The Diary of Dudley Ryder 1715–1716* (London 1939) p.363.

188 Harris *Passion for Government* p.120.

189 Ibid. p.219. All three children of the marriage died in infancy, and Sunderland himself died in 1722.

190 Christopher Hibbert *The Marlboroughs* (London 2001) p.314.

191 Churchill *Marlborough* VI p.645.

192 Ibid. pp.646–7.

193 Hamilton to Marlborough 5 June 1718 in HMC Stuart VI p.534.

194 Hibbert *Marlboroughs* p.318.

195 Ibid. pp.319–20.

196 Ibid. pp.321–2. Sadly, the last quote seems apocryphal.

197 Ibid. p.325.

198 Iris Butler *Rule of Three: Sarah, Duchess of Marlborough, and her Companions in Power* (London 1967) p.325.

199 Hibbert *Marlboroughs* pp.348–9.

200 Sarah Duchess of Marlborough *Letters at Madresfield Court* p.xviii.

201 Harris *Passion for Government* p.348.

202 V.G. Kiernan 'George Macartney' in *New Dictionary of National Biography* Vol. 35 p.25.

203 Ingoldsby to Marlborough 31 December 1706 in BL Add Mss 61157 ff.44–6.

204 Colonel Hugh Boscawen 'Over the Hills and Far Away: Marlborough: Blenheim and Ramillies – A Reconnaissance' in *British Army Review* No. 142 Summer 2007 p.81.

205 Chandler *Robert Parker* p.115.

206 Harris *Passion for Government* p.107.

207 Bevan *Marlborough* p.294.

SELECT BIBLIOGRAPHY

ARCHIVES

British Library

MARLBOROUGH AND DUCHESS OF MARLBOROUGH
Add Mss 9094–9113 Marlborough's correspondence
Add Mss 9114 Journal of campaigns (usually attributed to Chaplain General Francis Hare, though the earlier material is probably the work of Josias Sandby, secretary to General Charles Churchill and chaplain to the artillery train)
Add Mss 9118–9122 Letters and Papers of the Duchess of Marlborough
Add Mss 61101 Letters from Queen Anne to Marlborough
Add Mss 61119–61122 Letters to Marlborough from Sir Charles Hedges
Add Mss 61125 Letters to Marlborough from Harley (later Earl of Oxford)
Add Mss 61132 Letters to Marlborough from St John (later Viscount Bolingbroke)
Add Mss 61133 Letters to Marlborough from William Blathwayt
Add Mss 61157 Letters from Lord Portmore to Marlborough
Add Mss 61163 Letters from Lieutenant General Richard Ingoldsby to Marlborough
Add Mss 61363 Letters from the Duke of Buckingham and Knightley Chetwode to Marlborough
Add Mss 61366 Letters from Charles Davenant to Marlborough
Add Mss 61368 Letters from William Godolphin, Viscount Rialton (later Marquess of Blandford) to Marlborough
Add Mss 61270 Letters from Duke of Berwick to Marlborough
Add Mss 70938–70943 Marlborough to Sir Charles Hedges, William Blathwayt and Dutch officials
Add Mss 70944 (formerly Philipps Mss 11539) Orders of battle with watercolour illustrations 1703–1712
Add Mss 70945 Miscellaneous correspondence

WILLIAM CADOGAN
Add Mss 22196 Cadogan to Lord Raby (later Earl of Strafford)

ADAM DE CARDONNEL
Add Mss 28917–8 Letters from Cardonnel to John Ellis, under-secretary of state
Add Mss 42176 Letters from Cardonnel to deputy judge advocate general John Watkins

JEAN DE ROBETHON
Stowe Mss 222–231 includes correspondence with Cadogan and Marlborough

National Archives

WO 5/1 Secretary at War, Marching and militia orders

National Army Museum

6909/4 Account and map of the action at Elixheim (Lines of Brabant) 1705

Cadogan Papers, Cadogan Estate Office

Assorted correspondence of William Cadogan, much of it duplicating letters in
   BL Add Mss 22196, but including some original material
Unpublished Mss biography 'William, 1st Earl Cadogan' by Patricia Dickson

Published Collections of Papers

Beatrice Curtis Brown *Letters and Diplomatic Instructions of Queen Anne*
   (London 1968)
The Private Papers of William First Earl Cowper (Eton 1833)
William Coxe (ed.) *Private and Original Correspondence of Charles Talbot, Duke of
   Shrewsbury* (London 1821)
Sir John Dalrymple *Memoirs of Great Britain and Ireland* (3 vols, London
   1790)
H.C. Foxcroft (ed.) *The Life and Letters of Sir George Savile, First Marquess of
   Halifax* (2 vols, London 1898)
S.R. Gardiner (ed.) *Constitutional Documents of the Puritan Revolution
   1625–1660* (Oxford 1962)
The Correspondence of Sir Thomas Hanmer Bart (London 1838)
Philip Yorke, Earl of Hardwicke *Miscellaneous State Papers from 1501 to 1726*
   (2 vols, London 1778)
Sarah Duchess of Marlborough *Private Correspondence of the Duchess of
   Marlborough* (2 vols, London 1838)
Sir George Murray (ed.) *Letters and Dispatches of John Churchill . . .* (5 vols,
   London 1845)
Reports of the Royal Commission on Historical Manuscripts
   Bath
   Buccleuch
   Cathcart
   Cowper
   Dartmouth
   Downshire
   Le Fleming
   Northumberland
   Portland
   Somerset
   Spencer
   Stuart

Henry L. Snyder (ed.) *The Marlborough–Godolphin Correspondence* (3 vols, Oxford 1975)

B. van 'T Hoff *The Correspondence 1701–1711 of John Churchill and Anthonie Heinsius* (The Hague 1951)

E.M. Thompson (ed.) *Correspondence of the Family of Hatton* (2 vols, London 1878)

G.M. Trevelyan *Select Documents from Queen Anne's Reign Down to the Union with Scotland* (Cambridge 1929)

François Eugène de Vault and Jean Jacques Germain, baron Pelet *Mémoires relatifs à la succession d'Espagne . . .* (11 vols, Paris 1835–62)

The Wentworth Papers (London 1883)

Books

Donald Adamson (ed.) *Rides Round Britain: John Byng, Viscount Torrington* (London 1996)

Earl of Ailesbury *Memoirs of Thomas, Earl of Ailesbury* (2 vols, London 1890)

Sir Archibald Alison *Life of John, Duke of Marlborough* (2 vols, London 1852)

Anon *The Lives of the Two Illustrious Generals* (London 1713)

Maurice Ashley *Charles II* (London 1873)

C.T. Atkinson *Marlborough and the Rise of the British Army* (New York 1921)

Brigadier General Colin Ballard *The Great Earl of Peterborough* (London 1929)

Correlli Barnett *Marlborough* (London 1974)

Mark Bence-Jones and Hugh Montgomery-Massingberd *The British Aristocracy* (London 1979)

Memoirs of the Marshal Duke of Berwick, Written by Himself . . . (2 vols, London 1774)

Bryan Bevan *Marlborough the Man* (London 1975)

— *King William III, Prince of Orange: The First European* (London 1997)

Sir William Beveridge et al. *Prices and Wages in England from the Twelfth to the Nineteenth Century* (London 1939)

Matthew Bishop *The Life and Adventures of Matthew Bishop of Deddington in Oxordshire* (London 1744)

Lieutenant Colonel John Blackader *The Life and Diary of Lieut. Col. J. Blackader of the Cameronian Regiment* (Edinburgh 1724)

William Bray (ed.) *The Diary of John Evelyn FRS* (London 1890)

Major General J.M. Brereton *History of the 4th/7th Dragoon Guards* (Catterick 1982)

Richard Brooks *Cassell's Battlefields of England and Ireland* (London 2005)

Anthony Bruce *The Purchase System in the British Army 1660–1871* (London 1980)

Gilbert Burnet *Bishop Burnet's History of His Own Times* (6 vols, Oxford 1833)

Ivor F. Burton *The Captain-General* (London 1968)

Iris Butler *Rule of Three* (London 1967)

John Callow *King in Exile: James II, Warrior, King and Saint* (Stroud 2004)

Captain George Carleton *Military Memoirs* (London 1929)

The Memoirs of Captain George Carleton and the Life and Adventures of Mrs Christian Davies, commonly called Mother Ross (London 1840)

Thomas Carter (ed.) *Historical Record of the Twenty-Sixth or Cameronian Regiment* (London 1867)

Gérard Chaliand (ed.) *The Art of War in World History* (Berkeley, California 1994)

David Chandler (ed.) *A Journal of Marlborough's Campaigns . . . by John Marshall Deane, Private Sentinel in Queen Anne's First Regiment of Foot Guards* (London 1984)

David Chandler (ed.) *Military Memoirs: Robert Parker and the Comte de Mérode-Westerloo* (London 1968)

David Chandler et al. (eds) *Military Miscellany II* (Stroud 2005)

David Chandler et al. (eds) *Blenheim Preparation* (Staplehurst 2004)

David Chandler *The Art of Warfare in the Age of Marlborough* (London 1976)

— *Marlborough as a Military Commnader* (London 1973)

Edwin Chappell (ed.) *The Tangier Papers of Samuel Pepys* (London 1935)

Philip Dormer Stanhope, Earl of Chesterfield *Letters* (5 vols, London 1892)

G.K. Chesterton *A Short History of England* (London 1917)

John Childs *The Army of Charles II* (London 1976)

— *The Army, James II and the Glorious Revolution* (Manchester 1980)

— *The British Army of William III* (Manchester 1979)

Winston S. Churchill *Marlborough: His Life and Times* (6 vols, New York 1938)

J.S. Clarke (ed.) *The Life of James II* (2 vols, London 1816)

Anne-Marie Cocula (ed.) *Mémoires de Monsieur de la Colonie, Maréchal de Camp des Armées de l'Electeur de Bavière* (Paris 1992)

G. Cokayne et al. (eds) *The Complete Peerage of England, Scotland, Ireland, Great Britain and the United Kingdom . . .* (13 vols, London 1910–59)

André Corviser *La Bataille de Malplaquet 1709* (Paris 1997)

W.J. Coxe *Memoirs of the Duke of Marlborough* (3 vols, London 1896)

The Craftsman (Collected Edition, London 1757)

Charles Davenant *Works* (London 1771)

Ian Davidson *Voltaire in Exile* (London 2004)

Louisa Stoughton Drake *The Drake Family in England and America 1360–1895* (Boston 1896)

Peter Drake *Amiable Renegade: The Memoirs of Captain Peter Drake* (Stanford, California 1960)

Christopher Duffy *The Fortress in the Age of Vauban and Frederick the Great* (London 1985)

J.F. Dutems *Histoire de Jean Churchill, Duc de Marlborough* (3 vols, Paris 1808)

Ralph Dutton *English Court Life* (London 1963)

H.J. and E.A. Edwards *A Short Life of Marlborough* (London 1926)

James Falkner *Great and Glorious Days: Marlborough's Battles 1704–9* (London 2002)

— *Marlborough's Wars: Eyewitness Accounts 1702–1713* (Barnsley 2005)

Ophelia Field *The Favourite: Sarah Duchess of Marlborough* (London 2002)

C.H. Firth *Cromwell's Army* (London 1962)

Kate Fleming *The Churchills* (London 1975)

J.W. Fortescue *A History of the British Army* (20 vols, London 1910)

Marian Fowler *Blenheim: Biography of a Palace* (London 1989)

H.C. Foxcroft *A Supplement to Burnet's History of My Own Time* (Oxford 1902)

Antonia Fraser *King Charles II* (London 1979)

— *Love and Louis XIV* (London 2006)

Matthew Glozier *The Huguenot Soldiers of William of Orange and the Glorious Revolution of 1688* (Brighton 2002)

Matthew Glozier and David Onnekink (eds) *War, Religion and Service: Huguenot Soldiering, 1685–1713* (Aldershot 2007)

Sicco van Goslinga *Mémoires relatifs à la Guerre de Succession de 1706–1709 et 1711* (Leeuwarden 1857)

Edward Gregg *Queen Anne* (London 1980)

Eric Gruber von Arni *Hospital Care and the British Standing Army 1660–1714* (Aldershot 2006)

Henry Hanning *The British Grenadiers* (London 2006)

Frances Harris *A Passion for Government: The Life of Sarah Duchess of Marlborough* (Oxford 1991)

Simon Harris *Sir Cloudesley Shovell: Stuart Admiral* (Staplehurst, Kent 2001)

Tim Harris *Revolution: The Great Crisis of the British Monarchy 1685–1720* (London 2006)

R.M. Hatton *Charles XII of Sweden* (London 1968)

Nicholas Henderson *Prince Eugène of Savoy* (London 1964)

Christopher Hibbert *The Marlboroughs* (London 2001)

George Hilton Jones *Convergent Forces: Immediate Causes of the Revolution of 1688 in England* (Ames, Iowa 1990)

J.A. Houlding *Fit for Service: The Training of the British Army 1715–1795* (Oxford 1981)

John Hussey *Marlborough* (London 2004)

Jens Harald Fibiger Jahn *De danske Auxiliairtropper . . .* (2 vols, Copenhagen 1840–41)

Richard Kane *Campaigns of King William and Queen Anne from 1689 to 1712; also a new system of Military Discipline . . .* (London 1745)

John Keegan and Andrew Wheatcroft *Who's Who in Military History* (London 1976)

O. Klopp *Der Fall des Hauses Stuart* (14 vols, Vienna 1875–1888)

The Diary of Dr Edward Lake (London 1846)

J. Laperelle *Marshal Turenne* (London 1907)

Robert Latham (ed.) *The Shorter Pepys* (London 1985)

Thomas Lediard *The Life of the Duke of Marlborough* (London 1736)

A. Legrelle *La Diplomatie Française et la Succession d'Espagne* (6 vols, Paris 1892)

Sir Tresham Lever *Godolphin, His Life and Times* (London 1952)

Thomas Babington Macaulay *History of England* (8 vols, London 1858)

Derek McKay *Prince Eugène of Savoy* (London 1977)

Catharine MacLeod and Julia Marciari (eds) *Painted Ladies: Women at the Court of King Charles II* (London 2001)

Peter McPhee *A Social History of France 1780–1880* (London 1993)

M. de la R. Manley *Secret Memoirs and Manners of Several Persons of Quality of both sexes from the New Atlantis, an Island in the Mediterranean* (London 1741)

Sarah Duchess of Marlborough *An Account of the Conduct of the Dowager Duchess of Marlborough from her first coming to court to the year 1710* (London 1742)

— *Letters . . . from the originals at Madresfield Court* (London 1875)

William Matthews (ed.) *The Diary of Dudley Ryder 1715–1716* (London 1939)

Brian Miller *James II: A Study in Kingship* (London 1978)

Sergeant John Millner *A Compendious Journal* (London 1733)

B.R. Mitchell *Abstract of British Historical Statistics* (Cambridge 1962)

Michael Orr *Dettingen 1743* (London 1972)

John Paget *The New 'Examen'* (London 1934)

Liza Picard *Restoration London* (London 1997)

Diane W. Ressinger (ed.) *Memoirs of Isaac Dumont de Bostaquet, a Gentleman of Normandy* (London 2005)

Captain J. Revol *Turenne: Essai de Psychologie militaire* (Paris 1910)

Philip Roberts (ed.) *The Diary of Sir David Hamilton 1709–14* (Oxford 1975)

N.A.M. Rodger *The Command of the Ocean* (London 2004)

A.L. Rowse *The Early Churchills* (London 1956)

Jules Roy *Turenne, sa vie, les institutions militaires de son temps* (Paris 1884)

K.W. von Schöning (ed.) *Das General-Feldmarschalls Dubislaw Gneomar von Natzmer: Leben und Kriegshaten* (Berlin 1938)

Major R.E. Scouller *The Armies of Queen Anne* (Oxford 1966)

Philip W. Sergeant *My Lady Castlemaine* (London 1912)

Frederick Shobel (ed.) *Memoirs of Prince Eugène of Savoy Written by Himself* (London 1811)

S.W. Singer (ed.) *The Correspondence of Henry Hyde, Earl of Clarendon* (2 vols, London 1828)

Anne Somerset *The Affair of the Poisons* (London 2003)

Charles Spencer *Blenheim: Battle for Europe* (London 2004)

Graham Stewart *Friendship and Betrayal: Ambition and the Limits of Loyalty* (London 2007)

C. Sturgill *Marshal Villars and the War of Spanish Succession* (London 1965)

Arthur Symonds (ed.) *Sir Roger de Coverly and other essays from The Spectator* (London 1905)

J.W. Sypesteyn *Het leven van Menno baron van Coehoorn* (Leeuwarden 1860)

John Tincey *Sedgemoor 1685: Marlborough's First Victory* (Barnsley 2005)

G.M. Trevelyan *England Under Queen Anne: I Blenheim*

— II *Ramillies and the Union with Scotland*

— III *The Peace and the Protestant Succession* (London 1946)

— *English Social History* (London 1948)

Norman Tucker (ed.) 'The Military Memoirs of John Gwyn' in *Military Memoirs: The Civil War* (London 1967)

Walter C.T. Utt and Bryan E. Straymer *The Bellicose Dove: Claude Broussan and Protestant Resistance to Louis XIV 1647–1698* (Brighton 2002)

John Van Der Kiste *William and Mary* (Stroud 2003)

A.J. Veenendaal *Het Engels–Nederlands Condominium in Zuidelike Nederlanden . . .*
(Utrecht 1945)

Maureen Waller *1700: Scenes from London Life* (London 2000)

J.N.P. Watson *Marlborough's Shadow: The Life of the First Earl Cadogan*
(London 2003)

Stephen Saunders Webb *Lord Churchill's Coup* (New York 1995)

Margaret Whinney and Oliver Millar *English Art 1625–1714* (Oxford 1957)

Major General Barney White-Spunner *Horse Guards* (London 2007)

John B. Wolf *Louis XIV* (New York 1968)

Field Marshal Viscount Wolseley *The Life of John Churchill, Duke of
Marlborough . . .* (2 vols, London 1894)

Alan Wykes *The Royal Hampshire Regiment* (London 1968)

Peter Young (ed.) 'The Vindication of Richard Atkyns' in *Military Memoirs:
The Civil War* (London 1967)

Articles and Pamphlets

C.T. Atkinson 'Queen Anne's Army' in *Journal of the Society for Army Historical
Research* No. 36 1958

— 'A Royal Dragoon in the Spanish Succession War' *Journal of the Society
for Army Historical Research* No. 60 1938

Colonel Hugh Boscawen 'Over the Hills and Far Away: Marlborough:
Blenheim and Ramillies – A Reconnaissance' in *British Army Review*
No. 42 2007

Lieutenant General the Hon Sir James Campbell of Lawes 'A Scots Fusilier and
Dragoon under Marlborough' in *Journal of the Society for Army Historical
Research* No. 58 1936

H.H.E. Craster (ed.) 'Letters of the First Lord Orkney' in *English Historical
Review* XIX 1904

H.G. Farrer 'Kettledrums as Trophies' in *Journal of the Society for Army Historical
Research* Vol. 26 1948

Sir John Fortescue 'A Junior Officer of Marlborough's Staff' in *Historical and
Military Essays* (London 1928)

Edward Gregg 'Marlborough in Exile, 1712–1714' in *Historical Journal*
No. 15 1972

Frances Harris 'The Authorship of the Manuscript Blenheim Journal' in
Bulletin of the Institute of Historical Research LV 1982

Geoffrey Holmes and William Speck 'The Fall of Harley in 1708
Reconsidered' in *English Historical Review* LXVI 1965

'The Letters of Samuel Noyes, Chaplain of the Royal Scots 1703–4' in *Journal
of the Society for Army Historical Research* No. 37 1959

The *London Gazette* Assorted reports and announcements

Ian A. Morrison 'Survival Skills: An Enterprising Highlander in the Low
Countries with Marlborough' in Grant G. Simpson (ed.) *The Scottish Soldier
Abroad* (Edinburgh 1992)

'Review of a late Treatise entitled an Account of the Conduct of the Dowager
D_____ of M_____' (London 1742)

Henry L. Snyder 'The Duke of Marlborough's Request of his Captain-Generalcy for Life: A Re-examination' in *Journal of the Society for Army Historical Research* Vol. 45 1967

H. Fitzmaurice Stacke, 'Cavalry in Marlborough's Day' in *Cavalry Journal* October 1934

A.J. Veenendaal 'The Opening Phase of Marlborough's Campaign of 1708 in the Netherlands' in *History* February 1950

S. Wynne 'The Mistresses of Charles II and Restoration Court Politics, 1660–1685' unpublished PhD thesis, University of Cambridge

INDEX

NOTE: Titles and ranks are generally the highest mentioned in the text